THE GREEKS
IN
BACTRIA & INDIA

THE GREEKS
IN
BACTRIA & INDIA

by

W. W. TARN

GYAN

Published by

GYAN

Gyan Publishing House
5, Ansari Road
Daryaganj, New Delhi-110002
Phone: 011-47034999, 9811692060
E-mail: books@gyanbooks.com

Distribution Network
gyanbooks.com
India, USA, Canada, UK, Australia, France

ISBN : 978-81-212-9958-9 (PB)
First Published, 1922

2nd Impression 2021

Printed at: Gyan Press, Delhi.

The Greeks in Bactria & India
Author: W. W. Tarn

THE GREEKS
IN
BACTRIA & INDIA

by

W. W. TARN
LITT.D., F.B.A., Hon. LL.D. (Edinburgh)

CAMBRIDGE
AT THE UNIVERSITY PRESS

To

MY BEST CRITIC

CONTENTS

PART I. (INTRODUCTORY)

THE BACKGROUND IN THE MIDDLE EAST

PART II

BACTRIA AND INDIA

PREFACE TO THE FIRST EDITION

I HAVE dreamt of this book for forty years; it is fortunate for me that I had no opportunity of taking it up earlier. No Greek historian has yet attempted to handle the subject as a connected whole or to put it in its right place as a lost chapter of Hellenistic history. What needs saying about the book itself and its plan is given in the Introduction, which is meant to be read first; but I may here anticipate two obvious criticisms. I am aware that it is very reprehensible to write a book where you have to depend in part on second-hand information, as I have had to do on the Oriental side. But it is time that somebody with some knowledge of the Hellenistic world tried to get the more important Greek side into order, for one sees how often the Orientalist is hampered by not knowing what there is; and it is no use waiting for a scholar who shall have a proper and *critical* knowledge of both sides, or rather of all the sides, for he has not yet been born. And even in using a translation one need not entirely abandon one's common sense. I am also aware that history should be written impersonally. But to write this book impersonally was not possible; much of it is spade-work, and it had to get written as best it could, other considerations being subordinated to an effort to make the bearings of the rather complex collection of little details clear to the reader. I hope that the numerous cross-references may be of use here, for often it has been necessary to refer forward for the evidence for some statement, sometimes even on a large scale; for example, Chapter VIII presupposes a knowledge of Appendix 16, and the attempt in Chapter II to get the outline of the lost work of the historian whom I have had to call 'Trogus' source' presupposes a knowledge of the whole book.

My manifold debts to the published work of others are acknowledged in the notes, but one thing calls for special mention—the brilliant chapters in volume I of the Cambridge History of India (1922) in which, for the first time, Sir George Macdonald and the late Professor E. J. Rapson got the subject into a shape which one could understand and which offered a basis for future progress. If, as I venture to hope, I have been able to take the matter further than they left it, it must largely be because I have had the privilege, in Bentley's phrase, of standing on their shoulders.

PREFACE TO THE SECOND EDITION

As circumstances have made it impossible for me, cut off from libraries, to prepare a full revision of the text of this book, and as a simple reprint would have been unfair to readers, I have added some notes (*Addenda* 1950) to the reprint, in order, as far as I could, to indicate the advance of knowledge; some are really revisions of the text. They represent, not what I would, but what I could; and in two subjects at least, the peoples of the nomad invasion of Bactria and new coin-finds, my knowledge is sadly deficient. To friends who have helped me I am most grateful. One new book has recently appeared which covers the whole field and a good deal more, Professor Franz Altheim's *Weltgeschichte Asiens im griechischen Zeitalter* (2 vols., 1947, 1948), a book of vast learning that is not always matched by the use made of it; for my preliminary chapters on the Seleucid Empire Professor M. Rostovtzeff's great work *The Social and Economic History of the Hellenistic World* (3 vols., 1941) is now indispensable. My best thanks are due to the Syndics of the Cambridge University Press for reprinting this book and permitting me to include the 1950 *Addenda*, and to the Staff of the Press for the way in which it has been carried out.

W. W. TARN

MUIRTOWN HOUSE
INVERNESS

January 1950

To acknowledge all my more personal obligations is almost impossible, for so many people have kindly helped me in one way or another; some are mentioned in the notes. I desire here to thank Monsieur Jean Babelon of the Bibliothèque Nationale in Paris for particulars of the Indo-Greek coins in the unpublished Hackin collection; Dr L. D. Barnett of the British Museum for the translation used in Appendix 4; Professor E. H. Minns for procuring and making for me a synopsis of the Russian study mentioned in Appendix 10; Mr J. Allan of the British Museum for a cast of the coin which is no. 7 on the Plate, and also for giving me a proof of the Introduction to his *Indian Coins* many months in advance of publication, which saved me a great deal of trouble; and also, for help of various kinds, Sir Aurel Stein, Professors H. W. Bailey, Fr. Cumont, E. Herzfeld, and F. W. Thomas, and Messrs E. J. Gadd, H. Mattingly, E. S. G. Robinson, and Sidney Smith, of the British Museum. To three of my friends I owe a very special debt. Professors H. M. Last and A. D. Nock each read a good deal of the book in MS. and gave me not only numerous references and suggestions but also (a thing which meant much more to me) some greatly needed encouragement at a critical time. Professor F. E. Adcock read most of the book in MS. and gave me the benefit of his great editorial knowledge, beside much other help; he also most generously undertook the thankless but beneficent task of reading a proof. I desire to thank the Syndics of the Cambridge University Press both for undertaking the publication of the book and also for permitting me to use again the beautiful reproductions of the Bactrian coin-portraits made for the Cambridge History of India, and to thank the staff of the Press for the way in which the publication has been carried out. Lastly, I would take this opportunity to pay a tribute of gratitude, long overdue, to my daughter, to whom this book is dedicated, and whose critical sense and clear judgment have been my unfailing help in everything I have written for many years.

W. W. TARN

MUIRTOWN HOUSE
INVERNESS

ABBREVIATIONS

(It has not seemed necessary to list the ordinary abbreviations of classical periodicals and collections. In general, I follow those given in the Cambridge Ancient History.)

ASI *Reports of the Archaeological Survey of India.* (For some years there is a preliminary volume entitled Part I, which is so cited.)

BEFEO *Bulletin de l'École française d'Extrême-Orient.*

Berlin SB *Sitzungsberichte d. preuss. Akademie d. Wissenschaften zu Berlin.*

Berthelot A. Berthelot, *L'Asie ancienne centrale et sud-orientale, d'après Ptolémée.* 1930.

BMC *Catalogue of coins in the British Museum: Greek and Scythic kings of Bactria and India*, by P. Gardner. 1886.

BMC India Ditto: *Coins of Ancient India*, by J. Allan. 1936.

BMC Parthia Ditto: *Parthia*, by W. Wroth. 1903.

BMC Sel. Ditto: *The Seleucid kings of Syria*, by P. Gardner. 1878.

BSOS *Bulletin of the School of Oriental Studies.*

CAH *Cambridge Ancient History.*

CHI *Cambridge History of India*, vol. I. 1922.

CII *Corpus Inscriptionum Indicarum*, vol. II, I: *The Kharoshthi Inscriptions, with the exception of those of Açoka*, by Sten Konow. 1929.

Cumont, *Fouilles* Fr. Cumont, *Les fouilles de Doura-Europos*, 1922–3. 1926.

Cunningham, *Geog.* General Sir Alexander Cunningham, *Ancient Geography of India* (1871), edited by S. N. Majumdar (Surendranath Majumdar Sastri). 1924.

de Groot J. J. M. de Groot, *Chinesische Urkunden zur Geschichte Asiens*: zweiter Teil, *Die Westlande Chinas in der vorchristlichen Zeit.* 1926. (Published after the author's death by O. Franke.)

de la Vallée-Poussin L. de la Vallée-Poussin, *L'Inde aux temps des Mauryas et des barbares, Grecs, Scythes, Parthes et Yue-tchi.* 1930. (*Histoire du Monde*, vol. VI, I.)

Demiéville Paul Demiéville, *Les versions chinoises du Milindapañha. BEFEO* XXIV, 1924 (pub. 1925), p. 1.

Ep. Ind. *Epigraphia Indica.*

Foucher A. Foucher, *L'Art gréco-bouddhique de Gandhāra.* Vol. I, 1905; vol. II, 1918 and 1922.

Foucher, *Afghanistan* A. Foucher, *Notes sur l'itinéraire de Hiun-Tsang en Afghanistan*, in *Études asiatiques publiées à l'occasion du 25e anniversaire de l'École française d'Extrême-Orient*, vol. I, 1925, p. 257.

Foucher, *Gandhāra* A. Foucher, *Notes sur la géographie ancienne du Gandhāra.* 1902. (English trans. by H. Hargreaves, *Notes on the Ancient Geography of Gandhāra*, 1915.)

Franke O. Franke, *Beiträge aus chinesischen Quellen zur Kenntniss der Türkvölker und Skythen Zentralasiens. Abhandlungen d. preuss. Akad. zu Berlin*, 1904, no. I.

Griffith G. T. Griffith, *The Mercenaries of the Hellenistic World.* 1935.

Grousset R. Grousset, *Histoire de l'Extrême-Orient*, vol. I. 1929.

Gutschmid A. von Gutschmid, *Geschichte Irans.* 1888.

Herzfeld, *Sakastan* E. Herzfeld, *Sakastan: Archaeologische Mitteilungen aus Iran*, IV, 1931–2.

Hirth Fr. Hirth, *The story of Chang K'ien.* Translation of chapter 123 of the Shi-ki of Ssu-ma Ch'ien. *JAOS* XXXVII, 1917, p. 89.

IHQ *Indian Historical Quarterly.*

Ind. Ant. *Indian Antiquary.*

Isidore Isidoros of Charax, *Παρθικοὶ Σταθμοί.*

JA *Journal Asiatique.*

JAOS *Journal of the American Oriental Society.*

JASB *Journal of the Asiatic Society of Bengal.*

JBORS *Journal of the Bengal and Orissa Research Society.*

JEA *Journal of Egyptian Archaeology.*

JIH *Journal of Indian History.*

JRAS *Journal of the Royal Asiatic Society.*

Lahore Cat. *Catalogue of the coins in the Punjab Museum, Lahore*, by R. B. Whitehead, vol. I. 1914.

Lassen Chr. Lassen, *Indische Altertumskunde*, 1847–61.

Lévi, *Quid de Graecis* *Quid de Graecis veterum Indorum monumenta tradiderint theseim... proponebat Sylvain Lévi.* 1890.

McDowell, *Stamped objects* R. H. McDowell, *Stamped and inscribed objects from Seleucia on the Tigris.* 1935.

McDowell, *Coins from Seleucia* R. H. McDowell, *Coins from Seleucia on the Tigris.* 1935.

MDP *Mémoires de la Délégation en Perse.*

NC *Numismatic Chronicle.*

NNM *Numismatic Notes and Monographs.*

Otto, *Zeit d. 6. Ptolemäers* W. Otto, *Zur Geschichte der Zeit des 6. Ptolemäers, Abhandlungen d. bayerischen Akad. d. Wissenschaften*, 1934.

Pliny C. Plinius Secundus, *Naturalis Historia.*

Przyluski, *Açoka* J. Przyluski, *La légende de l'empereur Açoka (Açoka-Avadāna) dans les textes Indiens et Chinois.* 1923.

Rhys Davids T. W. Rhys Davids, *The Questions of King Milinda.* Translation of the Pali text of the Milindapañha, in *Sacred Books of the East*, vols. XXXV, XXXVI (1890, 1894).

Rostovtzeff, *Seleucid Babylonia* M. Rostovtzeff, *Seleucid Babylonia: Bullae and Seals of Clay with Greek Inscriptions. Yale Classical Studies* III, 1932, p. 1.

Sav. Z. *Zeitschrift der Savigny-Stiftung, Romanistische Abteilung.*

Susemihl Fr. Susemihl, *Geschichte der griechischen Literatur in der Alexandrinerzeit*, 2 vols. 1891, 1892.

Tarn, *Hell. Civ.*[2] W. W. Tarn, *Hellenistic Civilisation*, 2nd ed. 1930.

Tarn, Military Developments W. W. Tarn, *Hellenistic Military and Naval Developments*. 1930.

Tarn, *SP Stud.* W. W. Tarn, *Seleucid-Parthian Studies. Proceedings of the British Academy*, 1930, p. 105.

Tscherikower V. Tscherikower, *Die hellenistischen Städtegründungen von Alexander dem Grossen bis auf die Römerzeit. Philologus*, Supp. Band XIX, 1, 1927.

V. A. Smith[4] V. A. Smith, *Early History of India*, 4th edition after his death by S. M. Edwardes, 1924.

Warmington E. H. Warmington, *The Commerce between the Roman Empire and India*. 1928.

Whitehead, *NC* R. B. Whitehead, *Notes on Indo-Greek Numismatics. NC* 1923, p. 294.

Whitehead, *NNM* R. B. Whitehead, *Pre-Mohammedan Coinage of North-Western India. NNM* 13, 1922.

Wien SB *Sitzungsberichte d. Akad. d. Wissenschaften in Wien.*

Winternitz M. Winternitz, *Geschichte der indischen Literatur*, 3 vols. Vol. II, 1920; vol. III, 1922.

Winternitz, Eng. trans. M. Winternitz, *A history of Indian Literature*, trans. by Mrs S. Ketkar, with the author's revisions. (Practically a second edition. Vol. II, 1933; vol. III not yet published.)

Wylie A. Wylie, *Notes on the Western Regions*: translation of chapter 96 part 1 and chapter 61 fols. 1–6 of the Ch'ien-han-shu (Annals of the Former Han) of Pan-ku. *Journal of the Anthropological Institute*, vol. X, 1881, p. 20.

Wylie, part 2 Translation of chapter 96 part 2 of the above. *Ib.* vol. XI, 1881, p. 83.

Z. *Zeitschrift.*

Newell, *ESM* E. T. Newell, *The Coinage of the Eastern Seleucid Mints from Seleucus I to Antiochus III*, 1938.

Rostovtzeff, *SEH* M. Rostovtzeff, *Social and Economic History of the Hellenistic World*, 3 vols. 1941 (consecutive paging).

Tarn, *Alexander* I, II W. W. Tarn, *Alexander the Great*, vol. I Narrative, vol. II Sources and Studies, 1948.

Tarn, *Tarmita* *Two Seleucid Studies: II, Tarmita*. *JHS* LX, 1940, p. 89.

Whitehead, *NC* 1940 R. B. Whitehead, *Notes on the Indo-Greeks*. *NC*, 5th series, XX, 1940, p. 1.

Whitehead, *NC* 1947 R. B. Whitehead, *Notes on the Indo-Greeks* Part II. *NC*, 6th series, VII, 1947 (pub. later), p. 28 [1].

INTRODUCTION

It may be well to begin with a statement of the plan of this book.[1]

Asia under Greek rule, as matter of political history and not of distinctions of race or civilisation, may be divided into three parts. The first division consists of the countries west of the Euphrates and of the Syrian desert, Asia Minor and Syria, which were to become Roman and were for centuries to be dominated by Graeco-Roman civilisation before they ultimately returned to the East; with this division this book has nothing to do except by way of an occasional illustration. The second division, roughly speaking, consists of the countries between the Euphrates and the Persian desert, which were subsequently to form the kingdom of the Arsacids, known to Greeks and Romans as Parthia; from the Greek point of view it may be called the Middle East. The third division, which I call the Farther East, comprises Iran east of the Persian desert and India so far as it was under Greek rule. This division by the Persian desert is a real one, and very old; it is found in one of Darius' lists of the provinces of his empire.[2] This book is really concerned only with the Farther East, the story of eastern Iran and northern India under Greek rule; it is an attempt to recover what can be recovered of the history of a lost dynasty and of a rather extraordinary experiment. This story begins with Chapter III, and from that chapter to the end the book (except for art) is meant to be as complete as I can make it.

But every story has a background, and the background to mine is the Middle East; it has seemed advisable therefore to add to the book

[1] In this book, the name Demetrius alone always means Demetrius of Bactria, and Demetrius II alone always means his son; every other Demetrius, including the Seleucids Demetrius I and II, always has some distinguishing word unless the context renders the meaning unmistakable. Seleuceia alone always means Seleuceia on the Tigris. The word 'Greeks', east of the Euphrates, includes Macedonians, unless the latter are particularised; probably by the second century B.C. the two were indistinguishable, and anyhow there are no means of distinguishing them. The term 'Indian scholar' (on the analogy of 'Greek scholar') means one engaged in Indian studies and has nothing to do with nationality.

[2] Persepolis e §2 (F. H. Weissbach, *Die Keilinschriften der Achaemeniden* 1911), which after the western provinces gives specifically 'the lands in the East', those east of the desert.

an introductory part, Chapters I and II, which shall sketch certain aspects of that background and will, I hope, make it easier to see the connections between the story of the Farther East and that of the Seleucids. This introductory part has not, and is not meant to have, any claim to completeness, except perhaps as regards the account of the Greek literature in Chapter II. It is not an account of the Seleucid realm; it is a sketch only, designed to bring out certain points which bear upon facts utilised later, and may be a help to the understanding of them; these points are, chiefly, the Seleucid administrative divisions, the nature of the Seleucid settlement, the Greek literature of the Middle East (which is important on the question of our sources), and the relations between Greeks and Asiatics.

The world east of the Euphrates was the scene of the interaction of Greek civilisation with three other civilisations, those of Babylonia, Iran, and India. Of these, India, and Iran in part, belong to my subject. But Babylonia does not, and I am not giving an account of Babylonia under Greek rule, which would call for a separate study and special qualifications. I use Babylonia to illustrate certain matters; that is all.

It is unfortunate that in Britain, and I think everywhere, the story of the Greeks in India has been treated as part of the history of India alone. For in the history of India the episode of Greek rule has no meaning; it is really part of the history of Hellenism, and that is where its meaning resides. It is one of the misfortunes of ancient history that we become hypnotised into writing as though the importance of a thing were somehow proportionate to the amount of information about it which has survived; the papyri, for instance, tend to make the Ptolemies seem more important than the Seleucids. If we can manage to avoid this perversion of thinking, we shall recognise that any history of the Hellenistic states with the Farther East omitted is a sadly mutilated history; for there were not four Hellenistic dynasties—Seleucids, Ptolemies, Antigonids, Attalids—but five, and on any showing the Euthydemids, both in the extent of their rule and in what they tried to do, were vastly more important than the Attalids, the protégés successively of Egypt and of Rome. The Greek empire of Bactria and India was a Hellenistic state, with many of the usual characteristics of such states but with one very important one of its own, and its history was a branch of Seleucid history, just as the Euthydemid dynasty was on the distaff side a branch of the Seleucid line; as a Hellenistic state it must be treated, and I hope that this book may do something towards bringing it back into the sphere to which it belongs.

This book does not go beyond the end of the Hellenistic period. The conventional end of that period in the West is the occupation of Alexandria by Augustus in 30 B.C., and by a curious coincidence the last Greek kingdoms in India fell about the same time; and anything later than the Christian Era is only noticed for its possible bearing on what goes before. But the period which I have sought primarily to reconstruct is comparatively a short one; it comprises about two and a half generations, from 206 B.C., the year in which Antiochus III quitted the East, to somewhere between 150 and 145 B.C., the death of Menander; one may call it the first half of the second century B.C., and it is covered by three reigns, the latter part of that of Euthydemus and those of his son Demetrius and of Demetrius' son-in-law Menander. That half-century is the important matter, and on the success or otherwise of my reconstruction of those years everything else must depend.

A word must be said here about the sources, though they will sufficiently appear as the book proceeds. They are of course very scrappy. But they were not always scrappy. There was once a Greek history which covered the Farther East generally, apparently down to 87 B.C. (pp. 45 *sqq.*), and there was another Greek history which also dealt with the Farther East, though seemingly only as an appendage to the history of Parthia (pp. 44 *sq.*); and the same thing has happened with regard to the Farther East as has happened with regard to another story whose historians have perished, that of the early third century in the Greek world about the Aegean: the scraps tend to combine, not into other scraps, but into at least the outline of a whole. There will be something to be said about this later (p. 46), but, as there was once a tradition, it is somebody's business to attempt to recover the outline of it; one is not labouring in a vacuum. Our evidence is of many different kinds. On the Greek side, there are fragments of the lost historians preserved in several later writers, notably Strabo, Trogus-Justin, Plutarch, and Ptolemy the geographer (on whom see Chapter VI); various notices and indications in extant Greek and Latin writers, book VI of Pliny's Naturalis Historia in particular containing much valuable Hellenistic material; and in place of the third-century inscriptions an almost unique wealth of coins, which give much more historical information than is usually the case with Greek coins. On the

Indian side, there are some inscriptions and a little numismatic material, a bit of perhaps contemporary chronicle embedded in a later work (App. 4), indications of various sorts in literature (including Chinese and Thibetan translations of lost Indian writings), the excavations at Taxila, and the Milindapañha, which does not look quite the same to the Greek as to the Indian scholar and to which I have had to give a long Excursus. Towards the end we get a little real history, a rare blessing, in the Chinese historians Ssu-ma Chien and Pan-ku (App. 20); had China made the acquaintance of the 'western countries' a couple of generations earlier than she did, how thankful we should be.

At present, coins apart, it seems to be only from the Indian side that fresh information can be looked for, and I must bear grateful testimony to the fact that (so far as I can see) the Indian material has been far better prepared for the Greek historian than the Greek material has ever been for the Indian; I can only hope that I have not missed too much of it, but the main task is to get the Greek side into some sort of order and to try to establish a framework which may be of use to others. The coins of course are all-important, and one cannot overpraise the work done on them by generations of numismatists; it seems to me one of the wonders of scholarship. But the numismatist as such has sometimes been unable to place or explain the facts which he has elicited; naturally so, for he is not expected to be a Hellenistic historian. Again I can only hope that I have not missed too much; with one or two exceptions, my knowledge of the coins has, of necessity, been confined to printed publications and the unrivalled collection in the British Museum; one is never safe from the unpublished coin in private hands, and it has proved impossible to ascertain what, if anything, there may be at Tashkent. Naturally I am not concerned with the coins as coins, but only as material for history.

It is no part of my purpose to write about art; I am not qualified, and the book is long enough as it is. Artistic material is only treated where, as in the case of the Buddha-statue in Chapter IX, it has some definite bearing on Greeks and their activities. Much has been written of late years, and much more will be written, about those mixed arts of the East which originated in the Hellenistic period and especially about 'Parthian' art, the art which grew up in Iran under the rule of the Parthian military aristocracy; we are meeting names unknown a few years ago, like 'Graeco-Bactrian' and 'Graeco-Sacan' art. All these phenomena, except the art of Gandhāra (which stands on a different footing), appear to have one common characteristic: they are native arts which borrowed, and sometimes misapplied, a certain modicum of Greek form and ornamentation.[1] They furnish a subject of very great interest in itself; but they have little to do with the history of the Greeks of the Farther East, and even less with the Greek spirit.

[1] This theme runs through Professor Herzfeld's *Archaeological History of Iran* 1934; see *e.g.* p. 50, 'only the most superficial features of foreign' (*i.e.* Greek) 'art are taken over; the essential ones are missed'; and p. 75, 'it neither really understands nor assimilates the spirit of Hellenism'.

PART I

THE BACKGROUND IN THE MIDDLE EAST

CHAPTER I

THE SELEUCID SETTLEMENT

THE Seleucids, whatever from time to time they held or did not hold in the countries bordering on the Mediterranean, were Alexander's heirs in Asia. He had not greatly modified the Persian empire which he had conquered: he might separate the three powers in the satrapies—civil, military, and financial—but they remained the huge Persian satrapies, though they might be governed by men of a different nationality. The Seleucid empire in its turn was still, in outward shape, very much the empire of Persia under different rulers; the great satrapies still remained, their military nature emphasised by the governor of a satrapy being no longer called satrap but *strategos*, 'general'. But something was done to tighten up the reins of satrapal government, for in all the lands east of the Euphrates the Seleucids had a more complete system of internal subdivision; it was a threefold division[1]—satrapy, eparchy, hyparchy—corresponding roughly to the threefold division in Ptolemaic Egypt of nome, topos, village, the nome, like the satrapy, being under a *strategos* or general. This threefold administrative division in each of the two empires must, one supposes, have had a common origin, but what it was is unknown. As the smallest administrative unit was in Egypt the village and in the Seleucid East the hyparchy—a district which would comprise a number

Note. There is a good modern account of the Seleucid empire by M. Rostovtzeff in *CAH* VII Ch. V (1928), but the subject has now to be studied in special works; the excavations at Doura, Susa, and Seleuceia are important. The relevant bibliographies in *CAH* VII and VIII cover much of the ground. In this introductory sketch I am not always putting notes to well-known matters where touched on.

[1] For all that follows about the eparchies see Tarn, *SP Stud.* § IV. Cf. M. Rostovtzeff in *Yale Class. Stud.* II p. 48 n. 1.

of villages—the organisation of the Seleucid East was of necessity much looser than that of Egypt; the hyparchy, however, for purposes of land registration, was again subdivided into fortified posts called *stathmoi*[1]—originally post stations on the main roads, the Seleucids having taken over the Persian postal system—each *stathmos* being the centre of a subdivision comprising so many villages.

The important thing in the Seleucid administrative division was the eparchy, of which each satrapy included a certain number; Appian's 72 Seleucid satrapies mean eparchies, for he is using the terminology of a later day, though it does not follow that the number 72 is correct. So far as is known at present, the eparchy was a Seleucid innovation. It *may* have been Achaemenid, for *a priori* the common source of the Ptolemaic and Seleucid subdivision should have been Persian, but the actual evidence is very dubious,[2] and the Alexander-historians know nothing about eparchies; they do very occasionally use an eparchy name, but that again is probably only the common case of late writers using the accustomed nomenclature of a later day. When the Seleucid empire broke up, it was the eparchy, not the satrapy, which survived; the Seleucid administration was imitated over a large part of Asia, and it was imitated on the basis of the eparchy. In the Seleucid Succession states, like Bactria, Parthia, Elymais, the eparchies became the satrapies, *i.e.* the primary administrative divisions, of the new kingdoms, while states which were not properly Succession states but were copying Seleucid (or, what comes to the same thing, Parthian) organisation gave their satrapies eparchy names; so universal was the practice that it was followed even by little states like Adiabene and Characene, which had themselves only been Seleucid eparchies. One reason for the emergence by the first century B.C. of the eparchy as the general unit of the organisation of a new Asia was that it had often been a natural division,

[1] The evidence for the *stathmoi* is from the Parthian period, notably Isidore and *Avroman Pg.* 1 (E. H. Minns, *JHS* XXXV, 1915, p. 22); but Strabo XV, 723 (see p. 55 n. 1) may show that they were Seleucid.

[2] Tarn, *SP Stud.* p. 32; add that in Darius' Behistun inscription, 38–9, Margus, *i.e.* Margiane, is under the satrap of Bactria. The question of subordinate governors of provinces under Persian satraps has since been discussed by O. Leuze, *Die Satrapienteilung in Syrien* 1935 pp. 163–5, for Syria and Babylonia, who decides that no conclusion is possible. It has, however, been suggested to me that the -ηνη termination in the East might have some connection with the Assyrian -anu; should that ever be substantiated, the connection could only be *via* Persia. The existence of old Greek city-names in -ηνη would not affect the (possible) adoption of the form in the East under other influences and for other purposes.

dictated by the lie of the ground, while the great satrapies were not; examples are the Bactrian satrapy, which had included northern Sogdiana and Merv, countries not geographically connected with Bactria, and the varying arrangements for the government of the hill land and the plain land which had both been included in the Persian satrapy of Arachosia (App. 9). The eparchies naturally varied greatly in size, as do English and Scotch counties, and it is possible that the eparchies of a satrapy did not always account for the whole of its geographical content; Ptolemy, who is careful over eparchy names, gives tribes in some satrapies as well as eparchies, and though one cannot press this, seeing that he so often mixes up items from different periods, still we do hear of unconquered hill peoples, like the Elymaeans of Susis, and the great satrapies may have included territory which was informally a sort of native reserve, the general of the satrapy being responsible for keeping the hill tribes in check. This may be why the Seleucid *strategos* retained his military status while his Ptolemaic counterpart became a civil official.

The great satrapies almost always bore names ending in *-ια*, Persis being the only exception, unless Susis be reckoned; the eparchies most often bore names ending in *-ηνη* or, after iota, *-ανη* (*-ιανη*). Two other forms do also occur among the primary administrative divisions of the Succession states, names (very occasionally) in *ια* and some in *-ῖτις*, which may be old eparchy forms; a third form in *-υαια* is merely a variant of *-ηνη* when preceded by upsilon, the two being used indiscriminately, as Parthyaia—Parthyene, Gordyaia—Gordyene.[1] The eparchy names had many sources; they might be taken from a city name, as Gabiene, Rhagiane; from a tribal name, as Paraitakene; or from some district name whose origin is lost, as Margiane from Margus (these are probably the majority); in Armenia some fanciful names are found, like Xerxene, Cambysene. And though other forms might sometimes occur, it was the *-ηνη* (or *-ιανη*) form which was the typical one and which spread all over Asia; and it is this form which has enabled the identification of a number of the Greek satrapies in India (Chap. VI). To make that identification valid, it is of course not

[1] Parthyaia and Parthyene indiscriminately in Strabo and Josephus. Gordyene always in Plutarch; both forms in Strabo, but usually Gordyaia. So even in personal names: the astronomer Naburiannu is *Ναβουριανός* in Strabo XVI, 739, but *Ναβουριναν* (acc.) in a Babylonian text written in Greek: W. S. Schileico, *Arch. f. Orientforschung* v, 1928, p. 11.

enough to show that the majority of eparchies had names in *-ηνη* or *-ιανη*; it must also be shown that these names, in Greek writers, regularly meant either Seleucid eparchies or the primary administrative divisions of a Seleucid Succession state or of a state copying the Seleucid organisation; this is done in Appendix 2, the one or two exceptions being negligible among the mass of names extant; in fact, looking at the Greek dislike of technical terms, the result is rather notable. It must be emphasised that in speaking of the eparchy organisation I am speaking only of the lands east of the Euphrates (see on this App. 2), though the countries between the Euphrates and the Halys copied it.

The Seleucid empire was nothing organic, in the sense that the Roman state, up to a point, was organic. The latter resembled a vertebrate animal; it expanded outwards from a solid core, the city of Rome. The Seleucid empire resembled rather a crustacean, not growing from any solid core but encased in an outer shell; the empire was a framework which covered a multitude of peoples and languages and cities. What there really was to the empire, officially, was a king, an army, and a bureaucracy—the governing and taxing officials in the several satrapies. It had no imperial citizenship, as the Roman empire had; it hardly even had a unified state worship, for each satrapy had its own cult of the deified kings. Even before the final dissolution, any satrapy could easily set up for itself, as Bactria did for good and Media spasmodically, without endangering the life of the rest; and in the general break-up even eparchies, like Osrhoene, Adiabene, Mesene, easily became little kingdoms, because the governor of an eparchy, just as much as the governor of a satrapy, had an organisation ready to his hand, even to a *basileion* or palace residence,[1] while the Greek cities or settlements in his territory were only separate units and not parts of a whole. What actually held the empire together was the personality of the quasi-divine monarch, for the army was his and the officials were in his hand; how this might work out will be seen when we come to Antiochus Epiphanes. It had one advantage; the king—commander-in-chief, head of every service, the fount of law—stood high above the clash of nationalities or creeds; he could hold the balance level, for he had the power, and in particular he could if he chose hold it level

[1] *Βασίλειον* of Gabiene at Gabae, Strabo XV, 728; of Parthyene at Susia-Tōs, Artemidorus in Steph. *s.v.* *Ὑσία*; of Hyrcania (the Parthian not the Seleucid province) at Tambrax, Polyb. X, 31. These may suffice.

between the Greek and the Asiatic. But it was not precisely of a level balance that the Seleucid kings were thinking.

Such was the theoretical outline of the monarchy; and it was very well understood by the two capable men, Seleucus and his son the first Antiochus, who made of the empire what it was to be. They knew the weakness of their position over against their vast and strange inheritance, and set to work to remedy it in their own way, by filling Asia with Greek settlements. I see no reason to believe that they had any deliberate intention of hellenising Asia; their object was not to spread Greek culture or turn Asiatics into Greeks, but to make of their unwieldy empire a strong state. Certainly they were hard-working, conscientious men who meant to govern as well as they could according to their lights; but their lights were the commonplace Greek lights of Plato and Aristotle—the barbarian was a person who was to be kept in his place and ruled by Greeks, though the Seleucid kings added *well* ruled. Alexander had gone far beyond that, and we shall hear something later about his ideas and their consequences, but to Seleucus a strong state meant the support of his own people: on them the state must be founded. The Seleucids did get the support of their own people; the dynasty was popular, and the abiding loyalty of the Graeco-Macedonian settlers to the person of the reigning Seleucid became notorious (Chap. v).

The Greek settlement of Asia was one of the most amazing works which the ancient world ever saw, for it was not the natural result of an overspill of population, as had been the early Greek colonisation of the shores of the Mediterranean; it was undertaken deliberately, and though there *was* an overspill it was the kings who used and directed it. The Seleucid idea was to give to the framework of their empire substance and strength by filling it out with Greeks; Greeks were to supply its lack of living tissue. Indeed it is conceivable that the early kings dreamt of a day when the empire should no longer be a framework at all but should have become a complex of contiguous and quasi-autonomous city states, the whole under a quasi-divine king who managed policy and saw to security. This is the period we want to know about, the period from 312 to 262 B.C. when Seleucus and his son were settling Asia; and we hardly know anything. Some light has been thrown upon the Middle East in recent years by excavations, but the light has all fallen upon later times, usually the Parthian period; the first half of the third century is still almost a blank, and we have to deduce what happened as best we can.

The basis of the Seleucid settlement was the military colony and not the Greek city, the *polis*.[1] The first two kings did not, as one used to be told, fill Asia with Greek cities directly; it was largely done indirectly. This was what enabled it to be done at all, for only the king could found a *polis*, and there is a limit to the work one man can do, especially under a system where delegation of power is imperfectly understood. Greek tradition remembered that Seleucus was a hard worker;[2] but even the foundation of a single *polis* meant for the king hard work.[3] He had to find land for the city, build the wall, supply food, seed-corn, cattle and tools to give the people a start, remit taxation until the city had found its feet, and decide personally innumerable housing, economic and social questions; give a constitution and get political life started; and settle the city law. As to the last, he probably ordered the adoption of some well-known Greek city code, with any modifications required to suit local circumstances; but doubtless a city colonised for the king by some old Greek city, as it kept the gods of its mother-city,[4] kept its code also. For while the king also had to find settlers, we should undoubtedly see, if we had the complete story, that in this he was greatly helped by the old Greek cities of Ionia. What is known is that Magnesia on the Maeander colonised Antioch towards Pisidia[5] and Antioch in Persis[6] for the Seleucids, that Miletus when under the rule of Ptolemy II colonised for him Ampelone in Arabia,[7] and that the Greek populations of Susa and Uruk-Orchoi must have come from Ephesus, for the city-goddess of Susa, Artemis-Nanaia (p. 29), annexed the bee of Artemis of Ephesus for her own symbol, as did Artemis-Ishtar at Uruk.[8]

The military colony[9] goes back to Alexander. Traditionally he founded 70 'cities'; but comparatively few can be identified, and the

[1] It was the great merit of Tscherikower's book (pp. 121 *sqq.*) to bring this out, though he hardly went far enough. No reliance of course can be placed on the use of the word *polis* in many writers. Isidore (the Parthian survey) is always accurate, and Strabo usually so; I would not care to commit myself further.

[2] Plut. *Mor.* 790 A. Somewhat similar sentiments were attributed, doubtless with truth, to Gonatas (Stob. *Flor.* 7, 20; 49, 20) and Doson (Justin XXVIII, 3, 13).

[3] Ditt.[3] 344 gives the best idea of the work which fell on a king. See also Holleaux, *BCH* XLVIII, 1924, p. 1 on *SEG* II, 663; Rostovtzeff, *CAH* VII pp. 178 *sqq.*; *Sardis* VII, i, no. 2 (1932).

[4] *OGIS* 233 l. 40, κοινοὺς θεούς.

[5] Strabo XII, 577.

[6] *OGIS* 233.

[7] Tarn, *JEA* XV, 1929, p. 21 on Pliny VI, 159.

[8] On the bee see Allotte de la Fuye, *MDP* XXV, 1934, pp. 9 *sq.*

[9] Oertel, *Katoikoi* in PW; Tscherikower *loc. cit.*; Rostovtzeff, *CAH* VII p. 180; and the excellent account in Griffith pp. 147 *sqq.*

number, right or wrong, includes his military colonies; the same is true of many of the 'cities' attributed to Seleucus.[1] The first Antigonus continued Alexander's system, as did the early Seleucids, and it is only rarely that we know under which king any particular colony was founded. The places called Alexandropolis, for example, must be military colonies which claimed to go back to Alexander;[2] Doura and Orrhoë are recorded to have been founded under Antigonus I;[3] but the majority probably belonged to the Seleucid settlement. A military colony was settled either with time-expired troops, sometimes mercenaries, or with men able and willing to serve; normally, though by no means always, it was located at or beside a native village, and was usually, it seems, perhaps always, founded by the provincial governor on the king's order, as some of the names show (p. 11); the king had to provide the land and money required, but he could and did delegate the actual work to a subordinate, whereas a subordinate could not found a *polis*. Each settler received a *cleros*, an allotment of land which carried with it the obligation to serve in the army when called upon; hence the name cleruch, one who had a *cleros*, the regular name in the Hellenistic period for a settler in a military colony.[4] The succession law of Doura[5] shows that the allotments there were at the start grouped

[1] App. *Syr.* 57.

[2] No evidence; but Alexander could not, without reason, have altered his regular name (Alexandria) in just two or three cases.

[3] Doura (Isidore 1) was founded by Nicanor, who was the well-known general of the upper satrapies under Antigonus I (Tarn, *CAH* VI p. 430, and independently Tscherikower p. 88), though most writers still persist in calling him an official of Seleucus, no such Nicanor being known. The same Nicanor (Pliny VI, 117) founded Orrhoë, later Antioch-Edessa called Arabis (*ib.*); this Antioch Arabis is not Nisibis, as Tscherikower thought p. 89, for Pliny had previously given Nisibis (VI, 42), and the Orrhoei (*v.l.* Orroei and see VI, 129) extended to Orrhoë. There is no Greek authority for the name Ὀῤῥόη, but it follows from the Syriac form Ōrhāi, which ultimately came back and on which see A. R. Bellinger and C. B. Welles, *Yale Class. Stud.* V, 1935, p. 96 n. 8.

[4] The Hellenistic use of *cleros* is to be distinguished from the classical use (Lenschau, κλῆροι in PW), in which *cleros* refers to the division of the city land of a new city among the citizens and has nothing to do with military service. This *may* have still obtained in those new Hellenistic cities which were founded directly as *poleis*, if the Emperor Julian's reference to 10,000 κλῆροι at Antioch on the Orontes, cited by Cumont, *JRS* XXIV, 1934, p. 188, be not a piece of archaising.

[5] B. Haussoullier, *Rev. hist. du droit français et étranger* 1923 p. 515; P. Koschaker, *Sav. Z.* XLVI, 1926, p. 297 (belongs to the first days of the colony before families were well established); D. Pappulias, Ἀκαδημία Ἀθηνῶν 28 Nov. 1929, given by L. Wenger, *Arch. f. Pap.* X, 1932, p. 131.

together into larger units; it cannot be said whether this system was general or not, but the name given in that law to these larger units, *hekas*,[1] has not occurred elsewhere. The reason for this arrangement is unknown, but it had nothing to do with the one-time system of land-ownership by the *genos* (the clan, or family in the widest sense), for at first the *genos* did not exist at Doura;[2] it might conceivably point to some system of collective farming under a head man. The same law shows that from the beginning the *cleros* could, on failure of the male line, pass to and be held by a woman; doubtless in that case she had to provide a man for the army. This elasticity in the law of inheritance, and the *hekas* (if it existed at other places), differentiated the Seleucid *cleros* in the third century B.C. from the better-known Ptolemaic *cleros*, and may have been one reason, though not the principal one, why the cleruch system was so much more successful in Asia than in Egypt.[3]

The purpose of the military colony was primarily defence; there was a chain of seven across Asia Minor to prevent the Galatians attacking Ionia;[4] those in Bactria-Sogdiana, started by Alexander, were to safe-guard the frontier against the nomads (Chap. III); those in Media were to bridle the hill tribes;[5] but those in normally quiet districts like northern Syria served the double purpose of settling Macedonians and Greeks in Asia and constituting an army reserve. Naturally they were walled. At some places in Asia Minor, and presumably everywhere, the military colony called itself a *koinon*,[6] that useful word which did duty for almost any form of association from a League to a dining club; a village in old Greece might also call itself a *koinon*,[7] and by analogy a military colony might be referred to as a village.[8] The elected officials therefore of a military colony, like those of any private *koinon*, must have tended to copy city officials so far as might be, and it had some

1 A *hekas* is also mentioned in *Doura Pg.* 1; Fr. Cumont, *Fouilles* pp. 287 *sqq.*

2 This follows from Koschaker *op. cit.* p. 300; see further p. 37.

3 See Griffith pp. 162–3 on the fact and the reason.

4 Names in Tarn, *Hell. Civ.*[2] p. 134.

5 Polyb. X, 27, 3.

6 *BCH* 1887 p. 466 n. 32, [*Οἱ π*]*ερὶ Θυάτειρ*[*α Μ*]*ακέδονες*; *OGIS* 290, [*Οἱ περὶ Νά*]*κρασον Μακέδονες*; *οἱ περὶ* is a usual expression indicating a *koinon*. L. Robert, *Villes d'Asie Mineure* 1935 p. 75, would restore *"Α*]*κρασον* for *Νά*]*κρασον* in *OGIS* 290, but this does not affect it as evidence for a *koinon*. For examples of a *katoikia* being called a *koinon* see Oertel, *Katoikoi* in PW col. 10.

7 *SEG* III, 12.

8 Steph. *s.v. Σύνναδα*: Docimeum a *κώμη*. Many instances in Oertel, *Katoikoi* in PW col. 8.

power of managing its internal affairs. It was a planned foundation and had something which may be called a written charter;[1] perhaps a stereotyped form existed. In the Mediterranean countries the great majority, if not all, of the settlers were no doubt Greeks or Macedonians, but east of the Euphrates this element tended to become thinner. There were cases in which Greeks, if there were any at all, can only have been a small minority, as at Avroman in Kurdistan, where the settlers named in the parchments are all Asiatics;[2] Mysia in the Parthian satrapy[3] and Pterion in Media[4] must have been primarily settled with Anatolian mercenaries, Mysians and Cappadocians of Pteria; Thracian colonies are recorded east of the Tigris,[5] and we shall meet a colony of Pisidian mercenaries in India (p. 250); but probably Greek was always the *official* language, as it still was in the first century B.C. at Avroman.

The aim of every military colony was to become a full *polis*, which in the East meant a city, not necessarily of Greek nationality, but of Greek organisation and civic forms; there was a steady upward growth of the colony into the *polis*, and it was this which before the end of the second century B.C. had filled Asia with 'Greek' cities. It is difficult to define the minimum distinction between a military colony and a *polis*; the real matter was the greater autonomy of the latter. The wall was there in any case. It may I think be taken that, to constitute a place a *polis*, there would have to be, at the least, a Council, an Assembly, a division of the Greek population into tribes with consequent rotation of prytanies[6] and the other phenomena of that division, an elected magistracy, and almost certainly a gymnasium (p. 17). How the change-over from military colony to *polis* took place is not known.[7] There were cases where the king of set purpose enlarged some colony and formally made it a *polis*, but usually the settlement itself must have outgrown the *koinon* form and petitioned for the change: mere permission from the king probably sufficed, but was certainly needed (p. 31).

[1] *Avroman Pg.* I, ἐν τῇ παλαιᾷ συγγραφῇ; see E. H. Minns, *JHS* XXXV, 1915, p. 52; L. Mitteis, *Sav. Z.* XXXVI, 1915, p. 428.

[2] Minns *op. cit.* p. 45.

[3] Ptol. VI, 5, 3.

[4] Steph. *s.v.*

[5] Diod. XIX, 27, 5.

[6] Common in Asia Minor. An identifiable case, from its name (p. 11), of a military colony which became a *polis* with prytanies is Themisonium, Michel 544.

[7] On the very peculiar case of the colony at Magnesia-under-Sipylos, *OGIS* 229, see now Griffith pp. 154 *sq.* In the Roman period a place might be allowed to *call* itself a city as a favour; I know of no evidence that this is Hellenistic.

In Asia Minor there are supposed also to have been some Greek civil colonies;[1] there is not the material for detecting such forms in the East, and their existence there is not very probable. But civil colonies of another people are heard of. Where the Greek went the Phoenician trader followed, as he had followed Alexander to India: two important cities, Seleuceia and Antioch-Merv (p. 15), contained large bodies of 'Syrians', and their presence can be deduced at Susa (p. 29); doubtless there were 'Syrians' in every city important for commerce. But, quite apart from their presence in Greek cities, foundations of their own are recorded. Eddana on the Euphrates, south of Doura, is mentioned as a Phoenician colony;[2] another is given in Arabia;[3] and they founded a Tyre, probably a small one, in India itself.[4] There are names too which imply civil colonies of other Asiatic peoples, doubtless founded as trade settlements; such are Nisibis in Aria,[5] which must have been settled from Antioch-Nisibis in Mesopotamia, and Elymaide (if the record can be trusted) in India,[6] a colony from Elymais. As these two colonies took the native and not the Greek names of their places of origin, it is not likely that they were military colonies, though it is not impossible.

The military colony at first had no name but that of the native village where it was founded, and many kept their native names throughout, even when they became *poleis*, as for example Nacrasa, where this is proved by inscriptions;[7] this was the case with the *poleis* with native names given by Isidore in eastern Iran. But if most of the settlers came from one place they often renamed the colony themselves after their mother-city; the numerous colonies or cities in northern Syria and elsewhere with Greek or Macedonian place-names had all named themselves.[8] Every Greek or Macedonian place-name in Asia implies a

[1] Oertel, *Katoikoi* in PW cols. 7–8. The evidence is from Roman times, but some were presumably Hellenistic.

[2] Steph. *s.v.*

[3] Ptol. VI, 7, 3, *Φοινίκων κώμη*.

[4] Steph. *s.v.* *Τύρος*. Unfortunately no source is given, but it can hardly be a made-up name from Dionysius' *Bassarica*, for it does not occur in Nonnus; and Nonnus has so much to say about Tyre itself that had he found an Indian Tyre in the *Bassarica*, his regular source, he was almost bound to mention it.

[5] Ptol. VI, 17, 7.

[6] Peutinger Table (K. Miller, *Itineraria Romana* 1916 p. 787).

[7] Before becoming a *polis*, *OGIS* 290 (see however p. 8, n. 6); after, *ib.* 268, which is Attalus II, not I, see Griffith p. 151 n. 4.

[8] Tscherikower pp. 123 *sqq.*; to me conclusive. It must have been universal.

military colony at the start, and the same is true of Anatolian names in the East; the name Europus, Seleucus' birthplace, has been thought to be an exception,[1] but there is no reason to suppose that it is, or that Seleucus ever founded *poleis* of that name. East of the Euphrates Greek and Macedonian place-names become more rare; Tanagra[2] and Maitona (Methone)[3] in Persis, Thera, Rhoetea, and possibly Argos in Bactria-Sogdiana (p. 120), Arethusa, Larisa and Chalcis on the Arabian side of the Persian Gulf,[4] the two Cretan names in India (p. 250), are about all which chance has preserved. Other names besides place-names were also possible for a military colony. The names ending in -polis, like Alexandropolis, Dionysopolis, Macedonopolis, are almost certainly names assumed by the settlers themselves, either to claim that they went back to Alexander or to honour their god or themselves; and any place bearing a non-dynastic man's name,[5] like Docimeum, Zenodotium, Menedemium, Themisonium,[6] was once a military colony which had named itself after the official who founded it. But unless there are inscriptions or coins, which one does not get east of the Euphrates, it is difficult to detect a military colony which retained its native name, and there were far more of such settlements in the East than are recorded. The mutations which a name might pass through can be illustrated from Nicanor's two foundations already noticed (p. 7, n. 3). Doura at first had only the native name; Seleucus sent new Greek settlers, who in his honour renamed it Europus;[7] subsequently some Seleucid allowed it to become a *polis*, which kept the name Europus; in Roman times the native name Doura came back, as native names usually did sooner or later. Orrhoë had only the native name till Seleucus sent fresh Macedonian settlers, who renamed it Edessa after

[1] Tscherikower pp. 123 *sqq*.

[2] Ptol. VI, 4, 4.

[3] *Ib*. VI, 4, 6; see Herzfeld, *Klio* VIII, 1908, p. 16; Tarn, *JEA* XV, 1929, p. 11 n. 4.

[4] Pliny VI, 159; see p. 66 n. 2. Not, strictly speaking, east of the Euphrates.

[5] To be distinguished from foundations made by little dynasts, like Lysias and Philomelium in Phrygia; see A. Wilhelm, *Neue Beiträge* I p. 48; Holleaux, *RevEA* 1915 p. 237; L. Robert, *Villes d'Asie Mineure* 1935 p. 156 n. 2.

[6] All are in Tscherikower but Menedemium, which is Ptol. V, 5, 6; for the epigraphic evidence as to Docimeum and Docimus see L. Robert, *Rev. Phil.* LX, 1934, p. 267. It is at best doubtful whether the Themison who founded Themisonium *was* the minister of Antiochus II, as given in all the books, most recently by W. Ruge, *Themisonion* in PW; there is no evidence at all. *Prima facie*, Paus. X, 32, 4 shows that Themisonium existed in 277, but possibly the name is there used proleptically; see A. Wilhelm, *Πρακτικὰ Ἀκαδ. Ἀθηνῶν* VI, 1931, pp. 323–4.

[7] Given plainly in Isidore 1.

their home town; then some Seleucid made it a *polis* and officially named it Antioch on the Kallirhoë; under the Roman empire the name Antioch vanished, and the Syriac Ŏrhâi came back alongside the Roman name Edessa.

It has been mentioned that the Ionian cities settled whole new cities for the Seleucids, and that many military colonies named themselves after their mother-towns. The two processes in combination went further, for the new cities themselves sometimes sent out colonies of the same name; there were foundations upon foundations. A clear case is Artemita on the Arabian side of the Persian Gulf,[1] which must have been settled from the well-known Artemita in the Apolloniatis; another is 'Calliope' in India, which must have had *some* settlers at any rate from 'Calliope' in Parthia (p. 246); Carrhae on the Persian Gulf[2] was presumably settled from Carrhae in Mesopotamia. Unmistakeable, though not Seleucid, is Ouranopolis in Pamphylia;[3] it was a colony from Ouranopolis in Chalcidice, the city founded by Cassander's brother Alexarchus (p. 210), for two people could never have hit upon that extraordinary name independently. One may suppose that these places were military colonies, anyhow at the start; perhaps the Seleucids supervised the process. How far it went cannot be said; but the fact that some new cities themselves were able to send out colonies is obviously important (p. 70).

The recorded nomenclature of the cities has never really been considered, and it is important for the Farther East. Putting aside for a moment the Alexandrias (p. 18) and the foundations of Antiochus IV (p. 186), the only places which were founded directly as *poleis* from the start were *some*, probably the majority, of those which bore the four Seleucid dynastic names—Antioch, Seleuceia, Apamea, Laodicea—and perhaps (we do not know) one or two towns named after some god, like Heracleia or Artemita. By the middle of the second century B.C., however, every place which ultimately bore a Seleucid dynastic name had received that name and become a *polis*. But no city was ever *officially* named Antioch or Seleuceia alone; the confusion would have been impossible, and some geographical designation was always part of the city's official name,[4] so that *e.g.* a Greek of Susa in a formal

[1] Ptol. v, 19, 7. [2] Steph. *s.v.* [3] Ptol. v, 5, 6.

[4] *OGIS* 231, Antioch in Persis; *ib.* 233 l. 100, several cities; Susa, *SEG* VII, 1; Seleuceia on the Tigris, *OGIS* 233 and the coins (McDowell, *Coins from Seleucia* pp. 94 *sqq.*); a number of cities on coins of Antiochus IV, *BMC Sel.* pp. 40–42. Much other evidence.

document would call himself not a Seleuceian but a Seleuceian-on-the-Eulaeus. It was a very clumsy system, and naturally led in popular speech to many cities getting secondary or popular names, which may be comprehensively called nicknames; these were convenient and found their way wholesale into literature, with the result that east of the Euphrates we know the nicknames better than the official names, which have often been ousted altogether. These nicknames[1] were of many types; they might allude to some historical event, as Prophthasia (p. 14) or Zetis (App. 12); to some peculiarity of construction, as Hekatompylos; to virtues and vices, as Charis, Stasis, Apate;[2] to some feature of the population, as the ethnic names (p. 15); to something in the city worship, as Calliope and Soteira;[3] even to material objects, as Kibotos (the ark),[4] Aspis (the shield),[5] Perikephalaia (the necklace),[5] Syrinx (the mine),[6] where the allusion is for us completely lost. As even stranger nicknames occur in India, it is necessary, before reaching that country, to understand what was happening. One must of course distinguish from nicknames those cases in late compilers where they copied from their sources the description of a place as though it were a name; such are Diadochou, 'the city of the Successor';[7] Ionaca polis, 'Greek town';[8] Portus Macedonum, 'the harbour-town of the Macedonians';[9] Asylum Persarum, 'the asylum of the Persians';[10] and even Komopolis, 'a village-city'.[11]

It is worth looking at some of these nicknames in eastern Iran, though some lie outside the course of my main story. How completely they came to dominate literature is shown by a statement of Appian[12] that five new cities—Soteira, Charis, Calliope, Hekatompylos, Achaea—were named after Greek cities. There were no such Greek cities; his *statement* refers to the real names, but what he has *given* is not the real names but the nicknames; the real names of the first four are lost. Achaea and Calliope I shall come to. Hekatompylos, prior to Mithridates I, was the Parthian capital; but the word only occurs in Greek as Homer's stock epithet for Thebes 'of the hundred gates', and means

1 Many of these will be noticed later.
2 Charis, App. *Syr.* 57; Stasis, Steph. *s.v.*; Apate, Pliny VI, 55.
3 Soteira *might* refer to Soter, the title of Antiochus I.
4 The well-known Apamea Kibotos in Phrygia. Not used separately.
5 Steph. *s.v.* Ἀσπίς.
6 Polyb. X, 31; see pp. 15, 20.
7 Steph. *s.v.*
8 Ptol. VI, 4, 2; see p. 418.
9 Pliny VI, 110; see App. 12.
10 Pliny VI, 135.
11 Ptol. VI, 1, 5.
12 App. *Syr.* 57.

that the place had more gates than the stereotyped four of Hellenistic town-planning; its real name is unknown, and 'Hekatompylos' in our late Alexander-historians is only a case of the usual proleptic use of names of a later day. Whether the city stood at Damghan or Shahrud need not be discussed here; only excavation can decide.

Another very important city whose name is lost is Prophthasia in Seistan (Drangiane or Zarangiane), though in this case the name can be recovered. The old Persian capital of Seistan, known as 'The Zarangians',[1] was on or near the Hamun lake; Alexander founded a city at 'the Zarangians' to be the capital of Seistan[2] when he detached it from Arachosia, but the old name, as was usual, came back again; the place is Zarin of Isidore, Aris of the Peutinger Table[3] whence several roads started, the mediaeval Zarang. Prophthasia, 'Anticipation', was only a nickname, in allusion to Philotas' conspiracy; the official name, Alexandria, has been preserved by the Chinese historian Pan-ku, who called Seistan O-ik-san-li, a word which has been shown to be Alexandria (see p. 347). That Prophthasia did stand on or near the Hamun lake and not at Farah is both certain[4] and important (p. 49).

[1] Arr. III, 25, 8, and all analogy.

[2] Arr. *ib.*

[3] Tomaschek, *Wien SB* CII, 1883, p. 206.

[4] I gave this in *CAH* VI pp. 389–90, but necessarily without explanation. Modern writers locate Prophthasia at Farah, though Droysen long ago proved that this was impossible (*Hellenismus*[2] III, 2, p. 216). Pliny VI, 61, after the bematists, gave the distance from Herat to Prophthasia as 199 Roman miles, say about 185 English miles; Eratosthenes, using the Seleucid survey (p. 55 n. 1), gave 1600 stades, say some 200 English miles (Strabo XI, 514), while others (*ib.*) made it 1500 stades, say 187½ English miles; these figures agree well enough with a site on the Hamun lake, but absolutely exclude Farah, which modern maps make about 140 English miles from Herat. Farah is Isidore's Phra, capital of the Anauoi satrapy; this is from the Parthian survey, but Isidore has added a note that the Anauoi country was once part of the (undivided) satrapy of Aria; Farah therefore (this is the point) was never in Zarangiane-Seistan at all. Farah-Phra is Propasta of the Peutinger Table, a word which has nothing to do with Prophthasia; it may be a Persian term meaning 'seen from afar', Tomaschek, *op. cit.* p. 213. Stephanus, *s.v.* *Φράδα*, says that the old name of Prophthasia was Phrada, which I suppose is Persian (cf. Autophradates), and was presumably the Iranian name of the village where 'the Zarangians', *i.e.* the Persian satrap's palace and fortress, were located; it is not Phra. The later Zarang is said to be represented by the ruins at Nad Ali (Herzfeld, *Sakastan* p. 3); but it does not follow that Nad Ali was the actual site of 'the Zarangians' and Prophthasia (it seems rather far south), for names sometimes moved a considerable distance, and the Hamun lake has altered its size and shape greatly from time to time.

Next, those nicknames which are ethnics. Antioch 'the Syrian' (Merv),[1] and Heracleia 'the Achaean',[2] refer to large elements of those peoples among the settlers, but whether Antioch 'the Arabian'[3] (Edessa in Osrhoene) refers to an Arab element in the population (it was known as 'the half-barbarian')[4] or only to the fact that it stood in Arab country may be doubtful, and the same doubt applies to the important nickname of this class, Seleuceia (on the Tigris) 'the Babylonian',[5] for it had an enormous Babylonian population (p. 61). This nickname has been a curse to scholarship, for it contributed to the process whereby Seleuceia was sometimes called Babylon[6] and Seleuceians more often than not were called Babylonians;[7] indeed a Greek called a 'Babylonian' generally means a Seleuceian, though after Antiochus IV refounded Babylon as a Greek city it is sometimes impossible to say which city is meant.[8]

It was not only later writers who used nicknames by themselves, for Polybius sins in the same way with his 'Calliope'[9] and 'Sirynx'; he says expressly that the latter name is a nickname.[10] It is obviously meant to sound like Syrinx, which means either a covered gallery[11] or a mine used in attacking a town. Antiochus III, coming eastward by the main Ecbatana-Hekatompylos road toward Bactra, as soon as he entered Hyrcania came to a town Tambrax, unfortified and containing a palace (*i.e.* the seat of the Parthian governor of Hyrcania), and close to it,

[1] Pliny VI, 47, Syriam, which may be an adjective or perhaps equally well a substantive: as Heracleia 'the Achaean' (next note) is twice referred to simply as 'Achaea' (Strabo XI, 516; App. *Syr.* 57), so this Antioch could have been called 'Syria', precisely as some English writers have called districts in London 'Alsatia' or 'Bohemia'.

[2] Pliny VI, 48, Heraclea called Achaiis. Strabo XI, 516, by mistake included 'Achaea' in a list of cities named after their founders, which has given much trouble.

[3] Pliny VI, 117, Arabis; see p. 7 n. 3.

[4] Malalas XVII, 418, *ἡ μιξοβάρβαρος*; he implies that the epithet belonged to the Seleucid period.

[5] Pliny VI, 122.

[6] Steph. *s.v.* *Βαβυλών*; Eustathius in *GGM* II p. 390.

[7] Strabo XVI, 743, the people are called Babylonians from the *χώρα, ἀπὸ δὲ τῆς Σελευκείας ἧττον, κἂν ἐκεῖθεν ὦσι.*

[8] Prior to Antiochus IV a Greek called a Babylonian must, it would seem, be a Seleuceian, like Dromon son of Phanodemus at Andros in the third century, *IG* XII, 5, 715.

[9] In Steph. *s.v.* So App. *Syr.* 57.

[10] Polyb. X, 31, 6, *τὴν προσαγορευομένην Σίρυγκα πόλιν.*

[11] Polyb. XV, 30, 6.

οὐ μακράν, a *polis* Sirynx, a very strong place; this account puts out of court the suggested and attractive identification of Sirynx with Sarakhs.[1] Sirynx was indeed strong, for it had three great ditches[2] to keep off siege machines, and Antiochus, to take the place, had to use all the resources of Hellenistic siege-craft, gradually sapping his way in behind his 'tortoises'.[3] Many cities had one ditch outside the wall, but only very great fortresses, like Syracuse, had three;[4] what kind of town was this unknown place in Hyrcania that it should be fortified on such a scale? I shall come back to Sirynx, for it helps to solve one of the problems of the eastern cities.

The statements often found in late writers that some king had given its nickname to this or that city are merely ridiculous, with one possible exception—the name Bucephala given to Alexandria on the Jhelum (p. 245), traditionally founded by Alexander on the spot where Bucephalus died. Alexander certainly had much affection for the famous charger which had carried him across Asia,[5] and it is conceivable that he did mean the city to be Bucephalus' monument and gave the name himself, much as T'ai Tsong, the virtual founder of the T'ang dynasty, was to set up a monument in honour of the six chargers he had ridden in battle.

The towns of the East which ranked as *poleis*, cities with Greek organisation, appear to have fallen into two distinct classes. Those of the first class were, it would seem, really Greek cities, though they may have contained more foreigners than a city in old Greece; the decree

[1] By Herzfeld: *Arch. Mitt. aus Iran* I pp. 109–10; *Sakastan* pp. 38, 62. Sarakhs is far away on the lower Arius and not in the Parthian satrapy of Hyrcania at all; it was the chief town of Sirakene, Ptol. VI, 9, one of those Parthian satrapies which do not come in Isidore because the main road did not pass through them. The old name of Sarakhs may have been Sirax or Sirak, but it is not Isidore's Sirok, which was in Parthyene; the same name in two or more places is common enough, and all these names, like the better-known Sirakene in Armenia, must be due to an invasion and settlement of Siracians (on whom see Rostovtzeff, *CAH* XI p. 94), whether before the Greek period or as part of the Saca invasion of 129 B.C. If the Greek spelling of Syrinx as Sirynx be due to the place having been another Siracian settlement, then their invasion (or infiltration) had taken place long before the Saca invasion of 129; P. Kretschmer, *Sirakes* in PW, makes it part of the great invasion of the seventh century B.C.

[2] Polyb. X, 31, 8.

[3] Shields to cover sappers; see Tarn, *Military Developments* p. 109.

[4] At Syracuse the outer ditch has been partially traced: E. Schramm, *Röm. Mitt.* XL, 1925, p. 3.

[5] Arr. V, 19, 4–6.

of Antioch in Persis,[1] on the Gulf of Bushire, is no more distinguishable from the decree of an old Greek city than are the decrees of the new Greek cities in Asia Minor,[2] and a whole group of cities is known which passed similar decrees,[3] decrees which, having the same object, would follow a common model; they are Seleuceia on the Tigris, Apamea on the Seleia (Silhu) in southern Babylonia, Antioch in Sittakene, Alexandria (Charax) at the mouth of the Tigris, and the three Seleuceias in Elymais—Susa (Seleuceia on the Eulaeus), Seleuceia on the Hedyphon, and Seleuceia on the Erythraean Sea, *i.e.* the Persian Gulf (p. 43). These cities may be taken as representative of those in the East with dynastic names, and all were really Greek; there was a Council and Assembly at Antioch in Persis, and the Council of 300 at Seleuceia on the Tigris is explicitly mentioned,[4] as is the popular Assembly;[5] there was the usual organisation by tribes, as there was at Seleuceia in Pieria,[6] shown by the mention of prytanies at Antioch in Persis[7] and of a deme (with a Macedonian name) at Alexandria-Charax.[8] At Seleuceia in Pieria the magistrates formed a board or college of *archontes*,[9] as was beginning to be the case in old Greek cities; and as the same thing is found at Susa (p. 27), it may be taken to have been the same in all the cities of this class. At Susa there was a gymnasium and a stadium,[10] at Greek Babylon a gymnasium[11] and a theatre,[12] and the same inscriptions show that games were held in both cities: we may suppose therefore that cities of this class in the East usually possessed a theatre, for in Asia Minor a theatre and games were part of the ordinary equipment of a city with a Seleucid dynastic name,[13] and it is certain that they would

[1] *OGIS* 233; on its location Tarn, *JEA* XV, 1929, p. 11 n. 4.

[2] *E.g.* Michel 543, decree of Laodicea on the Lycus.

[3] *OGIS* 233 l. 100, Ὁμοίως δὲ ἔδοξεν (the list follows). The names of Seleuceia on the Hedyphon and Alexandria-Charax are mutilated but are certain from the grouping.

[4] Tac. *Ann.* VI, 42; see Streck, *Seleukeia am Tigris* in PW, and on the coins struck at Seleuceia with the legend Βουλῆς McDowell, *Coins from Seleucia* pp. 104, 224–6.

[5] Sua populo vis (Tac. *Ann.* VI, 42) can only mean this.

[6] *SEG* VII, 62; see Holleaux, *BCH* LVII, 1933, p. 61.

[7] *OGIS* 233 ll. 10, 87.

[8] Pliny VI, 138, pagum Pellaeum.

[9] *SEG* VII, 62; see Holleaux *op. cit.* p. 22.

[10] *SEG* VII, 3.

[11] Haussoullier, *Klio* IX, 1909, p. 352 no. 1.

[12] R. Koldewey, *Das wieder erstehende Babylon*[4] 1925 pp. 293–9, with inscription.

[13] Michel 543, Laodicea on the Lycus; *I. Magnesia* 90, Antioch in Caria.

possess a gymnasium, seeing that in Asia Minor even a *polis* with a native name would have a gymnasium.[1] We know the importance attached to the gymnasium by the Greeks in Egypt; we know that Alexander's Greek settlers in the East complained at first that his system was not 'Hellenic life and training';[2] and for a Greek city in the East a gymnasium, the centre of both physical and intellectual training for the common man who did not specialise in the higher learning, must have been all-important.

All these Greek cities must have contained many non-Greeks within the wall, even if the local natives largely lived in suburbs outside the wall, and the question is how the non-Greeks within the wall were organised. I have supposed elsewhere,[3] on the analogy of Alexandria in Egypt, that they were organised according to nationalities in quasi-autonomous bodies or corporations called *politeumata* or *catoeciae* (*κατοικίαι*), the latter perhaps the more usual name in the Seleucid sphere,[4] though the name *politeuma* was not confined to the Ptolemaic sphere, as there was one of Syrians at Seleuceia.[5] If this be correct, the system goes back to Alexander; indeed it may be doubted whether his Alexandrias in Asia, at the start, were properly speaking *poleis* at all and not rather a collection of *politeumata*, the Greek one being merely the most important; it has been seen that his system was strange to his Greek settlers (p. 18 n. 2). In any case, however, the Alexandrias became *poleis* under the Seleucids.[6] One may take it that, in any city where there were enough Greeks, they were the citizen body who really constituted the city, provided the magistrates, and were known by the city name, Alexandrians or Seleuceians or what it might be; certainly that was so at Seleuceia on the Tigris and also at Susa, where the inscriptions, which go down to A.D. 21, represent it as a Greek city with the usual forms, though it is known to have had many other inhabitants.

[1] As Prymnessus in Phrygia, Michel 545; 2nd century B.C.

[2] Diod. XVIII, 7, 1 (from Hieronymus), of the revolted Greeks: *ποθοῦντες τὴν Ἑλληνικὴν ἀγωγὴν καὶ δίαιταν.*

[3] *CAH* VI p. 430; *Hell. Civ.*[2] p. 129; based on *Dikaiomata* (*P. Hal.* 1) and the discussions to which it has given rise.

[4] *OGIS* 238; *Inscr. Hierapolis* no. 212; Strabo XIII, 625; Oertel, *Katoikoi*, and Swoboda, *κώμη*, in PW.

[5] Jos. *Ant.* XVIII, 372 (and cf. 378), *Σύρων οὐκ ὀλίγων τὸ ἐμπολιτευόμενον*, which is the verb of *πολίτευμα*, not of *πόλις* or *πολίτης*. Josephus, where he has no axe to grind, is often well-informed on details of the Greek and Parthian East.

[6] The only direct evidence is *OGIS* 233 l. 114, and *Ἀλεξάνδρεια πόλις* in Isidore 18 (really 19, see p. 471). But it was inevitable.

In contrast with the Greek cities of the first class are the cities of the second class, which only had native names; Isidore gives a number of them, chiefly in eastern Iran, which must all have been evolved from military settlements with the same native names. A *polis* in the West with a native name might be Greek, like Nacrasa and other places in Asia Minor; Nacrasa, when a *polis*, claimed to be Macedonian,[1] but then the original military colony there had seemingly consisted of Macedonians.[2] But east of the Euphrates there were military colonies which were mixed or even non-Greek, and some at least of the *poleis* in the East with native names can have had little that was Greek about them but the civic organisation and the use of Greek as an official language; the latter was taken over from the military colony where, as Avroman shows, Greek was the *official* language even when the settlers were Asiatics. The type of one of these non-Greek cities is probably exhibited by an invaluable inscription of the first century B.C. from a native town in Cappadocia, Anisa,[3] which had become a *polis*; though not evolved from a military colony, and probably the creation of one of the Cappadocian kings, it must have followed the standard model of a non-Greek *polis*. Anisa had a Council, an Assembly which held monthly and yearly meetings, and prytanies, which show that it was organised by tribes; there was the usual college of magistrates, one of whom named the year; decrees were passed in Greek, showing that Greek was the official language; and the city worshipped two gods with Greek names. But its record office was its temple of 'Astarte' (here probably Mā or Anaïtis), and there was so little that was Greek about it that even those of the citizens mentioned in the inscription who had Greek and not Cappadocian names had fathers with Cappadocian names; the custom of giving children Greek names evidently only started when the place was made a *polis*.

The interest of this non-Greek type of *polis* is that, judging by Anisa, it shows that Asiatics were attracted by Greek city-forms and used them on a considerable scale, and that the Greek language was a very powerful *official* instrument. There seems nothing to show that the Seleucids ever created or licensed such a *polis*, though they might sanction towns of old renown, like Tyre or Sardis, turning themselves into *poleis*, naturally with a citizen body which was primarily Asiatic;

[1] *CIG* 3522.
[2] *OGIS* 290, but see p. 8 n. 6.
[3] Michel 546; see Fr. Cumont, *RevEA* XXXIV, 1932, p. 135; *CAH* XI p. 608.

but, speaking generally, one associates the non-Greek type of *polis* with the non-Greek king. Those known in the East are only heard of in the Parthian period (though this may be due to the defects of our tradition); it is thought that some king of Cappadocia gave Anisa her constitution;[1] and Josephus describes the creation by Herod the tetrarch of a *polis*, Tiberias on the sea of Galilee, which had no Greeks in it at all.[2] The excavation of some *polis* of this non-Greek type in the Farther East, should circumstances ever permit, would probably throw much fresh light on the hellenisation (or otherwise) of the Asiatic; a good one to choose might be Isidore's Nië in the Anauoi satrapy, for the Hellenistic city should lie beneath the great mediaeval ruin-field at Neh.[3]

Meanwhile we appear to have some description of a *polis* of this type, containing only a few Greeks, in the already noticed Sirynx of Polybius; one cannot rely on Polybius' use of the word *polis*, but the fortifications of the town show that it cannot well have been anything less. The defeated Parthian army sought refuge in Sirynx, and the natives opened the gates to them; the Greeks, assuming that they favoured Antiochus, were therefore not numerous enough either to prevent this or to open a gate in turn to the king. When the city was about to fall, the Parthian troops massacred all the Greeks and broke out; the Greeks therefore were too few to resist successfully, and they were not in control of the citadel (as they would have been in a Greek *polis*, p. 22), which would have given them a refuge. At the same time, it was the Parthian troops and not the townspeople who massacred the Greeks, and as those troops had fought Antiochus' phalanx face to face they were not Parthians (who only fought on horseback) but mercenaries, condottieri of any race, who had got out of hand. Native towns are known farther west where a small body of Greeks lived among the natives in a Greek quarter;[4] some of these eastern cities, but for their *polis* forms, may have had some analogy to this system, but the Greeks (this is the point) must have lived under the local government of Asiatics. The Seleucids of course had not dug the three ditches at Sirynx, for under their rule the only possible enemies were raiders, hill-men or nomads, and it did

[1] Cumont *op. cit.* p. 137.

[2] Jos. *Ant.* XVIII, 37–8; see Rostovtzeff, *Social and Econ. Hist. of the Roman Empire* p. 568 n. 30.

[3] On these ruins see Sir P. Sykes, *Ten thousand miles in Persia* p. 14.

[4] *P. Cairo Zen.* I, 59034 (an unknown Syrian coast-town): ἐν τῆι Ἑλληνικῆι (sc. μερίδι). Also at Memphis: *P. Lond.* I, 50, ἐν τῶι Ἑλληνιῶι; see Schubart, *Klio* X, 1910, p. 63 n. 2, and Wilcken, *Grundzüge* I p. 18.

not need three ditches to stop *them*; the ditches were for defence against a siege-train, and Sirynx had been fortified to meet a Seleucid attack by Greek engineers in Parthian service.[1]

We have seen, in the steady evolution of military colonies into *poleis*, that under Seleucid rule the level of Asia, as regarded civic forms, tended to rise; and these non-Greek *poleis* show that the rising level was carrying with it a considerable number of Asiatics. Asia must have been affected by a sort of Greek *atmosphere*; nothing very tangible, perhaps, but an outlook on life which made many Asiatics desire the Greek *polis* form, whether merely because it was the fashion or because they thought it good in itself. To what extent Greek forms of city life may have become modified in the process cannot be said: on all analogy the probability would be that Asia took the form but not the spirit.

In these eastern cities with native names the citizens must largely have been Asiatics, or there would have been no citizens, but the question of Asiatic citizenship in the truly Greek cities of my first class is not easy; indeed the real distinction between the two classes of *poleis* in the East may have been, Was the citizen body primarily Greek or primarily Asiatic? It would be tempting to suppose that the two classes were represented by the expressions *polis* and *polis Hellenis*, 'Greek city', in Isidore, but this is certainly not so, for Isidore's usage shows that both expressions meant to him exactly the same thing;[2] the Parthian survey accurately entered every town with Greek organisation as a *polis*, and why Isidore himself occasionally added 'Greek' is obscure. The Greek cities must have admitted selected Asiatics to citizenship, because even in the third century B.C. old Greek cities were sometimes doing that;[3] but the question is what happened to the generality of the Asiatics within the wall, the *politeumata*. Logically, a *politeuma* should ultimately have received citizenship and become a new

[1] On Parthian adoption of Greek siege technique compare the quarrels for the fortress catapults found at Parthian Doura: *The Excavations of Dura-Europos, second preliminary Report* 1931 p. 73, where they are called arrows for hand-bows. But they are heavy.

[2] The five called πόλις Ἑλληνίς are Ichnae, Nicephorium, Artemita, Chala, Alexandria-Ghazni; among those called πόλις only are Apamea at Zeugma, Apamea in Choarene, Rhaga (Europus) in Rhagiane, and Alexandropolis-Kandahar. How could Chala be 'Greek' and not Rhaga, or Ghazni and not Kandahar?

[3] *E.g.* Aspendus (A. Wilhelm, *Neue Beiträge* IV p. 61; M. Segre, *Aegyptus* XIV, 1934, p. 253) and Sparta (Alexander of Aetolia in *Anth. Pal.* VII, 709).

city tribe; but whether this took place may be doubted. Certainly in a number of cities in the West one *politeuma*, the Jewish, did receive potential rights of citizenship, rights however which could not be transmuted into actual citizenship because that would have entailed worship of the city gods, *i.e.* apostasy;[1] but the way in which Jewish writers speak of their privilege suggests that it was not shared by the *politeumata* of other peoples. There is said to have been a Babylonian tribe at Charakmoba (Kir of Moab) in Syria;[2] but the known coinage of Charakmoba belongs to the reign of Elagabalus,[3] so this may be outside the Hellenistic period, and in any case 'Babylonian' more probably refers to Greeks from Seleuceia. Stratonicea in Caria certainly had some Carian demes, but this was part of a most peculiar and complicated arrangement[4] to which no parallel is known elsewhere and which cannot be used as evidence for other cities. On the other hand, the Syrian *politeuma* at Seleuceia was still a *politeuma* and not a tribe in the first century A.D. (p. 18 n. 5), and this agrees with what happened at Alexandria in Egypt, where the Phrygian *politeuma* was still only a *politeuma* at some period of Roman rule.[5] The conclusion from the Middle East can only be the negative one that the evidence, such as it is, does not prove that the *politeumata* ever became tribes;[6] that implies that if a city was Greek the Greeks meant to keep it Greek, and it agrees with this that in a Greek city the Greeks kept the citadel in their own hands,[7] which gave them a certain control and a refuge if required. It is unfortunate that the long and fruitful excavations at Doura and Susa have thrown no light on this obscure question of Asiatic citizenship in a Greek *polis*; for more definite evidence we must wait till we reach India, though that is not evidence for anything but India itself.

Besides cities definitely founded as *poleis*, and military colonies located at some village, there was a third type of settlement, apparently employed where a large Oriental town was to be hellenised. An

1 A large literature. See Tarn, *Hell. Civ.*[2] pp. 192 *sq.*

2 Steph. *s.v.* Ἀδάρου πόλις. No source given.

3 Sir G. F. Hill, *BMC Arabia etc.* pp. xxx, 27; the coins exhibit the city's Fortune.

4 A description in Tarn, *Hell. Civ.*[2] p. 136, from Strabo and the inscriptions.

5 *OGIS* 658.

6 That at a very much later time Arab clans were called φυλαί in Edessa (A. R. Bellinger and C. B. Welles, *Yale Class. Stud.* v, 1935, p. 133) does not bear on the question.

7 At Susa: *SEG* VII, 13, Polyb. v, 48, 14. At Greek Babylon: *OGIS* 254. Apamea in Syria, Polyb. v, 15, 10, is hardly in point.

inscription shows that about the Christian Era there were Greek cleruchs at Susa,[1] though the town was a Greek *polis*. What must have happened, therefore, was that a Greek military colony had been planted in Susa, with control of the citadel; ultimately the colony grew, or was enlarged by some king, sufficiently for Susa to be turned into a Greek *polis*, but the cleruchies remained, the point being that the cleruchs, though now citizens of a *polis*, would still be liable to be called up for military service.[2] The rule then was, once a cleruch always a cleruch, or better perhaps, once a *cleros* always a *cleros*, the obligation to serve running with the land;[3] and that meant that in every city which had grown out of a military colony—and they were certainly the majority—there was a body of men who had to serve in the army when required. This will partly answer the question whether a Seleucid king could call out the citizens of the new cities. It has sometimes been assumed that he could, but there is no direct evidence either way;[4] it can now be seen that he could at any rate call out *some* men in the *majority* of the cities, the men who represented the original cleruchs and were in possession of their allotments. It throws no light on the general question whether the king could call out the citizens of any new city; it is hard to believe that at cities like Seleuceia or Antioch the capital he could do so without the city's consent.[5] But it will explain both the new cities and the enlarged phalanx of Antiochus IV (pp. 186 *sq.*).

There is no need for my purpose to consider the relation of the Seleucid kings to the old Greek cities of Asia Minor; at the start it was officially a symmachy or alliance, but the amount of freedom the cities enjoyed seems to have varied greatly with circumstances, though occasionally it might be fairly complete.[6] As to the new cities, the

[1] *SEG* VII, 13; see Fr. Cumont, *CR Ac. Inscr.* 1931 p. 242.

[2] On a man being at the same time κάτοικος and πολίτης see Griffith p. 155.

[3] The *cleros* retained the name of its first owner: *Doura Pg.* 1, Cumont, *Fouilles* p. 290.

[4] W. Otto, *Zeit d. 6. Ptolemäers* pp. 42, 43 n. 1, makes the regents Eulaeus and Lenaeus call out the citizens of Alexandria in Egypt. His reasons have not convinced me; but even if correct it is not evidence for Asia.

[5] The natural supposition would be that the new cities had an alliance (συμμαχία) with the king, entitling him to call upon their troops as technically 'allies'; but there is no evidence on the subject (p. 24 n. 1). I cannot believe that, if the king could not call out the citizens of (say) Magnesia without their consent, he could without their consent call out the same men when Magnesia had transferred them to (say) Antioch in Persis, even if consent could not easily be withheld.

[6] The restoration of freedom by Antiochus II to the Ionian cities, *OGIS* 226,

kings when founding them could impose any terms they chose; but their position is obscure, and it is not known if they were technically 'allies',[1] though that supposition would remove one difficulty (p. 23 n. 5). The king could issue rescripts which became part of the city law, and he could express a wish, tantamount to an order, which a city could hardly disobey; but the instances known are small matters—a grant of citizenship to some one or the erection of a statue. The new cities were not of course sovereign states; they could neither have a policy nor interfere in affairs; none is heard of taking a line of its own with the Seleucids as Seleuceia was sometimes to do with the Arsacids, or even playing the part which Smyrna played towards Seleucus II. But neither were they municipalities of the empire, as they were to be of the Roman empire; they were a sort of half-way house. They sent ambassadors to the king,[2] as being states even if subject ones; and it is unlikely that the kings interfered much with their internal autonomy. One is familiar in the Antigonid realm with the royal *epistates* or city governor, who represented, and was directly responsible to, the king in some Greek city. Certainly the *epistates* is met with in the Seleucid realm also; but only three cases are known,[3] none are earlier than Antiochus III, and it cannot just be assumed that they were a regular institution or that they existed under the early Seleucids; we do not know. The Antigonid *epistates* might sometimes control the Assembly,[4] that is, he really did govern the city for the king; but whether this was really the function of the Seleucid *epistates* seems to me very uncertain, for I think there is no evidence for the Assembly being controlled in any of the new cities.

Jos. *Ant.* XII, 125 *sqq.*, must have been complete enough for a time, witness Smyrna under his son Seleucus II, *OGIS* 229; Tarn, *Hell. Civ.*[2] p. 151. There is a good examination of the position of these cities under Antiochus III by E. Bickermann, *Hermes* LXVII, 1932, p. 47; but I have doubts about his whittling down (p. 59) of the original symmachy.

[1] The only evidence seems to be *OGIS* 221 l. 45, which could equally well mean that some were or that none were.

[2] *SEG* VII, 62.

[3] Seleuceia in Pieria, *SEG* VII, 62; Seleuceia on the Tigris, Polyb. V, 48, 12; and Uruk-Orchoi (pp. 25 *sq.*). Those at Jerusalem and Gerizim (U. Kahrstedt, *Syrische Territorien* p. 53 n. 1) seem to have been something else. See generally Holleaux, *BCH* LVII, 1933, pp. 27 *sqq.*

[4] *IG* XI, 4, 1053 (Thessalonica); see generally Tarn, *CAH* VII p. 200. The sign of control is that the city's decrees bear at their head the name of the *epistates* or (if he governed several cities) of his lieutenant in the city in question.

There is in fact another possibility. The inscriptions from Seleuceia in Pieria have suggested that the business of the Seleucid *epistates* was rather to collaborate with the Greek magistrates than to govern the city;[1] and a reason can be seen for this. Every new city contained, beside Greeks, a number, often a large number, of people of other nationalities. In certain respects the Greek magistrates might no doubt act for the entire community; the *agoranomos* would feed Greeks and non-Greeks alike, the *astynomos* would cleanse all the streets without regard to who lived in them; and the non-Greeks were subject to the πολιτικὸς νόμος, the city law.[2] But if it came to trouble, it is hard to see what control the Greek magistrates could have had over the non-Greek *politeumata*, or how they were going to enforce order, save by club-law; and the primary reason for the Seleucid *epistates* may have been to ensure that there was someone in the city who, if occasion arose, stood above all the nationalities (for he represented the king) and had behind him legitimate force. This suggestion might be supported by two things. It was common under Parthian rule for the city governor to be called, not *epistates*, but '*strategos and epistates*',[3] *strategos* meaning here the highest magistrate,[4] not a military general; that is, the Arsacids endowed the chief Greek magistrate with powers which *did* give him authority over the non-Greeks as well, perhaps an example of their Philhellenism. Also, of the three Seleucid *epistatai* known, the one at Uruk, under Seleucus IV, was a Babylonian, Anu-uballit also called Kephalon; he is called in a cuneiform inscription 'city lord of Uruk', which, as generally supposed, can hardly mean

[1] The suggestion is that of Holleaux, *op. cit.* p. 31 (on *SEG* VII, 62). But he is not responsible for my suggested reason which follows in the text. It has recently been maintained (G. Daux, *Delphes* 1936 pp. 219 *sq.*) that part of the business of the Aetolian governor (*epimeletes*) in Delphi, during the period when Aetolia controlled that cosmopolitan city, was to act as arbiter between Delphians and non-Delphians and preserve social peace, which if correct would be a valuable parallel to my view. Cf. the decree for an Attalid governor in Aegina, *OGIS* 329.

[2] *Dikaiomata* (*P. Hal.* 1) shows this for Alexandria in Egypt, and on the analogy of metics in old Greece it must have been universal.

[3] Doura: *SEG* II, 784, 811, 815; VII, 361; for other instances see J. Johnson, *Dura Studies* 1932 §II, and Bellinger and Welles, *Yale Class. Stud.* V, 1935, p. 129. Babylon: *OGIS* 254. Nineveh: *SEG* VII, 37. See generally Holleaux *op. cit.* p. 29; Rostovtzeff and Welles, *Yale Class. Stud.* II p. 54.

[4] W. Schwahn, *Strategos* in PW Supp. Bd. VI, 1935, gives a tremendous list of Greek towns where one or more magistrates were named *strategos*. But for the Seleucids he has not the recent material.

anything but *epistates*.[1] Uruk, under the name Orchoi, ranked as a Greek city;[2] but the Babylonian element was very strong (p. 58) and may have far outnumbered the Greeks. A Seleucid king could not have put the Greek citizen body under the direct rule of a Babylonian; so long as things went well, Kephalon, who doubtless possessed special influence with his own people, must have been meant to co-operate with the Greek magistrates and help to maintain good relations between the two peoples. One need not therefore suppose that the Seleucid *epistates*, where he existed, interfered much with the internal autonomy of the city: the machinery of democracy was in no sense destroyed and remained ready to act, for when Parthian rule replaced that of the Seleucids the cities seem to have had rather more freedom than before (p. 30).

One thing, as regards the new cities, seems tolerably certain. Though in theory the Seleucids were autocrats, they could not afford to ride roughshod over the Greeks, and the popularity of the dynasty shows that they did not do so. The Antigonid, with the Macedonian army behind him, could treat Greek cities as he pleased; the Ptolemy, with his army of mercenaries, was not dependent on the Greeks scattered about Egypt; but the force at the disposal of the Seleucids was largely supplied by the Greeks whom they had settled in Asia, and that put them in quite a different position. Whatever that position might be in political or philosophic theory, in actual fact their power was anything but autocratic; it was limited by the necessity of respecting the rights of the cities and colonies which they themselves had founded.

[1] J. Jordan, *Uruk-Warka* 1928 p. 41; see Holleaux, *op. cit.* p. 30, and Rostovtzeff, *Seleucid Babylonia* p. 6, who suggested that Kephalon might have been chief magistrate, *strategos*, as well as *epistates*; but a Babylonian magistrate in a Greek city would open up such a vista that the idea could not be entertained without express evidence (see p. 27 n. 3). Jordan's date made the inscription fall in the reign of Seleucus IV, but Professor Rostovtzeff tells me that a fresh examination (*Fünfter Bericht* p. 25 n. 1) has shown that the date is really 110 Sel. (201 B.C.), in the reign of Antiochus III.

[2] Greek: a great number of Greek sealings found, Rostovtzeff, *Seleucid Babylonia passim*; a Seleucid wall has been discovered dividing two temple precincts, A. Nöldeke, *Siebenter Vorläufiger Bericht über die Ausgrabungen in Uruk-Warka*, *Berlin Abh.* 1935 no. 4 p. 40; a long Greek dedication (unpublished) of the second century A.D. was found in 1934, J. Bidez, *Mélanges Capart* 1935 p. 69. Many known Greek names are listed by O. Schroeder, *Kontrakte der Seleukidenzeit aus Warka* 1916; and see A. T. Clay, *Babylonian Records in the library of J. Pierpont Morgan* II p. 17. McDowell, *Stamped objects* pp. 172–3, argues that under the Seleucids Orchoi had more autonomy than Seleuceia.

It may be useful to give here what sketch is possible of one of the new Greek cities in the East, Susa, the 'city of lilies', though most of our knowledge belongs to the Parthian period; for it is most probable that two of the Greek centres in the Farther East, Bactra and Pushkalāvatī the capital of Gandhāra, were cities of the same general type as Susa, though they did not start as military colonies. The inscriptions of Susa[1] range from the reign of Antiochus III to A.D. 21; there are none before Antiochus III, nor is the official Greek name Seleuceia on the Eulaeus found earlier, so it looks as if Susa only became a *polis* in that king's reign; the earlier military colony there has already been noticed. Much of our information comes from a letter[2] written in A.D. 21 by the Parthian king Artabanus III to Susa, which quotes at length a decree of the city. It is addressed to 'Antiochus and Phraates, the magistrates and the city', this last a common phrase for the Council and the People together. Antiochus no doubt was the *epistates*, who according to Parthian practice would be a citizen; the Parthian Phraates, as he is named second, was of less importance,[3] and was probably the Parthian official in charge of the great Achaemenid palace,[4] which must have been extra-territorial, so to speak, as the burden of its upkeep could never have been thrown on the Greek *polis* and must have been borne by the king.

The letter shows that there was at Susa a Council and Assembly who passed decrees; that magistrates were proposed by the Council but elected by the People; that no magistrate could be elected till after the usual δοκιμασία or scrutiny of his qualifications; and that the office of

[1] *SEG* VII, 1–34. I draw largely on M. Fr. Cumont's exhaustive studies in *CR Ac. Inscr.* 1930, 1931, 1932, 1933.

[2] *SEG* VII, 1. See Fr. Cumont in *CR Ac. Inscr.* 1932, p. 238; M. Rostovtzeff, *Scientia* LIII, 1933, p. 120; C. B. Welles, *Royal Correspondence in the Hellenistic Period* 1934 no. 75 p. 299; A. Wilhelm, *Wien Anzeiger* 1934 p. 45; A. G. Roos, *Mnemosyne* 1934 p. 106. I have been unable to see Wilhelm's study.

[3] He cannot therefore be satrap of Susiana, as Cumont suggested. C. B. Welles, *Royal Correspondence* p. 303, would see in Antiochus and Phraates the eponymous archons of the city, though in fact they are distinguished from the *archontes*. This raises the same question as Professor Rostovtzeff raised over Kephalon at Uruk, p. 26 n. 1; and it cannot be supposed that a Parthian was a magistrate of a Greek city unless there be direct evidence. The same consideration applies to Rostovtzeff's statement that 'it is evident that Zamaspes was commander of the garrison of Susa', the Greek cleruchs (*CAH* XI p. 117). Zamaspes was a Persian and apparently in Parthian service; one would indeed need clear evidence for this arrangement.

[4] A Seleucid official in charge of the palace is known, *SEG* VII, 4, on which see Cumont, *CR Ac. Inscr.* 1932 pp. 273–4.

City Treasurer could be held a second time only after an interval of three years. One is familiar in Greece, notably in the Achaean and Aetolian Leagues, with offices which could be held again only after an interval; and the interval shows, as the *δοκιμασία* shows, that there was no dearth of suitable citizens at Susa to fill the offices. The stadium, gymnasium and games have already been mentioned (p. 17); and the city set up honorary statues, with metrical dedications on their bases, in the regular Greek form.[1] A prominent citizen, Hestiaeus, is praised in the city's decree for having gone on embassies for the city at his own expense,[2] one of the regular services to the state in old Greek cities in the Hellenistic period for which prominent men received decrees of thanks;[3] and it is interesting to find in the East the added laudation, which has its parallels in honorary decrees in the West, that Hestiaeus had neglected his own affairs for the public good,[4] for it points to a single culture-sphere (of which we shall find other indications) extending from Greece to Susa; all decrees everywhere follow the same forms. An embassy might have been sent by Susa either to another city or to the Parthian king, as the embassy mentioned in the decree of Seleuceia in Pieria was sent to the Seleucid king;[5] it proves that Susa was a state, even if a state subject to Parthia. Though the Parthian king himself dated by the Arsacid Era,[6] Susa still dates by the Seleucid Era,[7] though she also dates by the eponymous magistracy, as was customary in older Greek cities; but she exhibits the unique phenomenon of dating, not by one eponymous magistrate, as was usual, but by two.[8] No Greek city did this; but it was the custom at Rome, where the two consuls were the eponyms, and presumably the custom was introduced at Susa by Antiochus IV as one of his imitations of Rome (p. 186).[9]

1 *SEG* VII, 1, 13.
2 *SEG* VII, 1, l. 5.
3 Instances are *OGIS* 339; Ditt.^{3} 591; *SEG* I, 366; *I. Priene* III, 121.
4 *τὴν ἐπιμέλειαν τῶν ἰδίων ἐν οὐδενὶ θέμενος καὶ τὰ τῆς πόλεως προυργιαίτερα ἡγούμενος*. There are parallels to this in *IG* IV^2, 65 (Epidaurus), *Ath. Mitt.* 1907 p. 261 l. 12 (Pergamum), *OGIS* 339 l. 12 (Sestos), Ditt.^{3} 591 l. 14 (Lampsacus).
5 *SEG* VII, 62 l. 10.
6 It was this letter which proved that the Arsacid Era was a real Era.
7 The date of the receipt of the letter is given in both Eras, that of the erection of Hestiaeus' statue in the Seleucid alone.
8 Petasus and Aristomenes, ll. 9, 12.
9 Two eponymous *strategoi* at Edessa occur in the Syriac contract of sale of A.D. 243, and similar cases of two archons are said to be common in the Roman period; see Bellinger and Welles, *Yale Class. Stud.* V, 1935, pp. 131, 132 n. 47, who compare the Edessa *strategoi* to the Roman *duoviri*.

So far we are in a purely Greek city; but other inscriptions show that foreign peoples shared Susa with the Greeks. One Greek makes a dedication to the Cappadocian goddess Mā,[1] whose presence attests that of Anatolians; the vocative θεέ in Herodorus' ode (p. 39), elsewhere confined to Jewish and Christian texts and to magical texts where it probably shows Jewish influence,[2] reinforces the known fact[3] that there was a Jewish community; a Babylonian woman frees one of her slaves;[4] and a Greek epigram addressed to Apollo by the Syrian title of Mara, 'Lord', and praising a Persian inhabitant of Susa, Zamaspes, for something he had done in Parthian service, shows that the city included Syrians and Persians.[5] But the borrowing from the native Elymaeans was more important. The gods of the Greek settlers had been Apollo and Artemis the Twins;[6] and if Apollo had got himself a Syrian title, he was still at bottom Apollo, who had appeared in person to two Greek women of Susa to deliver them in some trouble.[7] But Artemis had ceased to be anything Greek and was merely a name for the Elamite goddess Nanaia; Nanaia's great temple, called τὰ Ἄζαρα, which had financial autonomy like the great Greek temples,[8] stood at Susa, though possibly outside the wall (App. 7), and Artemis-Nanaia had become the city-goddess of the Greeks, as other mother-goddesses did from Ephesus to Pushkalāvatī under the name of Artemis; on some coins of Elymais of the first century A.D. she does actually appear as the city-goddess,[9] radiate like Artemis-Anahita at Bactra (p. 115); the symbol of the Ephesian Artemis, the bee, was transferred to her (p. 6 n. 8); and the Greeks of Susa manumitted their slaves in her temple (pp. 68 *sq.*).

[1] *SEG* VII, 10.

[2] A. D. Nock, *JEA* XV, 1929, p. 223; *Harvard Theolog. Rev.* XXVII, 1934, p. 100.

[3] *Acts* ii, 9.

[4] *SEG* VII, 26.

[5] *SEG* VII, 12. Another Persian, Goras, is mentioned in *SEG* VII, 13 l. 13, where his son has a Greek name, Ariston. Cumont thought this meant that Goras had married a Greek woman; if so, it would be of importance that the son was named, against the rule, from the mother's side. But it probably only means that Goras had adopted Greek culture; compare the men with Greek names but Cappadocian fathers at Anisa, Michel 546 (p. 19), and the common custom of Asiatics under Roman rule giving their sons Latin names.

[6] *SEG* VII, 17, 183 B.C., Ἀπόλλωνι καὶ Ἀρτέμιδι Δαίτταις; on this word in *OGIS* 244 see Cumont, *CR Ac. Inscr.* 1931 pp. 282–3, and compare Ἀρτέμιδι καὶ Ἀπόλλωνι ἀρχηγοῖς at Doura, *SEG* VII, 352.

[7] *SEG* VII, 11.

[8] Shown by the terms of the manumission documents. See Cumont, *CR Ac. Inscr.* 1932 p. 284.

[9] Sir G. F. Hill, *BMC Arabia* pp. clxxxiii, 253, Pl. XXXIX nos. 14 *sqq.*

Susa, like Seleuceia, may have had more autonomy under the Arsacids than under the Seleucids,[1] and the relations of these cities to the Parthian kings may be noted. At Susa, when the magistrates and the people differed as to the legality of the election of Hestiaeus to a second term of office as city Treasurer, they referred the matter to the arbitration of the Parthian king;[2] and as the *epistates* did not interfere and the king acted as arbitrator and did not use his powers, it looks as though internal autonomy was subject to little restriction. Hestiaeus himself was both a city magistrate and a 'Friend' and 'Bodyguard' of the Parthian king;[3] his Court titles gave him an established position should he go to Ctesiphon or the king come to the palace at Susa. Seleuceia coined the Parthian king's money for him and, besides putting Greek legends upon it, she dated it by the Seleucid Era which *she* used and not by the Arsacid Era which the king used; and she sometimes played a part in politics, it being apparently her practice in Parthian dynastic quarrels for her mercantile aristocracy to support the established line while the people, who sometimes had the co-operation of the Syrian and Jewish communities in the city, sided with the pretender. It is quite impossible, military reasons apart, to suppose that when Mithridates I of Parthia conquered Babylonia he *took* Seleuceia; after conquering the rest of Babylonia he went northward and only appears as lord of Seleuceia a year later;[4] there must have been a treaty, and Seleuceia must have accepted his lordship upon terms. It probably paid the Arsacid well, in the financial sense, to give good treatment to the great mercantile city; and the extraordinary fact has recently come to light that during the latter part of the great reign of Mithridates II Seleuceia was issuing a coinage of her own,[5] which must have been a privilege granted by the king. Susa also may have made terms; the

[1] For Seleuceia see McDowell's argument, *Stamped objects* p. 171.

[2] *SEG* VII, 1; see Welles, *Royal Correspondence* p. 304, following a reading of Rostovtzeff's.

[3] For other Greek citizens with Court titles under the Arsacids see *Doura Pg.* 10 l. 3 (Rostovtzeff and Welles, *Yale Class. Stud.* II p. 54) and *SEG* II, 815 for Doura; *SEG* VII, 3 and perhaps 8 for Susa.

[4] Evidence in Tarn, *CAH* IX p. 580.

[5] McDowell, *Coins from Seleucia* p. 96 type 128; the dates run, with gaps, from 103–2 to 84–3 B.C. If Mr McDowell gives an explanation I have missed it; but looking at what is known of the reign of Mithridates II it cannot, one would suppose, mean that Seleuceia was independent, even though the Fortune of the city carries a Victory on her hand. I would sooner connect the privilege in some way with trade; in 106 the first through caravan from China had reached Parthia.

Greeks continued to hold the citadel. Neither city was 'free': absolute freedom meant armed revolt, as Seleuceia once revolted for seven years;[1] but both seem to have had about as much freedom as was possible under the rule of a king. It is likely, as will be seen, that their position afforded a sort of precedent for that of Greek cities in India when under Saca or Parthian rule.

I must conclude this sketch of the Seleucid settlement with some notice of the land system which lay behind that settlement, though some of it is well known.[2] The greater part of the land in the empire was, *in theory*, the possession of the Seleucid king for the time being; Seleucus must have claimed that Asia, so far as it had been Persian, was 'spear-won territory',[3] precisely as Ptolemy claimed Egypt.[4] The exceptions were the lands of the old Greek cities of Asia Minor which had been there before the Persians, and perhaps the lands of some hill tribes who had never acknowledged Persian rule; but it would seem that the Seleucids claimed to be overlords of the temple states, old as they were. Most of the Seleucid cities and colonies were of necessity founded on King's Land, thus greatly diminishing its extent; but one city, Antioch towards Pisidia, stood on land taken from a too powerful temple state, the vast domain of the god Mēn,[5] and there may have been others. The Seleucids, unlike the Ptolemies, also sold land out and out on condition that it was joined to the territory of some city,[6] which helped further to diminish the area of King's Land. In the case of the allotments (*cleroi*) made to the settlers in a military colony, the succession law of Doura (p. 7), dating from the earliest days of the colony and undoubtedly laid down by the king, shows that the king retained a right of escheat on failure of heirs. He did not therefore entirely part with the ownership of the allotment, but as when he sold land to be joined to city territory he did entirely part with the ownership the city territory must have been in the same position; that is to say, it looks as if one of the distinctions between the *polis* and the military colony was that in the case of the former the king retained no interest in the land, while so long as a place was a military colony he did retain an interest.

[1] Tac. *Ann.* XI, 8–9.

[2] The foundation work was Rostovtzeff's *Geschichte d. römischen Kolonats* 1910, especially pp. 240–68, 305–9. See also E. Kornemann, *Domänen* in PW.

[3] For parts of Asia Minor as δορίκτητα see Polyb. XVIII, 51, 4.

[4] Diod. XVIII, 43, 1 (from Hieronymus): δορίκτητος.

[5] References, Tarn, *Hell. Civ.*[2] p. 309 n. 5.

[6] *OGIS* 221, 225, 335 l. 133.

Much of the land, however, was not in the king's own hand, but was held by great landowners, sometimes probably under grants which long antedated Persian rule, the king being their feudal superior. These men lived in castles or strongholds[1] on their estates, which were cultivated for them by a serf peasantry, and maintained bodies of mounted retainers, who had supplied the cavalry for the Persian armies. It seems that in Asia Minor some of them lost their estates and were sometimes replaced by Greeks;[2] but nothing of the sort is known in the East, nor is it known that any city or settlement was ever founded on their lands. So far, however, as these landowners were Iranians—and taking the Seleucid empire as a whole the majority would be Iranians—it would seem that the Seleucids never won their confidence; this is clear from the very small amount of Iranian cavalry in the Seleucid armies.[3] That cavalry was the best in Asia; if the Seleucids did not use more of it, it can only have been that they dared not. Alexander had seen that one of the great problems was how to include in one polity the Greek city and the Iranian baron, and he had refused to acquiesce in the belief that Hellenism and Iranism were 'perpetual and instinctive enemies'.[4] But the Seleucid kings, for good or ill, had not followed Alexander's lead but had come down heavily on the side of the Greek city and of their own nationals. There will be more to say about this when we come to Bactria, but these few words may serve to indicate the problem which faced the Greeks, men from cities who were not familiar with feudal systems, though these were less strange to their Macedonian rulers.

But toward the peasantry[5] the attitude of the Seleucid kings, to their honour, was rather different. Speaking generally, the peasantry throughout the Persian empire were serfs, tied to the soil, bought and sold with the land, living in their own villages without any corporate organisation, a class which rarely changed though conquerors might come and

[1] Xen. *Anab.* VII, 8, 13; Plut. *Eum.* 8; *OGIS* 225 iv l. 36 (baris) = Welles, *Royal Correspondence* no. 18 l. 2; Jos. *Ant.* XIII, 36.

[2] Plut. *Eum.* 8; *Sardis* VII, i no. 1.

[3] The only formations mentioned are 1000 Median horse of Antiochus III at Magnesia (Livy XXXVII, 40), and the corresponding 1000 *ἱππεῖς Νισαῖοι* of Antiochus IV (Polyb. XXX, 25); but some of the cataphracts of either king might have been Iranian. As to Raphia, Polyb. V, 79 gives no information.

[4] The phrase is that of M. Cumont.

[5] Besides Rostovtzeff's *Kolonat* see E. Kornemann, *Bauernstand*, and H. Swoboda, *κώμη*, in PW.

go; much of the peasantry must have been there long before the Persians, though they probably received an Iranian admixture. The peasants in the Persian homeland of Persis itself may have been free men belonging to the ruling Persian race, just as the Macedonian peasants were free men, for otherwise the Persian foot-archers, the mainstay of their early armies, cannot be accounted for;[1] Babylonia too may have had some system of its own; but the actual cultivation of most of the soil of the empire was done by the serfs, whether for king or landowner or city. Even before Alexander some of the Greek cities of Asia Minor had begun to improve the condition of their serfs: there were places where they were ceasing to be serfs and becoming *catoeci* (κάτοικοι), hereditary settlers.[2] The Seleucids carried on the work. They could not free the serfs in the mass, even had they wished to; for one thing, Greek civilisation itself was based upon and made possible by slavery, and for another the whole land system of Asia would have fallen to pieces. But something really was done. The system of special judges for the peasants on the King's land,[3] though only mentioned in Aeolis under Attalus I, must have been Seleucid. The Seleucid foundations and sales of land turned King's land into city land on a considerable scale, and, once land became city land, the peasant had a fair chance of ceasing to be a serf. But, apart from the cities, the unorganised native village began to approximate to the organised and quasi-autonomous settlement,[4] and the large walled village, with all that it implied, began to appear. Consideration of these walled villages and what they meant may be deferred till we come to Bactria (p. 121), but it may be noted here that the growth of the native village into the settlement shows the same features as the growth of the military colony into the *polis*; under Greek rule the level of Asia was slowly but steadily tending to rise.

[1] Tarn, *Military Developments* p. 52. The semi-nomad tribes in Persis could hardly furnish *foot-archers*.

[2] *I. Priene* no. 1; cf. *JHS* 1904 p. 21 (Cyzicus).

[3] Athen. xv, 697 c, d.

[4] On the development of the village in Asia Minor see especially Swoboda, κώμη §iii in PW.

CHAPTER II

LITERATURE AND SOCIAL CONTACTS

WHAT kind of people now were these Greeks whom the Seleucid settlement scattered throughout Asia? For the third and much of the second centuries B.C. the answer is simple: just Greeks, with all that that implies. Most certainly they were not, as it was once the fashion to suppose, a people of Eurasians and Levantines. I have said elsewhere what I have to say about Greek 'decadence' in the Hellenistic period;[1] there is small sign of it down to about the middle of the second century B.C., and I trust that, as regards the Farther East, readers of this book will come to the same conclusion. But the later period may need some special consideration, for in the latter part of the second century much of the Greek and Greek-speaking world lost its political independence. In 168 Macedonia fell to Rome. Between 163 and 141 Iran and Babylonia passed out of Seleucid hands into those of the Parthians. In 146 Greece itself became a Roman province, and in 133 Rome took over the Attalid kingdom of western Asia Minor. About 130 the Graeco-Bactrian kingdom fell to the Yueh-chi, and by about 110 or even earlier the Saca invasion of Greek India had begun. We might therefore expect to find some alteration in the first century B.C., and to a certain extent we do. Leaving the Roman provinces aside, there was a change in Egypt in the direction of mixture of blood and of social ideas; but Egypt was not a land of Greek cities and offers no analogy with Asia. There was, we shall see, a change in India; but the circumstances in India which mattered were special to that country and cannot be used as an argument for anything else. What concerns us at present is the Middle East under Parthian rule, and there, so far as can be seen, the loss by the Greeks of their political background had the somewhat unexpected result of instilling fresh vigour into them and leading to a stronger assertion of their Greek-hood, if we may judge by what happened in the sphere of literature and learning; and to talk much about Greek decadence prior at any rate to the Christian Era would, as I see it, give a very false impression.

Greek decadence in Asia has usually been assumed off-hand as an

[1] In *Hellenistic Civilisation*.

inevitable result of intermarriage between the Greek and the Asiatic, and it may be well to look at this question of mixed marriages. When we talk of the unfortunate consequences of mixed marriages as they affect the children we are usually thinking of the mating of the European with some totally different stock, for example the negro. Such a thing did not, and could not, come within the purview of the Greeks of the Middle East: intermarriage between Greeks and the Asiatic peoples there had much more resemblance to intermarriage between members of two European peoples to-day, though the analogy goes a little too far. But, even so, long-continued intermarriage on any scale would have resulted in the absorption by Greeks of non-Greek ideas and outlook. With Greek settlements scattered throughout Asia, there must always have been occasional mixed marriages, marriages of inclination; but that is unimportant when one is considering the race generally, and the question is, how much intermarriage was there? The answer once given was that it must from the first have been, if not universal, at any rate widespread, the evidence adduced being Alexander's settlers and a couple of sentences in two speeches in Livy purported to be made by Roman generals to their troops before action.[1] I need not linger over this, for no one to-day would quote those particular speeches as evidence for anything: they are Livy's own dramatisation of what he thought would be useful arguments to put into the mouths of Roman consuls engaged in screwing up their men's morale; and in fact Livy himself in a more serious speech, that of the Rhodians before the Senate in 190, has recorded a precisely opposite view (p. 37 n. 2). Alexander's settlers in the East certainly married native women;[2] but by 301 their numbers had been greatly reduced by Peithon's massacre (p. 72) and by the long wars of the Successors, and the settlement of Asia as we know it was essentially Seleucid. To-day, I suppose, the

[1] Livy XXXVI, 17, 5 (191 B.C.): Syri et Asiatici Graeci, vilissima genera hominum et servituti nata; XXXVIII, 17, 11 (189 B.C.): Macedones, qui Alexandriam in Aegypto, qui Seleuciam ac Babyloniam, quique alias sparsas per orbem terrarum colonias habent, in Syros, Parthos, Aegyptios degenerarunt. Note 'Parthos'; it took some courage to write that after Crassus and Antony. Servituti nata is merely taken from Aristotle, *Pol.* III, 14, 1285 a l. 21 (cf. I, 2, 1252 b l. 9), Asiatics are slaves by nature; written before Alexander.

[2] V. Chapot (*Mélanges Glotz* I, 1932, p. 179 n. 3) has attributed to me the amazing statement that Alexander sent out (fit expédier) new colonists, especially women. What I did say (*CAH* VI p. 429) was that he 'probably meant to send out further settlers, and above all European women'. Only he died.

evidence adduced would more probably be the inscriptions from Doura,[1] which reveal some mixed families and also, beside the Greek names, a welter of non-Greek names in the city, drawn from half the languages and religions in Asia. That these inscriptions give a picture of a city in decay is true enough; but they belong to the first and second centuries A.D., and the picture they give is of a Parthian rather than of a Greek city. Doura had once, no doubt, been a Greek *polis*. But the Doura we know was not exactly a Greek city under Parthian rule, like Susa or Seleuceia; the Parthians had occupied and rebuilt it[2] as a frontier post towards Rome, and much of Greek civic and family life alike had broken down in the process. It may be doubted whether Doura is much evidence for anything but itself, though it affords certain material which will be noticed later (pp. 37 *sq.*); but with what happened at that late time this book is not really concerned, and for the Hellenistic period we must look for other indications.

One point is that Greeks, with their dominant civilisation and language, could and did absorb a good deal of foreign blood without losing their Greekhood.[3] Cyrene, for example, was a great Greek city—no one will deny the title to the city of Callimachus and Eratosthenes—but all the original Greek settlers had taken Libyan wives, and the Greek women of Cyrene and Barca continued to observe some of the taboos of their Libyan ancestresses.[4] Miletus was a great Greek city, but it was full of Carian blood. No one calls Themistocles a half-breed, or that great organiser Antiochus I, but both had foreign mothers. The saying that nationality depends chiefly on the mother is at best barely a half-truth. What happened at Cyrene must have happened to Alexander's settlers, for where the father is of a higher civilisation than the mother the children are apt to follow his language and civilisation; there is a notorious modern instance and that in an isolated community.[5] In any case the Seleucid settlement, speaking generally, was undoubtedly a settlement of men *and* women. When late in the third century Miletus

[1] *SEG* II, 754–824 (= Cumont, *Fouilles* pp. 355 *sqq.*); VII, 331–800.

[2] Beside the Reports, cf. N. C. Debevoise, *Amer. J. of Semitic Languages* XLVII, 1931, p. 73.

[3] Note how Plato (*Menexenus* 245 D), through the mouth of Socrates, boasts that Athenians are pure Greek and not half-breeds at bottom (μιξοβάρβαροι) like some cities.

[4] See *CAH* IV p. 109.

[5] The children of the mutineers of the Bounty by Tahitian mothers and their descendants all spoke, and became, English.

issued a request to the Greek world for colonists to resettle Myus, the men who came brought their women and children,[1] and the Seleucid settlement must have been of that nature; this is supported by the Susa inscriptions, in which, though late, every woman's name but one is Greek. No doubt a time was to come when many Greek communities in Asia, outside of Rome's sphere, would take in more foreign blood than they could absorb and would ultimately merge in the Asiatic world about them, but that process, though there must have been many local variations, did not begin till after the Christian Era and belongs essentially to a much later period than the Hellenistic.

Another point is that though Greeks had not the faintest objection to any kind of mixed marriage in itself, they had a great deal of pride in their Greekhood, and efforts to keep that Greekhood intact, both in blood and civilisation, can be traced: Polybius[2] bears witness to this generally for the early second century B.C., and Tacitus[3] and Pliny[4] are explicit about Seleuceia as late as the first century A.D. An inscription from Doura of the year 33–2 B.C. has revealed the existence of *genearchs*,[5] heads of the *gene* (the *genos* may be called a clan, or family in the widest sense); they have been compared to sheikhs,[6] but the inscription is too early for that, and in any case they had not always been sheikhs. For the succession law at Doura (see *ante*, pp. 8, 31), which dates from the inception of the colony and is primarily Athenian law, ignores altogether the claim which in Athenian law the *genos* would in certain contingencies have had to the land;[7] there were therefore, it would seem, no *gene* at the start at Doura. They were adopted from the practice of old Greece after the settlement was well under way, and one of the functions of the *genearch* must have been to

[1] *Milet* I, 3, nos. 34–93.

[2] Livy XXXVII, 54, 18 (190 B.C., from Polybius): non, quae in solo [modo] antiquo sunt, Graecae magis urbes sunt quam coloniae earum, illinc quondam profectae in Asiam; nec terra mutata mutavit genus aut mores. Phrygia and Pisidia are explicitly included, *ib.* 54, 11. The speech need not be Polybius' own composition: the matter was important to Rhodes, and the gist of the actual speech of the Rhodian envoys might have been preserved by one of the Rhodian historians whom Polybius used.

[3] Tac. *Ann.* VI, 42, neque in barbarum corrupta, sed conditoris Seleuci retinens.

[4] Pliny VI, 122, libera hodie ac sui iuris Macedonumque moris.

[5] *SEG* II, 818; on the date see Bellinger and Welles, *Yale Class. Stud.* V, 1935, p. 133 n. 50.

[6] Cumont, *Fouilles* pp. xxii, 344.

[7] P. Koschaker, *Sav. Z.* XLVI, 1926, p. 300 n. 5.

maintain the Greekhood of the *genos*, for *genos* and *genearch* cannot have been artificially introduced for any other purpose.[1] For even at Doura toward the end of the first century A.D., amid all the mixture of nationalities and beside the vulgarised Greek of the lower classes, the writing and speech of the upper class, the old Graeco-Macedonians, show (as has recently been said) that after two centuries of Parthian rule they still proudly clung to their nationality and their traditions.[2]

Finally, we have the rare blessing of one quite definite and conclusive piece of evidence on this matter. The well-informed writer, a Greek of Carrhae or Seleuceia, who was Plutarch's main source for the Parthian chapters of his Life of Crassus and who wrote between 50 and 36 B.C. (see p. 51), recorded that the Parthian general Surenas had two half-breeds with him;[3] these men are not only called by a special name, *μιξέλληνες*, 'mixed Greeks', but are definitely ranked with the 'barbarians'; and they make *proskynesis* (obeisance) to Crassus, a Persian habit, not a Greek one. The very rare word *μιξέλληνες* (I have only found three other instances of it) had been used either as an expression of contempt[4] or to denote some half-breed community who were not reckoned as Greeks and who might possess a special name of their own,[5] like the Griquas in Cape Colony, who were not reckoned as Afrikanders; and this means that in Mesopotamia, or in some Mesopotamian cities, as late as 50 B.C., those men of mixed blood who were becoming orientalised were not reckoned as Greeks at all but formed a class apart with a special and contemptuous designation. The importance of this fact for the question in hand needs no discussion,

[1] On this aspect of the *genos* at Doura see F. Chapouthier, *L'influence grecque à Doura-Europos*, *RevEA* XXXIV, 1932, p. 74; and cf. Polybius' reference to the *genos* above (p. 37 n. 2). That *γενεάρχης* was used at a much later time to translate a Persian term (Herzfeld, *Sakastan* p. 54) has no bearing on its original institution.

[2] C. B. Welles, *Sav. Z.* LVI, 1936, p. 101: 'Offenbar haben die Makedonen... noch an ihren stolzen Ursprung und ihren Traditionen treu festgehalten.'

[3] Plut. *Crassus* 31: *πρῶτοι δὲ τῶν βαρβάρων ἀπήντησαν αὐτῷ δύο μιξέλληνες, οἳ καὶ προσεκύνησαν κ.τ.λ.* They *may* have been two of Surenas' interpreters; but the *δίγλωττος* actually mentioned (*ib.* 28) was an ordinary interpreter for *Latin*.

[4] Polyb. I, 67, 7: among the Carthaginian mercenaries were a number of *μιξέλληνες*, mostly deserters and slaves.

[5] Hellanicus, *F.Gr. Hist.* I p. 125 fr. 71 a, a community of *μιξέλληνες* on Lemnos called *Σίντιες*, whom Hellanicus refers to as Thracians; Ditt.[3] 495 l. 110, a separate community in the territory of Olbia. The correlative term, *μιξοβάρβαροι*, is used by Xenophon (*Hell.* II, 1, 15) to describe the half-breeds who formed the population of *Κεδρεῖαι* in Caria.

and there I may leave it: in the Middle East the Greek of the first century B.C. did not essentially differ from the Greek of the third.

The sketch of Susa given in the last chapter purposely omitted what, to my thinking, is the most important thing about that city, the existence of Greek poems; one still recalls the thrill of learning that Greek poetry was being written east of the Tigris near the Christian Era. Four poems are now known. Three are metrical epigrams; one celebrates the already mentioned Epiphaneia of Apollo,[1] while the other two,[2] which are of fair length and praise a certain Zamaspes of Susa, furnish some pretty historical problems; the later of the two is dated, A.D. 1–2. The fourth poem[3] is a lyric ode in an intricate metre addressed to Apollo by his Syrian title Mara, and is now thought to have been written not later than the first century B.C.[4] The poem may be of importance for the history of religion—it has been thought to be an early expression of the later belief that all deities merge in the Sun—but what is material here is that it is an acrostic, the first letter of each line giving the author's name, 'Herodorus son of Artemon a Seleuceian on the Eulaeus'. A number of poems are known in the West which give the author's name in an acrostic in a similar way;[5] in this respect Herodorus' ode is one of a *class*, and that shows once more that a single culture-sphere extended from the Adriatic to the Zagros. In view of the freedom of intercommunication across Asia in the Hellenistic period it would be astonishing had it been otherwise; we may find reason to suppose that in the second century B.C. that culture-sphere extended to Greek India.

Susa brings us naturally to the Greek literature and learning of the

[1] *SEG* VII, 11.

[2] *Ib.* 12, 13 (dated).

[3] *Ib.* 14.

[4] Cumont's revised opinion, in a letter to M. P. Nilsson, *Arch. f. Religionswiss.* XXX, 1933, p. 164 n. 3.

[5] The initial letters of the first 23 lines of the *'Αναγραφὴ τῆς 'Ελλάδος* of Dionysius son of Calliphon (*GGM* I p. 238; Dionysius 115 in PW) give *Διονυσίου τοῦ Καλλιφῶντος*; professedly early third century B.C. There are two acrostics, ll. 109–34 and 513–32, in the *Οἰκουμένης περιήγησις* of Dionysius (*GGM* II p. 103; Dionysius 94 in PW col. 917; Graf, *Akrostichis* in PW, who also mentions some others); Hadrian's time. See further J. U. Powell, *New Chapters in the history of Greek literature*, third series, 1933 p. 202, who cites two good specimens from Kaibel, *Epigrammata Graeca* nos. 979 (late first century B.C.) and 1096. I may add two more: (1) the Hymn of Maximus from Talmis in Ethiopia (*BCH* 1894 p. 150; Kaibel, *Berlin SB* 1890 p. 781; G. Manteuffel, *Eos* XXXI, 1928, p. 181; cf. A. D. Nock, *Harvard Theolog. Rev.* XXVII, 1934, p. 59), where ll. 1–22 give *Μαξίμος Δεκουρίων ἔγραψα*; (2) a Latin Hymn to Apollo from Talmis, Bücheler, *Carm. Lat. Epigr.* 271, cf. Nock *op. cit.* p. 61.

Middle East;[1] science apart, it produced four serious writers of some importance, three of whom will be frequently referred to as sources in this book. The reproach has often been brought against the Seleucid empire that it produced little literature, which in one sense is true: when the Middle East began to produce writing which was worth while it was no longer Seleucid. What happened in Asia Minor and Syria under Seleucid rule happened in the Middle East also: all men of real importance migrated, as did Poseidonius of Apamea in Syria to Rhodes and Diogenes of Seleuceia to Athens, and most of the lesser men followed their example; two Stoics, Apollophanes of Antioch-Nisibis[2] and Apollodorus of Seleuceia,[3] went to Athens to study under Ariston and Diogenes respectively; Agathocles of Seleuceia,[4] called 'the Babylonian', lived at Cyzicus and wrote that city's history; Euphranor of Seleuceia[5] became a pupil and perhaps a successor of Timon the Sceptic. Only two men of any learning are known in the Seleucid period who did not move to some old Greek city: Apollophanes of Seleuceia,[6] body-physician to Antiochus III, and a certain Diogenes of Seleuceia, a sort of Epicurean, probably identical with the voluminous writer of the same name who lived at Tarsus in the second century B.C. and who went from city to city improvising a lecture or a poem on any theme given him;[7] he spent some time at the court of Alexander Balas,

[1] No real study exists. There are brief sketches in V. Chapot, *Les destinées de l'Hellénisme au delà de l'Euphrate*, *Mém. soc. nat. des antiquaires de France* LXIII, 1904, pp. 241 *sqq.*, and in Ed. Meyer, *Blüte und Niedergang des Hellenismus in Asien* 1925 pp. 24 *sqq.*

[2] Susemihl I p. 75; v. Arnim, *Apollophanes* 13 in PW. Stephanus, *s.v.* Ἀντιόχεια no. 3, shows that his Antioch was Nisibis.

[3] Susemihl I p. 84. V. Arnim, *Apollodoros* 66 in PW, doubts his identity with Ἀ. ὁ Ἔφιλλος of Diog. Laert. VII, 39.

[4] Susemihl II p. 383; *FHG* IV p. 288. E. Schwartz, *Agathokles* 24 in PW, puts him before Alexander, which is impossible because (1) 'the Babylonian' means from Seleuceia, (2) fr. 8 treats the Aeneas legend, which makes him Hellenistic, and (3) Athen. XIV, 649 f (fr. 6) discusses a rare word used at Alexandria. If he *was* Zenodotus' pupil he was third century B.C.

[5] Susemihl I pp. 115 n. 541, 116; v. Arnim, *Euphranor* 6 in PW.

[6] Polyb. V, 56, 58; Susemihl I p. 822; Wellmann, *Apollophanes* 15 in PW.

[7] Susemihl's reason (II pp. 258–9) for identifying the two seems conclusive. V. Arnim, *Diogenes* 46 in PW, identifies Diogenes the Epicurean, known from Diogenes Laertius, with the writer of Tarsus, but makes a separate person of Diogenes of Seleuceia (*ib.* no. 47); it was however very common for a man to be attributed to two cities, meaning that he was born in one and worked in and probably became a citizen of the other; see Tarn, *Hell. Civ.*[2] p. 80.

who collected philosophers and apparently found him amusing.[1] There had been much valuable scientific and geographical work done under the first two Seleucids, but of the known names Berossus was a Babylonian priest writing at the request of Antiochus I, and Megasthenes, Patrocles, and Demodamas were Greeks or Macedonians from the West who had no successors. The famous Stoic of the second century B.C., Diogenes of Seleuceia, called 'the Babylonian', became head of the Stoic school at Athens, and his reputation drew to that city many other Greeks from Asia[2]—Antipater and Archedemus from Tarsus, Boethus from Sidon, the before-mentioned Apollodorus from his own city of Seleuceia; among his pupils was Panaetius of Rhodes, who was to surpass his teacher. What is noticeable about this list, so far, is that even our very fragmentary tradition has remembered the names of six men from Seleuceia who were interested in learning in one way or another; the great city was not entirely given over to money-making, and one may recall that its councillors, even at a much later date, were chosen for wisdom as well as for wealth.[3]

One other Greek who is earlier than the Parthian period must be noticed here, the grammarian Herodicus of Babylon;[4] in his case this means Babylon and not Seleuceia (pp. 252 *sq.*). He migrated to Greece, and took part in the controversy between Aristarchus of Samothrace at Alexandria and Crates of Mallus at Pergamum; this dates him to the reign of Ptolemy VI Philometor, and that in turn shows that he must have been one of the settlers of Antiochus IV when that king refounded Babylon as a Greek city; he can hardly therefore be claimed as a Greek of the Middle East, but in his well-known epigram[5] he said that he had two homes, Hellas and Babylon, which is further evidence that the Greek culture-sphere embraced Babylonia. His other writings were perhaps no great matter, but his epigram may have had the honour of being quoted in a poem attributed to Virgil,[6] and it con-

[1] Athen. V, 211 a *sqq.* The actual story of the singing girl may or may not be true, like that of the philosopher Persaeus and the singing girl; they rather suggest a cliché.

[2] Diogenes and his pupils: Susemihl I pp. 82 *sqq.*, II pp. 62 *sqq.*; primarily from Diogenes Laertius.

[3] Tac. *Ann.* VI, 42, opibus aut sapientia delecti.

[4] Susemihl II p. 24, who put him too late; Gudemann, *Herodikos* in PW; Christ-Schmid, *Gr. Literaturgesch.*[6] II, 1, 1920, p. 271.

[5] Athen. V, 222 a.

[6] In *Catalepton* II: Bücheler, *Rh. Mus.* XXXVIII, 1883, p. 507; Christ-Schmid *loc. cit.*; Gudemann *op. cit.* See however Susemihl's argument against this, II p. 25

tains a most recondite allusion which will be of use in a later chapter (p. 253).

So far, save for the Babylonian Berossus, no actual literary production in the Greek Middle East has been met with; and this corresponds to what happened in Syria, where native Greek literature only started with Meleager and Philodemus in the anarchy of the last Seleucids, while its effective period belongs entirely to the time when Syria was a province of the Roman empire.[1] But once the Middle East had become Parthian, a process completed when in 141 B.C. Seleuceia accepted the rule of Mithridates I, things began to change; it must be supposed that the loss of their political background called out in these Greeks a more strenuous assertion of their Greekhood, a matter quite irreconcilable with any belief in their decadence or orientalisation. Migration to the West seems to have ceased; perhaps Syria under the last Seleucids and Greece and Asia Minor under the Roman Republic were not so attractive to literary men as they had been. So far we have had names from two cities only besides Seleuceia, Antioch-Nisibis and Babylon; a number of others now come into the picture—Susa, Artemita, Antioch in Mesene (Charax Spasinu), Seleuceia on the Persian Gulf, very likely Carrhae; and it must be emphasised once more that we only possess chance fragments from a lost tradition. The process began, in the generation that saw the Parthian conquest, when Diogenes' pupil Archedemus returned from Athens to Babylonia—the tradition says to Babylon, but it must mean Diogenes' home city, Seleuceia—and established there a Stoic school 'with succession',[2] that is, a parallel in the East to the schools at Athens and Rhodes (if the latter yet existed) in the West; how long the succession lasted is unknown, but Plutarch's few jejune words conceal what must have been one of the most important events in the history of the Greek East. A generation later a rhetorician, Amphicrates, visited Seleuceia, and the people begged him to stay and set up a school of rhetoric there;[3] the impertinence of the unimportant man's reply, 'A dish will not hold a dolphin', is not bettered by it being a quotation from Euripides,[4] but what is known of Amphicrates' style, the Asianic style at its worst,[5]

[1] See Cumont's brilliant account, *CAH* XI pp. 640 *sqq*.

[2] Plut. *Mor*. 605 B: *εἰς τὴν Πάρθων μεταστὰς ἐν Βαβυλῶνι Στωϊκὴν διαδοχὴν κατέλιπε*.

[3] Plut. *Lucullus* 22; early first century B.C.

[4] Dindorf, *Poetae scenici Graeci*[6] p. 712 fr. 1062 (237). I have not seen it given elsewhere.

[5] Susemihl II p. 373.

may suggest that Seleuceia did not lose much. But though this story presupposes that in the second century B.C. there was no school of rhetoric at Seleuceia, it seems certain, from the correct Greek and good style of Greek scribes down to a late period (and perhaps one should add from the emergence of Greek historians, p. 44), that under Parthian rule proper training in grammar and rhetoric could be obtained in some of the Greek cities.[1]

Production began in the second century with the astronomer Seleucus,[2] of Seleuceia-on-the-Erythraean-Sea,[3] which stood on the north-east shore of the Persian Gulf somewhere between Charax Spasinu at the mouth of the Tigris and Antioch in Persis (p. 17) on the Gulf of Bushire. Strabo calls him a Chaldean,[4] but it is incredible, if so, that Greek tradition did not preserve his Babylonian name, as it did that of every other Babylonian astronomer it knew—Kidenas, Sudines, Naburian. Those Greeks, like Artemidorus of Parium, Epigenes of Byzantium, Apollonius of Myndus, who came from the West to study astronomy and astrology in the Babylonian schools used to call themselves Chaldeans as a sort of title of honour;[5] and this no doubt is what the word means, though it is always possible that the Greeks of Seleuceia on the Persian Gulf were called Chaldeans to distinguish them from those of Seleuceia on the Tigris who were called Babylonians, the designation in either case being territorial; but however that may be, Seleucus was almost certainly a Greek. His precise date cannot be given, but he must at any rate have overlapped the Parthian conquest. He spent his life maintaining, against Hipparchus, the theory of Aristarchus of Samos that the earth went round the sun;[6] but apparently he had not mathematics enough to correct (as Hipparchus could and should have corrected) Aristarchus' mistaken

[1] M. Rostovtzeff, *CAH* XI p. 125; cf. C. B. Welles, *Sav. Z.* LVI, 1936, pp. 100–1.

[2] The classical references are set out in Susemihl I p. 763; for modern literature see J. Bidez, *Les écoles chaldéennes sous Alexandre et les Séleucides*, Mélanges Capart 1935 pp. 81–2.

[3] Fr. Cumont, *Syria* 1927 p. 83 (quite certain). Modern writers have usually called it Seleuceia on the Tigris, as W. Kroll in PW Supp. V still does.

[4] Strabo XVI, 739.

[5] Bidez *op. cit.* p. 76. Bidez lays stress on the astrology; but Vettius Valens (ed. Kroll, 1908), *Anth.* IX, 11, p. 353, names Apollonius as an astronomical source in company with Kidenas, Sudines, and Hipparchus, and the fragments of Epigenes given by P. Schnabel, *Berossos* pp. 109 *sqq.*, are serious enough; it rather looks as if astrology were only a second string.

[6] Plut. *Mor.* 1006 C.

belief that the earth's orbit was a circle instead of an ellipse. He studied the tides of the Persian Gulf, and his theory of *how* the moon made the tides[1] is of great interest, for he seems to have been groping after something which might with luck have led him to the discovery of gravitation, especially as Babylonian astronomers already had some idea of the sun's attraction;[2] but more important for my purpose is the light which he and his work throw upon the nature of this forgotten Greek city on the Persian Gulf.

I come now to the four writers of the Middle East in the Parthian period who are of importance to the modern student, three historians and a geographer. The earliest in time seems to have been the historian Apollodorus of Artemita,[3] a Greek city east of the Tigris where the main road eastward from Seleuceia bifurcated, the more important branch going northward by Ecbatana to Bactria and north-western India, the other going southward by Susa to Seistan and the lower Indus. Apollodorus wrote a history of Parthia in at least four books,[4] which included the story of Greek Bactria down to the nomad conquest and also the Greek conquest of India; how much more it may have included cannot be said, but the story of the Bactrian Greeks seems only to have been incidental to the story of Parthia,[5] just as a history of England must include a good deal of the history of France. He had evidently travelled widely,[6] and he was presumably competent, as he was Strabo's regular source for the Farther East in the second century B.C. after Eratosthenes ended; there is much more of him in Strabo than the named fragments,[7] and his account of the Greek advance to the

[1] Aëtius p. 383, Diels; see Tarn, *Hell. Civ.*^{2} p. 270.

[2] Bidez *op. cit.* p. 78.

[3] Fragments in *FHG* IV pp. 308 *sq.* (not yet in *F. Gr. Hist.*). Münzel, *Apollodoros* 58 in PW; Susemihl II p. 385.

[4] Fr. 7 = Athen. XV, 682c.

[5] This follows from Strabo's phrasing, XV, 686 = fr. 6: *Ἀ. ὁ τὰ Παρθικὰ ποιήσας, μεμνημένος καὶ τῶν τὴν Βακτριανὴν ἀποστησάντων Ἑλλήνων*. This fragment as given in *FHG* is far too long, and should stop at *ὑφ' ἑαυτοῦ ἔχειν*; the rest (as the sense shows) is Strabo, who is here citing Aristobulus (p. 144 n. 3).

[6] Strabo XI, 508, where the writer on Parthia who knew more of countries and peoples than the Alexander-historians *because he had seen more* is obviously Apollodorus. Münzel rightly made him travel.

[7] Two writers have recently, and justly, emphasised the fact that the named fragments of a lost historian are no more than a starting point for reconstruction: H. Strasburger, *Ptolemaios und Alexander* 1934 p. 16: E. Kornemann, *Die Alexandergeschichte des Königs Ptolemaios I von Aegypten* 1935 p. 42.

Ganges and Pātaliputra can now be compared with an early Indian account (App. 4 and Chap. IV). His date must fall between the conquest of Bactria, *c.* 130 B.C. (Chap. VII), and the death of Mithridates II of Parthia in 87 B.C. The latter terminus is certain from this, that the classical writers we now possess know practically nothing of Parthia between Mithridates II, down to whose reign they had the Greek historians of the East, and the completion of the reconsolidation of the empire by Phraates III in 66 B.C., in whose reign contact with Rome was well established, Parthian history thenceforth running regularly in Roman channels. The Parthian king Sinatruces (77–70 B.C.) is indeed just mentioned from the Roman side when he made contact with Rome,[1] but otherwise this period is a blank,[2] merely characterised as one of confused civil wars;[3] only in modern times have the bare names of the forgotten kings who filled it been recovered from cuneiform documents. There is no reasonable doubt that Apollodorus belonged to the flourishing period of the reign of Mithridates II, somewhere round about 100 B.C., the period that saw the Parthian survey of their empire (p. 55), made of course by Greeks; as two of Strabo's named citations from Apollodorus deal with distances,[4] it is conceivable that he himself had something to do with the survey.

The second historian on our list is more important than Apollodorus, and we shall meet him pretty often in this book. It is certain that he is not identical with Apollodorus; the two have different accounts of the nomad conquest of Bactria,[5] and while Apollodorus called a certain nomad people Asii, the substantival form, our historian used the (Iranian) adjectival form Asiani (see pp. 284, 292). Neither his name nor his city is known; his very existence has been forgotten, and I have to refer to him throughout by the clumsy appellation of 'Trogus' source', meaning the source used by Trogus Pompeius for Parthia and the Farther East. But he survived in other works besides Trogus, and there is no doubt that he wrote a comprehensive history of the whole

[1] On the mention of him in Pseudo-Lucian, *Macrobii* 219, see p. 54 n. 4.

[2] G. Rawlinson in 1873 headed the tenth chapter of his *Sixth Great Oriental Monarchy* 'Dark period of Parthian history'. Except for the mere names from the cuneiforms that is still true.

[3] Plut. *Lucullus* 36; cf. Trogus, *Prol.* XLII.

[4] Strabo XI, 519 = fr. 3; XI, 514, omitted in *FHG*.

[5] Sections 2 and 3 of Strabo XI, 511 are Apollodorus beyond question, though he is not named; for there is no alternative.

of the Greek and Parthian East.[1] I have already mentioned in the Introduction the way in which the fragments of our tradition tend to combine into a whole, like the fragments in the early third century B.C. Now this phenomenon in the West was certainly due to the presence behind the broken fragments of our tradition of a great lost historian, Hieronymus of Cardia, and similarly there must once have been in the East, behind our broken fragments, a definite and a comprehensive historian, who can be no one but 'Trogus' source'. For it is, I think, a sound canon of historical method in dealing with ancient history that sources are not to be multiplied beyond necessity; and this is especially true of the Farther East, where one cannot postulate many Greek historians. From 'Trogus' source' then must ultimately come also, but not at first hand, the notices of the Farther East in Plutarch and many scattered items in late Hellenistic writers; and on one point the parallel with the influence of Hieronymus holds close. Hieronymus gave to the world the gazetteer or satrapy-list of Alexander's empire,[2] and it can only have been 'Trogus' source' who gave to the world the satrapy list, of which such valuable fragments remain in Claudius Ptolemy (Chap. VI), of the Indian empire as it existed under either Demetrius or Menander; in the case of each historian there is the same doubt whether he reproduced an official document or whether, as a historian might, he made the list himself.

Certain facts in our historian's life can be ascertained. He had travelled widely; he had seen and admired the first Parthian capital, Dara in Apavarktikene,[3] and he had spent some considerable time in India. The proof of this is a curious one. Chandragupta the Maurya seized the throne of Magadha soon after Alexander's death in 323, and if, as usually supposed, his helper Parvataka was Porus, it must have been before 318, by which year Porus had been killed by Eudamus;[4] about 321, the last year in which Porus is mentioned as alive,[5] is likely enough.[6] But Justin, *i.e.* 'Trogus' source', says that Chandragupta got his kingdom at the time when Seleucus was laying the foundations of his

[1] Justin XLIII, 1, 1: Parthicis orientalibusque ac totius propemodum orbis rebus explicitis. Said of Trogus; but it applies to the source he was following.

[2] Diod. XVIII, 5 and 6; Tarn, *JHS* XLIII, 1923, p. 93.

[3] Justin XLI, 5, 2–4 is obviously from the description of one who had seen it.

[4] Diod. XIX, 14, 8.

[5] *Id.* XVIII, 39, 6.

[6] This is the date taken in *CHI* p. 698.

future greatness;[1] that is the year 312, the year in which Seleucus returned to Babylon, the starting-point of the Seleucid Era.[2] Now one Indian sect, the Jains, had a version of their own about Chandragupta's accession which made the year either 312 or 313 (the tradition varies);[3] 'Trogus' source' therefore knew of the Jain dating, and can only have got it from some Greek in India who read Jain literature, unless, as is quite conceivable, he could read Sanscrit and Prakrit for himself (p. 381). For Plutarch's story about Menander[4] shows that 'Trogus' source' not only understood what a stupa was (p. 135 n. 3) and not only knew the story of Buddha's death as told in the Book of the Great Decease, but also knew that stupas were raised to dead Chakravartins (see on this p. 264); he knew therefore a great deal about India and must have lived there for some time; probably to him too goes back the introduction into Western literature of the name of the Pāndus of the Mahābhārata (App. 19). Indeed it seems to me an open question whether he was a Greek of Parthia who had lived for some time in India, or whether he was not rather a Greek of India who, perhaps late in life, settled in one of the Greek cities of Parthia to write his book.

As regards Parthia,[5] his history ran from the origins to the death of

[1] Justin xv, 4, 20: Sic adquisito regno Sandracottus ea tempestate qua Seleucus futurae magnitudinis fundamenta iaciebat Indiam possidebat cum quo facta pactione Seleucus...in bellum Antigoni descendit. The form of the second mention of Seleucus shows that ea tempestate goes with adquisito regno and not with Indiam possidebat, as taken by Sourindra Nath Ray, *IHQ* XI, 1935, p. 211 and by H. C. Raychaudhuri, *Indian Culture* II, 1936, p. 559, who are using McCrindle's translation, not always a safe guide. But it was a letter from Mr S. N. Ray in 1934 which set me on enquiry.

[2] One cannot take it as 321 (Ray *op. cit.*) or hesitate between the dates (Raychaudhuri *op. cit.*) for two reasons: (1) because in the preceding sentence in Justin Sandracottus gets his kingdom after a war with the Macedonian satraps, and the last one, Peithon of Gandhāra, did not leave India till 316; and (2) because from 316 to 312 Seleucus was a homeless fugitive, a captain in Ptolemy's service who owned nothing but his sword. Incidentally, the passage proves that the Seleucid Era known to 'Trogus' source', *i.e.* that used in Bactria and India, was the Macedonian form which began in autumn 312.

[3] *CHI* p. 698; N. K. Bhattasali, *JRAS* 1932 p. 273, who quotes some Jain works, p. 284. The two datings mean that Chandragupta seized the crown of Magadha *c.* 321 and completed the conquest of his empire by 312; compare the two dates for the accession of Phraates III, Tarn, *CAH* IX p. 587.

[4] Plut. *Mor.* 821 D, E; not at first hand, for he makes Menander king of Bactria. See Chap. VI pp. 249, 264.

[5] From here onward I am compelled to assume that the reader knows what comes later, especially Chapter VIII.

Mithridates II in 87 B.C., for the panegyric on that monarch epitomised by Justin[1] must have come from him and have been the formal conclusion of his book, just as Arrian's panegyric on Alexander is the formal conclusion of his Anabasis; it shows also that he was living in Parthia when he wrote. Further down than 87 B.C. his history cannot have gone, for the reasons given in Apollodorus' case, but equally the panegyric could hardly have been written during Mithridates' lifetime; the date of the completion of his history may then provisionally be supposed to have been shortly after 87 B.C. As regards Bactria, it went down to the end of the nomad conquest, with an account of the nomads:[2] the latest incident mentioned by Trogus is the 'perishing' of the Sacaraucae, of which the date is discussed elsewhere (p. 306),[3] and our historian is not likely to have continued the story of Bactria under Kushan rule. In India, the latest thing mentioned in Trogus' prologues is the *res gestae* of Menander,[4] though the Plutarch passage mentions Menander's death and the distribution of his ashes; but the history may not have stopped there, for though Trogus mentions nothing further, his prologues are too brief to prove a negative. Menander died between 150 and 145 (p. 226), and if the provisional placing of the completion of our historian's book soon after 87 B.C. be correct (and it cannot be *earlier*), then his sojourn in India must have been a good deal later than 145; he was in India at some time during the reigns of the two kings who divided northern India in the last third of the second century (see Chap. VIII), Antialcidas, who ruled everything between the Hindu Kush and the Jhelum from *c.* 130 to *c.* 100 or possibly rather later, and Menander's son Strato I, who ruled the Greek possessions east of the Jhelum from Menander's death to *c.* 100 B.C. or a little later.

There is a passage in Plutarch[5] which bears all this out; the collocation of names, if not the whole passage, must go back to 'Trogus' source', since he is the only possible source for the very peculiar knowledge displayed, and the passage shows that our historian included at least a sketch of the period after Menander's death in his

[1] Justin XLII, 2, 3.

[2] Trogus, *Prol.* XLI, XLII.

[3] Probably it followed upon the Parthian capture of Merv, between 124 and 115 B.C.

[4] Trogus, *Prol.* XLI.

[5] *De Alexandri fortuna aut virtute* 328 F; not at first hand, as is shown by the blunder Σογδιανή for Δραγγιανή (or conceivably Σακαστηνή).

history and that my provisional date for the completion of that history is approximately correct. Plutarch says that, but for Alexander's career, five Greek cities in the Orient would not have existed, namely Alexandria in Egypt, Seleuceia on the Tigris, Prophthasia, Bucephala, and Alexandria of the Caucasus. Prophthasia (*i.e.* Alexandria in Seistan, p. 14) is never mentioned elsewhere subsequently to its foundation, and this is the one hint in Greek literature of its importance. The only way to make sense of this perplexing list is to suppose that the last three names are *in pari materia* with the first two, and that what are being given are the capitals, or chief Greek cities, of different kingdoms at some particular period; and this seems to be true. Alexandria of the Caucasus (*i.e.* Alexandria-Kapisa, see App. 6) was the capital of the western Greek kingdom under Antialcidas when, *ex hypothesi*, 'Trogus' source' was in India; after Antialcidas' death his kingdom was divided (Chap. VIII). Bucephala appears later as (probably) the capital of the eastern Greek kingdom in India (p. 326); either the change from Menander's capital Sāgala was already made by Strato, or else Bucephala is given for the same reason as Seleuceia—the official capital Sāgala was an Indian city and not a foundation of Alexander. Seleuceia is given as being the greatest Greek city in western (Arsacid) Parthia, the actual capital in the first century B.C., Ecbatana, having been an Oriental capital long before Alexander. Finally, Prophthasia was the capital of the Suren's realm of Seistan, eastern Parthia (Chap. VIII), which was later to expand into Indo-Parthia; the Suren cannot well have become a (virtually) independent ruler till Mithridates II died, but the troubles in which that monarch's kingdom broke up had started some years before his death,[1] and we must suppose that 'Trogus' source' contained some allusion to the new kingdom. What are being given, then, are the four civilised kingdoms which at the beginning of the first century B.C. occupied what had once been Greek Asia east of the Euphrates, nomads being omitted; and that this was written soon after 87 B.C. is clinched by the extraordinary fact that the Greek city which was only second to Alexandria in Egypt, the Seleucid capital Antioch on the Orontes, is not mentioned. To one writing soon after 87 the omission of Antioch was only too natural, for it was no longer capital of anything; the surviving fragments of what had been the Seleucid realm in northern Syria were in complete anarchy, and in 83

[1] Tarn, *CAH* IX pp. 586–7.

Tigranes of Armenia was to step in. Everything fits; and there is certainly no other period in history that it *will* fit.

The history we are considering was then completed shortly after 87 B.C.; and the *terminus post quem non* is a simple matter. Ptolemy's (temporary) kingdom of 'Indo-Scythia' must be from 'Trogus' source' (p. 233); it can be dated to about the generation from *c.* 110 to *c.* 80 B.C., and as the Sacas were in Taxila before but only shortly before *c.* 77, the latest date for the beginning of their advance up the Indus from Abiria would be *c.* 80.[1] But that advance was unknown to Ptolemy, *i.e.* to our historian; the *terminus post quem non* for the completion of his history is therefore *c.* 80 B.C. On the other hand, the Parsii had reached Kabul at some time prior to 87 B.C. and Ptolemy's knowledge of their presence in the Paropamisadae (Chap. VIII), which *might* come from our historian, is consistent with the above dating. The limits of the lost history we have been considering are therefore now pretty well blocked out,[2] and the date of its completion is to be put round about 85 B.C.

It is unfortunate for us that our knowledge of this historian depends to a certain extent on Justin's Epitome of Trogus. Certainly Justin on the East is not quite the same thing as Justin on the West, because he ultimately goes back or may go back to a good source and one has to weigh carefully what he says. But he has the same faults; he does not always summarise correctly, he has no interest in history as such and omits whole chapters of Trogus on the Farther East which to us would be invaluable, for Trogus himself gave a comprehensive account;[3] and accuracy to him is of small importance compared with the chance of drawing a moral lesson. Certainly 'Trogus' source' has had hard measure from Fortune. He may not have been a great historian; but he is a great loss.

The third historian of the Middle East is the unknown Greek who was Plutarch's main source in his Life of Crassus for Crassus' Parthian expedition and who has already been cited. He has been called a Greek of Mesopotamia,[4] and certainly the number of names which he gives

[1] See Chapter VI p. 233, Chapter VIII pp. 320 *sqq.*, and Appendix 16.

[2] The general account of the Parthians in Justin XLI, 1 to 3, is partly from 'Trogus' source' and partly Roman material; I need not analyse it here.

[3] Justin XLIII, 1, 1 (see p. 46 n. 1), and the Prologues.

[4] K. Regling, *De belli Parthici Crassiani fontibus* 1899 pp. 8–11, first effectively investigated this writer and called him an Asiatic Greek, but brought in the now discredited Timagenes theory; W. Otto, *Hyrodes* in PW, rightly discarded Timagenes and said a Greek of Mesopotamia.

of citizens of Carrhae, and his knowledge of the advice given by two of them to Publius Crassus in the battle just before his death,[1] point strongly to Carrhae as his city; on the other hand, his dislike of Surenas and his account of Surenas' mock triumph at Seleuceia, which suggests an eye-witness, may point to Seleuceia; one cannot say for certain. His date is fixed within narrow limits: he wrote after the battle of Carrhae in 53 B.C., with which he was clearly contemporary, and before Antony's Parthian expedition of 36 B.C., which he could hardly have avoided mentioning more than once had he known of it. His work, so far, has not been shown to be part of any comprehensive history;[2] it may have been simply a monograph on the Roman invasion of Parthia, just as Demetrius of Byzantium had once written a monograph in thirteen books on the Galatian invasion of Asia Minor. As a historian he must take high rank. He is very well-informed, and gives us a better account of the battle of Carrhae and its preliminaries than we possess of most battles of antiquity; also we know what *both* sides were doing. He is quite impartial, in that he dislikes the Romans and Surenas[3] about equally, but he does not belittle either Surenas' military genius or the dignity of Crassus' end; and there is some interesting psychology, though that might partly be Plutarch. The appearance in a Greek city of the Middle East about 50 B.C. of a man with such a large measure of the historical sense throws a good deal of light on the nature of those communities.

It is however advisable to be sure that Plutarch's source *was* a Greek and not, as has been suggested, king Artavasdes of Armenia,[4] which if true would mean that a king of Armenia in the first century B.C. might possess the historical sense, a thing difficult to believe. The theory has never been examined. Plutarch says that Artavasdes wrote Greek

[1] Plut. *Crassus* 25, Hieronymus and Nicomachus.

[2] I am not going to speculate on the identity of the unknown of Livy IX, 18, 6.

[3] In *CAH* IX p. 611 I said Rome and *Parthia*; I think now it was not Parthia but Surenas. See *Crassus* 21, the silly story of the train of concubines with his army, the whole point being mobility; 24, his effeminacy and foppishness; 30, he tricks Crassus; 32, the shameful mock triumph (note θηλύτητα, answering θηλύτητα in 24); 33, the mutilation of Crassus' body. He does not belittle Surenas' real qualities (21), but adds what he can to his discredit; while in 21 he defends Orodes for taking the Armenian front himself.

[4] Put forward, very briefly, by A. H. L. Heeren, *Vermischte historische Schriften* III, 1821, p. 412. M. Cumont suggested to me that I ought to examine this possibility, which modern writers dismiss offhand.

tragedies and histories;[1] it would be strange, if he himself were using one of those histories, that he did not here say so; but it is not impossible, and in fact most of the story will fit Artavasdes as well as a Greek. The historian's dislike of Surenas fits him better, for he was the brother-in-law of Orodes' son Pacorus and as such would sympathise with the party of the nobility whom Pacorus represented rather than with that of the common man who looked to Surenas;[2] but it is not conclusive, for any Greek might have disliked Surenas, who had taken Seleuceia when Mithridates III stood a siege in it. On the other hand the account of Surenas' mock triumph at Seleuceia seems to be from an eye-witness; but Artavasdes could have got the story from one. Plutarch's statement that the Arsacid kings were the sons of Greek courtesans[3] would of course be conclusive against Pacorus' brother-in-law if it came from the source we are examining; but it is certainly a much later insertion, possibly Plutarch's own, for the earlier Arsacids married their half-sisters or other princesses, and the first king whose mother was a Greek concubine was Vologases I, A.D. 57–77; the statement cannot be *earlier* than his reign.[4]

We want some decisive point, and there appear to be two, both decisive against Artavasdes. One is that our historian, as already noticed, knew of the advice given by two named citizens of Carrhae to Publius Crassus in the battle just before his death; it seems impossible that Artavasdes could have known this. The second comes in the story of the performance of a scene from the Bacchae at Artavasdes' Court,[5] when Crassus' head was brought in and the Agave, Jason of Tralles, took it in his arms instead of Pentheus' mask. This story is the reason why Artavasdes was ever thought of, for he was there and our Greek could not have been; yet it seems decisive against him. Our historian shows that the choragus altered half a line of Euripides to agree better with the new situation.[6] Granted that Artavasdes would have read the

[1] Plut. *Crassus* 33.

[2] On the two parties in Parthia see Tarn, *CAH* x pp. 49, 50, 71.

[3] End of *Crassus* 32; this carries with it the abuse of Surenas just before.

[4] So the mistaken statement in *Crassus* 17 that Seleuceia was always hostile to the Parthians must be later than that city's revolt, A.D. 37–43.

[5] *Crassus* 33.

[6] *Ib.*, substitution in l. 1178 of the direct *τίς ἐφόνευσε* for *τίς ἁ βαλοῦσα πρώτα*, the reading of the single MS (Vaticanus), which was inapposite. The choragus is echoing Agave's last words in l. 1177, (*Κιθαιρὼν*) *κατεφόνευσέ νιν*, perhaps on the spur of the moment; but he might have thought of it beforehand, if Artavasdes really arranged the incident of the head to please Orodes.

Bacchae, a king could hardly be such a professed and close student of the play that he would detect, and record, this trifling and unimportant alteration in the performance of a work in a foreign language. The people who did notice it would be the Greek actors, who knew the text by heart. Among the actors all the limelight falls on Jason, the only one mentioned by name, and he must be the source of the whole account; probably it was his best story for years. He was a strolling player; any Greek might have met him or sought him out. But though Artavasdes (not necessarily in person) gave Jason a present of money, would the king of Armenia at the same time have sought personally from a strolling actor another and more minute version of an incident which he himself had just witnessed and perhaps even arranged? I do not think so.

The fourth writer is the geographer Isidore of Charax; that is Charax Spasinu (Charax of Hyspaosines),[1] the Greek city at the mouth of the Tigris which had been successively an Alexandria and an Antioch and which in the first century B.C., as the capital of Characene, was one of the great trading ports of the East, with a motley population of many races and languages, as the names of its kings attest; Isidore himself knew Aramaic.[2] His traditional date is shortly before the Christian Era, and this has recently been confirmed by a fresh examination of the material.[3] He refers to the second attempt of Tiridates to seize the crown of Parthia from Phraates IV in 26–5 B.C.,[4] and he mentions that the Parthians called Arachosia 'White India', which, it has been pointed out, is only sense if Arachosia was at the time part of some Indian kingdom;[5] in fact the statement can only belong to the time of the Azes dynasty (Chap. VIII), from *c.* 30 B.C. to A.D. 19, and as Isidore was a well-known man in 1 B.C. his writings must fall in the last quarter of the first century B.C. There is however an apparent difficulty. Pseudo-Lucian, speaking of the kings of Characene, quotes 'Isidore of Charax the historian'[6] as mentioning either the eleventh or

[1] For Hyspaosines see Tarn, *CAH* IX p. 578; for Charax, Andreas' account in PW.

[2] J. Kennedy, *JRAS* 1912 p. 1015: he translates φαλίγα (by μεσοπορικόν), §1.

[3] Herzfeld, *Sakastan* pp. 5–7, who shows that Pliny knew and used Isidore's *Σταθμοί*. This is independent of his argument p. 8 from the kings of Characene (see p. 54 n. 1).

[4] See Tarn, *Mélanges Glotz* II pp. 832 *sq.*

[5] Herzfeld, *Sakastan* p. 98: 'der Teil des indischen Reichs mit den weissen Bewohnern, der zu Indien gehört.'

[6] Ps.-Lucian, *Macrobii* 218–19.

the tenth[1] king of Characene, Artabazus. No Artabazus is known to the coins; and as the dated coinage of the kings goes down to A.D. 71–2, followed by a gap down to 100–1, Artabazus if historical should come in that gap,[2] which would put Isidore late in the first century A.D. He has recently in fact been so dated;[3] but this seems impossible, quite apart from Pliny's knowledge of him, for in the Stathmoi he knows nothing later than Phraates IV (died 3–2 B.C.), and the expression 'White India' can only belong to the period *c.* 30 B.C.–A.D. 19. Pseudo-Lucian's source on the kings of Characene was a late work on Characene which passed under the name of Charax' greatest citizen—a thing common enough in Hellenistic times—and which ought to be cited as Pseudo-Isidoros;[4] what it does prove is that Isidore's city was Charax Spasinu and not Charax in Media.

Isidore wrote a geographical account of the Parthian empire, which is lost, and the invaluable little work called Παρθικοὶ Σταθμοί, 'Parthian Stations', which has survived; it is a sort of guide to the two great routes across the empire, the one running from Zeugma on the Euphrates by Seleuceia to the Parthian outpost of Merv, the other going south from Merv by Herat to Seistan and thence north-east to Alexandria-Ghazni,[5] 'to which Parthian rule extended'. This had been so under Mithridates II, but was not true for Isidore's own day; the vassal-kingdom of the Surens in Seistan created by Mithridates II had become practically independent on that king's death in 87 B.C., and Alexandria-Ghazni—perhaps all Arachosia—was in the hands of the Spalirises-Azes Saca (Parsii) dynasty (Chap. VIII), whence Isidore's 'White India'. Isidore is, then, reproducing an older document of the reign of Mithridates II, and there can be no doubt what it was, for

[1] On the possibility of two different reckonings see Sir G. F. Hill, *BMC Arabia etc.* pp. cxcvi *sqq.* Herzfeld, *Sakastan* p. 8, makes Artabazus seventh of the dynasty, which cannot be right, from the context; Ps.-Lucian says *Τίραιος ὁ μεθ' Ὑσπαοσίνην τρίτος*, followed by *Ἀρτάβαζος ὁ μετὰ Τίραιον ἕβδομος*; had he meant 7th of the dynasty he must, *in that context*, have reckoned from Hyspaosines and not from Tiraios.

[2] M. Rostovtzeff, *CAH* XI, 1936, p. 126, cf. p. 118; for a different theory of Artabazus see Hill *loc. cit.*

[3] Rostovtzeff *ib.*

[4] Weissbach (*Isidoros* 20 in PW) suggested that there must have been two Isidores. There is no need to suppose that Pseudo-Lucian's references to kings other than those of Characene (Sinatruces, Goaisos) come from the false and not from the true Isidore, *i.e.* from his account of Parthia; on Goaisos see Appendix 12.

[5] Ghazni, not Kandahar; see Appendix 9.

'Stathmoi' was almost a technical term for a book founded on an official survey; he is reproducing part of an official survey of the Parthian empire made in the great period of Mithridates II, say *c.* 110–100 B.C., after Parthia had acquired Merv (by 115 B.C., p. 281), no doubt in imitation or correction of the Seleucid survey.[1] He has added some instructive notes of his own; but it is the official survey which accounts for his peculiar precision in the use of technical terms—*polis* (city), *kome* (village), *komopolis* (a native town too large for a village but without Greek *polis*-organisation). We shall blunder sadly if we do not distinguish the survey he is commenting on from his own comments made the better part of a century later.

A few words must now be said on the relations between Greeks and Asiatics. Whatever impression the Greeks made, and they made a good deal, on the peoples of Asia Minor and Syria, in the Middle East they faced two civilisations which, in their different ways, were too strong for them to affect, the Iranian and the Babylonian. It has been mentioned how the Seleucids failed to win the confidence of the Iranian landowners; they never in fact secured any real hold upon Iran at all, as is shown by the manner in which it fell away from them almost automatically as soon as the Parthians made it possible; indeed, it is conceivable that it was as a bulwark against Iranism that the Seleucids favoured Babylonia. The Parthians were only a small military aristocracy; but they had the sense to adopt the Mazdean religion of Iran from the start, they spoke a related language, and Iran recognised them as kinsfolk; that sufficed. Realisation of the admitted failure of the Seleucids in Iran itself is necessary for understanding what the Euthydemids accomplished in one part of Iran, Bactria, and how it came about that while the Parthians had no difficulty, so far as the Seleucids were

[1] Alexander's bematists, Baeton and Diognetus, wrote *Σταθμοὶ τῆς Ἀλεξάνδρου πορείας* (Athen. x, 442b), founded on their measurements of his march across Asia; these were also the foundation of the book of Amyntas, variously alluded to as *Σταθμοὶ Ἀσίας*, *Σταθμοὶ Περσικοί*, and simply *Σταθμοί* (references Susemihl I p. 54). Eratosthenes used the later Seleucid survey in the form of *Ἀσιατικοὶ Σταθμοί*, Strabo xv, 723; Kiessling, *Hekatompylos* in PW col. 2794, showed that in places this survey differed from the measurements of the bematists, and fragments of it have been identified in the Peutinger Table (Tomaschek, *Wien SB* CII, 1883, p. 145). In *CAH* IX p. 586 n. 3 I suggested that some of the discrepancies in measurements between Eratosthenes-Strabo and Pliny might reflect differences between the Seleucid and Parthian surveys; on Pliny's use of Isidore, *i.e.* the Parthian survey, see now Herzfeld, *Sakastan* pp. 5 *sq.*

concerned, in securing the huge satrapy of Media, they never succeeded in holding one foot of ground in Bactria itself.

Conditions in Babylonia were very different, for Babylonian civilisation was a city civilisation like the Greek and not a country one like the Iranian; and if it is necessary to keep Iran in mind when we come to Bactria, it may be useful to remember Babylonia when we come to the city civilisation of India. The Babylonians had welcomed Alexander; and after the preliminary troubles of the wars of the Successors, in which some Babylonian cities suffered,[1] the country settled down contentedly enough under Greek rule, and there was a religious and literary revival, aided by the policy of the early Seleucids, following Alexander's lead, in restoring native temples.[2] Though Babylonian kings had once claimed dominion over the four quarters of the world there was no political hostility to the Seleucids, like the native revolts against the Ptolemies in Egypt; all that Babylonia now wanted was to lead her own life, to keep her own civilisation and laws, to trade and to study. She was ready to adopt such Greek practices as might be useful to her: she would reckon time by the Seleucid calendar, in a form adapted to her own year (p. 64), because it was a better system for business than reckoning by the regnal years of kings; Babylonians would add a Greek name to their own[3] and learn Greek,[4] even to writing Babylonian in Greek letters,[5] for all these things were useful to merchants in a world where Greek was not only the official language but a widely spread medium of commerce; they would add the rescripts of the Seleucid kings to their own laws,[6] as was proper for subjects to do; they might even write books in Greek, for it gave a wider public.

In fact they went far beyond this; they put at Greek service the material they had accumulated and the discoveries they had made in

[1] See their complaint: J. Oppert, *CR Ac. Inscr.* 1901 p. 822.

[2] See R. Campbell Thompson, *CAH* III p. 246; Tarn, *Hell. Civ.*[2] p. 118. The recovered chronicles are given by Sidney Smith, *Babylonian Historical Texts* 1924. A temple library formed at Uruk: E. F. Weidner, *Studia Orientalia* I (Tallquist Festschrift), 1925, p. 347.

[3] A. T. Clay, *Babylonian Records* IV p. 54 no. 58; P. Koschaker, *Sav. Z.* XLVI, 1926, p. 296; M. San Nicolò, *Beiträge zur Rechtsgeschichte im Bereiche der Keilschriftlichen Rechtsquellen* 1931 p. 58.

[4] Tablets for the use of Babylonians learning Greek: T. G. Pinches, *Proc. Soc. Biblical Archaeology* XXIV, 1902, p. 108 (notes by A. H. Sayce *ib.* p. 120 and F.C. Burkitt *ib.* p. 143); cf. *CAH* III p. 147, IX p. 720.

[5] W. G. Schileico, *Arch. f. Orientforschung* V, 1928, p. 11.

[6] San Nicolò *op. cit.* p. 84, citing a document of 218 B.C.

their own special science, astronomy; some Babylonians translated Babylonian astronomical texts into Greek for Greek use,[1] and it is now well known that Hellenistic astronomy was not purely Greek but essentially Graeco-Babylonian,[2] even if some details are still matter of acute controversy.[3] That astronomy is perhaps the one instance in antiquity of true scientific co-operation between different peoples; and by that, even had there been nothing else, Alexander was justified of his work. It must for a time have looked as if Babylonia was going to be hellenised or at any rate was hellenisable, and as if her future might lie with the West and not with the East; and some Romans from Caesar to Trajan dreamt of pushing forward the frontier from the Euphrates to the Tigris and incorporating Babylonia in the Roman empire.

But this was only on the surface; beneath it the Babylonian kept his civilisation and his religion unaltered and untouched by Greece. That civilisation was too ancient and had set too hard to be modified: for unnumbered centuries Babylonia had been the home of the highest culture in Asia, and Babylon had been to an older world what Rome was to become to a newer one. Babylonian law was the one law in Western Asia which was untouched by Greek law,[4] and that law still governed her commercial transactions; no Greek word so far has been found in the mass of Babylonian commercial documents of the Hellenistic period,[5] though the Greek system of registration of documents[6] was imposed upon or adopted by Babylonians.[7] The cuneiforms lasted till 7 B.C. in spite of Greek and Aramaic writing;[8] there is even a case in

[1] Fr. Cumont, *Astrology and Religion among the Greeks and Romans* p. 11, and further references in Gundel (next note), especially p. 101.

[2] Modern literature down to 1933 in W. Gundel's Bericht on *Astronomie, Astralreligion, Astralmythologie und Astrologie* 1907–33 in Bursian-Münscher, *Jahresberichte* vol. 242, 1934, ii, pp. 1–153; add Bidez *op. cit.* (*Mélanges Capart*) pp. 71 *sqq.* and a good summary in Professor D'Arcy Thompson's Presidential Address to the Classical Association of Scotland, 2 Nov. 1935 (*Proceedings* of the Association, 1936, p. 38).

[3] The main dispute has been as to whether Hipparchus did discover the precession of the equinoxes or whether he took the discovery from the Babylonian Kidinnu (Kidenas), *c.* 300 B.C. I need not go into this; see P. Schnabel, *Berossos* pp. 237–9, and the literature in Gundel *op. cit.* pp. 25, 26, 98–9, 101; for later references see last note. On balance, opinion now verges toward the claim of Kidinnu.

[4] San Nicolò *op. cit.* p. 57, cf. p. 253, and *Sav. Z.* XLVIII, 1928, p. 247; Koschaker *ib.* XLIX, 1929, pp. 195 *sq.*

[5] San Nicolò *op. cit.* (*Beiträge*) p. 24.

[6] Rostovtzeff, *Seleucid Babylonia* pp. 57–74.

[7] San Nicolò *op. cit.* p. 147.

[8] P. Schnabel, *Z. f. Assyr.* 1925 p. 66.

the Seleucid period of Aramaic being written in cuneiform.[1] Documents from Uruk have shown that the ritual of the old gods continued unmodified in all its complexity.[2] Even in astronomy itself, though the Babylonian gladly gave to Greece, it is not actually known (on the assumption that Seleucus the astronomer was a Greek) that he took anything from her. It was not Greece that affected Babylonia but Babylonia that affected the Greeks, perhaps the only Asiatic civilisation which did, if religion be put aside. The total effect was not great, save for astrology; but the unique phenomenon is interesting, and merits a few words.

That the Greeks of Seleuceia, though they kept the megaron type of house, built it to face north like a Babylonian house instead of south like a Greek one[3] would probably have happened anyhow in that climate, but that they should bury their dead in the walls or under the floors of their houses was simply a copy of Babylonian practice;[4] it is believed that Babylonians did this because the arable land was too valuable to be used for cemeteries, but this could hardly apply to Seleuceia, which must in any case have imported, and could easily import, food for some part of its enormous population. The Greeks adopted the Babylonian system of the double document, with the original sealed up in a clay cylinder for reference if required and the duplicate outside the cylinder for current use,[5] though in Babylonia itself the double document in this form had been extinct for some three centuries;[6] they met it somewhere else, perhaps in Syria, brought it back to Babylonia, and proceeded to spread it in some form or other all over the East. Though Babylonian law was not affected by Greek law, it is a matter of discussion whether Greek law was not affected by Babylonian; a mortgage deed from Doura,[7] which provides for the enslavement of the debtor if in default, has been pronounced to be an example of Graeco-Hellenistic law taking up into itself its Oriental

[1] Cited by R. P. Dougherty, *JAOS* XLVIII, 1928, p. 133.

[2] F. Thureau-Dangin, *Rituels accadiens* 1921.

[3] *Second Preliminary Report upon the excavations at Tel Umar* pp. 29 *sq.* (N.E. Manasseh).

[4] *Ib.* pp. 34, 60 (S. Yeivin).

[5] Rostovtzeff, *Seleucid Babylonia*, Introduction; San Nicolò *op. cit.* pp. 124 *sqq.*

[6] San Nicolò *op. cit.* pp. 127–30.

[7] *Doura Pg.* 10; see Rostovtzeff and Welles in *Yale Class. Stud.* II p. 3, and on the juristic questions arising see especially P. Koschaker, *Abh. Sächs. Akad.* XLII, 1931, no. 1 pp. 2–68.

parallel and moulding it to its own forms of thought.[1] Babylonian gods travelled far, and entered Greek cities like Doura. It has been claimed that the architecture of the temple of Anu at Uruk, built under Antiochus III, shows the influence of Babylonia upon Greece,[2] but it seems to be only the ordinary case of Oriental architecture adopting some Greek forms; however, a Greek at Uruk did imitate Babylonian practice by dedicating a girl-child in a native temple that she might learn a handicraft.[3] It does not appear, however, that any Hellenistic Greek became acquainted with Babylonian history or literature; normally Greeks took little account of the literatures of Asiatic peoples, and Berossus was as unable to interest them in the older history of Babylon as was Manetho in that of Egypt. Callimachus knew of one Babylonian fable, though probably not at first hand;[4] but the earliest trace of any Greek knowledge of the Gilgamesh epic seems to be the use which was made of one or two episodes by the Alexander-Romance, and that belongs to a later time.

But the real effect which Babylon produced upon Greeks, as upon every people with whom it came in contact, was through its astrology. Berossus' book had lived for Greeks not because of its history but because of its astrology and the school of astrology which he set up upon Cos (if indeed that story be true);[5] Greeks who went to study in the Babylonian schools went partly for the sake of astrology (p. 43 and n. 5); a number of horoscopes have been found at Doura,[6] and there was a Greek reading public for astrology in the East, as is shown by the book of the Babylonian Zachalias[7] on the astral affinities of precious stones, and by the book of the 'Babylonian' Teucros,[8] whose great

[1] Koschaker, *Sav. Z.* LI, 1930, p. 429, and more fully *Abh. Sächs. Akad.* XLII p. 62. But another jurist (E. Schönbauer, *Arch. f. Pap.* X p. 210; *Sav. Z.* LII, 1932, pp. 340–2) has argued that it is purely Greek and shows the great cultural strength of Greek Hellenistic law in the East.

[2] J. Jordan, *Uruk-Warka* 1928 pp. 70 *sqq.*

[3] A. T. Clay, *Babylonian Records* II no. 53.

[4] E. Ebeling, *Die babylonische Fabel* 1927.

[5] Vitruv. IX, 6, 2; but see Schnabel's discussion, who doubts it, *Berossos* pp. 10 *sqq.*

[6] *SEG* VII, 363–70.

[7] Pliny XXXVII, 169; Susemihl I p. 867. Possibly there were other writers on this subject (see Susemihl's list under *Steinkunde* I pp. 856 *sqq.*) connected with Babylonia.

[8] Fr. Cumont, *Rev. Arch.* 1903, i p. 437, reviewing Fr. Boll, *Sphaera*, and in *L'Antiquité Classique* IV, 1935, p. 18; W. Gundel, *Teukros* and *Sternbilder* in PW.

influence lasted into the Middle Ages and who in place of the old constellations introduced a host of barbaric astrological figures which for long ruled the skies of Asia. In one sense the astrology which flooded the Greek lands was merely one of the half-worlds that have always attached themselves to science, and some Babylonian astronomers would not touch it;[1] in another sense it was a religious system, with its star-gods and its doctrine of correspondence between heaven and earth. But whatever way men took it, behind it loomed the gigantic and terrible figure of the Babylonian Fate, immutable and inexorable, neither loving nor hating, which ruled the Universe and before which gods and men were alike puppets playing their predetermined parts, a figure which outraged the Greek sense of freedom till the history of Hellenistic religion might almost be summed up as a series of attempts to find a way of escape. It may be worth while, when we come to India, bearing in mind the difference for Greeks between the teaching of Babylon and the teaching of Buddha.

The most important thing in Babylonia was Seleuceia,[2] the greatest of all the Seleucid foundations in the East, so often referred to in this book. Few cities in history have ever dominated the trade of a continent as Seleuceia dominated the trade of Asia in the Hellenistic period. The city had been built to replace ruined Babylon, and as a centre of commerce it more than replaced it; Seleucus displayed Alexander's own insight in his choice of a site for his first name-city. It is now known that the ruins with the great double wall which used to be called Seleuceia are really those of Parthian Ctesiphon, on the east of the Tigris, for the Tigris then flowed farther to the westward than it does to-day, and formed a natural lake; Seleuceia stood not on the river but on the lake, which was her harbour and received shipping coming up the Tigris; though far inland, the city was a deep water port,[3] and

cols. 2423 *sqq.* The date of Teucros is unknown; probably not before the Christian Era. Gundel, following Eisler, thinks he may have come from Babylon near Memphis in Egypt, as his work has Egyptian affinities; if so, he must have been far later than usually supposed, for in Strabo's own day, XVII, 807 (under Augustus or Tiberius), this Babylon was only a fortified post; all other references to it are late, see Sethe, *Babylon* in PW col. 2700. Probably 'Babylonian', as usual, means Seleuceian.

[1] Strabo XVI, 739.

[2] For the older literature, M. Streck, *Seleukeia und Ctesiphon*, and *Seleukeia am Tigris* in PW. The site as now known: O. Reuther, *Antiquity* 1929 p. 434; L. Waterman, *First Preliminary Report upon the excavations at Tel Umar* 1931.

[3] Strabo XVI, 739.

into the lake debouched also the old Royal Canal, Nahr Malik, which gave a waterway to the Euphrates.[1] It has been thought that the harbour was controlled directly by the Seleucid kings and not by the city magistrates.[2] Whether all ocean-going ships could come up, or whether cargo had sometimes to be transhipped at Antioch-Charax at the mouth of the Tigris,[3] is unknown; but the later importance of Charax as one of the great trading ports of the southern seas rather belongs to Roman times, when Seleuceia and Charax were in different kingdoms and Charax had direct trading connection with Palmyra,[4] cutting Seleuceia out. Essentially a Greek city, Seleuceia had an enormous Babylonian population outside the wall and in the contiguous Opis, the old Babylonian town on the Tigris whose place it had taken[5] and which in the usual way was not destroyed but became its 'village';[6] unhappily the excavations at Tel Umar did not go far enough to show whether Seleuceia and Opis were united or were separate entities like Demetrias and Pagasae (p. 98), and we have no knowledge of how the Babylonian population was governed; but the traditional number of inhabitants in the Parthian period, 600,000,[7] is perfectly possible if it refers to Greater Seleuceia with its Babylonian population, including Opis, the suburbs, and the harbour, for Opis too must have flourished, as it was the centre for the local trade.[8]

In Seleuceia, like a nerve centre, met all the great routes across Asia south of the Caspian and of the steppes; the most important, which traversed the whole breadth of Asia from the Ganges to the Aegean and which is well known from Greek and in parts from Chinese and Indian sources, may be noticed here once for all. Starting from the Mauryan capital Pātaliputra (Patna) on the Ganges, it ran across northern India by Mathurā (Muttra) on the Jumna, Sāgala (Sialkot), and Taxila (near Rawal Pindi) to Alexandria-Kapisa under the Hindu Kush, and thence, turning the mountains (p. 139), to Bactra, and so by

[1] Pliny v, 90; vi, 122; and for the Greek name Polyb. v, 51, 6.

[2] McDowell, *Stamped objects* p. 174.

[3] The Shatt-el-Arab did not then exist, and the Tigris and the Euphrates entered the Persian Gulf by separate mouths.

[4] Fr. Cumont, *CAH* xi pp. 631 *sq*.

[5] For the inscriptions with the name Ak-sak (*i.e.* Opis), which settled this, see *First Report on Tel Umar* p. 6. Most scholars (not all) had recognised for some time that Xenophon had misplaced Opis.

[6] Strabo xvi, 739, κώμη.

[7] Pliny vi, 122.

[8] Strabo *ib.*, ἐμπόριον τῶν κύκλῳ τόπων.

Hekatompylos, Ecbatana, and Artemita to Seleuceia; the main route from Seleuceia westward sometimes varied, but normally it crossed the Euphrates and ran up the west bank by Doura to Nicephorium at the mouth of the Belik, where it crossed again and then crossed once more at Zeugma; one branch went southward to Damascus and the Phoenician towns, another to the Seleucid capital, Antioch. From Antioch westward the road was identical with the old Persian Royal Road, across the Taurus and through Asia Minor to the great seaports of Ionia; while in the first century B.C. there came into use a short cut across the Syrian desert from Doura by Palmyra to Damascus and Phoenicia. There also came to Seleuceia a road down the Tigris from Armenia and northern Mesopotamia, and a route from the lower Indus by Kandahar, Seistan, Persepolis, Susa, and Artemita, though this latter was less important than the sea route from India up the Persian Gulf and the Tigris (App. 12). Yet another main route came from south Arabia: the Gerrhaeans[1] brought incense and spices by caravan to Gerrha on the inner Persian Gulf and thence by sea to Seleuceia. Gerrha was never Seleucid, but was Seleuceia's trade partner in Arabia; even Antiochus III, though at one time he thought of incorporating Gerrha in his empire, finally realised the disadvantages of disturbing an arrangement which must have been highly lucrative to both cities.[2] It seems probable that no commercial changes of importance could take place anywhere in Asia without exerting some reflex action upon the great city on the Tigris (see especially p. 261 and n. 3).

If we survey the vastness of the Seleucid experiment as a whole, it is difficult to believe that it can have failed, but fail it ultimately did, except where Rome salved it. Of course, as regards the Middle East, it produced a good deal of effect for a time. Many Asiatics acquired a knowledge of and apparently a liking for Greek civic forms (p. 19), and many must have picked up a certain amount of Greek, the official language of city and settlement alike; that did not mean much, but there are traces of a real knowledge of Greek among the upper class, and some wrote in it, beside the Babylonian writers on astronomy and astrology and apart from the possibility of Jewish writings in Greek in Mesopotamia no less than in Palestine;[3] Artavasdes of Armenia wrote

[1] Tkač, *Gerrha* in PW; Tarn, *JEA* XV, 1929, p. 22. [2] Polyb. XIII, 9, 4–5.

[3] Professor Rostovtzeff has deduced a work written by a Jew of Mesopotamia with special reference to Adiabene, used by Josephus (*CAH* XI p. 126); but this must have been later than the Christian Era.

histories and tragedies in Greek (p. 52), a certain Pharnouches of Antioch-Nisibis wrote a history of Persia,[1] and one Sudines, who may or may not have been the astronomer, wrote what may have been a serious and not an astrological treatise on precious stones, notably those of Carmania.[2] The attempt to write Babylonian in Greek letters was to have a parallel later in the East, for when the Saca language of the Kushans was reduced to writing it was written in Greek letters (p. 305), though in fact this had already been done with Lycian. Greek temples, more or less Greek in architecture, rose in some Graeco-Iranian towns, like the one at Conchobar (Kaṇgivar) in Media; the renascent art of Iran ('Parthian' art) adopted a certain amount of Greek form. What we do *not* find is the 'culture-Greek' as known in Syria and Asia Minor—the Asiatic who not only took a Greek name and spoke Greek but 'went Greek', so to speak, and adopted Greek culture as his own;[3] but this may merely be due to lack of information. It is difficult to believe that in the Greek cities the gymnasia and all that they stood for produced no effect; but that again might largely depend on whether non-Greeks were admitted to the gymnasium and the ephebe training as Italians were at Delos in the first century B.C., and as to that nothing is known.

The Greek city however stood for law as opposed to mere force, and many Asiatics came under, and were affected by, Greek law; there are legal documents from Doura (p. 58 n. 7) and Avroman (p. 9 n. 1) which are Greek though the parties were Asiatics, but Greek law as a whole seems to have produced no such effect upon native law in the Middle East as it did in Syria, where the later Graeco-Syrian law book bears witness to its great cultural strength. But it must just be noticed here, though it is foreign to my subject and is in any case a matter for experts, that the Hellenistic law of Asia has of late years given rise to what is much the most important question connected with the Greek East; much has been written on it by jurists and much more I suppose will be. It is a question which concerns the law of Imperial Rome, the foundation of so much modern law, and it has been briefly stated thus:[4] the final question about Roman law is, which was stronger, the Italian law of Rome itself or the Hellenistic element; and as to the latter, which was stronger, its Greek or its Oriental component.

[1] Steph. *s.v.* Ἀντιόχεια no. 3. [2] Susemihl I p. 862; often cited by Pliny.

[3] Conceivably Goras at Susa (p. 29 n. 5) was one.

[4] L. Wenger, *Arch. f. Pap.* IX, 1930, p. 259.

Two things however seem certain, and one is the enormous success of that great invention the Seleucid calendar, which swept Asia; it was the first attempt on a comprehensive scale to reckon time from an Era, a fixed event (in this case Seleucus' return to Babylon in October 312 B.C.), instead of by the regnal years of kings or by annual magistracies in cities. The Macedonian or Syrian form of the calendar, with the Macedonian months, began 1 Dios (October) 312; Babylonia had a form suited to her own year, with the Babylonian months, which began on her New Year's Day, 1 Nisan (March–April) 311.[1] The Seleucid calendar was adopted in many countries; beside the Seleucid Succession states, like Characene,[2] Elymais,[3] Adiabene,[4] Osrhoene,[5] it was used in Bithynia and Pontus, Armenia, Cappadocia, Judaea, Nabataea, and Palmyra;[6] to some extent it was used in Parthia; its fortunes in India will be noticed later (p. 359). As the Macedonian months were lunar months, any system of lunar months could be fitted to the new calendar; Babylonia, Judaea, and Osrhoene used the Babylonian months, Armenia, Cappadocia, and perhaps other country districts besides Kurdistan,[7] used the Persian. It used to be taken for granted that, where the names of the Macedonian months occur, the Macedonian form of the calendar was in use, but recently it has been strongly argued that the calendar in use at Seleuceia was a mixed form, with the Macedonian months but the Babylonian year, and that this, and not the Macedonian form of the calendar, was the form used by Seleuceia on the Parthian coinage which she minted;[8] and this view might perhaps be supported by the fact that at Nineveh later the

[1] The two forms have been clearly explained by F. K. Ginzel, *Handbuch der mathematischen und technischen Chronologie* I, 1906, p. 137; see also W. Kubitschek, *Grundriss der antiken Zeitrechnung* 1928 p. 70 (in Müller's *Handbuch*), and especially W. Kolbe, *Beiträge zur syrischen und jüdischen Geschichte* 1926 pp. 1 *sqq.*, who argued that the Babylonian form was the original one; I gather from *Rev. E. G.* XLVIII, 1935, p. 598 that E. Bikermann in his forthcoming *Études sur l'administration séleucide* will maintain that there was only one calendar, the official Macedonian one beginning in autumn, though Orientals might begin with 1 Nisan. Naturally the questions involved cannot be discussed here.

[2] E. T. Newell, *NNM* 26, 1925, p. 12.

[3] The coinage.

[4] The Macedonian months in *CIG* 4672.

[5] Bellinger and Welles, *Yale Class. Stud.* V, 1935, p. 96.

[6] Ginzel *op. cit.* III pp. 314–16. For Judaea see also W. Kolbe *op. cit.*

[7] *Avroman Pg.* 1, if the dating be Seleucid and not Arsacid; see p. 65 n. 5.

[8] McDowell, *Stamped objects* pp. 157–61; *Coins from Seleucia* pp. 148–53.

Macedonian months were fitted to yet another year, the Roman.[1] The question cannot be discussed here; but whatever the case as regards Seleuceia in Babylonia, it seems incredible that the Seleucid foundations generally should have used anything but the form used by their Macedonian creators, while it was certainly the Macedonian calendar beginning in October 312 which the half-Seleucid kings of Bactria, as was natural, took to India (p. 47 n. 2).

The Parthian kings imitated the Seleucid Era with one of their own, the Arsacid Era from which they themselves reckoned,[2] the initial year being 248–7 B.C., the date of the establishment of the kingdom of Tiridates; but even under Parthian rule both Babylonia and the Greek cities kept to the Seleucid dating, though in Babylonia regularly[3], and among Greeks sometimes, both calendars were used as double dating, the Arsacid in that case being called by Greeks 'as the king reckons' and the Seleucid 'by the former reckoning';[4] no Babylonian or Greek document has yet been found which is certainly dated by the Arsacid Era alone,[5] and there is no trace so far of the Arsacid calendar in India, which means that it was probably not used in the east Parthian kingdom of the Surens. The tenacity of the Seleucid calendar was remarkable: Doura used it when under Roman rule and Jews down to the eleventh century, and it is said to have still been in use among Syrian Christians at the beginning of the present century.[6]

The other thing which appears to me to be certain is the general rise

[1] *CIG* 4672. [2] *SEG* VII, 1; see p. 28 n. 6.

[3] List of Babylonian double datings, E. H. Minns, *JHS* XXXV, 1915, p. 33; see also especially F. X. Kugler, *Sternkunde und Sterndienst in Babel* II, ii, 1912, §B pp. 438 *sqq*.

[4] *SEG* VII, 1, 25, 39, 40 (*Inscr. BM* IV, ii, 1052); *Doura Pg.* 10 (*Yale Class. Stud.* II pp. 4, 39), and 21 (*Sav. Z.* LVI p. 101). The phrase 'the former reckoning' occurs as late as A.D. 243 in the Syriac contract already mentioned, *Yale Class. Stud.* V p. 96.

[5] One Babylonian document, Strassmaier, *Z. f. Assyr.* III p. 129 no. 1 = J. Kohler and A. Ungnad, *Hundert ausgewählte Rechtsurkunden* no. 94, is dated by the Arsacid Era alone, but is one of such a numerous class of double-dated documents that this is certainly a scribe's omission. The arguments for the Greek *Avroman Pg.* 1 being dated by the Arsacid calendar are strong (M. Rostovtzeff, *Yale Class. Stud.* II pp. 41–2) but cannot amount to certainty in the absence of any Greek document certainly dated by the Arsacid Era alone. Professor C. B. Welles, *Royal Correspondence* p. 302 n. 8, has claimed *SEG* VII, 1 (Artabanus' letter to Susa) as such a document. But it is not a Greek document; it is a Parthian one, the letter of a Parthian king who naturally used his own dating; his secretary might just as well have been writing in Pahlavi as in Greek, had the addressees spoken Pahlavi.

[6] Kubitschek *op. cit.* p. 70.

in the level of Asia, not merely the evolution of the settlement into the city and of the village into the settlement, but the kind of intangible Greek atmosphere, already noticed, which affected many Asiatics; it has left one literary monument of itself, Ecclesiastes, whose Greek atmosphere has been the despair of those scholars who have sought to pin it down to some definite source. Even so, in the actual world, that atmosphere cannot be pinned down to definite data, but it can be felt and occasionally its effects can be seen. Two instances may be given. Where the Kurdistan hills come down to the Tigris there had lived in Xenophon's day a savage people, the Karduchi. The country became successively the Seleucid eparchy of Gordyene and then a little Succession kingdom; as no Greek settlements are known there the Greeks in it must have been few, but by the first century B.C. the Karduchi had become the comparatively civilised Gordyeni[1] whom we meet in Plutarch, merely because a better way of life was in the air and they felt it. Another instance, though outside the actual Seleucid bounds, is furnished by the Nabataeans, who in the third century B.C. were pirates and who by the Christian Era had become a civilised state.

Many causes can be adduced for the ultimate failure of the Seleucid settlement of Asia, east of the Roman boundary. Some provinces were not adapted for the kind of life Greeks liked to live, and there is a hint of homesickness in the recurring complaint in Strabo that this or that district produced everything needful *except olives*. Very many districts had no access to the sea, and a Greek without the sea was a lost creature. All the rulers knew this. This was why the Seleucids, following out one of Alexander's ideas, took such trouble to colonise the inner Persian Gulf in spite of the heat; even our all but vanished tradition reveals nine cities or settlements there: in the east Antioch in Persis (Bushire), Seleuceia on the Erythraean Sea, and Antioch-Charax; on the Arabian side Arethusa, Larisa, Chalcis, Artemita; and two whose situation is unknown, Carrhae and Trapezus.[2] This too may be one

[1] Pliny VI, 44, Carduchi quondam dicti, nunc Cordueni.

[2] Larisa, Chalcis, Arethusa: Pliny VI, 160; Tarn, *JEA* XV p. 11. Trapezus: Steph. *s.v.* The others have already been mentioned. L. Robert, *Villes d'Asie Mineure* 1935 p. 154, makes Larisa, Chalcis, Arethusa on the Persian Gulf in Pliny VI, 160 duplicates of the towns of the same name in North Syria which are scattered through Pliny V, 81–2. I fear that I cannot agree. Pliny makes strange blunders and has strange duplicates, as this book will show, but in this case his source knew certain things about these three towns in Arabia which he summarises as deleta variis bellis; and that does not apply to the towns in Syria. A duplicate implies a confusion behind it, and he could hardly confuse the well-known North Syria with peninsular Arabia.

reason why, in India, Demetrius was to lead the advance to the sea himself but was to entrust that to the capital, Pātaliputra, to a general. Again, the Greek race was getting old and very civilised, too old and too civilised perhaps for successful colonisation. And though the number of Greeks east of the Euphrates must have been much greater than used to be supposed, there were not enough for ruling so vast a country permanently, while the Seleucid kings for over a century dissipated their strength in a senseless struggle with Egypt, though, to be fair, Ptolemy II was the original aggressor. Yet again, the Greek colonisation began at the wrong end for inland districts: it began with cities and potential cities, as though the whole country had been sea-coast. But a land, at any rate in antiquity, belonged essentially to those who worked the land; conquerors might come and go over their heads, but at the end the children of the soil remained. To make a really permanent settlement the Greeks would have had to go on the land, as did the Angles and Saxons in Britain; that they never did, and once the cities had lost their political background and nexus and had become enclaves in the Parthian empire the end was certain. Some cities made a good fight for their Greekhood and delayed the end for centuries; but it had to come, and the destruction of Seleuceia by the Romans[1] in A.D. 165 may have been a symbol rather than a cause.

But perhaps the most potent reason was the failure of the Greeks—I am speaking of the Middle East—to produce any real effect upon the civilisations of Asia; Iran in particular, backed by a great religion, was too strong for them. Individual exceptions apart, the Asiatic remained, at bottom, unaffected by Greek civilisation; he had no wish to become a Greek, though he might take what Greeks could give him; he did not regard Greek culture as his culture or Greece as his spiritual home. And if the Greeks could not hellenise Iran, and were not numerous enough to rule her, and were not going to take her into partnership, it was obvious what must happen. Considered broadly, what the Asiatic took from the Greek was usually externals only, matters of form; he rarely took substance—civic institutions may be an exception—and never spirit. For in matters of the spirit Asia was quite confident that she could outstay the Greeks; and she did.

I feel no certainty, however, that (putting India aside for the present) the Oriental *religions* had as much to do with the Greek failure as has sometimes been supposed. One sees the strength of the appeal made

[1] McDowell, *Coins from Seleucia* p. 234, argues that the damage done was less than the literary sources would suggest.

by those religions when they invaded the Mediterranean world, but it is only an assumption that they would have exercised the same influence over Greeks who, far from the Mediterranean, were fighting to maintain their Greekhood. Of course these Greeks worshipped Asiatic deities; in a polytheistic society you naturally worshipped the god who knew the way of the land. And of course many of the names of Greek deities met with do not mean Greek deities at all: Artemis usually meant the mother-goddess in one of her numerous forms, Heracles might be the rider-god of the cave shrine at Kerefto,[1] and so on; even in a temple at Persepolis the Persian gods received Greek names.[2] But Greeks had worshipped an Asiatic mother-goddess for several centuries at Ephesus and Magnesia, and were none the less Greek for that. There are things which should make one a little cautious about believing that Greeks made such a complete surrender to the religions of the East that it tended to orientalise them. For example, there was one Greek deity, Athena, who in the Hellenistic period practically never represented or was equated with anything Asiatic,[3] but always remained herself. She had played no great part among the Greeks of the Nearer East, except at Pergamum. But there were found at Seleuceia a large number of sealings made by the signets of the Greek mercantile community; the device on a man's signet probably did express his personal taste or feelings, and much the commonest device was Athena,[4] which may mean that the owners were holding fast to their own religion.

Again, there are the Susa manumissions.[5] There was an old form of quasi-manumission in Babylonia and Elam (practically a gift) by which the owner dedicated the slave to some god and the slave became the god's property.[6] That had once been so in Greece also;[7] there grew out

[1] Tac. *Ann.* XII, 13; forthcoming publication by Sir A. Stein.

[2] E. Herzfeld, *Archaeological History of Iran* 1934 p. 44.

[3] In the temple mentioned in the last note Anaïtis is said to appear as both Artemis and Athena; but this does not really affect my statement, for that Anaïtis was usually Artemis is undoubted. At a later time Athena was identified by the Nabataeans of Petra with their warrior-goddess Allath; but that is immaterial here.

[4] McDowell, *Stamped objects* p. 226, and Table p. 224.

[5] *SEG* VII, 2 and 15 to 26; see P. Koschaker, *Abh. sächs. Akad.* XLII, 1931, pp. 74 *sqq.*; M. San Nicolò, *Sav. Z.* LII, 1932, p. 464; L. Robert, *Rev. Phil.* LXII, 1936, pp. 137 *sqq.*, and p. 149 on *SEG* VII, 2.

[6] Koschaker *op. cit.* pp. 74 *sqq.*

[7] Thalheim, *Freigelassene*, and Hepding, *Hierodulí*, in PW; Dareste-Haussoullier-Reinach, *Inscr. juridiques grecques* II p. 234; Koschaker *op. cit.* p. 69. These gifts never died out; there is one at Susa, *SEG* VII, 24, and a number to Mā at Edessa in Macedonia, Roman period, Ἀθηνᾶ XII, 1900, pp. 70–3.

of it in Greece (the process is unknown) that form of manumission (ἀνάθεσις-manumission) in which, though words of dedication were still used, the god became not the owner of the slave but only a quasi-trustee, so that the slave went free and the god guaranteed his freedom; and this form of manumission was still sometimes used[1] even after it had been largely superseded in the second century B.C. by manumission through a fictitious sale to the god. The Greeks of Susa treated Nanaia as their city goddess and manumitted their slaves in her temple, but they altered the old form to which Nanaia had been accustomed and which had made the slave her property; they imposed upon her their own more civilised practice of freeing the slave,[2] fitting on to the words of dedication[3] the appropriate Greek clause in that behalf; and Nanaia, for all her power, had to acquiesce in the loss of what would once have become her own property, and did in her new position of quasi-trustee guarantee the slave's freedom very effectually, judging by the heavy penalties which she was entitled to exact from wrongdoers. That is to say, Nanaia's Greek worshippers, far from being orientalised by her, compelled her most thoroughly to serve their own purpose, a purpose purely Greek. Similarly we shall find, in India, that the one permanent mark which Greeks set upon Asia was nothing secular but was a mark set upon an eastern religion.

I must conclude by asking a question which every reader will ask sooner or later: where did all the Greeks come from? At present there is no answer; certain points alone can be indicated. The old cities of

[1] On the ἀνάθεσις-manumissions see A. Calderini, *La manomissione* 1908 pp. 86 *sqq.* and list p. 438; add a series, Hellenistic, at Coroneia, Ἀρχ. Δελτ. II, 1916, pp. 218–24. Even at Delphi there are instances among the sales: *SGDI* II, 2071, 2097; *SEG* II, 307.

[2] Now certain: Koschaker *op. cit.* pp. 70, 74, 83; Robert *op. cit.* p. 146. The three complete manumissions of a slave girl give her age in every case as 'about 30', ὡς ἐτῶν λ'. I fear that I cannot agree with Robert that this is coincidence. It was unusual, though not unknown, to give the slave's age in manumission documents, for nothing turned on it; there must have been a reason why the age was always given at Susa, and in my view these identical ages point to a legal fiction; if we could explain it we should know the process by which at Susa the Greeks turned dedication into manumission.

[3] The operative word at Susa, ἀφιέρωσεν—'consecrate' instead of 'dedicate'—seems unknown in Greece; it is not given in Calderini's table, *op. cit.* p. 438, though on p. 442 he quotes a formula at Chaeronea, τὰν ἀνάθεσιν ποιούμενος, in which ἀφιέρωσιν is sometimes substituted for ἀνάθεσιν, and though occasionally in ἀνάθεσις-manumissions the slave is expressed to become ἱερὸς καὶ ἐλεύθερος instead of ἐλεύθερος alone. Perhaps ἀφιέρωσεν has no especial significance; but might it not be a relic of the old Oriental form at Susa?

Asia Minor were probably more populous than used to be believed,[1] and they certainly played a large part in the settlement. The long Seleucid peace in the interior must have enabled a rapid growth of population, especially if, as is possible, there was for a time little or no infanticide; for though one regards infanticide as the general rule in antiquity,[2] it always depended on the food supply, and in the vast empire of the Seleucids, with many provinces sparsely populated, food can hardly have been a problem. Also, as has been seen, there were cases of new cities themselves planting colonies, which shows that the Greek population *did* grow rapidly. But this is not enough; neither is it enough to say that people like Thracians, who hellenised easily, would probably be reckoned with Greeks.[3] We cannot get away from the supposition that for a generation before and a generation after 300 B.C. there must have been a much greater Greek population available for settlement than we had any idea of; a recent examination of mercenary service[4] points, I think, on other lines, to the same conclusion. It may even turn out that the Macedonia of the Antigonids was never more than a shadow of the Macedonia of Alexander, and that war and emigration had bled that country too severely for it ever to recover.[5] One does not envy the man who shall undertake the revision of current notions of the population of the Hellenistic Greek world; but it is beginning to seem inevitable that such a revision will have to be made.[6] It is a sound rule in ancient history to take the lowest figure that will do the work; but it must do the work.

With this much of prelude I may turn to my main subject.

[1] The inscription in Wiegand, *Siebenter Milet-Bericht* 1911 pp. 26 *sqq*. From it he calculated the population of Miletus early in the second century at nearly 100,000, while Beloch, *Gr. Gesch.*[2] IV, 1, p. 272 n. 2, made it 'about 40,000 at least'. I once recalculated it in my own way and got a result near to Wiegand's.

[2] A. M. Carr-Saunders, *The Population Problem* 1922.

[3] *E.g.* the non-Lycian population of Apollonia-towards-Pisidia seems to have been largely Thracian; Sir W. M. Ramsay, *JRS* XII pp. 184–6.

[4] G. T. Griffith, *The Mercenaries of the Hellenistic World* 1935.

[5] Perfectly possible. The Highlands of Scotland have never recovered from the great emigration when the land was cleared for sheep.

[6] Another pointer beside Miletus (above) is M. Cumont's recent conclusion, *JRS* XXIV, 1934, p. 189, that Beloch's figures for Syria were far too low; see further *CAH* XI p. 628. He gives the citizen body of Apamea in Syria (*ib.* p. 621) in Augustus' reign as 117,000 of both sexes, exclusive of slaves and the labouring classes.

PART II

BACTRIA AND INDIA

CHAPTER III

EUTHYDEMUS AND BACTRIA

HAD the story of the Bactrian Greeks survived, it would be considered one of the most remarkable of a remarkable time; but though it was treated by two Greek historians of the Farther East (Chap. II), nothing has come down to us directly but some fragments and scattered notices and the coins. And there is not even the help which can be got in India from Indian literature and inscriptions and from archaeological research; nothing seems known of any native Bactrian literature at this period, and though the brief Chinese account of the country is invaluable China did not get into touch with Bactria till Greek rule had just ended. Moreover, the situation of the country, which to-day forms the northern part of Afghanistan, has always precluded archaeological research. There is said to be a certain amount of archaeological material in the museum at Tashkent, but if so it has never been made available to European scholars generally. A French archaeological mission was able to visit the upper Kabul valley in 1923, and permission was obtained for a brief visit to Balkh; a trench was sunk in a mound believed to represent the citadel of Bactra, but it got no further down than the fifteenth-century city, the Balkh of the Timourids.[1] The ruin mounds on the plain of Balkh are said to extend for 16 miles,[2] and the excavation of Bactra alone would occupy many years; that of Susa has been going on for over a generation, and it was

Note. On the sources generally see the Introduction, and on the principles followed with regard to the coins see Appendix 1.

[1] *BEFEO* XXIV, 1924, p. 647.

[2] This figure is from W. (V. V.) Barthold, *Turkestan down to the Mongol invasion* 1928 p. 78. The first chapter of this book gives a valuable survey of Bactria-Sogdiana in Arab times.

not till 1928 that Greek inscriptions began to be found. While light upon Greek rule in India has been slowly growing, it is unlikely that for many years yet much new material will be available about Bactria; but that does not mean that there is nothing more to be learnt from critical handling of what does exist. An attempt will be made in this chapter to put together what little can be made out about Bactria under Greek rule, prior to the invasion of India.

When in the middle of the third century B.C. Bactria began to break loose from the Seleucid empire there were obviously many Greeks settled in the country, but it is not clear how they got there. Alexander had left large forces of mercenaries in the Bactrian-Sogdian satrapy—at one time 10,000 foot and 3000 horse—and was supposed to have founded there eight, or twelve, unnamed 'cities', *i.e.* military colonies; but if 23,000 of his settlers in the Farther East, as is supposed, had been massacred[1] in the defeat of the great Greek rising after his death, his whole system of settlement should have tottered; certainly one place, Alexandria in Margiane (Merv), was destroyed by nomads.[2] Yet some twenty years later the satrap Stasanor was able to make a fight against Seleucus;[3] and as few settlers can have gone out during the wars of the Successors, when the contending generals in the West were enlisting every available man, it is a possibility that the massacre of 23,000 Greeks (by only 3800 Macedonians) is a mere mistake in Diodorus' transcript, and that the number of killed given elsewhere,[4] 3000, is the correct one. Certainly the early Seleucids must have encouraged settlement, for by the latter part of the second century the country had changed from one almost devoid of towns to one whose great number of towns had become a proverb. This will be considered later; it suffices to say here that when Diodotus, satrap of Bactria-Sogdiana, gradually began to outgrow Seleucid authority he must have had a considerable body of Greeks under his control.

The tradition that Diodotus of Bactria revolted against Antiochus II in 250 B.C. has long been discarded, and his gradual progress to independence has been traced from the Seleucid coinage.[5] The coins furnish no direct evidence that he ever took the royal title; but there seems no reason to doubt Justin's statement that he did,[6] and if the

[1] Diod. XVIII, 7, 2 and 9.
[2] Pliny VI, 47.
[3] Justin XV, 4, 11.
[4] Diod. XVII, 99, 6.
[5] *CHI* pp. 435–8; another coin, Sir G. F. Hill, *NC* 1925 p. 20 no. 62.
[6] Justin XLI, 4, 5 and 8.

cult-name Soter, which he bore after death,[1] was used by him as his title before he died, then at the end he must have been king, though he has left no named coins, the Diodotus coins being those of his son Diodotus II. It cannot be made out that he ever ruled more than his own satrapy of Bactria-Sogdiana; the idea that he also ruled Arachosia-Seistan and that Antiochus III had to reconquer these provinces seems mistaken.[2] It has been thought that the monogram Dio on certain Seleucid coins of the period when he was reaching out towards independence stands for his name.[3] A monogram is usually that of the moneyer; but in this case a theory that Dio stands for Diodotus might be supported by a reference to those ambitious governors, Aspeisas satrap of Susiana[4] and Nicocles king of Paphos,[5] who put their names on the Alexander-coinage with results disastrous to themselves. Diodotus had better fortune; far from being destroyed by Antiochus II he married his daughter. This quite certain fact, and the equally certain fact that Euthydemus married a daughter of Diodotus,[6] enable us to get some dates. In 206 Euthydemus' eldest son Demetrius was *νεανίσκος*—about 19 to 20, not more;[7] Euthydemus therefore married about 227, or possibly even a year or two later, and his wife, Diodotus' daughter by the daughter of Antiochus II, need not have been born till 243 or even a little later, though of course she might have been a little older. This makes it clear under what circumstances Diodotus married the Seleucid princess. Antiochus II died late in 247, and his son Seleucus II was at once faced by tremendous difficulties, including civil war; in 246 his capital was in the hands of Ptolemy III and the Egyptian king was making a military parade to Seleuceia to secure the eastern satrapies for the party he supported.[8] Seleucus II then, about 246, gave

[1] The Diodotus coins in the pedigree series of Agathocles and Antimachus (App. 3), and the *Διοδότου Σωτῆρος* coin given *CHI* p. 451 (p. 201).

[2] Herzfeld, *Sakastan* p. 38. But Justin XLI, 4, 5, totius Orientis populi...defecere, is only a hyperbole for Parthia, as the next sentence shows; and Strabo XI, 515 shows that the movement was confined to those north of (*ἔξω*) the Taurus, *i.e.* Bactrians and Parni, as he says.

[3] *CHI* p. 437, and an unpublished study by Professor C. A. Robinson Jr.

[4] E. S. G. Robinson, *NC* 1921 p. 37.

[5] E. T. Newell, *NC* 1919 p. 64.

[6] Shown by Agathocles' pedigree coin-series, see Appendix 3.

[7] Polyb. XI, 34, 9. It means one who has ceased to be a boy, *παῖς*, but is not yet a man, *ἀνήρ* (Plat. *Rep.* 413E), and on ordinary Greek reckoning a youth was *ἀνήρ*, a full warrior, when he had finished his ephebe training (19th and 20th years).

[8] *CAH* VII p. 717.

one of his sisters to Diodotus to secure his allegiance, just as he gave two other sisters about the same time to the kings of Pontus and Cappadocia to secure their alliance.[1] It was common enough in all the dynasties for kings to use their daughters or sisters as pawns in the game, but these Macedonian girls were often anything but nonentities, and the pawns sometimes queened with surprising results; Cleopatra VII of Egypt was only the last of a long line who had done what they could with lesser opportunities than hers.

In 246, then, Diodotus was still a Seleucid satrap. His son Diodotus II, who took the royal title, was on the throne in 228 or 227,[2] so Diodotus' death cannot be put later than about 230; he had been satrap under Antiochus I[3] and was not young. His coins show Diodotus II as a young man,[4] but the dates make it almost certain that he was not a son of the Seleucid princess; he must have been Diodotus' son by a former marriage. He reversed his father's policy and allied himself with Tiridates of Parthia,[5] the enemy of the Seleucids, who was then at war with Seleucus II; with Seleucus' sister at Diodotus' Court as his father's widow the situation must have followed well-known lines. The queen-widow married her own daughter to Euthydemus, presumably one of Diodotus' satraps,[6] and Euthydemus killed Diodotus II,[7] probably with popular support (for the alliance with Parthia cannot have been popular with the Greeks), and took the crown. At the moment he may have appeared to be acting in the Seleucid interest; he told Antiochus III later that he was no rebel, but that he had killed the son of a rebel.[8]

The story of independent Bactria is, in its great period, essentially that of Euthydemus and his eldest son Demetrius. Euthydemus was a Greek from one of the Magnesias; it has been thought that Magnesia-under-Sipylos is the more likely because one of his coin-types resembles the type of certain cities in the neighbourhood of this Magnesia (not, be it noted, of Magnesia itself);[9] but it is hard to believe that Polybius would call a man from the less important of the two cities a 'Magnesian'

[1] Euseb. (Schöne) I p. 251; Justin XXXVIII, 5, 3.

[2] When Seleucus II went eastward, Justin XLI, 4, 9; on the date see *CAH* VII p. 722.

[3] *CHI* pp. 435–7.

[4] *BMC* Pl. I, 4–8; *CHI* p. 440.

[5] Justin XLI, 4, 9, foedus.

[6] Why de la Vallée-Poussin, p. 233, and Grousset, p. 53, make him satrap of *Sogdiana* I do not know.

[7] Polyb. XI, 34, 2; see *CHI* p. 440.

[8] Polyb. XI, 34, 2.

[9] *CHI* pp. 440, 443.

without any qualification,[1] and probably Euthydemus came from the great city on the Maeander which had already sent so many of her sons to the East (p. 6). A fine portrait-bust of him, thought to have been set up in his native Magnesia, is (or was) in the Torlonia museum in Rome;[2] it shows the strength of the man towards the end of his life, but not so successfully as the wonderful coin-portrait of him taken in old age. One has only to look at his face to see why he seized the crown: he meant to rule because he could.

It will be well to consider here the Euthydemid relationships of the earlier period, and the portraits on coins struck in Bactria are such fine work that it ought to be possible to use them as evidence.[3] Three of these Bactrian heads, in their stark truth and realism, stand out from the rest—that of Euthydemus in old age and those of his son Demetrius wearing the elephant-scalp and of a certain Antimachus wearing a flat kausia, both men in the prime of life;[4] Greek art has bequeathed to us no finer portraits. These three are certainly the work of one man, whom I may call *X*, and cannot be very far apart in time. Antimachus then belongs to the same generation as Demetrius, and his portrait shows a feature which I believe to be all but unique in Hellenistic art, a peculiar half-mocking smile, as of one who did not take himself very seriously; those who wish may trace a resemblance to the smile of Monna Lisa. It has nothing to do with the vacuous smile, resembling the archaic smile, common in late Seleucid portraits; it is an essential part of the man. Now that smile occurs once again in Greek art; it occurs in the portrait of Euthydemus[5] on one of Agathocles' pedigree coins (App. 3). This coin is the work of a later artist—let us say school of *X*—who was portraying Euthydemus some twenty years after his death; but he remembered the smile, though he could not render it with the same subtlety with which *X* had rendered that of Antimachus. So far as I know, that peculiar smile never occurs again anywhere—certainly not in the East. Antimachus therefore was a son of Euthydemus and a younger brother of Demetrius.

[1] Polyb. XI, 34, 1, ἦν ὁ Εὐθύδημος Μάγνης.

[2] R. Delbrück, *Antike Porträts* Pl. 29.

[3] Not those struck in India, which can only be used to corroborate something else. I have checked the Bactrian heads here used with the coins, as is very necessary if portraiture be in question, and they are accurate. For a contrary instance, which might deceive any one, see p. 77 n. 7.

[4] See the Plate of coin-portraits in this book, hereinafter referred to as Plate, nos. 1, 3, 4.

[5] Plate no. 2.

Now I need not have deduced this from the portraits, because it is known from other evidence; part of Antimachus' own pedigree exists (App. 3) and it shows that he *was* a son of Euthydemus. But as I am going to use Bactrian coin-portraits throughout this book as evidence, I gave this deduction of a fact otherwise known just to show that one is on firm ground in using them.

Whether Euthydemus had a third son beside Demetrius and Antimachus is purely matter of speculation, for Apollodotus has left no portrait of himself. He belonged rather to Demetrius' generation than to the next (Chap. IV), and the confidence which Demetrius obviously felt in him (p. 166), and the fact that Demetrius' grandson Strato I imitated his regular coin-type,[1] would fit well enough with a belief that he was Demetrius' youngest brother. But there is nothing to show. He cannot have been a mere general, for his regular coin-type on his bronze money is the Seleucid type[2] of Apollo and tripod, and he therefore presumably claimed Seleucid descent; if not Demetrius' brother, we must suppose that at any rate he was a collateral of the royal house. But as such a collateral would hardly be a Seleucid, his Seleucid type makes it much more probable that he was Demetrius' brother.

Of the second generation after Euthydemus we are now moderately well informed; and there are good portraits of Demetrius' four sons, though not done by *X*—call them 'school of *X*'. It has never been doubted that Euthydemus II, on the ordinary rules of nomenclature, must be the eldest son of Demetrius, and this is now certain, for a comparison of his face[3] with that of Agathocles[4] would alone suffice to prove that they were brothers; Agathocles' face is practically that of Euthydemus II a few years older. But the new coin of Agathocles' pedigree series acquired in 1934 by the British Museum, which bears the head of Demetrius,[5] proves conclusively that Agathocles, already known to be a grandson of Euthydemus, was a son of Demetrius (App. 3). Of the two extant portraits on Pantaleon's rare coinage one

[1] Square bronze with Apollo and tripod; *BMC* p. 42; *CHI* Pl. VI, 5 and p. 552.

[2] Head of Apollo and tripod-lebes appear on bronze of Seleucus I, III and IV and Antiochus II (*BMC Sel.* pp. 7, 15, 23, 32), and the type was imitated by Achaeus (*ib.* p. 30).

[3] Plate no. 5. Cf. the coin given by Svoronos, *J.I.d'A.N.* XV, 1913, Pl. XVIII, 7.

[4] Plate no. 9.

[5] J. Allan, *NC* 1935 p. 1 and Pl. III, 1: obv., head of Demetrius in elephant-scalp with legend *Δημητρίου ἀνικήτου*; rev., Demetrius' type of Heracles standing and crowning himself, with legend *βασιλεύοντος Ἀγαθοκλέους δικαίου*.

is extremely like Euthydemus II,[1] though the face on the other is rather heavier.[2] But Pantaleon, the rarity of whose coins points to a very brief reign, cannot be separated from Agathocles, as except for one series of Agathocles their coinages are practically identical; Pantaleon therefore is another brother, and as the coins show that one must have taken the other's place and as Agathocles was king when Eucratides arrived (Chap. v), it must have been he who took Pantaleon's place, and Pantaleon was therefore the elder. The fourth brother is Demetrius II.[3] His features have no very great resemblance to those of the other three brothers; it has been supposed that he was a son of Demetrius because his rare Bactrian coinage belongs to that period and because, on the rules of nomenclature, Demetrius' second son should have been named after himself. This can now be confirmed. The Bactrian coins of Demetrius II bear the legend *Βασιλέως Δημητρίου*, 'Of King Demetrius', and are distinguished by a peculiar treatment of the floating ends of the diadem.[4] In 1923 Mr Whitehead published a unique bilingual tetradrachm,[5] now in the British Museum, which shows on the obverse the head of a young prince, wearing the same flat kausia as Antimachus wears, and with the ends of the diadem (as he pointed out) treated in the same way as those on the Bactrian tetradrachms of Demetrius II. The head has usually been called Demetrius;[6] but though the coin was struck in India and though one cannot rely upon portraits struck in India, the coin is good as Graeco-Indian coins go and the face does not bear the least resemblance to the well-known features of Demetrius, beside being far too young; it is to me quite certain that it can only be meant for Demetrius II,[7] apart from the diadem ends, which are really

[1] Whitehead *NC* Pl. XIV, 3. [2] Plate no. 8.

[3] Plate no. 6 (two specimens in the British Museum). This king was discovered by Sir G. Macdonald, *CHI* p. 448. [4] *CHI* p. 448. It is very marked.

[5] Whitehead, *NC* p. 317 no. 2, Pl. XIV, 2: obv., bust of a young king, diademed, in flat kausia, with legend *Βασιλέως ἀνικήτου Δημητρίου*; rev., Zeus standing facing, thunder-bolt in r. hand and long sceptre in l., with Kharoshthi legend Maharajasa aparazitasa Demetriyasa. It is Plate no. 7.

[6] Whitehead, *NC loc. cit.*; C. T. Seltman, *Greek coins* 1933 p. 235; J. Allan, *NC* 1935 p. 2.

[7] If the head on Pl. XIV, 2 in Whitehead *NC* were correct it would be one of the most beautiful things in antiquity; but it has little resemblance to the coin. I examined the coin itself together with tetradrachms of Demetrius and Demetrius II, and Mr E. S. G. Robinson, who was with me, agreed with me that the face must be meant for Demetrius II, apart from the diadem ends. The face is liker those of the other brothers than is the Bactrian portrait of Demetrius II.

conclusive. The coin then was struck by Demetrius II, and the type, which is not one of Demetrius' types, is his own; but the legend 'Of King Demetrius the Invincible' is Demetrius' legend, as is proved by the new 'Demetrius' coin in Agathocles' series (p. 76 n. 5). Demetrius II then struck this coin on behalf of Demetrius, putting on Demetrius' name and legend but his own head and type;[1] he was therefore at the time Demetrius' sub-king,[2] that is (from the ages) his son, as the names imply. I shall return to this coin and what it means; I only want here to get the relationships.

The four sons of Demetrius, in order of age, are then Euthydemus II, Demetrius II, Pantaleon, and Agathocles. In addition, Menander's queen Agathocleia (Chap. VI) was probably his daughter.[3] It has long been known from her use of Euthydemus' coin-type of Heracles seated on a rock that she must have been descended from him, and on the dates that can only mean that she was his granddaughter; but if Agathocles and Agathocleia were both grandchildren of Euthydemus their names are strong to show that they were brother and sister. If Apollodotus was a son of Euthydemus it would be conceivable that she was Apollodotus' daughter, for her son Strato I uses Apollodotus' type of Apollo and tripod; but he may have used it, not because it had been used by Apollodotus, but because it was Seleucid, and in default of exact information it will be assumed in this book that she was the daughter of Demetrius. One point to notice about Demetrius' family is that his eldest son Euthydemus II looks rather younger on his coins than any of his brothers (which means that he coined several years before they did), and that none of the four unless perhaps Demetrius II can have reached the age of thirty; these facts must be accounted for in the reconstruction.

One other relationship of this period is now known. The publication in 1929 of the great Bajaur hoard showed that the Graeco-Indian king Antimachus II Nikephoros, whose place and date had been utterly uncertain, belonged at latest to the generation after Demetrius;[4] it may therefore be taken for granted that he was a son of Antimachus.

[1] Similarly some rare Seleucid coins struck by Antiochus I when joint-king bear his own name but the head of his father Seleucus; Bunbury, *NC* 1883 p. 67 and Pl. IV, 1; Head[2] 758.

[2] On sub-kings see p. 90.

[3] Rapson, *Corolla Numismatica* 1906 p. 249 n., suggested that she was a daughter or niece of Demetrius.

[4] On this king and the evidence see pp. 229 *sq.*

Before coming to the kingdom of Euthydemus, it may be useful to give some slight indication of the nomad background which always threatened Greek Bactria and ultimately destroyed it. That kingdom, while it lasted, was to play the same part in shielding the settled world of Iran from the semi-barbarism of the northern steppes as Antigonid Macedonia played in Europe in shielding Greek civilisation from the barbarism of the Balkan peoples. The true home of nomadism was the vast Eurasian steppe, extending from the Danube through Russia and the plains north of the Caspian far to the eastward, a reservoir of peoples which, as the world then went, seemed inexhaustible. Every nomad horde had its own territory within which it moved, pasturing its flocks and herds; of various blood and speech but identical way of life, hordes easily coalesced or broke up again, though on the whole the tendency seems to have been for the greater hordes to absorb lesser ones. This world of nomads had offshoots in more than one direction, and the offshoot which concerned Bactria was that which extended southward into the great gap between the Aralo-Caspian water system and the mountain barrier of the Pamirs and its contiguous ranges. This offshoot seems to have been entirely composed of peoples who spoke some form of Iranian; I must follow general usage and call them Iranians, but it will be understood that that refers to a common inheritance of language and custom and not to blood, which cannot be traced. Through this gap between mountain and sea the Iranian peoples had once poured southward;[1] Medes and Persians, Bactrians and Arachosians, had long since conquered and settled the lands of the Iranian plateau, the Ariana of Eratosthenes, and had forgotten that they were ever nomads; but behind them there remained layers of the less developed peoples of the Iranian name, still largely in the nomad stage, for whom Persians and following them Greeks used the general designation 'Saca', though Greek writers were apt improperly to call them 'Scythians', really the name of a particular Iranian people in South Russia. One of the brilliant results of the explorations of recent years in Central Asia has been the discovery and identification of the Saca language,[2] belonging to the North Iranian group which includes Sogdian and Pahlavik (Parthian Pahlavi). The history of the Sacas, so far as they had any before the second century B.C., had consisted in a great attempt made in the

[1] The most recent account is in E. Herzfeld, *Archaeological History of Iran* 1935 pp. 7 *sqq*.

[2] First identified by H. Lüders, *Berlin SB* 1914 p. 94.

seventh century B.C. to follow their kinsmen southward; it was a far-reaching effort and one or two of its details will be noticed later.

When Eratosthenes said that the Jaxartes separated Sacas and Sogdians[1] his statement was only true for the Chodjend district at the great southward bend of that river; for though in his day and later there were Saca peoples north of the Jaxartes, a considerable proportion of the Saca name lived to the south of it, and these were the people with whom the Bactrian Greeks were primarily concerned. Bactria's defence against the nomads, until the arrival of the Yueh-chi, was a domestic matter, a defence against those backward Iranian tribes in the steppes to the west and north-west who were perpetually attracted by the rich settled lands; it was not altogether a conflict between the desert and the sown, for some of the Sacas were now only semi-nomads. The peoples south of the Jaxartes who principally came in question, and of whom more will be heard later, were essentially three, the Dahae, Massagetae, and Sacaraucae. The Dahae, who originally came from the Jaxartes steppes,[2] were a comparatively small confederacy of three tribes now living on the Caspian northward of Hyrcania[3] and only semi-nomad; they occupied some oases, including Dihistan (which long bore their name), and though primarily horse-archers were also known as good fighters on foot. They had not appeared in Darius' province-lists, but had been subject to Xerxes;[4] whether they were still subject to Persia when Alexander came cannot be said.[5] Their importance to history was that one of their three tribes, the Parni, had in 248–7, according to their own reckoning, founded a kingdom in the Hyrcanian-Parthian satrapy, but when Euthydemus came to the throne there was nothing to suggest that 'Parthia' would ever be more than a local principality. The Sacaraucae, the Sacas of 'Saca-land beyond Sogd' which Darius I had ruled, will be described later (p. 291); they occupied the country south of the Jaxartes from the Chodjend district westward toward the Oxus, but as Ptolemy knows of other Saca peoples between the lower Jaxartes and the lower Oxus the Sacaraucae, as we shall meet them later, were probably also a confederacy of several tribes. Most important to the

[1] Strabo XI, 514 (Eratosthenes), 517 (probably not Apollodorus but Strabo's own addition).

[2] Arr. III, 28, 8 and 10.

[3] Justin XLI, 1, 10; Strabo XI, 508, 511.

[4] Xerxes' province-list from Persepolis l. 26, dahā: E. Herzfeld, *Arch. Mitt. aus Iran* VIII, 1936, pp. 56, 61.

[5] That he recruited Dahae is consistent with either supposition.

Greeks were the Massagetae, whose name is now supposed to signify 'the great Saca horde'.[1] They were a huge confederacy of tribes, lords of the Caspian steppes northward from the Great Balkan mountains to the lower Oxus and the Aral; eastward of the Aral they may or may not have extended to the mouth of the Jaxartes, westward of it they stretched northward for an unknown distance, possibly to the Aorsi at the head of the Caspian. Five of their tribes are recorded—Derbices,[2] Apasiacae (p. 91), Attasii, Chorasmii,[3] Augasii;[4] and we shall meet another later.[5] What their confederacy really meant is unknown; the tribes apparently often acted independently.[6] Some of the Massagetae fought on foot,[7] which means that they were agriculturalists; but the majority still led a pastoral life and fought on horseback after the universal fashion of the nomads, horse-archers led by an aristocracy of mailed warriors on mailed horses.[8] They ruled various subject races, including primitive 'fish-eaters' in the swamps at the river mouths and along the sea shores, some of whose peculiar customs were transferred by Greek writers to their Saca overlords;[9] they had slain the great Cyrus and had defied Alexander.[10]

One fertile country, a great island in the Saca steppes—Chorasmia (Kwarizm) on the lower Oxus—at a later day the seat of a powerful monarchy, raises such a difficult problem that it is considered in an

[1] A. Christensen, *Die Iranier* 1933 p. 250 (in *Kulturgeschichte des alten Orients*, dritter Abschnitt, ed. W. Otto, as part of Müller's *Handbuch*); E. H. Minns, *Scythians and Greeks* 1913 p. 111, had previously interpreted it as 'belonging to the great (horde)'. The old interpretation, 'Fish-eaters', merely perpetuated the partial confusion in Herodotus and Strabo of the primitive fish-eaters with their Saca overlords.

[2] A. Herrmann, *Massagetai* in PW 1930, col. 2127.

[3] Strabo XI, 513 (both tribes).

[4] Steph. *s.v.*; probably they are the Augaloi of Ptol. VI, 12, 4.

[5] For the Parsii see pp. 292 *sqq.* and Appendix 9.

[6] Thus Bessus expected the help of the Chorasmii, Curt. VII, 4, 6; and that people gave asylum to Spitamenes, as did the Apasiacae to Tiridates I of Parthia, Strabo XI, 513.

[7] Strabo *ib.*, ἀγαθοὶ ἱππόται καὶ πεζοί.

[8] See Tarn, *Military Developments* pp. 73 *sq.*

[9] Notably promiscuity and the stock accusation φανερῶς μίσγεσθαι, Strabo XI, 513; Greeks, who were not anthropologists, called all primitive peoples promiscuous, as Agatharchides in *GGM* I pp. 130, 133, 143, 153. For a similar transfer of primitive customs to other Iranians see Plut. *Mor.* 328C, Alexander taught the Hyrcanians marriage.

[10] Herrmann *op. cit.* without any warrant makes them subject to Alexander.

Appendix (11). I shall have a conjecture to make about it later (pp. 293 *sq.*), but it cannot be more than a conjecture.

With this sketch of the background, one can now turn to Euthydemus and Bactria. So long as the Seleucids were strong, Euthydemus confined himself to the rule of what had been the Bactrian satrapy, Bactria and Sogdiana; Polybius shows that when Antiochus III attacked him in 208 he held nothing east of the Hindu Kush, and his western boundary was still the lower Arius (Ochus) river.[1] I need not elaborate the oft-told story of that expedition,[2] as given by Polybius, though some of the details will be useful later. Euthydemus tried and failed to hold the lower Arius against Antiochus with 10,000 Bactrian horse, and then seemingly stood a two years' siege in Bactra; if the fortifications of the capital bore the relation to those of Sirynx (p. 16) which the relative importance of the two places demanded, it is readily understandable why Antiochus failed to take it after a siege with which only one other in the third century can compare for length, the Roman siege of Syracuse;[3] Euthydemus had turned Bactra into one of the greatest fortified places known. Finally Euthydemus threatened to call in the Sacas (p. 117) and pointed out the general disaster which would ensue; and Antiochus wisely made peace, left him his kingdom, and concluded an alliance. The Polybius fragment does not give the one thing which matters, whether Euthydemus acknowledged Seleucid suzerainty or not; but as the first overtures toward peace came from him, and he surrendered his elephants, probably he did,[4] though it soon became a dead letter. Antiochus is said to have promised him a daughter for his son Demetrius; but she can only have been a little child at the time, and it is quite certain that whomever Demetrius married it was not a daughter of Antiochus (p. 201 n. 1). The interesting thing is that Antiochus should have thought that he saw in Demetrius, young as he was, one who both by his bearing and his address was worthy to be a king.[5]

The common belief that Euthydemus died about the time of the battle of Magnesia, 189 B.C., cannot be far wrong; his portrayal in old age on one of his coins, conjoined with the date of his marriage, shows

[1] Doubtless the traditional boundary, for Mithridates I when powerful still treated it as the frontier.

[2] See in the last place M. Holleaux in *CAH* VIII pp. 138 *sqq.*

[3] The Roman siege of Capua was only a blockade.

[4] The *συμμαχία* of Polyb. XI, 34, 10 is not against this.

[5] Polyb. XI, 34, 9.

that he cannot have died much earlier, and, had he lived longer, the city founded by Demetrius in Arachosia (see pp. 94, 471) must have been named Euthydemia and not Demetrias. After the departure of Antiochus III in 206 he began to develop his kingdom in such directions as were open to him without inviting a fresh attack by the Seleucid; the last phase prior to the invasion of India, the incorporation of some Seleucid provinces, did not take place till Antiochus' power had been broken at Magnesia, and was due to Demetrius; but it may be taken that (India apart) such traces of expansion outside the Seleucid realm as exist belong to the reign of Euthydemus, for after Magnesia Demetrius' hands were full with other matters. A connected story of Euthydemus' reign is impossible; one can only take the kingdom as it existed when Demetrius crossed the Hindu Kush and go through the several provinces. It will be convenient to take the outlying parts first and leave Bactria itself, the kernel of the kingdom, to the end, for Bactria leads naturally to such account of the nature of Euthydemus' rule as it may be possible to give.

To the northward, Euthydemus, besides Sogdiana, ruled Ferghana, a province which in the Greek period was as highly cultivated as Bactria itself (App. 10); whether its population were Sacas, Sogdians, or something older,[1] they had definitely ceased to be nomads, if they had ever been so. The boundaries of Seleucid Sogdiana are not known, and Ptolemy's Sogdiana, which includes Chorasmia (never under Greek rule) and does not include Ferghana,[2] is a patchwork of different periods which gives no help; but whether or no Ferghana had ever been part of the Persian empire, it was certainly not part of it in Alexander's day (App. 10). But it was undoubtedly in Greek hands before Euthydemus died, whether its acquisition was due to him or to the Seleucids; we hear of a mysterious Antioch in Scythia,[3] which might have been the capital of the province, whatever it was, and if so the conquest may have been made by Demodamas during the joint reigns of Seleucus and Antiochus I, the period which saw the exploration of

[1] Marquart, *Untersuchungen z. Gesch. von Eran* I p. 30 n. 136, made its people the Barkanioi (O. P. Varkāna), which he thought the same word as Ferghana. But Stephanus *s.v.* definitely makes this tribe neighbours of the Hyrcanians; and they appear in the army of Darius III (Curt. III, 2, 6), who certainly did not rule Ferghana. Herzfeld has located the Paricani in Ferghana, p. 285 n. 3.

[2] Berthelot pp. 191, 195.

[3] Antioch no. 10 in Stephanus. But conceivably it was only Alexandria-Eschate refounded.

the Caspian and the walling-round of the Merv oasis, for Demodamas is known to have been active on the Jaxartes.[1] The Persian road which Alexander had followed from Samarcand only went to Cyropolis and the loop of the Jaxartes; but in 128 B.C. Chang-k'ien, coming from the east, travelled through Ferghana on 'postal roads' and found it full of 'walled towns',[2] and Greek rule over the province is not in doubt (App. 10), though it cannot be said if they ruled the whole of Chang-k'ien's Ta-yuan, which seems to have been larger than the later Ferghana; in his day its then Saca lords held the river valleys up to the watershed on the Pamirs (*ib.*). The route through Chinese Turkestan to the West most favoured at a somewhat later time passed through Kashgar and thence ran, skirting rather than crossing the Pamirs, to Irkishtam, where it bifurcated, one branch crossing the Terek pass and reaching Ferghana, the other, the later Silk Route, holding on down the Alai valley and so ultimately to Bactra;[3] with Bactria and Ferghana in his hands Euthydemus held the ends of both forks of the easiest route into Chinese Turkestan.

There seems no doubt that he conquered and held some part of that country. Apollodorus says that the conquests of the Greek kings of Bactria extended to the Seres and Phryni,[4] which however does not necessarily mean that the two peoples were close together. The Seres will be considered later. The Phryni are mentioned again, under the name Phuni, by Pliny at a later period in association with the Tochari,[5] *i.e.* the Little Yueh-chi (p. 276) who settled in the Tarim basin somewhere between 174 and 160; there has been so much confusion about this that it may be well to repeat[6] the elementary fact that Apollodorus does not mention the Tochari because they were not in the Tarim basin in *c.* 200 B.C., the period he is talking about, and Pliny does mention them because they had arrived there in the interval between *c.* 200 and the date of his source. Who the Phryni or Phuni were cannot be said; most certainly they were not the Hiung-nu, whose power was not

[1] Pliny VI, 49.

[2] See Chapter VII p. 307 and also Appendix 10, where the references are given.

[3] See Sir A. Stein, *On ancient tracks past the Pāmīrs*, *Himalayan Journal* IV, 1932, pp. 20 *sqq.* and map.

[4] Strabo XI, 516.

[5] Pliny VI, 55, Phuni et Focari; see also Kiessling, *Hunni* in PW cols. 2595–6. Gutschmid p. 45 n. 1 emended Focari to Thocari, but it may be doubtful if this was really necessary; see Appendix 21.

[6] Tarn, *SP Stud.* p. 9.

extended into Chinese Turkestan till after 174.[1] The Ch'ien-han-shu gives the names, in the first century B.C., of a great number of peoples and states in Chinese Turkestan, none of which seems to represent Phryni; but before they had more exact knowledge the Chinese had lumped together the peoples of the Tarim country on their western border under the general name of Ki'ang, and in the same way Phryni may be a general term for the peoples of the Kashgar-Yarkand or the Khotan country. Whether any Greek ever crossed into Chinese Turkestan by the more difficult southern route from Badakshan across the Pamirs[2] may depend on what follows.

In some of the Kharoshthi texts of the third century A.D. brought by Sir A. Stein from the Khotan district in Chinese Turkestan there occur two Greek words for coins, stater and drachma, and a word milima, which is thought to be medimnos (a bushel);[3] also the word Yonu or Yona (*i.e.* 'Greek') used as a proper name.[4] These seem certain. Two others have been suggested; one is that a word khi is derived from χοῦς,[5] another measure of capacity, and the other that a word hinajhasya is a translation of στρατηγός, 'general',[6] which has however been thought too conjectural to be accepted.[7] One cannot suppose that these words were brought by traders from Roman Asia in Imperial times, as many of the Greek seals from the Khotan country were (pp. 365 *sq.*), for it is impossible to see how they can have brought the word stater. But though no Greek king later than Eucratides coined staters, the word survived in India as a measure of *weight*; it occurs, together with drachma, in two Kharoshthi inscriptions from Taxila of about the Christian era;[8] and another Kharoshthi inscription on a silver saucer from Taxila, early

[1] Tomaschek, *Wien S.B.* CXVI, 1888, p. 769, proposed to read *Φοῦνοι* = *Οὖννοι* of Cosmas = Huns. I do not know of anyone who has accepted this; the word *Οὖννοι* is many centuries later than Apollodorus, and the Hiung-nu were not in the Tarim basin till some time between their final defeat of the Yueh-chi, 176 or 174, and 138, when they caught Chang-k'ien; see p. 279 and also Herzfeld, *Sakastan* p. 14.

[2] Stein *op. cit.* pp. 1 *sqq.* and map.

[3] F. W. Thomas, *JRAS* 1924 p. 671, 1926 p. 507; for milima, *JRAS* 1930 p. 204, and see T. Burrow, *BSOS* VII, 1935, p. 785.

[4] Thomas, *JRAS* 1924 p. 672.

[5] Burrow, *JRAS* 1935 p. 669.

[6] Burrow, *BSOS* VII, 1935, p. 514; cf. Sten Konow, *Indian Culture* II, 1935, p. 195, who thought it might even be earlier than the third century.

[7] Thomas, *BSOS* VIII, 1936, p. 789.

[8] *CII* no. XXXVII, 3 and 4 (pp. 98–9); see Sten Konow, *Acta Orientalia* VI, 1928, p. 255.

in the first century A.D., gives the signs of all three coins, stater, drachma, and obol.[1] Now a piece of silk, with a trader's memorandum written on it in Brahmi, which was discovered at a ruined watch-station on the old Chinese *Limes*, is said to show that traders from India, coming for silk, had already reached the *Limes* in the latter part of the first century B.C.,[2] while in the first three centuries A.D. there were settlements of Indian-speaking people in the Khotan country (p. 365); it is possible therefore that these Greek words thus passed into Chinese Turkestan from India in the course of trade,[3] in the same way that coins of some of the Greek kings—Hermaeus and probably Menander—passed into the same country from India.[4]

But though this must always be a possible view, I doubt if it be the true one. In 1935 Professor F. W. Thomas discovered in these Kharoshthi documents from the Khotan district two occurrences of the word παρεμβολή, camp.[5] This word cannot well have been brought by Indian traders, but points to Greek military occupation, just as -chester (castra) in English points to Roman military occupation; one recalls the παρεμβολαί near Barygaza (p. 148), and it is possible that παρεμβολή survived in India as a place-name,[6] like Chester. It may be therefore that all these Greek words in the Khotan country are a deposit from Euthydemus' conquest. The time-gap is considerable, but hardly a real objection; putting -chester aside, it has been pointed out that old names of coins may survive for a very long time, and a case has been cited of the use of Ἀττικαὶ (δραχμαί) in Egypt three and a half centuries after the last Attic drachma had been coined and over six centuries since the last drachma on anything which could be called the Attic standard had been struck in Egypt.[7] One cannot assert that these Greek words do

[1] *ASI* 1929–30 pp. 62 no. 46 and 63: Aspavarmasa strategasa Sa. 10. 1. Dra. 2. O. 2. (Too late for inclusion in *CII*.) The known name of the *strategos* Aspavarma dates this inscription to near the end of the Azes dynasty.

[2] Sir A. Stein, *Asia Major*, Hirth anniv. vol. 1923, pp. 367–72.

[3] This seems to be the view of F. W. Thomas, *Acta Orientalia* XIV, ii, 1935, p. 109. I had thought so myself prior to Thomas' discovery of παρεμβολή, *ib.*

[4] A silver coin of Hermaeus from Karghalik, Sir A. Stein, *Serindia* III p. 1340; not counting his 'Chinese' copper coin (p. 338). A coin probably Menander's: R. Hoernle, *JASB* LXVIII, 1899, pt. 1, extra no. 1, p. 27.

[5] *Acta Orientalia* XIV ii p. 109.

[6] Professor Thomas suggested to me that the name Παραβάλει, a town on the Indus, Ptol. VII, 1, 61, might be παρεμβολή. Alexander had left some garrisons along the Indus, Arr. *Anab.* VI, 17, 1.

[7] J. G. Milne, *JEA* XX, 1934, p. 193; the Ἀττικαί he cites are from *P. Oxy.*

date from Euthydemus' conquest; but of the two possibilities this view seems to me at present the more probable one.

One result of this conquest of Euthydemus, wherever it extended to, was that nickel, which was not isolated in Europe till 1751, began to appear in Bactria. The Chinese used several alloys in which nickel was combined with other metals; and since chemical analysis has shown that the composition of the Bactrian 'nickel' coins is almost identical with that of the alloy known to the Chinese as 'white copper'[1] there can be no doubt that the Bactrian nickel came from China, whether it came as an alloy or otherwise. But Euthydemus himself did not coin nickel; and as all the nickel coins known were struck by sub-kings of his son Demetrius—Euthydemus II, Pantaleon, and Agathocles—it seems that the penetration of Chinese Turkestan must be placed towards the very end of Euthydemus' reign. Whether he was seeking touch with China, ruled since 201 by the enterprising Han dynasty, cannot be said.[2] There was certainly no *direct* trade with China during the Greek period, for through caravans from China to Iran only started in 106 B.C. as a consequence of Chang-k'ien's missions;[3] such exports from China as reached Greek Bactria were passed along from one people to another, as they always had been; in this way came the nickel, and in this way the bamboos and cloth from Szechuan which so astonished Chang-k'ien when he saw them in Bactria.[4] But when in 128 B.C. Chang-k'ien first reached Ferghana it is recorded that the people there were overjoyed, because 'they had tried in vain to communicate with China';[5] presumably therefore attempts to open up through communication had been made from the Greek side, though it was the Chinese who finally succeeded in doing it.

In the west, at some time subsequent to 206 Euthydemus crossed the Arius and took from Parthia the Parthian satrapies of Astauene and

2113 (A.D. 316). Cf. Mdlle. C. Préaux, *La chronique d'Égypte* no. 20, 1935, *Bibliog. Papyrologique* p. 416, for some modern instances: in Belgium the 20 franc piece is still called a Louis. One might compare some English nautical terms, like starboard, fo'c'sle.

[1] W. Flight, *NC* 1868 p. 305. White copper, neglecting decimals, is 79 per cent. copper, 16 per cent. nickel, and 4 per cent. iron; the Bactrian coins are 77 per cent. copper, 20 per cent. nickel, 1 per cent. iron, and a little cobalt, tin, and sulphur. The other known Chinese alloys of nickel contain a good deal of zinc.

[2] The Ciñas who appear among the retinue of Bhagadatta-Apollodotus in the *Mahābhārata* (B. C. Law, *Ind. Culture* III, 1937, p. 731) can hardly be Chinese.

[3] Hirth, pp. 103, 135; Wylie pp. 69, 70. [4] Hirth p. 98. [5] Hirth p. 94.

Apavarktikene and perhaps part of Parthyene, which became (with a different division) the Bactrian satrapies of Tapuria (or Tapuruaia) and Traxiane,[1] Tapuria being the country of the Tapuri about the upper Atrek and Traxiane the Kasaf-rud valley with its capital at Susia-Tōs and probably extending northward. The conquest is reflected in Apollodorus' statement that the Arius flows *through* Bactria,[2] and it implies a war with Parthia, though the occasion is unknown. The two new satrapies, with the outlying Bactrian satrapy of Margiane (Merv) and the country between the Margus and the lower Arius (which may have been part of the Merv satrapy) to connect them,[3] were formed into a sub-kingdom for Euthydemus' second son Antimachus;[4] his seat was probably Antioch-Merv, as his kingdom appears to have been generally known as Margiane. Cunningham, who knew more about the find-spots of coins than anybody, has recorded that he would have put Antimachus' kingdom in Margiane[5] but for his own theory of the Bactrian mints, which has never been accepted by anybody and may now be left out of the question (App. 1); and this kingdom of Margiane appears in Ptolemy, who, as will be seen later (Chap. VI), has preserved a good deal of information about the second century from 'Trogus' source' (p. 45). Ptolemy's divisions of Asia, speaking generally, are the old Achaemenid-Alexander satrapies, but he makes Margiane (VI, 10) a separate division of Asia as though it had been a satrapy. This it never was; under Darius I the Merv district (Margus in Old Persian) was part of the Bactrian satrapy and when it revolted it was the satrap of Bactria who was entrusted with its reduction;[6] Alexander continued this arrangement (all his satrapies are known and Margiane is not among them), and there is nothing to show that the Seleucids ever did otherwise. The name Margiane, from its form, must be that of a Seleucid

[1] Strabo XI, 517, τήν τε 'Ασπιώνου τήν τε Τουριούαν, on which see Tarn, *SP Stud.* pp. 20–4.

[2] Strabo XI, 518 with 509; see Kiessling, *Hyrkania* in PW cols. 492–3.

[3] This follows from Ptolemy's Gouriane in Margiane (VI, 10, 4) being identical with Polybius' *Ταγουρίαν* (x, 49; Gutschmid's conjecture *τὰ Γουρίανα* is certain), which was somewhere east of the lower Arius; see Tarn, *SP Stud.* p. 24; *CAH* VIII p. 141 n. 1.

[4] The facts connected with Antimachus' pedigree brought out in Chapter V pp. 200 *sq.* amply confirm this.

[5] *NC* 1869 p. 39.

[6] Behistun 38–9 (F. H. Weissbach, *Die Keilinschriften der Achaemeniden*, 1911): Darius ends with 'This is what I did in *Bactria*'. The name Margus does not occur in any of Darius' lists of provinces.

eparchy (App. 2), the eparchy of Merv proper (not Ptolemy's Greater Margiane); like the other Seleucid eparchies of Bactria, it became under Euthydemus a satrapy of the Bactrian kingdom (p. 113) and at a later time a satrapy of the Parthian kingdom.[1]

Now Ptolemy in Iran never notices or reflects either the Bactrian or the Parthian reorganisation, but gives eparchy names everywhere as what they originally were, subdivisions of the old satrapies; his usage is consistent throughout. The Parthians took Merv in the reign of Mithridates II some time between his accession in 124 and 115,[2] as part of the liquidation of the great Saca invasion which began in 129; and as no place can be found for Ptolemy's Greater Margiane after that date, its existence must lie somewhere between the reorganisation of Bactria by Diodotus or Euthydemus on the one hand and the Parthian conquest of Merv on the other, which means that Greater Margiane was either the kingdom of some Bactrian king or a short-lived Saca kingdom somewhere between 129 and 115. But the nomad or semi-nomad Sacas were hardly likely to have carried out a comprehensive reorganisation during their brief occupation of the country, though they possibly set up a transient kingdom in Traxiane (p. 295); it seems certain enough that Greater Margiane must belong to the Bactrian period, and, if so, no king comes in question but Antimachus.[3] Besides, as will be seen (Chap. v), he must have ruled somewhere westward of Bactria itself, as he was one of the two sub-kings who bore the first brunt of Eucratides' attack; and he cannot have been far away, as the coin-portrait for his tetradrachms was engraved by the artist *X* (p. 75), who must have worked in Bactra, and some of his money was seemingly coined in Bactra (App. 1). Ptolemy (VI, 10) includes in his Greater Margiane the Tapuri, that is the new satrapy of Tapuria, and Gouriane (p. 88 n. 3) between the lower Arius and Margus rivers. He also includes the Dahae, which *may* mean that Antimachus had, or claimed, rule over

[1] Isidore 14.

[2] Tarn, *SP Stud.* pp. 15–18, *CAH* IX p. 585. By 115 I mean the date (Hirth's) of Chang-k'ien's second mission, which Herzfeld puts in 118, *Sakastan* p. 16.

[3] I do not mean that Ptolemy's Margiane necessarily gives the correct boundaries, but that it shows there was such a kingdom; see also p. 90 n. 2. Of the scanty occurrences of the word Margiane, Pliny VI, 46 and Strabo XI, 516 = II, 73 are the Seleucid eparchy; Strabo II, 72, Isidore 14, Justin XLI, 1, 10, and the Parthian *Μαργιανή* coin (*BMC Parthia* p. 40) are the Parthian satrapy; Strabo XI, 515, a reference to the oasis, might be either; Curtius VII, 10, 15 and IX, 7, 4 are merely unsafe emendations.

the southern part of the Caspian steppes.[1] Ptolemy makes the schematic boundary of his Greater Margiane touch the Caspian just north of Hyrcania; but it certainly did not reach the Caspian, or reach it to any purpose. This Greater Margiane was also known to one of Pliny's sources.[2]

We have now got the rough outline of the kingdom of Antimachus, and it gives several pieces of information. Undoubtedly he was a sub-king under his father Euthydemus, and subsequently under his brother Demetrius (Chap. v). The Seleucids had never employed a system of sub-kings of their own race; when the heir-apparent governed the East he was in theory joint-king with his father of the whole kingdom and Babylon dated by the two jointly. Euthydemus introduced a new state-form, in which a younger son might rule a definite part of the realm not as joint-king or as satrap but as sub-king, with the right of coining. We shall meet many such sub-kings again; they explain that standing numismatic puzzle, the large number of kings in the early period. The Parthians, those supreme imitators, may have borrowed the idea of sub-kings; Mithridates III was seemingly for a time a sub-king of his brother Orodes II,[3] and it seems that some of the great Parthian feudatories were practically sub-kings in their own districts.[4]

Antimachus' regular coin-type of Poseidon and trident on his various issues has rightly been held to indicate a naval victory. It was certainly not won on the Indus, for he had no connection with India,[5] and as this type was his regular coin-type from the start the victory must have been won early in his reign, long before the invasion of India; it may indeed have been the occasion of the grant to him of the royal title.[6] And certainly no Bactrian king reached or used the 'unnavigated' Caspian; for one thing, Parthia lay between them. A unique bronze coin of Antimachus from Seistan,[7] showing on one side an Indian elephant (the usual adoption of a Seleucid type, p. 213) and on the other Nike bearing a wreath and standing on the prow of a galley, one of the

[1] It *might* merely reflect the fact that the Dahae were in Xerxes' empire (p. 80).

[2] Because Pliny VI, 47 refers to *mountains* in Margiane: ab hujus excelsis.

[3] H. Dressel, *Z. f. Num.* XXXIII, 1922, p. 175.

[4] Herzfeld, *Sakastan*, *passim*.

[5] Cf. Cunningham, *NC* 1869 p. 38.

[6] As he was the first sub-king, he may for a time have been only a governor before he received the royal title.

[7] *BMC* p. 164 no. 2.

numerous imitations of the Victory of Samothrace, must refer to the same victory; but it was not won on the Hamun lake, for at this time Seistan was Seleucid and the presence of this one coin there is an accident of trade, like his coins from Baluchistan (p. 94). The only place where the ruler of Merv can have won a naval victory is on the Oxus; and what Antimachus did was to defeat a fleet of the Sacas (Massagetae). The use made of Sacas on Xerxes' fleet shows that among them were people acquainted with the water;[1] and one tribe of the Massagetae, the Apasiacae, which is Apa-saka, 'Water-Sacas',[2] are said to have lived about the middle reaches of the Oxus,[3] north-westward of the effective boundary of the Bactrian kingdom. A century later, when Sacas had invaded India, the naval symbolism on the coins of Maues and Azes shows that they had fleets and fought battles on the Indus and the Jhelum (Chap. VIII); similarly the Water-Sacas would have shipping on the Oxus,[4] presumably combining trade and piracy in the usual way. It must be remembered that the Massagetae were not all nomads (p. 81).

But the startling thing on Antimachus' coins is that he calls himself Theos, 'the god'.[5] No king of any of the western dynasties called himself Theos on his coins till Antiochus IV, and though Antimachus overlapped the first few years of Antiochus (Chap. V), his regular coinage had certainly begun long before 175, when Antiochus ascended the throne; if there was borrowing, which seems unlikely, it was done

[1] See A. Herrmann, *Sakai* in PW cols. 1780, 1784.

[2] Apa-Saka was Tomaschek's interpretation, *Wien SB* CII, 1883, p. 218. It is undoubtedly right, and is supported by the form Psacae in Pliny VI, 50, which in Ptolemy VII, 12 has become *Πάσκαι*.

[3] Strabo XI, 513, *Ἀρσάκης τὸν Καλλίνικον φεύγων Σέλευκον εἰς τοὺς Ἀπασιάκας ἐχώρησε. φησὶ δ' Ἐρατοσθένης τοὺς Ἀραχωτοὺς καὶ Μασσαγέτας τοῖς Βακτρίοις παρακεῖσθαι πρὸς δύσιν παρὰ τὸν Ὦξον.* That the meaningless *Ἀραχωτοὺς* should be *Ἀπασιάκας* is clear from the context. Polybius in Stephanus *s.v.* *Ἀπασιάκαι* is a little more precise than Eratosthenes; they are an *ἔθνος* of the Massagetae, who live on the middle Oxus. Cf. Polyb. X, 48.

[4] Patrocles called the Oxus *εὔπλους* (App. 14; Polyb. X, 48 *πλωτός* only copies), which *might* have been suggested by native shipping on it. His *εἰσπλέοντι* (Strabo XI, 507)—the point of view of a man sailing into the Caspian down the gulf which stretched towards the Aral—may also indicate native shipping, for the use of *εἴσπλους* just before may show that the word means more than simply *εἰσιόντι*. And on the Persian side the *Mihr Yast* §14 refers to the 'broad navigable waters' of the Oxus; Christensen *op. cit.* p. 216. (See however p. 479 n. 7.)

[5] *BMC* p. 12, *βασιλέως θεοῦ Ἀντιμάχου*. So on his pedigree coins, *ib.* p. 164, *βασιλεύοντος Ἀντιμάχου θεοῦ*.

by the Seleucid. There is also a Parthian 'beardless' coin on which some Parthian king called himself Theos,[1] a title not used again officially by any Parthian king, though Greeks gave it unofficially to Phraates IV;[2] Wroth tentatively attributed this coin to Phriapitius because his son Artabanus II (Wroth's Artabanus I) called himself *θεοπάτωρ*, 'son of a god', but, whichever of the early Arsacids it may have been, the title Theos was borrowed from Antimachus. Why did Antimachus, a younger son who was only a sub-king of his father Euthydemus when he settled his coin-types, adopt this title? So far as is known, the Euthydemid kings were not gods during life, though Euthydemus was deified after death,[3] perhaps with the usual state-cult, and one has only to look at Antimachus' face to see that there is no overweening pride there; he is rather amused at himself. Now Alexander in private had been ironical about his divinity; once when wounded he had said to those who called him a god: 'This, you see, is blood and not "ichor such as flows in the veins of the blessed gods".'[4] And there had been irony enough in the snub once administered by Antigonus Gonatas to the poet who called him god;[5] I need not cite later cases.[6] And irony might be the explanation of Antimachus' adoption of the divine title: this is what the great kings think, so let a small king say it. Indeed one small king had practically said it before, though not in irony; Alexarchus of Ouranopolis (p. 210) had called himself the Sun and had put the Sun on his coins. The more that strange man is considered the more important he grows as a forerunner of later ideas; we shall meet a king presently (p. 210) who may have had him in mind, and one cannot say that his example may not have suggested to Antiochus IV the assumption on his coins of the radiate crown of Helios the Sun-god and to Antimachus the assumption on his coins of the divine title. However it be, there are the coins of Antimachus the god; and strange enough it is.

I come now to the south. It has already been mentioned that Demetrius' conquest of the Seleucid provinces of eastern Iran cannot have been made till the battle of Magnesia (189) and the following

[1] *BMC Parthia* pp. xxix, 5, *βασιλέως θεοῦ 'Αρσάκου.*

[2] In the Zamaspes poems from Susa Phraates IV is *θεοῦ παγκράτορος*, *SEG* VII, 12, 13.

[3] *Εὐθυδήμου θεοῦ* on one of Agathocles' pedigree coins, *BMC* p. 10.

[4] Plut. *Mor.* 341 B, cf. 65 F.

[5] *Ib.* 360 C.

[6] The most famous is Vespasian's 'Vae, puto, deus fio'.

peace of Apamea (188) had rendered Antiochus III powerless to interfere, and that Euthydemus must have been dead before the attack was made, or Demetrias in Arachosia would have been named Euthydemia.[1] Certainly a few copper coins of Euthydemus were once found in the Indus at Attock,[2] but what they show is what his numerous copper coins found in Seistan show,[3] not that he was alive when Demetrius conquered Seistan, still less when he invaded India, but that Euthydemus' money, like that of Eucratides (p. 217) and probably several other kings, continued to be struck after his death. The coin-types are important here. Euthydemus' regular type was Heracles seated on a rock, resting after his labours; doubtless it was settled after Antiochus III retired, and meant that Euthydemus had made of Bactria an important kingdom. But Demetrius' regular type was Heracles standing and crowning himself; the new king envisaged fresh labours and conquests, and may even have thought from the start of invading India just as Alexander had of invading Persia. Somewhere between 187 and 184 or thereabouts Demetrius annexed to his kingdom three Seleucid provinces, Aria, Arachosia, and Seistan.[4] With Seistan he acquired the focus of a number of important routes which radiated from that centre; one going eastward by Kandahar to the Lower Indus; one going north-eastward by Ghazni and Kabul to the Paropamisadae, where it joined the main Bactra-Kapisa-Taxila route; one going northward by Herat to Merv and across the Oxus to Bokhara; and two main routes to the west, the land road by Persepolis and Susa to Seleuceia and Babylonia and, perhaps more important, the route which came to the sea at the Gulf of Ormuz (App. 12).

Demetrius certainly never conquered Carmania, but Gedrosia presents a problem, for though it is not in Justin's list it is possible that he held the eastern part; but if so it was probably not annexed till after the

[1] Demetrias in Sind (p. 142) is practically conclusive that Demetrias in Arachosia was named after Demetrius himself and not after some supposed father of Euthydemus. His father's name is unknown.

[2] Cunningham, *NC* 1869 p. 136. The belief that copper never travels far from its place of origin is unfounded; see Appendix 1.

[3] *Ib.* p. 138; *CHI* p. 442. Imitated by the Sacas of Seistan; Rapson, *JRAS* 1904 p. 675 no. 5.

[4] Justin XLI, 6, 3, a list of the provinces taken by Eucratides from Euthydemid sub-kings (p. 199). Strabo XI, 515 attributes the conquest of *τὴν ἐγγὺς αὐτῆς* (Bactria) *πᾶσαν* to *οἱ περὶ Εὐθύδημον*, but this phrase is quite consistent with the conquest of the north by Euthydemus and of the south by his son.

conquest of Sind. For among the peculiar notices relating to Gedrosia which we possess (p. 260), one says that Patalene was in Gedrosia[1] and another that the Gedrosians performed the tragedies of Euripides and Sophocles,[2] which implies some important urban centre; and the only way to make sense of these notices is to suppose that eastern Gedrosia[3] had been annexed to the satrapy of Patalene (p. 233) and was governed not from Demetrias in Arachosia but from Demetrias in Sind (p. 142). If so, this was done for the sake of the spice trade. For barren as much of Gedrosia was, it produced one of the things which all Greeks coveted—spices;[4] and the Bactrian coins found in Baluchistan[5] for the period prior to its annexation by Mithridates I of Parthia—coins of Demetrius, of his brother Antimachus, of his sons Euthydemus II and Pantaleon, of his conqueror Eucratides—may attest a trade in the export of spices to Bactria and the West.

In Arachosia Demetrius founded a city which bore his name, Demetrias;[6] it was a sign that Seleucid suzerainty over the Euthydemids, if it had existed, was at an end, for to found a city bearing your own name was a proclamation of independence (p. 208). Isidore, *i.e.* the Parthian survey, places Demetrias on the main route from Seistan by Alexandria-Ghazni to Kabul, and somewhere between Seistan and Ghazni.[7] The old Persian capital of the combined Seistan-Arachosia satrapy, known as 'the Arachosians', had been somewhere in the neighbourhood of Kalat-i-Gilzai, convenient for governing both the Seistan plain and the hill country of Arachosia; but Alexander had detached Seistan from Arachosia and had left the hill land as a separate satrapy, with its capital at his new city of Alexandria-Ghazni. But in Demetrius' scheme Seistan was again to be united with the Arachosian hill land under one sub-king, and therefore neither Alexandria-Prophthasia (pp. 14, 347), Alexander's capital of Seistan, nor Alexandria-Ghazni was suitably placed for the ruler's seat; there can be little doubt that he founded Demetrias to be again a joint capital and therefore founded it at, or as representing, the old Persian centre, 'the Aracho-

1 Marcianus I, 32 (*GGM* I p. 534); from some Hellenistic source.

2 Plut. *Mor.* 328 D.

3 On the natural division of Gedrosia into two halves and the greater importance of the eastern half see Kiessling, *Gedrosia* in PW. Stephanus *s.v.* Arabis implies that at some period eastern Gedrosia was autonomous; I do not know what it means.

4 Arr. VI, 22, 4; Strabo XV, 721.

5 Rapson, *NC* 1904 pp. 319–21.

6 Isidore 19.

7 For the whole of this paragraph see Appendix 9.

sians'; in the first century B.C. the old town-name, as happened so often, came back in the form Arachosia. It was not a retrograde step, for the division of the land into at least three Parthian satrapies later[1] shows that Arachosia-with-Seistan formed at least three separate satrapal governments (representing the Seleucid eparchies) under the Euthydemid sub-king, Arachosia forming one satrapy and Seistan at least two—Zarangiane, the Hamun lake country, and Paraitakene, the lower Helmand, afterwards Sacastene; there may have been a third, Tatakene.[2]

There is no real evidence as to who was Demetrius' sub-king in Seistan-Arachosia till we come to Pantaleon and Agathocles (Chap. IV), who show that these provinces were a unit of government; but as Demetrius cannot have employed his two younger sons before the two elder ones, whose dates are reasonably certain, there must have been an earlier sub-king. Since the only alternative to Apollodotus would be to invent an unknown prince who has left no trace in the coinage, that sub-king can only have been Apollodotus; his coins have been found there,[3] but apparently Euthydemus' copper was still struck as the copper currency of the new provinces. What happened to Aria (Herat) is uncertain, but it is more probable that it was joined to Antimachus' kingdom than to Seistan-Arachosia; for when the colleague of Mithridates II, *i.e.* the Suren, drove the Saca invaders northward he recorded on his coins the conquest of Aria, Traxiane, and Merv,[4] which may mean that he was clearing Antimachus' one-time kingdom before dealing with Seistan-Arachosia. What is tolerably certain is that, when Eucratides arrived, Antimachus and Agathocles between them were ruling all the Iranian provinces westward of Bactria and India, however divided (see further Chap. V).

This finishes the outlying provinces of the Bactrian realm; but before coming to Bactria itself something must be said about the extremely important country which under the Persians and Alexander had been the satrapy of the Paropamisadae,[5] though it may not have been acquired

[1] Isidore 17, 18, 19. It must be remembered that he does not give *all* the Parthian satrapies. [2] Ptol. VI, 19, 3.

[3] Cunningham, *NC* 1869 p. 146, 1870 p. 78; *BMC* p. xxxvii; *CHI* p. 548.

[4] Tarn, *SP Stud.* pp. 16–18. For the identity of my 'king of the campaign coins' with Herzfeld's Suren see Appendix 16.

[5] I follow Strabo's spelling; Arrian's Parapamisadae looks like an obvious Greek alteration. The forms Paropanisadae and Parapanisadae also occur. All I want is the name by which Greeks knew the country; which form is likeliest to be correct is guess-work.

till after Euthydemus' death. Certainly it lay on the Indian side of the Hindu Kush; but at this time it belonged very definitely to the Iranian and not to the Indian system, which I understand accords with the physical nature of the country. This satrapy had once extended to the Indus,[1] but in the second century B.C., as doubtless since Alexander's time, it only reached from the Hindu Kush to the Kunar river, comprising the country which was to be one of the Greek strongholds for a century after the loss of Bactria itself—the valleys of the Panjshir and Ghorband rivers under the Hindu Kush, some part of Kafiristan, and also Laghman, Kabulistan, and the country about the Kabul (Kophen) river to the frontier town towards Gandhāra, Ptolemy's Nagara-Dionysopolis, represented to-day by Jalalabad. (See Map 3.)

The Paropamisadae, to-day part of Afghanistan, has sometimes been politically part of India, but throughout the Macedonian period it had been considered to belong to Iran, even though Indian or semi-Indian races might extend north and west of the Kunar river; the mixture of races is reflected in the fact that the satrapy had no racial name like Media or Bactria, but was only known to Greeks as 'the Paropamisadae', the peoples of the Paropamisus or Hindu Kush; if it had an official name it is lost. Alexander had appointed a succession of Iranian satraps to the country—Proexes, Tyriaspes, Oxyartes;[2] Eratosthenes had expressly distinguished it from India;[3] a number of the old local names are said to be Iranian;[4] and it had received the regular organisation of a Seleucid satrapy, the division into eparchies.[5] Most of the eparchy names can be recovered. Pliny (VI, 92) gives the name Kapisene, with Kapisa as its capital; it included the Panjshir valley and Kafiristan, or part of it. Stephanus gives the name Opiane[6] with its capital Alexandria;

[1] Eratosthenes *ap.* Strabo XV, 723–4. He made the Indus the western boundary of India (Strabo XV, 689; Pliny VI, 56), a statement repeated by other ancient writers.

[2] H. Berve, *Das Alexanderreich*, under the several names.

[3] Strabo XV, 723–4.

[4] A. Foucher, *JA* 216, 1931, p. 358.

[5] The names, like the corresponding names in Gandhāra (p. 237), represent Demetrius' division into satrapies, but, unlike Gandhāra, they must have been Seleucid eparchies first. That they would be small compared to those of (say) Media is naturally no objection: Rutland is a county as much as Yorkshire.

[6] Alexandria no. 5, *ἐν τῇ Ὀπιάνῃ κατὰ τὴν Ἰνδικήν*. Opiane is the regio referred to in Pliny VI, 92, deinde cujus oppidum Alexandria a conditore dictum; the clause, often misunderstood, is quite complete as it stands, regio being understood after deinde from the clause before. Pliny's sixth book is only a collection of notes very briefly transcribed; but VI, 92, the Paropamisadae, is good stuff if properly construed.

the connection of Opiane with the ruins of Opian near Charikar seems obvious, and presumably it also included the country to the southward about Ak Serai. Kabulistan was Kophene, with its capital Kophen (Ortospana-Kabul), origin of the Chinese Ki-pin (App. 9). The fourth eparchy was the Ghorband valley with Bamyan, extending to the boundary of Bactria, wherever it was. Its name is unknown, but it is given in Pliny as the regio (province) about Cartana, north of Opiane and opposite Bactria,[1] an unmistakable description of the district through which ran the main route (p. 139) between Bactra and Alexandria in Opiane. Last comes Strabo's Bandobene,[2] a name found again on the Bactrian side of the mountains (p. 114); it must be Laghman, as no other district is left. To call all this country the upper Kabul valley, as is often done, is misleading, especially as in the Greek period Kabul was of very secondary importance, and in default of better I shall keep the clumsy but expressive Greek name 'the Paropamisadae'.

There was a good deal of Greek settlement in the country, and there was one city of considerable importance, the double city Alexandria-Kapisa,[3] capital of the Paropamisadae and gateway of India, which stood at the 'τρίοδος from Bactra', the point where the three routes over the Hindu Kush (p. 139) from Bactria met; roughly speaking, the τρίοδος was about the junction of the Panjshir and Ghorband rivers. Alexander had founded Alexandria of the Caucasus, the 'Queen of the Mountains' of the Alexander-Romance, on the west side of the united Panjshir-Ghorband river near their confluence in what was afterwards Opiane, facing the old native town of Kapisa on the east side in what was afterwards Kapisene. Alexandria was the Greek city, and must have had a substantial Greek population, but the chief god of the combined city, as the coins show, was the elephant-god of Kapisa who lived on Mount Pīlusāra and was graecised as Zeus (pp. 138, 213). The two towns must have formed one city, but their political relationship cannot be guessed. The Hellenistic world was familiar with double

[1] Pliny VI, 92; coming from the north, Cartana oppidum...haec regio est ex adverso Bactrianorum. Opiane (see preceding note) immediately follows.

[2] Strabo XV, 697, a confused passage; his 'Choaspes', flowing through Bandobene and Gandhāra, must here mean, not the Kunar, but the united Panjshir-Ghorband river. Writers sometimes treated one river of the Paropamisadae system as the main river, sometimes another (A. Foucher, *BSOS* VI, 1930–2, p. 347); hence a good deal of confusion.

[3] On this and what follows see Appendix 6.

cities, like Demetrias-Pagasae,[1] but it is hardly possible that Kapisa should have been a deme of Alexandria as Pagasae was of Demetrias; it may have ranked in Greek eyes as its 'village', but we really know no more how the native city was part of Alexandria than we do how Babylonian Opis was part of Seleuceia on the Tigris. But if a modern theory be correct,[2] there was a close parallel to Alexandria-Kapisa in Seleuceia-Ctesiphon (Old Ctesiphon), which was also one city though divided by the Tigris, and which may have been copied from the older foundation. Native Ctesiphon must have received some Greek settlers, and, though at first a 'village', perhaps ultimately became, or called itself, a *polis*.[3] There is nothing to show that Kapisa ever became a separate *polis*; but as it was the capital of Kapisene there must have been some Greek settlement there. It would be natural to suppose that the palace and government buildings, and also the mint, were in the Greek city; but though Alexandria had doubtless been the satrapal seat, it does not follow that it was the seat of the Euthydemid sub-kings who from time to time governed the Paropamisadae. Given the Euthydemid native policy, which we shall come to, there are many reasons why these sub-kings might have preferred to live in the native city: Demetrius, we shall see, built what was virtually an Indian city to be his capital, and Menander, who carried on the Euthydemid tradition, took for his capital the Indian Sāgala and not the Greek Bucephala; and apart from policy the same motives of convenience may have come into play as those which led the later Parthian kings to make Ctesiphon and not Seleuceia their capital. Towards the close of Greek rule Alexandria and Kapisa, again like Seleuceia and Ctesiphon, were not always, it seems, under the same government; and there must have been a branch of the mint in both towns, normally using the same types, but each able on occasion to function independently. If we could distinguish the two mints, which at present seems impossible, it would be a great help towards reconstructing the story.

Cartana, nicknamed Tetragonis, must also have been a Greek city,

[1] On the situation of these two towns, one on either side of the river Lagororema, see now *Pagasai und Demetrias* by Fr. Stählin, Ernst Meyer, and A. Heidner, 1934 (map at end).

[2] McDowell, *Coins from Seleucia* pp. 177 *sqq*.

[3] Ctesiphon a κώμη, Strabo XVI, 743; a πόλις Ἑλληνίς, Jos. *Ant.* XVIII, 377. The two city-Fortunes holding hands on some coins of Seleuceia, first century A.D., have been thought to be Seleuceia and Ctesiphon; Allotte de la Fuye, *MDP* XX, 1928, p. 39 no. 24; McDowell *op. cit.* pp. 100, 177–9.

a native place rebuilt on the Hellenistic model,[1] for *tetragonos* is practically a technical term for a city laid out on the Hellenistic plan described by Polybius,[2] four-square with two main roads intersecting at the centre of the city. Pliny puts it in the Ghorband eparchy (p. 97) and there can be little doubt that it was Bamyan;[3] the great Buddhist sculptures found at Bamyan attest its importance later, and it must have been equally important in the Greek period from its position on the principal route (p. 139) from Bactra to Alexandria-Kapisa and so to India. Another Greek city, Nicaea, perhaps founded by Alexander, is mentioned once, somewhere near and apparently south of Alexandria;[4] but it cannot be identified and may no longer have existed in the Greek period. Alexandria, Cartana, and Nicaea are the only places which can be figured as Greek cities; but there must have been a Greek settlement in the frontier town of Nagara-Dionysopolis (p. 159), and also at Kophen-Kabul (App. 9) on the road which ran from Alexandria-Kapisa by Alexandria-Ghazni to Seistan, though the French mission found Kabul disappointing. There must of course have been some military settlements, though they would usually be concealed under native names. One of Cretans, Asterusia, is recorded;[5] an unnamed foundation ascribed to Alexander[6] would be another; Menander, who was a Greek of the Paropamisadae, may have been born in one (p. 141); and Pliny gives a tribe Cataces or Cateces, which is only one of his usual mistaken transliterations from the Greek and is really *κάτοικοι* (*catoeci*), settlers.[7]

[1] Pliny VI, 92, postea Tetragonis dictum, shows it was rebuilt.

[2] Polyb. VI, 31, 10, *τετράγωνον*; Strabo XII, 566, *ἐν τετραγώνῳ σχήματι*. See pp. 419 *sq.*

[3] *If* it be Ptolemy's Carsana, as Cunningham thought (*Geog.* p. 32), then Ptolemy's unnamed river is the Ghorband.

[4] Arr. IV, 22, 6; he of course uses the later name Nicaea proleptically, which has been misunderstood (as by Tscherikower p. 104) but is common enough in Greek (*e.g.* Hekatompylos in the Alexander-historians) as in English. Nicaea *might* be the 'other city', a day's journey from Alexandria, of Diod. XVII, 83, 2; I do not see how it could be Kapisa.

[5] Stephanus *s.v.*

[6] Pliny VI, 92, ad Caucasum Cadrusi, oppidum ab Alexandro conditum. This has been much misunderstood, and Cadrusi has been called a city (Tscherikower p. 104; Kiessling, *Gedrosia* in PW, 902). Certainly there were town-names in India ending in -i, which Greeks sometimes transliterated by iota and sometimes by eta. But had Pliny meant a town, he would have written, as he regularly does, oppidum Cadrusi, and on his usage the meaning is clear enough: 'the Cadrusi (and among them) a city founded by Alexander.' The Cadrusi are otherwise unknown; Kiessling thought it the same word as Gedrosi.

[7] Pliny *ib.* For a rough list of similar mistakes see p. 482 n. 3.

The Paropamisadae was not among the provinces ceded by Seleucus to Chandragupta. Extravagant views have been put forward as to what Seleucus did cede,[1] but there is a passage from Eratosthenes, usually neglected, which seems plain enough.[2] It says that, before Alexander, the Paropamisadae, Arachosia,[3] and Gedrosia all stretched to the Indus; the reference is to the Achaemenid satrapies, and it implies that in Persian times the Paropamisadae and Gandhāra were one satrapy. Alexander (it continues) took away from Iran the parts of these three satrapies which lay along the Indus and made of them separate κατοικίαι (which must here mean governments or provinces); it was these which Seleucus ceded, being districts predominantly Indian in blood. In Gedrosia the boundary is known; the country ceded was that between the Median Hydaspes (probably the Purali) and the Indus, as is shown by a later mention of the Hydaspes[4] as the boundary of Iran in this direction. Of the satrapy which Eratosthenes calls Paropamisadae Chandragupta got Gandhāra, the land between the Kunar river and the Indus; this is certain, because Eratosthenes says that he did not get the whole, while the thorough evangelisation of Gandhāra by Asoka shows that it belonged to the Mauryas. The boundary in Arachosia cannot be precisely defined; but, speaking very roughly, what Chandragupta got lay east of a line starting from the Kunar river and following the watershed to somewhere near Quetta and then going to the sea by Kalat and the Purali river; that will serve as an indication. The Paropamisadae itself was never Chandragupta's.

When Alexander died, the satrap of the Paropamisadae was his

[1] The worst has been that of V. A. Smith (App. F in the 4th ed.), who gave Chandragupta the satrapies of Gedrosia, Arachosia, Paropamisadae *and Aria* on the strength of Pliny VI, 69, a historical absurdity of unknown origin.

[2] Strabo XV, 724; I gave it briefly in *CAH* VI pp. 413–14. The whole passage is from Eratosthenes, from his name in 723 onwards; this is shown by the Indus being the boundary of India.

[3] For Arachosia there is ample confirmation; Darius I got ivory from it (inscription from the Apadāna at Susa l. 43, see p. 103 n. 5) and Darius III elephants, Arr. III, 8, 4 and 6.

[4] Kiessling, *Hydaspes* 2 in PW. Orosius V, 14, 6 (Mithridates I conquers from the Hydaspes to the Indus), from Livy, shows that it was the boundary of Iran, though the conquest may have been transferred to him from the later 'Indo-Parthians'. Herzfeld, *Sakastan* p. 40, says there was no Hydaspes in Iran and would read in Orosius Choaspes (near Susa), which makes no sense; moreover the name graecised as Hydaspes seems to be not Indian but Iranian: *CHI* p. 568; J. Charpentier, *JRAS* 1927 p. 115.

father-in-law, the Bactrian Oxyartes; he must have become virtually independent during the wars of the Successors, though he or his successor finally accepted the overlordship of Seleucus. One of the best numismatic authorities on these eastern borderlands has held that the name Vakhsuvar on a famous coin dated in the year 83 of some era is a transcript of Oxyartes and that the era cannot be the Seleucid;[1] his deduction that Oxyartes founded a dynasty whose members all bore the same name and that this is a coin of the dynasty struck in a year between the limits 253 and 244 is very attractive, for such a dynasty has a certain probability in itself and would agree with Asoka's inscriptions. Another of Alexander's Iranian satraps, Atropates, founded a similar dynasty in Azerbaijan, 'Media of Atropates', which lasted long and at one time played some part in history;[2] and there is another case beside that of Oxyartes where only a single coin remains to testify to a lost kingdom (p. 484). The Oxyartes dynasty (if it existed) must have remained Seleucid vassals down to the time of this coin, the time which saw the hand of the Seleucid slacken in the East and Asoka the Maurya at the height of his power. Asoka has recorded that he sent missionaries to Greeks on his frontier, which, from their being coupled with the Kambojas of Kafiristan (Kapisene), means the Paropamisadae; but whereas at first he calls these Greeks a frontier people,[3] he afterwards treats them as included within his dominions.[4] It looks as though, soon after the date of the coin, the Oxyartes dynasty ended and Asoka established some form of rule or suzerainty over the Paropamisadae, for when Antiochus III crossed the Hindu Kush, far from re-establishing Seleucid suzerainty over the province, he renewed friendship with Asoka's descendant the Maurya Sophagasenos (p. 130) and merely used the occasion to raise the number of his elephants to 150, an overwhelming force which, properly handled, should have saved the battle of Magnesia by preventing Eumenes from charging. It cannot be said whether either Euthydemus or Demetrius acquired this important province prior to 184 (Chap. IV), for that Menander, a Greek of the Paropamisadae, had already been in Demetrius' service for some time before that date (p. 141) proves nothing; it is possible, but the history

[1] Allotte de la Fuye, *Rev. Num.* 1910 pp. 290 *sqq.*, 1925 p. 31. There are other explanations of the word.

[2] For Atropatene see Herzfeld, *Sakastan* p. 55 and *passim*; also the story of Antony.

[3] Rock Edict 5.

[4] Rock Edict 13.

of the Paropamisadae is a blank between 206 (Antiochus III) and Demetrius' invasion of India.

I come now to the kernel of Euthydemus' kingdom, Bactria itself, including southern Sogdiana, the Samarcand country; for the natural line of division is said to be the mountains north of Samarcand, and whatever the political boundaries might be southern Sogdiana belonged to the Oxus basin and northern Sogdiana (*para Sugdam*) belonged with Ferghana to the basin of the Jaxartes. Apollodorus says that what made the Bactrian Greeks so powerful was the fertility of the country.[1] We have to think, not of the Afghanistan of to-day, but of a second Babylonia;[2] a land of irrigation canals, where the Oxus and each of its tributaries were utilised to the utmost for cultivation, where Merv was the centre of one vast garden, and where the Samarcand district, said to be the most fertile land in Central Asia, was such a rich complex of water-courses and husbandry that its river, from which most of the water was drawn off before it could reach the desert, was known to Greeks as Polytimetus, 'the most precious'; a land comparatively thick with settlement, whatever the nationality of the settlers; a land called by Greeks the Jewel of Iran.[3] The goddess of the land, Anahita 'the undefiled' (Anaïtis), who in an old description has a thousand arms and a thousand canals, and streams mightily down from the mountains to the Aral Sea, was originally the personification of the mighty Oxus itself;[4] Bactria almost *was* the Oxus, in the sense that Egypt was the Nile.[5] It has been pointed out that, as a general thing, the deserts in north-eastern Iran given by Ptolemy are too small to accord with those now existing, that in Margiane he locates towns where to-day is only sand, and that remains of towns, villages, and cultivated land have been found beneath the Kizil-Kum desert in Sogdiana,[6] as they have beneath the Taklamakan, the moving desert of Chinese Turkestan. The Achaemenids had always paid great attention to the maintenance and development of irrigation,[7] a thing inculcated by the Zoroastrian religion,[8] and parts of Iran, which otherwise would have been useless,

[1] Strabo XI, 516. [2] Cf. Berthelot p. 182.

[3] Apollodorus' phrase (Strabo *ib.*), τῆς συμπάσης Ἀριανῆς πρόσχημα.

[4] Ed. Meyer, *Anaïtis* in Roscher. See also on Anaïtis O. M. Dalton, *The treasure of the Oxus*, 2nd ed. 1926 pp. xxvii *sqq.*, 26 no. 103, 52 no. 198.

[5] The Russians to-day claim that the Oxus silt has the higher fertilising value of the two.

[6] Berthelot pp. 180 *sqq.* and *passim.* [7] Polyb. x, 28, 3 *sq.*

[8] Fr. Cumont, *CR Ac. Inscr.* 1931 pp. 249 *sq.*

were kept in cultivation by a system of underground channels which brought water down from the hills, known to Greeks as ὑπόνομοι[1] and to-day called Karezes;[2] Greeks, as was vital, continued the Persian policy, and two of the most important of the Greek inscriptions from Susa allude to the restoration or amelioration of the irrigation channels on its territory.[3]

But the wealth of Bactria lay in, and not below, its soil. Certainly in the Middle Ages there were three famous mine-fields in north-eastern Iran; but I do not know whether the ruby mines of Badakshan were being worked in the Greek period,[4] though they were under the Yueh-chi; and though the turquoise mines of Khorasan were presumably worked they were anyhow in Parthia, not in Bactria.[5] The lapis lazuli mines[6] in Sogdiana (Yamghan), which were of great antiquity, were at work, for Darius I, as his invaluable inscription from the Apadāna at Susa shows, had got lapis from Sogdiana for that building,[7] and as the Greeks continued to work them[8] they were doubtless a source of income; the same inscription may show that Sogdiana produced carnelian, much used for seals. Badakshan to-day produces some copper and iron, and may always have done so; but Bactria in Greek times was

[1] Polyb. x, 28, 3 *sq.*

[2] See on these Sir A. Stein, *J. R. Anthrop. Inst.* LXIV, 1934, pp. 188, 196.

[3] *SEG* VII, 12, 13.

[4] I have failed to find out how old the balas ruby is. The earliest I have met with are those on the Bimarān casket, which was found with coins of Azes I and is probably not *earlier* than *c.* 30 B.C.; some ruby beads from Taxila are also not earlier than Azes, *ASI* 1915–16 p. 5. For Roman times see Warmington, p. 249, who tells me he has not met with the balas ruby in Hellenistic or Greek times. Yet it is hard to believe that the mine was first opened by the Yueh-chi.

[5] One interpretation of l. 39 of Darius' inscription from the Apadāna at Susa (V. Scheil, *MDP* XXI, 1929, p. 9) makes him get turquoise from Chorasmia (R. G. Kent, *JAOS* LI, 1931, pp. 189 *sqq.*; LIII, 1933, p. 1); but other interpretations are haematite (Scheil) and grey amber (Herzfeld, *Arch. Mitt. aus Iran* III, 1931, pp. 29 *sqq.*), and anyhow Chorasmia, whatever it meant at this time (see App. 11), was not in the Bactrian kingdom. There is a good deal of turquoise paste in the jewelry found at Taxila. Pliny XXXVII, 110 speaks of turquoise coming from the Sacas; but the notice cannot be dated, so it is impossible to say what it means.

[6] See Marco Polo I, Chapter XXIX, with Yule's note, 2nd ed. p. 170 (3rd ed. p. 162).

[7] Darius' inscription, l. 37. Kent's article of 1933 (n. 5, *above*) gives the literature.

[8] A ring of gold and lapis engraved with a Hellenistic warrior and ascribed by Marshall to the second century B.C. was found at Taxila, *ASI* 1912–13 p. 27. Most of the lapis from Taxila belongs to the great mass of jewelry of the first century A.D.; *ASI* 1914–15 ii p. 18, 1915–16 p. 24, 1924–5 p. 49 no. 2, 1929–30 p. 60 no. 15.

seemingly poor in precious metals. In Arab times there were rich mines of silver at Anderab and also mines in Wakhan,[1] but it seems improbable that they were worked or much worked in the Greek period, for there are signs that Euthydemus was short of silver; many of his tetradrachms were struck upon old coins already in circulation,[2] and he attempted at the end of his life to import nickel from China. East of the Hindu Kush, however, the silver mines on the Panjshir river,[3] which were to supply the mint at Alexandria-Kapisa, were doubtless working to some extent—one of the things which made that city such a desirable acquisition.

As to gold, Bactria-Sogdiana did not produce any, and the fact that in Darius' inscription no gold came from Sogdiana shows that the Greek name for the Zarafshan river, Polytimetus 'the most precious', referred not to gold-washing but to its value for irrigation. Now the first and best-known sign of independence, in king or country, was to coin gold. Both Diodotus and Euthydemus struck a few gold staters, but they are said to be rare[4] and these coinages cannot have been large; those of Euthydemus were struck early in his reign[5] and may have only meant the putting into circulation of the accumulated reserve which must have existed in Bactria as in every satrapy. But after Euthydemus no king of or in Bactria, not even Demetrius, ever coined gold: the 20-stater memorial piece of Eucratides and his solitary gold stater (p. 208) were probably struck from the gold he brought from the west in his war-chest. There was no real supply of gold in Bactria or coming to it, and even in India no Greek or Saca king coined gold;[6] one gold coin of Taxila, presumably pre-Greek, is known, the only gold coin of ancient India itself.[7] A true gold coinage first occurs with the Kushans; that is much later than the period I am considering, and their gold was imported from the Western world.[8]

[1] W. Barthold, *Turkestan down to the Mongol invasion* 1928 pp. 65, 67. Marco Polo also refers to silver mines in Badakshan in his day.

[2] Allotte de la Fuye, *Rev. Num.* 1910 p. 299.

[3] Yule *op. cit.* I, p. 170 (3rd ed. p. 162).

[4] Whitehead, *NC* p. 300: the known total of both kings cannot amount to 30.

[5] The heads on his three gold staters in the British Museum are about the youngest heads of him extant.

[6] There is a gold stater in the British Museum, without any legend, which shows a badly executed owl and might therefore conceivably be Menander's; but Whitehead, *Lahore Cat.* p. 5 n. 1, considers it impossible to make any attribution.

[7] *BMC India* pp. cxxxviii, 236 no. 169. But Whitehead, *NC* p. 299 n. 5, says there are two or three.

[8] Long known. See now Warmington p. 299.

The gold question in Bactria and India is so peculiar and so illuminating for one point in the history of Euthydemus that it merits closer examination. For in the past Bactria had been, in legend and in fact, a golden land; from Bactria the Persian empire had drawn its gold, as is illustrated by the golden Treasure of the Oxus of the fifth and fourth centuries B.C.[1] Bactria's neighbours the Massagetae had also in the fifth century possessed gold in such abundance that they used it to make bits and trappings for their horses,[2] as the Turdetani in Spain made their horses' mangers of silver.[3] The Bactrian gold supply is epigraphically attested in the inscription already referred to, in which Darius I listed the countries which supplied the various materials for building the Apadāna at Susa; the gold, he says (l. 35), came from Sardis and Bactria, the silver (l. 40) from Egypt. But Egypt has never produced an ounce of silver from one end of its history to the other; it was transit silver, Egypt being the middleman, and Darius' statement means that the satrap of Egypt sent the silver; where it originated is not said.[4] In the same way the satraps of Sardis and Bactria sent gold; the gold of the Pactolus in Lydia is well known, but Bactria, like Egypt, was only a middleman.

There is no mystery as to the source of the Bactrian gold; it came to Bactria, as it came to South Russia, from Siberia[5]—the 'griffin-gold' whose guardian griffin adorned the coinage of Panticapaeum. This was the main Asiatic source of supply; it furnished the gold for the mass of Siberian and South Russian gold-work which is the glory of the Hermitage Museum in Leningrad. The gold is usually said to have come from the Altai mountains, known to the Mongols as 'the mountains of gold'; at the beginning of the present century, however, the mines of the Altai proper were not producing gold, though to the northward in the Kusnetsk region, now being developed as a coalfield, there were said to be many alluvial deposits.[6] But both in antiquity and in the Middle Ages mining, in the absence of machinery, was a primitive and laborious business, and far more gold was obtained from river-washings than from mines;[7] even at the beginning of the present

[1] Dalton *op. cit.* p. xvi. In the British Museum.

[2] Herod. I, 215.

[3] Strabo III, 151.

[4] The obvious source is Spain, *via* Carthage; but if so one would have expected it to go to Tyre, not to Egypt.

[5] See generally Dalton *op. cit.* pp. xvii–xx.

[6] *Enc. Brit.* 1911 *s.v.* Altai.

[7] On this point Strabo III, 146 is as explicit for Spain as is Marco Polo II chaps. 47–58 for Yunnan.

century the main Siberian source of supply was from the washings on the Lena and Amur,[1] and most of the recent discoveries have been in the Lena country.[2] The Lena may be too distant to have ever supplied Iran, and doubtless the bulk of the gold came from washings on nearer rivers; both the Obi and Yenisei systems originate in the Kusnetsk country, and new gold fields are said to have been discovered about the head waters of both rivers.[3] Probably gold was obtained over a very large district; to the ancient world the supply seemed inexhaustible, and it was only a question of being able to tap it; it is claimed to-day that Siberia possesses greater resources in gold than any other country.[4] The antiquity of the Siberian washings is shown by the discovery at Tepé Hissar near Damghan of a gold treasure, with five gold mouflon heads, dating from about 1500 B.C.[5] In Achaemenid times there must have been a definite 'gold route' to Bactria, and all or most of the gold would come in the form of gold-dust.

So far the matter is simple; in Darius' day the Siberian gold was coming to Bactria, in Euthydemus' day it was not. But when we turn to India the question is more complex. According to Herodotus, Darius received every year at Susa 4680 talents in gold-dust as the tribute of his Indian satrapy, a tribute utterly out of proportion to that paid, in silver or in kind, by any other satrapy.[6] How came it then that the Greeks found no gold worth mentioning in India, and that Darius sent to the distant satrapies of Sardis and Bactria to get gold for his Apadāna instead of using the great amount which reached Susa every year from India? For he did not use Indian gold; the inscription is specific that India only contributed ivory (l. 43) and Gandhāra (l. 34) Yakā-wood.[7] In Herodotus' story, which he got from Persians who had got it in turn from Indians, the Indian gold was 'ant-gold', dug up by ants in the burning Thar desert,[8] *i.e.* just beyond the world he and

[1] *Enc. Brit.* 1911 *s.v.* Siberia. It seemed unnecessary to look up the reports of the Lena Goldfields Company.

[2] See the map in N. Mikhaylov, *Soviet Geography* 1935 p. 29.

[3] *Ib.*

[4] Mikhaylov *op. cit.* p. 90. His text, perhaps intentionally, is very sketchy as to what the Soviet Government *have* discovered. But the Russian gold production is already (1937) greater than that of any country except South Africa.

[5] *Rev. Arch.* 1933 i p. 108.

[6] Herod. III, 94 *sq.* The tribute of the rest of the empire was valued at 9540 talents, the largest single payment, Babylonia, being 1000 talents.

[7] On the various interpretations see Kent *op. cit.* 1933 p. 17.

[8] Herod. III, 102–5.

the Persians knew. Megasthenes too was told of 'ant-gold' by his Indian informants, but, as he knew Rajputana, the ants were shifted to Dardistan,[1] to the upper gorges of the Indus, *i.e.* just beyond the world *he* knew. The reference to 'ant-gold', *pipilika*, in the Mahābhārata shows, as these stories show, that the name was current among Indians and was not a Greek or Persian invention. The name in fact came with the gold; it has been shown that the ant-gold was only the Siberian gold again and that the name is known in Mongolian and Thibetan sagas.[2] It has been suggested that the name arose from a confusion of the name of a Mongolian tribe with the Mongolian word for ant;[3] but how old these words may be I do not know, and as the gold in question was gold-dust I would rather suppose that the name was derived from the well-known class of folk-tales in which the ant-king and his subjects, to help the hero, collect for him a mass of little grains of something which he cannot collect for himself;[4] for it was this meaning which ultimately lay behind the story told to Herodotus of the ants extracting the grains of gold from the sands of the desert. The *application* of the name to the gold was no doubt due to the middlemen on the gold route, who wished to prevent their clients discovering the source of supply.[5] Indians did not know the source of supply, but they knew how the gold came to them (whether it came through Bactria or across the difficult passes into Gandhāra or Kashmir), and they in turn were ready to tell any story which might put too inquisitive westerners off the scent; hence the fairy-tale told to Herodotus of the ants digging up grains of gold in the desert, while some skins of the ants were exhibited

[1] Strabo xv, 705 *sq.*; Arr. *Ind.* 15, 5 *sq.*

[2] B. Laufer, *Die Sage von den goldgrabenden Ameisen*, *T'oung Pao* IX, 1908, p. 429. Laufer admitted (p. 444) that on chronological grounds the name *might* have travelled from India to Mongolia and not *vice versa*; but Darius' Susa inscription has now made this impossible and has confirmed his view. There is no need now to refer to the stock explanation of the 'ants', going back to Humboldt and given by many writers, most recently by R. Hennig, *Rh. Mus.* LXXX, 1931, p. 331; once the facts are sorted out it is impossible, for two separate reasons.

[3] Laufer *op. cit.* p. 451, Shiraighol and shirgol (an ant).

[4] For two ant-stories of the sort from Khalatse near Leh see A. H. Francke, *Asia Major* I, 1924, p. 67. He was also shown a large live ant which was called a 'gold-digger'. The name may have sprung from folk-lore; or again it may mean no more than the name of the tiny spider which in Britain is called a 'money-spinner'.

[5] Laufer *op. cit.* pp. 430, 451. The story of the griffins was no doubt told by other middlemen on the route to South Russia; it has been suggested that the idea of 'griffins' was due to South Siberian art, R. Hennig, *Klio* XXVIII, 1935, p. 249.

to the honest Nearchus, who said that they were very like the skins of leopards.[1]

Not one ounce of ant-gold ever originated in India, and the Greeks got no gold worth mentioning in north-west India because there was next to none there[2] and the Siberian supply had stopped; the only native Indian gold of any account came from the washings on the upper Ganges and its tributaries which are referred to by Megasthenes[3] and Pliny[4] and probably (later) by the Brihat Samhitā.[5] In fact Indians knew next to nothing about gold-mining; Alexander's mining engineer Gorgos, who opened a silver mine[6] in the Salt Range in Sopeithes' kingdom whence came Sopeithes' unique silver coinage, said that Indian ideas of mining and refining were elementary,[7] and Megasthenes said that they did not even know how to separate gold from dross.[8] Essentially, India's gold was imported and so had to be paid for like other commodities; the North-West got its gold from Siberia, the East probably imported some gold from the very rich river-washings in Yunnan and the neighbouring provinces,[9] in either case in the form of gold-dust; there were no other sources of supply,[10] unless in China, and in the first century A.D. northern and western India sought to offset the loss of the Siberian supply by importing bullion, or coins used as bullion, from the Roman world.[11] Darius' Indian satrapy *may* have paid its tribute in imported gold-dust, but the prodigious amount mentioned by Herodotus could never have been paid for; it is irreconcilable with the facts and with Darius' inscription, and cannot be true.

[1] Strabo xv, 705, cf. Arr. *Ind.* 15, 4.

[2] Explicitly stated for Alexander's day, Arr. v, 4, 4.

[3] Strabo xv, 711.

[4] Pliny xxxiii, 66; see Warmington p. 258.

[5] This is the north-eastern *kanaka* or 'gold region' of the topographical list in that work; J. F. Fleet, *Ind. Ant.* xxii, 1893, p. 171. Its topographical indications are said to be none too accurate, but it gives another 'gold region' in the western division, in Aparānta (east coast of the Gulf of Cambaye), which can only refer to the imported gold of the Roman period, when, besides coin from the Roman Empire, Barygaza was importing gold from Omana (p. 483), whether Arabian gold re-exported (*Periplus* 36) or gold from the Hyctanis in Carmania (Pliny vi, 98).

[6] Strabo xv, 700; the mine is called silver and gold, but obviously it produced little gold.

[7] *Ib.* 700.

[8] *Ib.* 706.

[9] Marco Polo, ii, chaps. 47–58; merchants came to fetch the gold (53). Chang-k'ien found cloth from Yunnan and Szechuan passing through India to Bactria, p. 87.

[10] Arr. *Ind.* 8, 13 and Pliny vi, 17 are only references to Megasthenes' ant-gold.

[11] Bullion, *Periplus* 36; coins, Warmington pp. 279–92.

The bearing of this on the most obscure of the few facts recorded about Euthydemus, his expedition to the Seres, seems clear. Somewhere between the reigns of Darius I and his own the influx of gold from Siberia into Bactria and India had practically ceased,[1] not because the source of supply had failed, but because some movement of peoples in Central Asia had cut the route and destroyed the accustomed machinery of the gold trade, just as the old amber route from the Baltic to the Mediterranean was cut early in the Greek period and not restored till the reign of Nero;[2] the golden road to Samarcand was no longer golden. Now if Euthydemus, late in life, made conquests in the Tarim basin, it is natural to suppose that, being short of precious metals, he would have first tried to deal with a much more important matter, the restoration of the import of gold from Siberia and the re-establishment of the gold route; this meant getting into contact with whoever had been the middlemen for southern Siberia, as he could not hope to reach the source of supply itself, and this is the meaning of Apollodorus' statement, which I deferred considering (p. 84), that the Greek kings of Bactria (which we saw could only mean Euthydemus) made conquests as far as the Seres. Euthydemus then made an expedition from Ferghana into Siberia along what had been the gold route. Since the Koslov expedition to Mongolia it has been established that in the second and first centuries B.C. there was a northern trade route to China running through Mongolia and quite independent of the routes through Chinese Turkestan, and evidence now exists of artistic influences exercised by Hellenism on the art of Siberia in the second and first centuries B.C. which can only have originated in contact with the Greeks of Bactria,[3] while in the latter century Greek, Iranian, and Chinese products and art motives all met in distant Mongolia.[4] The south-western end of this northern trade route, which must have reached the Greek sphere in Ferghana, must have been closely connected, if not identical, with the old gold route, and it was Euthydemus' expedition which started

[1] The account of the gold of the Massagetae in Strabo XI, 513 is merely copied from Herod. I, 125, and does not refer to anything later than the early fifth century B.C.

[2] Blümner, *Bernstein* in PW.

[3] Dalton *op. cit.* p. li, and the discoveries of the Koslov expedition, published only in Russian; on these see W. P. Yetts, *Burlington Magazine* 1926, pp. 168, 174; M. Rostovtzeff, *Mon. Piot* XXVIII, 1925–6, pp. 171 *sqq.* Some articles found are thought to have been made in Bactria; see p. 363.

[4] Yetts *op. cit. passim.*

Hellenic influences and products travelling along this road. But what he himself was seeking was obviously the Seres.

The passage in Apollodorus is the earliest known mention of this word.[1] The name Seres in the sense of the silk-producing people of the extreme East, the Chinese, does not occur before the time of Julius Caesar and Augustus;[2] knowledge in the West of the Chinese was one of the consequences of the opening up of through trade between China and Iran in 106 B.C., due to Chang-k'ien's discoveries. But Pliny (VI, 88) has preserved one notice of 'Seres' which, as has long been known, has nothing to do with China[3] and is taken, he says, from a Ceylonese who had visited them: they were a very tall race with red hair and blue eyes, living north of the Himalayas (montes Hemodos), whose speech was unintelligible and who traded by silent barter in the usual way. The conventional location of Pliny's blonde Seres has been in the Tarim basin, a view which has been developed in modern times[4] by calling them the Tochari (Little Yueh-chi) on the strength of von Le Coq's identification of the Tochari with the people who have red hair and blue eyes in the much later art of Turfan;[5] but one need not go to the Tochari, for a wedge of blondness stretched far into Central Asia from Europe, and, while Hippocrates recorded a red-haired strain among the Scyths of Russia, one of the tribes of the Hiung-nu (Huns) were blondes,[6] there is said to have been a blonde strain in the Wu-sun, and there was a red-haired Sarmatian horde called Roxolani, 'blonde

[1] *Σηρικά* in Strabo XV, 693 is not from Nearchus but is Strabo's own comparison (see also Arr. *Ind.* 16, 1). A. Herrmann, *Seres* in PW, assigns Strabo's Serica to Nearchus and Apollodorus' Seres to Strabo, creating complete confusion in the dating.

[2] Seres as Chinese first in Augustan literature. The earliest mentions of Chinese silk are Caesar's alleged silk awnings, the Parthian silken banners at Carrhae, and Cleopatra's silks (Lucan, *Phars.* X, 141–3). Before this all silk in the West came from the wild silkworm of Western Asia; *Hou-han-shu* chap. CXVIII, tr. E. Chavannes, *T'oung Pao* VIII, 1907, see p. 184; Blümner, *Serica* in PW; Tarn, *Hell. Civ.*[2] pp. 224 *sq.*

[3] Pliny's notice comes from the father of a man who was an envoy to the Emperor Claudius, and is therefore, at earliest, later than the application by Romans of the name Seres to the Chinese; but that is not incompatible with the accepted view.

[4] R. Hennig, *Z. f. Rassenkunde* II, 1935, p. 90; A. Herrmann, *ib.* III, 1936, p. 200, *one* of his two components of Pliny's account; and previously in *Seres* in PW.

[5] A. von Le Coq, *Auf Hellas Spuren in Ostturkestan* 1926 *passim.* (Eng. Trans. *Buried Treasures of Chinese Turkestan*, 1928.) See now Chap. VII.

[6] E. H. Minns, *Scythians and Greeks* 1913 p. 45.

Alans'. I feel little doubt that the Seres of Apollodorus and of Pliny, the two mentions of the name which are not the Chinese, are connected, though they are far apart in time. Professor Herrmann's conjecture that Pliny's Seres might be the Wu-sun, or that section of the Tochari-Yueh-chi who had remained behind in the Wu-sun country,[1] has much to commend it. The Wu-sun country at the time seems to have been the district about Lake Issyk Kul and the plains north of the Alexandrovski range;[2] and to a Ceylonese 'north of the Hemodi mountains' could just as well mean beyond the Tien-shan range as in the Tarim basin south of it. Pliny's informant must have called the people he saw Seres because they were in a country where he expected to find Seres, *i.e.* the country of Apollodorus' Seres, and traded by silent barter in the same way. Who Apollodorus' Seres were cannot be said, because the Chinese information does not go back to *c.* 200 B.C.;[3] but if they lived in the Lake Issykul country and were the nearest middlemen to the Bactrian Greeks for the Chinese as well as the Siberian trade, it is easy to see how, at a later time, the name of the middlemen on the route was transferred by Greek or Greek-speaking merchants to the silk-producing people at the end of it.

Presumably therefore Euthydemus' expedition was from Ferghana to the Lake Issykul country, which was feasible enough; Seleucus' general Demodamas had crossed the Jaxartes before him,[4] but there is no hint of how far he went. Apollodorus indeed shows that Euthydemus reached his objective, the Seres, but he certainly did not manage to restore the gold route; the Seres can only have been one of a chain of middlemen, and the disturbance must have been farther to the north-east; naturally he had no chance of reaching the gold-producing country itself about the head waters of the Yenisei system.

Having failed in the north, Euthydemus turned eastward to the Tarim basin, as already related. His expedition to that country was a quest for any metal available; what the Greeks first got was a certain supply of nickel originating in China, but later they managed to get

[1] *Z. f. Rassenkunde* III p. 200 (the second component); and see Chap. VII. Berthelot p. 239 seemingly located Pliny's Seres in Siberia, but made them metal-workers.

[2] See Herrmann, *Τάπουρα ὄρη* in PW, and App. 21.

[3] The Yueh-chi found there a Saca people called Sai-wang (Chap. VII), but it does not follow that they were there in 200 B.C.

[4] Pliny VI, 49.

from China some bullion, both gold and silver.[1] One of the reasons, but a very subordinate one, for the Euthydemid invasion of India was probably to secure precious metals, but India was as disappointing as the north had been; no Greek king in India was able to coin gold, and the relative scarcity of the larger silver coins, the tetradrachms,[2] may suggest that even silver was never too plentiful.

These seem to be all the indications which can at present be got about the trade of Bactria with Siberia and China in the reign of Euthydemus; the general question of the Chinese trade will be considered later (pp. 363 *sq.*). But from the beginning the trade with India must have been of considerable importance, for Bactria lay across the most used route from India to the West, and just after Greek rule ended Chang-k'ien called attention to the great markets and bazaars in Bactra itself,[3] which did not grow up in a day; the capital must, under the Greeks, have been a clearing-house for the Indian trade, as it was later for the Chinese trade under the Kushans. In the first century B.C. Merv was another gateway for imports from the Far East (p. 364 n. 4), and *may* have been one much earlier. From Bactra the caravan trade followed the great road (p. 61) which ran by Hekatompylos and Ecbatana to Seleuceia and so to the West. One thing, however, the Indian trade did not do: it did not, in Hellenistic times, go down the Oxus into the Caspian and thence up the Cyrus river and down the Phasis. There must have been an active trade of some sort down the Phasis to the Black Sea, for in the third century B.C. Dioscorias on the Black Sea coast was one of the most polyglot of ports;[4] but it cannot be said if the Caspian, which Strabo called 'unnavigated',[5] came into this at all. Some of the trade which passed through Media[6] *may* have gone by sea along its western coast from the mouth of the Kizil Uzen at the south-western angle of the Caspian to that of the Cyrus, but the only reason for supposing this would be that Patrocles had followed that coast from the mouth of the one river to the other, and against it of course is the vital fact that no harbour towns at the mouth of either river are known. As to the supposed Oxo-Caspian trade route from Bactria westward, the so-called

[1] Hirth p. 109; Wylie p. 46.
[2] Whitehead, *NC* pp. 303–4, *NNM* pp. 25–6.
[3] Hirth p. 98.
[4] Timosthenes of Rhodes in Pliny VI, 15; Strabo XI, 498.
[5] Strabo XI, 509, ἄπλους τε οὖσα καὶ ἀργός.
[6] For Indian trade passing through Media northward see Strabo XI, 506.

'northern route' from India which has played such a part in text-books and in theories,[1] there is no evidence that it ever existed and no reason whatever for supposing that it did. What happened was that Patrocles, sent to explore the Caspian, mistook the mouth of the Atrek, seen from the sea, for that of the Oxus,[2] and, believing that the Oxus flowed into the Caspian, reported to Antiochus I that such a trade route could easily be made; in due course his report was turned into a statement that it existed. The proof is given in Appendix 14.

With the vanishing of the Oxo-Caspian trade route there vanishes the only reason which ever existed for believing that in the Greek period the Oxus flowed into the Caspian and that consequently the river-system of Bactria and the neighbouring countries was very different from what it is to-day. The whole thing originated in the already mentioned mistake of Patrocles; the Ochus (lower Arius) became confused with the Atrek and the Ochus-Atrek with the Oxus,[3] producing a tangle which Strabo could not unravel and I shall not attempt to.[4] Strabo himself, though he duly quotes Patrocles, knew that the Oxus entered the same sea as the Jaxartes, *i.e.* the Aral;[5] and some valuable Persian evidence has recently been emphasised[6] which shows that in the second century B.C. the Oxus flowed by Chorasmia (Khiva) as it does to-day. No competent person now believes that the Oxus ever discharged bodily into the Caspian, though the belief will die hard in semi-popular literature; but there is a widespread and very lively theory that both in the Hellenistic period and long afterwards the river sent a *branch* into that sea. I have considered this theory in Appendix 15; here I need only say that it is a question for science, not for scholars.

The Greek kings divided Bactria-Sogdiana into a number of satrapies,[7] the satrapies being the Seleucid eparchies, a more manageable arrangement; and their example was followed by every Seleucid Succession state, including Parthia, and by states which, though never Seleucid, fell

[1] As recently as 1923 its importance was made one of the foundations of W. Schur's *Die Orientpolitik des Kaisers Nero*, on which see now J. C. C. Anderson in *CAH* x pp. 880, 884.

[2] Kiessling, *Hyrkania* in PW col. 467.

[3] Strabo XI, 518.

[4] A good specimen of the confusion, if read carefully, is Polyb. x, 48.

[5] Strabo *ib.*, *εἰς τὴν αὐτὴν τελευτῶν θάλατταν*. The Jaxartes could only change by running up-hill.

[6] E. Benveniste, *BSOS* VII, ii, 1934, pp. 271–2.

[7] Strabo XI, 516.

within the sphere of Seleucid or Parthian influence; the Greek kings of Bactria were in fact the originators of what became the almost universal organisation of Asia in the first century B.C. (pp. 2 *sq.*). It is possible that the new organisation in Bactria itself might date from Diodotus, but as it is not known for certain that he took the royal title this must be very doubtful. It certainly antedated the organisation of the Parthians, who copied it, but here again it cannot be said whether that organisation began with Mithridates I or was solely the work of Mithridates II; but even Mithridates I was later than Euthydemus, and the probabilities are that it was Euthydemus' work. The Bactrian satrapy-list, unlike those for Cappadocia, Armenia, and (to some extent) Parthia, has not been preserved; the only satrapy names known are Tapuria and Traxiane west of the Arius[1] and Bubacene somewhere in Sogdiana;[2] but it is possible that the name for Badakshan was Bandobene[3] and that Bandobene in the Paropamisadae (p. 97) was taken from it.[4] It is tolerably certain, from the analogy of India (p. 241), that the satrapies were governed by generals, *strategoi*, on the Seleucid model, and the administration, speaking generally, must have been modelled on that of the Seleucids; but of what modifications may have been introduced we know nothing.

Bactra, 'Mother of cities' and 'Paradise of the earth', represented by the modern Balkh, was the capital, but it has never been excavated and little enough is known about it; probably we should think of a city of the type of Susa (p. 27). It was the traditional home of Zoroastrianism, and its other name, Zariaspa,[5] may represent that of its great fire-temple, Azar-i-Asp;[6] as Strabo (XI, 516) says that it stood on both sides of the river Bactrus, the united stream of the Band-i-Emir and the Darrah which then reached the Oxus, it is possible that the second name

[1] Strabo XI, 517 and the Traxiane coin, *BMC Parthia* p. 40; see Tarn, *SP Stud.* §III.

[2] Curtius VIII, 5, 2 (the name as usual used proleptically).

[3] If this be the meaning of *Οὐανδάβανδα* in Ptolemy VI, 12, 4.

[4] Cf. the two eparchies called Paraitakene, in Media (Strabo XV, 723, 726, 744) and in Drangiane-Seistan (Isidore 18).

[5] The identity is certain from Eratosthenes (Strabo XI, 514) and Apollodorus (*ib.* 576). Arrian made of them two different places because one of his sources used the name Bactra and another Zariaspa and he did not know they were the same place. Ptolemy often makes two places out of one, pp. 231 *sq.*

[6] Cunningham, *NC* 1868 p. 107. Tomaschek, *Baktriane* in PW, referred the name to 'gold-coloured' horses.

Zariaspa was the name of one definite part of it. It had been refounded by Alexander as an Alexandria, a name which curiously enough was used by Chinese historians though not by Greek ones;[1] it must therefore by the time of Euthydemus have possessed full Greek city forms and, besides being an important clearing-house of trade, had become a very great fortress, while the temple of its native goddess Anaïtis probably formed a centre for the native population in the same way as did E-sagila at Babylon and Nanaia's temple at Susa. The old goddess of the Oxus had now developed into a goddess of fertility on the Babylonian model, and had acquired Babylonian elements and become equated with Ishtar; her worship had been officially promulgated throughout the Persian empire by the Achaemenid Artaxerxes II, together with her festival the Sacaea during which a mock king held rule, also derived from Babylon.[2] In her temple in Bactra stood a famous cult-image of her wearing a golden crown with eight rays and a hundred stars[3] and clad in the skins, dear to Persians, of thirty beavers 'of the sheen of silver and gold';[4] she and her crown of rays figure on coins of Demetrius,[5] which must mean that she was the city-goddess of Greek Bactra as she subsequently was of Greek Pushkalāvatī (p. 135) and as Nanaia was of Greek Susa.

There is a story told by Onesicritus[6] that the people of Bactra had once reared dogs known as ἐνταφιασταί, 'entombers', who were trained to devour the dying, and that Alexander had abolished the custom. It might, I suppose, be taken from some real trace of something pre-

[1] Lan-chi (Alexandria) was the capital of the Ta-hia *i.e.* Bactria (Hirth p. 98) and subsequently, after they occupied Bactria, of the Yueh-chi (*Hou-han-shu* chap. 118, tr. Chavannes, *T'oung Pao* VIII, 1907, p. 187). Probably it is Stephanus' Alexandria no. 11, κατὰ Βάκτρα. E. Specht, *JA* 1897 pp. 159–61, first saw that Lan-chi was Alexandria. De Groot p. 96 makes it Pan-ku's Kam-si, which he then interprets and locates by the aid of very much later Chinese works, a doubtful method. Why Chavannes, *loc. cit.*, and Konow, *CII* p. liv, should put the Bactrian capital in Badakshan I cannot guess. Historically, Lan-chi cannot possibly be anything but Bactra.

[2] Strabo XI, 512; Ed. Meyer, *Anaïtis* in Roscher; S. Langdon, *JRAS* 1924 p. 65; Dalton *op. cit.* pp. xxvii *sq.* and 26 no. 103; *CAH* IV pp. 192, 211, VI p. 21.

[3] Clem. Alex. *Protr.* p. 57; *Ābān Yast* §§ 126–9 (Darmesteter's translation of the Zend Avesta in *Sacred Books of the East* XXIII p. 82, cf. p. 53). Many have noticed that the description was taken from a temple image.

[4] Cf. Dalton *op. cit.* p. xxxi. Presumably the skins known to the trade as 'golden beaver'.

[5] *BMC* Pl. III, 1; called 'Artemis radiate'.

[6] Strabo XI, 517.

Iranian;[1] but the man who deliberately invented the Queen of the Amazons story cannot complain if one distrusts every other story he has to tell,[2] and it may be that he met with, and did not understand, a word translated to him as ἐνταφιασταί (whatever it really meant) and made up a story[3] out of this word, the pariah dogs, and his own Cynic principles; for it was Cynic doctrine that what happened to a man's corpse did not matter and that no care need be taken over its disposal.

The first business of every Greek king of Bactria was to hold the gateway of Iran against the semi-barbarism of the north and north-west, a task they successfully accomplished till the great upheaval of the peoples caused by the migration of the Yueh-chi. The pressure upon them came principally from two quarters, from the north across the Jaxartes and from the north-west up the line of the Oxus. As to the Jaxartes, the Persian government and subsequently Alexander had built and maintained a number of fortified places both to hold the river line at the great southward bend by Chodjend and to protect the Chodjend country from the nomads of the lower Jaxartes steppes to the westward; these the Greek kings of course maintained and perhaps added to, and if, as seems certain enough, Euthydemus ruled Ferghana, the line he had to hold was longer but perhaps easier. Whether under Euthydemus there was much pressure on this frontier cannot be said; it must at first have been a matter of local peoples only, such as those whom Alexander had found there; the movements which finally brought fresh hordes of nomads across the river and ended Greek rule in Bactria belong to a later period (Chap. VII). The real pressure at first must have come from the north-west, where there was no natural barrier like the Jaxartes, the Oxus only providing a roadway; and the frontier on the west and north-west must have been a chain of military colonies and of fortified posts, some of the latter anyhow going back to Persian

[1] Like the parallel story, Plut. *Mor.* 328C: Alexander taught the Sogdians not to kill their fathers. See p. 81 n. 9.

[2] For his repute as a liar see in the last place H. Strasburger, *Onesikritos* in PW, who thinks (doubtless correctly) that the purpose of the story was to represent Alexander as a bringer of civilisation.

[3] Porphyry, *de abstinentia* IV, 21 is not independent evidence. He uses this story and others to prove a point, which is always suspicious; he introduces the sentence with ἱστοροῦνται γοῦν, 'anyhow the story goes that', showing that he was merely copying, not affirming; and his statement that Alexander's ὕπαρχος Stasanor tried to stop the custom is definitely wrong, for Stasanor did not become satrap of Bactria till two years after Alexander's death, Diod. XVIII, 3, 3; 39, 6. It is a hash-up of Onesicritus.

times.[1] The enemy here was primarily the great Saca confederacy known as Massagetae, and secondarily the Sacaraucae (p. 291); ultimately they were to break through, but this was not yet. It does not appear that the Greek kings ever attempted to subdue the Massagetae and hold Chorasmia and the line of the lower Oxus, as the Parthians were to do for a little while under Mithridates II;[2] they had the Alexander-tradition firmly in mind and their thoughts of expansion turned in another direction. Also these peoples might supply mercenaries, as the Dahae had done to Alexander and as, farther west, the Galatae were doing to any Greek king who would pay them; indeed, if things were really desperate, the nomads might be used as allies, as Nicomedes and Hierax had used the Galatae, though the danger was great; we shall meet a strange story of this later (p. 342). This was the threat which Euthydemus had used to induce Antiochus III to make peace. Naturally the Massagetae were watching the siege of Bactra from the frontier, in case there might be opportunities, and Euthydemus threatened that, if he were driven to it, he would admit them and destroy Antiochus, even if he destroyed himself in the process.[3] Antiochus could not foresee that, when their day did come, the Sacas would kill two Parthian monarchs and all but master Parthia; but he had at this time a sense of what was possible, and he gave way.

The nomads had been accustomed to put the settled lands to tribute on a plan of their own: they granted immunity from casual raids on terms that they might plunder unhindered at stated times,[4] much as (it is said) pilgrims to Mecca used to engage a sheikh to protect them against unlicensed marauders on terms that he himself should plunder them decently at the end. Naturally the Greek kings would stop this; but raids must have been a perpetual danger, and it was to meet the risk of these that Antiochus I had surrounded the oasis of Merv with a wall 187 miles long.[5] This wall may not have been the only one. At a later time large tracts of country round Bokhara, Samarcand, and Balkh

[1] Euthydemus spoke of *admitting* the Sacas, as though through some barrier, Polyb. XI, 34, 5. One of these fortified posts on the Bactrian frontier is mentioned by Arrian, IV, 16, 4 *sq.*; another on the Sogdian-Massagetae frontier, *ib.* IV, 17, 4.

[2] Tarn, *SP Stud.* p. 19.

[3] The word *προσδέχωνται*, 'admit', in Polyb. XI, 34, 5 proves that this was Euthydemus' real meaning: he was not, as usually supposed, expressing a general fear of the nomads.

[4] Strabo XI, 511, *τακτοῖς τισι χρόνοις*.

[5] Strabo XI, 516; cf. Pliny VI, 47.

(Bactra) were enclosed by similar vast walls;[1] it is likely enough that this may go back to the Greek period.

New settlers must have continued to arrive in Bactria throughout the third century: Euthydemus was not the only Greek who came from the West. The process is lost, but the consequences of the two centuries of Greek rule are well attested: Alexander in 326 found a land of open villages, Chang-k'ien in 128 found a land of walled towns;[2] to the Greeks of the Farther East the 'thousand cities of Bactria' became a proverb, though perhaps not till after the destruction of Greek rule.[3] What proportion of all this settlement was Greek or European (for people like Thracians would soon have become indistinguishable from Greeks, as they did in Ptolemaic Egypt) cannot be said, but the story of Eucratides (Chap. v) shows that it was substantial: in spite of their power and their Indian armies, the position of the Euthydemids was not proof against the defection of the Graeco-Macedonian military colonists. There are however very few indisputably Greek cities known. The record is miserably defective, but for what it is worth the only names recorded by Greek writers in the Euthydemid home kingdom are, in Bactria, Alexandria-Bactra and (later) Eucratideia;[4] in Sogdiana, Alexandria-Eschate[5] on the Jaxartes (Chodjend) and the rather dubious Alexandria of the Oxus;[6] possibly an Antioch in Ferghana (p. 83), if it be not Alexandria-Eschate refounded; and Antioch-Merv. It is however tolerably certain that Demetrius founded a name-city Demetrias in Sogdiana, for a Sanscrit work, existing only in a Thibetan translation, recorded a city Dharmamitra,[7] and Dharmamita is the (Prakrit) form given to Demetrius' name in the Yuga-purāna (App. 4 and p. 178). The Thibetan translator has added that this name was the original of Tarmita, which is Termedh,[8] represented by the modern Termez, on

[1] Barthold *op. cit.* p. 112. Pre-Muslim mud walls with watch-towers round the oases of Bokhara and Samarcand are said to have been recently excavated, but I have no details.

[2] Hirth p. 97, of the Ta-hia: 'the people have fixed abodes and live in walled cities and regular houses'.

[3] Apollodorus, Strabo xv, 686; 'Trogus' source', Justin XLI, 1, 8; 4, 5.

[4] Strabo XI, 516; Ptol. VI, 11, 8. See pp. 208 *sq.*

[5] Arr. IV, 4, 1; Curt. VII, 6, 26; Justin XII, 5. Appian, *Syr.* 57, probably shows that it was existing in Seleucid times.

[6] Ptol. VI, 12, 6 (in Sogdiana).

[7] S. Lévi, *JA* 1933 p. 27 n. 1.

[8] Lévi's identification of Tarmita with Termedh is certain, but he did not notice that Dharmamitra must be Demetrias, or that Tarmita is twice mentioned from the

the north bank of the Oxus; the river of Bactra, the Bactrus, then entered the Oxus,[1] and there is some later evidence that when it did so it was at a point opposite Termedh.[2] Termedh, where the railway from Samarcand now comes to the river, was also the location of the crossing on the main route from Samarcand and the north to Bactra—Hsüan Tsiang crossed at this point;[3] there is an island here in the river, and possibly the Greeks had a bridge of boats, as there was at a later time; and Greek coins are often found in the ruins of the oldest city.[4] Demetrias therefore was well placed to gather up both the trade from the north and that which came down the Bactrus, as well as the local river traffic, which was doubtless important on the Oxus just as it was on the Nile. The complete shipwreck of our Greek evidence is illustrated by the fact that, of the three cities named Demetrias, two—those in Sogdiana and in Sind—are only known now from Indian sources; and no one can say that another may not come to light.

As however the invasion of India and the events to be recorded in Chapter v would be incomprehensible without a considerable Greek population, it must be supposed that, if there were few Greek cities, there were numerous military colonies: Alexander's unnamed group of foundations in Bactria and Sogdiana must have been of this type.[5] It has already been shown (Chap. I) that the military colony and not the city, the *polis*, was the basis of the settlement of Asia beyond the Euphrates; but the military colony often defies detection, for normally it kept the native name of the village in which it started and might keep that name, as Isidore shows, even after it had grown into a city. In Parthia east of the Persian desert some of these names are known from Isidore, but his work naturally did not include Bactria, so his invaluable help is lacking. There can, however, be no doubt about the general outline: the Greek settlement of Bactria was carried out principally by means of military colonies, and some of these places grew into cities

Greek side: (*a*) by Stephanus, *s.v.* *Ἄρμα· Ἄρματα, πόλις Ἰνδική*, doubtless a confusion of Demetrias-Termedh with Demetrias in Sind; and (*b*) in the Peutinger Table, where Antioch Tharmata or Tarmata (*v. ll.* Tarinata, Tramata) is another confusion, possibly a conflation of Antioch-Merv and Demetrias-Termedh which has been misplaced (on Antioch Tharmata see K. Miller, *Itineraria Romana* 1916 cols. 795, 798; Tscherikower p. 111).

1 Strabo XI, 516.

2 Ritter, *Erdkunde*, Part 8, book 3, p. 219.

3 Foucher, *Afghanistan* p. 278 and his Map 3 facing p. 278.

4 W. Barthold, *Turkestan down to the Mongol Invasion*[2] 1928 pp. 75–6.

5 Strabo XI, 517 (eight); Justin XII, 5, 13 (twelve; Ruehl prints Gutschmid's conjecture seven in the text).

though they retained their native names. Two with Greek names are known, Thera in Sogdiana and Rhoetea in Bactria,[1] colonies named after their homes by the mercenaries settled there; possibly Argos in 'Scythia' may be another;[2] but only one other place-name which looks as if it might be European has been preserved.[3]

But this does not end, or even explain, the matter, for the number of military colonies can only have been a limited one. Their chief use was to form a military frontier, a *limes*, against the Massagetae and to guard the natural frontier of the Jaxartes. The Seleucids in Asia Minor had formed just such a military frontier to guard the Ionian cities against raids by the Galatae, and seven colonies had sufficed (p. 8); granted that the Massagetae were stronger and far more numerous than the Galatae, still the analogy shows the kind of thing the frontier must have been, supported of course by a squadron on the Oxus (p. 91). And the Greeks in Bactria, even though *relatively* numerous and even if the term included Europeans generally, can only have been a strictly limited body in actual fact. But we have to account for the thing already noticed which, in the latter part of, or at the end of, the second century B.C., is attested both from the Greek and the Chinese side: our two well-informed Greek sources call Bactria the land of a thousand cities, and Chang-k'ien, an eye-witness and a shrewd observer, says that the people dwelt in walled towns. To talk in an easy fashion of mixed communities and a Eurasian population is worse than useless. A military colony in the East was no doubt apt to be mixed in a sense; it might for example, beside Greeks and Europeans, contain Anatolians (p. 9) or possibly men from local hill-tribes, as at Avroman, and possibly some of the original settlers might marry native women; but how far that takes us has already been discussed (p. 35), and the number of military colonies was totally inadequate to afford an explanation of the thousand cities. And there seems little question of a number of mixed cities, that is cities whose citizens were partly native Bactrians.[4] For what was a

[1] Stephanus under these names. [2] Argos no. 8 in Stephanus.

[3] Menapia, Ptol. VI, 11, 8. I cannot explain it, for I do not propose to bring Menapii from the North Sea to Bactria, even though Goths from the Vistula have been brought to India (p. 257 n. 2). Certainly a column with an Indian inscription and reliefs was dug up at Ostend in 1793 (Baron de la Pylaie, *Rev. Arch.* 1848 ii p. 456); but doubtless the suggestion that it was the discarded ballast of a modern ship is correct.

[4] Any Greek city in the East would probably contain 'corporations' of other nationalities (p. 18) like the omnipresent Syrians (Phoenicians); but that is not what I am referring to.

native Bactrian? The country possessed the ordinary Iranian feudal system (p. 32); the land, other than King's land with its serfs, was in the hands of those Iranian barons or landowners who play such a part in the Alexander-history, men who lived in their own strongholds, kept a body of mounted retainers of their own race, and had their lands cultivated by a serf peasantry living in villages, who were probably in part at least pre-Iranian in blood.[1] To settle Bactrians in cities on any scale would have implied either the existence of a free Iranian peasantry, which we have no grounds for postulating anywhere except in Persis (though some think it did exist in Bactria), or of a middle class of some sort, for there could be no question of settling the serfs. And the only germs of a middle class were the merchants who conducted the caravan trade—they might be and probably were settled—and the barons' retainers; it is not so long since there was no middle class in large parts of the Highlands of Scotland, apart from the small and scanty towns. As the Greek kings were to make Indians full citizens of the Greek cities in India (p. 257)—in India they had large town populations to draw upon—it must be supposed that they gave the franchise to what Bactrians they could; but these can, relatively, only have been few.

The explanation of the thousand cities must be sought on other lines, of which the beginning can be detected in those measures of the Seleucid kings which tended gradually to raise the status of the serfs and the serf villages (p. 33). Chang-k'ien is not speaking of Greek cities or military colonies; what he means is that in Bactria every native village of any size had been walled. After all, he is explicit enough: his description of the Ta-hia is that of an Iranian or Iranianised population, as is clearly shown by the reference to their beards and their language.[2] He describes exactly the same thing in the small kingdom of Ferghana (Ta-yuan), once a Bactrian province, and there he gives the number of walled towns as 'fully 70';[3] but if half-a-dozen military colonies had been planted there to watch the Jaxartes frontier, that is all there would be in that distant land. Alexander had started the system of walling-in villages by establishing fortified posts throughout Sogdiana in his struggle with Spitamenes,[4] which meant fortifying villages at strategic points, and doubtless the Seleucids, who built the great wall of Merv,

[1] For the possible survival of a pre-Iranian custom or trait see p. 299.

[2] Hirth p. 108 §§ 101, 102. See p. 298.

[3] *Ib.* p. 95 § 19.

[4] Arr. IV, 16, 3; 17, 4.

built little walls also; the invaluable Parthian survey which Isidore has preserved shows the gradual emergence in Media and eastern Iran of the large walled village, for the scanty villages noted in the survey are of course walled villages only; were it otherwise, some provinces of Iran would according to Isidore have possessed no country population at all.[1] But the Greek kings of Bactria, partly no doubt under the ever-present threat of the nomads, had carried out this policy on a scale which at the time had no parallel elsewhere. If Chang-k'ien knew of 70 such walled villages in the little province of Ferghana, a round figure of 1000 for Bactria and Sogdiana, though perhaps exaggerated, might be no such great exaggeration, especially as the native population had increased considerably during the two generations of the Seleucid peace; even after Eucratides' wars and the nomad conquest Chang-k'ien gives the number in Bactria itself (without Sogdiana) as over a million.[2] These large walled villages were meant to protect the peasantry from nomad raids till the troops of the king or satrap could intervene, and they would accustom the serf population to the use of arms in self-defence. But they also acted in another way, which was more important: they enabled the germs of communal life to take root and grow.

And those germs did grow, till by the time that Greek rule ended the villages of Bactria had sufficient organisation to be capable of a considerable degree of self-government. Chang-k'ien, who saw the country when it was derelict, just after the overthrow of the Greek government and before the victorious Yueh-chi had established their own government (see generally Chap. VII), said that the people 'have no great king or chief but everywhere the cities and towns have (or "set up") their own petty chiefs';[3] and by towns he meant, as we have seen, the walled villages. Of course any native village in any country might have some sort of a head man, like the komarch of the Armenian

[1] Five villages apiece in three Median satrapies; then Rhagiane 10, Comisene 8, Hyrcania 11, Astauene 12, Parthyene 1, Apavarktikene 2, Margiane none, Aria 4, Anauoi none, Zarangiane none, Sacastene none but six near, *i.e.* in Arachosia. Note the contrast between the northern frontier provinces and the security of Seistan. So Marcianus 1, 22 gives only 17 cities and villages together in Susiane (Elymais), *GGM* I p. 530.

[2] Hirth p. 98 §50.

[3] Hirth p. 97 §48. So in the *Ch'ien-han-shu:* Wylie p. 40 'were accustomed to set up petty chiefs over their cities', de Groot p. 95 'Die Städte setzten vielfach kleine Obmänner ein', which makes it even clearer that some form of magistrate is meant.

village who plays a part in Xenophon's story;[1] but Chang-k'ien would know this well enough, and it is not this that he troubled to record. What he means—and it is a great tribute to his powers of observation that he should have detected it—is that the villages of Bactria had some system, each under a single head, which was enabling each one to carry on for itself (at the time) without a central government, and even to continue trading (p. 298); the country had reached a point in which the absence of a central government did not (for a time) spell anarchy. It is known that at a later time, in one part of Syria under the Roman Empire—Batanea, Auranitis, Trachonitis—the native villages had acquired an organisation which in many ways imitated that of a Greek or Graeco-Roman city;[2] they had Assemblies and perhaps occasionally Councils, communal income and expenditure, boards of officials to superintend finance and public works, and in some cases they had at their head a single official who was known by different names—*komarchos*, *protokometes*, *strategos*;[3] the *strategos* might even give his name to the year, like the eponymous magistrate of some old Greek city. In the late Hellenistic period *strategos* had often been the title of the chief magistrate of a Greek city, and undoubtedly this village organisation goes back in origin, though probably in less elaborate form, to Hellenistic times;[4] it was the outcome of the Seleucid policy of raising the status of the serf population and so of their villages. It is on these lines that one must seek to understand the Bactrian villages which Chang-k'ien called walled towns: the serf village had become a fortified and quasi-organised township. How far the organisation had progressed naturally cannot be said, but it was far enough to enable the villages to carry on for themselves under their own officials after the central government had perished. The numbers already considered show that by the end of the second century B.C. Bactria was in this respect far ahead of any country east of the Euphrates, possibly of any country in Greek Asia; and if the Seleucids started the process, the credit for the thoroughness with which it had been carried out must be

[1] *Anab.* IV, 5, 10 and *sqq.*

[2] G. McL. Harper Jr., *Village Administration in the Roman Province of Syria*, *Yale Class. Stud.* I, 1929, pp. 105 to 168, and especially p. 116 to end (with a bibliography of the earlier literature); A. H. M. Jones, *JRS* XXI, 1931, pp. 270 *sqq.*

[3] Strategos: Harper *op. cit.* pp. 120–1; see J. Johnson, *Dura Studies* 1932 p. 29. Jones *op. cit.* pp. 270–1 makes the strategos the supreme magistrate in the second and early third centuries.

[4] So Swoboda, κώμη in PW, Supp. Band IV, 967.

given to Euthydemus and his son. I make no apology for having dealt with this subject at length, for the evolution of the serf village into the organised and quasi-autonomous township was the most important work done by the Greeks in Asia; this it was which really affected the mass of the native population, for it must have meant a considerable improvement in their conditions of life. And this, as I understand it, and not mixed cities or anything else, was the real gift of the Greek world to Bactria.

One thing is certain about the Euthydemids: to do what they did, they not only had a large population behind them, but they had the support, perhaps the hearty support, of the native Bactrians, without which Euthydemus might have met the fate of Molon; for purposes of external policy that would mean the landowners, who with their retainers supplied the famous Bactrian cavalry. Euthydemus' 10,000 Bactrian horse sufficiently witnesses to the increase in the population during the Seleucid peace; for the trustworthy figures supplied by Hieronymus of Cardia as to the amount of native cavalry in the Farther East after Alexander's death show that in the time of the Successors the Bactrian satrapy could not have raised anything approaching that figure.[1] And the fact that Euthydemus sought to hold the line of the Arius against Antiochus III with the Bactrian horse alone, though that was not the way to hold a river line, if it shows (as it probably does) that he had learnt from Molon's fall and was afraid of trying to use the Greek settlers against their lawful king (though some may have been guarding the Massagetae front), also shows that he knew that he could count on the loyalty of the Bactrians. Iran had always been the Seleucids' failure (pp. 32, 55), and they had never secured any real hold on the country, which had fallen away to the Parthians at the first opportunity; but though Parthia, when her time came, might lop off outlying parts of the Bactrian empire, she never permanently got one foot's breadth of the soil of Bactria itself. It must mean that in some way Euthydemus had really secured for his house the loyalty and co-operation of the Bactrian aristocracy, the thing which Alexander had tried to do by his

[1] Tarn, *Military Developments* p. 153. The satraps of Persis and of every satrapy east of Media, after raising 8000 horse for Peithon (Diod. XVIII, 7, 3), could only raise another 4600 for a life or death struggle against him (*ib.* XIX, 14, 8), a total of only 12,600 for Persis and the whole East, even if the numbers do not overlap. The total cavalry at Ipsus, with all Asia contributing, was 20,500, or only twice what Bactria alone gave Euthydemus, and some of it was certainly European.

marriage with Roxane, and that he went nearer than anyone else to solving the problem of how to combine in one polity the Greek city and the Iranian baron, the problem which, as Alexander had seen, lay at the root of governing Iran. The one name of a satrap of Euthydemus which has survived, Aspiones, is Bactrian;[1] Menander later had a Bactrian on his Council (Excursus, p. 422); and it was apparently during the Greek occupation that the Sogdian language of the Bactrians, a north Iranian speech akin to Pahlavi, was reduced to writing (p. 304).

We must imagine something like a double state: a state in which the Bactrian landowners, while continuing to manage their estates, also came to the Court and had their share of the administrative posts, and prospered considerably, for that 10,000 horse means a considerable increase in the number of their retainers. We have to work with rather slight indications, but about the general position there can be little doubt, for the policy of the dynasty in Bactria cannot have differed radically from that which it was to follow in India. Alexander had finally decided that the only way to rule Iran was frankly to take her into partnership, and Euthydemus in some form took Bactria into partnership; it is our loss that we do not know by what means he and his son managed to secure the co-operation of the landowners while they were at the same time transforming the condition of the serfs. It is unfortunate too that the Indian material does not enable us to trace the Bactrians who must have borne their part in the Greek invasion of India; Indian writers would usually class them with Greeks under the name Yavana, while as the word Bāhlīka (Bactrian) was already in use in India for some of the semi-foreign peoples of the Indian North-West (p. 169), its occasional occurrence in inscriptions gives no clue as to what kind of Bactrian is meant.[2]

Connected with this attitude of the Euthydemids may be the fact that Euthydemus, besides his tetradrachms on the Attic standard, struck

[1] Strabo XI, 515; see Tarn, *SP Stud.* pp. 20–2.

[2] I know only two inscriptions which may mention Bactrians. (1) *CII* no. XXVII pp. 70, 77 (Kushan period) = *ASI* 1913–14, i, p. 13, Urasaka son of Lotafria (or whatever the name is) the Bāhlīka (Bactrian). His ancestor might have come with the Kushans, *or* with the Greeks, *or* he might just have been a Bhalla (p. 169). (2) *CII* no. XXIV p. 65 (*c.* 42 B.C., see p. 391 n. 2), Datiaputrena Thaidorena (Theodoros), which Bühler (*Ind. Ant.* 1896 p. 141) and Senart (*JA* 1899 p. 531) translated 'son of Dati', the Iranian name Datis (and therefore a Bactrian). But F. W. Thomas in *Festschrift Ernst Windisch* p. 364 gives it as 'son of Datia', while Konow in *CII ad loc.* says there is no certainty that Datia is a personal name.

lighter ones on a standard which has been called Persian,[1] Phoenician,[2] and purely arbitrary.[3] It might have been due to scarcity of silver or some other economic reason;[4] but it has also been attributed to a desire to please a native population accustomed to coins of lighter weight than the Attic.[5] His successors all followed his policy, and ultimately a lighter standard was to become universal among the Greek kings in India.

The conclusions here come to are not contradicted by the history of art. This book is not concerned with art as such, but some slight indication must be given here of recent developments and their bearing on the general position. Two things, as regards Bactria, have to be distinguished, and the first is the art of the Greeks. The great art of the coins with their wonderful portraiture is not only purely Greek but bears eloquent witness to the vitality of the Graeco-Bactrian State; it shows no trace of deterioration down to the Yueh-chi conquest, when it is suddenly cut off and never reappears, in India or anywhere else; the school of Greek engravers in Bactria was wiped out (p. 301). But it is inconceivable that a man with the gifts of the artist whom I have called *X* should have done nothing in his life but engrave three coin-portraits; there must have been a corresponding school of purely Greek sculpture, of which nothing can ever be known[6] till northern Afghanistan, and especially Bactra, be excavated (for the bust of Euthydemus was carved in Asia Minor); it cannot be deduced from the Greek pieces found at Taxila (though perhaps the child with its finger to its lips is good enough to have been an importation from Bactria), because the coin-portraiture shows that none of the great Bactrian artists ever reached India; those who did go to that country, whether with Demetrius or later, were the second-rate.

The other thing is the native Bactrians. It used to be pointed out,

[1] P. Gardner in *BMC* p. lxviii.

[2] Allotte de la Fuye, *Rev. Num.* 1910 p. 329.

[3] Whitehead *NC* pp. 297–8.

[4] Whitehead *ib.* thought they made a profit by debasing the currency; Cunningham *NC* 1888 p. 217, who however dated the new standard too late, more plausibly suggested that it was due to a rise in the value of gold. I have already discussed the scarcity of gold.

[5] Allotte de la Fuye *loc. cit.*

[6] Conceivably the moulds used for casting the heads of the late statues from Hadda, which look like good Hellenistic work (see p. 398 n. 9), are going to bear on this.

rightly enough, that as regards art they might not have existed during the period of Greek rule; and we still have no actual *knowledge* to the contrary,[1] for the one Iranian work of art described for us, the statue of Anahita at Bactra (p. 115), has Babylonian affinities and might have been made for Artaxerxes II by a Persian artist. But since Sir A. Stein's discovery of Kūh-i-Khwāja, the 'castle of Rustam' on the sacred Mount Ushidão on an island in the Hamun lake in Seistan,[2] with its Hellenistic ornamentation, a theory has been put forward by Professor Herzfeld in a preliminary lecture[3] of a Graeco-Bactrian school of mixed art, or rather of an Iranian art coloured with Hellenistic ornaments and motives; it is a sort of parallel to 'Parthian' art but is, he thinks, based primarily on painting, and though he indicates other remains, Kūh-i-Khwāja is essentially the expression of this art. The question is in its infancy, and the layman must tread cautiously; Kūh-i-Khwāja is not yet fully published, and ultimately there will have to be considered its relationship to that form of Graeco-Iranian art which Professor Rostovtzeff has called 'Greco-Sakian'[4] and of which the earliest examples are connected by him with Bactria.[5] It seems to be becoming clearer that, in the Parthian period, from the Euphrates to the Indus a considerable revival took place of Iranian art mixed with Hellenistic elements, the relationships and the relative importance of the two components not being always the same but naturally witnessing to the long contact between the Greek and the Iranian which is known to have taken place; but any specific connection of Kūh-i-Khwāja with the Greek kingdom of Bactria must, it seems to me, for the present be very much in the air. Herzfeld dates Kūh-i-Khwāja in the first century A.D.[6] and compares its (unpublished) painted figures with the portraits on the Kushan coinage, which cannot begin earlier than about 50 A.D. (p. 352) and go on into the second century A.D.; and in this connection one is bound to remember that Seistan was ruled by the Bactrian Greeks for precisely one generation and no more, from 187 B.C. at the very earliest (p. 93) to *c.* 155 B.C. at the very latest (p. 223), and that it is even doubtful if they ever coined there; and those dates are two cen-

[1] For a hypothesis as to metal-work see Rostovtzeff on 'Greco-Sakian' art, n. 4 below.

[2] *Innermost Asia* II chap. XXVIII, 'The sacred hill of Seistan'.

[3] *Archaeological History of Iran* 1935 (Schweich Lectures for 1934) pp. 58–75.

[4] *Seminarium Kondokovianum* VI, 1933, pp. 170–85.

[5] *Ib.* p. 171.

[6] *Op. cit.* p. 74.

turies earlier than Herzfeld's dating of Kūh-i-Khwāja. It seems certain enough that an art current started by a people or kingdom may go on working long after that people or kingdom has come to an end; but it is hazardous work going backwards and deducing anything about art in a certain kingdom (nothing else being known about it) from an art current two centuries later, however much one would naturally like to believe that Graeco-Bactrian art has been discovered. Connecting links may be found; certainly there will be much more to be said about Graeco-Iranian art before the subject can crystallise. Its interest is great, but it is an interest in and for itself and for the history of art; it seems to me to possess small importance for an attempt, such as is made in this book, to recover the outlines of the political and social story of certain peoples and places, unless we are going to be able to detect in it (as in the Graeco-Indian art of Gandhāra) the working of some definite idea which has happened to find its expression in art but might equally well have found it in some other way, say in literature.

For let it be supposed for a moment, since nothing can be known for certain about the art of Bactria under the Greeks till Bactria be excavated, that (the view has been taken) there was therefore no art there at all and the coins are just a freak—the most extreme view possible. Even this would not, as I see it, affect in the least anything I have written; it does not go to the question of the political, military or social values of either Greeks or Bactrians, for ability to carve a statue is not the only, or the most important, test of a man. A handful of Macedonians conquered and ruled half Asia, and in peace the race was so efficient that they fetched, both men and women, a higher price in the slave market than any other people, even Italians;[1] but not one of Alexander's Macedonians could have engraved a coin or carved a statue to save his life. What the Greek kings did in Bactria, if we could see it, was probably rather extraordinary, just as we *shall* see, even if dimly, that what Demetrius and his lieutenants nearly did in India was extraordinary; one has only to look at the strength of the faces of Euthydemus and Demetrius to realise that they were no common men. Those who still believe in Greek 'decadence' in the third and second centuries B.C. may find them somewhat of a stumbling-block.

[1] Statistics in Tarn, *Hell. Civ.*[2] p. 97.

CHAPTER IV

DEMETRIUS AND THE INVASION OF INDIA

GREAT changes had taken place in India since Alexander's day. He had found a number of disconnected states and peoples in the North-West, and had had no relations with, even if he had heard of, the most powerful of the Indian kingdoms, that of Magadha on the Ganges. Soon after his death the Maurya Chandragupta had seized the crown of Magadha, and, perhaps by 312, had extended his rule to embrace all India north of the line of the Vindya mountains and the Nerbudda river. He was succeeded first by his son Bindusāra and then by his grandson Asoka, under whom the Mauryan empire was expanded to include a considerable part of peninsular India; but the southern conquests were only temporary and were apparently lost after Asoka died, and the empire was essentially a North Indian empire; the capital was Pātaliputra on the Ganges. The Seleucids and the Mauryas were always on friendly terms, and Greeks knew a good deal about the Mauryan empire as it had been under Chandragupta through the account of it given by Megasthenes, Seleucus' ambassador at his Court; probably they knew as much about it as they had known about the Persian empire in Xenophon's day, while Indians in turn knew a certain amount about the Greeks of the Seleucid East, whom they called Yavanas or Yonas (p. 417). It is however of some importance to the subsequent story to note that the Mauryan empire as most Greeks knew it was that of Chandragupta and not that of Asoka, that is, it was an empire of Northern India. Asoka made one other very great change in India. He became a convert to Buddhism, and through his encouragement and missionary efforts that religion attained a position in India such as it never held again, though Brahmanism remained strong; in particular, he successfully evangelised a good deal of the North-West. Had the Mauryan empire continued powerful it might perhaps have done something to create a sense of Indian nationality in the loose complex of subordinate states and peoples which went to form it, but after Asoka's death it began to suffer the common lot of Oriental empires and gradually to decline; little however is really known of his successors, and it is not even certain whether the whole empire remained in one hand, or whether the two extant lists of names mean that the dynasty had divided into two lines,[1] one ruling in Pātaliputra and one in the North-West, or merely reflect the fact that one list is Brahman and one Buddhist. Certainly the Sophagasenos whom Antiochus III met in the Paropamisadae (p. 101) was no local rajah but a Maurya,[2] a powerful ruler[3] with whom he renewed the traditional friendship of the two houses. It was the ultimate break-down of the Mauryan empire which gave Demetrius his opportunity.

Demetrius, when he crossed the Hindu Kush, was the third foreign conqueror whom north-west India had seen in historical times, not counting the unrecorded tribes, proto-Bactrian and other, who prior to the Achaemenid period had made their way over the passes and settled in the country. Darius I had conquered Gandhāra, Sind, and part of the Punjab; whether he had any plan beyond the enlargement of his empire is not known, but there seems to have been a good deal of Iranian blood in the North-West, which may have had some bearing on his actions. These Indian provinces were finally lost in the reign of Artaxerxes II; Artaxerxes III (Ochus) was very hazy about the geography of the Indus,[4] and Alexander met no Persian officials east of the Hindu Kush. Alexander himself had a double plan: to conquer what Darius I had held, which he achieved, and to reach the Eastern Ocean which he thought quite close, a thing now known to have been impossible. His success was far more evanescent than that of Darius; a few years after his death the only traces left of his rule, not counting the Paropamisadae, were two or three of the cities he had founded, islands now in an Indian sea. Demetrius' invasion was a different matter. It followed a plan which neither Darius nor Alexander had known enough about India even to dream of, and employed methods which Alexander had indeed dreamt of but had only begun, very tentatively indeed, to practise when he died, and which might have provided possibilities of permanence in advance of previous attempts; in distances traversed, in territory acquired, the Bactrian Greeks far surpassed both the Persian and the Macedonian, and came near to

[1] *CHI* pp. 511–12; de la Vallée-Poussin pp. 163–8.

[2] Hemchandra Raychaudhuri, *JASB* 1920 pp. 305, 310. Polyb. XI, 34, 11 calls him τὸν βασιλέα τῶν Ἰνδῶν, which on Greek usage (p. 154) ought to mean a Maurya.

[3] Cf. J. Allan in *Camb. Shorter Hist. of India* 1934 pp. 54, 63.

[4] Aristot. *Liber de inundacione Nili*, Rose[3] fr. 248.

success in an undertaking hardly less ambitious and far-reaching than had been Alexander's conquest of the Persian empire. What this plan was will have to be elucidated by events. But it was a plan which could only have originated in some definite man's brain, and that man was quite certainly Demetrius.

One thing however must be noticed here which will be elaborated later. The Greek 'conquest' of India was hardly a conquest in the ordinary sense of the word, the sense in which Alexander conquered Persia. But in the earlier part of this chapter I shall for convenience use the conventional language of conquest, and shall consider in the latter part what it was and what it meant.

That Demetrius was quite consciously (up to a point) copying Alexander—that he regarded Alexander not merely as his supposed ancestor (App. 3) but as his model—comes out clearly from his coins, and is of the first importance for the story. On his own coins[1] he wears the elephant-scalp. As elephants live in India, it was inevitable that the elephant-scalp should have been taken to refer to his Indian conquests; but it is certain that it does not, for not only does it appear on his Bactrian coinage from the beginning of his reign, but it had been used as a head-dress for Alexander on early coins of both Ptolemy I[2] and Seleucus I;[3] yet Ptolemy I had no connection of any kind with India—he neither ruled it nor aspired to rule it—and Seleucus had ceded all his Indian possessions to Chandragupta. The tradition behind this portrayal of Alexander is unknown, but the elephant-scalp itself must be a symbol of power—power far extended, as his had been; for both Ptolemy and Seleucus had every object in representing themselves as successors of the man who had reached the summit of human greatness. The representation of Demetrius in the elephant-scalp then means that he had himself portrayed in the guise of Alexander;[4] and in fact, apart from the general resemblance of his portrait (features excepted) to that of Alexander on Ptolemy's coins, the elephant-scalp on the two is identically treated,[5] as opposed to its later treatment in art. There will be more to say about the elephant-scalp later (pp. 189, 206); but meanwhile

[1] *BMC* pp. 6, 163, Pl. II, 9–12; see Plate no. 3.

[2] *BMC Ptolemies*, pp. 1–3, Pl. I nos. 1, 2, 5, 6, 8.

[3] On some anonymous double staters (Head[2] 756) and on a rare copper coin in the collection of E. T. Newell, figured by M. Rostovtzeff, *Seleucid Babylonia* Pl. VI, 3.

[4] Cf. Rostovtzeff *op. cit.* p. 53.

[5] Best seen in *BMC Ptolemies* Pl. I no. 1.

this suffices. Again, Demetrius, presumably after crossing the Indus, took the title ἀνίκητος, 'the Invincible'; it has already been mentioned that he is so called on the bilingual Indian tetradrachm of Demetrius II and on the Demetrius coin of Agathocles' pedigree series, and the same title occurs on those rare bilingual copper coins of 'King Demetrius the Invincible' which have been supposed to be his copper coinage for India.[1] No king anywhere before him had assumed this title. It is a poetical word, known in Hesiod and the tragedians, but it is occasionally used in prose and was so used in a famous story: when Alexander visited the oracle of Delphi, the Pythia hailed him ἀνίκητος,[2] and this story must be the origin of Demetrius' title. He wore then the symbol of Alexander's power and used the title conferred upon him by Apollo; he was to be a second Alexander.

Before considering the course of the invasion, one must fix the chronology, as near as may be. It has been seen that Demetrius' conquest of the Seleucid provinces in eastern Iran, which naturally antedates the invasion of India, could not have been begun till after the battle of Magnesia, 187 being the most probable year; how long it took cannot be said, but Demetrius cannot have crossed the Hindu Kush till very distinctly later than 187. The other terminal point is given by the account in the Yuga-purāna[3] of the Gārgī Samhitā, which says that, after the occupation of Pātaliputra, the Greeks would not stay in the Middle Country (say roughly the district between Mathurā and Pātaliputra) because of a terrible civil war which would break out among themselves; the reference is of course to the invasion of Eucratides (Chap. v), because there is no other civil war to which the words 'an awful and supremely lamentable strife' can refer. It was therefore Eucratides' invasion which caused the abandonment of Pātaliputra. I must anticipate here what will be proved in the next chapter, that Eucratides' dates are certain within very narrow limits; he set out most probably in 169, though early in 168 may be possible, and had conquered everything west of the Hindu Kush by the end of 167; the most probable date for the evacuation of the Middle Country is there-

[1] *BMC* p. 163 no. 3, Pl. XXX, 3.

[2] Plut. *Alex.* 14, ἀνίκητος εἶ, ὦ παῖ. See Diod. XVII, 93, 4; *Anth. Pal.* VII, 239.

[3] Translations and discussion of the material sections of this work are given in App. 4. Being embedded in an astrological work, it is given in the form of a prophecy; but the Yavana sections appear to reproduce an older document of the nature of a chronicle.

fore some time in 168, with a possible year's margin either way. The statement that the Greeks will not stay in the Middle Country means of course that they will not stay long; and reasons will be given later (p. 156) for supposing that a date of *c.* 175 for the occupation of Pātaliputra cannot be far wrong.

That gives the end of the conquest; it remains to date the beginning a little more closely. The date given in the Purānas for the end of the Maurya dynasty, 184, has been generally accepted by historians of India;[1] that is the year in which Pushyamitra the Sunga, hereditary ruler of Vidisā (East Malva) and general of the last Maurya king, assassinated his master and seized the vacant throne. Whether the Maurya dynasty had split into two lines and, if so, what were their relationships is too obscure a matter to warrant any deductions; we can only take 184, the year of Pushyamitra's accession, as signifying the end of the Mauryan empire.[2] In the tradition (p. 177) Pushyamitra proceeded to make his power felt, first near the capital, and then at Sāgala (Sialkot) in the eastern Punjab, subsequently Menander's capital, which must imply some intermediate steps; the Greeks then did not take Sāgala for an unknown period after 184, say two or three years at the least. On the other hand, there are reasons, which need not be anticipated here, for connecting Demetrius' enterprise with the end of the Mauryan empire and the accession of a usurper in 184, a thing which fits very well with the dates already obtained for Demetrius; if then it be supposed that he crossed the Hindu Kush about 183 or 182, that date cannot be very far out. In any case, the whole of the events to be recorded down to the death of Demetrius (Chap. v) must lie between 184 and 167 as their terminal points.

The story has been rendered meaningless by the custom of dating Menander either in the second half of the second century or, even worse, about 125–95 B.C.[3] One of the many merits of the late E. J. Rapson's work in the Cambridge History of India was to place

[1] There seems to be a variant, 185.

[2] For later descendants of the Mauryas see *CHI* p. 513.

[3] Von Gutschmid's date (*Gesch. Irans* p. 104), though he himself called it an unsafe calculation. He was going on the list in the *Vayū-purāna* which gives eight Greek kings of India—Demetrius, Eucratides, Apollodotus, Strato I, Strato II, Zoilus, Menander, Dionysius—and puts Menander two generations after his great-grandson. The sooner this worthless list is allowed to die the better. Even later dates for Menander have been suggested; see Winternitz, Eng. Tr. II p. 174 n. 2. I need not consider them.

Menander in his correct period;[1] this has not been followed by subsequent writers,[2] but is so obviously right that it is needless to argue it afresh;[3] everything that follows will bear it out. Menander's chronology, like that of the Victory of Samothrace, has been an instructive instance of the danger of dating historical events by considerations drawn from artistic style. Because his coins are much inferior in style to those of Demetrius and his successors in Bactria, who could be approximately dated from Polybius, it was concluded that he must be late, so as to give time for the art to become 'debased'; whereas in reality it means that the artists at his disposal in the rather remote eastern Punjab were inferior in skill to those who worked in Bactria. It is as though some historian in the distant future should place the reign of George V in the Aurignacian period on the strength of some of Epstein's sculpture.

Demetrius had to make arrangements for the government of Bactria during his absence, and he left his eldest son Euthydemus II as king in Bactria-Sogdiana; Euthydemus II put his own name and portrait on his silver coins,[4] but on his nickel and bronze issues he used a Seleucid type, the head of Apollo and a tripod-lebes.[5] The common Hellenistic practice when a king was absent had been to leave a son merely as governor (p. 218 n. 1), but a parallel to the kingship of Euthydemus II can be found later among the Ptolemies: when Ptolemy VI Philometor invaded Syria and expected to be in that country for some time he left his son Ptolemy Neos Philopator as king in Egypt.[6] As Bactria was Demetrius' home kingdom, it is probable that Euthydemus II was not a sub-king—that would hardly have suited the circumstances—but a full joint-king with his father on the Seleucid model; this would agree with what happened later (p. 221). The western provinces of the empire in Iran, as already noticed, were under the rule of Antimachus in the north and Apollodotus in the south.

Demetrius took to India with him his second son Demetrius (II),

[1] *CHI* pp. 543 *sqq.*: contemporary with Demetrius.

[2] The editor of V. A. Smith[4] pp. 229, 239 (his invasion 156–3); Grousset p. 39 (155 B.C.); Przyluski, *Açoka* p. 166 (150 B.C.). No evidence exists for such a dating; see p. 146 on Patañjali.

[3] Apollodorus makes him contemporary with Demetrius, Trogus with Apollodotus, and some coin indications (*CHI* p. 551) with Eucratides.

[4] *BMC* p. 8, Pl. III, 3, 4; *CHI* pp. 447–8; J. N. Svoronos, *J.I.d'A.N.* xv, 1913, p. 186.

[5] *BMC* p. 8, Pl. III, 5, 6.

[6] Otto, *Zeit d. 6. Ptolemäers* p. 128 n. 4.

and also his general Menander, of whom much will be heard later. It is just possible that the Paropamisadae were his already (p. 101); anyhow he took Gandhāra, crossed the Indus, and occupied Taxila, which had been Alexander's advanced base and must have been his also. It may be taken as certain that he occupied Taxila himself, because the line of conquest there bifurcated, and had he left Taxila to be occupied by Menander, it and not Sāgala must have become Menander's capital.

Gandhāra,[1] the country between the Kunar river and the Indus, comprising the modern Bajaur, Swat, Buner, the Yusufzai country, and the country south of the Kabul river about Peshawur, was to be one of the strongholds of Greek power; it has been called a kind of new Hellas.[2] Asoka had converted much of the country, and it became to Buddhists a second Holy Land, where rose three of the four great stupas[3] which recorded Buddha's charity with his own body in earlier incarnations, those of the Body-gift at Manikyala, the Flesh-gift at (probably) Girarai in the hills between Peshawur and Buner, and the Eye-gift; this last may have towered aloft on the acropolis of what was to be the Greek capital, Pushkalāvatī (Charsadda), rendering, as has been said, 'still more striking its resemblance to its more famous Athenian counterpart'.[4] But Pushkalāvatī, like Taxila, was only partially Buddhist; Siva was still powerful enough there for his humped bull to become the coin-type of the Greek mint,[5] while the Greeks were to worship Artemis as their city goddess.[6] But she was not the Greek Artemis; she was Anaïtis (Anahita) of Bactra, for Anaïtis and her crown of rays appear as Artemis radiate on coins of the Saca king Maues[7] which are shown by the humped bull on them to have been struck at Pushkalāvatī,

[1] In the *Jātakas* Gandhāra includes Taxila; but in this book I use the term in its strict sense. On Gandhāra see Foucher, *Gandhāra*; R. Grousset, *Sur les traces de Bouddha*, 1929, chap. VI.

[2] Grousset *ib.* p. 96.

[3] A stupa was a Buddhist shrine, circular and domed, usually but not always enclosing a relic. Buildings, even of stupa form, which did not enclose a relic were usually called chaityas: de la Vallée-Poussin p. 149. See on stupas, archaeology apart, Foucher I chap. I, and the long study by P. Mus, 'Barabudur', *BEFEO* XXXII, 1932, pp. 269–439, XXXIII pp. 577–980, XXXIV pp. 175–400.

[4] Foucher, *Gandhāra* p. 15.

[5] This certain fact (*CHI* p. 557) is confirmed by Siva being known to Greeks as the god of Gandhāra: Hesychius, Γάνδαρος· ὁ ταυροκράτης παρ' Ἰνδοῖς.

[6] Copper coins of Peucolaos, obv. Artemis, rev. the Fortune of some city with mural crown; *Lahore Cat.* p. 324 no. 20, see *CHI* p. 558. What identifies the city of these coins with Pushkalāvatī is Maues' coins (next note).

[7] *BMC* Pl. XVI, 4; *Lahore Cat.* Pl. X, 10; *ASI* 1929–30 p. 89 nos. 24, 25.

just as in Bactra itself she had appeared as Artemis radiate on a coin of Demetrius (p. 115). Unfortunately it is not known whether the Greek invaders brought her with them from Bactra, which would throw light on Greek relations with Asiatic deities, or whether she had arrived long before with one of the earlier streams of invaders whom Indians comprehensively called Bāhlīkas, *i.e.* Bactrians (p. 169); the latter possibility would, if correct, imply an Iranian element at Pushkalāvatī, again as at Taxila. But, unlike Taxila, Pushkalāvatī became a Greek *polis* (doubtless somewhat of the type of Susa, p. 27), as is shown by the Fortune of the city on kings' coins;[1] the solitary coin of the city itself[2] which exists to prove that it was once for a time completely independent (p. 336) shows, beside Siva's bull, the Fortune of the 'city of lotuses' with her mural crown, holding in her hand the lotus of Lakshmī. Evidently Pushkalāvatī, when a Greek *polis*, was no less proud of her alien deities than was Ephesus of her alien Artemis, and Siva's bull is a parallel to Artemis' bee on the coins of the Ionian city. Pushkalāvatī stood at what was probably then the junction of the Swat and Kabul rivers,[3] and as it and not Purushapura (Peshawur) became the Greek capital, the regular Greek line of communication westward probably did not run through the Khyber pass but by the route which Alexander had followed more to the northward; it seems unlikely that the Khyber was in *regular* use till the Kushans made Peshawur their capital.[4]

With Gandhāra in his hands, Demetrius would be well informed of Buddhist feeling, a matter which was to be of great importance; but from the military and political point of view the acquisition of Taxila was of more moment. The great city was even more important than it had been in Alexander's day, for it had long been the seat of the Mauryan governor of the North-West; though near it stood the fourth great stupa, that of the Head-gift, it was only partially Buddhist[5] and

[1] Those of Peucolaos (above). On the Greek name of Pushkalāvatī see p. 237 n. 5. Many of the city Fortunes on the Saca coinage (p. 353 n. 1) are probably Pushkalāvatī.

[2] *CHI* p. 587 and Pl. VI, 10.

[3] Foucher, *Gandhāra* p. 11.

[4] See Foucher, *BSOS* VI, 1930–2, pp. 344–5, and plan p. 343. A correspondent, however, sent me a sketch of the masonry of some old block-houses above and commanding the Khyber pass, which he suggested was Greek. It looks to me more like the Kushan masonry at Taxila; but it is a matter which requires investigation on the spot by an archaeologist.

[5] There are Buddhist inscriptions of the Saca period, *CII* nos. II, XIII, XXVII, XXXI, XXXII.

Vishnu was strong there (p. 406); with its famous University, of which the buildings have been excavated,[1] sought by students from many quarters, its merchant guilds who struck their own city coinage,[2] the Iranian element in its population with their Towers of Silence,[3] its balance of religions, its feeling of independence which had led it to withstand Porus and to revolt against the Maurya, it seemed destined to be the capital of the foreign invaders. So Demetrius thought. The city he found is now represented by the latest stratum of ruins on the Bhir mound; he presently built a new city on Sirkap, now buried beneath the remains of the later Parthian city (p. 179). To it he transferred the population of Old Taxila, as Hellenistic kings in the West would transfer the population of some Greek town to one of their new foundations, and the city on Bhir came to an end;[4] the Taxila henceforth mentioned throughout this book is the city on Sirkap, which will be described later.

Demetrius left his son Demetrius II as his sub-king to govern the Paropamisadae and presumably Gandhāra also, that is, all the country between the Hindu Kush and the Indus; his also must have been the task of securing and perhaps improving the communications with Bactria. That he had the royal title is shown by his putting his own portrait on the bilingual tetradrachm already referred to (p. 77). It is certain enough (p. 158) that his seat was Alexandria-Kapisa, the capital of the Paropamisadae (App. 6), from which Gandhāra also could be governed, as it was from Kapisa in Hsüan Tsiang's day. Many reasons contributed to the importance of the capital beside its wonderfully fertile plain, which has led to it being called a little Kashmir without the lake.[5] It was near the silver mines of the Panjshir valley and was thus

[1] Sir J. Marshall, *A guide to Taxila* 1918 p. 72.

[2] E. J. Rapson, *Indian coins* 1897 p. 14; C. J. Brown, *The Coins of India* 1922 pp. 15–19; J. Allan, *BMC India* pp. cxxv, cxxviii, and see *post* p. 161 n. 1.

[3] Aristobulus saw there corpses exposed to vultures, which he saw nowhere else in India, Strabo xv, 714. The Aramaic inscription found there (L. D. Barnett, *JRAS* 1915 p. 340; A. Cowley, *ib.* p. 342), though much earlier, may support this; and a tutelary Yaksha in the region of Taxila had an Iranian name, S. Lévi, *JA* 1915 p. 75.

[4] Sir J. Marshall thinks that Bhir came to an end with the Greek conquest, the two latest strata being Mauryan, *ASI* 1930–4 p. 149. Sirkap was therefore certainly Demetrius' foundation, even if he did not finish it, for there is nothing beneath the two Hellenistic strata.

[5] Foucher, *Afghanistan* p. 266 (of Kapisa). But as he thought Kapisa is represented by Begram, I fancy that the plain he describes must be that of Alexandria.

well suited to be the principal mint of the province; Kapisa was the outlet for Kafiristan, the land of the Kambojas, who were possibly a valuable support to the Greeks (p. 170)—indeed it has been thought probable that Kapisa and Kamboja are the same word;[1] and the dual city was nearer to Bactra than any other important city and commanded the three routes. The reverse type on the bilingual tetradrachm of Demetrius II is Zeus holding a thunder-bolt. Zeus, one of the three deities of the Alexander coinage, had not before been used by any Bactrian king, and it is almost certain, from the types on the silver coinages of Pantaleon and Agathocles (p. 158), that the Zeus of this tetradrachm is meant for the elephant-god of Kapisa. A few years later the god of Kapisa began to be regularly represented as Zeus enthroned;[2] but the reason for representing him as *enthroned* (p. 213) was due to other circumstances which had not yet arisen, while the reason for representing him as Zeus was a compelling one. For the elephant-god had his abode on the mountain Pīlusāra;[3] and to Greeks a god who lived on a mountain-top could not well become anything but Zeus.[4]

Demetrius II then ruled and coined in Alexandria-Kapisa. But he coined for his father, not for himself, as Antiochus I had once done:[5] this is shown by his putting his father's title 'Of King Demetrius the Invincible' on his tetradrachms, while on his square bilingual copper coins (which were struck by him and not by his father)[6] he put not only his father's title but his father's head, the well-known head wearing the elephant-scalp. The tetradrachms would circulate principally among Greeks, who understood the position; hence his own head. But the copper coins would circulate, or so it was hoped, among Indians, who might not understand; hence his father's head. But the real matter was the introduction on the coinage of a Prakrit legend, written in Kharoshthi, beside the Greek legend. The great importance of this step will be considered later; here I need only say that this radical development in policy could only have been due to Demetrius himself, not to any sub-

[1] S. Lévi, *JA* 1923 ii p. 52. [2] Eucratides' coin, see p. 212.

[3] *CHI* p. 556 (from Hsüan Tsiang). The mountain appears on Eucratides' coin.

[4] Zeus Kasios is perhaps the best-known instance, but there are many; see A. B. Cook, *Zeus* II, App. B, 'The mountain cults of Zeus'.

[5] Coins with Antiochus' legend and Seleucus' head: E. H. Bunbury, *NC* 1883 pp. 67–71; Head[2] p. 758.

[6] Because the reverse type (*BMC* p. 163 no. 3) is the winged thunder-bolt, which appears in Zeus' hand on the tetradrachm and symbolises Zeus, and is therefore the type of Demetrius II, not of his father.

king, and proves yet again that Demetrius II was coining to his father's instructions. Demetrius himself struck no coins in India; his coins nearly all come from Iran, and are practically never found east of the Indus,[1] though one has come from the excavations at Taxila.[2]

One word as to Demetrius' communications. The Hindu Kush, which has never prevented anyone from invading India who had a mind to, is said to be a less formidable barrier than it seems; and it has been pointed out that the whole story of the Greeks in India presupposes fairly easy communication between Taxila and Bactra.[3] There were three routes across the Hindu Kush into Bactria,[4] all of them commanded by Alexandria-Kapisa at the junction of the Panjshir and Ghorband rivers. The central route, over one of the lofty Kaoshan group of passes, does not come in question; it rises too high, though local tradition believes that Alexander used it for one of his crossings. The north-eastern route commanded by Kapisa, up the Panjshir and across the longer but lower Khawak pass, had been used by Alexander on his other crossing; but though it may have occasionally been used by the Greeks, it led primarily to Badakshan, and made the road to Bactra itself very long. The south-western route commanded by Alexandria, generally used to-day, furnished the most direct road between the capital of the Paropamisadae and Bactra; it runs up the Ghorband by Bamyan and across the Kara Kotal pass to the Darrah, the river of Bactra, thus turning the Hindu Kush rather than crossing it; the road crosses three passes, but all are much lower than the Khawak.[5] This was the regular route in Hsüan Tsiang's day, though the pilgrim himself, perhaps for variety, went home by the Khawak; and the great Buddhist sculptures found at Bamyan attest the importance of the place subsequently to the Greek period.

The French archaeological mission had no doubt that the Bamyan

[1] Cunningham, *NC* 1869 p. 141; *BMC* p. xxv; Whitehead, *NNM* p. 15.

[2] One from Bhir, *ASI* 1920–1 Part I p. 21. Also one of Euthydemus from Sirkap, *ib.* 1927–8 p. 60. In the Pearse collection in the Indian Museum, Calcutta, is a silver coin ascribed to Demetrius, *ASI* 1928–9 p. 139 no. 4, Pl. LVI, no. 4: obv. youngish head of king, diademed and uncovered; rev. Apollo on omphalos, with legend *βασιλέως Δημητρί[ου] [σώ]τηρος*. It is obviously the Seleucid Demetrius I.

[3] A. Foucher, *CR Ac. Inscr.* 1927 p. 117.

[4] Cunningham, *Geog.* p. 28. On the routes of the Paropamisadae see also E. Trinkler, *Afghanistan*, Petermanns Mitt. Supp. Bd. 196, 1928, pp. 57 *sqq.*

[5] On the Bamyan route see Foucher, *Afghanistan* p. 257 and his Map 3 facing p. 278.

route was the usual Greek route,[1] though apparently no archaeological remains, such as foundations of block-houses, were found. I do not know their reasons, but there are two pieces of evidence which are very strong: one is the passage from Varro to be presently cited, and the other the fact that Pliny, speaking as though approaching from the north, names first the Bamyan-Ghorband eparchy and then Opiane (p. 97 n. 1), that is, he speaks from the point of view of someone approaching Alexandria by the Bamyan route. If this were the usual route, it would explain why Alexander founded Alexandria on the opposite bank of the river to Kapisa instead of utilising the latter city, and would explain two other things also: the small importance in Greek times of Kabul, cut off from this road by the Koh-i-baba range between Kabul and the Ghorband valley, and the tradition of the hardships endured by Alexander's army in crossing the Khawak; for though Persian armies had invaded India before him, if they had used the Bamyan route his crossing of the Khawak in force may have been pioneering work. It may be supposed that the Greek kings did all they could—road improvement, shelters, depôts of provisions suggest themselves—to make the route between Alexandria and Bactra as easy as might be, and there is one curious bit of evidence that they succeeded. When Pompey called for a report on the feasibility of making a trade route from India via Bactria and the Caspian to the Cyrus river, Varro says that the report stated that goods could be brought in seven days from India (presumably Alexandria-Kapisa) to the river of Bactra;[2] one need not insist on the seven days, but it shows that the transit was considered tolerably easy, and also that the regular route was that by Bamyan to the Darrah river.

Once in possession of Taxila, Demetrius had two possible lines of advance, on either side of the Indian desert: one south-eastward along the great road across the Punjab and by the Delhi passage to the Ganges and the Mauryan capital Pātaliputra, the other southward (at first south-westward) down the Indus to its mouth and whatever might lie beyond. Alexander had attempted the two lines successively; Demetrius took them concurrently. His own sons, as their portraits show, were as yet too young to lead a great advance; but he was fortunate in commanding the services of two lieutenants who must have been very able men, his brother or kinsman Apollodotus and his general Menander. The two

[1] Foucher, *Afghanistan* pp. 280 *sqq.*; cf. *CR Ac. Inscr.* 1927 p. 117.

[2] Pliny VI, 52; see App. 14.

are twice coupled in the classical tradition,[1] which indicates some close connection between them,[2] but in each case Apollodotus is named first, which suggests that he was the more important; doubtless the reason is that he was connected with the royal house, while Menander was not. Who Apollodotus was has already been considered (p. 76); for Menander I must refer to the Excursus (pp. 420 *sq.*). He was a Greek from the Paropamisadae, and certainly a commoner; his birth in a village *might* mean that his father was a great landowner, successor to one of those Iranian barons who figure so largely in the Alexander story,[3] and that he was born in his father's stronghold to which the village was ancillary, but it more probably means that he was merely the son of a cleruch in a military settlement; in either case he had risen by his own abilities. As he died between 150 and 145 (p. 226), and as his latest coins (so far as portraiture can be relied on in Graeco-Indian coins) show a man of advanced years,[4] he must have been nearer to the generation of Demetrius than to that of his sons; and he had certainly seen fighting, for Demetrius would not have put an unproved man in command of the advance to Pātaliputra. His portraits,[5] for what they are worth, confirm the fact that he was not a Euthydemid; he has a different type of face, and the Euthydemid bull-neck is conspicuously absent. An Indian writer remarked later that among the Yavanas slaves could rise to be kings;[6] doubtless he used 'slaves' in the Persian sense of everyone not royal (p. 355 n. 6), and was thinking primarily of the career of the most famous of the Yavana monarchs. But it must be emphasised that at the time of the invasion Menander was only Demetrius' general, a fact, it would seem, better understood by Indian writers of the period (p. 166) than by modern scholars.

Our two primary Greek sources, taken together, ascribe the conquest of Northern India to three men, Demetrius, Apollodotus, and Menander. At first sight indeed it looks as if Apollodorus ascribed the conquest to Demetrius and Menander,[7] 'Trogus' source' to Apollodotus and Menander;[8] but these brief notices in a fragment of Apollodorus and in

[1] Trogus *Prol.* XLI; *Periplus* 47.

[2] As E. J. Rapson has noticed: *Ancient India* 1914 p. 128; *CHI* p. 547.

[3] See p. 32. It is not however known that this ever happened in the Farther East.

[4] *Lahore Cat.* p. 59 n. 1.

[5] Whitehead *NNM* Pl. VII, 1 is about the best.

[6] Lévi, *Quid de Graecis* p. 23.

[7] Strabo XI, 516.

[8] Trogus *Prol.* XLI: Indicae quoque res additae, gestae per Apollodotum et Menandrum reges eorum.

Trogus' prologue to a chapter which Justin did not excerpt are inclusive, not exclusive; they mean, not that Apollodorus excluded Apollodotus or 'Trogus' source' Demetrius, but that these were the three men who between them carried the conquest through. As however the secondary sources, Strabo and Trogus, while one selected Demetrius for mention and the other Apollodotus, both name Menander, and as there were certainly two lines of advance, we are justified in taking it to mean that one line of advance was Menander's and that the other was shared by Demetrius and Apollodotus; it will appear that the evidence agrees with this.

Demetrius himself was responsible for the conquest of Sind. A scholion to the grammarian Patañjali[1] (p. 146) mentions a town Dattāmitrī among the Sauvīras and says that it was founded by Dattāmitra, who is named in the Mahābhārata as king of the Yavanas and Sauvīras and is undoubtedly Demetrius; and the existence of this Demetrias in Sind is confirmed by an inscription.[2] It was certainly not the Arachosian Demetrias between Seistan and Ghazni (see App. 9), for the Sauvīra-Sindhus had nothing to do with Arachosia; at this time they were on the lower Indus and occupied its Delta (p. 171). This Demetrias is not likely to have been a completely new city. Alexander had begun to build great docks at Patala and must have left a colony there; what Demetrius found there is unknown, but Patala was the natural port and centre, and undoubtedly Demetrias was Patala refounded and renamed;[3] Demetrius may have had in mind the creation of a port on the Indus which should correspond to that of Seleuceia on the Tigris. Demetrius then followed Alexander's track down the Indus to the sea. Alexander had gone by water; Darius I before him had sent a fleet down the Indus; Demetrius too must have followed the easy and natural course of going by water, which would mean that on reaching the sea there was a fleet at his disposal. The trident on one of his coins[4]

[1] Given by A. Weber, *Indische Studien* v p. 150 n.

[2] No. 19 of the Nasik cave inscriptions (p. 257 n. 3). Weber *ib.* pointed out that the term Dattāmitriya used in another scholion to Patañjali for an inhabitant of Dattāmitrī is only the Sanscrit form of the Prakrit Damtāmitīyaka of the inscription, for which he suggested Datāmitīyaka; since then E. Senart has in fact read the word in the inscription as Datāmitīyaka, *Ep. Ind.* VIII, 1905–6, p. 90 no. 18. See also on the identification of the towns of the scholion and the inscription N. R. Ray, *IHQ* IV, 1928, p. 743. It seems free from doubt.

[3] This will be confirmed by the section on the pepper trade in chap. IX (pp. 370 *sqq.*).

[4] *BMC* p. 7 no. 14.

must imply naval power, but it is a Bactrian coin and not likely to refer to a fleet on the Indus; probably it is connected with the symbolism of Antimachus' coins (p. 90) and refers to the squadron which every Bactrian king must have maintained on the Oxus as part of the country's system of defence.

Demetrius himself can have gone no farther. Like the Antigonids, the Euthydemids were tied to their northern frontier; as Macedonia was the shield of Greece against the barbarism of the Balkans, so Bactria was the shield of Iran against the nomads who, as Euthydemus had told Antiochus III, were perpetually threatening her; and who were one day to overwhelm her; no Bactrian king, for his own safety, dare neglect this responsibility. Demetrius, even though he had left a young son to guard Bactria, had taken some risk in going himself to Sind. He had done what Alexander had done; he must now have handed over the command of the advance southward to Apollodotus and returned to Taxila. Apollodotus, coming from the Arachosian Demetrias, may have joined him on his way down the Indus, or may have been annexing eastern Gedrosia, which was seemingly governed from Sind (p. 94).

Menander's advance to the south-east is attested both from the Greek and the Indian side. Some writers indeed, with no clear idea of the two lines of advance, have ascribed all the Indian conquests to Menander, a thing which time, space, and Trogus' mention of Apollodotus alike forbid. It is a proof of Cunningham's penetration that he saw something of the truth as long ago as 1870,[1] when he said that the campaigns of Apollodotus and Menander were contemporary but distinct, that of Apollodotus being directed from Sind against Rajputana; but nothing came of his illuminating suggestion, because he put both kings much too late and numismatists subsequently saw that Apollodotus, who still coined on the Attic standard and some of whose coins were overstruck by Eucratides, must be a very early king. The first thing is to consider exactly what Apollodorus *does* say, before coming to the Indian account.

He says in one passage that the Greeks conquered more of India than the Macedonians (Alexander) had done,[2] and in another that they became (imperfect tense; that is, they were for a time) masters of 'the Indians'; they overthrew more peoples than Alexander had done (*i.e.*

[1] *NC* 1870 p. 85.

[2] Strabo xv, 686: *πλείω τῆς Ἰνδικῆς ἐκείνους* (the Greeks) *ἢ Μακεδόνας καταστρέψασθαι λέγων.*

Alexander in India) and most of all Menander, some himself and some Demetrius.[1] As the words 'they overthrew' (aorist; that is, one point of time) apply to *both* men, we get two facts: that Demetrius and Menander were acting in concert, and that Menander went farther than Demetrius. Strabo adds to this excerpt a note of his own, showing that (like some moderns) he found it hard to believe: 'at least if Menander really crossed the Hypanis (Beas) toward the east and went as far as the Isamos',[2] which implies that Apollodorus had said he did, and incidentally implies that Demetrius did not go so far and did *not* cross the Hypanis. Most of the Alexander-historians call the Beas, where Alexander turned back, the Hyphasis; but one of them, Aristobulus, preferred the form Hypanis,[3] and that is the form always used by Strabo. For the unknown name Isamos the most usual conjectures are the Iomanes (Jumna) or the Soamos (Sōn); if there really be a Prakrit name Issumai for the Jumna[4] it settles the matter, but it is not very material. For there is one more passage of Apollodorus, or rather of Strabo paraphrasing Apollodorus in his own words, which has too often been overlooked:[5] it says that those who came after Alexander advanced beyond the Hypanis to the Ganges and Pātaliputra.[6] The language used imports a military expedition and imports also that

[1] Strabo XI, 516: *τῆς τε Ἀριανῆς ἐπεκράτουν καὶ τῶν Ἰνδῶν, ὥς φησιν Ἀπολλόδωρος ὁ Ἀρτεμιτηνός, καὶ πλείω ἔθνη κατεστρέψαντο ἢ Ἀλέξανδρος, καὶ μάλιστα Μένανδρος, τὰ μὲν αὐτὸς τὰ δὲ Δημήτριος.*

[2] *Ib. εἴ γε καὶ τὸν Ὕπανιν διέβη πρὸς ἕω* (Menander) *καὶ μέχρι τοῦ Ἰσάμου προῆλθε.*

[3] In XV, 686 Strabo contrasts Apollodorus with some unnamed writer who uses the form Hypanis and exaggerates city numbers in round thousands (Alexander had 5000 cities between Hydaspes and Hypanis). In 693, a named fragment of Aristobulus (= *F. Gr. Hist.* fr. 35, 19), a similar exaggeration of city numbers in round thousands occurs (the shifting of the Indus made over 1000 cities desert). Therefore the unnamed writer of 686, who uses the form Hypanis, is Aristobulus, though the passage is not given as his in *F. Gr. Hist.* It is morally certain that the Hypanis of 700 is from Aristobulus also. Strabo took the form from him.

[4] K. H. Druva, *JBORS* XVI, 1930, p. 34 n. 25. But I cannot make out if Issumai be a real name or if the writer is only suggesting that it would be the Prakrit form of Isamos.

[5] It is not given among the fragments of Apollodorus in *FHG* IV, p. 308, but there can be no question about it. Apollodorus is not yet given in *F. Gr. Hist.*

[6] Strabo XV, 698: we know India within the Hypanis *καὶ εἴ τινα προσιστόρησαν οἱ μετ' ἐκεῖνον* (Alexander) *προελθόντες μεχρὶ τοῦ Γάγγου καὶ Παλιβόθρων.* The word *προελθόντες* shows that a military expedition is meant and excludes the possibility of the reference being to Megasthenes, who anyhow could not be classified under Alexander's successors (*οἱ μετ' ἐκεῖνον*).

Pātaliputra was taken; Strabo could not have put it in that form had Apollodorus said that they had tried to take the capital and failed.

The advance of the Greeks to Pātaliputra is recorded from the Indian side in the Yuga-purāna (p. 132); translations of the material sections are given in full in Appendix 4, with such discussion as is necessary. It remains to take the outline (we cannot get more) of Menander's advance and see the way in which the Greek and Indian sources agree with and supplement each other, a conclusive proof that the story is true.

In the tradition (p. 177) Pushyamitra's power reached anyhow to Sāgala (Sialkot between the Chenab and the Ravi); it is possible, as will be seen, that the halt at Taxila, while the ground won was being consolidated and Demetrius' fleet was being built, was used to prepare Menander's way with a little propaganda (p. 178). Menander first occupied Sāgala, known from the Milindapañha to have been his capital later (see Excursus), and then, as Apollodorus says, crossed the Beas, where Alexander had turned back. The Yuga-purāna then mentions the Yavanas at Mathurā (Muttra) on the Jumna; here comes in Apollodorus' statement about the Isamos, if it be the Jumna. The Yuga-purāna then records the Yavanas at Sāketa (in Oude) and in the Pañchāla country (the Jumna-Ganges doab), which is followed by Apollodorus' statement that the Greeks reached the Ganges. Finally both Apollodorus and the Yuga-purāna record the occupation of the capital. The latter document says that the Greeks first took Kusumadjava, which is Kusumapura, the old name of Pātaliputra, but which at this time must have been separate from, or a suburb of, the Mauryan town, and then took the Mauryan capital itself, which was defended by a mud wall, necessitating the use of their siege train, as Alexander had had to use his siege train against the high mud wall of Cyropolis; it is said that the excavations at Pātaliputra have brought to light a mud wall of the Mauryan period 14 feet thick and flanked with wooden palisades.[1] The Yuga-purāna subsequently treats the Greeks as masters of the country: they command, and the kings disappear.

One point in this account, the taking of Sāketa, is further confirmed from the Indian side by a statement of the grammarian Patañjali (made merely to illustrate the right tense to use for an event which has just

[1] K. P. Jayaswal, *JBORS* xiv, 1928, p. 417.

happened), 'The Yavana was besieging Sāketa.'[1] Patañjali's date has generally been put about 150 B.C. on the strength of his supposed reference to Pushyamitra's horse sacrifice as a contemporary event, and the dating so reached has been used to date Menander's advance to about 150. There is nothing in this, for it is generally admitted that Patañjali's grammatical examples are, or in any particular case may be, not necessarily his own composition but traditional examples, put together before his own time;[2] in fact a recent authority, I venture to think conclusively, puts him much later than 150.[3] What Patañjali does show is that the Greek invasion produced such an impression that it could be used as a commonplace illustration in grammars.

Before passing on, one or two points in connection with the Greek advance to Pātaliputra must be noticed. One need not waste time over the belief of some writers that the Greek kings were condottiere and their conquests raids, beyond hoping that such writers have clear ideas of what a 'raid' from Rawul Pindi upon Patna would mean; but the view held in defiance of Apollodorus, that it was Demetrius and not Menander who led the advance south-eastward, must be considered. It was first put forward as a guess in 1911 by Professor D. R. Bhandarkar,[4] because he very properly saw that the advance must have taken place much earlier than the late date which he believed to be that of Menander; his reasoning was sound, but now that Menander's true date is known it has no further application.[5] Subsequently in 1923 Dr Sten Konow[6] based a similar theory upon a passage in the Hāthigumphā inscription of Khāravela, which is supposed to state that Demetrius withdrew (from Pātaliputra) to Mathurā, and this has found some acceptance. It

[1] Cited in many works: see Lévi, *Quid de Graecis* p. 16; *CHI* p. 544. Weber, *Ind. Studien* XIII p. 304, pointed out that the verb in the sentence, *arunad*, means 'besiege' and nothing else.

[2] Weber *op. cit.* XIII pp. 312, 315, 319; de la Vallée-Poussin p. 200.

[3] De la Vallée-Poussin pp. 199–202, based on Patañjali's mention of the Sacas. See on these Sacas the theories of Bhandarkar, *Indian Culture* I, 1934, p. 275, and Konow, *ib.* II, 1935, p. 189, with de la Vallée-Poussin's reply, *ib.* II, 1936, p. 584. His argument is unanswerable, *unless* the mention of Sacas in Patañjali be a later interpolation, which no one has suggested.

[4] *Ind. Ant.* XL, 1911, p. 11 n. 5.

[5] The same thing applies to the adoption of this theory by H. Raychaudhuri, *The Political History of Ancient India* 1923 pp. 204 *sqq.*, 209. I have been unable to see this book, and take the information from L. D. Barnett, *Calcutta Review* X, 1924, p. 250.

[6] *Acta Orientalia* I, 1923, p. 27.

is fully discussed in Appendix 5; apart from some uncertainty as to what the inscription does say on the matter, it is abundantly clear that it has no bearing at all upon the Greek *invasion* or who led it, though it may be important for later events (p. 166). Let me assume that the passage means what Dr Konow and the late Dr Jayaswal say it means (though they do not altogether agree) and then put the matter in general terms. Some king, carrying on widespread operations over an enormous territory, is said to have abandoned a certain conquered province. This does not imply that he conquered the province in person or abandoned it in person or ever set eyes upon it; it may, and probably will, refer only to his orders to his generals or governors. *Qui facit per alium facit per se.*

We may now leave Menander at Pātaliputra and return to Sind and Apollodotus. The evidence for what he did is not so clear as that for Menander, the Yuga-purāna being only concerned with Pātaliputra, but rather more is known about the ultimate consequences. Doubtless he first conquered the coastal provinces where a fleet could help him, and the notice of him in southern Rajputana comes later; we may suppose that he went round the Rann of Cutch, then possibly a sea-gulf, and so southward. Ptolemy (VII, 60) knows of a Greek city Theophila in those parts (p. 234), and his co-ordinates, for what they are worth, place it eastward of the Indus delta; he seems to have figured it as on the route from Patala to Ujjain,[1] and its foundation—it must have been an Indian town refounded—would belong to Apollodotus' activity. A woman's name means a dynastic name, which implies a Greek *polis*; Theophila might have been Demetrius' queen, but the likeliest guess would be that Apollodotus *was* Demetrius' youngest brother (p. 76) and that Theophila was their mother, the half-Seleucid consort of Euthydemus. Apollodorus says of this advance that not only did the Greeks occupy Patalene (the Indus delta country) but also, of the rest of the coast land, the kingdom called of Saraostos and the kingdom of Sigerdis.[2] The former has long been certain; it was Surāshtra, Kathiawar.[3] There seems to have been a foreign element in the province, at any rate in the seaports, a thing in favour of the Greeks; Asoka's governor in Surāshtra had had an Iranian name, Tushaspa, and had

[1] See the map in Berthelot facing p. 264.

[2] Strabo XI, 516: *οὐ μόνον δὲ τὴν Παταληνὴν κάτεσχον ἀλλὰ καὶ τῆς ἄλλης παραλίας τήν τε Σαραόστου καλουμένην καὶ τὴν Σιγέρδιδος βασιλείαν.*

[3] *CHI* p. 542 and every writer.

been called a Yavana,[1] and Ceylonese tradition knows of a missionary, Dhammarakkita, sent by Asoka to Aparānta (Gujerat), who is called a Yona.[2] The other kingdom, that of Sigerdis, is unknown, but can only mean the country between Patalene and Surastrene, including Cutch;[3] the provinces however will be discussed later (pp. 233 *sqq.*) and I only want here to get the outline of the conquest.

The next notice of Apollodotus is in the anonymous Periplus Maris Erythraei (referred to throughout as the Periplus), in connection with the great seaport of Barygaza (Broach) in Gujerat, on the east coast of the Gulf of Cambaye facing Kathiawar. The merchant who wrote the Periplus in the middle of the first century A.D.[4] is not always clear about the interior of India, which he did not know; but for the things he personally knew and had seen—the coast and the ports—he is good authority. He says that in the country about Barygaza there were still mementos of Alexander's expedition—old shrines, foundations of permanent camps (or barracks), and very great wells.[5] Alexander of course was never near Barygaza. Some of the Alexander-stories belong to Islam; but it has often been suspected that some are reminiscences of the Greeks, and this one, from its date, is certain: the objects referred to are mementos of the Greek (Apollodotus') conquest and of the subsequent Greek occupation. The camps are interesting, as showing that the troops were camped outside, and not in, a city, but more interesting are the wells. Few countries could exist without knowing how to dig wells; what the Periplus means is that Greek engineers could dig deeper wells than the people of India could. One recalls that

[1] The Rudraman inscription, *Ep. Ind.* VIII, 1905–6, p. 46.

[2] *CHI* pp. 499, 603, from the *Mahāvamsa*.

[3] This, and Theophila, preclude the idea that Apollodotus might have gone by sea to Kathiawar; though he may have had a fleet co-operating.

[4] On the date of this work see now J. G. C. Anderson in *CAH* X, 1934, p. 882, whose reasoning is conclusive against the later date often adopted; equally conclusive against any date near the end of the first century A.D. is it that the Kushans are still in Bactria and have not yet occupied Gandhāra (*Periplus* 47). Anderson's date, the early part of the reign of Malchus II of Nabataea, A.D. 40–71, may for practical purposes be called the middle of the first century A.D., as I have done throughout; it agrees fairly closely with the date, 50–65 A.D., taken by M. P. Charlesworth, *C.Q.* XXII, 1928, p. 92, who rightly said it *could* not be later.

[5] *Periplus* 41: *Σώζεται δὲ καὶ ἔτι νῦν τῆς Ἀλεξάνδρου στρατιᾶς σημεῖα περὶ τοὺς τόπους, ἱερά τε ἀρχαῖα καὶ θεμέλιοι παρεμβολῶν καὶ φρέατα μέγιστα.* On *παρεμβολαί* see p. 86.

Alexander had a well-digging expert with his army,[1] and that when the Chinese attacked Ir-shi in Ferghana in 101 B.C. the citadel was saved by a 'man from Ts'in' who knew how to dig (deep) wells (see pp. 310 *sq.*).

The Periplus further shows that Apollodotus ruled Barygaza—that is, it was in his realm—for some years, in the statement that his coins and those of Menander were still circulating in that town in the first century A.D.[2] This is of the first importance. One numismatist has indeed denied that the word in question means 'circulating' and thinks it means 'come to light',[3] but fortunately there is exact evidence about the word which leaves no loophole for doubt;[4] it means circulating as current coin for buying and selling. One may dig up a king's coins in places where he did not rule, coins brought thither by merchants, changed at the money-changer's, and ultimately buried or lost; but if, long after a king's death, his money was still current in trade in some town—which *may* mean that the town had gone on issuing copies of it[5]—then he must have ruled that town during his lifetime long enough to make his coinage a well-accepted medium of exchange.[6] Consequently Apollodotus' rule in Barygaza cannot be in doubt.

[1] Gorgos ὁ *μεταλλευτής* (Strabo XV, 700) was presumably not only a mining engineer but also a water engineer, like the *μεταλλευτής* charged to open up the choked outlets of Lake Copais, *id.* IX, 407. On Alexander's well-digging see Arr. *Anab.* VI, 18, 1.

[2] *Periplus* 47: *Μεχρὶ νῦν ἐν Βαρυγάζοις παλαιαὶ προχωροῦσι δραχμαί, γράμμασιν Ἑλληνικοῖς ἐγκεχαραγμέναι ἐπίσημα τῶν μετ' Ἀλέξανδρον βεβασιλευκότων Ἀπολλοδότου καὶ Μενάνδρου.* This means that the writer had seen them.

[3] Whitehead, *NC* p. 306 n. 16.

[4] Sext. Empir. *adv. Math.* I, 178: *ὥσπερ γὰρ ἐν πόλει νομίσματός τινος προχωροῦντος κατὰ τὸ ἐγχώριον ὁ μὲν τούτῳ στοιχῶν δύναται καὶ τὰς ἐν ἐκείνῃ τῇ πόλει διεξαγωγὰς ἀπαραποδίστως ποιεῖσθαι, ὁ δὲ τοῦτο μὲν μὴ παραδεχόμενος ἄλλο δέ τι καινὸν χαράσσων ἑαυτῷ καὶ τούτῳ νομιστεύεσθαι θέλων μάταιος καθέστηκεν.* This is conclusive for the meaning of *προχωρεῖν*. It never means 'come to light'.

[5] Old coins might also have been sent there; but the deduction would be the same.

[6] Whitehead *loc. cit.* makes the objection that before the war Indian rupees were accepted in parts of the Levant, but that did not mean that the Levant was an appanage of the Indian empire. I see no connection between the two things. The rupees (if not taken merely to melt down) were accepted because behind them was the credit of the Government of India. But Apollodotus' kingdom was long extinct; the acceptance of his money was 'use and wont', and that could only have originated in his rule. I note as a curiosity that about 1841 H. H. Wilson found Kushan copper coins in circulation in various Indian cities (*Ariana Antiqua* p. 349); and the receipt among small change of a copper coin of Cleopatra VII has recently been recorded from the French Riviera.

This is the known limit of Apollodotus' advance southward—Kathiawar and part of Gujerat, *i.e.* Barygaza and presumably Surat. There are indeed the cave inscriptions from the country behind Bombay, which will be considered in their place, but they do not go to proving Greek rule. More important is the manner in which his advance is confirmed by the fragments of a list of the provinces (satrapies) of the Greek empire in India preserved by Ptolemy; but I want to deal with Ptolemy's invaluable evidence as a whole, and these fragments will be considered in Chapter VI. But one remark may be made here about Apollodorus' phrase, the 'kingdom called of Saraostos'. Greeks adopted from Indians the habit of calling a king by the name of his country or his capital: Saraostos is 'King Surāshtra', the king of Kathiawar; Taxiles of the Alexander-historians is 'King Taxila', his personal name being Ambhi; the 'King Palibothros' of Strabo (XV, 702) is the Mauryan emperor for the time being, whose capital was Palibothra (Pātaliputra); two fresh Indian instances, on coins of the Andhra dynasty, have recently been recorded.[1] The usage is notorious. But Patañjali's 'The Yavana' (p. 146) is not in this category, for Yavana is not a territorial designation; the phrase does not mean 'King Yavana', but merely 'the Yavana chief'. There is a similar use in English.[2]

With Barygaza Apollodotus had reached what must have been one of the Greek objectives, the great port which could give them good trade communication by sea with the West; but he had also reached something else, for Barygaza was the terminus of the main road which ran from west to east across India by Ujjain and Vidisā (Bhilsa) to Kosambī on the Jumna, and so to the Ganges and Pātaliputra.[3] It is known that he turned inland, for Patañjali gives one more notice, 'The Yavana was besieging Madhyamikā',[4] a place identified by its coins with the strong fortress of Nagarī near Chitor in southern Rajputana.[5] It seems certain that he not only besieged but took it, for its coins show that in the middle of the second century B.C. it was peopled by

[1] J. Przyluski, *JRAS* 1929 p. 276.

[2] Cf. 'The Percy' and 'The Douglas' of the old ballads, or a title like 'The Mackintosh' to-day, which is said to be English, not Gaelic.

[3] On this route and the Deccan route (p. 151) see T. W. Rhys Davids, *Buddhist India* 1903, pp. 36, 103; *CHI* p. 517; de la Vallée-Poussin p. 173.

[4] P. 146 n. 1. Confusion used to be caused by the *Brihat Samhitā* mentioning a *people* called Madhyamikas in the Middle Country (Fleet, *Ind. Ant.* XXII, 1893, p. 170), but the coins have cleared that up.

[5] V. A. Smith[4] p. 227 and refs., and see now *BMC India* p. cxxiv.

Sibi,[1] whose own country was about Jhang in the southern Punjab with their capital at Shorkot, 'Sibi-town',[2] and who must, it seems, have been settled at Madhyamikā by Apollodotus; there is no question of the whole people having moved, for the known coins come from a very circumscribed area, Nagarī and Chitor.[3]

At Madhyamikā he was only some 80 miles north of Ujjain, the capital of Avanti (West Malva), and at Barygaza he had been on the great road running eastward to Ujjain. He could no doubt have reached Madhyamikā across country, leaving Ujjain on his flank; but Alexander had always followed the main routes where they existed, as no doubt any army in Asia normally did, and the common-sense of the matter is that Apollodotus would follow the main highway and occupy Ujjain; indeed one can go further and say that it is inconceivable that his principal objective can have been anything but that city.[4] For Ujjain was in the west very much what Taxila was in the north, an important seat of learning and one of the chief commercial centres of India: situated at the junction of two main routes, the Barygaza-Kosambī road to the capital and the road that came north from the Deccan, it gathered up and forwarded the trade between the Ganges valley, Southern India, and the western sea. In one way it was more than Taxila, for it was one of the seven sacred cities of India, whose meridian was to be taken as the base for India by the astronomers of a later day;[5] and like Taxila it had been the seat of a Mauryan viceroy. That Apollodotus could have passed it by is impossible; but it must be emphasised that this is only a deduction. There is no direct evidence of his occupation, for though Ujjain appears in Ptolemy (VII, 62) with a Greek name, Ὀζηνή, this is only a rendering in Greek letters of the sound of the Indian name Ujjahini and might have been made at any time. But there is the indirect evidence of the rule there later of the Saca Western Satraps (pp. 243, 335); for the Sacas merely followed where the Greeks had led.

[1] The coins (*ib.*), found at Nagarī, bear the legend 'Of the Sibi people of Madhyamikā city'. These must be the Sibi whom the list in the *Brihat Samhitā* places in the south division, with Barygaza (Fleet *ib.* p. 171).

[2] Sivipura = Shorkot, V. A. Smith[4] p. 97 n. 2, from an inscription, *Ep. Ind.* XVI pp. 15–17.

[3] *BMC India* pp. cxxiv–v.

[4] Cunningham, who sometimes had flashes of intuition in advance of the knowledge of his day, actually made this suggestion (*NC* 1870 p. 85), but nothing came of it.

[5] V. A. Smith[4] p. 163; E. J. Rapson, *Ancient India* 1914 p. 175; *CHI* p. 531.

We can now see where we are going and what Demetrius was aiming at. The Mauryan empire proper, north of the line of the Nerbudda and the Vindhya mountains, had pivoted upon three great cities: Pātaliputra the capital and seat of the emperor, Taxila the seat of the viceroy of the North-West, and Ujjain the seat of the viceroy of the West; these two viceroys had usually been princes of the blood, and Asoka himself had been viceroy in Ujjain under his father Bindusāra. Certainly Asoka when king had given the empire a great extension southward;[1] but the new possessions had been lost again after his death, and it must be remembered that Greek ideas of the empire were largely taken from Megasthenes' account of the empire of Chandragupta, and that to Greeks the Mauryan empire essentially meant Northern India. Now, with Menander at Pātaliputra, Apollodotus at Ujjain, and himself in occupation of Taxila, Demetrius held the three cardinal points of that empire, the three centres of the administration; the occupation of what remained might seem a mere matter of time and detail. One cannot, as will be seen later, call it the 'conquest' of the Mauryan empire; rather, Demetrius' aim was to restore that huge derelict empire, but under Greek rule and with himself on the throne of Asoka. That was his plan, a plan hardly inferior in scope and audacity to Alexander's plan of conquering the Persian empire. One may suppose that he meant to govern his empire from his new city of Taxila, with Apollodotus and Menander as his viceroys in Ujjain and Pātaliputra, that is, to govern in a direction the reverse of the Mauryas; for from Taxila he could keep in touch with Bactria, which must necessarily have remained the basis of his power.

Perhaps one curious speculation may be permitted here. It has recently been suggested[2] that Asoka was grandson of the Seleucid princess, whoever she was, whom Seleucus gave in marriage to Chandragupta.[3] Should this far-reaching suggestion be well founded, it would not only throw light on the good relations between the Seleucid and Maurya dynasties, but would mean that the Maurya dynasty was descended from, or anyhow connected with, Seleucus. But Demetrius

[1] He had two new viceroys for the southern conquests, one in Tosali over the Kalingas (Kalinga Borderers Edict, Dhauli version) and one in Savarnagiri for the south (Minor Rock Edict I, Brahmagiri version).

[2] J. Allan in *The Cambridge Shorter History of India* 1934 p. 33.

[3] See p. 174 n. 3. The suggestion of K. H. Druva, *JBORS* XVI, 1930, p. 35 n. 28, that on the dates she was more probably married to Chandragupta's son Bindusāra, Asoka's father, is worth considering.

was a Seleucid on the distaff side; and when the Mauryan line became extinct, he might well have regarded himself, if not as the next heir, at any rate as the heir nearest at hand. His plan to revive the Mauryan empire would then really have meant that he proposed to enter upon his inheritance. Should this be true, then he must have crossed the Hindu Kush with his plan ready formed; otherwise one might conjecture that that plan only took final shape at Taxila, after he had learnt more about Indian feeling and the possibilities of the situation, just as it was not till after Issus that Alexander definitely envisaged the conquest of the whole Persian empire.

There are two other matters which bear out Demetrius' plan. The author of the original document or chronicle which must stand behind the Yavana sections of the Yuga-purāna (App. 4), in recording the Greeks at Pātaliputra, was thinking all the time about the Mauryan empire; 'all provinces will be in confusion', he says, meaning the provinces of that empire, and when the Yavanas command 'the kings will disappear'; as his story centres throughout on Pātaliputra, he means that there will be no more Indian kings in the Mauryan capital as aforetime. But more important is the meaning at this time of the words 'India' and 'Indians' to Greeks of the East like Apollodorus and 'Trogus' source'. There is no direct evidence, but the evidence from analogy is too strong to be set aside. In Alexander's day the word 'Asia' was habitually used in the sense of the Persian empire,[1] that is, it was used as a political term and not merely as a geographical one. Some indeed knew that there were bits of the Asiatic continent, like the spice-land of Arabia, which were not within the Persian bounds; but such lands were shadowy things, outside the range of the politics of the day. When the Seleucid empire replaced the Persian, the word 'Asia' was transferred to signify that empire, though it was now well known that considerable sections of the continent were outside the Seleucid bounds: Seleucus was 'King of Asia',[2] and the term 'Stations of Asia'[3] applied to the Seleucid survey of their empire, and the title 'Saviour of

[1] By Alexander himself: Arr. *Anab.* I, 16, 7 (dedication in 334), II, 14, 8 (political manifesto in 333, 'King of Asia'), *Lindian Chronicle* c. 103 (dedication in 330, 'Lord of Asia'), Arr. *Anab.* IV, 15, 6 (in speaking, 329–8). By Nearchus: Arr. *Ind.* 35, 8 ('in possession of all Asia', 325). By others: Arr. *Anab.* III, 9, 6; 18, 11; 25, 3; Plut. *Alex.* 34; Ditt.[3] 303. Officially in 311: Diod. XIX, 105, 1. In common parlance in 307–6: Ditt.[3] 326, l. 23.

[2] App. *Syr.* 60, ὁ τῆς Ἀσίας βασιλεύς.

[3] Strabo XV, 723, ἐν τοῖς Ἀσιατικοῖς σταθμοῖς; see p. 55 n. 1.

Asia' given to Antiochus IV,[1] are sufficient proof. To Alexander, when he crossed the Hindu Kush, 'India' meant only the Indus country which Darius had ruled;[2] but since then Greek knowledge of India had been enormously enlarged by Megasthenes. But Megasthenes, though he knew of the existence of peninsular India, had only described the Mauryan empire of Chandragupta, and the only part of India with which Greeks had been in contact since Alexander's death was the Mauryan empire, just as the only part of Asia with which they had been in contact before Alexander's birth was the Persian empire; Southern India was as shadowy a land as Southern Arabia had been. It is therefore inconceivable that 'India' should not also have had a political meaning, just as 'Asia' had always had; as 'Asia' was used in the sense first of the Persian and then of the Seleucid empires, so 'India' must have been used in the sense of the Mauryan empire. Consequently when Trogus' well-informed source called Demetrius (the Greek equivalent of) *Rex Indorum*,[3] 'King of the Indians', he meant exactly what Alexander meant when in 330 he called himself 'Lord of Asia':[4] Demetrius was monarch of the Mauryan empire. Alexander in 330 had not completed the conquest of the Persian empire, but he held the great centres, and after Gaugamela what was to come seemed a foregone conclusion. Similarly, Demetrius had not yet completed the conquest of the Mauryan empire, but with the three great centres in his hand what was to come might well seem a foregone conclusion also; the one statement was as true as the other. Where Chaucer's 'grete Emetrëus, the kyng of Inde' came from is unknown;[5] but for a moment it had seemed true, and legend remembered where history has forgotten.

[1] *OGIS* 253; see p. 195.

[2] Tarn in *CAH* VI p. 402.

[3] Justin XLI, 6, 4, Demetrii regis Indorum. Cf. Apollodorus' phrase (Strabo XI, 516), ἐπεκράτουν τῶν Ἰνδῶν.

[4] *Lindian Chronicle* c. 103.

[5] *The Knight's Tale* l. 1298. The affinity of some of Chaucer's Tales with Indian stories is notorious: the last section of the *Pardoner's Tale* is the *Vedabha Jātaka*, though Chaucer cannot have known the Indian story (see the ed. of 1929 by A. W. Pollard and M. M. Barber, Introduction pp. viii–xi; H. T. Francis, *The Vedabha Jataka compared with the Pardoner's Tale* 1884); for the literature on the Indian and Chinese analogies to the *Franklin's Tale* see J. Schick, *Studia Indo-Iranica, Ehrengabe für W. Geiger* 1931 p. 89. But the lineage of *The Knight's Tale* (see A. W. Pollard's ed. of 1903) goes back through Boccaccio's *Teseïde* to Statius, and Boccaccio does not mention Emetrius; and Chaucer's phrase in the preceding line, 1297, 'in stories as men fynde', is said to be his way of mystifying his readers as to his source. Seemingly he has succeeded.

For a few brief years Demetrius was lord of a realm which in mere size probably surpassed that of the first Seleucus; he ruled from the Jaxartes to the Gulf of Cambaye, from the Persian desert to the middle Ganges. Put into modern terms, and speaking roughly, his kingdom included Afghanistan and something more, the northern and probably also the southern part of Baluchistan, most of Russian Turkestan with some extension into Chinese Turkestan, and in India part of the North-West Frontier, the Punjab with southern Kashmir, much of the United Provinces with a small slice of Bihar, Sind, Cutch, Kathiawar, and the northern part of Gujerat, with apparently some extension into Rajputana. What can be made out about the Indian provinces in detail will be considered later, when everything that remained after the abandonment of Pātaliputra and Ujjain had passed into the hands of Menander; but it may be noticed here that the later legend which carried Alexander's victorious arms to the Ganges and Magadha (Pātaliputra),[1] and the saying attributed to Chandragupta that Alexander had all but secured for himself his (Chandragupta's) empire of Northern India,[2] alike spring from the victorious progress of Demetrius.

To return to Apollodotus. Whether he went beyond Madhyamikā cannot be said. It is conceivable that he was aiming at Ajmer, the Eragassa Metropolis of Ptolemy, to secure the Ujjain-Mathurā route; at Madhyamikā he was more than half-way thither on the road from Ujjain, his coins have been found near Ajmer,[3] and Cunningham, who knew India well, thought that any conqueror in that part of the country *must* try to take Ajmer.[4] But in fact nothing is known about Rajputana except that the Greeks called the Aravalli mountains 'The vengeance of Heaven' (p. 253); Apollodotus at Madhyamikā may only have been clearing his flank of an inconvenient garrison of Pushyamitra's, in preparation for the final move. For the final move must have been meant to be that Apollodotus from Ujjain and Menander from Pātaliputra should join hands along the great road and complete the circuit

[1] Strabo XV, 702; Diod. II, 37, 3; XVII, 108, 3; Plut. *Alex.* 62; Justin XII, 8, 9; see Tarn, *JHS* XLIII, 1923, p. 100.

[2] Plut. *Alex.* 62, Chandragupta *λέγεται πολλάκις εἰπεῖν ὕστερον* (*i.e.* after he was king of Northern India) *ὡς παρ' οὐδὲν ἦλθε τὰ πράγματα λαβεῖν 'Αλέξανδρος*, where *τὰ πράγματα* means the Mauryan empire. The king who 'just missed' that empire was not Alexander but Demetrius.

[3] At Pushkar; Cunningham, *NC* 1870 p. 85.

[4] The Saca Great Satrap Nahapana ruled in Ajmer (V. A. Smith[4] p. 221), and the Sacas were usually copying the Greeks.

of Northern India. Between them lay Pushyamitra's home kingdom of Vidisā, where they might expect some serious fighting. But, so far as is known, it was never attempted; though they held Vidisā as it were between the jaws of pincers, the pincers had no strength to close. Whatever fighting the Greek leaders had had or had not had, the wastage of their armies in garrisons and settlements must have been severe; for the time being both had shot their bolt. Doubtless Demetrius would presently have reinforced them with fresh troops for the final stage; he cannot yet have been fifty when he crossed the Hindu Kush, and there seemed plenty of time.

But at some period which cannot be precisely indicated he had to return to Bactria, and had among other things to carry out a reorganisation of his sub-kings. His return to Bactria seems certain from the coinage. His coins struck in India are rare and seem to have all been struck by Demetrius II west of the Indus (p. 138). But his great new empire in India needed an abundant coinage, and had he stayed in India he, as supreme ruler, must have supplied it; this he never did, and though India received a plentiful Greek coinage it was struck by Apollodotus and Menander. His reorganisation may not all have been done at once, but it can only be indicated as a whole. I suggested before that somewhere about 175 might be a likely date for the termination of the advance; it cannot well be put later, as ten to twelve years at least must be allowed for Apollodotus' money to establish itself in Barygaza (though it may have continued to be struck or copied long after his death); and it cannot well be put earlier, because a fair interval must be allowed between the appointments of Euthydemus II and Agathocles to allow for Agathocles' coin-portraits looking slightly older than those of his eldest brother.

Probably the first step was the appointment by Demetrius of his third son Pantaleon to be sub-king of Seistan and Arachosia in place of Apollodotus, whose hands were full in India. Pantaleon's own coins[1] are too rare to indicate where he ruled, but their practical identity with those of Agathocles, which will presently be discussed, shows that it was the same country, that is, that he was also sub-king of and coined in the Paropamisadae; it is conceivable that he never coined at all in Seistan but continued to strike Euthydemus' money there, and that he got the Paropamisadae later than Seistan. This of course implies the

[1] *BMC* pp. 9, 164; Cunningham, *NC* 1870 p. 41, found chiefly about Ghazni and Kabul (*i.e.* along the Seistan-Alexandria road); Whitehead, *NC* p. 318 no. 3.

transfer of Demetrius II from the Paropamisadae. It is known that he was governing Bactria when Eucratides arrived (*below*); therefore Euthydemus II was dead, and this is borne out by the fact that all the coins of the latter show a very youthful portrait. It may have been the death of Euthydemus II, or troubles from the north, or both, which recalled Demetrius from India; the Euthydemids were no less tied to their northern frontier than the Antigonids, though for Bactria the record is lost prior to the final conquest by the nomads, just as it is lost for Macedonia prior to Philip V. Demetrius made Demetrius II his joint-king in Bactria in his brother's place, which shows that he himself intended to return to India. Demetrius II in the Paropamisadae, as has been seen, had simply coined for his father; but henceforth in Bactria he struck his own tetradrachms with his own portrait and type and his own legend 'Of King Demetrius',[1] just as Euthydemus II had done; it is the Seleucid bead and reel moulding on one of his tetradrachms in the British Museum which shows that he was king when Eucratides came (p. 201). Pantaleon, as the rarity of his coins indicates, can only have had a short reign and must have soon died, for before Eucratides came he had been succeeded by the fourth brother, Agathocles,[2] who has left an amount of both information and problems out of all proportion to his political importance. It will be best to finish with Pantaleon and Agathocles before returning to India.

Like the other sons of Demetrius, these two kings did not take any distinctive title on their regular silver coins, but put on them their own portraits, royal title, and types, each using as type Zeus seated and holding in his hand a three-headed Hecate. It may be taken that Zeus is the elephant-god of Kapisa, as he was later, and that they successively coined in Alexandria-Kapisa; a sub-king of the Paropamisadae, being in charge of communications, could not well have his seat anywhere else but in the capital, and doubtless Seistan and Arachosia were actually administered by their satraps. It is also noteworthy that the portraits of these two kings on their silver issues are good Bactrian portraits of the 'school of X', and, as the portrait of Demetrius II on his bilingual

[1] *CHI* p. 448. His own type, shown on his Bactrian tetradrachms, was Athena, which confirms that the Zeus of his Indian tetradrachm (p. 77) *was* the god of Kapisa.

[2] His coins: *BMC* pp. xxvii, 10, 164, Pls. IV, 1–7, XXX, 5; J. Allan, *NC* 1935 p. 1. Cunningham, *NC* 1870 p. 41, says common about Kabul and Begram (Alexandria) and found in Seistan and Arachosia; *i.e.* along the Seistan-Alexandria road, like Pantaleon's.

Indian tetradrachm struck at Alexandria-Kapisa is not (in my judgment) 'school of X', but distinctly inferior, this may mean that Pantaleon brought a Bactrian artist with him; but the monogram on two of Agathocles' silver coins seems to show that they were struck for him in Bactra (App. 1), and therefore all the silver of both kings *may* have been.

But the important figure on these coins is the three-headed Hecate; she has never been explained, but she is the key to several things. She is Hecate of the Three Ways, *τριοδῖτις*, who was worshipped at a *τρίοδος*, a place where three roads met; and only one *τρίοδος* can come in question here, the one in the Paropamisadae given by Alexander's bematists and twice mentioned by Eratosthenes (App. 6), where met the three routes across the Hindu Kush from Bactria. Alexandria-Kapisa stood at the point of junction and doubtless Hecate of the Three Ways was worshipped there; and the fact that she stands on the hand of Zeus proves, as has already been deduced, that the Zeus of these coins *was* the god of Kapisa, that therefore Alexandria-Kapisa at the *τρίοδος* *was* the seat of Pantaleon and Agathocles, and that they *were* therefore successively sub-kings of the Paropamisadae. It also follows from this, almost with certainty, that the Zeus on the bilingual tetradrachm of Demetrius II was also the god of Kapisa and that consequently the deduction (p. 137) that at one time Alexandria-Kapisa had been the seat of that sub-king is sound.

Hecate may perhaps give some help in elucidating the types on the nickel and bronze issues of Pantaleon and Agathocles. The nickel[1] and round bronze coins show a bust of the young Dionysus and on the reverse a panther; as they are not bilingual, they were intended for Greeks, and Dionysus is simply Dionysus and has nothing to do with Siva. The square bronze coins,[2] which are bilingual and intended for Indians, show a 'dancing girl' in Indian dress holding a flower (? lotus) with a panther on the reverse. The panther of Dionysus, then, is common to the two series and both therefore ought to refer to the same thing; it is difficult to suppose that the same reverse type was used with two different significations, and that seems to exclude any idea that the panther on the square bronze coins might be the lion which is so common on coins of Taxila. The 'dancing girl' has been a problem. It has been suggested that the flower is a lotus and that she is the goddess

[1] *BMC* pp. 9, 1; 11, 6; Pl. IV, 6.

[2] *BMC* pp. 9, 3–5; 11, 9–14; Pls. III, 9, IV, 9.

of the 'city of lotuses', Pushkalāvatī;[1] but one cannot imagine the Fortune of a city without her mural crown and dancing, and on the solitary autonomous coin of Pushkalāvatī she wears her mural crown,[2] which seems decisive, apart from the panther. The same reason seems fatal to the suggestion that she might be the city goddess of Taxila, comparing her with a female figure on coins of Taxila which indeed holds a flower but stands stiff and upright;[3] moreover there is no reason to suppose that Taxila was ever a *polis*—it is tolerably certain that it was not—or that Agathocles ever ruled there (pp. 160 *sq.*). The figure in fact cannot be interpreted apart from the panther. Now the Zeus-Hecate silver coins refer to the gods of a particular city, Alexandria-Kapisa, and the explanation of the types on the nickel and bronze issues should therefore be that they also refer to some particular town; this, from the Dionysiac types, can only be Nagarahāra near Jalalabad, the frontier town towards India, which appears in Ptolemy as 'Nagara, also called Dionysopolis'.[4] Very few places east of the Hindu Kush have a Greek name, so the town must have been important; the form of the name Dionysopolis shows that a Greek military colony had been planted there (p. 11), one of the usual methods of hellenising an existing Oriental town (p. 22); whether, like Susa, the place had become, or ever did become, a Greek *polis* cannot be said. The settlers were devoted in some especial way to the worship of Dionysus; hence the panther, probably the city type. The 'dancing girl' on the bilingual coins should then stand in the same sort of relation to the Indian community of Nagara as the head of Dionysus does to the Greek community, and she is presumably a Yakshī or something of the sort with a special connection with the city; there would be no objection, from the point of view of a Buddhist community, to representing her as dancing, for the Yakshīs at Mathurā, with their voluptuous coquetry, come from a Buddhist monument.[5] We shall meet a similar case later (p. 400) of two coins of Maues, linked by a common obverse type, which refer to the two religions of a particular town. If Nagarahāra, whose site has been

[1] H. K. Deb, *IHQ* x, 1934, p. 581.

[2] *CHI* p. 587, Pl. VI, 10; see p. 336.

[3] *BMC India* p. cxxvii; the Taxila figure is given on p. cxxxiv, h.

[4] VII, 1, 42; Foucher, *Afghanistan* p. 279. Ptolemy assigns it to Gandhāra, but it was the frontier town and may have been governed from either capital at different times.

[5] J. Ph. Vogel, *La sculpture de Mathurâ* 1930 (*Ars Asiatica* xv) p. 32, Pls. XVIII, XIX.

identified, be ever excavated it may be possible to be more precise; but what is both interesting and important is that these two Euthydemid princes on their money treat the Greek and Indian communities in the town as on a level.

In addition to the above, Agathocles (not Pantaleon) issued a series of square bronze coins[1] which have no Greek legend at all, but a Prakrit legend on both obverse and reverse, the only instance of the sort among Greek kings in India. It was for long believed that the symbolism on these coins was Buddhist, but it seems certain now that it is not. The type on the reverse which used to be called a stupa is quite certainly a hill,[2] a type extremely common on the Mauryan currency (the punch-marked coins) and on coins of Taxila; while the obverse type, a tree in a rail, is one of the commonest types on early Indian coins all over India.[3] The reverse bears Agathocles' name, and the obverse a word which used to be read *Hidujasame*; there were many interpretations of it,[4] the most attractive of them, comparing the title δίκαιος on Agathocles' pedigree coins, being 'Just to Indians', which made it look like a propaganda coin. It is now said to be certain that the true reading is Hirañasame, 'The Golden Hermitage',[5] and that the coins are copied from a coin of Taxila which shows the same reverse but on the obverse, instead of the tree in a rail, a plant with the legend Hirañasame; Agathocles, it has been said, in copying the type replaced the plant by a tree in a rail,[6] but a specimen of this coin at Lahore which has the plant[7] and used to be called Agathocles' really belongs to Taxila. The Golden Hermitage has been taken to be the name of some district which issued coins as (practically) part of the Taxila coinage;[8] there is however a specimen of the coin from Taxila which omits the word Hirañasame.[9]

The connection between some of Agathocles' coins and coins of Taxila has naturally led to the view that he must have ruled there, but that seems impossible (apart from his being a younger son), for it is certain enough that it was Apollodotus whom Demetrius put in charge of Gandhāra (p. 163) which lay between Taxila and the sub-kingdom

[1] *BMC* p. 12 no. 15, Pl. IV, 10; *Lahore Cat.* p. 18 nos. 52–3.
[2] *BMC India* p. xxiv; one gets animals and trees on it, see p. xxv.
[3] *Ib.* Introduction *passim.*
[4] Versions collected, *Lahore Cat.* p. 18 n. 1; Tarn, *JHS* 1902 p. 273 n. 26.
[5] *BMC India* pp. cxxxi *sq.*
[6] *Ib.* p. cxxxii.
[7] *Lahore Cat.* p. 18 no. 51.
[8] *BMC India* p. cxxx.
[9] *ASI* 1929–30 (pub. 1935) p. 86 no. 4.

of Agathocles. That sub-kingdom lay primarily in Iran, and Agathocles' connections ran along the road from Alexandria-Kapisa to Seistan and not along the road from Alexandria-Kapisa to India. The explanation of the resemblances between bits of the two coinages seems simple. Many of Taxila's coins had been explicitly issued by the merchant guilds of the city and for trade purposes;[1] also no other Indian coinage is known further to the north-west except the coins bearing the name Vatasvaka, a name connected with the Asvaka (Assaceni) of Swat and now thought to be probably another of the districts whose coinage was (practically) part of the Taxila coinage.[2] That coinage then had served the trade of the whole North-West; and Agathocles at Alexandria-Kapisa sat in the gate of the West, through which all overland trade with the world beyond India had to pass. What he was doing was putting into circulation under his own name[3] more coins of types known and acceptable to the merchants of Taxila and the North-West.

It is unfortunate that the coinage of Taxila[4] does not help us to understand the position of the great city under Greek rule. That coinage, though abundant, is thought only to have begun late in the third century B.C. and to have ended 'with the Greek conquest before the middle of the second century';[5] that is, it belongs to the period when the Maurya power was failing and Taxila could assert itself. But it seems unlikely that Demetrius, who, apart from any views of his own, was bound by the circumstances of his conquest to be conciliatory where he could, should have begun by abolishing his own city's coinage, especially as his hands were too full at the time to put anything in its place; and the relationship between the coinages of Taxila and Agathocles may suggest that Taxila was still coining when Agathocles was governing the Paropamisadae,[6] that is, during the latter

[1] The coins with the legend negama, 'mercantile money token issued by traders', and those with the legend Pamcanekame, 'The five guilds', are specific: *BMC India* pp. cxxvi, cxxviii, 214, 216.

[2] *BMC India* pp. cxxx, cxxxiii, cxlvi. Rapson, *Indian coins* 1897 p. 14, following Bühler, made the word not a place-name but a division of the Asvaka. The coin-legends are written in Brahmi, *BMC India* p. 264.

[3] I find it difficult to believe (*BMC India* p. cxxxv) that he may himself have struck certain variants of the 'elephant and lion' coins of Taxila on which the lion is replaced by a horse and star, seeing that they do *not* bear his name.

[4] *BMC India* pp. 214–38.

[5] *Ib.* p. cxxxix.

[6] For the possibility of some Taxila coins being later than Agathocles see *ib.* p. cxxviii. The stratification of the coins found at Taxila in 1928–9 would put the Taxila issues between the Indian punch-marked (Mauryan) coins and the Greek,

part of the reign of Demetrius (died 167). Indeed the end of the city's coinage might be connected with the invasion of Eucratides (165 or 164) or with the capture of the city by his son Heliocles; but the whole matter is too uncertain to enable any conclusions about the amount of autonomy which Taxila may or may not have possessed under different Greek rulers.

A peculiar feature of Agathocles' coinage is that the Prakrit legends are often written in Brahmi instead of Kharoshthi, which Demetrius II had already used and which was to be used by every subsequent Greek king; Agathocles and Pantaleon are the only two to use Brahmi. Brahmi, believed to have come by sea from Babylonia, would no doubt have become the universal writing of India, as it did later, but for the subsequent intrusion of Kharoshthi, a script derived from Aramaic, the common writing in Persia for official use in Achaemenid times, which is supposed to have reached India about 500 B.C. in the train of Darius' conquests; it drove like a wedge into the Achaemenid provinces of the North-West and became the usual writing in Gandhāra and Taxila. But we hardly know the position in the Paropamisadae; for though Kharoshthi inscriptions have been found in abundance in Gandhāra and the Taxila country, none have come from westward of the Panjkora river,[1] though this may in part be due to lack of facilities for exploration. It is now believed that where Brahmi and Kharoshthi are both employed (as on Agathocles' coins) a dialectical difference is indicated,[2] and the natural explanation of the use of Brahmi by Pantaleon and Agathocles is that in the Paropamisadae there were districts whose dialects were normally written in Brahmi, as were the legends on the already mentioned Vatasvaka coinage from Swat, and on some of the coins of Taxila;[3] but as no other Greek king in the Paropamisadae used Brahmi they must have overestimated its importance in relation to Kharoshthi, a mistake easy enough for strangers to make.

When Demetrius returned to Bactria he handed over to Apollodotus as his sub-king everything in India outside Menander's sphere except

ASI 1928–9 p. 64; but one is warned (*ib.*) not to rely too much on the stratification, and the coins have often been found together with those of Greek kings, even kings of the first century B.C.; see generally *ASI* 1929–30 p. 71.

[1] See a valuable map of the find-spots of Kharoshthi inscriptions in *CII* facing p. xiv.

[2] *BMC India* p. cxxix, on the coins of the Audumbharas and Kunindas which have Brahmi on one side and Kharoshthi on the other.

[3] *Ib.* pp. cxxvi–cxxix.

the Paropamisadae; this follows from the fact that Apollodotus, besides being king in Barygaza, was also king in Gandhāra, and therefore must have ruled everything between the two. His rule in Gandhāra is proved by the appearance of the humped bull of Siva on both his round and square silver coins,[1] for the two types which are certain are the Zeus of Kapisa and the humped bull of Pushkalāvatī, the capital of Gandhāra.[2] He must also have ruled Taxila and the kingdom between the Indus and the Jhelum of which Taxila was the capital, for Menander's sphere did not come west of the Jhelum, Bucephala being his most westerly town (p. 245). But one of the great difficulties in reconstruction has been that the coin-type used by the Greeks for Taxila was unknown. The modern view is that it was the *pilei* (caps) of the Dioscuri;[3] but even if this be true—it seems very conjectural—it cannot apply to the period before Eucratides, whose coinage first introduced the Dioscuri and their *pilei* into India as coin-types. The Taxila type ought to be discoverable on Taxila's own coinage. That coinage uses several types, among them the lion and the humped bull, but infinitely the commonest type is the elephant;[4] indeed the elephant, though a common type on early Indian coins, is so particularly associated with two towns, Eran and Taxila, that it has been thought to possess a local significance.[5] Now Apollodotus' round silver coins show on one side Siva's humped bull, with the 'footprint of Nandi' on its hump,[6] and on the other an elephant, and the conjunction of these two types is imitated by subsequent kings who ruled both Gandhāra and Taxila—Heliocles and the Sacas Maues, Azes, and Azilises[7]—and I suggest that the elephant here is the missing type of Taxila on Greek coins and signifies that Apollodotus, as he must have done, ruled that kingdom as well as Gandhāra.

[1] *BMC* p. 34; Pl. IX, 8, 9.

[2] *CHI* p. 557. Certainly the humped bull had long been a wide-spread emblem, and appears on the autonomous coins of several Indian cities, including Ujjain (see Rapson's list in Rhys Davids' *Buddhist India* pp. 321–2, and *BMC India* pp. cxliv, 258–60) and occasionally Taxila (*ASI* 1914–15 p. 28 no. 2; *BMC India* p. 235), but the imitation of Apollodotus' 'humped bull and elephant' type by Heliocles (p. 271 n. 2) shows that only Pushkalāvatī can be meant. See p. 135 n. 5.

[3] *CHI* pp. 556, 558, 591; H. K. Deb, *IHQ* x, 1934, p. 515.

[4] See especially *BMC India* pp. 218 to 228 and 234, as compared with other types.

[5] *Ib.* p. xxvi.

[6] *BMC* p. 34 no. 10; see A. B. Cook *Zeus* I p. 637.

[7] Heliocles, *BMC* p. 24 nos. 30–1; Maues, *ib.* p. 71 no. 25; Azes, *ib.* p. 90 nos. 188–9; Azilises *ib.* p. 97 no. 41.

There is indeed a difficulty about invoking the aid of the elephant, for any particular elephant might merely be the well-known elephant of the Seleucid coinage, as is certainly the case with the elephant on the unique copper coin of Antimachus (p. 90), and Apollodotus did use the Seleucid type of 'Apollo and tripod' on his bronze money; but the fact that Apollodotus' humped bull and elephant type became a regular type of the Saca kings may show that it had a local significance.[1]

There is a story which may bear on the elephant of Taxila. It is now known that Philostratus, when he wrote the Life of Apollonius, had before him a pretty accurate description of Parthian Taxila by some one who had visited it (p. 360); and he says that at Taxila there was a very old elephant, once belonging to Porus, whom Alexander had dedicated in the temple of the Sun and had named Aias, and whom the people used to anoint with myrrh and adorn with fillets.[2] Philostratus attributes many things to Alexander and Porus, but the story might really be evidence for the existence at Taxila of a sacred elephant, the elephant of the coins; the bell round the elephant's neck on the elephant-head coin-types of Demetrius,[3] Menander,[4] and Maues[5] would support this. More than a suggestion it cannot of course be.

Apollodotus on his appointment must have returned to the north and fixed his seat at Pushkalāvatī or Taxila, probably the latter; presumably he governed the southern provinces through *strategoi* (p. 241). There is indeed an obscure Greek king Theophilus, whose coins are very rare indeed,[6] and whose name might suggest 'King Theophila' (cf. p. 150); but the square theta in his coin-legend shows that he is much later, and Theophilus is far too common a Greek name for any connection with Theophila to be postulated. What seems fairly certain is that, though the coastal provinces south of Patalene remained Greek, Apollodotus' inland conquests, including Ujjain, were soon lost, for Pushyamitra subsequently appears as ruler of Ujjain and Avanti

[1] If this be correct, Apollodotus did not coin silver till he became king in Gandhāra; if he coined at all when king in Seistan-Arachosia, it was his common 'Apollo and tripod' bronze. But very likely, in Seistan, he continued to strike Euthydemus' bronze, as did Agathocles after him; it was so common there (Cunningham, *NC* 1869 p. 138; *CHI* p. 442) that it was subsequently imitated by the Sacas of Seistan (Rapson, *JRAS* 1904 p. 75 no. 5).

[2] Life of Apollonius II, 20.

[3] *BMC* Pl. III, 2.

[4] *Ib.* Pl. XII, 6.

[5] *Ib.* Pl. XVI, 1.

[6] *BMC* p. 167 nos. 1, 2; also one found at Taxila, *ASI* 1915–16 p. 32 no. 6. He used the Euthydemid Heracles as type.

generally;[1] whether he reconquered them when Apollodotus went north, or whether like Pātaliputra they were abandoned when Eucratides came, cannot be said; the latter alternative seems more probable, and would give time enough for Pushyamitra's rule there. They do not appear in the province-list in Ptolemy, but as we only possess fragments of that list that means nothing.

Apollodotus, like Demetrius, appears in the Mahābhārata as a king of the Yavanas under the name Bhagadatta,[2] and the wide extent of his rule is attested in general terms by the wide diffusion of his abundant coinage; the range of find-spots is said far to exceed that of any other Greek king except Menander, and the number of monograms on his money suggests that he coined in other places beside Pushkalāvatī and Taxila. It is unfortunate that Cunningham, with his unrivalled knowledge of find-spots, a knowledge which no one now can ever acquire again, never drew up a complete list of the places in India where within his knowledge Apollodotus' coins had been found; putting together the indications he left[3] and omitting Seistan-Arachosia and the Paropamisadae, he refers to finds in the Lower Punjab, Sind, Gujerat, Karnal near Delhi, Roh, and Pushkar near Ajmer; add to these Amarkot near Dera Ghazi Khan,[4] Bajaur,[5] Mathurā,[6] Bundelkhund south of the Jumna,[7] Dudial in Hazara,[8] and of course Taxila; apparently too they circulated among the Kunindas (p. 325), and certainly in Barygaza. Probably this list is nowhere near complete, but it covers most of Greek India. The presence of his coins in Menander's sphere attests a lively trade; it can hardly be taken to mean that at the end of his life he was Menander's suzerain. Why, unlike every other Greek king except Antimachus II and Telephus, he never put his portrait on his coins is a mystery; that, and the great amount of power delegated to him by

[1] *CHI* pp. 531–2, at some period Pushyamitra lost Ujjain to the Andhras; he had therefore recovered it from the Greeks. On the Andhra chronology, which is no obstacle to the view I have taken, see de la Vallée-Poussin pp. 210 *sqq.*

[2] Von Gutschmid's identification. Endorsed by A. Weber, *Berlin SB* 1890 p. 906, and cf. p. 87 n. 2, *above*.

[3] *NC* 1870 pp. 78, 85.

[4] W. Vost, *JASB* v 1909, Num. Supp. xi; 221 silver coins of Apollodotus I and II.

[5] M. F. C. Martin, *ib.* xxiii, 1927, Num. Supp. xl p. 18; 95 silver coins of Apollodotus I in the Bajaur hoard.

[6] Whitehead *NNM* p. 45.

[7] V. A. Smith, *Ind. Ant.* xxxiii, 1904, p. 217; 34 coins.

[8] Whitehead *NC* p. 342; a few coins.

Demetrius, which implies complete confidence, may support the view that he really was Demetrius' youngest brother (p. 76) and that the relations between them were those between Antigonus Gonatas and his half-brother Craterus. But indeed one obvious feature of the whole story is the manner in which the early Euthydemids trusted one another; there is no hint anywhere, such as one overstriking another's coins, that that trust was ever misplaced, and we shall see the way in which they acted as a family against Eucratides. The phenomenon is a well-known feature of two other Hellenistic dynasties, the Antigonids and the Attalids; but clearly those two houses had no monopoly of family loyalty.

The amount of power delegated to Apollodotus may show that Demetrius did not expect to be able to return from Bactria to India for some time, and it is unfortunate that there is no hint to be got of what it was which kept him in Bactria. At the same time, the appointment of Demetrius II to take his brother's place as joint-king in Bactria itself is proof that Demetrius did intend to return to India sooner or later; it was obvious that he would have to, if his plan was to be carried out to its conclusion. Whether he really did return can hardly be said with any confidence; the question depends on the much defaced Hāthigumphā inscription of Khāravela (App. 5), which throws an uncertain light. But if it says what some scholars claim that it says, then he did return and was somewhere in Menander's sphere in the south-east, perhaps at Mathurā, when the news came of Eucratides' attack in 168; and certainly it would fit in very well with Eucratides' story if we suppose that Eucratides rather had things his own way at the start and that Demetrius did not come on the scene in Bactria till late in 168 or even 167, especially as it is just possible (p. 200) that he brought Indian troops. If so, what took Demetrius to the south-east was either that Menander was being attacked and needed reinforcements, or else he came to arrange the final campaign in which Apollodotus and Menander were to join hands; in either case he can have had no suspicion of the plans of Antiochus IV. But there is nothing certain except that, as the Yuga-purāna shows, it was Eucratides' attack which caused the Greeks to abandon the Middle Country.

The fact has already been emphasised that Menander at this time was only Demetrius' general, as Indian writers well understood: in the Yuga-purāna it is Demetrius who is supreme at Pātaliputra, in the Hāthigumphā inscription (if it really bears on the matter) it is Demetrius who orders the withdrawal, and in the Mahābhārata, while Demetrius and Apollodotus appear as kings of the Yavanas, Menander is not mentioned. Doubtless Menander was meant to be, and was, governor or viceroy for Demetrius of all the conquests south-eastward of the Jhelum, the line of division between the spheres of Apollodotus and himself; but it is quite uncertain when he became king. It was one thing for Demetrius to confer the royal title and a great measure of power upon Apollodotus, who was his brother or kinsman, and quite another to confer that title upon a general, a thing as yet without any precedent anywhere.[1] It is unlikely that Menander's sphere was ever subject to Apollodotus, and it may be that Demetrius, from sheer necessity, made Menander king when he himself returned to fight Eucratides; though more probably Menander took the title himself when Demetrius was killed, in the usual form of a vote by his army. We simply do not know when the most famous of the Yavanas received, or assumed, the diadem.

. . . .

So far I have used the conventional language of conquest; the attempt must now be made to show what the conquest really meant and how it happened that a not too numerous body of Greeks came into possession of a large part of Northern India and were apparently able to do so much more than Alexander had been able to do; for even if the armies of Apollodotus and Menander were, as they probably were, Indian armies with Iranian cavalry and only a nucleus of Greek infantry as a spear-head, you cannot lead a native army till you have raised it. As usual, one must start from Alexander.

Alexander, after much fighting west of the Indus, had reached Taxila and made it his advanced base for the conquest of the Punjab. He had a veteran and ever-victorious army; his infantry was of finer quality than anything Demetrius was likely to possess; he was drawing on the same regions of Iran as Demetrius for cavalry; he himself was among the greatest of known commanders. He fought his way across the Punjab as far as the Beas; by the time he reached that river half his remaining force was on his communications with Taxila and he was using Porus' troops for the necessary garrisons,[2] while the difficulty of the advance and the severity of the fighting had been such that the morale of his veterans broke at the Beas and they refused to go farther. If the reader will look at the distance on the map from Taxila to the Beas, and then

[1] But not impossible; Napoleon's Marshals. [2] Tarn in *CAH* VI p. 410.

at the distances from Taxila to Pātaliputra on the one hand and to Kathiawar and Barygaza on the other, he will see at a glance that the Greeks were most certainly not fighting their way through a consistently hostile land, as Alexander had tried to do; whatever their conquest meant, it did not mean *that*.

It is unlikely that Alexander's own conquest was of much help to his Greek successors. Leaving out of account the Paropamisadae, as belonging rather to the Iranian than to the Indian system, almost everything he did in India was wiped off the map within seven years of his death; the last Macedonian satrap, Peithon, quitted Gandhāra in 316,[1] and the whole of his Indian dominions fell into the hands of Chandragupta. If Indian literature remembered him at all it was only in the form of a bogey called Skanda, used to frighten naughty children;[2] many stories about him are found in the North-West, but the majority, where not modern, are probably due to Islam, which made him one of its heroes, though a few may be real reminiscences of the Bactrian Greeks. Of the cities he founded, the two Alexandrias on the Indus[3] left no trace; it does not even follow that they were ever completed. Nicaea on the Jhelum may have weathered the storm, though that is purely conjectural (p. 328 n. 1). The only city which is recorded to have survived is Alexandria Bucephala on the east bank of the Jhelum,[4] though there is no reasonable doubt about the Alexandria at the junction of the Chenab and the Indus (p. 247). Demetrius may also have found a few Greeks at Patala, or at one or two places in Gandhāra;[5] that is about all. But if some of Alexander's settlements did survive, we do not know in what shape they survived; clearly many of his Greek settlers must have quitted India with Eudamus and Peithon. What Alexander's career did give to the Greek kings was not so much

[1] Diod. XIX, 56, 4.

[2] Weber, *Berlin SB* 1890 p. 903. A writer of the seventh century A.D. has a reference to the Alexander-Romance: S. Lévi, *IHQ* XII, 1936, p. 131; but that is a different matter.

[3] Arr. V, 29, 3; VI, 15, 4.

[4] Perhaps still a city as late as the first century A.D., *Periplus* 47. It is also named in the Peutinger Table and the Ravenna *Cosmographia*, but I do not know the date of their information.

[5] Arigaion (Arr. IV, 24, 7) and perhaps Nysa (Arr. V, 1, 1), which is not Ptolemy's Dionysopolis. The garrisons left in Swat—Massaga, Ora, Bazira, Orobatis (Arr. IV, 25, 4–5)—did not necessarily become military colonies. (To V. Chapot, *Mélanges Glotz* 1932 p. 173, all Alexander's foundations were essentially garrisons. The greater number were really military colonies; see pp. 6 *sq.*)

material help as an inspiration, the same inspiration as it had given to Chandragupta.

Alexander had found a country divided between local kings and 'free peoples' (Āratta) under their own oligarchic rule. With the kings accommodation was possible to him, for he understood kings, but it was not common: Taxiles joined him and Porus became reconciled to him, but three others—Sambos, Musicanus, and the second Paurava king, the 'bad Porus'—were irreconcilable, and one, Abisares, held aloof. But the free peoples—the Asvaka of Gandhāra, the Cathaei between the Ravi and the Beas, the Mālavas (Malli) of the lower Ravi—all fought him desperately; he did not understand them and they did not understand him. Subsequently this whole complex of states became part of the Mauryan empire, but that empire was nothing organic, merely a covering framework; it functioned while the central power was strong, but easily fell back into its component parts when it became weak, though the component parts might have altered meanwhile. The Greeks met with local kings in Cutch and Surastrene, as has been seen, and at Mathurā (p. 259); but though in the case of many of the Indian peoples to be mentioned it cannot be said whether there was a king or not, there are two districts, Taxila[1] and the Madras (p. 171), where the kingship which had existed in Alexander's day had certainly been lost, and it seems as if the relative importance of the free peoples may have increased. However that may be, it seems probable that the attitude of the free peoples to the Greeks and the Greek attitude to them was something quite other than it had been in Alexander's day.

Many of the peoples of the North-West had been immigrants, from Iran or elsewhere, and some were not yet fully Indianised; some north-Iranian names occur in the Alexander-story,[2] traces of foreign words are found even in the Punjab, and Indian writers classed all these semi-foreign peoples together as Bāhlīkas (Bactrians),[3] a term which in a narrow sense meant the Bhallas west of the Jhelum.[4] I must run through the principal peoples; the difference in nomenclature since Alexander's day may sometimes be accounted for by migrations or by supposing that we hear of peoples instead of kings, though the important Āratta

[1] The absence of kings on Taxila's coinage is conclusive.

[2] The hill ruler Arsaces, Arr. *Anab.* v, 29, 4, and the Sogdoi on the Indus, *ib.* vi, 15, 4.

[3] J. Przyluski, *JA* 1926 pp. 11–13; de la Vallée-Poussin pp. 13–14.

[4] Przyluski *loc. cit.* p. 11.

people Cathaei are not mentioned again. The most foreign of all, unless the Abhīras, were the Kambojas[1] of Kafiristan, the country behind Kapisa, which city perhaps bore their name (p. 138 n. 1); Asoka's Edicts class them definitely with Greeks,[2] like the Greeks they were regarded as degenerate Kshatriyas, and they spoke a language which was either half Indian and half Iranian or anyhow had an infusion of Iranian words.[3] The importance of Kapisa as a Greek centre, and the legend, which like other Alexander-descents (p. 302 and App. 3) should really go back to the Greek period, that the 'White Kafirs' of Kafiristan were descended from Alexander's Macedonians, show that there was little hostility here. The Asvaka (Aspasii and Assaceni) of Bajaur and Lower Swat, who had fought hard against Alexander, had since been converted to Buddhism by Asoka; in his edicts he classes them, under the name of Gandhāras, with Greeks and Kambojas,[4] and Gandhāra became a Greek stronghold; there can have been little hostility here. The Sibi of the Lower Punjab had been spared by Alexander for sentimental reasons (he thought they were descended from followers of his ancestor Heracles); now they contributed troops to the Greek armies, for the only explanation of a settlement of Sibi at Madhyamikā as early as the middle of the second century B.C. must be that it was made by Apollodotus (p. 151). Statements in some modern writers that the Sibi were a very primitive race are merely reproductions of a mistake in, or rather perhaps of a false impression given by, the Alexander-historians;[5] they were at least as civilised as their neighbours, as is shown by the Greek praise of their capital,[6] by their coinage at Madhyamikā, and by the story in the Sibi-Jātaka of the charitable Sibi king who was the hero of the Flesh-gift and was reincarnated as Buddha.

Most instructive of all are the Madras,[7] a people between the Chenab

[1] The relevant passages in Indian literature are collected by B. C. Law, *Some Kshatriya tribes of Ancient India* 1923 pp. 232 *sqq*. Lévi, *JA* 1923 ii p. 54 n., suggested that they might be the Tambuzi of Ptol. VI, 11, 6.

[2] Edicts 5 and 13.

[3] Sir G. Grierson, *JRAS* 1911 p. 802.

[4] Edict 5. Literature in Law *op. cit.* pp. 253 *sqq*.

[5] The Greek material in Wecker, *Sibi* in PW. Greek writers perhaps confused them with some backward tribe in their territory, as Herodotus and Strabo ascribed to the Saca clans of the Massagetae some of the customs of the primitive fish-eaters whom they ruled.

[6] Diod. XVII, 96, 2, ἐπιφανεστάτης πόλεως.

[7] Law pp. 216 *sqq*. For their entry into India, Przyluski *op. cit.* p. 13.

and the Ravi who had entered India shortly before the Persian period; they are sometimes classed among 'barbarians' like the Yavanas, and there seems to be some evidence for non-Indian customs among them.[1] The name of their principal town, Sāgala (Sialkot), does not appear to be Indian; it has been suggested that it is 'Saka-town'[2] and that it points to some old invasion or infiltration of Sacas prior to Alexander, which would explain why Indians sometimes classed the Madras among 'barbarians'. They had been the people of the 'bad Porus', irreconcilable to Alexander. But now they were Buddhists[3] and had lost the kingship;[4] and the best testimony we have to a change of attitude in these peoples is that Menander selected Sāgala to be his capital instead of the Greek city Bucephala. The peoples between the Madras and Mathurā will be noticed later (pp. 238 *sqq.*)

Two peoples on the Indus remain to be mentioned. The Sauvīras or Sauvīra-Sindhus[5] (the names are never separated) had entered India shortly before the Persian period and had worked southward. In the Mahābhārata they are on the Upper Indus; by the beginning of the Maurya period they were on the Lower Indus, and their capital Roruka, supposed to be Alor, was in the tradition destroyed by natural forces about the time that Pātaliputra became important, one man alone escaping to found Barygaza;[6] in the second century B.C. they were occupying the Indus Delta with an unknown extension eastwards, and the second part of the Milindapañha accordingly places them on the sea.[7] Two Greek cities, Demetrias and Theophila, were founded among them, and in literature they were classed with the Bāhlīkas and the Yavanas;[8] we shall see that they supplied some citizens to Demetrias (p. 257). The Abhīras were the latest comers of all; it seems that they

[1] Law p. 249; he however thinks they had become 'barbarised', which appears to reverse the facts.

[2] J. Przyluski, *JA* 214, 1929, pp. 315–17, who also discusses the Indian name of Sāgala.

[3] This is why the *Mahābhārata* (see Fleet, *JRAS* 1913 p. 966) calls them irreligious and impure.

[4] There could not have been an Indian vassal-king in Menander's capital Sāgala.

[5] Best in H. Lüders, *Berlin SB* 1920 pp. 54–6, who however has not seen that the different localities in which they are mentioned must mean that they were moving southward.

[6] See, beside Lüders, Lévi, *JA* 1915 p. 75, and on the transference of the name Roruka to Chinese Turkestan Konow, *Acta Orientalia* XII, 1934, p. 136.

[7] Rhys Davids II, 269 (359).

[8] *Brihat Samhitā* (Fleet, *Ind. Ant.* XXII pp. 170–1).

only entered India during the confusions after Alexander's death.[1] There will be something to say about them later; at present they were on the Indus north of the Sauvīras, where they gave their name to the Greek satrapy of Abiria (p. 235). Their advance down the Indus must have caused, or been made possible by, some displacement of peoples, and the Malli, so prominent in the Alexander story, are not heard of again; the likeliest of the theories about them is that they had gone, or been driven, southward and that they were the Mālavas who gave their name, Malva, to Avanti.

It seems then that, speaking generally, these semi-foreign peoples were probably a help rather than a hindrance to the Greek advance. The Euthydemids had behind them, as Alexander had not, much experience of successful conciliation of the native Bactrians; doubtless they applied the same methods to the Bāhlīkas, and, it would seem, just as satisfactorily. But we require to find a much wider and deeper reason for the sweeping successes of the Greeks than anything so far indicated, and fortunately there can be little doubt what it was. It lies in the position of Buddhism with regard to the circumstances of the moment when the Greeks came; and it needs putting with some care, if it is to be rightly understood. Under Asoka Buddhism had become the official religion of the empire; the religion itself had been spreading along the two great roads north-westward and westward,[2] and a great deal of the North and West had genuinely become Buddhist. But in the second century B.C. Buddhism was not quite the victorious faith which it had been under Asoka. More than one of his successors, in the tradition, had fallen away; Brahmanism had remained strong, though it was ceasing to be Vedic Brahmanism, for it had known how to assimilate the new forces which had been at work since *c.* 300 B.C. or earlier and which were making of Vishnu and Siva personal and all-embracing deities. The new Vishnuism and its effects will be noticed later.[3] But Siva, though he appears in the Vedas under the name Rudra, was pre-Vedic and pre-Aryan and immensely old, and his worship had been widely spread throughout the Indo-Iranian borderlands long before history began.[4] It is possible therefore that he appealed with special

[1] N. G. Majumdar, *Ind. Ant.* XLVII, 1918, p. 35: at least by 300 B.C. (It had been put much later.) A good deduction, seeing that he did not know Ptolemy. H. Jacobi, *Festschrift Wackernagel* 1923 p. 124, also says *c.* 300.

[2] Przyluski, *Açoka* pp. 72–3.

[3] See on all this Chap. IX p. 406.

[4] The discovery of Siva and his humped bull at Mohenjodaro is now famous. Sir A. Stein has found the humped bull and other emblems of Siva at various sites

force to the half-foreign peoples of the North-West, one of the Buddhist strongholds; certainly in the Greek period he was firmly established in Pushkalāvatī, the capital of the Holy Land of Gandhāra, and had apparently a footing in Taxila also.[1] What was going on may in one aspect be called a counter-reformation; that the Brahmans should have enlisted the aid of a non-Aryan deity like Siva is a fact of considerable interest.

Now the Brahman was the natural enemy of the Greek invader, not of course on religious but on patriotic grounds: no one who studies the history of Alexander can miss the fact that the Brahmans had been his most determined opponents.[2] For the Brahman was under the necessity of proving himself. It is too early yet to talk of 'castes' in India, but the four 'colours' existed[3]—warriors (Kshatriyas), priests (Brahmans), husbandmen (Vaisyu), proletariat (Sūdras). The Kshatriyas, to whom the kings usually belonged, had long held the first place,[4] but a silent struggle was now in progress between warrior and priest for social primacy,[5] a struggle to be settled centuries later in favour of the Brahmans. Now Indian writers assigned the Greeks, as they did many foreign invaders later, to the Kshatriya 'colour'; they could hardly do otherwise, for the Greeks came as fighting men, not as priests or peasants or labourers. The assignment indeed was often qualified by saying that the Greek was an inferior sort of Kshatriya, half Kshatriya half Sūdra by descent, or else a Kshatriya who had degenerated through neglect of the Brahmans,[6] obviously a Brahman definition; but a Kshatriya of some sort he was, and as such a member of the 'colour' opposed to the Brahmans. Greeks must have known this well enough, for the Sacas who came after them knew it, as is shown by their adopting

of the chalcolithic period in Gedrosia, *Journ. R. Anthropological Inst.* 1934 pp. 184–5, 190–2.

[1] Humped bull on a single-die coin of Taxila, *ASI* 1914–15 p. 28 no. 2.

[2] Arr. VI, 7, 4–6; 16, 5; 17, 2; Diod. XVII, 103. The notice in Plutarch *Alex.* 59 is probably tendencious; see 64, and Excursus p. 429.

[3] T. W. Rhys Davids, *Buddhist India* 1903 p. 53; D. R. Bhandarkar, *Ind. Ant.* XL, 1911, p. 7 (all castes were mixed); E. Senart, *Les castes dans l'Inde*, 2nd ed. 1927; *CHI* p. 209.

[4] Rhys Davids *ib.* p. 61. Cf. de la Vallée-Poussin p. 147: a burial mound was higher for a Kshatriya than for a Brahman.

[5] Rhys Davids *ib.* pp. 61, 151, 158–9.

[6] The Indian references are given in Lévi, *Quid de Graecis* pp. 20–1; Law *op. cit.* p. 239. Cf. N. R. Ray, *IHQ* IV, 1928, p. 740. Yavanas, Sacas, and Kambojas are all classed together.

Kshatriya name-endings like -varman and -datta;[1] indeed a theory has been put forward that the ἐπιγαμία included in the treaty between Seleucus and Chandragupta meant a grant by the Indian king to the Greeks of the right to intermarry in the Kshatriya 'colour', that is, that he formally recognised them as Kshatriyas.[2] This theory cannot be supported, either from Strabo[3] or in substance, for there seems to have been no *jus connubii* in India or any difficulty at this time in the marriage of persons of different 'colours';[4] but the classification of Greeks as Kshatriyas was one more element in the opposition of Greek and Brahman, an opposition, it must be repeated, which had nothing to do with the Brahman *religion*. But it had something to do, indirectly, with the Buddhist religion; for that religion, though it cared nothing for race or 'colour', had in fact happened to make a special appeal to that Kshatriya 'colour' to which Gautama himself had belonged. Buddhism in fact at this time seems to have been something more than a monastic religion; it was also to some extent the creed of a warlike aristocracy,[5] and it is of some importance for what follows to note that one cannot

[1] *CHI* p. 577; Ray *op. cit.* p. 744.

[2] Foucher II p. 450 (on the meaning of ἐπιγαμία he follows Bouché-Leclercq, *Hist. des Séleucides* I pp. 29–30). See de la Vallée-Poussin pp. 59 *sq.*, and next note.

[3] Because συνθέμενος ἐπιγαμίαν in Strabo XV, 724 is said of Seleucus, not of Chandragupta, which is conclusive. For the rest, Strabo certainly uses ἐπιγαμία elsewhere in both its meanings (XI, 523 matrimonial alliances; V, 231 *jus connubii*); but there was no *jus connubii* in India (next note) and it certainly means here a matrimonial alliance, as Appian understood the same original to mean (*Syr.* 55, Seleucus κῆδος συνέθετο). The objection that Seleucus' only recorded daughter Phila II was not yet born is idle; he could have had daughters by Apama or an earlier wife without our fragmentary sources mentioning them; we know very little about the daughters of *any* Seleucid, and this book alone has rescued from oblivion two Seleucid princesses unknown to the literary record (pp. 73, 196). Besides, it might have been a niece; Antiochus Sidetes on his Parthian expedition did take a niece with him, and Phraates II married her after his death. How scholars like Droysen and Beloch (see Stähelin, *Seleukos I* in PW col. 1216) can have persuaded themselves, against Strabo's text, that it means that Seleucus married a daughter of Chandragupta I cannot guess; when did a conqueror in the East ever give a daughter to the conquered?

[4] Rhys Davids *op. cit.* pp. 53 *sqq.*; *CHI* p. 209.

[5] Cf. the essay of R. Fick, *Die Buddhistische Kultur und das Erbe Alexanders d. G.*, Morgenland 25, 1934, on the earlier Buddhist culture as that of the warrior. It has been pointed out that the mass of donations to Buddhism between *c.* 300 B.C.–A.D. 100, compared with the paucity of those to Brahmanism, show that Buddhism was the creed of the upper classes: Sir C. Eliot, *Hinduism and Buddhism* II, 1921, p. 69.

apply, or can only apply with great caution, to the second century B.C. the view, drawn from later times, that Buddhism tends to render unwarlike the peoples who profess it.

Something of this sort was the position when a Brahman, the Sunga Pushyamitra,[1] murdered the last Maurya and seized the crown, as already related. But he was more than a Brahman; he was a convinced, perhaps even a fanatical, devotee of the Brahman religion, which he therefore naturally desired to see restored as the religion of his realm. The matter at once became of concern to every Buddhist in India; they had no desire to be under the rule of a very earnest Brahman. Probably too there were people who did not desire to be under his rule for more mundane reasons; there was no national feeling in India, and to many men Pushyamitra, the Sunga from the south, would seem hardly less a foreigner than Demetrius, the Yavana from the north. The Greek leaders saw that they could use these feelings. Of course they fought Pushyamitra, not because he was a Brahman, but because he wanted what they wanted and was in their way; both sought control of the huge derelict empire, and war between them was inevitable. Obviously therefore anyone who, for whatever cause, was an enemy of Pushyamitra might become a friend to the Greeks. Both Apollodotus and Menander on their coins, the former exclusively, the latter down to his latest issue, called themselves *Soter*, 'the saviour'. The title still had its full value in the Greek world. It had only been used twice before in history: Ptolemy I had been *Soter* because he had helped to save Rhodes from Demetrius the Besieger, and Antiochus I because he had saved Asia Minor from the Gauls; in the same way, Apollodotus and Menander were *Soteres* because they professed to come to Indians as saviours, to 'save' them from Pushyamitra. It was entirely a political matter; but it happened that the people to be 'saved' were in fact usually Buddhists, and the common enmity of Greek and Buddhist to the Sunga king threw them into each other's arms.

I want to be clear as to the meaning of this, lest any one should suppose that I am talking of an alliance of the Greeks with Bud-

[1] For his history see *CHI* pp. 517 *sqq.*; V. A. Smith[4] p. 208; R. C. Mazumdar, *IHQ* 1925 pp. 91, 214; Rai Bahadur Ramaprasad Chanda, *IHQ* 1929 p. 393; de la Vallée-Poussin pp. 172–82 (very full). Mazumdar p. 214 argues that he was *not* hereditary king of Vidisā; but he could hardly have recovered himself as he did without an assured kingdom of his own to fall back upon, so I follow the usual view.

dhism,[1] the Buddhist religion. Such a thing is, to my mind, impossible. It would presuppose a state of war between Brahmanism and Buddhism which did not exist, though there may have been a good deal of tension;[2] and it would run counter to the deepest feelings of Hellenism. No Hellenistic king would ever have supported one religion against another, for one of the cardinal tenets of Greeks in the Hellenistic centuries was that no man's religion was any one's business but his own, and except by Antiochus IV the rule never seems to have been broken; it seems certain enough now that we never find Buddhist symbolism on the coins of the Greek kings[3] (that was left to Sacas and Kushans), or indeed any Indian religious symbolism except that relating to the god or gods of some particular city on the coins minted in that city. Naturally Hellenistic kings were clear enough as to the distinction between a religion and the temporal power of its priesthood: the early Ptolemies did not touch the Egyptian religion but they circumscribed the power of its priests; the early Seleucids did not touch the strange matriarchal religions of Asia Minor but they sometimes curtailed the territory ruled by the priest-kings. But in purely religious matters these kings never interfered; all the religions of India were safe enough in Greek hands, and indeed we shall meet Greeks later who were devotees of Brahmanism (p. 391). It must be remembered that reconstructing history from coins is like restoring a dinosaur from a fossil bone; the coin also was once clothed in flesh and blood—proclamations, speeches, acts of state. The word *Soter* on the coins of Apollodotus and Menander may really imply a manifesto issued by Demetrius to the peoples of India on the lines, though not in the sense, of the famous proclamation of Antigonus I that all Greeks should be free, a proclamation which for years was a main motive power of Hellenistic history. And if the Mauryas really had Seleucid blood (p. 152), he must also have proclaimed that he came as kinsman and heir of the extinct dynasty.

Pushyamitra himself may have played into the hands of the Greeks, if there be anything in the story of his persecution of Buddhists. A

[1] The converse, an alliance of the Buddhist religion with the Greeks, has been definitely suggested by Grousset p. 57. He may be right; but I do not see it like that myself.

[2] Something of the sort is necessitated by Patañjali using sramana-brahmana as an instance of things in eternal opposition: Weber, *Ind. Stud.* XIII p. 340.

[3] For Agathocles see p. 160 and for Menander pp. 262 *sq.*

usual view among historians of India has been that, though the story is greatly exaggerated, it must have had *some* basis in fact; and indeed several other persecutions of Buddhists in India are known.[1] But the story comes from a source which, at best, is only quasi-historical: the Asoka-Avadāna[2] or Acts of Asoka. An Avadāna is the story of the doings of some great man—Greeks might have said his ἀριστεῖα—and the Asoka-Avadāna stands in much the same relation to the real history of Asoka as the Alexander-Romance does to the real history of Alexander. But it is much nearer in time—it is supposed to have been written at Mathurā about 150–100 B.C.,[3] which might make its author a younger contemporary of Pushyamitra; and even the late Alexander-Romance contains *some* truth. Putting together the different notices,[4] the full story about Pushyamitra is that, as Asoka had built 84,000 stupas and he himself did not feel equal to doing so much, he resolved to rival him by destroying 84,000 stupas; he started at Pātaliputra, where the great Kukkuta-ārāma monastery was saved by a miracle, and then went on to Sāgala (represented as under his rule) where he massacred the members of the Buddhist Order, offering a gold piece for the head of each Arhat; but in the north-west he was checked, so he turned southward towards the southern ocean, where he was destroyed by supernatural agency. Naturally this is not history: there is said to be no trace of any destruction of stupas at this time, there were many Buddhists and Buddhist buildings in Pushyamitra's own kingdom of Vidisā, and he himself had a long reign.[5]

But I have given the story for the sake of a strange feature which has never been noticed. Pushyamitra's route is from Pātaliputra to Sāgala, thence north-west, and thence to the southern ocean. But at the end of the Greek advance the Greek dominions lay as a great horse-shoe round the desert, from Pātaliputra to Sāgala, thence north-west, and thence to the southern ocean at Patalene and Surāshtra; and what the story does is to take Pushyamitra right round the Greek horse-shoe,

[1] List in V. A. Smith[4] p. 214 n. 1.

[2] This work, though extracts exist in Sanscrit and have been published, is only known in its entirety from a Chinese translation called *A-yu-wang-tchouan* made about A.D. 300 by the Parthian Fa-kin. A complete translation of the Chinese work is given by Przyluski, *Açoka*. For other Chinese versions see, beside this work, Demiéville pp. 44 *sqq*.

[3] Przyluski, *Açoka* p. 166.

[4] *Ib.* pp. 90, 93, 301–4; cf. Demiéville p. 46.

[5] In the usually accepted Purāna chronology he reigned 36 years, from 184 to 148.

persecuting as he goes. This cannot be accidental coincidence. Greeks, *i.e.* Greek propaganda, had something to do with this story; and that becomes almost a certainty when it is noticed that the only town mentioned by name, after leaving Pātaliputra, is Sāgala, and Sāgala was just about to become Menander's capital. One need not postulate religious persecution; but if some people who did not desire Pushyamitra's rule *were* killed at Sāgala, that would have given Demetrius, whose general Menander was about to invade the eastern Punjab, an opportunity for propaganda among the Madras which he would indeed have been blind to neglect: Menander was coming to save them from the oppression of the Sunga king. But the Madras killed at Sāgala had doubtless in actual fact been Buddhists, and, even if this were accidental, it might well be interpreted by Buddhists generally as religious persecution; the Greek leaders might think that they were helping Pushyamitra's enemies, but to the Buddhist world it meant that they were helping Buddhists;[1] would they or would they not, the Greek kings, in Indian eyes, inevitably became champions of Buddhism.

A strange touch in the Yuga-purāna, of great importance, bears this out. The late author of this Sanscrit document as we have it, of Brahman sympathies and disliking the foreigner, might say that the effect of the Greek conquest (if indeed he refers here to the Greek conquest) was to turn the world upside down, confound the castes, and make Jack as good as his master;[2] and doubtless the Greeks did take little account of the four 'colours' and made use of anyone willing to support them. But he has also preserved traces of a very different view, probably from the original Prakrit chronicle or document on which the sections of our Yuga-purāna dealing with the Yavanas are based (see App. 4). For Demetrius appears as Dharmamita,[3] that is, the name has been 'adjusted' to bring in the word Dharma and to make it signify 'Friend of Justice', and one can hardly mistake the reason: it is meant to recall the traditional Dharmaraja, the ideal King of Justice of Indian literature (see p. 256). There were, then, Indians to whom

[1] A very similar misinterpretation had occurred in 225 in the story of Cleomenes III of Sparta; the peoples of the Peloponnesian cities believed that he was championing social revolution, while *he* saw in social revolution an opportunity to get them on to his side as against Aratus. See Tarn in *CAH* VII pp. 755–7.

[2] Whether §6 of the *Yuga-purāna* really belongs where the MSS place it may be doubtful; see App. 4.

[3] The Prakrit termination. The Sanscrit Dharmamitra appears in another place as the name of Demetrias in Sogdiana, p. 118.

Demetrius appeared, not as a foreign conqueror, but as the King of Justice.

In this connection must be noticed the new Taxila[1] which Demetrius built on Sirkap to be his capital and to which he transferred the population of Old Taxila (p. 137). It was a strange foundation to be made by a Greek king, for what Demetrius built was not a Greek city but an Indian one, and an Indian city it remained; there is no indication that it ever became a Greek *polis* or bore Demetrius' name. The ground plan was fairly regular, so far as the lie of the ground permitted, and may show Hellenistic influence;[2] one large and well-planned house has been uncovered,[3] and apparently some bare walls of other houses;[4] but 'there is nothing typically Greek about the buildings, nor are there any remains of temples altars public monuments or statues such as the Greek fancy ordinarily delighted in'.[5] The city had not even that indispensable feature of a Greek city, a stone wall; it had only the mud wall of an Indian town, and a stone wall was first built by the Sacas.[6] No trace was found of a distinctive Greek quarter, or of a palace; the 'palace' may just have been a large house, like the Attalid 'palace' at Pergamum. Even more noteworthy, there was no indication of a citadel, though Susa and Babylon have shown that Greeks liked to keep the citadel in their own hands; apparently it cannot be said if there was a citadel at Sirkap at all,[7] though later the Parthians may have fortified an area within the wall, as was their custom. The transference of the population of Old Taxila, even to their University and their gods, seems to have been so complete that there was no real break in the continuity of the city's life, especially if it be the case that the Indian city coinage continued to be struck throughout the reign of Demetrius (p. 161). If there was no Greek quarter, Greek and Indian must have lived side by side; one may recall Demetrius' sons treating the Greek and Indian communities in another town as on a level (p. 160). Above all, the mud wall and the absence of a citadel show that the Greeks had no fear of an Indian attack, whether from without or within; they were among friends.

[1] Sir J. Marshall's excavations have been published yearly in *ASI*; see also his *Guide to Taxila* 1918. He is publishing an exhaustive monograph on Taxila.

[2] *ASI* 1927–8 p. 63. [3] *Ib.* 1928–9 p. 62.

[4] *CHI* p. 646.

[5] Marshall in *ASI* 1930–4 (pub. 1936) p. 151.

[6] *ASI* 1928–9 p. 62.

[7] Marshall, *A Guide to Taxila* p. 5.

We can now, I think, see what the Greek 'conquest' meant[1] and how the Greeks were able to traverse such extraordinary distances. To parts of India, perhaps to large parts, they came, not as conquerors, but as friends and 'saviours'; to the Buddhist world in particular they appeared to be its champions; some provinces must have welcomed them precisely as Egypt and Babylon, and in India Taxila, had welcomed Alexander. They may have had comparatively little fighting till their achievement was half finished; they may even have had none at all except with the actual troops of Pushyamitra and in districts in the South where he was strong; the places where fighting is recorded—Mathurā, Sāketa, Pātaliputra, Madhyamikā—are all places which he would be bound to try to hold. Whatever allowance be made for adventurers and mercenaries from the West (p. 251), the Greeks and Westerners actually engaged in the enterprise cannot have been too numerous, and in each province when occupied the Greeks must largely have retained whatever native organisation existed (Chap. VI), merely seeing that power was in the hands of their friends and probably leaving a handful of Greeks to help in administration. The instance of the Sibi at Madhyamikā may show that points which had to be held for military reasons were settled with native troops from a distance, whose isolation might guarantee their loyalty. Questions of towns and settlements will be considered later; but it may be said here that the only districts in which Greeks really settled to any extent were Gandhāra and the northern Punjab, and perhaps the western seaports and parts of Surāshtra. Over large parts of Greek India we need not think of Seleucid analogies.

There is no doubt that the policy followed by the Greek leaders was the policy of Demetrius; his lieutenants, especially Menander, may have entered wholeheartedly into his scheme, but his was the brain which conceived it and his the will which so nearly carried it through. For there is one unmistakable piece of evidence. Whether we believe or disbelieve the stories of Asoka's conversions of Greeks to Buddhism,[2] he had at any rate converted Gandhāra and preached to the Greeks of the Paropamisadae;[3] and this means that Demetrius was well informed

[1] A once famous 'conquest' which was not a military conquest is that of Ptolemy III; but the reasons were very different. See Tarn in *CAH* VII, 717; W. Otto, *Beiträge zur Seleukidengeschichte* 1928 pp. 48 *sqq*.

[2] The Ceylonese chronicles make Asoka convert great numbers of Yonas and also send a Yona missionary Dhammarakkita to Aparānta (coast of Gujerat); *CHI* p. 499.

[3] Rock Edicts 5 and 13.

about the position by the time he reached Taxila, even if he had not been so when he crossed the Hindu Kush. And his first step, as has been noticed, was to cause his son Demetrius II, his governor west of the Indus, to issue in his name a bilingual coinage with a Greek legend on the obverse and a Prakrit legend written in Kharoshthi on the reverse. As every succeeding Greek king in India copied him, the bilingual coinage has become such a commonplace that the tremendous significance of its first introduction has been obscured. It was *not*, as is sometimes said, issued for the benefit of Indian subjects who knew no Greek. Many Hellenistic kings, both before and after Demetrius, ruled over subjects who knew no Greek; but no Seleucid ever put Iranian or Babylonian legends on his coinage, no Ptolemy ever put Egyptian; the Arsacids of Parthia did not enquire if their subjects could read their Greek legends, any more than any British Government has ever troubled itself about its Latin ones. What Demetrius was doing was expressing the very basis of the conquest he meditated, the policy which made some Indians see in him the traditional King of Justice, the policy which had led him to rebuild his destined capital as an Indian rather than a Greek city (p. 179), and had led him, contrary to what appears to have been the Seleucid practice with regard to Greek cities with dynastic names, to admit Indians as citizens of Demetrias in Sind (p. 257). His realm was to be a partnership of Greek and Indian; he was not to be a Greek king of Indian subjects, but an Indian king no less than a Greek one, head of both races. There will be more to be said about this when we come to Menander's kingdom; it may be the most important thing about the Greek empire in India. It has already been shown that Demetrius was consciously copying Alexander; but in this matter his inspiration was not the Alexander who had cut his blood-stained way to the Beas but the Alexander who had imagined something better, the man who had prayed at Opis for a joint rule of the Macedonian and the Persian, the man whom Eratosthenes had called 'reconciler of the world'[1] and who had dreamt of a union of peoples in a human brotherhood.[2] It is to the lasting credit of the Euthydemids that they made an attempt to put this into practice; an attempt imperfect enough, no doubt, and one whose motive force may have been

[1] διαλλακτὴς τῶν ὅλων, Eratosthenes *ap.* Plut. *Mor.* 329C.

[2] Tarn, *Alexander the Great and the unity of mankind*, *Proc. Brit. Acad.* XIX, 1933, p. 123; W. Kolbe, *Die Weltreichsidee Alexanders des Grossen* 1936 p. 18. *Contra*, M. H. Fisch, *A. J. Phil.* LVIII, i, 1937, pp. 59, 129.

largely ambition; but still an attempt. And that was more than was done by any other Hellenistic dynasty.

It has already been argued that Demetrius must have meant to make a final effort, in which Apollodotus and Menander should join hands, settle with Pushyamitra, and complete the Greek circuit round Northern India. The Greek leaders now had command of large revenues,[1] and were in a position, should they so desire, to raise native armies of overwhelming strength; they could not have failed. How long the Greeks with their scanty numbers could have continued to sit on the throne of the Mauryas; whether men who had done what Apollodotus and Menander had done would have been content to remain subordinates, as Agrippa was to be content to serve Augustus; these questions are unprofitable speculations, for the final effort was not destined to be made. Why it was not made will be told in the next chapter.

[1] Illustrated by the enormous coinages of Apollodotus and subsequently of Menander. The *Yuga-purāna may* refer to Demetrius' tax-collectors, App. 4.

CHAPTER V

ANTIOCHUS IV AND EUCRATIDES

THE invasion of India had been the work of three men, whose far-reaching plan had come within a very little of complete success; that success was prevented, at the last moment, by two other men, who were also working on a far-reaching plan of their own. Dimly as we discern the outlines of their several schemes and actions, the magnitude of them gives us the feeling that the age of giants had come again and that we are back among the men who fought for the heritage of Alexander. For though Greeks could change their sky they could not change their souls. The gods had given them every gift save one, the gift of combination; and they tore each other to pieces beneath the shadow of the Hindu Kush with the same enthusiasm which Greek city-states and Macedonian generals had always put into the business round the Aegean home-sea. This chapter is concerned with the story of how and why Demetrius failed to secure the Mauryan empire, the story of the Seleucid Antiochus IV, called Epiphanes, and his cousin Eucratides.

Antiochus IV has often had hard measure from his historians. Some have repeated the Hellenistic gossip which made of him half a fool—vain, silly, theatrical; it is worth precisely what any Hellenistic gossip is worth, and the less that serious history has to do with it the better. To others, he is little but the king who persecuted the Jews; that story can be read in many books, and I need only say here that, whatever he did to the Jews, they have had an ample revenge. The latest and ablest account of him,[1] while recognising his ability, has drawn a brilliant picture of his later life as that of a man broken by the 'day of Eleusis' when Rome ordered him out of Egypt, half hysterical and perhaps verging on madness, the result of whose career was to end the days of his empire as an international force. But one feature is common to every account: certain well-attested details of his reign are either omitted altogether or, if noticed, are explained away somehow—anyhow—because they will not fit the writer's picture, whatever it may be. Why, in the spring of 166, did he hold that great review of his army at

[1] Otto, *Zeit d. 6. Ptolemäers.*

Daphne, the Hellenistic equivalent of the Roman triumph, two years after a Roman envoy with a walking-stick had turned him out of Egypt? Why, three months later, did he celebrate a Festival of Deliverance at Babylon, and why was he hailed Saviour of Asia? Why did Diodorus (reproducing Polybius) say that in 165 he was stronger than any other king? Why did Jason of Cyrene, who loathed his memory, say that his power seemed irresistible? And why, above all, did Mithridates I of Parthia, the able and ambitious monarch who created the Parthian empire, make no move till the broken nervy Seleucid was safely dead? One could easily add to the list; and it has to be considered whether we may not here possess the débris of a lost chapter in the life of this king which has never been written. We shall, I hope, find reason to believe that this is true.

Fortunately a starting point was provided years ago, though in a place where historians concerned with the West would hardly look for it. In 1922 Sir George Macdonald threw out, as 'pure speculation', a suggestion that Antiochus IV might have been behind Eucratides.[1] He did not follow it up, and still regarded Eucratides as a rebel against Demetrius; but the association of the two names was the first ray of light in the darkness, for, once the idea was mooted, it was easy to see that there was ample evidence to support it and that several facts whose meaning was heretofore obscure would now automatically fall into place. If, however, I were to start by examining that evidence it would mean writing this chapter twice over, and it will be more comfortable for the reader to travel in the reverse direction from that in which I travelled myself: that is, the story will be told in the form into which analysis ultimately brought it, and the evidence given as we go along. Meanwhile I am not concerned to maintain that Antiochus either was or was not a statesman, or anything else about him; it has always been known that he had ideas. All I want to do is to get the outline of certain facts which ought to show the plan on which he was working and which may of themselves modify our conception of his character. It is worth trying; for, right or wrong, he was no small man. I must begin by briefly sketching his story as I see it.

Antiochus IV, third son of Antiochus III, had spent part of his early life in Rome and had acquired rather an excessive admiration for Rome's power and methods. His brother Seleucus IV died in 175, leaving two

[1] *CHI* p. 454: 'Possibly it was in his interest and with his encouragement that Eucratides first raised the standard of revolt. That of course is pure speculation.'

young sons; one of them, apparently also named Antiochus,[1] was made king, and Antiochus (IV) was installed in Antioch by Rome's friend Eumenes II of Pergamum as regent for the boy and (as is now fairly certain) married the boy's mother, his brother's widow Laodice.[2] Laodice, a daughter of Antiochus III, had successively married her eldest brother (another Antiochus who died in 193), and then her second brother Seleucus IV; when she married her third brother Antiochus (IV) she cannot have been very young. After a short interval during which coins were struck in the boy-king's name,[3] Antiochus the regent took the crown as Antiochus IV, just as Antigonus Doson in Macedonia was for a little while regent for Philip (V) and then himself took the crown;[4] and Antiochus IV married the boy-king's mother to secure the boy's succession, just as Antigonus Doson married 'Chryseis', the mother of Philip V, and as Attalus II of Pergamum married his brother's elderly widow Stratonice to secure the succession of his brother's son (her son by adoption) Attalus III.[5] In fact, Antiochus IV went further in the path of correctness than either of the other two kings; while Philip V and Attalus III did not become kings till after the deaths of their respective kinsmen, the boy-king Antiochus was and remained joint-king with Antiochus IV, Babylonian documents being dated by their joint names. But in the winter of 170–69 the boy-king was murdered by one Andronicus, and Antiochus IV, having executed the murderer, remained sole king.

Seleucus IV had seen that, if the empire was to recover from the disaster of Magnesia, a period of peace was absolutely necessary; there were no wars during his reign, and Antiochus IV followed his policy down to 169. By that time 20 years had passed since the great defeat; a new generation of boys had grown to manhood and the treasury was again full. Much could be done in twenty years, as Philip V had shown, especially if infanticide were stopped; it is possible that among the

[1] W. Otto, *Heliodoros* in PW; E. R. Bevan in *CAH* VIII pp. 497 *sqq.*, 713. If this be well founded, Epiphanes was Antiochus V, not IV; but it is too late to alter the numeration.

[2] An old conjecture, now seemingly borne out by inscriptions from Susa, *SEG* VII nos. 17, 24, on which see Fr. Cumont, *CR Ac. Inscr.* 1931 pp. 284 *sq.*, 1932 p. 285. For a coin-portrait of Laodice see Allotte de la Fuye, *MDP* XXV, 1934, p. 21 no. 9.

[3] This explains why the coins of the boy-king all seem to belong to one year, *CAH* VIII p. 714.

[4] *CAH* VII p. 751; S. Dow and C. F. Edson, Jr., *Harvard Stud. in Class. Philology* XLVIII, 1937, p. 127.

[5] Tarn, *Hell. Civ.*[2] p. 37.

Greeks of Asia at this time there was little or none to stop (p. 70). To the beginning of Antiochus' uneventful five years must belong his imitations of Rome, a passing phase which culminated in the building of a temple at Antioch to Juppiter Capitolinus;[1] more important was the use made of this period of quietude to strengthen the Greek element in the empire, a process perhaps begun by Seleucus IV.[2] It has often been supposed that Antiochus' alleged hellenisation of a number of Oriental towns was no real hellenisation, in the sense of a reorganisation by the introduction of Greek settlers, but was only a change of names meant to minister to his vanity;[3] but though, apart from Babylon, details are not to be obtained, there is one general consideration which is strong to prove a real hellenisation.[4] The best index to the number of Graeco-Macedonian settlers in the Seleucid empire is the phalanx, which was exclusively recruited from them.[5] The phalanx of Antiochus III at Raphia in 217 had numbered 20,000, that at Magnesia in 189, 16,000, the hypaspists in either case being Asiatics. But the phalanx of Antiochus IV at Daphne in 166 again numbered 20,000, together with 5000 Graeco-Macedonian hypaspists,[6] and this is far more significant than the mere figures indicate, not merely because the phalanx at Magnesia had been cut to pieces and one of the two great centres of Graeco-Macedonian settlement in Asia, Asia Minor, had been lost, but also because the troops at Daphne must have been drawn from the west of the mutilated empire alone; they cannot, as we shall see, have included settlers from the sphere of the general of the upper satrapies—Media, Babylonia, Susiana.

This seems conclusive for a considerable new influx of Greek settlers; and as the population of many districts of old Greece was now stationary or falling, the increase must primarily have come from Asia Minor and the cities of Thrace. By the treaty of Apamea in 188 Rome had forbidden the Seleucids to recruit mercenaries in Asia Minor west of the new boundary or to receive deserters;[7] but she had no direct control

[1] Livy XLI, 20, 11.

[2] Seleuceia on the Pyramos (Mopsuestia) might be his (see W. Ruge, *Mopsu(h)estia* in PW), though the name first appears under Antiochus IV; see p. 188 n. 1.

[3] Most recently by Ruge, *Tarsos* in PW. An exception is Ed. Meyer, *Ursprung und Anfänge des Christentums* II, 1921, p. 140, who took these names to signify a deep change in the nature of the community.

[4] Griffith pp. 152–3. [5] *Ib.* pp. 161 *sqq.*

[6] Tables in Griffith pp. 143–6.

[7] Polyb. XXI, 43, 15, μηδ' ὑποδέχεσθαι τοὺς φεύγοντας; so App. *Syr.* 39. Livy XXXVIII, 38, 10 substitutes 'voluntarios' for φεύγοντας, but one must follow Polybius.

and it does not appear how she could prevent voluntary leakage, apart from the fact that introducing settlers was not recruiting mercenaries. The Seleucids had always been popular with the Greek element, while Eumenes II of Pergamum, whom Rome had put in control of Asia Minor, was not; the leakage into Seleucid territory, especially among young men, may have been considerable, and would explain the intensive settlement in Seleucid Cilicia. As Antiochus could call up his new settlers, they must have been cleruchs; he therefore dealt with the Oriental towns which he hellenised as Susa had been dealt with (p. 23), by planting military colonies in them.[1] But as his new foundations appear as cities, he must have run together the two processes which at Susa may have taken some time: as soon as his cleruchs were planted in some place he made it a *polis*, the liability to military service remaining. This disposes of the belief that his was no real hellenisation. He was in a hurry, of course; he may conceivably have known years before his death that he could expect no long life (p. 215).

But if Antiochus made no move during his first five years that does not mean that he made no plans. Fortunately his coins[2] afford a means of dating certain indications, for to this period belong the coins on which the legend is only 'Of King Antiochus' and the type the common Seleucid type of Apollo seated on the omphalos.[3] The first indication is his refounding of Babylon as a Greek city.[4] It is not known what happened to Babylon under the earlier Seleucids,[5] but though Strabo's description of it as a desert[6] belongs to his own day, the same passage shows that it was anything but flourishing; nothing is known of any Greek colony there, but there must have been a considerable native Babylonian population grouped round E-sagila, the rebuilt temple of Bel. Antiochus made of Babylon a regular Greek city, with a theatre[7] and at least one gymnasium.[8] But one thing about it was unique in

[1] Griffith p. 152.

[2] See generally *BMC Sel.*; E. Babelon, *Rois de Syrie* 1890; E. T. Newell, *The Seleucid Mint of Antioch* 1918.

[3] Newell *op. cit.* p. 17 (down to 170–69).

[4] *OGIS* 253; he is *κτίστης τῆς πόλεως*.

[5] McDowell, *Stamped objects* pp. 202–6, has given what can be given.

[6] Strabo XVI, 738, *νῦν*.

[7] R. Koldewey, *Das wieder erstehende Babylon*,[4] 1925, pp. 293 *sqq.*, with the Greek inscription found there.

[8] B. Haussoullier, *Klio* IX, 1909, p. 352, no. 1, inscription giving a list of victors, both ephebes and *νέοι*. But whether the building which has been excavated be the gymnasium has recently been doubted: G. E. Kirk, *Iraq* II, 1935, p. 223.

Seleucid history: it kept its native name, as literary allusions show. Any large Oriental city refounded by a Seleucid invariably received a dynastic name, and Antiochus himself followed the rule elsewhere, as he showed at Ecbatana;[1] but at Babylon he did not. And this was no accident; for there are coins of his of this period, *i.e.* with the legend 'Of King Antiochus' only, which show his head with the radiate crown of Helios (*below*) and on the reverse the Fortune of Babylon—that is, the personification of Babylon itself—*enthroned* like Zeus, and like Zeus holding Victory on her hand.[2] No other city had ever been enthroned on any king's coinage;[3] there may be a reference to this in the Greek story of the nymph Babylon Thronia, Babylon 'of the throne' or 'enthroned' (p. 253). Taken together, these facts can only mean that Antiochus intended Babylon ultimately to be his capital; and he kept the old name because, under that name, it had been the destined capital of Alexander. Antiochus was then going to play Alexander; and if he were going to sit in Alexander's seat it is a fair inference that he thought of restoring Alexander's empire. What that means will be considered presently; two other indications must first be noticed. One is that on some of these early coins he wears the crown of rays which was the crown of Helios the Sun-god.[4] No Seleucid had worn it before him, though it had been adopted by Ptolemy III of Egypt. Doubtless its primary meaning was that the king's reign would bring prosperity;[5] but it is difficult to dissociate the crown of Helios from some con-

[1] In fact, omitting the two called Hierapolis (Castabala and Bambyce) and Seleuceia-Mopsuestia, which may not be his (p. 186), all Antiochus' cities, great or small—6 Antiochs and 5 Epiphaneias—were named from himself. List in Tscherikower p. 176.

[2] *BMC Sel.* p. 36 nos. 23–30, Pl. XII, 1–4; *Brit. Mus. Quarterly* VI, 1931, p. 14 no. 3; see Rostovtzeff, *Seleucid Babylonia* p. 39. That this coin-type refers to Babylon is not in doubt.

[3] There is a much obliterated Saca coin of a later time of which Cunningham gave the type as female figure with turreted headdress seated on throne, *NC* 1890 p. 154 no. 6, Pl. VIII, 6. But one cannot on the plate make out either turrets or throne, merely a female figure seated on *something*.

[4] On his radiate crown see Rostovtzeff *op. cit.* pp. 26, 28. A. Alföldi, *Röm. Mitt.* L, 1935, pp. 139–42, thinks that, as regards Hellenistic kings, if the crown of rays be combined with the diadem it was not the Sun's crown but a working of the Hvareno idea. One can think of cases where this might be true, *e.g.* the radiate king in a *biga* on a coin of the Iranian Maues; but I cannot believe it in the case of kings like Ptolemy III (whom he cites) or Antiochus IV, who did not adopt Iranian ideas.

[5] Tarn, *JRS* XXII, 1932, pp. 146 *sqq.* and literature there cited.

nection with world-rule, and that in turn, in men's minds, from some connection with Alexander. The other is furnished by a seal from Babylonia published by Professor Rostovtzeff, on which some Seleucid king wears the elephant-scalp.[1] He himself did not identify the portrait, which is clearly idealised; but he mentions a suggestion made to him[2] that it is the Seleucid Demetrius II, as he does wear the elephant-scalp on one of his coins. But this suggestion seems impossible, for the features of the king on the seal do not bear the least resemblance to the strongly individualised features of the Seleucid Demetrius II;[3] on the other hand, they do bear a resemblance to some portraits of Antiochus IV[4] and would do very well for an idealised portrait of him. It has been noticed already (p. 131) that the elephant-scalp was the symbol of Alexander's power, and (with all necessary reserves) that must be what Antiochus had in mind; his adoption later of Alexander's coin-type 'Zeus enthroned' bears this out.

I must explain in passing what I mean by restoring Alexander's empire. Antiochus III had meant to restore the empire of Seleucus I,[5] but no more; he had neither attempted to make conquests in India nor to take possession of defeated Egypt, but he had risked and finally suffered war with Rome for the sake of a few cities in Thrace, because they had belonged to Seleucus. The crash at Magnesia had greatly curtailed his realm; and the position which faced Antiochus IV was that most of Asia Minor was lost, the once vassal state of Parthia had recovered her independence and had succeeded in reaching out to the Caspian Gates, if not to the Nesaean fields,[6] and Demetrius of Bactria had annexed all the Seleucid provinces east of the Persian desert and

[1] *Op. cit.* Pl. VI nos. 1, 2; see pp. 45, 53.

[2] By E. T. Newell, *ib.* p. 45.

[3] His portraits: *BMC Sel.* Pls. XVII, XVIII, XXI. They have a peculiar look in the eye, largely due to a highly arched, almost semicircular, eyebrow, which no artist could miss.

[4] The head in *BMC Sel.* Pl. XIII, 7 (p. 42 no. 86, a coin from Nisibis), and still more the head on a coin figured by Newell *op. cit.* p. 24 (allowing for idealisation). The features are not unlike those of the radiate head of Antiochus IV on a seal, Rostovtzeff *op. cit.* Pl. V, 2.

[5] See Holleaux, *CAH* VIII p. 184.

[6] See generally Tarn, *CAH* IX p. 577. At one moment, which must be earlier than the conquest of Media by Mithridates I, Parthia was bounded on the west by an otherwise unknown Median people called by Pliny (VI, 113) Pratitae, *i.e.* the people of the *pratum* or 'meadow', the Nesaean fields; no doubt a translation of some Iranian name. The Nesaean fields were still Seleucid under Antiochus IV, Polyb. XXX, 25, 6 (his Nesaean horses, 166 B.C.).

like his father, cannot be said; for whatever his plan was, it was deranged by the regents in Egypt, Eulaeus and Lenaeus, who in the spring of 169 declared war upon him with the object not only of recovering Coele-Syria but of destroying himself.[1] Antiochus' war with Egypt was a thing he could not avoid. He mastered Egypt in 169 and was crowned at Memphis; but circumstances compelled him to return in 168, and that summer Rome warned him off. Now, granted that he was forced to fight, it would have been a possible course to defeat Egypt, exact an indemnity, and leave it at that; he decided instead to incorporate Egypt in his empire, for that is what his actions meant, however that meaning might be disguised as a protectorate over Ptolemy Philometor. As I have said, I am not seeking to prove that Antiochus was a statesman, and this was not the act of a statesman; it was merely the kind of 'forward' policy, common enough, in which one thing is allowed to lead to another with insufficient consideration of the ultimate consequences. He knew that Rome could hardly stand aside, and he was determined to have no breach with Rome; why did he do it? One possibility is that he miscalculated the strength of Perseus and thought that the Macedonian king might hold Rome off till, in weariness, she might accept his protectorate over Egypt as an accomplished fact; another is that, in vulgar parlance, he was just 'trying it on' to see how far he could go. In either case, as soon as he heard of Perseus' defeat at Pydna he must have known that Rome would act; it is possible that when on the 'day of Eleusis' Popillius Laenas handed him the Senate's ultimatum ordering him to quit Egypt he was the one man there who was not astonished. But Popillius, a 'new man' anxious to prove himself, presented the ultimatum in a way which outraged every decency of international intercourse; and Antiochus, the king whom even a bitter enemy called 'fiery, born of the lightning',[2] at the head of a strong and victorious army, swallowed the insult, accepted the ultimatum, and went. That was not the act of a man hysterical or half insane; to overlook the insult so as not to risk his plans meant great self-control and long views. For of what he had meant to do he had lost nothing; he had acted foolishly in Egypt, and by his self-control on the 'day of Eleusis' he had put it right.

Egypt occupied the years 169 and 168; 167 was taken up with the troubles in Judaea. By the end of the year, however, that country

[1] Otto, *Zeit d. 6. Ptolemäers* pp. 24–36, and especially p. 30 n. 4.

[2] *Oracula Sibyllina* III, 389.

seemed secure: the governing party were his friends, Jerusalem was safe, and the worship of Olympian Zeus was established;[1] if next year Judas Maccabaeus and his guerillas began to give trouble, guerillas were not unknown in great empires and were a thing one left to one's provincial governor. For world-history his dealings with the Jews were of great importance owing to their reaction upon Jewish religious conceptions; but for Antiochus, which is all that I am concerned with here, their only importance was lest they might furnish Rome with a pretext for interference. He himself possibly regarded his marriage with Atargatis,[2] the great goddess of northern Syria, as a much weightier matter. It was not a device to secure a temple treasure; it was a perfectly serious political measure. A god must have a divine consort;[3] but his marriage to Atargatis was a guarantee to the native religions of the empire,[4] always provided that people were willing to accept the overriding unification of the worship of Olympian Zeus, which was no difficulty to men of any religion but the Jewish. His insistence on his divinity and his marriage to Atargatis may or may not witness to a flaw in his mind;[5] but I want to stress the fact that the whole thing was political and that he was in earnest.

It has been necessary to go through Antiochus' career in some detail in order to understand his actions in the crucial year 166. In the spring of that year he held his great festival at Daphne,[6] a parallel to the

[1] Cf. E. R. Bevan in *CAH* VIII pp. 507–8 and especially 513.

[2] Granius Licinianus, p. 5, Flemisch: se simulabat Hierapoli Dianam ducere uxorem. The marriage is given as later than the 'day of Eleusis'.

[3] It must be remembered that if Antiochus were Zeus he would also be Atargatis' consort Hadad.

[4] If Otto's deduction be right (*op. cit.* p. 55; it could be supported by Diod. XXX, 14) that Antiochus during his rule in Egypt sought to win over the native Egyptians, this would be a very important confirmation of his attitude; he would have been anything but the blind helleniser which he is represented to be in Jewish history. Rostovtzeff's view (*Seleucid Babylonia* pp. 6, 7) that Antiochus stood behind the hellenised Babylonian Kephalon when he built the great Anu-Antum temple at Uruk would have been in point here, but it was due to a misreading of the date, see p. 26 n. 1; it appears now that the king was Antiochus III.

[5] It is possible that the reason why some people called Antiochus mad was, not because he called himself a god, but because he identified himself with a *particular* god, Zeus. On the distinction see M. P. Charlesworth, *Harvard Theolog. Rev.* XXVIII, 1935, pp. 15 *sqq.*

[6] Polyb. XXX, 25, 1 *sqq.*; Büttner-Wobst in his edition prints with it the Athenaeus and Diodorus passages. The date, 166, is certain: Niese III p. 215; W. Kolbe, *Hermes* LXII, 1927, p. 238; Otto *op. cit.* p. 83.

festival of Ptolemy II in Alexandria described by Callixenus.[1] The conventional explanation is that he was fond of ostentation and that he desired to surpass the show given by Aemilius Paullus,[2] the conqueror of Macedonia, at Amphipolis in 167, which had greatly impressed the Greek world. Likely enough both explanations are true, though the precisely similar ostentation of Ptolemy II had not prevented that monarch from being in fact as much a realist as any modern captain of industry; but even if true they are minor matters. The main feature of the show at Daphne was the review of Antiochus' strong army; it recalls the similar review of his army by Ptolemy II, but while at Alexandria the march past of the army came last, at Daphne it came first of everything.[3] Such a review was the Hellenistic form of triumph, and marked the end of a victorious and successful war;[4] that point needs no elaboration. Antiochus had not himself been waging any successful war. But neither had Ptolemy II: whichever war he was actually celebrating,[5] it had been won by his generals. We must look then for a war won by some general of Antiochus, precisely as at a later time an Antony or an Octavian might take the title *Imperator* for successes won by his legates. That this interpretation of the show at Daphne is correct is amply borne out by Antiochus' coins, for in the same year, 166, he began to issue his third series and added to his coin-legend the title *νικηφόρου*, 'The Victorious';[6] and the head of Zeus now begins to exhibit his own features.[7]

After Daphne Antiochus went to Babylon, and a most important dated inscription,[8] so far unexplained, gives the needed key. It records

[1] Athen. v, 197 c *sqq.*
[2] Athen. v, 194 c says this.
[3] On the significance of this see F. Caspari, *Hermes* LXVIII, 1933, p. 407.
[4] Otto, *Beiträge zur Seleukidengeschichte* 1928 pp. 6 *sqq.*; *Zeit d. 6. Ptolemäers* p. 83 and note 6; Tarn, *Hermes* LXV, 1930, p. 447 n. 2; *JHS* LIII, 1933, pp. 59–60; Caspari *op. cit.* p. 407; E. Kornemann, *Die Alexandergeschichte des Königs Ptolemaios I* 1935 p. 225 n. 22.
[5] It is immaterial for the principle here stated whether the war was the first Syrian (Otto, preceding note and *Philol.* XXXVI, 1931, p. 414 n. 27) or that of 280–79 (Tarn, preceding note).
[6] Newell's third series, *op. cit.* p. 28, which he connects with Daphne. He dates Daphne wrongly in 167, and therefore the series; the date 166 for the series follows automatically on the true date for Daphne.
[7] *BMC Sel.* p. 36 no. 22, Pl. XI, 9; see *CAH*, Vol. of Plates III p. 12 *i*. For other references see Rostovtzeff *op. cit.* p. 26 no. 2, and add J. de Foville, *Les monnaies gr. et rom. de la collection Prosper-Valton: Catalogue* p. 100 no. 493.
[8] *OGIS* 253.

a gift made to Antiochus by one Philippus, who may or may not be the Philippus who was Antiochus' minister 'for affairs';[1] he calls Antiochus 'Saviour of Asia', and the inscription shows that in August-September 166 Antiochus celebrated Charisteria at Babylon. The political connotations of the word Asia have already been discussed (p. 153); at this time it meant the Seleucid empire. The term Charisteria signified a sacrifice of thanksgiving for something which the celebrant considered a deliverance;[2] usually it seems to have consisted of a single celebration, but two annual Charisteria are known at Athens, a thanksgiving for Marathon[3] and another for the deliverance from the Thirty Tyrants through the return of Thrasybulus and the exiles from Phyle in 403 B.C.[4] The Charisteria of Antiochus, it may be supposed, were a single celebration, and he must have attached great importance to holding them at his destined capital, or he would never have gone to Babylon in the hot weather; they were obviously a thanksgiving for the 'saving' of Asia. But, once again, Antiochus personally had done nothing to 'save' Asia; the reference is to the victorious war waged by a general which had been celebrated at Daphne shortly before. To 'save' a place was well-known Hellenistic terminology for expelling your opponent and bringing the place over to your own side or under your own power. From what opponent then had Asia, that is, the Seleucid empire, been 'saved'? Not from Parthia; Parthia had not as yet been touched, and the little state hardly seemed a threat to anybody. Not from barbarians; there had been no barbarian invasion. Only one meaning is possible; the reference is to Demetrius, who had annexed the Seleucid East and built up an empire hardly if at all inferior in extent to the Seleucid. Antiochus then had 'saved' Asia—the Seleucid empire—from Demetrius; that was his successful war. But the actual overthrow of Demetrius was the work of Eucratides—that is matter of history; Eucratides therefore was Antiochus' general, the general who had waged the war celebrated at Daphne. The proof seems as complete as may be, though we shall meet another not less cogent. I must now turn to Eucratides, whose career will fill out the details.

[1] *II Macc.* xiii, 23.

[2] Ditt.[3] 398 l. 17; Arr. VI, 28, 3; Polyb. XXI, 1, 2; Diod. XX, 76, 6. Antiochus' Charisteria are called an ἀγών, which would include sacrifice.

[3] E. Pfuhl, *De Atheniensium pompis sacris* 1900 pp. 34–6; L. Deubner, *Attische Feste* 1932 p. 209.

[4] Plut. *Mor.* 349 F; Deubner *op. cit.* p. 39.

It had more than once been suggested that Eucratides had some connection with the Seleucids,[1] but the first definite proof (though it is far from being the whole proof) that he himself was a Seleucid was given in 1922 by Sir George Macdonald in the work already quoted,[2] who relied on two things: that Eucratides on his coinage used the Seleucid bead and reel moulding introduced by Antiochus III, and that on the coin which figures his parents, Heliocles and Laodice,[3] Laodice wears the diadem while Heliocles does not and was therefore a princess of a reigning house, which from her name should be the Seleucid. Let me add that when Eucratides represented himself on his coins as helmeted he put on his helmet the badge of the founder of the dynasty, the bull's horn and ear which had appeared on the helmet of the first Seleucus.[4] This must suffice for the moment; the most decisive proof must be left to its right place (p. 202). I may notice here that no one now doubts that the Heliocles and Laodice coin represents his parents, and as he was a Seleucid he can only have been such through his mother,[5] who was therefore certainly a Seleucid princess; and her diadem shows that she was the daughter of a king, not of some collateral. This gives, in passing, two interesting facts about Seleucid princesses: one is that the conjecture that the unmarried princesses, like those of the Ptolemies, were officially called βασίλισσα, 'queen', is certainly correct, as Laodice wears her diadem in her own right;[6] the other is that it was evidently Seleucid practice to marry superfluous daughters, for whom no royal bridegroom was at hand, to great commoners, as Seleucus II (we have already seen) gave a sister to Diodotus, *strategos* of Bactria (p. 73).

Who exactly then was Eucratides? On his Bactrian coins[7] of *c.* 165 B.C., whose portraiture can be trusted, he appears as a man in the

[1] I suggested this in *JHS* 1902 p. 271, but did not then know enough to work it out. R. B. Whitehead in 1922 (*NNM* p. 17) said he 'appears to be some connection of the royal house of Seleucus', but gave no reasons.

[2] *CHI* p. 454.

[3] *BMC* p. 19 nos. 1, 2, Pl. VI, 9, 10; *CHI* Pl. IV, 3.

[4] *BMC Sel.* p. 4 nos. 36–40. Cunningham noticed this, *NC* 1869 p. 237, but curiously enough thought it had 'no special significance'. Had he followed it up, Eucratides might have been put in his right place long ago. (See Plate no. 11.)

[5] This excludes the possibility of Laodice belonging to the royal house of Pontus, where the name was also at home.

[6] In popular speech any king's daughter was βασίλισσα: Arr. IV, 15, 3, a Scythian. Cf. the ἄνασσαι in Cyprus: Suidas, *s.v.* ἄνακτες καὶ ἄνασσαι.

[7] Eucratides' coins: Cunningham, *NC* 1869 pp. 217 *sqq.*; *BMC* pp. 13, 165; Whitehead *NNM* p. 17; *CHI* pp. 453, 554.

prime of life, say about 40 to 45; he was therefore born somewhere round about 210–205. As his mother Laodice was married to a commoner, she can hardly have been married till well over twenty, till it was certain that she was not needed for a marriage of high policy; she was therefore born round about 235–225—not later—with a preference for the earlier part of the period. This makes her a daughter of Seleucus II; Seleucus III (226–223 B.C.) is just possible, but as he only reigned three years and is not known either to have married or to have left children, Seleucus II is practically certain, and this is confirmed by the fact that Eucratides on his coinage adopted, though he modified, one of the types of Seleucus II, the Dioscuri.[1] Laodice was therefore a sister of Antiochus III, and Eucratides was first cousin of Antiochus IV. Heliocles must have been general of some satrapy; Antiochus III could hardly have given his sister to a lesser man, and there is the precedent of Diodotus. It would be most natural to suppose that he was, not merely the general of a satrapy, but governor of the upper (eastern) satrapies; but though he might have been so after 193, down to 193 that office must have been filled, in accordance with Seleucid custom, by Antiochus, eldest son of Antiochus III and joint-king with him till his death that year. That Eucratides was governor of the upper satrapies under Antiochus IV goes without saying in view of his selection to reduce the East to obedience; for that was that official's business, if the king was not going to command in person.

Eucratides' chronology, India apart, seems certain within very narrow limits. It has been usual, following von Gutschmid, to place his 'revolt' about 175, on the ground that that is the date of the accession of Mithridates I of Parthia and that Justin says that the two men came to the throne 'about the same time'.[2] This is quite unfounded. No one knows the year of Mithridates' accession, and a whole range of dates, from 175 to 160, have been proposed by various scholars; the only thing certain is that his activity did not begin till after the death of Antiochus IV in 163. And Justin's vague phrase might cover an interval of some years, and only means that the two men were roughly contemporaries, as they were. Antiochus' review at Daphne in spring 166

[1] In the type of Seleucus II (*BMC Sel.* p. 18 no. 28) the horses are prancing, in that of Eucratides galloping. On the Dioscuri type see H. Mattingly and E. S. G. Robinson, *The date of the Roman denarius*, *Proc. Brit. Acad.* 1932, and especially Appendix 3 to that work.

[2] Justin XLI, 6, 1, eodem ferme tempore.

and his Charisteria at Babylon that summer show that 'Asia'—the Seleucid empire—had been 'saved' by the end of 167, which means that Eucratides had conquered everything up to the Hindu Kush; and as the conquest could not be called complete while Demetrius lived, the latter part of the campaigning season of 167 is the date of the final defeat and death of Demetrius. It agrees with this that Plato's dated coin struck in 165 B.C. is copied from a coin of Eucratides' second series, which was issued in 166 after his final victory (p. 203), contemporaneously with the issue in that year of Antiochus' third series. As to the start. *A priori*, Antiochus might have dispatched him any time after his own accession in 175; but it will appear that any idea of a long protracted war in the eastern provinces of Iran is out of the question, while the first five years of Antiochus' reign were years of quiescence. He can hardly have dispatched Eucratides before 169, and, as Egypt interfered, probably not till after he had mastered or knew that he could master Egypt and would not need his brilliant general in the west; Eucratides most probably left Babylonia late in 169 and wintered in Seistan; it might be just possible that he did not leave Babylonia till early in 168, but there is a reason (p. 201 n. 2) which makes this unlikely. As it was certainly all over by the end of 167, this would mean that a couple of campaigning seasons sufficed to overthrow the powerful empire of the Euthydemids in Iran. If one considers the time taken by Alexander and Antiochus III to conquer the same territory as did Eucratides, against opposition which on paper should have been less formidable, and if one also considers that Eucratides' army cannot have been large, it is clear that (if I am right) some convincing explanation of the speed of his conquest is needed. Not only is there such an explanation, but it is one which, I think, forbids us to imagine several years of protracted warfare.

For Eucratides cannot possibly have taken a very large force with him, seeing that the main Seleucid army, 55,500 strong,[1] was with Antiochus in Egypt and was reviewed by him at Daphne. Presumably he had his own troops as governor of the upper satrapies, with some additional mercenaries; though no guess can be made at its strength, it can hardly have seemed an army adequate to overthrow Demetrius. But Eucratides was not altogether relying upon his own sword. His story has been obscured by modern writers persistently calling him a rebel against Demetrius, a statement devoid alike of authority and possibility. He was not a rebel; but he raised a rebellion.

[1] Polyb. xxx, 25: 46,000 foot, 9500 horse.

It cannot be guessed what Antiochus' plan would have been had Egypt not intervened, but the plan subsequently followed can be deduced from events: Eucratides was to clean up the East and Antiochus the West, and at the end they were to take Parthia between two fires; the result could not have been in doubt. Though neither of them lived to carry it out, the plan for a combined attack on Parthia seems to follow from the fact that an attempt was made to put it into operation a generation later, when Demetrius II of Syria attacked Parthia from the west and his Bactrian allies (presumably Eucratides' son Heliocles) co-operated from the east;[1] but by that time Parthia had become strong enough to defeat the coalition.

Eucratides had the choice of two routes eastward from Babylonia; the northern road by Ecbatana and Hekatompylos to Bactria which Antiochus III had taken, or the southern road through Susiana to Seistan. In 169 the Parthians were across the northern road, with their capital at Hekatompylos and a firm hold on the strong pass of Sirdarra, the 'Caspian Gates'; he could no doubt have fought his way through, but with much loss of time and perhaps of men, and it is fairly certain that he took the southern route to Seistan and from that province advanced northward by the great road from Seistan by Herat to Merv and Bactria, the route subsequently taken by the colleague of Mithridates II of Parthia in liquidating the Saca invasion.[2] His conquests included Seistan, Arachosia, Aria, Bactria, and Sogdiana; Justin gives the list, though not in chronological or geographical order.[3] It is unfortunate that the chapter in Justin which deals with Eucratides is Justin at his very worst, for he is trying to summarise an unfamiliar piece of history which he did not understand and which he considered of no importance;[4]

[1] Justin XXXVI, 1, 4, in 141 B.C.

[2] Tarn, *SP Stud.* pp. 16–18; *CAH* IX p. 585. See p. 499.

[3] Justin XLI, 6, 3: 'Bactriani...Sogdianorum et Arachotorum et Drangarum et Areorum Indorumque bellis fatigati ad postremum ab invalidioribus Parthis... oppressi sunt.' 'Sogdianorum' shows that the reference cannot be to the campaigns of Demetrius in Iran; moreover his wars did not end in his being conquered by the Parthians. The reference is therefore to the campaigns of Eucratides, because there is nothing else that it can refer to, and 'Bactriani' therefore means Eucratides' following and in a sense Eucratides himself. Indeed the next sentence proves it: 'Multa *tamen* Eucratides bella magna virtute gessit'; that is equivalent to saying: 'His end was to be conquered by the Parthians; however, he fought well first.' This will be important later.

[4] Shown by his omitting all the other chapters in which Trogus dealt with the Farther East. He only gave the Eucratides chapter because it was Seleucid history.

but there was ultimately a good and understanding source behind him (p. 50), and one has to try to restore the real sense. If the above view of Eucratides' operations be correct, then the two sub-kings who had to bear the first shock of the invasion were Agathocles in Seistan and Arachosia (or rather his provincial governors, for his own seat was Alexandria-Kapisa, p. 158) and Antimachus in Herat and Merv; and as these are the two sub-kings whose propaganda is known, my view probably *is* correct.

It is possible, but not certain, that Demetrius himself was in the Middle Country in India when Eucratides arrived (App. 5), and that during the campaigning season of 168 Eucratides only had to deal with sub-kings. Wherever Demetrius was, he ordered Menander to abandon Pātaliputra and all the Middle Country south of Mathurā (p. 227) and he himself hurried to Bactria to meet Eucratides, for it is clear from Justin and from the Yuga-purāna that their duel was fought out west of the Hindu Kush and that Eucratides did not invade India till later;[1] whether Demetrius was able to take the field in 168 or not, 167 was the critical year. Justin may show that the struggle was not without its vicissitudes, but his one story[2]—that Demetrius with 60,000 men besieged Eucratides with 300 and the latter after frequent sorties broke out—has little chance of being true as it stands. The figure 300 is probably correct, as it is the normal figure for the *agema* (bodyguard) of one in Eucratides' position;[3] and the story presumably means that at one point Demetrius cut off Eucratides from his army, but the latter got away. The figure 60,000 is naturally untrustworthy; but if Demetrius was really able to employ a large force it *might* mean that he brought and used Indian troops. The end of course was the death of Demetrius;[4] otherwise it would not have been the end. Presumably Antimachus was also killed, though all that there really is to go upon here is that by the time Eucratides died there was no one left who could seriously

[1] Justin XLI, 6, 4 gives the order of the two events explicitly enough. The *Yuga-purāna* locates the civil war in 'their own country', *i.e.* not India but Bactria (App. 4).

[2] Justin XLI, 6, 4.

[3] In the campaign of Antigonus (I) against Eumenes of Cardia the bodyguards of both Antigonus and Eumenes, and the joint bodyguard shared by Antigenes and Peucestas, all numbered 300 men; Diod. XIX, 28, 3; 29, 5 (from Hieronymus of Cardia). A king's *agema* might be larger.

[4] Implied in Justin's word *liberatus*; but he gives the sequence of events quite clearly.

challenge Menander's rule in India, and Menander was not a Euthydemid.

I come to the explanation of how it was done, which is furnished by the 'memorial' coin-series of Agathocles and Antimachus. These coin-series are the pedigrees of these two kings, *i.e.* of the Euthydemid house (see App. 3); they show that the Euthydemid kings were Seleucids and (by means of the fictitious pedigree) claimed to descend from Alexander. They are propaganda against Eucratides,[1] or rather they are the dead bones of what was once propaganda, and they were therefore issued in 168 or possibly 167;[2] the matter was naturally made plain by manifestos and speeches, but we can still see the central fact, that when the blow fell it seemed to the Euthydemid princes a vital matter to prove to their people that they were Seleucids.[3] The other kings north of the Hindu Kush did the same thing. A strange coin exists which seems to be all that now remains of a similar pedigree series issued by Demetrius himself;[4] his last coins also have the Seleucid bead and reel edging,[5] and one of the two Bactrian tetradrachms in the British Museum struck by his son Demetrius II, his joint-king in Bactria itself, also has the bead and reel edging,[6] the proof that he was joint-king when Eucratides came. Eucratides' answer was simple; it was the coin figuring his parents, already noticed, which showed that his mother was the Seleucid princess Laodice; naturally he would issue proclamations also.

Now why were the Euthydemid princes so desperately anxious to

[1] So *CHI* p. 453, 'manifestos against Eucratides'. Incidentally they show that Demetrius did *not* marry a daughter of Antiochus III, or Agathocles could just have pointed to his mother, as Eucratides did.

[2] They would take a little time to prepare; probably therefore Eucratides did winter in Seistan in 169–8, and they were engraved during that winter.

[3] Nothing turns on the Alexander-descent, which had no propaganda value; the Euthydemids, in claiming it themselves, equally claimed it for their Seleucid opponents. The cult-names borne by Diodotus and Euthydemus in the series may point to an organised state-cult, and if so Alexander may have been brought in because in the state-cult his name headed the list, as in Egypt.

[4] *CHI* p. 451 (Pl. III, 9), tetradrachm with obv. conventional head and no legend, rev. Zeus thundering and legend *Διοδότου σωτῆρος*; monogram ⏀. The reasons given in *CHI* for believing it to be a 'memorial' (*i.e.* pedigree) coin, struck by Demetrius, appear to me to be conclusive. On the date of the monogram (see App. 1) the only alternative to Demetrius would be Demetrius II, and he I think would have necessarily (like Antimachus and Agathocles) put on the coin the word *βασιλεύοντος* and his name.

[5] *CHI* p. 447.

[6] *Ib.* p. 448.

prove to the world that they were no less Seleucids than Eucratides? Every historian has noticed one thing about the Seleucid empire, the abiding loyalty of the Graeco-Macedonian settlers, when they got the chance, to the person of the reigning Seleucid. When the general Molon revolted against Antiochus III part of his army went over the moment it saw Antiochus himself;[1] when Achaeus marched against Antiochus III, the settlers in his army refused to go on as soon as they guessed against whom they were marching,[2] though Achaeus was collaterally a Seleucid; there are other instances later.[3] That is the explanation of the speed of Eucratides' conquest: the Greek settlers in the East revolted and joined him wherever he appeared—in one case, that of the two mint-masters in Bactra, this can apparently be traced (App. 1)—and the propaganda of the Euthydemids was a desperate attempt to hold them by showing that they themselves were just as good Seleucids as Eucratides. Eucratides was not a rebel, but he raised and led a rebellion. The most important thing, however, is not that he raised a rebellion, but that the comparatively small force he brought with him proves that he knew beforehand that he *could* raise and lead such a rebellion—that he would find troops to his hand when he arrived. But he was only a Seleucid collaterally, just as his opponents were and just as Achaeus had been; whence came his knowledge? It could only have come in one way: he held Antiochus' commission, and could proclaim 'Who fights against me fights against the Lord's Anointed.' Once the pedigree coin-series of Agathocles and Antimachus be understood they seem quite conclusive for two things: that Eucratides was a Seleucid and that he came as the representative of Antiochus.

It is also probable that another factor was at work among the Greek settlers, reinforcing that of loyalty to Antiochus; Eucratides probably knew about it beforehand. More than once Alexander had had trouble with those of his Macedonians who disliked what they considered his pro-Persian policy. The policy of the Euthydemids towards the native peoples of Bactria and India has already been explained so far as evidence permits, and there must inevitably have been among the Greeks of Bactria some, perhaps many, who disliked what they considered the

[1] Polyb. v, 54, 1.

[2] *Ib.* v, 57, 6, where *τὸν κατὰ φύσιν βασιλέα* means the legitimate king of the blood royal according to the rules of heredity.

[3] See Griffith p. 168.

pro-native policy of the dynasty and would have preferred to keep the 'barbarian' in his place; they would regard the hellenising Antiochus as a better representative of the Greek world in Asia. Demetrius' fall was doubtless assisted by his ideas being too far in advance of those of a number of his Greek subjects.

Eucratides' position with regard to Antiochus can be deduced from his coins. It seems fairly certain now that what used to be called his first series, with the type of the Seleucid Apollo, belongs to a later Eucratides (pp. 271 *sq.*); his first series was really the coins with the Dioscuri type and the simple legend 'Of King Eucratides'.[1] His second series, on which he is 'Great King', can be dated, for one of the pieces was copied by Plato's dated coin of 165, and Eucratides' second series therefore began to be issued in 166 after his victory, contemporaneously with the third series of Antiochus on which he is 'The Victorious'. The first series of Eucratides, then, is earlier than 166; that is, he began coining as soon as he reached the East. Antiochus then had conferred upon him *before he started* the royal title in the provinces he should conquer. But he was not joint-king. The Seleucid realm had been familiar with joint-kings who governed the eastern provinces from Seleuceia; but they had always been sons or brothers of the reigning Seleucid, and though in fact they governed the East, in theory they were joint-rulers of the whole empire, and Babylon always dated by both names, those of the reigning Seleucid and of the joint-king. But Babylon did not date by Eucratides; after the death of the boy who was joint-king with Antiochus IV till 170–69 she dated by Antiochus IV alone.[2] Eucratides then was Antiochus' sub-king; Antiochus was copying the Euthydemids, just as Parthia did later when Mithridates II appointed the Suren to take charge in the East (p. 499), with all the consequences which followed. Antiochus' action meant that, in plain English, there were in future going to be *two* Seleucid realms, with himself ruler of one and suzerain of the other; doubtless he intended to supervise both from his seat in Babylon. Again Parthia copied. The Parthians were the supreme imitators of the ancient world; except in warfare, where they could be original enough, they never invented anything themselves but always copied from the Greeks, whether of the West or the East; Parthian analogies, therefore, are legitimate illustrations, and in the first century B.C. there were

[1] *BMC* p. 13 nos. 6, 7, Pl. V, 6. Some issues have the *pilei* of the Dioscuri only.

[2] Babylonian tablet of 168 B.C. in the possession of Mr E. T. Newell; see his *Seleucid Mint of Antioch* p. 21.

similarly two Parthian realms, one in the west governed by the Arsacids which Romans knew and called Parthia, and one in the east governed by the Surens,[1] at first nominally vassals of the Arsacid, with its centre originally in Seistan and subsequently on the Indus. It is obvious that Antiochus' innovation was a dangerous one, as the conferring of special powers on a general usually was; but Antiochus had no grown son or brother to employ, Eucratides was his first cousin, and to give him the royal title meant at least that he would not revolt in order to seize it, like Achaeus. The amount of risk in fact depended on Eucratides' character, about which Antiochus knew more than we do.

The bearing on the matter of Eucratides' Dioscuri type must be noticed. The Dioscuri were a known Seleucid type; their heads had been used on a bronze issue of Seleucus I,[2] but the first adoption of the complete figures was due to Antiochus II[3] and had been continued by his son Seleucus II;[4] doubtless it was connected with the successes of these two kings against the Ptolemies and, in the case of Antiochus II, with his acquisition of Samothrace, home of the Cabeiri. Eucratides' type of the Dioscuri galloping was new, and it appears also on a sealing from Babylonia,[5] which had been his sphere before he went eastward; but it was a development of the type of his grandfather Seleucus II in which the horses are prancing, and naturally has no connection with the type on the Roman denarius. Now the Dioscuri were, in a very special sense, *the* saviours (*Soteres*), and Eucratides' use of the type meant that he had come to the East as *Soter*, a 'saviour', just as Apollodotus and Menander had appeared in India as 'saviours' (p. 175). It must be repeated that neither the name nor the idea of *Soter* had yet become a commonplace, and in Eucratides' hands it was, and was meant to be, an invitation to the Greeks of the East to be 'saved', that is, to join him against their rulers; he had come to deliver the one-time

[1] Herzfeld, *Sakastan* pp. 70 *sqq.*; 101 *sqq.* See also on the Indo-Parthian kingdom *CHI* pp. 567 *sqq.*, and chap. VIII *post*. This kingdom, as generally supposed, was O-ik-san-li of the *Ch'ien-han-shu*. Herzfeld has argued that O-ik-san-li was a mythic realm in the west just beyond the known world, but it was real enough, even to the ostrich eggs; see generally pp. 14, 347.

[2] *BMC Sel.* p. 5 nos. 51–60.

[3] Mattingly and Robinson *op. cit.* (p. 197) p. 56 no. 15. This work includes a special study of the Dioscuri type.

[4] Mattingly and Robinson *op. cit.* p. 56 no. 16; the type differs slightly from that of Antiochus II.

[5] In the collection of Colonel Allotte de la Fuye; see Rostovtzeff, *Seleucid Babylonia* p. 21.

Seleucid East from the Euthydemids, and it was in consequence of his success as a 'saviour' that Philippus called Antiochus 'Saviour of Asia', a title possibly coined by Antiochus himself.

All this is straightforward; and hardly less straightforward would be the suggestion that Eucratides adopted the Dioscuri not merely because they were saviours, but because they were *twin* saviours—Antiochus and himself. For the Dioscuri, besides being saviours, were patrons of φιλία, of a close friendship between two men.[1] They appear on some tetradrachms of Eumenes II of Pergamum, where they symbolise the close relationship between himself and his brother Attalus (Attalus II),[2] two princes who came to typify brotherly love no less than the Dioscuri themselves;[3] but the idea could certainly be extended to other relatives (Antiochus and Eucratides were first cousins), for it appears later as extended to two men who were no relations at all: on a coin of Alexandria the Emperor Hadrian and Antinous appear in the guise of the Dioscuri.[4]

The Dioscuri then on Eucratides' coins in all probability typify Antiochus and himself, naturally with reference to the two Seleucid realms that were to be; and this in turn may explain a hitherto unexplained coin-type. Antiochus' successor, the Seleucid Demetrius I, struck coins on which the *pilei* (caps) of the Dioscuri were *enthroned*, each cap on a separate throne.[5] It may be uncertain whether cult of a throne in itself was or was not known to Greeks,[6] but the question cannot bear on this coin-type, for if it has anything to do with *cult* the cult could only be that of the Dioscuri, seeing that their symbols appear on the thrones.[7] But this in turn seems impossible, for no

[1] Evidence in F. Chapouthier *Les Dioscures au service d'une déesse* 1935 p. 240. I owe this reference to Prof. Nock.

[2] Chapouthier *op. cit.* pp. 242 *sq.* So the twins of Drusus' daughter Livilla were the New Dioscuri (inscription of Ephesus cited by S. Eitrem, *Symb. Osl.* x, 1932, p. 54).

[3] Plut. *Mor.* 489E, F; cf. 480C.

[4] Chapouthier *op. cit.* p. 64 no. 56; cf. p. 326.

[5] *BMC Sel.* p. 49 nos. 54, 55, Pl. XIV, 10.

[6] The idea of a cult of the empty throne was started by W. Reichel in *Vorhellenischen Götterkulten* for Mycenean times and strongly contested by H. von Fritze, *Rh. Mus.* LV, 1900, p. 588 (see however Usener's note pp. 602–3). Then H. Herter, *Rh. Mus.* LXXIV, 1925, p. 164 sought to extend the idea to Hellenistic times, citing the Alexander-tent and the *pompe* of Ptolemy II. I doubt if he proved his point; but it is not really material to me here. See further L. R. Farnell, *JHS* XLIX, 1929, p. 79; A. Alföldi, *Röm. Mitt.* L, 1935, p. 134.

[7] For kings' thrones with divine insignia upon them see Alföldi *op. cit.* pp. 134–6.

connection of the Dioscuri with thrones seems known elsewhere, either in numismatics or in art;[1] such a type as the Dioscuri enthroned does not exist. I suggest therefore that the two thrones typify the two Seleucid realms. It is probable that for some time after the death of Antiochus IV the Seleucid kings continued, though as a dead fiction, to claim suzerainty over the realm ruled by the descendants of Eucratides in the East; no other reason is apparent for the Seleucid Demetrius II wearing on one of his coin-issues the elephant-scalp of Alexander.[2] This is theory, not proof; but it will explain an unexplained coin-type.

Antiochus celebrated the recovery of his eastern provinces by the review of his army at Daphne, his Charisteria at Babylon, the title 'Saviour of Asia' (whether he assumed it or merely permitted others to give it him), and a new series of coins, on which Zeus sometimes has his own features and the word *νικηφόρου* appears in the legend, making his full title 'King Antiochus the god manifest, the Victorious'.[3] If he be really the king of the seal from Babylonia (p. 189), his adoption of the elephant-scalp of Alexander may belong to this period; certainly he put on the coins he issued at Tripolis in 166–5 the Saviour gods, the Dioscuri,[4] but as he could not very well adopt the type of his sub-king he adopted that of the Roman denarius: his Dioscuri are not merely galloping, like those of Eucratides, but charging with couched spears. Doubtless the adoption of the Roman type and of the elephant-scalp were intimations that Alexander's empire was reviving and that there might be a second Great Power in the world as a counterpoise to Rome. But such intimations were merely of local importance; if he desired the world to take notice he must do something to capture its imagination; that was why his show at Daphne was deliberately meant

[1] No instance except this coin is given in the articles on the Dioscuri in PW and Roscher, and no instance at all in the great collection in Chapouthier *op. cit.*, though association with beds, tables, and altars is known. Mr Mattingly, who with Mr Robinson specially studied the Dioscuri for their work above mentioned, tells me that they found no other case except this coin.

[2] *BMC Sel.* p. 61 no. 27; McDowell, *Coins from Seleucia* p. 26 no. 61; see Rostovtzeff *op. cit.* Pl. VI, 4. The elephant-scalp worn by the late Seleucid Alexander II (*BMC Sel.* p. 83 no. 28) is doubtless mere imitation, connected probably with his name.

[3] The altar at Pergamum may show that at this time the idea of Zeus as a conqueror had rather come into prominence.

[4] Mattingly and Robinson *op. cit.* p. 57 no. 18 (*a*).

to outrival that of Aemilius Paullus in its magnificence.[1] He did strike the world's imagination; Polybius said that he was stronger than any other king,[2] and Jason of Cyrene wrote that his power seemed irresistible.[3] Even Rome began to regret that she had never enforced the disarmament clauses of the treaty of Apamea (188 B.C.). She could easily have done so at any time down to 175, and as she did not it must be supposed that she then thought it did not matter; now she wished to and could not do it without a serious war; that she wished to and feared to is conclusively shown by the fact that she enforced these clauses the moment Antiochus was dead. He was stronger than Antiochus III; and after all there were men at Rome who knew very well, though they did not blazon it abroad, that had there been a competent general on the other side Magnesia would no more have been a Roman victory than was Heraclea or Asculum. We seem to have travelled some distance from the king with disordered nerves who was broken by the 'day of Eleusis'. It is one of the ironies of history that, though there *was* to be a counterpoise to Rome, it was not after all to be provided by the empire of Antiochus but by the little state whose destruction was to be the final item in his programme.

Eucratides on his side celebrated his success, possibly by founding in Bactria a city bearing his own name, Eucratideia,[4] and certainly by striking the largest Greek gold coin known, the 20-stater piece now in Paris,[5] and by beginning to issue his second series of tetradrachms, on which he is no longer merely 'King' but 'Great King',[6] a title he continued to use till his death. Had the danger imminent in Antiochus' experiment already taken shape, and was Eucratides already declaring himself an independent monarch? The title 'Great King' does not prove this. It was copied from Antiochus III,[7] in whose case the name, though it became his cult-name,[8] referred originally to his reconquest

[1] Diod. XXXI, 16 (from Polybius) correctly makes it a great advertisement of his kingdom.

[2] Diod. XXXI, 17a (from Polybius).

[3] *II Macc.* i, 13, ἀνυπόστατος δοκοῦσα εἶναι δύναμις.

[4] Ptol. VI, 11, 7.

[5] *BMC* p. 165 no. 1; certainly, from the style, struck in Bactria, not in India. Cf. the medal struck by Alexander after his victory over Porus.

[6] *βασιλέως μεγάλου Εὐκρατίδου.*

[7] It was also copied from Antiochus III on some Parthian 'beardless' coins, which Wroth (*BMC Parthia* p. xxix) assigned to Phriapatius and Phraates I, *i.e.* earlier than Eucratides. But Eucratides was not copying Parthia.

[8] *OGIS* 245, 246.

of the Seleucid East;[1] probably therefore the same is true of Eucratides,[2] and to that extent it was merely the expression of a fact: he *had* conquered the Seleucid East. Neither does his great gold coin prove this; for though to coin gold was a declaration of independence, this piece was only a commemorative one. One other gold coin of his is indeed known, a stater with a romantic history;[3] but it may not have been struck till Antiochus was dead. But the question of Eucratideia needs careful consideration.

It has sometimes been supposed that Eucratides founded a new capital; and to give a new capital your own name was, *prima facie*, the clearest form of declaration known that you were an independent king, just as the foundation of Demetrias in Arachosia by Demetrius as capital of his new conquest Arachosia-Seistan had been his definite repudiation of any Seleucid suzerainty. This principle had been illustrated very clearly by the actions of the dynasts in the wars after Alexander's death; Cassander had founded his name-city Cassandreia while Alexander IV yet lived as a proclamation that he repudiated the authority of the boy-king, who was his prisoner, while Seleucus and Lysimachus, though actually no less independent than Cassander, observed the decencies to the extent of not founding Seleuceia and Lysimacheia till the boy had been murdered. But in view of one thing which was to happen in India (p. 212) it is almost impossible to believe that Eucratides meant at this time to repudiate Antiochus' suzerainty; and there is nothing to show that Eucratideia, a place never mentioned except by Ptolemy, was meant to be a new capital, for Eucratides, as is shown by his moneyers (App. 1), coined in Bactra, and Bactra was certainly the capital of his son Heliocles. The most natural supposition would be that Eucratideia was only Demetrias on the Oxus (p. 118)

[1] E. R. Bevan, *JHS* XXII, 1902, p. 241; M. Holleaux, *BCH* XXXII, 1908, p. 266 (conclusive).

[2] C. Seltman, *Greek Coins* 1933 p. 235, says that *βασιλέως μεγάλου* on Eucratides' coins is only a translation of *Maharajasa*, which cannot be right; when the two legends corresponded, the Kharoshthi translated the Greek, not *vice versa*, and *Maharajasa* had already been used before Eucratides to translate *βασιλέως* alone on Demetrius' bilingual coins, both tetradrachm and bronze pieces; this became its regular use throughout the Greek period. On Saca and Kushan coins, however, a vassal or viceroy might call himself 'Great King'; so Spalirises (p. 346) and the Nameless king (p. 354).

[3] Formerly in the Montagu collection (*NC* 1892 p. 37) and now in that of Mr E. T. Newell. It is said to have originally been worn by an Afghan officer attached to a ring as a signet.

with the name changed and some fresh settlers, for Eucratides would hardly have cared to leave a city to bear the name of one who, in his eyes, was a rebel who had come to his proper end (though even so he might have renamed the town Antioch); but this supposition seems forbidden by the fact that Ptolemy puts Eucratideia among towns not on the Oxus, though a mistake on his part is possible. Another possibility would be that Eucratideia was merely a later foundation made by Heliocles. In fact, the mere name Eucratideia, which is all that we have, gives no safe ground for dogmatising, while it must be remembered that we know nothing of the actual arrangements between Antiochus and Eucratides, except that Antiochus *had* given him the royal title; he already possessed what the name Eucratideia *might* imply that he claimed. We are, I think, entitled to believe that, had Antiochus and Eucratides lived to crush Parthia, Antiochus would then have been able to maintain the unity of the two Seleucid realms, at any rate during his own lifetime, precisely as later, after the Suren had crushed the Saca invasion, Mithridates II was able during his lifetime or most of it to maintain the unity of what had in effect become two Parthian realms.

The portrait of Eucratides in his helmet upon the tetradrachms of his second series,[1] a portrait engraved after he was in possession of Bactra itself, is so striking, with its look of a British officer in a sun-helmet, that one is at first tempted to attribute it to the great artist whom I have called *X* and rank it as a fourth beside his portraits of Euthydemus, Demetrius, and Antimachus. But this can hardly be the case. One characteristic of the work of *X* is its uncompromising truth and fidelity to the facts, while this portrait of Eucratides is idealised, like the Alexander-heads on Lysimachus' money; this can be seen by glancing at the bare-headed portraits of his first series, by another engraver,[2] where his face is quite ugly and bears a strong resemblance to the ugly features of his son Heliocles[3]. There was evidently more than one great portrait-engraver in Bactra, and if their names are forgotten, forgotten also are the names of the men who worked for Lysimachus and of many another fine artist. Their names are forgotten; but their honour lives in their work.

Before coming to India I must notice Plato. His solitary coin,[4] dated in 165 B.C., is no longer unique, for a second specimen, from

[1] Plate no. 11. [2] *Ib.* no. 10. [3] *Ib.* no. 12.

[4] *BMC* p. 20, Pl. VI, 11; legend *βασιλέως ἐπιφάνους Πλάτωνος*.

Turkestan, was published in 1913.[1] The coins shew a helmeted head and on the helmet the Seleucid device worn by Eucratides, the horn and ear of a bull, and they have the Seleucid bead and reel border; the reverse type is the four-horse chariot of Helios, with the legend 'Of King Plato, (god) manifest'. Artistically, the head is a copy of the helmeted head of Eucratides on one particular coin of his second series,[2] and (though poorly executed) the resemblance of the features is so close that I do not know myself whether the head be meant for Eucratides or Plato; the deduction in either case must be the same, that Plato was a very near relative, which from the ages can only mean Eucratides' brother; the chariot of Helios may be a fanciful allusion to the name of their father Heliocles. It cannot be said for certain that Plato was not this king's real name, for (the philosopher apart) it is not an uncommon Greek name in inscriptions; but as the name of a Macedonian king of Seleucid descent it is certainly suspect,[3] and may have been assumed. As only two coins of his are known, his kingdom was either very small, or ephemeral, or both; his assumption of Antiochus' cult-name Epiphanes[4] may show not only that he claimed divinity but that he had a childish vanity; the chariot of Helios, perhaps inspired by Antiochus wearing the radiate crown of the Sun-god, is not far from evidence that the god he claimed to be was the Sun. A man with the name of a philosopher who had some close connection with the Sun and had a little kingdom irresistibly recalls another man who thought he was the Sun and who had dreams of philosophy and a little kingdom to play with—Cassander's brother Alexarchus,[5] whom Cassander established in a small principality where he could dream in security under his brother's shield. In the same way Eucratides may have given Plato a town or two to play with while he did the work.

Before leaving Plato, it must be noticed that the four-horse chariot (*quadriga*) of the Sun on his coin is of interest in another connection,

[1] I. N. Svoronos, *J.I.d'A.N.* xv, 1913, p. 187. Forgeries I believe are common.

[2] *BMC* Pl. VI, 1; the resemblance is extraordinary.

[3] The name occurs in Curt. v, 7, 12 as that of an officer of Alexander, where it is more than suspect; H. Berve, *Das Alexanderreich* II p. 429 no. 67.

[4] Whether the coins should be read *ἐπιφάνους Πλάτωνος* or *Πλάτωνος ἐπιφάνους* seems immaterial. Antiochus III was *μέγας 'Α.* in inscriptions (*OGIS* 230, 237, 239–40) and *'Α. μέγας* in cult (*ib.* 245–6).

[5] On Alexarchus see Tarn, *Alexander the Great and the unity of mankind*, *Proc. Brit. Acad.* XIX, 1933, pp. 141 *sqq.*; O. Weinreich, *Menekrates Zeus und Salmoneus* 1933 pp. 12 *sqq.*, 108 *sqq.*

quite apart from his personality. The Sun's *quadriga* had long been a feature of Greek art[1]—it had its place on the Parthenon—and had already appeared in the Greek East on coins of Andragoras and Vakhsuvar (? Oxyartes).[2] These coins, and especially that of Plato, supply one of the few definite instances (as opposed to assumptions) of a Greek artistic motive passing into Indian art through Bactria; they point the road which led to the relief on the Sūrya panel on a pillar at Bodh Gaya, dating from one of the kings of the Sunga dynasty and perhaps therefore not much later than Plato, on which 'the Sun-god appears driving a four-horse chariot, manifestly copied from a Greek model'.[3] The Sun's *quadriga* was now started on a long journey; it appears in a Parthian house in Babylonia,[4] in the art of Gandhāra and Central Asia,[5] and is said to be a favourite motive in Sassanian art;[6] very notable is the Sun's chariot (third century A.D.) with four winged horses in the vault over the great Buddha at Bamyan,[7] once a Greek city. Professor Herzfeld has derived all these representations ultimately from the art of Greek Bactria;[8] and Plato's coin supplies the missing link in his theory.[9] But Professor Rostovtzeff has traced the Sun's *quadriga* in the Iranian art of South Russia back to the fourth century B.C.,[10] and it still remains to be ascertained whether the original Greek and Iranian conceptions of that *quadriga* were independent of each other or, if not, how they were related. But however that may be, the coin-type of the unimportant Plato constitutes a most important nodal point in the travels of this artistic motive.

To return to Eucratides. Had he stopped at the Hindu Kush, there

[1] Jessen, *Helios* in PW 88–90, and Rapp, *Helios* in Roscher 2005 *sqq.*, will supply instances.

[2] *BMC Arabia etc.* Pl. XXVIII, 1 and 6.

[3] Sir J. Marshall, *ASI* 1907–8 p. 41, and see *CHI* p. 640.

[4] M. Rostovtzeff, *Yale Class. Stud.* v, 1935, p. 189.

[5] E. Herzfeld, *Arch. Mitt. aus Iran* II, 1930, pp. 130–1. He does not notice Bodh Gaya.

[6] Herzfeld *ib.* pp. 128 *sqq.*

[7] Herzfeld *ib.* p. 131 and Rostovtzeff *ib.* p. 169 n. 9 call the charioteer the Sun; R. Grousset, *Sur les traces de Bouddha* 1929 p. 82, calls him a Lunar Genius. But the Moon traditionally drove two horses only.

[8] Herzfeld *Arch. Mitt. aus Iran* II, 1930, p. 131.

[9] There is a *quadriga* on a Graeco-Bactrian engraved gem in the Pearse collection in the Indian Museum, Calcutta (*ASI* 1928–9 Pl. LV no. 4), but I do not know if it is meant for the chariot of the Sun.

[10] Rostovtzeff, *Yale Class. Stud.* v, 1935, p. 169 n. 9, citing his *Iranians and Greeks in South Russia* p. 105 and Pl. XXIII, 1.

is no reason why he should not have formed eastern Iran into a powerful kingdom with elements of permanence; but he proceeded instead to invade India, and that was his undoing. If I am right that the aim of Antiochus was to restore the empire of Alexander, it was of course intended that he should invade India. There is unfortunately not the same certainty for his chronology in India as in Iran. Whatever his energy, he must have needed a certain time to organise his conquests; at the same time, the subsequent troubles behind his back show that his settlement of Bactria was anything but thorough. He may have spent 166 at least in Bactria, and invaded India in 165 or 164. He was alive in 162, when Timarchus in Media copied his coinage (p. 218); and it will appear presently that his death almost certainly fell in 159 (p. 219), with early in 158 just possible; later than that it cannot be. His reign in Bactria-Sogdiana cannot have been a long one, for the nomad conquerors of Bactria did not imitate his coins, while imitations of those of Euthydemus and of Eucratides' son Heliocles are common (p. 303). Eucratides' time in India should therefore fall between the years 165 and 160.

Menander on his recall had abandoned everything south of Mathurā, had created a new frontier (pp. 227 *sq.*), and must soon have returned himself to the Punjab; the estimate of Demetrius and himself as to what could still be held in India must have largely depended on native circumstances and attitudes which are unknown to us. Apollodotus must have previously returned to the north (p. 164); doubtless he met Eucratides' invasion in Gandhāra, which is known to have been part of his realm. Eucratides, after crossing the Hindu Kush, took Kapisa from Agathocles, and presumably all the Paropamisadae; Agathocles must have met his death, as all his coins show a young head and had he lived he would have had a better claim to rule India than Menander. Eucratides' conquest of Kapisa is known from an invaluable issue made by him of square bronze bilingual coins with the type 'Zeus enthroned' and a legend in Kharoshthi, 'The god of the city of Kapisi'.[1] This issue is of great interest. In the first place, Zeus enthroned was the special type of Antiochus IV; this suggests that Eucratides still considered himself, or desired to be considered, a loyal vassal of Antiochus, and this may be borne out by the fact of his presently using this type to overstrike the coins of the defeated Apollodotus. In the second place

[1] *BMC* Pl. VI, 8; E. J. Rapson, *JRAS* 1905 p. 783 no. 1, and in *CHI* p. 555 and Pl. VII, 36.

it throws much light on some of the types used by Greek kings in India. The humped Indian bull on Graeco-Indian coins, for example, is certainly the bull of Siva and represents Pushkalāvatī (p. 135 n. 5), but it had been a common Seleucid type;[1] in the same way both the elephant and the elephant's head were common Seleucid types, and even Menander's ox-head occurs on coins of Seleucus II.[2] Evidently the Greek kings in India often took Seleucid types and fitted them, more or less modified, to other kingdoms and other gods. At Kapisa we see the whole process. The standing Zeus-types of both Demetrius II and Agathocles had probably been meant to represent the elephant-god of Kapisa who dwelt on Mount Pīlusāra (pp. 138, 158); but as Eucratides, perhaps to show his loyalty, desired to use Antiochus' type of Zeus enthroned for the god of Alexandria-Kapisa, and as this type was doubtless well known as being that of Antiochus, he modified it to represent the elephant-god by adding to it the forepart of a small elephant in front of Zeus and also a representation of Mount Pīlusāra. Finally, to remove any doubt, the somewhat naive explanatory legend was added; one only wishes there were more such legends.

Antiochus himself started in 165 to begin clearing up from the western end;[3] unless we suppose that the real beginning was his activity in Judaea in 167. He reduced Armenia, which had only been nominally subject to Alexander and had never acknowledged the suzerainty of a Seleucid except for a time that of Antiochus III. He is next heard of in Chaldaea, where he refounded Alexandria at the head of the Persian Gulf as an Antioch (later Charax Spasinu),[4] though this *might* belong to his visit to Babylonia in 166. Pliny takes him down the Arabian coast of the Gulf to Gerrha, but this is certainly a mistake for Antiochus III, as Pliny adds that that coast had not been explored before,[5] while it is known from Polybius that Antiochus III had gone as far as Gerrha.[6] Similarly the activity of Numenius, eparch of Mesene, in the

[1] *BMC Sel.*, Seleucus I p. 6 nos. 62–70 and App. p. 107, 63a, 67a; Seleucus II p. 18 nos. 32–4.

[2] *Ib.* Seleucus II p. 18 no. 31.

[3] On this campaign see generally Niese III pp. 216–18; Ed. Meyer, *Ursprung und Anfänge des Christentums* II, 1921, pp. 216 *sqq.*; W. Kolbe, *Beiträge zur syrischen und jüdischen Geschichte* 1926 pp. 155 *sq.*; Otto, *Zeit d. 6. Ptolemäers* pp. 85–8.

[4] Tscherikower p. 94; *quintus regum* of Pliny VI, 139 is certainly Epiphanes. Technically, he probably *was* Antiochus V (p. 185 n. 1).

[5] VI, 147, oram Epiphani primum exquisitam.

[6] Polyb. XIII, 9, 4–5.

Gulf, recorded by Pliny (VI, 152), belongs to the time of Antiochus III, for it is known that the eparch of Mesene at the end of Epiphanes' lifetime was Hyspaosines. In fact, except for the refounding of Antioch (Charax), there is nothing to connect Epiphanes with the Persian Gulf at all. The tradition next takes him to Elymais or Susa—it was in reality Susa—and late writers state either that he plundered the temple of Artemis-Nanaia or that he attacked it and was beaten off. This question is considered in Appendix 7; it will suffice to say here that the temple of Nanaia was at Susa, which was his own city; that he had some dealings with the temple authorities, the nature of which cannot now be ascertained but which were certainly peaceable; and that statements that he plundered or attacked the temple are demonstrably untrue. There may have been in late writers the same confusion of his actions with those of Antiochus III as there has been over Gerrha; but that is not really material.

After Susa he is next heard of at Gabae, which gives his route; he followed the main road from Seleuceia through Susa to Persepolis and then the main road from Persepolis which went by Gabae to Ecbatana.[1] If there was a king in Elymais at this time he was Antiochus' vassal (App. 7), while as to Persis there is nothing to show that her kings became independent till after his death[2]; probably all that he was doing was showing his power to his vassals on his way eastward. For at Gabae he was on the main road to Ecbatana and Hekatompylos, that is, he was on his way to attack Parthia.[3] Certainly Eucratides, involved in India, was not ready to co-operate, but possibly Antiochus had no trustworthy information about his position; one may recall how entirely Alexander when in India vanished from the purview of the West.[4] But Eucratides' governor in Bactria could have co-operated; not that it mattered, for Parthia at the time could no more have withstood

[1] On this route, Herzfeld, *Klio* VIII, 1908, 14; see my map in *CAH* VII facing p. 157, and my note *JEA* 1929 p. 11 n. 4. The otherwise worthless story in II Macc. ix, 1 *sqq*. (see App. 7) does record his presence at Persepolis and then takes him to Ecbatana, that is, it has the direction right.

[2] The stories of fighting in Persis (Polyaen. VII, 39, 40; Steph. *s.v.* Stasis) cannot be dated, but like Numenius (Pliny VI, 152) they may belong after Magnesia.

[3] On this, Tac. *Hist*. V, 8 is useless. Otto's note, *op. cit*. p. 85 n. 3, is certainly right: the hellenising king can only be Epiphanes, and *Parthis nondum adultis* refers to a time before the conquests of Mithridates I; but equally *Parthorum bello prohibitus* can only refer to Sidetes. Tacitus has mixed the two up.

[4] *CAH* VI pp. 416, 450.

Antiochus IV alone than she had withstood Antiochus III. But at Gabae Antiochus died prematurely of consumption of the lungs,[1] of which several kings of Macedonian blood—Cassander, his son Philip IV, and Antigonus Doson—had died prematurely before him. Consumption in the ancient world was incurable; but the disease often works slowly, and if Antiochus had known for some time that he was doomed that would explain the nervous haste (if it existed) which has been thought to characterise his last years;[2] it was the desire to get *something* done before the end came.

It has been said of Antiochus that he aimed at the impossible.[3] But his plan in Asia was possible enough: had he lived two years longer—he was not bound to calculate upon a premature death—and reached Bactria, there would have been no Parthian empire, Eucratides would not have been killed, and the two would have held Asia in their hands. After all, neither Alexander nor Napoleon did all that they meant to do. But Antiochus failed because he died. Certainly one result of the troubles which followed his untimely death was that the Seleucid empire was never the same again; but he can hardly be held responsible for dying. What he *was* responsible for—and it would seem that it must have happened even had he been completely successful—was a great weakening of the Greek position in the Farther East and the failure of a promising experiment in India.

Antiochus' death meant that Eucratides henceforth considered himself to be the independent king of his eastern kingdom and worked for his own hand. How far exactly he penetrated into India cannot be said. He must have conquered Apollodotus' kingdom of Gandhāra, or anyhow part of it, for some of his 'Kapisi' coins are overstruck on bronze money of Apollodotus.[4] For one king to overstrike the money of another is normally a proof of victory; it does not of course necessarily mean that the defeated king was killed, but Apollodotus cannot have

[1] His death: Polyb. xxxi, 9 (11). App. *Syr.* 66 says phthisis; usually I think accepted. The story in *II Macc.* ix means consumption of the bowels; but Jews were too fond of relating that their enemies were 'eaten of worms' for any credence to be attached to this, especially as the same book, i, 12 *sqq.*, has a totally different story. On the contradiction see Kolbe *op. cit.* p. 120.

[2] Otto *op. cit.* pp. 84 *sqq.* I do not see it myself, at any rate as regards the eastern campaign.

[3] *Ib.* p. 85, 'Kunst des Unmöglichen'.

[4] *BMC* p. xxxv; Whitehead *NC* pp. 302, 307. Rapson (*CHI* p. 555) points out that Eucratides' Indian issues are at least as late in style as those of Apollodotus.

lived much longer in any case. For a sufficient length of time (p. 149) has to be allowed after his death for Menander's money to become well established in Barygaza,[1] and as Menander died between 150 and 145 (p. 226), Apollodotus' death cannot be later than 160, and it would be better to put it about 163 or 162; he almost certainly therefore died fighting against Eucratides. In about seven years Eucratides had disposed of at least four Euthydemid kings; it must have looked as though he would exterminate the race altogether, which may have been his intention; to him they were just rebels. It has been mentioned that this period resembles the wars of the Successors; one may recall the number of prominent personalities—Perdiccas and Leonnatus, Craterus and Eumenes, Olympias and Eurydice, satraps without number—who came to a violent end within seven years of Alexander's death.

As Eucratides struck no coins with the humped bull of Pushkalāvatī, and as he overstruck Apollodotus' money with his 'Kapisi' issue, he must have governed all his Indian possessions from Alexandria-Kapisa; his measures in India were naturally only temporary. Strabo shows that he never crossed the Jhelum,[2] and it is quite uncertain if he even crossed the Indus; a few of his coins have been found in the Punjab,[3] but with his large coinage that means nothing; coins of Diodotus, for example, have been found in Seistan[4] and Taxila,[5] places where he never ruled and never even was. It is an inevitable deduction that Eucratides' further advance eastward was checked by Menander, most probably somewhere in the Indus district; indeed Menander must have recovered Gandhāra or most of it (p. 229). Every step took Eucratides farther from his base in Bactria, and he could no longer call on the Greeks in Antiochus' name, for he was outside the Seleucid empire and Antiochus was dead, while Menander was near his own base and must, if his legend has any meaning at all, have had the support of large elements among the Indian population. It has been pointed out that the

[1] Even if it was copied there after his death it must have been established during his lifetime.

[2] Strabo xv, 686. Strabo is trying to cast doubt on Apollodorus' statement that the *Euthydemids* conquered more of India than Alexander had done by saying that anyhow *Eucratides* only ruled 1000 cities while Alexander had 5000 between the Jhelum and the Beas alone (this from Aristobulus, see p. 144 n. 3). The implication that Eucratides had nothing east of the Jhelum is clear, and is not affected by the badness of Strabo's argumentation.

[3] Cunningham, *NC* 1869 p. 233, 'rare'.

[4] *JRAS* 1904 p. 675.

[5] *ASI* 1912–13 Part I p. 16.

resemblances between some of the bronze coins of Eucratides and some of those of Menander are so strong that they must have been issued in the same district at about the same time,[1] which may indicate a condition of stalemate between the two kings; certainly Menander was not damaged. All that is known of the end is that Eucratides returned to Bactria.[2] He must have made a treaty with Menander; Menander is subsequently found ruling Gandhāra (p. 229), but there is no real evidence that he ruled the Paropamisadae. It, like the rest of Iran, was probably left to Eucratides, for he almost certainly retained Alexandria-Kapisa: Masson found his coins about Begram in such quantities[3] that they must have continued to be struck after his death.[4]

Eucratides issued several types of bilingual coins in India,[5] which means that he was in the country for some little time; this bears out the chronology here adopted and the protracted nature of his struggle with Apollodotus and Menander. One of his square bronze issues, with the type 'Victory',[6] is of interest as an indication of what was now in his mind. In the Greek legend he is still only 'Great King', but the Kharoshthi legend adds to this the word *rajadirajasa*, 'King of Kings': he was to be the independent monarch of a great Graeco-Asiatic empire. It is no doubt true, speaking generally, that Graeco-Macedonians did not use the title 'King of Kings';[7] but apart from the fact that the last Greek king in India, Hermaeus, was for political reasons called *rajadirajasa* after his death (App. 17), there is another eloquent exception besides that of Eucratides—Antony's famous coin on which Cleopatra is 'Queen of Kings'. Now the title 'King of Kings' was the nearest equivalent a Greek knew to the Indian Chakravartin,[8] the 'king of the wheel' (p. 263), and as Menander in Indian eyes was a Chakravartin (*ib.*), Eucratides' title must have some connection with this fact and with his struggle with Menander. But the actual relationship is obscure, for it cannot be said when Menander was first regarded as a Chakravartin; chronologically, we do not know which title came first.

[1] *CHI* p. 551.
[2] Justin XLI, 6, 5, unde (from India) cum se reciperet.
[3] Cunningham *NC* 1869 p. 233.
[4] The belief however that his types were impressed on a much later coin of Antialcidas is merely a mistake, *CHI* p. 558 n. 3.
[5] *BMC* pp. 16, 165.
[6] *BMC* p. 166 no. 7, Pl. XXX, 12. See Cunningham *NC* 1869 p. 239.
[7] E. R. Bevan, *JHS* XXII, 1902, p. 241.
[8] *CHI* p. 567.

It does however show that Eucratides regarded Indian support of Menander as important and was going to make an effort to attract it to himself.

When Eucratides crossed the Hindu Kush, he may as was customary have left his eldest son Heliocles to govern Bactria in his absence; Heliocles certainly was his eldest son, as is universally supposed, since he bore his grandfather's name. But there is nothing to show that Heliocles was joint-king; that was *not* Hellenistic practice,[1] though it had been the practice of the Euthydemids. Judging by Eucratides' age, Heliocles in 165 must have been quite young, probably not over twenty, but none of his coins show so young a face; and as, if he had been joint-king, he would presumably have coined, his coins are evidence that, if he *was* left to govern Bactria (which is only a presumption), he did not coin and was therefore just governor in the ordinary way. The matter is one of some importance for what follows.

Before going further it will be well to try to establish the date of Eucratides' death, which can be done with the help of the chronology of Mithridates I of Parthia. Soon after the death of Antiochus IV in 163 his elder brother Demetrius (I), who had been living in Rome as a hostage, escaped to Syria, set aside Antiochus' young son (Antiochus V), and took the crown. He may have continued to claim to be Eucratides' suzerain (p. 206), but certainly Eucratides did not recognise him, and there was a complete breach between West and East, though the final step in the plan of Antiochus IV and Eucratides, the conquest of Parthia, still remained to be carried out. It was in these circumstances that Timarchus, the Seleucid general of the Median satrapy, revolted in 162 and took the royal title as king of Media and Babylonia; he called himself 'Great King' in imitation of Eucratides and issued money which was a copy of his.[2] Obviously there was some connection between him and Eucratides, perhaps an alliance; it may be that Eucratides, regarded without any favour by the Seleucid Demetrius I as a man who had thrown off his allegiance, had incited Timarchus to revolt in order that, when the time came, he might have someone in the west who would

[1] The regular practice was to leave the eldest son as temporary governor *de facto*. So Alexander once governed Macedonia in Philip's absence; Antigonus Gonatas' son Demetrius governed Macedonia while Gonatas was fighting the Chremonidean war; Seleucus, eldest son of Antiochus I, governed Asia Minor while his father was meeting Ptolemy II's invasion of Seleucid Syria.

[2] *BMC Sel.* p. 50, *βασιλέως μεγάλου Τιμάρχου*, with Eucratides' Dioscuri type. See *CHI* p. 457.

co-operate with him in an attack on Parthia.[1] Certainly Mithridates believed this: his actions show that he thought that his best chance was to anticipate any co-operation between the two while Eucratides was still involved in India. He at once struck with all his strength at Timarchus,[2] and after a severe struggle, which is said to have been protracted and may therefore have occupied 160 as well as 161, took all Media up to the Zagros, which doubled his own strength and left Timarchus comparatively powerless. He did not wait to finish him off (Demetrius I did that presently), but at once turned upon Eucratides' kingdom, attacked Bactria, and recovered the one-time Bactrian conquests west of the Arius, the satrapies of Tapuria and Traxiane (p. 88 n. 1);[3] Apollodorus shows that these satrapies were taken by force of arms and in Eucratides' lifetime.[4] The date of this conquest then, if not 160, is almost certainly 159 (it cannot be *later*), and it was the occasion, as will be seen, of Eucratides returning from India to meet his death; his death therefore falls almost certainly in 159, though early in 158 may just be possible. Later it cannot be: the conventional date, *c.* 155, is not supported by anything[5] and is quite impossible. For a reasonable time has to be allowed for Menander's undisturbed rule in India after Eucratides left, and Menander's own death must have taken place between 150 and 145 (p. 226).

As Eucratides left India without doing what he meant to do—he must at least have meant to secure the Punjab up to Alexander's frontier the Beas—it must have been serious trouble in Bactria which recalled him. The story of his death has to be reconstructed from a chapter of Justin which is one of the most confused and worst excerpted anywhere in that unsatisfactory writer, but with care it can be done. The first thing to notice is that Justin gives two different and mutually exclusive versions of Eucratides' death—that he was killed by his son and that

[1] R. H. McDowell, *Stamped objects* pp. 219 *sq.*, suggested that Bactria was behind Timarchus' revolt, as a measure against Parthia.

[2] Justin XLI, 6, 6 shows that Media was independent when Mithridates attacked it, which it never was except during Timarchus' brief rule, and mentions a protracted war. On the order of events see E. Breccia, *Klio* V, 1905, pp. 44–7.

[3] Justin XLI, 6, 7 shows that Mithridates' conquest of Media was followed at once (his viribus auctus) by a campaign in 'Hyrcania', which means the acquisition of these two satrapies; for their conquest see next note.

[4] Strabo XI, 517, *ἀφῄρηντο Εὐκρατίδην*; 515, *βιασάμενοι τοὺς περὶ Εὐκρατίδαν.*

[5] Professedly following von Gutschmid, though it is not what he said; he said 155 *at the latest*, *Gesch. Irans* p. 49. In fact, 155 is only Rochette's original guess, extremely creditable at the time, and repeated ever since in default of better.

he was killed by the Parthians. The formal story,[1] often repeated in modern works, is that he was killed on his way back from India by the son he had made joint-king (*socius regni*), who, as though he had slain an enemy and not a father, drove his chariot through the blood and gave orders that the corpse should be cast forth unburied. This piece of nonsense has usually been supposed to mean that Heliocles killed his father; but there is no chance whatever of it being true as it stands. A victorious king at the head of his army might indeed be assassinated by his young son,[2] but he would not be so assassinated without things happening, and the murderer would not have leisure to insult the corpse or the opportunity of giving orders that it should not be buried. In fact, as has been seen, there is no likelihood of Heliocles having been joint-king with his father, *socius regni*; and he succeeded his father and had a long reign, a thing quite inconsistent with Justin's story. Moreover, though Justin *calls* it assassination and parricide, he gives away the fact that it was really death in battle by saying that 'the son' was in a chariot and had ample leisure afterwards. Here comes in his second version, in which he has named the victors in the battle: after the list of provinces conquered by Eucratides—for that, as we have seen (p. 199 n. 3), is the meaning of his 'Bactriani'—he adds that the 'Bactriani'—meaning Eucratides—were finally crushed by the weaker Parthians,[3] which is a very different matter from being assassinated by his son. Putting the two versions together, what we get is that Eucratides was killed by the Parthians and was killed by 'a son'; and the story is perfectly consistent if we suppose either that Justin has misunderstood whose son it was or that a proper name—that of the son's father—has dropped out somewhere between Justin and the original source; the mistake once made, it was inevitable that Justin should seek to improve the occasion in his usual manner by making moral remarks about parricide. Eucratides was indeed killed by 'a son'; but it was by a son of one of the dead Euthydemid princes, with Parthian help.

[1] Justin XLI, 6, 5: unde (from India) cum se reciperet (Eucratides), a filio, quem socium regni fecerat, in itinere interficitur, qui non dissimulato parricidio, velut hostem non patrem interfecisset, et per sanguinem ejus currum egit et corpus abici insepultum jussit. Note that Justin does *not* say 'a filio ejus'.

[2] Seleucus I was successfully assassinated at the head of his victorious army by Keraunos; but Keraunos, a man of much military experience, was able to choose his time, and knew that if he escaped—he had a swift horse ready—he would have behind him a strong fortress, a still powerful army, and a great country.

[3] Justin XLI, 6, 3; see p. 199 n. 3.

Before going on, a word must be said about the chariot. A Greek king fighting from a chariot seems so strange that it has led to a suggestion[1] that the story of the chariot driven through the blood is merely a reproduction of the story of Tullia driving her carriage through the blood of Servius in Livy (I, 48, 7). But 'Trogus' source' is much earlier than Livy himself (p. 50), and though Livy doubtless got the story from some annalist, an eastern Greek is hardly likely to have read Roman annalists; and I am not prepared to say that the chariot story is untrue. Both Persians and Indians used war chariots; so did Seleucus I at Ipsus, and on his coins Athena fights from an elephant-chariot. There is a bronze issue of Antiochus IV on which Victory drives a two-horse chariot[2] (the war chariot); some coins of Maues, with one of the Telephus monograms and the type 'Zeus enthroned' and therefore struck at Kapisa (App. 16), show a two-horse chariot in which a radiate king with a spear or sceptre is being driven by a charioteer;[3] a century later a coin of Wima Kadphises, the conqueror of northern India, shows the king being driven in a two-horse chariot.[4] Finally, one of the coins of Mithridates I of the time when he was virtually master of Bactria (p. 222 n. 2) shows Victory in a two-horse chariot,[5] which exactly fits and may even refer to the battle in which Eucratides was killed.

A reconstruction of the main lines of the story can now be attempted. A too swift conquest may have its drawbacks, as Alexander himself had found in Bactria-Sogdiana; and though Eucratides had mastered the country, the Euthydemid party, which was probably favoured by the native Bactrians, had only been scotched, not destroyed. Justin's statement that 'the son' who killed Eucratides was joint-king with his father shows that he was a king, and as such should have left his mark on the coinage. It is just possible that we may be dealing with some unknown prince who has left no trace; but it is best to keep to what is known, and we do know a son, and only one, who had been made joint-king, *socius regni*, with his father, Demetrius' son Demetrius II, who was governing Bactria as his father's joint-king when Eucratides came (p. 201). If then a name has fallen out of Justin's text after *filio* it

[1] *CHI* p. 455.

[2] Babelon, *Rois de Syrie* p. 72 nos. 556–8.

[3] *BMC* p. 172, Cunningham *NC* 1890 p. 130 nos. 1–3; cf. Whitehead, *JASB* VI, 1910, Num. Supp. XIV p. 561.

[4] *BMC* Pl. XXV, 10; Cunningham *NC* 1892 p. 69 no. 7.

[5] *BMC Parthia*, Pl. II no. 9.

is that of Demetrius; if on the other hand, as is perhaps more probable, the mistake is due to Justin's own confusion, he has previously been talking of Demetrius and Eucratides together and has attributed 'the son' to the wrong man. I shall assume therefore, with all necessary reservations, that the son in question was not someone unknown but was Demetrius II, and that he had not perished with his father but had escaped to the hills and there rallied his party. One thing which Justin does bring out clearly is the intense hatred of 'the son' for his 'enemy' Eucratides. The family loyalty of the Euthydemids has already been alluded to (p. 166), and as Eucratides had been exterminating the family, the hatred felt for him by the survivor was only too natural. There is a hatred which will move Acheron itself for vengeance; and Demetrius II, unable to deal with Eucratides without external help, turned to the one quarter open to him, Mithridates I of Parthia.

Sacas too have to come into the story somehow (see App. 16); but though the Sacas were to Bactria what the Galatae were to the princes of Asia Minor—Spitamenes had called them in against Alexander, Euthydemus had threatened to do so against Antiochus III, Ferghana in 101 B.C. by the same threat was to secure decent terms from the invading Chinese (p. 310)—in this case they were not called in by Demetrius II but must have come with Mithridates. For though the strength of Mithridates had been greatly increased by his conquest of Media in 161–60, he had to conquer it before he could use it and it does not appear whence he originally got the strength to do so; the natural supposition is that he supplemented his own forces with a body of Sacas, whether as mercenaries or as allies.

It was Mithridates' subsequent attack upon Eucratides' kingdom of Bactria in 159 which gave Demetrius II his opportunity; like Diodotus II before him, he allied himself with Bactria's secular enemy, and Mithridates crossed the Arius. It was Mithridates' attack which recalled Eucratides from India. He may have hurried back with only part of his army;[1] in any case the allies met him and defeated and killed him, and Demetrius II in his hatred refused burial to the corpse. For a little while Mithridates was the real power in Bactria; Justin implies as much, and it has been deduced from some of his coins[2] that at some period he

[1] Justin XLI, 6, 5, he was killed 'in itinere'.

[2] Rapson, *Ancient India* 1914 p. 126. The coins had been collected by Wroth in *BMC Parthia* Pl. II and called 'time of Mithridates I'. Two, nos. 6 and 7, show an exact copy of Eucratides' Dioscuri type; Mithridates was claiming to be his successor.

was in possession of Bactria or anyhow of part of it, and no other time is possible; Justin too calls the Parthians the weaker,[1] which means that it must have been prior to the full establishment by Mithridates of his empire. Beside the coins, confirmation of Mithridates' rule in Bactria may perhaps be found in a town 'Surogana of Phraates' which Ptolemy gives in Bactria near the Oxus;[2] there seems no other time when a Bactrian town could have received a Parthian nickname. Doubtless 'Trogus' source' made the whole thing clear.

How and why Mithridates quitted Bactria is obscure. The proceedings of his Sacas, to be presently noticed, may have had something to do with it; but all that is known is that Heliocles finally recovered Bactria, Sogdiana (or southern Sogdiana), and presumably Merv, while Mithridates is found in possession of Seistan, Arachosia and Gedrosia.[3] It may be supposed that Mithridates left a governor in Bactria called Phraates (not his son Phraates II, who was not yet born) and himself passed on to the conquest of Seistan and Arachosia, and that a rally of Bactria to Heliocles as the one effective force, aided perhaps by the return of the rest of Eucratides' army from India, drove Phraates out. Demetrius II vanishes, and with him vanishes the last trace of Euthydemid rule in Iran. Somewhere about 155 B.C.[4]—a year or two either way—Mithridates either settled his Sacas on the lower Helmand in the province afterwards called Sacastene, or, as is much more probable, they settled themselves; he probably had as little choice in the matter as his namesake of Pontus had when he and Nicomedes of Bithynia settled the Galatae in northern Phrygia, for the Sacas were not settled on his frontier, as would have been customary, but secured a rich province in the interior. There they set up a kingdom, which was independent or virtually so from the start, as were the Galatae; it was to form a rallying point for their compatriots in the Saca invasion of

No. 9, Victory in a *biga*, has already been noticed (p. 221). Though meant for use in Bactria, they are not Bactrian work, and were doubtless struck in Media (Wroth *ib.* p. xxvi). All bear the simple legend *βασιλέως Ἀρσάκου*, that is, they come early in Mithridates' reign.

[1] Justin XLI, 6, 3, ab invalidioribus Parthis oppressi sunt.

[2] Ptol. VI, 11, 7, *Σουρογάνα Φράτου*.

[3] Justin XLI, 6, 8 makes his realm stretch from the Hindu Kush to the Lower Euphrates, which would at least include Arachosia and Seistan. Gedrosia seems certain, Orosius V, 4, 16; see Kiessling, *Hydaspes* (2) in PW. On Herzfeld's alteration of Hydaspes to Choaspes see p. 100 n. 4.

[4] For the following paragraph see App. 16.

Parthia in 129, and, so far as can be seen, was never really subject to Parthia till it was conquered for Mithridates II by the Suren somewhere between 124 and 115 B.C. as part of the liquidation of that invasion. From the inception of this kingdom *c.* 155 B.C. dated the old Saca Era, which was used by the first Saca Great King of Kings in India and appears in many Kharoshthi inscriptions.

Trogus, who knew more than we know, calls Eucratides, as he calls Mithridates, 'great';[1] and he was hardly thinking of the legends on their coins. The man who inherited a little kingdom and made of it the Parthian empire had a fair claim to the title, as the world then judged greatness; and perhaps, if Eucratides had stopped at the Hindu Kush, the man who in a couple of years overthrew a powerful monarchy and recovered the eastern part of the Seleucid empire might have put forward a claim, a claim which always seemed absurd when he was believed to have been a mere rebel. But at the end he attempted too much; no benefit was reaped by the Seleucid kings, and the one positive achievement of his career was the substitution of a new and short-lived dynasty in Bactria itself. The real results of his extraordinary expedition and his exhausting wars were the failure of the Euthydemid attempt to revive the Mauryan empire, the acquisition by the Parthians of much of the Euthydemid realm in Iran, and a great weakening of the Greek position in Bactria and eventually in India.

[1] Justin XLI, 6, 1, magni uterque viri.

CHAPTER VI

MENANDER AND HIS KINGDOM

MENANDER[1] was the most famous of the Yavana kings, and his legend attests the impression he made upon the world about him; and a sketch must now be attempted of the kingdom of the man who for a little while had held Asoka's capital and whose conquests were exalted by a Greek historian even above those of Alexander. The deaths of Demetrius and Apollodotus and the return of Eucratides to Bactria left him master of the position in India, and thenceforth to his death he, the one man who had successfully resisted Eucratides, ruled the whole of the territory still remaining to the Greeks in that country, excluding the Paropamisadae; if he had not the royal title before (p. 167) he must have taken it, presumably by a vote of his army, when Demetrius was killed. The growth of his legend, and the establishment of his coinage in Barygaza, postulate for him a reign of reasonable length; at the same time the fact that his son, Strato I, was too young to rule alone when he died sets a definite limit to that length. He legitimised his rule by marrying Demetrius' daughter Agathocleia; the evidence that she was his queen seems conclusive.[2] If cadets of the house of Euthydemus still survived,[3] they must have accepted his rule as the only security against Eucratides and his line; he never had any civil war—at least in all his vast coinage no coin seems known which has been overstruck by anyone else or upon anyone else's money.

It is not possible to get an accurate chronology for Menander's reign, but one must approximate as nearly as possible. Assuming that Agathocleia *was* Demetrius' daughter and not a daughter of Apollodotus (p. 78), she may have married her father's general directly after Demetrius' death and his own return from Pātaliputra, *i.e.* in 166, or she may not have married him till the death of Apollodotus left him the sole repository of power in India and sole effective support of the Euthydemid cause, say *c.* 161 at latest; a later date than 166 seems

[1] Menander of India is not included among the numerous Menanders in PW.

[2] Evidence: E. J. Rapson in *CHI* p. 552 n. 1. It is conclusive to myself, as to de la Vallée-Poussin, p. 236; this chapter I hope will show how other things make it inevitable.

[3] For Antimachus II see p. 229, and on the question of Apollodotus II p. 318.

probable, but it can hardly be supposed (since unmarried kings normally married on their accession) that Menander did not marry till he was rid of Eucratides in 159. On his death Agathocleia became regent for their son (or eldest son) Strato I; he was therefore a minor, and as it may be assumed that he would take the power at 18 at latest, he was under that age. Now Agathocleia's first coins as regent bear her own portrait alone, with Strato named only in the Kharoshthi legend; her second series shows jugate busts of herself and Strato; then comes Strato's coinage alone.[1] As she was regent long enough to issue two series of coins, and long enough for Heliocles, who overstruck some of her coins, to invade India during her regency, it appears that Strato cannot have taken the power till at earliest the third year after his father's death; that is, he was certainly not over fifteen when Menander died and may of course have been two or three years younger. If now we take one extreme—that Menander married in 166 and that Strato was only twelve when he died—it is possible to put Menander's death as early as 153, though that is very unlikely. If we take the other extreme—that Menander married about 161 and that Strato was fifteen when he died—it is possible to put Menander's death as late as 145. To say that Menander's son might not have been born till some years after the marriage (unlikely in that age) and to bring Menander's death down to *c.* 140 seems to me impossible, for the association of Strato's grandson Strato II with Strato as king cannot be later than *c.* 100 or soon after (Chap. VIII). It would seem then that Menander's death must lie between the limits I have indicated, preferably in the latter half of the period; I shall therefore, with all necessary reserves, treat his death as occurring between 150 and 145. This would give him an undivided reign of probably not less than twelve years and perhaps two or three years more; that suffices. It cannot be very far out; for the portraits on his silver *δίκαιος* coins show an elderly man (p. 262) and, as has been seen, he must have proved himself as a general before Demetrius invaded India (see Addenda).

There is no difficulty about these dates from Agathocleia's side. It was found possible in Chapter IV to give the approximate dates at which Demetrius' four sons were respectively given office as kings; they show that the eldest, Euthydemus II, cannot have been born very long after 204, say *c.* 202 at latest (it is known from Polybius that Demetrius

[1] For the coins of Agathocleia and Strato see Rapson, *Corolla Numismatica* 1906 p. 245; *CHI* p. 553.

was not yet married in 206), and that the youngest, Agathocles, cannot have been born too long after 195; 190 would hardly be possible. Agathocleia, from her name, should come next to Agathocles, whether before or after; her birth would then fall somewhere from *c.* 195 to *c.* 190. Again taking the two possible extremes, she might have been about twenty-four when she married or she might have been about thirty-four; probably she was not much, if at all, under thirty. There is precedent enough for Hellenistic princesses not marrying till thirty, or even later: putting aside the first Berenice, Ptolemais and Berenice II at once occur to the mind, even if the marriage of Cleopatra VII, who was thirty-three when she married Antony, be hardly in point; in Agathocleia's case it may well have happened that, unlike her sisters in the West, there was no one of suitable standing for her to marry. It is generally safe to assume that a princess marrying a commoner was not in her first youth.

A modern writer has stated comprehensively that Menander's empire extended from Mathurā (Muttra) in the east to Barygaza (Broach) in the west,[1] and this is substantially correct, allowing that in form it was a horse-shoe; but the details have to be considered. There is not much doubt about his south-eastern boundary. When he was recalled from Pātaliputra he abandoned a great stretch of the valleys of the Ganges and the Jumna and formed a new frontier to the south of Mathurā,[2] which remained the farthest town of importance toward the south-east held by the Greeks (p. 245); the Mathurā-Delhi country has produced many Greek coins.[3] Whether Pātaliputra was reoccupied after Menander's withdrawal by Pushyamitra has been disputed, but it seems probable that he reoccupied Ayodhya in Oude,[4] and if so he was, as his legend states (p. 177), in possession of the capital. It seems

[1] Przyluski, *Açoka* p. 167.

[2] On the historical importance of the 'Jumna march'—the Mathurā-Delhi district—as a natural frontier see A. J. Toynbee, *A Study of History* II, 2nd ed. pp. 130–1.

[3] For Mathurā itself, Whitehead *NNM* p. 45. For the great hoard from Sonipat near Delhi, Cunningham, *NC* 1872 p. 159; 883 coins seen. For the hoard found in Bundelkhund south of the Jumna, including 40 coins of Menander, V. A. Smith, *Ind. Ant.* XXXIII, 1904, p. 217.

[4] The much discussed Sunga inscription from Ayodhya (see in the last place D. R. Sahni, *Ep. Ind.* XX, 1929–30, p. 54) shows that a descendant of Pushyamitra, probably a son, was in possession of that town; it is probable therefore that Pushyamitra re-occupied Oude (see Grousset, I p. 39) which would entail possession of the capital.

uncertain whether Ayodhya and Sāketa were different towns or merely two names for one place, perhaps a double town;[1] but Menander had had to take Sāketa from Pushyamitra on his way to the capital and the Sunga king would certainly reoccupy it if he could. In the story of Pushyamitra's horse-sacrifice his grandson Vasumitra, who was guarding the horse, came to the south bank of the Sindhu and had a brush with some Yavana cavalry who were patrolling the northern bank;[2] this implies that the Sindhu was part of Menander's frontier. It may be uncertain whether the Sind or the Sindhu tributary of the Chambal be meant; probably the Chambal, south of Mathurā, was the frontier west of the Jumna. On the Purāna chronology Pushyamitra died in 148, and as it was his grandson who guarded the horse, the incident must belong to the very end of his life; it is usually put about 150. As Menander's death falls between 150 and 145, he and his opponent Pushyamitra must have died very close together. If Plutarch's story that Menander died in camp be true,[3] the reference must be to further fighting on this frontier, which may have had to be kept by the strong hand.

In the north, Menander's treaty with Eucratides had left Alexandria-Kapisa to the latter and presumably therefore the Paropamisadae (p. 217). Certainly numbers of Menander's coins are said to come into Begram,[4] but the amount of trade passing through that gateway of the West would account for a good deal, and with a coinage so enormous and widespread as his the mere presence of used coins is little guide; had he ruled wherever his coins have been found he would have been king in Pembrokeshire,[5] and his coins from Begram cannot compare

[1] Rhys Davids, *Buddhist India* 1903 p. 39. So the old name of Pātaliputra was Kusumapura; but the *Yuga-purāna* (App. 4) shows that after the Mauryan Pātaliputra was built Kusumapura continued to have a separate existence.

[2] The story comes from Kālidāsa's drama *Mālavikāgnimitra* (*CHI* p. 520) and is late, but most writers (not all) have accepted it as history; it makes little difference in any case, for it is certain that Menander held Mathurā, both from Ptolemy (p. 245) and from a hoard of 96 coins of his son Strato I found there (S. P. Noe, *A bibliography of Greek coin-hoards*, *NNM* 1925 p. 126), beside his own coins (p. 227 n. 3). Some have maintained that Kālidāsa's Sindhu was the Indus, which historically is nonsense; also the Indus has no south bank, though R. C. Mazumdar, *IHQ* 1925 pp. 214 *sqq.*, says that we must suppose it had in the second century B.C.

[3] *Mor.* 821 D, *ἀποθανόντος ἐπὶ στρατοπέδου.*

[4] J. Hackin, *JA* 226, 1935, p. 290. Curiously, there was no coin of his in a hoard of 97 tetradrachms, of ten kings, found in the Paropamisadae in 1917: Whitehead, *NC* p. 315.

[5] On his coin found at Tenby see V. A. Smith, *Ind. Ant.* XXXIV, 1905, p. 202. Warmington, p. 301, thinks it was brought to Wales by a trader; but more probably

with the vast numbers of those of Eucratides collected in that district. It is plain enough that he ruled from Mathurā to the Upper Indus; and his rule over Gandhāra is now proved also (see Addenda).

There never was much doubt that Gandhāra was part of Menander's realm, for 200 tetradrachms of his in mint condition have been found in Swat[1] and 721 drachmae, showing little signs of circulation, in the great Bajaur hoard;[2] coins in this condition have nothing to do with trade. At the same time he seems not to have used the Pushkalāvatī mint, for Siva's bull never appears on his money, so probably he ruled Gandhāra through a sub-king; presumably he had some sub-kings, but only in the case of Gandhāra is it possible to identify one.[3] The discovery of the Bajaur hoard put one obscure Graeco-Indian king, Antimachus II Nikephoros, in a new light, for the mass of almost new coins of his found there in conjunction with almost new coins of Apollodotus and Menander[4] proves that he was an early king contemporary with Menander[5] and that his kingdom must have been in Gandhāra. There can therefore be little doubt now that he was a son of Antimachus (not a grandson) who escaped to India from Eucratides' attack and fought for Apollodotus or Menander or both against Eucratides, and that, after Eucratides retired, Menander made him his sub-king in Gandhāra; if he hated Eucratides as heartily as did his cousin Demetrius II, he was the right man to guard the frontier province. His title Nikephoros, the Victorious, must refer to some success gained against Eucratides in Menander's war with him, the only occasion on which there could have been a Euthydemid success; this, and the fact that the treaty must have given Menander Gandhāra, are reasons for supposing that Menander may have recovered that province from

it was a legionary's mascot, just as Eucratides' unique gold stater was once an Afghan officer's signet. For some strange instances of mascots see S. Yeivin, *Ann. Serv.* XXXII, 1932, p. 152.

[1] Whitehead, *NC* p. 312.

[2] M. F. C. Martin, *JASB* XXIII, 1927 (pub. 1929), Num. Supp. XL p. 18.

[3] Zoilus Dikaios *may* have been another, see p. 319.

[4] Martin saw 969 coins (drachmae)—95 of Apollodotus, 721 of Menander, 152 of Antimachus II, and one of Zoilus—and believes that at least 1200 reached Peshawur. The man who *formed* a hoard was not necessarily the man who *buried* it; the Zoilus coin may have belonged to the subsequent owner of the hoard who buried it.

[5] This could almost have been deduced from a hoard found in 1877 in a village in Bundelkhund south of the Jumna (V. A. Smith, *Ind. Ant.* XXXIII, 1904, p. 217) which contained 34 coins of Apollodotus (Soter), 40 of Menander, and 21 of Antimachus II, together with 3 of Eucratides.

Eucratides by force of arms, for Eucratides' recall from India was so urgent that it would seem that his treaty with Menander can only have been one hastily arranged on the basis of each keeping what he had. What clinches the matter is that all Antimachus' four monograms are said to occur frequently on Menander's coins:[1] he was therefore Menander's sub-king, and his money, as was not unusual with sub-kings, was struck for him in his suzerain's mints. His two characteristic types are the Gorgon-head, used by Demetrius and Menander,[2] and a new type, 'King on prancing horse';[3] this latter was imitated by several later kings,[4] who might therefore perhaps be his descendants. He was only a younger son of a younger son, who can have brought Menander little but his sword; juridically he had no claim to rule India which could compare with that of Menander's wife Agathocleia, and it is likely enough that the suggestion that he was content to serve Menander as the one remaining bulwark against Eucratides[5] is correct. Like Apollodotus, he never put his own portrait on his coins: whether it is conceivable that we have his portrait from Seleuceia is discussed in Appendix 8.

In the south-west, Menander certainly ruled in Barygaza for a number of years, which may be taken to mean from Apollodotus' death to his own; the evidence is precisely the same as for the rule of Apollodotus (see p. 149) and need not be repeated. This implies that he ruled the whole of the Indus country and southward to Gujerat. But Ujjain and Avanti were now Pushyamitra's (pp. 164, 165 n. 1), which means that if they had belonged to Apollodotus they had been lost or abandoned just as Pātaliputra had been abandoned; if so, Madhyamikā must have been abandoned also and Greek rule confined to the coastal provinces. But here the important evidence is that of Claudius Ptolemy, which has been several times alluded to; and I must now turn to that writer.

We possess in Ptolemy some fragments of what must once have been a complete list of the provinces into which the Greek empire in India was divided.[6] These fragments have never been noticed, since it

[1] Martin *op. cit.* p. 19.

[2] Antimachus, *BMC* p. 55; Demetrius, *ib.* p. 7 no. 14; Menander, *ib.* p. 49 nos. 59–62.

[3] *Ib.* p. 55.

[4] Philoxenus, Hippostratus, Nicias, and the Hermaeus-Calliope coins: *CHI* p. 586. See Chap. VIII.

[5] Martin *op. cit.* p. 19.

[6] Ptol. VII, 1, 55 and 42; the latter includes two fragments.

was not possible to identify them till the -ηνη names in the Seleucid empire and its Succession states had been examined, and this was not done till 1929.[1] This matter has already been fully explained,[2] and it may be taken that, east of the Euphrates, names in -ηνη and -ιανη, the forms which provide a touchstone, are practically never used for anything but the Seleucid eparchies or the satrapal (*i.e.* primary) provinces of some kingdom which had either possessed the Seleucid organisation or was copying that organisation, whether at first or at second hand. In particular, the usage of Ptolemy himself with respect to the -ηνη names is both strict and consistent; and if therefore he locates a group of -ηνη names in India, a country where Greek had never before been used, it does not seem open to doubt that they are the provinces of a Greek kingdom (see further p. 240), especially as for Indian districts which were never ruled by Greeks he uses a different form of ending in -κη, as Larike, Anariake, Prasiake.[3]

A word must be said about Ptolemy's sources and methods.[4] As a geographer he was extremely painstaking but devoid of critical and historical instinct; he collected or had at his disposal a vast mass of material from every kind of source and of many different dates and set himself conscientiously to work everything in, somehow or other; he illustrates what a nuisance learning divorced from criticism can be. Many of his sources were itineraries compiled by merchants or other people; these he plotted out on his maps, deducting a regular percentage for exaggeration of distances, and located the places named accordingly. But itineraries were seldom exact, and different men may exaggerate differently or not at all; also they were of different dates and might call the same place by different names; he sometimes therefore arrived at the result of the same city existing in two places, and as he knew nothing about inner Asia himself he made two cities of it. Thus he makes Arsacia-Europus[5] and Bactra-Zariaspa[6] in each case two different cities,

[1] Tarn, *SP Stud.* § IV. [2] P. 3 and App. 2.

[3] So in Thrace (III, 11, 8–9) all his provinces end in -κη, because it never received the Seleucid organisation.

[4] I am speaking throughout only of the *ultimate* sources of the work we call Ptolemy's, without prejudice to the question of how much he took from Marinus and Marinus' painstaking collection of material (see Honigmann, *Marinos von Tyros* in PW) or of how the ultimate sources reached him; such questions do not affect my object, which is to bring out the Hellenistic material in the work.

[5] VI, 2, 16 and 17. Both are names of Rhagae, Strabo XI, 524.

[6] VI, 11, 7 and 9; see p. 114 n. 5.

things which have taken in some modern writers; he puts Isagouros near Taxila but the Isagouroi on the Pamir;[1] his finest example is in the well-known Transjordania, where Rabbath-ammon and Philadelphia have become different cities located in different subsections of his list, which shows that he was using two documents of different periods.[2] Naturally boundaries of provinces or kingdoms varied greatly at different periods, but all periods with Ptolemy go in on one flat plane; so we get things like the Astauenoi located both in Aria and Hyrcania,[3] because *at different times* that may have been true. One has therefore, over each separate bit of information, to seek the date of the ultimate source he is using. A good example is his extraordinary Margiane (p. 89), where the first question is, at what date can we find a province or kingdom which may have given rise to his account? Having plotted out the position of his cities from itineraries or what not, he then proceeded to determine the latitude and longitude of the position chosen; in inner Asia, at any rate, the only value of his co-ordinates is to indicate that a place probably stood *somewhere* in that locality or to give very roughly its *relative* position. The idea that he had at his disposal a number of towns whose latitude and longitude had been determined by somebody on the spot, because Hipparchus had expressed a hope that one day this might be done, is, at any rate for inner Asia, quite out of the question.[4]

Consequently, as regards the Greek provinces in India, the first thing to consider is the date of Ptolemy's information. Some of these provinces he locates in 'Indo-Scythia',[5] the kingdom of the Sacas in India, which stops part of the way up the Indus, Abiria being the northernmost province (I shall take the several provinces presently). His source here then dates from a time when the Sacas, who went *up* the Indus from Abiria, had not yet reached the Punjab; and this intermediate stage in the Saca advance must have been stable long enough for it to find its way into history. Now 'Indo-Scythia' belongs to the generation which centres on 100 B.C.; the Saca invasion of India may have begun any time after about 120, and the Sacas reached Taxila

[1] Lévi, *JA* 1915 p. 85, who adds that in the Hindu-Kush region Ptolemy often takes a name from two different itineraries without seeing that it is the same.

[2] He gives Philadelphia under the Syrian Decapolis (v, 15–23) but 'Ραβαθμών under Arabia Petraea (v, 17, 3), *i.e.* from a document of the period of Nabataean rule.

[3] VI, 9 and 17.

[4] Berthelot believed this, p. 117, and called it 'une vaste enquête'.

[5] Ptol. VII, 1, 55.

before *c.* 77 B.C. but only shortly before, since on the Taxila copper-plate of that date Maues is not yet, as he is on the majority of his coins, Great King of Kings;[1] one may say therefore that the latest date for the advance northward from Abiria would be *c.* 80 B.C. Ptolemy's kingdom of 'Indo-Scythia' will thus belong in the period *c.* 110 to *c.* 80 B.C., and *c.* 80 is the latest possible date for his ultimate source for the North-West, since in his north-western India the Sacas have not yet appeared. The Greek names of the provinces in his 'Indo-Scythia' were obviously not given to them by Sacas but by Greeks before the Sacas came; the names are therefore second century B.C., and in one case, Abiria, this can be proved from Patañjali (p. 235). But if the Greek names continued to be used in the Saca period, as they evidently were, then they were well-established names, that is, they go back some way into the second century. Now as the three fragments in Ptolemy which we possess belong to widely separated districts—Sind with Kathiawar, Gandhāra, and the eastern Punjab—there must once have been in existence a complete list of the Greek provinces in India, something like the list given by Hieronymus of Cardia of the satrapies of Alexander's empire (p. 46); and as the names in the list, as has been seen, go well back into the second century B.C., there is no reasonable doubt that the list, whatever the date of its compilation, referred to the flourishing period of Greek rule, whether before the death of Demetrius or during the reign of Menander. Whether the original was an official or a historian's list cannot be said, but there can be little doubt that the writer who reproduced the list if it was official or compiled it if it was not, and from whom bits of it ultimately reached Ptolemy, was the historian whom I have called 'Trogus' source' (see p. 46) and who completed his history round about 85 B.C. and included in it an account of the reign of Menander.

The first fragment gives the Greek names of certain provinces in Ptolemy's 'Indo-Scythia'.[2] It begins with Patalene, the Indus Delta country, a province whose name and location are well known from Strabo. North of Patalene lies Abiria. South of Patalene, past the mouths of the Indus and round the 'Kanthian Gulf', lies Surastrene. Ptolemy knows absolutely nothing of the coast line here; he does not

[1] See on the invasion Chap. VIII, pp. 320 *sqq.* and App. 16, especially p. 501.

[2] VII, 1, 55: *'Ινδοσκυθία, ταυτῆς δ' ἡ μὲν παρὰ τὸν διαμερισμὸν τῶν στομάτων* (of the Indus) *Παταληνή, καὶ ἡ ὑπερκειμένη αὐτῆς 'Αβιρία, ἡ δὲ παρὰ τὰ στόματα τοῦ "Ινδου καὶ τὸν Κανθικὸν κόλπον Συραστρηνή* (Renou's text).

know of the Rann of Cutch, of Cutch, or of Kathiawar; his 'Kanthian Gulf' extends in a flat curve from the Indus mouth to the coast of Gujerat,[1] and his Surastrene apparently extends northward to adjoin Patalene, which would make a province of unmanageable size and cannot possibly be right. Surastrene, Apollodorus' 'kingdom called of Saraostos' (p. 147), included both Kathiawar (Surāshtra) and, as the name has been preserved in the modern Surat, part of Gujerat also, *i.e.* the eastern coast of the Gulf of Cambaye with Surat and Barygaza (Broach); indeed the Periplus,[2] about the middle of the first century A.D. (p. 148 n. 4), says explicitly that Surastrene included part of Gujerat, and though, strictly speaking, this may not be evidence for the state of things two centuries earlier, Ptolemy leaves little room for doubting that the Sacas retained the Greek provinces. But Apollodorus mentions a second kingdom, also on the coast, that of Sigerdis (pp. 147 *sq.*), as held (imperfect tense, *i.e.* held for some time) by the Greeks; there must have been another province corresponding to this kingdom, and as it was on the sea it must have lain between Patalene and Surastrene and have included among other things Cutch; the only alternative would be to place it south of Surastrene, which need not be seriously considered. Now it was traditional at a later time that Sind should be divided into four provinces[3]—Upper and Middle Sind along the Indus, Lower Sind which was the Delta country and corresponded nearly enough to the Greek Patalene, and Chach (Cutch).[4] So Hsüan Tsiang found it; but Cutch, according to the dimensions he gives, was far larger than the peninsula of that name and was supposed by Cunningham to have also included the country north of the Rann,[5] and this supplies a *prima facie* reason for supposing that there was a Greek province whose name is lost between Patalene and Surastrene, roughly corresponding to the later province of Cutch. It has been seen that, beside Demetrias in Patalene, another Greek city with a (probably) dynastic name, Theophila, stood somewhere east of Patalene (p. 147): Greek cities in India were so scarce that Theophila must have been the capital of a province, and as it was much too far north to be the capital of Surastrene I take

1 See the map in Berthelot facing p. 312 and cf. p. 319.

2 *Periplus* 41, τὰ δὲ παραθαλάσσια (of his Ariake) Συραστρηνή.

3 Cunningham, *Geog.* p. 285.

4 Chach means 'sea-coast land', Mazumdar in Cunningham, *Geog.* p. 696.

5 *Op. cit.* p. 347, but see Mazumdar's note. See also on Chach T. Watters, *On Yuan Chwang's travels in India* II, 1905, p. 245.

it to have been the capital of the province corresponding to the later Cutch. This does not necessarily mean that Ptolemy was wrong; for the form of his sentence about Surastrene is such that the name of a province could easily have dropped out.[1] Theophila can no more have been a completely new Greek foundation than Demetrias in Patalene; it would be an Indian town resettled and was probably the later Minnagara, 'Min town',[2] a capital of the Parthians, which also stood somewhere eastward of the Indus Delta;[3] it is noteworthy that in the twelfth century an Arab writer recorded that a 'descendant of Alexander' was ruling in Minnagara,[4] which might be an Islamite legend but might also mean that Minnagara had once been Greek. The Greek names of both Patalene and Surastrene lasted long, as can be seen from Strabo and the Periplus; both provinces were therefore under Greek rule long enough for the names to become well established, and this is confirmed by the curious discovery that the women of Surastrene continued to use as a form of greeting the Greek *χαίρειν* or *χαῖρε*.[5] Whether Junagarh, the old capital of Kathiawar, be Yonagarh, 'Greek-town', as has been suggested, I do not know.

Ptolemy's third province, Abiria, northward of Patalene, is also a good Greek form and is named from the Abhīras. Patañjali locates this people, about the end of the second century B.C. (p. 146 n. 3), in Sindhudeça,[6] the 'country of the Indus', which supplies an additional

[1] This is not apparent in Renou's text (set out p. 233 n. 2), based on *X* (on the MSS see App. 13). But the note in Renou's apparatus, p. 25, shows that *Γ* and *ω* read *ἡ δὲ περὶ τὰ στόματα τοῦ Ἴνδου* for *παρὰ* of *X* (which cannot be right, as Patalene was *περὶ*) and that *Γ* also inserts a second *ἡ περὶ*, thus making a reading *ἡ δὲ περὶ* (read *παρὰ*) *τὰ στόματα τοῦ Ἴνδου καὶ ἡ περὶ τὸν Κανθικὸν κόλπον Συραστρηνή*, which certainly suggests the loss of a province-name after *Ἴνδου*. The name may have fallen out early and the lacuna been smoothed over in *X* and *ω*.

[2] Cunningham, *Geog.* p. 334, suggested that Min nagara was connected with Isidore's Min in Sakastene. Min should be Saca, while Minnagara was a capital of the Parthian Gondophares; but it may have been a Saca capital first. Herzfeld, *Sakastan* p. 4, notices the connection, but does not elucidate Min.

[3] *Periplus* 38, to one going eastward along the coast from the Indus Minnagara is *μεσόγειος*. Not to be confused with the other Minnagara between Barygaza and Ujjain, *Periplus* 41, Ptol. VII, 1, 62.

[4] Cunningham, *Geog.* p. 336.

[5] A. Weber, *Indische Studien* IV pp. 269–70, 349–50; IX p. 380; *Berlin SB* 1890 p. 911; he cites a Shikshā, but their dates vary enormously (Winternitz, Eng. Tr. I pp. 282–5) and I have no means of ascertaining the date.

[6] See A. B. Keith, *A History of Sanscrit Literature* 1928 p. 33, who however misplaces Patañjali's Sindhudeça; its natural meaning is in agreement with Ptolemy, and what Kālidāsa may have said some six centuries later does not affect the matter.

proof that the list of provinces behind Ptolemy's sources refers to the second century, for at a later time the Abhīras moved much farther southward and founded a kingdom in Avanti.[1] Ptolemy's Abiria must have corresponded in main outline to the later province of Middle Sind. But this only takes us part of the way up the Indus, and there must have been another Greek province between Abiria and the confluence of the Punjab rivers with the Indus, corresponding to the later province of Upper Sind. The name of this province has, I think, been preserved by Pliny (VI, 71), doubtless ultimately from the same list which lies behind Ptolemy's sources: he says that the Indus formed two islands, a very large one called Prasiane and a smaller one called Patala; and Prasiane, a properly formed eparchy name, should be the name of the Indus province north of Abiria. The explanation of this 'island', which only means a piece of land between two pieces of water,[2] is given by Aristobulus,[3] who says that when he was there the Indus had recently changed its course into 'the much deeper channel' to the eastward—doubtless the Hakra channel—and that an enormous tract of country was perishing for want of water. Presumably therefore, at the date of Pliny's information, the Indus was running in *both* channels and a long tract of country between them was fertile; Prasiane means 'the eastern country', *i.e.* east of the Indus channel proper, but the province would include far more than the actual 'island'. The strange view sometimes put forward,[4] that during the Greek period the Indus and

[1] Indian evidence in V. A. Smith[4] p. 290. They had moved southward before the time of the *Periplus* (41). The Paikuli inscription also puts them near Avanti, Herzfeld *Sakastan* p. 90 no. 2, and one of the Nasik cave inscriptions mentions an Abhīra king, *Arch. Survey of Western India* IV, 1883, p. 103 no. 12.

[2] Cunningham, *Geog.* p. 251 and map IX, thought that the Indus sometimes made a true island just north of Patalene; but this could not be Pliny's island, as it would be in Abiria, while Prasiane is an eparchy name itself. The word 'island' here must ultimately represent the Sanscrit *dvīpa*, doab, which means any tract of land between two rivers (cf. *CHI* p. 550), a usage common everywhere; Arab geographers called Mesopotamia *el jezireh*, 'the island' (J. Kirste, *Wien SB* 182, 1918, Abh. 2 p. 72), and compare the long peninsula in Scotland called the Black Isle of Cromarty.

[3] Strabo XV, 693, *ἐκτραπομένου* (the Indus) *εἰς τὸ ἕτερον ἐν ἀριστερᾷ κοιλότερον πολύ*. The definite article shows that two channels were well known. Jacoby in *F. Gr. Hist.* no. 139 fr. 35 prints a bad conjecture, *τι* for *τό*.

[4] *E.g.* Berthelot pp. 269, 271–3, and Ernst Meyer on the Beas, *Klio* XXI, 1927, p. 183. On the known changes see Cunningham *Geog.* pp. 253–6; R. B. Whitehead, *Ind. Ant.* 1932 p. 162; and for the Indus especially, H. Cousens, *Memoirs of the Arch. Survey of India* XLVI, 1929, who (pp. 3–6) concludes that there were many different channels, often altering, and that we do not really *know* anything. Doubt-

its tributaries ran precisely as they do to-day, hardly requires mention; Aristobulus and Pliny's source are evidence enough of changes within the period itself, which is all that concerns me here. Prasiane has of course nothing to do with the Prasii, the 'Easterners' of Magadha on the Ganges, whose country Ptolemy (VII, 1, 53) calls Prasiake.

South of the Punjab, then, the Greeks made five provinces, substantially according with later divisions of the country, their names from north to south being Prasiane, Abiria, Patalene, (Cutch), Surastrene, the Greek name of the fourth being lost. What sort of provinces they were will be considered later.

The second fragment of the list (VII, 1, 42) gives two names of provinces in the Gandhāra kingdom, Souastene (Swat) and Goruaia, which is the alternative form of Goryene (cf. p. 3). Souastene must be Lower and perhaps Middle Swat; how far up the river Greek rule extended cannot be said,[1] for though Ptolemy describes Souastene as below the sources of the Swat river, it does not follow that anyone knew where those sources were. Goruaia must be the province between the Gouraios (lower Swat river) and the Kunar, the modern Bajaur.[2] Omitting Gandaritis, which *might* only mean Gandhāra generally,[3] one other province of Gandhāra is known from Arrian, Peucelaïtis,[4] the province along and north of the Kabul river with the capital Peucela[5] (Pushkalāvatī, now Charsadda).

less V. A. Smith went too far the other way; but it is strange that no one has discovered the Aristobulus passage.

[1] Sir A. Stein, *On Alexander's track to the Indus* 1929, found Graeco-Buddhist art motives still freely employed in wood carvings, not only in Middle Swat (p. 64) but as far north as Branial (p. 93). But this does not mean that Greeks ever ruled there.

[2] Berthelot, p. 279, would derive the name Goruaia not from the river but from Ptolemy's town Gorya, the Gorys of Strabo XV, 697, which he places on the Kunar. The derivation seems probable; but Strabo is here most confused and it is impossible to be sure that his 'Choaspes' on which Gorys stands means the Kunar; most probably it is meant for the united Panjshir-Ghorband river (p. 97 n. 2). But Goruaia certainly extended to the Kunar, for Ptolemy makes it include Nagara-Dionysopolis, the site of which has been identified (near Jalalabad).

[3] See p. 445 for two cases of eparchy names improperly used.

[4] In Arr. *Ind.* 4, 11 nearly all the MSS give *Πευκελαΐτιδι* (for the district), which on the analogy of a number of province-names in *-ιτις* is preferable to the *Πευκελαῶτις* of Arr. *Anab.* IV, 22, 7. Various other spellings have been proposed. It was not of course called Peucelaïtis when Alexander arrived; Arrian, as so often, is using the later Greek name proleptically.

[5] The MSS of Arr. *Ind.* 1, 8 give the Greek name of the capital as *Πεύκελα* or *Πεύκελλα*, and later writers give for the inhabitants the forms *Πευκαλεῖς* and in

We know then three of the Greek provinces: Goruaia (Bajaur), Souastene (Swat), and Peucelaïtis (between Swat and the Kabul river); there must have been two others at least, Buner and the Peshawur country, whose names are lost, though conceivably one was Gandaritis. Still, taking the western part of Menander's realm from the Paropamisadae border to Surastrene, we are not badly informed about the province-names and can see the outline of the organisation.

But little is actually recorded of the country east of the Indus. A third fragment in Ptolemy (VII, 42) gives the names of two provinces in Menander's home kingdom east of the Jhelum: Kaspeiria,[1] which Ptolemy calls the upper valleys of the Jhelum, Chenab, and Ravi, and which would thus have corresponded to southern Kashmir; and Kulindrene, named from the Kulindas or Kunindas,[2] which he calls the upper valleys of the Beas, Sutlej, Jumna, and Ganges, a statement which cannot be correct as it stands. We can see from some of the other provinces, as Abiria (the Abhīras) and Patalene (the Sauvīras), that there was a natural tendency to make the province coincide with the tribe or people, precisely as in the Seleucid empire; and the Kunindas were only one of several peoples in the eastern Punjab who lay between Sāgala (the Madras) and Mathurā and who must have been included in the Greek empire, not only because of their geographical position but because they started coining at the time which saw the end of Greek rule and the establishment of their independence (pp. 324 *sq.*). This will be considered later; it need only be said here that there must have been other provinces south-east of Sāgala beside Kulindrene—the whole country down to Mathurā could not have been included in one province—though whether each of these peoples formed a separate

Latin Peucalei = *Ποκλάεις* of Ptol. VII, 1, 44; references collected in the Index to Renou, *La géographie de Ptolémée: l'Inde* s.v. *Ποκλάεις* (Peucolis of Pliny VI, 94 can however hardly be the same place). When Arrian, *Anab.* IV, 28, 6 (in the MSS), speaks of *πόλιν Πευκελιῶτιν* he is transferring the name of the province to the city, possibly because the Indian name for the city was Pushkalāvatī, which had become graecised as the *province*-name. But the Greek form Peucela finally affected the Indian form; on the unique autonomous coin of the city the Kharoshthi legend gives Pakhalavadi, *CHI* p. 587. To avoid confusion, I call the city Pushkalāvatī throughout, as that is usually done.

[1] Stephanus' *Κάσπειρος· πόλις Πάρθων προσεχὴς τῇ Ἰνδικῇ* is fictitious; Herzfeld, *Arch. Mitt. aus Iran* I p. 94, has pointed out that it does not come from Herodotus, as Stephanus says, but from the *Bassarica* of Dionysius.

[2] Kulinda usually in literature, Kuninda always on the coins: *BMC India* p. cxxxix. On the interchange of *l* and *n* see Lévi, *JA* 1915 p. 101.

province cannot be said. Unfortunately the topographical indications in the Brihat Samhitā are too generalised to be of use here, and these peoples can only be located by the find-spots of their coins—an unsatisfactory method, but there is nothing better to be had.

The find-spots show that the most northerly people were the wealthy Audumbaras,[1] whose country was on the upper Beas in the Gurdaspūr and Hosiarpur districts, with its centre perhaps about Pathankot; their location shows that Ptolemy has not only made Kulindrene too large but has placed it too far to the north. This people manufactured a fine cotton cloth, kotumbara, which they traded to Sāgala;[2] apparently they were Buddhists,[3] and some of their coins after Greek rule ended imitated Greek types, the 'elephant and humped bull' type of Apollodotus I[4] and the regular type of Demetrius, Heracles standing and crowning himself,[5] so freely imitated by the Sacas. Southward of the Audumbaras were the Trigartas,[6] between the Ravi and the Sutlej with their centre about Jullundur, and the Kunindas[7] eastward of the Trigartas, somewhere between the Sutlej (Ludhiana district) and the Jumna at Saharanpur in the United Provinces; their centre may have been about Ambala. The coins of the powerful Yaudheyas[8] have been found in many places in the Punjab, but especially between the Sutlej and the Jumna; large finds have been made at Sonipat a little north of Delhi, and many types are said to have come from near Saharanpur. Geographically, their territory can only have lain southward of the Kunindas, with whose coins some of their own have affinities,[9] and of the Trigartas, with whom they are connected in literature;[10] it may perhaps be called the Delhi country with a large extension northward and north-eastward. Lastly come the Ārjunāyanas,[11] somewhere between Delhi and Agra; they must have marched with the Yaudheyas, with whom they are connected both in literature and by coin-legends, and were presumably Mathurā's nearest neighbours.

[1] J. Przyluski, *JA* 1926 p. 1; *BMC India* pp. lxxxiii *sqq*.

[2] Przyluski *op. cit.* pp. 21–2.

[3] The regular type on their coins of the first century B.C. is a stupa, *BMC India* pp. lxxxiii, 122 *sqq*.

[4] *Ib.* pp. 123 nos. 12, 13; 125 no. 23. I take 'Apollodotus Philopator' on p. xv to be a slip.

[5] *Ib.* pp. cxxxiv–v.

[6] *Ib.* p. cxxxix.

[7] *Ib.* p. ci.

[8] *Ib.* pp. cxlvii *sqq*.

[9] *Ib.* p. cxlix.

[10] *Ib.* p. cxxxix.

[11] *Ib.* p. lxxxii.

Which, if any, of these peoples represent the Oxydracae of the Alexander-story, who lived between the Beas and the Sutlej, or whether the Oxydracae had gone south to Malva with their allies the Malli and lost their identity, cannot be said.

These peoples probably cover the whole of Menander's domain between the Madras and the frontier south of Mathurā.[1] No doubt it is unfortunate that Ptolemy's record is so imperfect, and not only in the east; we know nothing of the provinces, which must have existed, in the southern Punjab and in the important kingdom of Taxila. However, when one considers his complete ignorance of the Seleucid organisation and province-names in parts of eastern Iran, one must be very grateful that he has preserved as much as he has done about India.

Of the nine province-names east of the Paropamisadae thus recovered, six—Surastrene, Patalene, Prasiane, Souastene, Goruaia (Goryene), and Kulindrene—have names formed in the usual fashion of Seleucid eparchies, as have the four provinces known in the Paropamisadae (pp. 96 *sq.*); and the other three—Abiria, Kaspeiria, Peucelaïtis—have names of types regularly found among the provinces of Seleucid Succession states, probably also, in their time, Seleucid eparchies. That the Indian conquests therefore were organised in imitation of the Seleucid system, more or less, is obvious; but it is also obvious that these great provinces were not eparchies, that is, subdivisions of satrapies, but were full satrapies, with governors responsible only to the king. The Greek kings of Bactria had already turned the eparchies of Bactria-Sogdiana into satrapies of the Bactrian kingdom (p. 113), and to Greeks from Bactria, like the Euthydemids, it would be the natural thing to give eparchy names to the new satrapies they formed, just as was subsequently done by every Succession state; in both respects Bactria provided the model which Parthia and every other Succession state was ultimately to copy. But in one way these Indian satrapies were a new departure. The Achaemenid satrapies had often been too large to be properly controlled from the centre of the kingdom, and there are indications that Alexander had had some idea of breaking them up.[2] This was not actually done; but the Seleucids had subdivided these satrapies into eparchies, and it was the eparchies, not the satrapies,

[1] There is no means of knowing if or how far his rule extended into the northern part of the United Provinces. Ptolemy's reference to the Ganges *may* mean that it did.

[2] *CAH* VI p. 426.

which speaking generally survived to be the basis of the organisation of Asia when the Seleucid realm broke up. But in India we meet the great satrapies again without the threefold Seleucid subdivision, though the population was probably denser than the Iranian. It looks like a retrograde step; but I do not think that is the explanation. As the organisation of the Seleucid empire was necessarily, from its size, looser than that of Ptolemaic Egypt, so the Greek organisation of India was looser again than that of the Seleucids; and the reason, apart from the lack of sufficient Greeks, must be sought in the retention in large measure of the existing native organisations (p. 259). In both empires the satrapies increased in size as the distance from the centre increased; a Seleucid satrapy in western Asia Minor was a more compact affair than Media or Bactria-Sogdiana, and the Greek satrapies in Gandhāra were of more manageable size than Surastrene. A modern parallel can be seen in the great size of the Highland counties of Scotland as compared to the Lowland.

The Indian satrapies, as one would expect, were governed by generals, *strategoi*, like those of the Seleucids; this is clear from the use of the word *strategoi* on the coins of both Saca and Parthian kings in India.[1] It is perhaps not certainly known what term the Parthians themselves may have used for the governors of their satrapies, but Greek and Jewish writers and scribes as a rule called them satraps, though occasionally they translated the Parthian term by *strategos*, a word borrowed from the Seleucid organisation which they knew;[2] if therefore in the Kharoshthi legends on Saca and Parthian coins in India their moneyers used *stratega* as a translation, they too must have taken it from something *they* knew, which could only be the Greek organisation in India. This conclusion is not affected by the fact that the Sacas, who stepped into the shoes of the Greeks, also used the term

[1] The *strategoi* Aspavarman and Sasas are known from coins, the former under Azes and Gondophares, the latter under Gondophares and Pacores; see *CHI* p. 577; de la Vallée-Poussin p. 271; Herzfeld, *Sakastan* pp. 92, 101. The word is copied exactly, the Indian form (in the genitive) being *strategasa*. Aspavarmasa strategasa also in an inscription, *ASI* 1929–30 p. 62 no. 46.

[2] See the discussion in M. Rostovtzeff and C. B. Welles on *Doura Pg.* 10, *Yale Class. Stud.* II pp. 46 *sq.* and add to the references for 'satrap' Josephus, *Ant.* xx, 24, 54; *SEG* VII, 13 l. 6, on which see Fr. Cumont, *CR Ac. Inscr.* 1931 p. 245; and the Gotarzes inscription (text best in Herzfeld, *Sakastan* p. 80). But I feel no certainty that the *strategos* of *Doura Pg.* 10 was a satrap rather than a military commander in a group of frontier provinces.

satraps,[1] as an Iranian people naturally would. Whether there was any and what subdivision of the more remote satrapies cannot be said, but there was subdivision in the North-West, for inscriptions have revealed the existence there of meridarchs, 'governors of fractions'; of the two known, one[2] was a Greek and belonged to the later period of Greek rule in Swat, and the other,[3] who was certainly an Indian, belonged to the Taxila kingdom and seemingly held office under some Saca king, another proof of how closely the Sacas followed the Greeks. Meridarchs are not heard of in the Seleucid empire except in Palestine, and there only in Jewish writers; it is impossible to say what they mean.[4] In Ptolemaic Egypt the Arsinoite nome, the Fayûm, was, unlike others, divided into three *merides*,[5] but the purpose of this is obscure. It is strange therefore to meet meridarchs in India, and one cannot explain them more closely than as subordinate governors of parts of a satrapy; I imagine that the Greek kings adopted this word because, as they had not the triple Seleucid division of satrapy, eparchy, hyparchy, they could not use the Seleucid terms and only wanted some indefinite word which would express the subdivision of the satrapy into districts.[6] Incidentally it shows that they were acquainted with the Seleucid organisation in Palestine.

It will have been noticed that for the titles of the Greek officials we have largely to go to inscriptions of the Saca period. The Sacas in fact

[1] List of Saca satraps in de la Vallée-Poussin p. 268; see also *CII* p. xxxiv. It seems however that the Saca Great Satraps in Malva and Mathurā were really viceroys, corresponding perhaps to the Greek sub-kings.

[2] Theodorus the meridarch, *CII* no. 1; see F. W. Thomas, *Festschrift Ernst Windisch* 1914 p. 362, and Chap. IX p. 388. The name has recently been read as Theüdata = Theodotus (C. C. Dāsa Gupta, *JRAS* 1933 p. 403); Thomas however (*ib.* p. 405) says that Theodorus still seems to him certain.

[3] *CII* no. 11, from Taxila; the name of the meridarch, a Buddhist by birth, is lost. For his nationality see p. 358 n. 1.

[4] Jos. *Ant.* XV, 216; XII, 261, 264; *I Macc.* x, 65. The usual view is that the meridarch governed some subdivision of a satrapy, but the difficulties are great; see U. Kahrstedt, *Syrische Territorien in hellenistischer Zeit* p. 54, whose own view, that the meridarch was head of the *Selbstverwaltung*, raises other difficulties in turn. It really looks as if καὶ μεριδάρχης in *I Macc.* x, 65 is an unintelligent gloss.

[5] A possible third-century meridarch of the Πολέμωνος μερίς was suggested by B. A. van Groningen, *Aegyptus* XIII p. 21; see however U. Wilcken, *Arch. f. Pap.* XI, 1935, p. 125.

[6] There was an indefinite use; see Stephanus *s.v.* 'Ατροπατία, where Atropatene is called the second μερίς of Media as opposed to Media Magna, and cf. Strabo XVI, 749.

seem to have been no less imitative than their Parthian kinsfolk; though they came up the Indus instead of down, they followed where the Greeks had led, kept the Greek provinces, the Greek system of officials, the Greek coin-names (p. 85 n. 8), the Macedonian month-names (p. 359), and coined in the Greek mints with Greek moneyers.[1] This is not without its importance. The Saca satraps in Mathurā and Surastrene confirm the fact that Greeks had ruled there before them; and their western Great Satraps who, starting from the coastal provinces, at one time conquered and held Ujjain,[2] furnish an additional reason for supposing that Apollodotus, after securing the coastal districts, may have occupied that city, if only for a short time. Though the Saca Great Satraps became practically independent, the Saca system in theory was that of a king ruling in the North-West, with his seat apparently at Taxila, and two Great Satraps (viceroys), one in Mathurā for the east and one in Surastrene for the west; the resemblance of this arrangement to Demetrius' scheme of government as deduced in Chapter IV is patent, and I venture to think furnishes valuable confirmation of the correctness of that deduction.

The towns of the empire, Greek or non-Indian, must now be considered. Ptolemy has preserved a valuable list of those in Menander's home kingdom, but before coming to that one must notice what there is elsewhere. South of the Punjab only two Greek cities are known, Demetrias and Theophila, which have already been considered; there must have been a Greek centre in Surastrene, but it is not known what it was, unless it was Barygaza, the principal port of this period. Alexander's two Alexandrias on the Indus had either never been built or had failed (p. 168); part one of the Milindapañha only knows of one Alexandria, Alexandria of the Caucasus, which can be alluded to without any mark of distinction from others,[3] for Bucephala and Iomousa (*post*) were known by nicknames. Ptolemy's Parabalei on the Indus may perhaps mark a Greek settlement (p. 86 n. 6); but the other names sometimes cited have nothing to do with Greeks or Greek rule. Ptolemy's Pentagramma[4] is not a Greek name, though it may look like one;

[1] Shown by the Greek monograms on their coins.

[2] De la Vallée-Poussin pp. 281 *sqq.*; cf. *CII* pp. xxvii *sqq.* See p. 335.

[3] Trans. Rhys Davids I, p. 127 (82); the name Alasanda in the *Milindapañha* is fully considered p. 421 and n. 4.

[4] VII, I, 57. Pancagrāma has been suggested: Przyluski, *Bull. Soc. Linguistique de Paris* XXVII, 1926, p. 218.

it cannot be separated from names like Asigramma and Naagramma on the Indus[1] and Anouragrammon and Maagrammon in Ceylon,[2] and -gramma is only the Sanscrit -grāma, 'village', as seen in names like Rāmagrāma, Vāsavagrāma, and Udegram in Swat to-day. Similarly his Monoglosson Emporion[3] in Surastrene is only a nickname given by some merchant later to record his astonishment at finding a seaport where there was not the usual medley of tongues. Pliny gives in the Indus Delta a town Xylenopolis or Xylinepolis, founded by Alexander.[4] It was not founded by Alexander or anyone else; it is merely one of Pliny's so common mistakes in transliteration,[5] and in his original source was only ξυλίνη πόλις, 'a wooden town',[6] some native place built of wood instead of brick, as was the Indian custom if the place was liable to be flooded.[7] The ridiculous story given by Curtius (IX, 10, 3) that Alexander founded a number of cities in the Indus Delta, if it means anything, only means that one or two garrisons were left; Justin's Barce (XII, 10, 6) is not worth a thought, as the number of different MS readings shows.[8]

In Gandhāra, Ptolemy gives a town which has a Greek name, 'Nagara which is also Dionysopolis',[9] and which certainly contained a Greek settlement (p. 159); but though the site, a little south-west of Jalalabad, was identified by the French archaeological mission,[10] it was not excavated. The capital Pushkalāvatī, the 'city of lotuses', was organised as a Greek *polis* (p. 136) and has already been described. Its Greek name, Peucela (p. 237 n. 5), might be a Macedonian word, as two Macedonians named Peucolaos are given by Curtius.[11] But a Greek king Peucolaos is known from coins[12] whose name *may* be 'King

[1] Ptol. VII, 1, 57, 61.

[2] *Ib.* VII, 4, 10.

[3] *Ib.* VII, 1, 3.

[4] VI, 96, Xylinepolis ab Alexandro condita.

[5] A rough list of these p. 482 n. 3.

[6] A parallel is the village in Pisidia which Livy (XXXVIII, 15, 7) calls Xyline Come.

[7] Arr. *Ind.* 10, 2.

[8] If Barce be correct, it may be a reflection of the story of Darius I removing Barcaeans to the East.

[9] VII, 1, 42, *Νάγαρα ἡ καὶ Διονυσόπολις*. *Not* Nysa, which was far away.

[10] Foucher, *Afghanistan* p. 279, *CR Ac. Inscr.* 1927 p. 117; R. Grousset, *Sur les traces de Bouddha* 1929 p. 88. It is Nagarahāra, with many Buddhist ruins, 8 km. north of Hadda.

[11] Berve, *Das Alexanderreich* II p. 319 nos. 636, 637. No other ancient writer gives the name.

[12] *Lahore Cat.* p. 80; *CHI* p. 557; Whitehead, *NC* p. 324 no. 20.

Peucela'; and I feel the same difficulty over the Macedonian Peucolaos as over some other names in Curtius, which may have been taken from the Greeks of India and tacked on to the Alexander story.[1] It is more likely that Peucela is taken from the province-name Peucelaïtis, itself an attempt to graecise Pushkalāvatī; similar names of town and province in conjunction, like Tyana-Tyanitis, Gabae-Gabiene, are extremely common, and it is not certain that the town-name is always the original one.

In the Taxila kingdom, Ptolemy's Isagouros or Ithagouros, which looks Greek, seems in fact to be the Indian Jāguda,[2] and it is quite uncertain whether Alexander's Nicaea still existed (p. 328 n. 1). Taxila itself has already been described; it was certainly not a *polis*.

I come now to Ptolemy's list of the towns east of the Jhelum,[3] in Menander's home kingdom, which later was the kingdom of the Greek kings of the eastern group (Chap. VIII). It begins with Bucephala, Sāgala, and Iomousa, continues with a string of Indian and non-Indian names, and ends with Mathurā, to which a Greek phrase is attached. As Mathurā recovered independence somewhere about 100 B.C. (p. 324) the list must, at any rate in part, go back to the second century; this and the fact that Ptolemy has no other similar list suggest that the names of the Greek and Western towns and settlements came to him from a list in 'Trogus' source', just as did the satrapy names; the Indian names, or some of them, might be Ptolemy's own, from his usual materials. It is a commonplace that the whole list in Ptolemy is wrongly orientated, bringing Mathurā, whose position is certain (it is Muttra on the Jumna), down to near the Vindya mountains; but that is easily allowed for, and it does not affect the list itself, only the question of Ptolemy's co-ordinates. The list shows that Alexandria Bucephala, contrary to the usual belief, stood on the east and not on the west bank

[1] Plato (p. 210) and Daedala (pp. 249 *sq.*), as well as Peucolaos. O. Hoffmann, *Die Makedonen* p. 178, does his best to make Peucolaos a Macedonian name, but there is no real evidence. At the same time, if the Greek king was 'King Peucela', Peucelaos may have become Peucolaos because the latter *was* a known name.

[2] Ptol. VII, 1, 45; see Lévi, *JA* 1915 p. 19.

[3] Ptol. VII, 1, 46, 47. In 45 he has explicitly given the towns between the Indus and the Jhelum; 46 therefore starts from beyond (east of) the Jhelum, though his phrase *περὶ τὸν Βιδάσπην* obscures this. As the list runs geographically from Bucephala to Mathurā it certainly relates to Menander's home kingdom. Even Mr Whitehead, who would like to confine Greeks to the northern foothills, admits that Menander ruled Mathurā, *NNM* p. 45.

of the Jhelum; there is in fact other evidence to this effect.[1] It should be feasible to locate and excavate the site of Bucephala; not only would that settle the century-old controversy as to whether Alexander crossed the Jhelum at Jhelum or Jalalpur, but Bucephala would be the likeliest site to give some idea of what a Greek city in India was like. In dealing with this list I will take Iomousa (Ἰώμουσα) first, as it throws light on the question of Sāgala.

No city anywhere was ever officially named Ἰὼ Μοῦσα, 'Hail, O Muse'. The words are the first words of a lyric addressed to the Muse whose name was the name of the city, and the city must have been mentioned or praised in the lyric; the poem, we may suppose, was famous locally, and the citizens, or more likely their neighbours, nicknamed the city from it; I have myself seen the first words of another lyric used in a somewhat similar way.[2] The name of the Muse and her eponymous city was no doubt Calliope, chief of the Nine,[3] for the last Greek king in the Paropamisadae, Hermaeus, married a Calliope who is universally supposed, from the type on their joint coins, to have been a princess from one of the surviving Greek principalities east of the Jhelum (p. 337); the name was at home in Menander's kingdom. But there was another Greek city called Calliope in Comisene,[4] which in the time of Antiochus III was already subject to Parthia; and the natural connection of the two names would be that Calliope in India was started off with settlers from Calliope in Parthia, that is, that some Greek volunteers had quitted Parthia in order to follow Demetrius to India. The Muses had come into fresh prominence in Hellenistic times as goddesses of the Museum at Alexandria and of the philosophic schools at Athens; Muse-names occur in Asia later,[5] and one, a girl called Clio at Susa,[6] is earlier than Menander, but no Muse except Calliope ever gave her name to a city. But 'Calliope' in Parthia was only a popular

[1] The Alexander-historians are all ambiguous; but, beside Ptolemy, the Metz Epitome puts it on the east bank, at the spot where the battle was fought (ed. O. Wagner, *Jahrb. f. klass. Phil.* Supp. Bd. XXVI, 1901, p. 106 §62).

[2] I have known a distinguished man in a public address describe himself as 'a regular Scots-wha-hae Scot'.

[3] Hes. *Theog.* 79; Hymn to Calliope (von Jan, *Musici scriptores Graeci* p. 460 and Supp. p. 44), *Καλλιόπεια σοφὰ μουσῶν προκαθαγέτι τερπνῶν.*

[4] Tscherikower p. 101.

[5] Erato and Ourania, Cumont, *CR Ac. Inscr.* 1932 p. 277; Calliope, *SEG* VI, 803, VII, 296.

[6] *SEG* VII no. 11.

nickname (p. 13), and 'Calliope' in India therefore can have been no more than that; and as Ptolemy's co-ordinates put Iomousa near the confluence of the Chenab and the Indus, it was doubtless the city which Alexander had founded at the confluence of those two rivers;[1] its official name therefore was Alexandria, and it was presumably the capital of the southern Punjab. Iomousa proves for certain that Greek lyrics were being written in Menander's kingdom; it would be astonishing if they were not, seeing that we possess a Greek lyric ode written at Susa half a century or more later.[2]

Sāgala (Sialkot between the Chenab and the Ravi) was Menander's official capital, though doubtless the suggestion is correct that he must also have had a summer capital in the hills.[3] It was certainly not a Greek *polis*[4] but a great Indian city, the capital town of the Madras, though the actual description of it in the Milindapañha is merely that of a great Indian city at large; and though it has been suggested that there was probably a Greek palace quarter,[5] this is very unlikely, seeing that in the parallel case of Demetrius' Taxila no indication of a Greek quarter was found; Greeks must have lived in the Indian city as they did at Taxila. Ptolemy gives a meaningless Greek nickname, *Σάγαλα ἡ καὶ Εὐθυμηδία*, 'Sāgala, also called Euthymedia'. Discussion of the MSS readings has been relegated to Appendix 13, which I must take as read; I have no more doubt than I ever had that the real name was *Εὐθυμέδεια*, Euthymĕdeia. The name usually found in modern books, *Εὐθυδημία*, Euthydēmia, was a conjecture of Bayer, made at a time when knowledge was naturally not at its present level; it has been copied by the majority[6] of writers since, because that was the line of least resistance, and is now so consecrated by repetition that it may be doubtful if any reasoning can displace it; yet it is so impossible that even if it occurred in a MS of Ptolemy (it does not) it would have to be emended. The impossibility is that Euthydemia is a dynastic name and

[1] Arr. *Anab.* VI, 15, 2.

[2] Herodorus' Ode to Apollo, *SEG* VII, 14; see p. 39.

[3] Whitehead, *NC* p. 309.

[4] This would not be affected if Fleet were right (*JRAS* 1913 p. 966) in saying that the correct translation of the *Milindapañha* is 'a city of the Yonakas' and not (as Rhys Davids) 'in the country of the Yonakas'. The *Milinda* describes an Indian town.

[5] Foucher II p. 448.

[6] Of recent years, doubt has been expressed by Sir G. Macdonald, *CHI* p. 446, and Demiéville, p. 46 n. 2.

would therefore have to be a Greek *polis*, while Sāgala was quite certainly not a *polis*. That is conclusive; and another reason is hardly less so. Whenever Ptolemy mentions a preexisting town which had acquired a Hellenistic dynastic name he always puts the dynastic (*i.e.* the official) name first, as was proper, even if it never came into general use;[1] on his practice therefore 'Sāgala, also called Euthydemia' would be an impossible phrase; he would certainly have written 'Euthydemia, also called Sāgala'.

It remains to explain the word Euthymedeia (Εὐθυμέδεια), though it is tolerably obvious. It is a word invented for the occasion, but a properly formed derivative of the Homeric *μέδω, corresponding to a known class of women's names;[2] it may be recalled that the one-time Parthian capital also bore a Homeric nickname, Hekatompylos. But the known feminine names in -μεδεια all seem to be poetical; this fact, and the scansion, show that the word comes from a hexameter verse and is consequently derived from some poem (whether in hexameters or elegiacs), precisely like Iomousa; and the meaning of the word, '(The town of) the upright ruler',[3] shows both that it belongs to Menander's time (Plutarch alludes to the equity of his rule)[4] and that he probably came into the poem somehow. The word became a name for the city precisely as other similar phrases have done for other cities; a traveller from afar, visiting Scotland a century ago, might well have written 'Edinburgh, also called Auld Reekie'. As two inscriptions from Susa in Greek elegiacs, written more than a century later, both introduce compliments to Susa's overlord, Phraates IV of Parthia,[5] there is no difficulty on the technical side. It is possible enough that

[1] III, 16, 19, Ἀντιγόνεια ἡ καὶ Μαντίνεια; IV, 4, 4, Βερενίκη ἡ καὶ Ἑσπερίδες, Ἀρσινόη ἡ καὶ Τεύχειρα; III, 11, 12, Φιλιππόπολις ἡ καὶ Τριμόντιον.

[2] Greek proper names were originally formed from *μέδω on two lines: (*a*) the very common masculine names in -μεδων (list in Bechtel, *Die historische Personennamen der Griechen* pp. 301–2), with corresponding feminine in -μεδουσα, as Ἀστυμέδουσα, Εὐρυμέδουσα, Ἱππομέδουσα (Pape, *Griech. Eigennamen*); (*b*) a rarer masculine form in -μεδης, as Ἀλκιμέδης, Ἀριστομέδης, Διομέδης (Pape), Κλεομέδδεις (Bechtel *ib.*), to which corresponded a feminine, apparently poetical, in -μεδεια, as Ἰφιμέδεια (Pape), Χαλκομέδεια (Nonnus XXXV, *passim*), and the Nereids Πρωτομέδεια and Λαομέδεια in Hesiod, *Theog.* 249, 257; either feminine form might have a variant in -μεδη or -μεδα. Εὐθυμέδεια is therefore a properly formed feminine name.

[3] For εὐθυ- with an ethical sense in compounds cf. εὐθυδικία, εὐθυμαχία.

[4] *Mor.* 821 D; see p. 263.

[5] *SEG* VII, 12, 13.

the poet who coined the word had in mind the name Epiphaneia, '(the city of) the god manifest', given by Menander's enemy Antiochus IV to Ecbatana, now the Parthian capital, and thought that his own king's capital might be given a rival but more honourable title.

Fortunately we possess another word from a poem, presumably the same poem, which does not depend on Ptolemy. The legend on the coins[1] struck by Menander's widow Agathocleia when regent after his death is *βασιλίσσης θεοτρόπου Ἀγαθοκλείας*, 'Of the godlike Queen Agathocleia'. *Θεοτρόπος* is another unique[2] poetical coinage suitable for an hexameter verse, and the reason that the lady used this extraordinary word was that she had been so described in a poem and liked the phrase, which moreover exactly fitted her position (p. 265).[3] The poem in question might only have been some metrical dedication, like the Susa elegiacs, and the description of Agathocleia might be paralleled by the description of Phraates IV in those elegiacs as *παγκράτωρ*; but as both Menander's capital and his queen came into it the poem might also have been a regular Praise of Menander on the lines of Theocritus' Praise of Ptolemy; it is possible that Plutarch's allusion to the equity of Menander's rule ultimately goes back to this poem, though through the medium of 'Trogus' source' (p. 47).

The next name in Ptolemy's list to consider is Daidala (Daedala). There was a district named Daedala in the Rhodian Peraea bordering upon Lycia,[4] and over against it in Lycia a mountain Daedala;[5] a curious repetition of this is found in the Paropamisadae, for Curtius gives there a district Daedala,[6] apparently in or near Bajaur, while Justin, probably from the same source, calls it the Daedalian mountains.[7] Stephanus says the name in Lycia came from Daedalus the Cretan,[8] and Strabo says that the people of the near-by Caunus believed that they

[1] Rapson in *Corolla Numismatica* 1906 p. 245.

[2] Unique at the time. It occurs again in Heliodorus, five centuries later, *Carm. ad Theodosium* v, 250. It is not given in the new Liddell and Scott.

[3] I cannot follow Rapson's suggestion *op. cit.* p. 249 that the word might mean *quae regis vice fungitur* and refer to her regency; I think no Hellenistic coin referring to a regency is known. The word is only a parallel to such a phrase as *θεαῖς ἐναλίγκιος Αὔγη* (mother of Telephus) in a metrical epigram from Pergamum, cited by L. Robert, *BCH* LVII, 1933, p. 541.

[4] Strabo XIV, 651, 664. Ptol. v, 3, 2 puts *Δαίδαλα τόπος* in Lycia.

[5] Strabo XIV, 664–5; so Steph. *s.v.* *Δαίδαλα*.

[6] VIII, 10, 19.

[7] XII, 7, 9, montes Daedalos.

[8] *S.v.* *Δαίδαλα*, where however he wrongly calls it a *πόλις*.

had originally come from Crete;[1] Stephanus too had heard of Menander's Daedala in India, which he calls an Indo-Cretan city.[2] Menander's Daedala then was a military colony of mercenaries;[3] and as Stephanus knows of a settlement of Cretan mercenaries in the Paropamisadae[4] and as the Cretans at this time supplied more mercenaries than any other Greek people,[5] it is safest to follow Stephanus and to conclude that Daedala was a settlement of Cretan mercenaries, though Lycians are possible. But it must remain uncertain whether these mercenaries came to Menander from Crete, from Lycia, or from no farther afield than the Paropamisadae (if Curtius' Daedala really existed, which is none too certain); neither can it be said if Daedala had become a *polis*.

The next name to notice is Salagissa, somewhere east of the Sutlej, which is clearly Selgessos, the alternative name given by Strabo (XII, 569) for the well-known Sagalassos in Pisidia; Salagissa should therefore be a military colony of Pisidian mercenaries, who in the usual way (p. 10) had named the place after their old home. Most of the Anatolian peoples regularly occur as mercenaries,[6] but in the centuries between Alcetas and Labienus, who both raised large forces of Pisidians, this people does not seem to be named very often.[7] But no one will suppose that for three centuries the most warlike race in Asia Minor[8] was not fully utilised, and I have wondered whether the perplexing number of

[1] Strabo XIV, 652.

[2] Ἔστι καὶ Ἰνδικῆς καὶ Κρήτης ἄλλη (πόλις). This does not mean one in India and one in Crete, but 'there is another Daedala Indian-and-Cretan', *i.e.* Indo-Cretan, a Cretan community in India.

[3] A. Foucher has pointed out that some of the troops of Mara in the Gandhāra sculptures may represent Greek mercenaries, I pp. 402–3; II pp. 14–16, 448; figs. 202–4, 306.

[4] *S.v.* Ἀστερουσία; no source given.

[5] Griffith p. 245, and see his index under 'Cretans'.

[6] Material collected by Griffith pp. 134, 251 *sqq.* and see the army of Antiochus III p. 145. For Egypt see J. Lesquier, *Les institutions militaires de l'Égypte sous les Lagides* pp. 319 *sqq.*, with Heichelheim's additions in 'Die auswärtige Bevölkerung in Ptolemäerreich' (*Klio*, Beiheft 18) p. 14 n. 5. Ptol. VI, 5, 3 gives a town (? a military settlement) called Mysia in Parthia.

[7] In Asia I only recall the Aspendus inscription (A. Wilhelm, *Neue Beiträge* IV p. 61; M. Segre, *Aegyptus* XIV p. 253), three Pisidians on stelae from Sidon (L. Robert, *BCH* LIX p. 428), and the army of Antiochus III at Magnesia; but I have not made a search. Robert, *ib.* p. 429 n. 3, says that it is well known that they supplied many mercenaries to many Hellenistic monarchs; a list would have been useful.

[8] Livy XXXVIII, 15, 9, longe optimi bello.

'Mysians' in the armies and settlements of the period—the actual Mysians of Olympus cannot have been too numerous—may not mean that 'Mysian' was military *argot* for any Anatolian Highlander, as sailors to-day call any sailor from northern Europe a 'Dutchman'.

The town however which comes next to Salagissa in Ptolemy's list, Astrassos, raises a difficulty, for while no Astrassos seems known in Asia Minor, Ptolemy has some *-ss-* forms in India which cannot well be Anatolian, like Panassa in Orissa, Sabalassa a mouth of the Indus, and Eragassa Metropolis (? Eran) in Rajputana. Such search as was possible to me among undoubtedly Indian place-names has produced one *-ss-* form, a village Samkassa;[1] add, for what it may be worth, the name given in Greek as Agelasseis.[2] Any particular *-ss-* form might therefore, I suppose, be Indian; but it is to be wished that some philologist acquainted with the Indian languages would examine the *-ss-* forms in Ptolemy's account of India and say how the matter stands.

The conclusion is that the only military settlements of troops from the West made by Menander which can be identified are Daedala and Salagissa; there must have been others, but they would be concealed under native names in the usual way. But Ptolemy's list induces one interesting reflection. It is usually thought that the number of Greeks who joined in the invasion of India cannot have been great, as there must have been a limit to what Bactria could provide. But if, even now, we can trace Greeks who came from a city in Parthia and from Crete, and with them Anatolians from Sagalassos (whom Indians would class under Yavanas), there may well have been many more Yavanas in the armies of Demetrius and his two lieutenants than we should suppose; we may have to reckon with a considerable number of men, adventurers or mercenaries, from the West. Greeks had exaggerated notions of the wealth of India, and distance and difficulty have never hindered the quest for El Dorado.[3]

The last name of importance in Ptolemy's list is Mathurā, *Μόδουρα ἡ τῶν θεῶν*. This is generally rendered either as 'Mathurā of the gods' (which does not translate the Greek) or 'Mathurā the city of the gods',

[1] Cullavagga XII, 1, cited by Przyluski, *Açoka* p. 68.

[2] Diod. XVII, 96, 3.

[3] Compare the venturers to Somaliland for spices (U. Wilcken, *Z. f. ägypt. Sprache* LX, 1925, p. 86; second century B.C.) who comprised a Spartan, a Macedonian, an Italiote, a Massiliote, a Carthaginian, and two Gauls from Marseilles.

and attention is drawn to such things as that Mathurā was the traditional birthplace of Krishna, or was a centre for the diffusion of Buddhism, or was so full of Jain and Buddhist buildings that it looked like a holy city; one might add an inscription of much later date which says that the Vodva stupa at Mathurā was 'built by the gods'.[1] But 'city of the gods' cannot be the correct translation.[2] I can find no instance in Greek, and none has been cited, where with a definite article followed by the genitive of the person the omitted word is 'city'; it is always 'son' or 'daughter'—that is the regular Greek usage—and there is no reason for translating Ptolemy's phrase differently because the genitive of the person is plural and not singular; 'daughter of the gods' is good English[3] and good Latin,[4] and I think good Greek also,[5] especially when you are none too sure just which god it might be. 'Modoura daughter of the gods' would then be an allusion to some story about a goddess or nymph called Modoura, an eponym of the city;[6] Greeks were familiar with city-nymphs—the head of the nymph Cyrene on the coins of her city may be cited[7]—and no doubt Modoura was only the tutelary Yaksha[8] or Yakshī of the city in Greek guise.[9]

This view is supported by an exact parallel from another and greater eastern city, Babylon. A Babylonian Greek, the grammarian Herodicus (p. 41), alluded in an epigram to his city as *θεόπαις Βαβυλών*[10]—

[1] *CHI* p. 167; second century A.D.

[2] It would probably have been Theopolis, as Antioch was called later: H. Delahaye, *Cinq leçons sur la méthode hagiographique* 1934 p. 72. I owe this reference and that in note 5 to Professor Nock.

[3] Tennyson's *Dream of Fair Women.* [4] Virgil, *Ecl.* IV, 49, cara deum suboles.

[5] Hephaestion of Thebes, p. 65, 17 (Engelbrecht): *ὁ γεννώμενος ἐκ θεῶν σπαρήσεται*; cited by E. Norden, *Die Geburt des Kindes* pp. 21, 125.

[6] Lévi, *JA* 1915 p. 91, after noting the strangeness of the phrase, said that Ptolemy had rendered, in the only way possible in Greek, 'le titre de devaputra, fils de dieu, de la dynastie Kushan'. I hope I have shown that Ptolemy's list dates from long before the Kushans.

[7] Cf. *Σίδωνος θεᾶς*, 'the goddess Sidon', on bronze coins of Sidon after 111 B.C., and the stories of the city-nymphs Nicaea and Beroe (Berytus) in Nonnus books XVI and XLI.

[8] Deities might change their sex in foreign hands. Nanaia became male at Asshur, W. Andrae and P. Jensen, *Mitt. d. deutschen Orient Gesellschaft* LX, 1920, p. 21, and Selene on Kanishka's coinage, Cunningham *NC* 1892 p. 73 no. 7 (= *BMC* Pl. XXVI, 9), cf. p. 74.

[9] In the so-called Bacchanalian group from Mathurā, perhaps first century B.C., the drapery of the Yakshis is partially Greek: Ramaprasad Chanda, *ASI* 1922–3 p. 167.

[10] Athen. V, 222 a l. 6.

'Babylon child of a god' or 'of the god'. I understand that there is nothing about this in Babylonian legend or literature. But the Greeks had invented for the city an eponymous nymph, Babylon, who was mother of a certain Arabos,[1] and there was another version which made the mother of Arabos a nymph named Thronia, who is called a daughter of the supreme god of Babylon, Bel;[2] there is no doubt therefore that Thronia and Babylon were the same nymph—Babylon 'of the throne' or 'enthroned' (see p. 188)—that Babylon consequently was the daughter of Bel, and that this was the story to which Herodicus alludes,[3] treating the nymph as the personification of the city—the sort of recondite allusion dear to some Alexandrians. In the same way Ptolemy must witness to some lost story about a nymph Modoura who personified Mathurā and was really an Indian Yakshī.[4]

It is not the only case from India of a lost Greek story. There is a story in Pseudo-Plutarch[5] that every year on the Jhelum an old woman condemned to death was buried alive in a mound called Therogonos, from which serpents then issued. Therogonos has been identified with Theraguhā,[6] a grotto or sacred place near Nandivardana, and I suppose that the serpent story was not invented to explain Therogonos but that the Indian name was turned into Therogonos because of the serpent story; one is reminded of the poisonous serpents of Egypt who congregated at the tomb of the prophet Jeremiah,[7] but the story cannot be complete as we have it, whatever it means. And there is the second Greek name of the Aravalli mountains.[8] The first name, Apokopa, 'precipitous', is a commonplace, and was also given to a headland on the African coast south of Bab-el-Mandeb[9] and to an inlet in South Arabia;[10] but one would like to have the story which caused Greeks to call these mountains 'The vengeance of Heaven'.

[1] Pliny VII, 196. [2] Baumstark, *Babylon* (4) in PW.

[3] Stephanus *s.v. Βαβυλών* knows of a man Babylon son of Bel who was *κτίστης* of the city, but this cannot be what Herodicus had in mind, for a *κτίστης* cannot *personify* a city, while an eponymous nymph can; and it is the city, not its *κτίστης*, whom Herodicus calls *θεόπαις*.

[4] I do not know if it is possible that Modoura could represent the goddess Lakshmī, who appears very often on the coins of Mathurā.

[5] *De fluviis* I, 5. The references are bogus, Susemihl I, p. 865.

[6] Lévi, *JA* 1915 p. 80.

[7] Suidas, *ἀργόλαι*, and the Ethiopian legend of Jeremiah, cited by Ganshinetz, *Agathodaimon* in PW Supp. III.

[8] Ptol. VII, I, 19, *τά τ' Ἀπόκοπα ἃ καλεῖται Ποιναὶ Θεῶν*.

[9] Ptol. I, 17; IV, 7, 11; *Periplus* 15. [10] Marcianus I, 13 (*GGM* I p. 523).

It will be seen from the foregoing review that the actual number of Greek cities with Greek names known in Menander's empire was very small indeed, not more than half a dozen at the most; and though when Greek rule was breaking up and the autonomous city acquired an added importance the number of city-goddesses, *i.e.* the Fortune of some city, appearing on the late Greek and Saca coinage is considerable,[1] there is nothing to show that any places with native names (omitting Peucela-Pushkalāvatī) may have acquired Greek *polis*-organisation, as was certainly the case in Iran (p. 19); for all the city-goddesses on the coins appear to represent three cities only, Alexandria-Kapisa, Pushkalāvatī, and Bucephala. There is however one ray of light on the nature of a *Greek* city in India which is invaluable; it comes from one of the cave inscriptions, and these must now be considered.

In the caves at Nasik, Junnar, and Karli, in the country inland from Bombay, are a number of inscriptions recording religious gifts by Buddhist donors, of which nine are material here:[2] in these nine, seven of the donors call themselves Yavanas and have Indian names, one calls himself a Yonaka and has an Indian name,[3] and the ninth calls himself a Yavana but his name is not given, or has perished.[4] Archaeological considerations put the buildings, and therefore the inscriptions, at Nasik and Karli in the first century B.C.;[5] and it will be seen later that there are grounds for dating the important inscription Nasik 19 about 50–30 B.C. (p. 257 n. 3). Most writers known to me have said that these Yavanas were Greeks who had taken Indian names;[6] but this is as improbable as anything can well be.[7] Very many cases are known throughout Asia, notably in Palestine and Babylonia, of Asiatics who

[1] Philoxenus, *BMC* p. 57 nos. 11–17, Pl. XIII, 10; Hippostratus, *ib.* p. 59 nos. 1, 2, Pl. XIV, 1; Peucolaos, Whitehead *NC* p. 324 no. 20. For a list of the Saca coins see p. 353 n. 1.

[2] Burgess, *Arch. Survey of Western India* IV, 1883: Karli nos. 7, 10, pp. 90–1; Junnar nos. 5, 8, 16, pp. 93–5; Nasik no. 19, p. 114. Three more inscriptions from the Karli cave in which the donors call themselves Yavanas have since been found and published; they are collected, with references, by O. Stein, *Indian Culture* I, 1935, p. 348 nos. 6, 7, 8.

[3] Nasik 19.

[4] Karli 10.

[5] Sir J. Marshall in *CHI* p. 637.

[6] Lévi, *Quid de Graecis* p. 5, was a weighty exception. O. Stein *op. cit.* naturally calls them Indians, in accordance with his paradox that Yavana never means Greek; see p. 417 n. 1.

[7] Some Sacas did take Indian names (p. 174 n. 1), as did the Kushan Vasudeva; but that is not in point.

took Greek names, whether in place of or in addition to their own; but though one reads modern statements (without references) that Greeks took Asiatic names, I have only met with one dubious case, which could be taken either way.[1] And this is common sense; the conqueror does not adopt the nomenclature of the conquered. Possibly some low-class Greek, broken by circumstances, might occasionally 'go native', a fact which would leave no record; possibly some religious fanatic here or there might desire to be known by a name drawn from his adopted religion; these things happen to-day, and are part of human nature. But all these Yavanas were men of substance, able to confer large gifts—no doubt wealthy merchants; five give pillars,[2] one gives two cisterns,[3] another a hall-front,[4] another a refectory for the monastic community;[5] while the ninth, Indragnidatta, excavates a cave and equips it elaborately as a holy place for the worship of all the Buddhas.[6] As he does this for the sake of his parents, and as his father bears an Indian name, it would seem that, if a Greek, he had acquired not only an Indian name but an Indian father, which might be difficult. It is hardly worth arguing; there is no real doubt that these Yavanas were Indians, and what we want to know is why they called themselves Greeks.

Certainly they were not 'culture-Greeks'. One is familiar in Egypt and Western Asia with the 'culture-Greek', an Egyptian or Asiatic who adopted Greek culture, took a Greek name, and probably called himself a Greek; but these men have not taken Greek names, and the culture exhibited in their donations is not Greek but purely Indian.

The explanation is furnished by the nameless donor at Karli, who calls himself, not Yavana, but Dhammayavana.[7] The late Sylvain Lévi's

[1] Epitaph from Babylonia. Haussoullier, *Klio* IX, 1909, p. 362 no. 3 read *'Αριστέας ᾧ ἄλλο ὄνομα 'Αρδύβηλ Τέϊος*, a Greek from Teos who called himself Ardubel, 'servant of Bel'; so E. H. Minns, *JHS* XXXV, 1915, p. 60 n. 135, and W. Otto, *Kulturgeschichte des Altertums* 1925 p. 100 n. 201. Subsequently P. Koschaker, *Sav. Z.* XLVI, 1926, p. 296 n. 4, read *'Αρδυβηλτεῖος*, 'servant of Belit'; Cumont has followed this, and see now *SEG* VII, 38. If this be right, the only reason for supposing the man to be a Greek would be that when Babylonians took Greek names they always put their Babylonian name first, often with their patronymic, and here the order is reversed. The reason may or may not be valid; Babylonian double names usually come from formal contracts where accuracy was essential, while this epitaph is informal.

[2] Karli 7 and 10, and the three given by O. Stein.

[3] Junnar 5. [4] Junnar 16. [5] Junnar 8. [6] Nasik 19 (see p. 257).

[7] Karli 10, Dhenukakata Dhammayavanasa, 'of a Dhammayavana from Dhenukākā'.

translation was 'Yavanus secundum legem',[1] one who had been legally made a Greek (I presume he meant by a grant of citizenship): but, as I understand it, Dhamma (Sanscrit Dharma) is not 'lex',[2] and I am going to venture on another explanation, premising that of course the word here has nothing to do with the Buddhist Dhamma, the sum total of the spirit and precepts of Buddhism. I have read various discussions of the word, and take it to mean the whole duty of a man[3] according to the sphere in life which he occupies; the word always carries a sense of *obligation*[4] (in the legal meaning of that term). Now a common conception in Indian literature, whether Buddhist or non-Buddhist, is the Dharmaraja, the king who does the whole duty of a king; and by analogy Dhammayavana should mean a Greek who does the whole duty of a Greek. The duty of a king was a known thing—primarily to do justice;[5] but what was the duty of a Greek as a Greek? One can seek duty in three spheres, moral, religious, and social-political. Dhamma here does not apply to the moral sphere, for the simple basic moral principles without which civilisation cannot exist were common to every civilised people, to the Jew, the Persian, the Indian equally with the Greek. And it does not apply to the religious sphere, for a Greek as a Greek had no religious duties; no man's religion was anyone's business but his own, and any religious obligations which a Greek might feel were either personal to himself or were part of his duty to his city, *i.e.* not religious at all but political. So we come to the social-political sphere; and here a Greek *had* duties which differentiated him from other men. For normally he was a citizen of an autonomous city, and as such he owed a well-defined set of duties to that city and his fellow-citizens. The Dhamma of a Greek as a Greek, then, was his duty as a citizen of a *polis*, and the Indian who called himself Dhammayavana thereby claimed that he carried out the duties of a Greek *citizen*; that is, he was a citizen of a Greek *polis*. I have therefore reached

[1] *Quid de Graecis* p. 5.

[2] T. W. Rhys Davids, *Buddhist India* pp. 292–4. But I apprehend that he goes too far in saying that it never has 'any one of the various senses attached to the word Law in English'. 'Law' has many non-legal uses; Kipling's 'Jungle Law', for instance, would in Pali be 'the Dhamma of the Jungle'.

[3] The actual phrase is V. A. Smith's.

[4] Mrs Rhys Davids, *Sakya* 1931 pp. 66–7, 73; see the striking Indian commentary which she cites, 'Dhamma is the ought to be done of a doing'.

[5] I think the usual translation of Dharmaraja is King of Justice. See de la Vallée-Poussin p. 194.

by another route what I take to be Lévi's conclusion: this Indian called himself a Yavana because he was a Greek citizen. It is strange that, at the farthest point of the earth's surface which any Greek citizen can so far have reached, we should find these Indian citizens, when long years of excavation at Doura and in Babylonia have failed to throw light on the question of Asiatic citizens in the Greek cities in Asia (pp. 21 *sq.*). But the citizenship of Indians in Greek cities is independently attested by the Kharoshthi monograms on the coins of some of the later kings in the eastern Punjab,[1] which show that their moneyers were sometimes Indians (see pp. 356 *sqq.*).

It is hardly possible to separate these nine Yavanas and it must therefore be supposed that all were Greek citizens.[2] The dedication by Indragnidatta is instructive in this respect.[3] He says that he was a native of the north but dwelt in Datāmitī (*i.e.* Demetrias in Patalene, p. 142), of which city he was therefore a citizen; and he knows enough of the Greek of his day to describe himself, not by the usual Indian term Yavana, but by the current Hellenistic Greek form Yonaka.[4] The notable thing here is that Demetrias was a city with a dynastic name, and so far as can be seen citizenship in Seleucid cities with dynastic names was confined to Greeks (Chap. 1); the Indian citizens of Demetrias therefore constitute a wide departure from Seleucid practice and throw fresh light on Demetrius' policy (p. 181) of making his Indian empire a kind of partnership.

These inscriptions do not mean that the Greek conquest had extended to the latitude of Bombay, or that there was a Greek province

[1] Whitehead *NC* pp. 314, 321 no. 8.

[2] I cannot follow Konow's ingenious but purely philological theory, of which he himself points out one difficulty, that in Junnar 5 and 8 the Yavanas Irila and Çita 'of the Gatas' were Goths from the Vistula; and see O. Stein's criticism, *op. cit.* pp. 349–50. I have failed also to find why Konow calls the Junnar inscriptions second century A.D.; all these Yavanas should be about the same period, and Nasik 19 is earlier (next note). But I am not using Junnar as evidence for anything.

[3] Nasik 19; edited afresh by E. Senart, *Ep. Ind.* VIII, 1905–6, p. 90 no. 18. The material words are Damtāmitīyakasa (Datāmitīyakasa Senart) Yonakasa Dhammadevaputasa Indagnidatasa (Idragnidatasa Senart) 'Of Indragnidatta son of Dhammadeva, a Yonaka of Demetrias'. He called his son Dhammarakshita, the name of the Yona missionary sent by Asoka in the third century to Aparānta (which would include Nasik); he knew enough current Greek to call himself Yonaka, and Demetrias in Patalene still kept its Greek name. As Yonaka was still in use *c.* 50 B.C. (p. 340), while Demetrias had gone out of use in the Roman period, the date ought to lie somewhere between *c.* 50 and *c.* 30 B.C.

[4] See on this word the Excursus pp. 416 *sqq.*

south of Surastrene; these Yavana merchants had doubtless come south for the sake of trade, primarily pepper.[1] Of the donors in the Karli cave, seven, including the five Yavanas, come from an unknown town Dhenukākā, which has accordingly been supposed to be a near-by trading port on the coast; if there is anything in this, the natural location of such a port, looking at the relative positions of Karli, Junnar, and Nasik, would be somewhere about the Bombay inlet (see further p. 372).

In spite of the Greek satrapal organisation it is not difficult now to see what kind of an empire Menander's really was. Asoka's empire, except for his home country of Magadha, had been a loose collection of vassal kings and 'free' peoples under his suzerainty, with a few semi-autonomous[2] cities like Taxila which were strong enough to be able sometimes to take their own line. The empire of the Seleucids was also said to consist of kings, peoples, cities, and dynasts:[3] but the Seleucids had worked hard to modify its Oriental aspect by filling it with Greek settlements. Menander's empire must in reality have been a collection of vassal states and 'free' peoples rather similar to that of Asoka, with some attempt, at any rate in the North, to form settlements. We may suppose that each satrapy contained a small nucleus of Greek officials for purposes of administration and revenue, and that the general of the satrapy, if a Greek, would dispose of a few troops, mercenaries or Indians; there were, we have seen, some military colonies, and this or that strong point would be settled and held by native soldiers from some distant province, like the settlement of the Sibi at Madhyamikā, though Madhyamikā itself had probably been given up. The unifying element must have been similar to that in the Seleucid empire—the king, his mixed army, his Greek (or possibly mixed) bureaucracy; but the bands must of necessity have been looser even than they were in the loosely-knit empire of the Seleucids, and there was no possibility of founding Greek cities on any scale as the Seleucids had done; the only *poleis* actually certain, apart from the two in the Paropamisadae, are Pushkalāvatī (Peucela) in Gandhāra, Bucephala and Iomousa in the Punjab, Demetrias and Theophila in Sind; Nicaea in the Punjab and Dionysopolis in Gandhāra may be possibilities; east of Bucephala there

[1] This is fully discussed in Chap. IX.

[2] Megasthenes mentions some autonomous (? semi-autonomous) cities, Arr. *Ind.* 1, 12.

[3] *OGIS* 229 l. 12.

were only some military colonies. Menander's system then can have borne little resemblance to the Seleucid system of relying on large bodies of Graeco-Macedonian settlers established in cities and military colonies.

The stability of his realm must have largely depended on the co-operation of friendly native elements, and the existing native organisations must often have been retained unaltered. Only one vassal king is actually known, the ruler of Mathurā,[1] though there must have been others, and no doubt a vassal king would sometimes receive the title *strategos* as governor of his country, just as Alexander's vassal-kings Taxiles and Porus had ranked as his satraps;[2] but in such a native vassal-kingdom there *might* also be a military force under a Greek general, like Eudamus in the realm of Porus. Doubtless too there might be an Indian *strategos* over this or that satrapy, just as (not to mention Alexander) Iranian satraps are heard of not only in Bactria but in the kingdoms of Antigonus I and the Seleucids.[3] We get indications later which show that the native organisation of many Indian peoples must have persisted without much change; the peoples of the eastern Punjab were able, as soon as Greek rule ended, to set themselves up as independent kingdoms or republics and start coining (p. 324), and the same must be true of the Abhīras of Abiria, as after Greek rule had ended they moved south in a body and founded a kingdom. It may be taken, on the authority of the Milindapañha (see Excursus), that Menander's Council was composed of men of different races—Greeks, Bactrians, perhaps Anatolians—just as Alexander at the end had made some Persians his kinsmen and introduced them into the *agema*; and doubtless Bactrians (whom Indian writers might class as Yavanas) had some share in high positions. There was of course force behind the satrapal organisation if required, the force of the army; no doubt the western element in the army itself was kept as strong as possible, and even though Menander was cut off both from Bactria and from the possibility of recruiting more Iranian cavalry, the western element in

[1] Regal coinage throughout the second century B.C., *BMC India* pp. cviii *sqq.*, 169 *sqq.*

[2] Diod. XVIII, 3, 2–3.

[3] Bactria: Aspiones of Tapuria (p. 125). Antigonus I: Orontobates of Media, Diod. XIX, 46, 5; Aspeisas of Susiana, *ib.* 55, 1, and see E. S. G. Robinson, *NC* 1921 p. 37. Seleucids: Artabazos of Cilicia, Wilcken, *Grundzüge* I ii no. 1; Hyspaosines, eparch of Mesene, Tarn, *CAH* IX p. 578; Oborzos (? Orobazes) of Persis, Polyaen. VII, 40.

his army may have sufficed for the needs of an empire where the native peoples had no national feeling and where large elements among them were (at any rate for a time) friendly to the government. But his empire, it seems, was essentially an Indian empire with a small Greek ruling caste; it was not a Greek empire, as the Seleucid was meant to be, but something much more in the nature of a partnership, as Demetrius had intended (p. 181); this is further shown by the Indian citizens in the cities, and by Menander, like Demetrius, choosing an Indian city to be his capital. Doubtless the Greek hoped to be the predominant partner, but in actual fact the Indian element in the empire may have had the preponderance; to the bulk of the population it can have made little difference whether their king was named Menander or Asoka, except that we may hope that Greek rule was the milder. Nothing quite like this ever happened elsewhere in the Hellenistic world; it probably went beyond anything of which Alexander had dreamt.

Menander's enormous coinage, found in quantities from Kabul to Mathurā, attests both the size of his empire (since it cannot be supposed that, as sole king, he had a very long reign) and its flourishing commerce. In his time Barygaza was the great port for the sea trade between India and the West—the Red Sea for Egypt and the Persian Gulf for Babylonia; and it was no doubt partly for the sake of trade with the West that the Greeks held Surastrene and its ports. Shipping still had to follow the Gedrosian coast, as Nearchus had done, calling at Patala on the way to and from Barygaza,[1] and some curious allusions to these coasting voyages remain; one notice calls Barygaza 'a port of Gedrosia, very famous',[2] another puts Patalene in Gedrosia,[3] and a third states that 'Alexander forbad the fish-eaters (of Gedrosia) to eat fish',[4] which must mean that someone had sought to make these coasting voyages easier by trying to establish centres of agriculture along the dreary coast of the Mekran; farther west, the number of rivers in Carmania given by Ptolemy (VI, 8) suggests that the coast of that province was well known to voyagers. Trade from the Indian side was no doubt largely carried on in Indian bottoms. For Egypt the southern Arabs were the middlemen; and there must have been middlemen also for the

[1] Pliny VI, 100; see Warmington p. 45. Pliny's notice is from the point of view of the Egyptian trade, but from Carmania eastward it applies equally to that to and from Babylonia. See further pp. 367 *sqq*.

[2] Steph. *s.v.* Barygaza.

[3] Marcianus I, 32 (*GGM* I p. 534).

[4] Pliny VI, 95.

trade from India to Charax Spasinu and Seleuceia, or Graeco-Indian coins would sometimes be found in Babylonia,[1] and Seleucid coins would not be so rare in India. One intermediary would be the wealthy and enterprising Gerrhaeans (p. 62); but as regards coasting voyages they were on the wrong side of the Persian Gulf, and one would expect an exchange depot somewhere on the Iranian coast also. Even before Alexander's day there may have been a centre of maritime trade on the Gulf of Ormuz, the natural place for it, for Nearchus was able to get an Iranian pilot there who knew the coast between the Amanis (Minab) river and the Tigris;[2] and it is a possible hypothesis that, when after the battle of Magnesia the Seleucid empire began to break up in the lands about the Persian Gulf, a Greek state formed for a time in the same district, with its centre and harbour on the Gulf of Ormuz. This question is examined in Appendix 12, but it may be well to indicate here the enormous importance, in the second century, of the Indian trade to Seleuceia; the outburst of prosperity in that city between about the years 175 and 150, as attested by the heavy increase in the output of its mint,[3] coincides with the great period of Greek rule in India.

Menander's regular type on his coins was Athena striding and hurling the thunderbolt, a variant of the widespread Athena Alkis type of Macedonia; she had already been used by Demetrius II (p. 157 n. 1), but doubtless one reason for Menander's adoption of Athena was that she had been one of the three regular deities on the Alexander-coinage and that of the other two Zeus had become closely associated with Antiochus IV and Heracles with the Euthydemids; it may also be that, in adopting the one Greek deity who had practically never been equated with anything Oriental but had remained Greek (see p. 68), he intended to emphasise the fact that, in spite of the predominantly Indian character of his empire, he was still a Greek king. He used two of

[1] A coin of the Bactrian Heliocles was found in the Mandali hoard (p. 270 n. 1), but this would have come down the Hekatompylos-Ecbatana road. It is no objection that no such coins seem to have been found in south Arabia; no one has had the chance of looking. But four Alexander-tetradrachms with Aramaic and Himyarite legends, of about the second century B.C., have come from Susa, *CR Ac. Inscr.* 1934 p. 235; R. Dussaud, *Mélanges Cumont* 1936 I p. 143.

[2] Arr. *Ind.* 37, 2.

[3] McDowell, *Coins from Seleucia* pp. 51–2, with table of average rates of issue. McDowell's dating of this outburst of coining is an extraordinary confirmation of my dating in this book, which he did not know but which was settled and in draft long before his book appeared.

Demetrius' types, the elephant-head (which had been Seleucid)[1] and the head of the Gorgon;[2] his ox-head, another Seleucid type adapted to new conditions,[3] has been thought with some plausibility to signify the mint at Bucephala; his Bactrian camel might mean that he ruled some part of Rajputana with its sands,[4] but is a slender thread to hang theories on. In reality, the significance of the rather striking menagerie of animals on his coins[5] is quite obscure; no other Hellenistic king exhibits a menagerie except his contemporary, the Seleucid Demetrius I.[6] That these two enemies of Eucratides (p. 218) may at some time have entered into political relations with one another is likely enough *a priori*; but no guess can be given as to what the animal coins of these two kings mean.

It has however often been claimed that Menander's coinage displays Buddhist ideas, both in its use of the title δίκαιος, 'Just', and of the symbol of the eight-spoked wheel on one of his bronze issues;[7] but this view must, I think, be rejected. Menander's regular title on his coinage, already explained (pp. 175 *sq.*), was *Soter*; the coins with δίκαιος are very rare, and the elderly portrait on the silver issue shows that he only adopted this title toward the very end of his reign.[8] Certainly δίκαιος is

[1] Seleucid kings: *BMC Sel.* Pls. II, 10, X, 13, XIV, 15; p. 43 no. 1. Demetrius, *BMC* p. 7 no. 16, Pl. III, 2; Menander, *ib.* p. 50 nos. 67–72, Pl. XII, 6.

[2] Demetrius, *BMC*, p. 7 no. 14; Menander, *ib.* p. 49 nos. 59–62, Pl. XII, 2 and 3.

[3] Seleucus I, *BMC Sel.* p. 107 no. 71a; Seleucus II, *ib.* p. 18 no. 31.

[4] Herodotus had heard of the use of camels in the Indian desert, III, 102–5.

[5] *BMC* Pl. XXXI, 8–12: owl (also Pl. XII, 4), dolphin, Bactrian camel, ox-head (also Pl. XII, 5), elephant, boar's head; Pl. XII, 6, elephant's head; p. 50 no. 74, lion or panther.

[6] *BMC Sel.* Pl. XIV, 12–15: lion's head and boar's head, head of panther or hound, griffin's head and stag's head, elephant's head and head of bridled horse; Babelon, *Rois de Syrie* p. 94 no. 739, Pl. XVI, 13, dog's head and head of wild goat.

[7] *BMC* p. 50 no. 73, Pl. XII, 7; another type of this coin, *ASI* 1929–30 p. 65 no. 4. Grousset p. 58 goes further and would see in the elephant-head on one of Menander's coins the elephant of the Conception of Sakyamuni; but Demetrius had used the elephant-head before him (*BMC* p. 7 no. 16) and it was a common Seleucid type. For a possible explanation of these elephant-heads with a bell see p. 164.

[8] Silver issue (four coins known): Whitehead, *Lahore Cat.* p. 59 n. 1. Bronze issue, *BMC* p. 50 no. 74; said to be very rare, Cunningham *NC* 1870 p. 236. The late date is borne out by the monogram on the bronze coin in *BMC*, which is not otherwise known on Menander's coinage, but occurs on coins of his son Strato (*BMC* p. 40 nos. 1, 2) and on an Indian coin of Heliocles (*ib.* p. 23 no. 25). That Menander at the end of his life should have adopted a new title on a few pieces is so strange that one is tempted to suppose that the δίκαιος coins belong to another

translated by Dharmika in the Kharoshthi legend, but the Dharmaraja or 'King of Justice' has his place in Brahman no less than in Buddhist literature. The first Hellenistic king to use δίκαιος, Agathocles, had used it only on his pedigree coins, which were propaganda for Greeks and meant nothing to Indians; it signified 'just' and nothing more, and I see no reason for supposing that on Menander's coins it referred to the Buddhist Dhamma. To Indians it would indeed signify that, like Demetrius (p. 178), he was a Dharmaraja or King of Justice, but that was not specifically Buddhist; the tradition that he ruled with equity found its way even into Plutarch.[1]

But much more important is the wheel. It has often been supposed to be the wheel of the Buddhist Dhamma; but the other symbol on the coin, a palm-branch—the Greek palm of victory—has nothing to do with the Buddhist Dhamma, and the eight-spoked wheel had already occurred on Indian punch-marked coins, where its rarity suggests that it had no religious significance.[2] The palm of victory points inevitably to the other interpretation of Menander's wheel, which has never lacked support: it is the wheel of the Chakravartin[3] (originally a disk of gold placed behind a fire altar to represent the Sun),[4] and it means that Menander claimed, or others claimed for him, that he was a Chakravartin, a King of the Wheel, one of those supreme rulers who from time to time appeared here or there.[5] The power of a Chakravartin, though great, was not unlimited—the dragon-kings of Rāmagrāma had defied Asoka when he desired of them their portion of Buddha's ashes for his redistribution—but it had one constant feature: a Chakravartin

Menander, the missing son of Strato I and father of Strato II, noticing also that the bronze coin, unlike Menander's, uses a dot for omicron. But the elderly portrait is against this; and as the monogram of the bronze coin points to a mint which changed hands, as did Taxila (p. 271), and as the dot for omicron occurs again on coins of Archebius (*BMC* p. 33 nos. 7, 8) and Gondophares (*ib.* p. 103 nos. 3 to 7), it was probably a local experiment at Taxila, like some of the square letters later (p. 327 n. 7).

[1] *Mor.* 821 D, ἐπιεικῶς βασιλεύσαντος. Note the typically Hellenistic term ἐπιεικῶς.

[2] *BMC India* p. xxxii. The type of the coins of the Five Guilds at Taxila had been a sixteen-spoked wheel, *ib.* pp. cxxviii, 216.

[3] Cunningham *NC* 1870 p. 236; Demiéville p. 35; de la Vallée-Poussin p. 148.

[4] A. K. Coomaraswamy, *A history of Indian and Indonesian art* 1927 p. 41.

[5] On the Chakravartin see generally Przyluski, *Açoka* pp. 102, 152; de la Vallée-Poussin pp. 62–4; and cf. D. R. Bhandarkar, *Ind. Ant.* LVII, 1928, p. 117. The main point is well, though unconsciously, put by Appian about Seleucus: δυνατὸς ὢν βιάσασθαι καὶ πιθανὸς προσαγαγέσθαι (*Syr.* 55).

must be able to make—must indeed make—conquests not by the sword alone but by the power of persuasion or of his own attraction; one recalls how Asoka had exalted conquest by the Buddhist Dhamma above that by the sword,[1] and how in the tradition, when Taxila revolted, he reduced it peacefully without recourse to arms. An excellent example of a Chakravartin is T'ai Tsong, the virtual founder of the T'ang dynasty in China, who could subdue Turki invaders by riding forth and looking at them, a really useful accomplishment in a monarch. Now it has already been seen that the aim of the Greek invasion of India was to restore Asoka's empire and that the conquests of Demetrius and his two lieutenants had only very partially been conquests by the sword; Menander, Asoka's successor even if only in a limited sense, might well claim that the honour with which legend had invested Asoka ought to be his also, and that he was a King of the Wheel of Gold.

Two considerations confirm this. It has already been pointed out (p. 217) that Eucratides, when engaged in his struggle with Menander, called himself 'King of Kings' on a coin for his Indian subjects and that this must have had some connection with Menander being a Chakravartin, though it cannot be more exactly defined. But what seems quite conclusive is the story preserved by Plutarch[2] that after Menander's death the cities raised stupas (μνημεῖα) over his ashes. In Buddhist literature four kinds of men, and they only, are described as worthy of stupas[3]—Buddhas, Pratyeka Buddhas (solitary saints), disciples of a Buddha who have become saints, and kings who are Chakravartins; but the Buddhist stupas grew out of the older stupa of the Chakravartin,[4] and it has been shown how the story of the funeral of Gautama Buddha himself was developed in order to make him the equal of such a monarch until the ritual observed became, in the story, nothing but the funeral ritual of a Chakravartin king.[5] There is therefore no doubt about Menander: Plutarch's story means that after death he was believed to have received the honours which tradition said should be paid to a dead Chakravartin.[6]

[1] Rock Edict 13.

[2] Plut. *Mor.* 821 D, E, ultimately from 'Trogus' source' (p. 47).

[3] J. Przyluski, *JA* XV, 1920, p. 48; de la Vallée-Poussin p. 148; P. Mus, *BEFEO* XXXIII, 1933, p. 579.

[4] Mus *op. cit.* pp. 579 *sqq.*

[5] See Przyluski's study of Buddha's funeral in *JA* XI (1918) to XV, especially XI pp. 514 *sqq.* and XV pp. 35, 50; Mus *op. cit.* pp. 580, 582.

[6] Cf. Gutschmid p. 105.

But this was for his Indian subjects. It could not mean much to Greeks; yet there should have been something for them also, and perhaps one can detect what it was. Menander was not a god; indeed in the second century B.C. it was no great distinction to be a god. His queen Agathocleia also was not a goddess; but as we have seen (p. 249) she was 'god-like'. Here comes in Professor Rapson's discovery that some of the portraits of Athena on Menander's coins have the features of Agathocleia;[1] she was not Athena, yet in a sense she might seem to be, as in a sense Antiochus IV might seem to be Zeus. Now to 'woo Athena' had become almost a Hellenistic proverb for the acts of a man who claimed to be exalted above his fellows;[2] still more of course to 'wed Athena', the action attributed, probably without foundation, to Antony at Athens.[3] When Pentheus in Nonnus exclaims that, if the bastard Dionysus be a god, he will be a god too, and proceeds to recount his divine associations, his outburst includes the declaration 'Pallas is my concubine';[4] and though Demetrius the Besieger had *said* that Athena was his sister, Plutarch hints plainly enough that there was more behind.[5] Add that Menander's enemy Antiochus IV had wedded Atargatis, and that it was advisable that he should do no less than Antiochus. The Greek equivalent, then, of his being a King of the Wheel was that he had done what no Greek king before him had done and had wedded Athena, though in a sense to which few would object; for his Athena, portrayed on his coins, was his human wife.[6] Small wonder that, on her own coinage, Agathocleia had herself represented as Athena[7] and called herself 'godlike'.

I come at last to the Menander legend, though the important document for it, the Milindapañha, has had to be treated separately (see Excursus). There is no one concerning whom it is more difficult to distinguish fact from fiction; but the important matter is that he should

[1] *CHI* p. 552 n. 1.

[2] Rhianos l. 14 in Powell, *Collectanea Alexandrina* p. 9, *μνᾶται δ' εὔπηχυν Ἀθήνην*. Cf. the story of Cotys of Thrace in Theopompus, *F. Gr. Hist.* no. 115 fr. 31, and see generally O. Weinreich, *Hermes* LVII, 1932, p. 361; S. Eitrem, *Symb. Osl.* XI, 1932, pp. 13–15.

[3] Tarn in *CAH* X p. 53.

[4] Nonnus XLIV, 167 *sqq.*, 174, *Παλλὰς ἐμὴ παράκοιτις*.

[5] Plut. *Dem.* 24, *εἰ δ' ἄλλο μηδέν*. Living in the Parthenon, he was in modern parlance 'sharing her room'.

[6] In the same way Antony wedded Isis in the form of Cleopatra.

[7] *CHI* p. 589 and Pl. VII, 25.

have had a legend at all. A ruler, to acquire a legend, had to be someone who greatly struck the imagination of his contemporaries; and it is noteworthy that, among Alexander's more immediate successors, whatever their qualities—great rulers, fighters, administrators—not one became the subject of legend, not even Demetrius the Besieger, seemingly so well fitted to be a hero of romance. Of all Alexander's heirs in the West, there was only one with whom legend became busy, Cleopatra VII of Egypt;[1] and if Menander forms the third of a trio of which the other members were Alexander and Cleopatra, he must at the least have been a notable figure in his day. And whether my deduction (see Excursus) that the germ of the Milindapañha is to be found in a Greek document inspired by the Alexander-story be right or wrong, Menander was at any rate again the third, with Alexander and Ptolemy II, in another trio of Hellenistic monarchs who questioned learned men of the East. But though a Greek historian did connect his name with Alexander's (p. 143) and though Greeks may even have played a part in the formation of his legend, that legend, so far as it survives, is essentially Indian and Buddhist.

One standing feature of the mass of Alexander-legends is the attribution to him of acts and things which really belonged to others, whether they lived before or after his lifetime; and a similar feature in Cleopatra's legend is the attribution to her of the works of Alexander himself and of earlier Ptolemies. And in Menander's case, despite the small amount of material which has survived, we can still trace the transfer to him of stories originally told of the Buddha or of Asoka. That his ashes should have been entombed in a stupa or stupas was proper to a dead Chakravartin; but Prinsep recognised long ago that Plutarch's story[2] of his ashes being *divided* among the cities of his kingdom, each one of which raised a stupa over its portion, was a transfer to him of the story in the Book of the Great Decease that the relics of Buddha were divided among eight peoples and enshrined in eight stupas; though it is conceivable that behind the Menander story lay some real political contest for the honour of being his burial-place, like the contest for the corpse of Alexander. Similarly the story which concludes the second part of the Milindapañha, that he handed over his kingdom to his son, retired

[1] On her legend see *CAH* x pp. 36, 38.

[2] *Mor.* 821 D, E. Plutarch has chosen Menander as the true king to contrast with the tyrant Dionysius. But he has the story at many removes: Menander has become τις and rules in Bactria.

from the world, and became not only a Buddhist but an Arhat, is merely a transfer to him of the story that Asoka late in life became an Arhat; and certain preliminaries to the meeting of Menander and Nāgasena in the Milindapañha are supposed to be taken from the story of the meeting of Asoka with Tissa Mogaliputta.[1]

One little item in the first part of the Milinda is illuminating here. The number of Menander's Yonakas, *i.e.* his Council, is given as 500. As history, the number is absurd; the *comitatus* of Alexander has been estimated at something over 100[2]—it is rather guesswork—and certainly no other Hellenistic king can have had more, or even as many; probably the number was usually far smaller. But the Buddha, when he moved from one place to another, had (in Buddhist literature) invariably been accompanied by 500 Arhats,[3] and legend had also made 500 the number of Asoka's ministers, *i.e.* of *his* Council;[4] and the intention of the author of the first part of the Milinda, therefore, when he gave Menander a Council of 500, was that his hero should not fall behind either Buddha or Asoka; the number has been transferred to Menander from their respective legends. Perhaps it is worth adding one more parallel between Menander and Buddha: both in fact were born commoners, but legend soon made them both descendants of a line of kings.[5]

Though India, having no national consciousness, took little enough notice of her numerous foreign invaders, Menander's name, unlike Alexander's, somehow managed to survive, for the Kashmiri poet Ksemendra in the eleventh century A.D. has a story about him which (it has ingeniously been suggested) is a transfer to him of a story first told about the great Kanishka two centuries after his death.[6] It is interesting too that an Indo-Chinese tradition, possibly old, connects with Menander the origin of the most famous statue of Buddha in Indo-China, the statue of Buddha of the Emerald, which Menander's

[1] Demiéville p. 26.

[2] Berve, *Das Alexanderreich* I p. 30.

[3] *Dialogues of the Buddha*, trans. Rhys Davids, I pp. 1, 108, 144, 173, 288, 300, etc. They are mentioned in the *Milinda*, Rhys Davids I p. 298 (207).

[4] Przyluski, *Açoka* pp. 233, 235 (from the Asoka-Avadāna).

[5] For Menander see Excursus p. 421; for Buddha, T. W. Rhys Davids, *Buddhism: its history and literature* 1896 p. 92.

[6] Demiéville p. 43. I have been given very circumstantial details of another story, concerning the fruit of immortality, which was transferred to Menander from an unnamed king, but my informant had lost the reference, and I have been unable to find or verify it.

teacher Nāgasena made out of a magic emerald by supernatural power.[1] But the greatest testimony to Menander's legendary fame is the mere existence of the Milindapañha; the two unknown authors of the two parts of this work had a large choice of Buddhist monarchs whom they could have made protagonists in a Buddhist dialogue, but instead of selecting Asoka or some other Indian king as interlocutor both chose the Yavana Menander. And this brings me to the final question, the question of Menander's real attitude to the Buddhist religion, as opposed to the legendary figure in the Milinda of a great Buddhist monarch.

The idea that Menander ever became a Buddhist in the sense of entering the Order may be dismissed at once; it depends on the story in the second part of the Milinda, which is not history, for the historical Menander did not retire from the world and hand over his throne to his son, but died leaving a son who was a minor and for whom his widow at first ruled as regent. He had an enormous number of Buddhist subjects and he probably could not have maintained his power without their support; politically, therefore, he must have done whatever seemed advisable to ensure that support, for no other course was open to him. It was traditional among Hellenistic rulers to respect, and even to be helpful to, the various religions of the peoples they ruled; but, except for Alexander's relations with Ammon, perhaps the only case known prior to Menander in which they took any *personal* interest in those religions is that of the elder Stratonice, wife and widow of Antiochus I; she at one time belonged to a club in Smyrna whose members were associated for the worship of Anubis, conductor of souls to the land of immortality.[2] It is perfectly possible that Menander went further, politically, than the usual practice, and that he did take a personal interest in Buddhism in the same sort of way that Cleopatra VII was to take a personal interest in the religion of Egypt;[3] but there is no historical tradition. The Questions of Ptolemy II (see Excursus) do not prove that Ptolemy took a personal interest in Judaism, still less that he adopted that faith; and even if the germ of the Milindapañha be a brief Greek Questions of Menander, that would not prove that Menander took a personal interest in Buddhism, still less that he became a Buddhist, even in the sense of giving to that religion the same sort of intellectual assent that was given by many a layman; all it would prove would be that he

[1] G. Cœdès, *BEFEO* xxv, 1925, p. 112; xxx, 1931, p. 448.

[2] Michel 1223.

[3] *CAH* x pp. 36, 67–8, 110–11.

was a great king, one to whom stories might be attached. It is certain enough, of course, that some Indians were of opinion that he stood very close to Buddhism—the mere existence of the Milinda, and the transfer to Menander of stories told of Buddha and Asoka, prove that much, and it may be one reason why he does not appear in the Mahābhārata; but that does not answer the question whether the acts on which these opinions were based were dictated by personal feeling, by policy, or by the same mixture of both as is to be found in Cleopatra's case. No one can prove that Menander was *not* a Buddhist; but his adoption as his coin-type of the one Greek deity who was practically never equated with anything Oriental, Athena, is against it, and on what is known it seems to me quite unsafe to call him a Buddhist even in the limited sense in which Antigonus Gonatas, the nearest analogy, is sometimes called a Stoic. Further than this I do not see how to go.

CHAPTER VII

THE NOMAD CONQUEST OF BACTRIA

AFTER the death of Eucratides his eldest son Heliocles ultimately acquired control of the Bactrian kingdom. It may be supposed that the country rallied to him as the one effective force against the Parthians; the fact that the title on his coins,[1] δίκαιος, The Just, was adopted from the Euthydemids may conceivably mean that he tried to reconcile the Euthydemid partisans. Doubtless the return of the rest of Eucratides' army from India gave him an accession of strength; but whether Mithridates of Parthia was expelled or bought off, or whether the virtual defection of his Sacas (Chap. v) induced him to quit the hostile country which he could hardly have held, and make sure of Seistan and Arachosia which he *could* hold, does not appear. Certainly the outlying provinces of the Bactrian empire in Iran were lost; the Parthian frontier was again the Arius, and (though there is no evidence) Mithridates presumably retained Herat, or he would have had no through communication between Parthia proper and Seistan. Heliocles probably retained Merv; otherwise his kingdom was apparently reduced to Bactria and southern Sogdiana. What happened to northern Sogdiana, the plain of the Jaxartes, will be considered later.

Justin[2], speaking of the result of the wars of Eucratides, says that Bactria bled to death; the statement may be true, though it is put too early, for Heliocles' conquests in India show that the country must still have possessed a fair degree of strength; he would of course retain Eucratides' mercenaries. Heliocles had probably kept what Eucratides had had south of the Hindu Kush, Alexandria-Kapisa and the Paropamisadae, for, as has been seen, there is no real reason to suppose that Menander ever ruled that country; if so, Heliocles held the gateway into India and could, as he subsequently did, invade it when he pleased. Looking at what is now known, it seems that he ought to have conserved his strength for the coming shock from the north; but this may hardly have come into view by the time that he invaded India, and he

[1] *BMC* pp. 21 *sqq.*, p. 166; Whitehead *NC* p. 321. One of his was found in the Mandali hoard, east of the Tigris, which was buried *c.* 90–85 B.C., a long way for a Bactrian coin to travel: E. T. Newell, *NC* 1924 pp. 151, 160.

[2] XLI, 6, 3.

may have thought that the possession of north-west India would strengthen him; probably too he regarded Gandhāra, which his father had conquered and lost again, as his by right. The idea that he wanted India as a refuge against the day when he should be driven out of Bactria may be disregarded; Greek kings did not practise what in modern jargon is called defeatism. The beginning of his reign was probably occupied in getting rid of the Parthians, and in India he made no move while Menander lived; that monarch must have seemed, and perhaps really was, too strong to be attacked. But when he died, leaving his widow regent for his young son, Heliocles at once invaded Gandhāra; some of his coins are found overstruck upon those of Agathocleia's first issue as regent, and others upon those of Strato after he took over the rule.[1] This war then lasted three or four years at least, and its ultimate consequences were in every way disastrous; Heliocles, as the sequel shows, weakened rather than strengthened himself, while Menander's vast and loosely-hung realm began to break up; its maintenance had obviously depended upon his own personality. Heliocles, as his coin-types show, conquered and annexed Gandhāra and Taxila,[2] which drove Strato back upon Menander's original frontier, the Jhelum; and in northern India Strato retained only the eastern Punjab and the country south-eastward to Mathurā. It became more difficult for his government at Sāgala to communicate with Sind and Surastrene; whether he governed them by sub-kings or satraps, the southern provinces may gradually have begun to shift for themselves till they fell a prey to the Sacas; that Barygaza continued indefinitely to use or copy the coins of Apollodotus and Menander and nothing later is eloquent, but really nothing is known of the southern provinces.

Heliocles, when he invaded India, left the younger Eucratides (Eucratides II) to govern Bactria, with the royal title; whether he was his son or younger brother is unknown, but on the ages the latter is much more probable. He struck the coins with a youthful head remarkably like that of Heliocles and the type of Apollo with his bow, holding an arrow in his right hand, and the simple legend 'Of King Eucratides'.[3] These coins used to be called an early issue of

[1] Rapson, *Corolla Numismatica* 1906 pp. 246–7. The belief that Strato overstruck a coin of Heliocles is unfounded, *ib.*

[2] Square bronze bilingual coins with type of humped bull and elephant. The humped bull makes Gandhāra certain; on the elephant as representing Taxila see pp. 163 *sq.*

[3] *CHI* p. 460; see Pl. IV, 8 and 9.

Eucratides (I);[1] but it has been suggested that the face is too young and too like that of Heliocles to be meant for Eucratides himself,[2] and the matter seems settled by a unique coin which recently reached Germany from Russia.[3] The description of it gives the same reverse type, Apollo with his bow and arrow, but on the obverse a 'youngish portrait bust' and the unique legend *βασιλέως σωτῆρος* Εὐκρατίδου, 'Of King Eucratides, Saviour'. Had Eucratides really used the title *σωτήρ* at the start, it is inconceivable that he would have discarded it when he adopted the type of the Saviour gods, the Dioscuri; and this coin seems sufficient proof of the existence of a second Eucratides.

The question was long ago raised whether there was not also a second Heliocles, to whom the bronze bilingual coins struck in India would belong.[4] Certainly the face on the Indian coins is not much like that of Heliocles;[5] but little reliance can be placed on the portraiture upon coins struck in India, the types are those of Heliocles, and no one but himself can have been the conqueror of Gandhāra and Taxila. What would be conceivable, however, is that Heliocles was doing exactly what Demetrius had done; when he invaded India he might have left his eldest son Eucratides II to govern Bactria and then left his second son, another Heliocles, to govern the Paropamisadae, and the younger Heliocles might have coined for his father precisely as Demetrius II had coined for Demetrius, striking coins with his father's types and legend but with his own head. The difficulties in the way of believing this are however considerable. Heliocles' invasion of Gandhāra cannot be later than about 145, if as late, and it is unlikely (see p. 218) that he himself can have been old enough at that time to have had two sons of an age to govern; and even were he older than I have supposed, the head on the Indian coins is not that of a particularly youthful man.

As Menander's death occurred between 150 and 145, Heliocles' war with Strato probably takes us a good deal of the way to 141, when for the last time the Bactrian kingdom is mentioned in literature. While Heliocles was waging civil war, Mithridates I of Parthia had acquired

[1] *BMC* p. 13 nos. 1–5, Pl. V, 4 and 5.

[2] By Sir G. Macdonald in *CHI* p. 460.

[3] Auctioned by Schlessinger in Berlin, 4 Feb. 1935. The particulars are from the sale catalogue, communicated to me by Mr E. S. G. Robinson. I do not know who bought it.

[4] By P. Gardner in *BMC* p. 23.

[5] Plate no. 12.

and was consolidating a very considerable empire, embracing most of Iran (except Bactria) from the Caspian Sea to the Persian Gulf. Late in 142 he made himself master of Babylonia,[1] and in 141 the Seleucid Demetrius II attempted to form a coalition against Parthia to recover that country, his principal ally being 'the Bactrians', which presumably means Heliocles.[2] It is possible that Demetrius II of Syria still claimed to be Heliocles' overlord (p. 206); but if he did it was a claim which had long ceased to have any meaning, like *Fid. Def.* on the British coinage. What he and Heliocles were really attempting was to carry out the plan of Antiochus IV and Eucratides and crush Parthia by a combined attack on two fronts; but what might once have been a simple matter had become impossible, for Parthia was now far too strong and vital to be overthrown by kingdoms past their prime. Mithridates allowed Demetrius II to defeat his generals and recover Babylonia while he himself met Heliocles' invasion of Parthia proper; he was in 'Hyrcania' in December 141 and mastered the situation there quickly enough to allow him to return to Babylonia and defeat and capture Demetrius late in 140 or early in 139. How serious Heliocles' defeat may have been cannot be said, but it may be assumed that it did not do Bactria any good.

Heliocles is usually supposed to have been the last Greek king of Bactria because it was his coins which the nomad conquerors continued to copy, and no doubt he was the last king who effectively ruled the country; but it is possible—the suggestion has been made—that Antialcidas, who succeeded him in the rule of his Indian provinces between the Hindu Kush and the Jhelum (p. 313), may for a time have had some connection with Bactria. Most of Antialcidas' coinage, like that of every Greek king who reigned eastwards of the Hindu Kush, is bilingual, and the silver was struck on the reduced standard usual among the Greek rulers in India; but he struck one silver issue of good coins on the Attic weight-standard which are not bilingual but bear his Greek legend only, 'Of King Antialcidas the Victorious'.[3] It was not a Bactrian coinage; it was issued in India. But the Attic standard and the absence of a Kharoshthi legend may point to this coinage being intended for use in Bactria, and it might mean that,

[1] See Tarn, *CAH* IX pp. 579–80, where the chronology used in this section is discussed.

[2] Justin XXXVI, 1, 4.

[3] *BMC* p. 25 no. 1, βασιλέως νικηφόρου Ἀντιαλκίδου.

though Bactra and the mint there had been lost, he for a time retained some territory to the north of the Hindu Kush; the title *νικηφόρος*, 'The Victorious', might refer to some success against the nomad conquerors.[1] This silver issue is the last appearance of the Attic standard in the Farther East.

In 141 the curtain falls on Greek Bactria, to rise again in 128 upon new peoples and new names; somewhere between these two dates lies the end of the Greek kingdom. The latter date[2] is the year in which the Chinese Chang-k'ien, general and diplomat, was in Bactria, and it is his Report to his emperor which supplies such knowledge as we have of the country immediately after the conquest. It is our misfortune that that acute observer could not have visited Bactria fifty years earlier; in a small way he resembles Strabo, who also deals with a world—the world of the Hellenistic kingdoms—which had just passed away, but he had not Strabo's resource of drawing copiously upon his predecessors, for he had none; to China he was the discoverer of a new world. Though this book is meant to be Greek history, it is pertinent to give a few pages to the conquest and the conquerors of Greek Bactria;[3] the Greek evidence should help to straighten out the story.

Before coming to the details of that conquest one must just glance at the cause of the nomad invasion which swept away the Greek kingdom of Bactria and came near to overrunning Parthia also. It has been powerfully urged[4] that most of the historical invasions of the settled lands of Asia by nomads from the Eurasian steppes, including the one to be described in this chapter, followed fixed laws and were due, in whole or in part, to a regular climatic period,[5] an alternation of humidity and aridity which worked in 600-year cycles; the periodic increase in the fertility of the soil led to an increase in the nomadic

[1] It is no objection to this view that Apollodotus, who never ruled any part of Bactria, struck some silver on the Attic standard (*BMC* p. 34) which is shown by the humped bull on it to have been issued at Pushkālavatī; for this issue was bilingual while that of Antialcidas was not.

[2] I follow the Chavannes-Hirth dating for Chang-k'ien; but the year he spent with the Yueh-chi has also been given as 127–6 and 126. Nothing turns on this for my purpose.

[3] See Appendix 20 on the Chinese sources and the translations used.

[4] A. J. Toynbee, *A Study of History* III (2nd ed. 1935) pp. 395–452. He frankly gives the objections to his view.

[5] The theory worked out by Dr Elsworth Huntington in a number of studies, which has not escaped criticism; see the note by G. F. Hudson in Toynbee *op. cit.* pp. 453–4.

population,[1] and the subsequent decrease of fertility and consequently of the food supply forced the hungry nomads, whose grazing grounds no longer sufficed them, to invade the settled lands. But in the case we have to consider, the movements of the various Saca peoples we shall meet (except the Massagetae) are fully accounted for by the disturbances due to the advent of the Yueh-chi. No doubt the sequel in India shows that the Saca world *was* over-populated, but had it been underpopulated the movements would have been the same; for the ultimate reason why the Sai-wang and the Sacaraucae—one may add the Yueh-chi themselves, for that matter—came south was that they were driven by superior force. The Massagetae alone appear to have been free agents; Bactria and Khorasan had attracted them from the time of Euthydemus (p. 117) and doubtless earlier, and what brought *them* south was not compulsion but opportunity, an opportunity which they did not mean to leave entirely to others.

It would seem, then, that if the movement was really due to the operation of a climatic cycle, that cycle must have operated by starting the Yueh-chi on the long trek which was the cause of all the disturbance. But as the Yueh-chi and the Hiung-nu had long been neighbours, climatic changes which affected the one people should have affected the other; nevertheless the historical record (p. 276) is that the Yueh-chi had cared nothing for the Hiung-nu (*i.e.* were too strong for them) until in the final struggle they suffered a great defeat at their hands and were driven from their grazing grounds, which started the whole movement. The Hiung-nu followed this up by the creation of a regular empire, which might mean that *their* motive force was not so much hunger as imperialism; it looks, too, as if the cause of the final defeat of the Yueh-chi, previously the stronger horde, was not that the Hiung-nu were starving but that they had received a large accession of strength by incorporating some other people or peoples. I have neither the desire nor the knowledge to question either the fact or the potency of the climatic cycle, and the Saca peoples, who were not all nomads but included cultivators and oasis-dwellers, had obviously become too numerous for their lands and were ripe for trouble; I only wish to point out that the whole of the events to be described in this chapter *could* be accounted for quite simply by Hiung-nu imperialism, a foretaste of that of Chingis and his Mongols later, which would mean that

[1] On the ease with which a nomad population may increase, given favourable circumstances, see Prof. F. A. Lindemann in Toynbee *op. cit.* p. 436.

the whole thing originated not in natural causes but in the mental processes of some individual man or group of men.

I must now turn to the particular consideration of the conquest of Bactria. To Chang-k'ien, that conquest was the work of a single great nomad horde, the Ta Yueh-chi. The Yueh-chi[1] (the name is still unexplained) first appear in history in Kan-su, in the north-west of China, where apparently they had been for some time; a struggle between them and another great horde, the Hiung-nu, usually supposed (though it has been doubted) to have been the people known later to the western world as Huns, culminated in 176 or 174 B.C. in their complete defeat, and they quitted Kan-su and set out westward. Part of the horde, called by Chinese writers the Little Yueh-chi (Siao Yueh-chi,[2] in contrast to the larger body, the Ta Yueh-chi or Great Yueh-chi), unable or unwilling to follow, turned southward into the Tarim valley and settled among the Ki'ang, apparently a general term for the border peoples of China in that region; it used to be thought that they formed two kingdoms there, Turfan and Kucha,[3] but that may now be doubtful (see p. 289). The main horde, going westward, fell on the Wu-sun, killed their king, and must have attempted to occupy their grazing lands and been driven out again, presumably by the Hiung-nu. Still going westward, somewhere before 160 they attacked a people called Sai-wang[4] about Lake Issyk Kul and the plain northward of the Alexandrovski range and attempted to occupy their lands; the Sai-wang, or some part of them, fled southward (pp. 277 *sq.*). But in or just before the year 160[5] the Yueh-chi were again attacked by the son of the dead Wu-sun king with the help of the Hiung-nu and were driven out of the

[1] This story, primarily from Ssu-ma Ch'ien, is given, whether fully or otherwise, in many modern books. See especially E. Chavannes' translation of Ssu-ma Ch'ien, *Les mémoires historiques de Se-ma Ts'ien* vol. I, 1895, Introduction pp. lxx *sqq.*; Franke, p. 13 and *passim*; *CHI* pp. 565 *sqq.*; E. H. Minns, *Scythians and Greeks* pp. 92, 121 *sq.*; de Groot pp. 9, 16, 24; Herzfeld, *Sakastan* pp. 14 *sqq.*; Konow, *CII* pp. liii *sqq.* De Groot spells the name Goat-si.

[2] Hirth p. 97; Wylie p. 40. Notices collected by F. W. K. Müller, *Berlin SB* 1918 pp. 570–4.

[3] Grousset pp. 210, 213.

[4] I follow Konow in keeping the Chinese name Sai-wang (Franke's view), literally 'King of the Sai', so as to beg no questions as to who they were. De Groot, p. 25, would prefer to render the name Sak-ke or Sik-ke (*i.e.* Sacas), but admits that Franke may be right; Franke in a note maintains his view. All I want myself is a word which will distinguish this Saca people from others.

[5] This date, established by Franke p. 55, is now a fixed point.

Sai-wang country, of which the Wu-sun took possession; the main body of the Yueh-chi again went westward, though some remained and were ultimately absorbed by the Wu-sun, as were also some Sai-wang elements who had not joined in the flight southward.[1] After 160 the Yueh-chi vanish from view for a generation—a fact which has not been noticed—till we meet them again shortly before 128; their steady progress westward was doubtless primarily to escape from the Hiung-nu, but it is noticeable that they were retracing the road which, on one theory, the Tochari section of the horde may have originally followed from Europe (p. 290).

What ultimately turned them southward is not known. The brief Chinese statement that after the defeat of 160 they went westward and occupied Ta-hia (Bactria)[2] is really two separate statements with a whole generation in time between them, the second statement merely giving the end of a lost chain of events. All we know is that these lost years were occupied in fighting and in attempts to settle somewhere; for in 128 they told Chang-k'ien that they were weary of trekking and fighting and only wanted to live in peace,[3] and this does not refer to the story we know, for by 128 a new generation had grown up to whom the defeats of 174 and 160 were at most only memories of childhood. Sometime between 141 and 128—we shall see that it cannot have been much, if at all, before 130—they crossed the Jaxartes westward of Ferghana,[4] went southward, and put an end to the Greek kingdom of Bactria; in 128 the horde was camped somewhere between Samarcand and the Oxus,[5] not having yet moved across the Oxus into Bactria proper (Ta-hia), though it was theirs, *i.e.* tributary.

The defeated Sai-wang, who are supposed to have been Sacas of some sort, are said in the Ch'ien-han-shu to have moved southward to Ki-pin,[6] or 'over the Hanging Pass' to Ki-pin.[7] It has been sufficiently shown that no horde with its flocks and herds could ever have crossed

[1] Wylie part 2 p. 84; de Groot p. 125.

[2] Wylie p. 34; de Groot p. 87; cf. Hirth p. 97.

[3] Hirth p. 94.

[4] Wylie p. 40; de Groot p. 16; they passed Ta-yuan and attacked Ta-hia on the west. So Hirth p. 97; they crossed (the Jaxartes) to the west of Ta-yuan.

[5] Hirth p. 97; they were living north of the Oxus and subsequently had their capital there.

[6] Wylie p. 34, 'moved south and ruled over Ki-pin'; de Groot p. 87, 'moved south and made themselves masters of Ke-pin'.

[7] Wylie part 2 p. 84 (who translated it as 'Hindu Kush'); Franke p. 58; de Groot p. 125. For the Chinese accounts of the Hanging Pass see de Groot pp. 72, 76–7.

the Hanging Pass;[1] this is a mistake of Pan-ku's own, who knew that it became later the most direct route for Chinese envoys and traders. Also, in the middle of the second century B.C., there was no such place or thing as Ki-pin (see App. 9): it was Pan-ku's usual term for the later Saca realm in India, which did not come into existence on the Indus till somewhere about 110 B.C. and did not extend to northern India till somewhere about 80 B.C.[2] The statement, then, that at some date prior to 160 the Sai-wang went southward to Ki-pin is exactly like the parallel statement that in 160 the Yueh-chi went westward to the Ta-hia: it is two separate statements, of which the second represents the culmination of a long and a lost chain of events: the Sai-wang are, to us, lost to view for at least two generations, but some of them ultimately ended up in Ki-pin, which means that among the Sacas who subsequently invaded India were Sai-wang elements.

The flight of the Sai-wang southward (which probably from the lie of the land means south-westward) would take them across the Jaxartes, to Ferghana or Chodjend. But there was no vacant country south of that river for them to occupy; and as I understand that they are never again mentioned by name in Chinese literature[3] they must have ceased to exist as a separate horde. Some might have joined a horde called K'ang-kiu, whose grazing grounds were the Tashkent plain;[4] but those who subsequently went to Ki-pin must have joined the Sacaraucae[5] (p. 291), who occupied the country about Chodjend and the steppes to the west of it, for it does not appear how otherwise they could have reached India. A horde (or a fraction of a horde) which joined another may sometimes have preserved its separate identity for a considerable time; this supposition is necessitated by (for example) the two components of the Yueh-chi horde (p. 286) and by Ammianus sometimes calling the Alans Massagetae after they had, at two removes, absorbed part of the latter people (p. 307).

The remainder of the Sai-wang horde apparently seized the Greek province of Ferghana (p. 83 and App. 10), their name to Chinese writers becoming merged in that of the province, Ta-yuan. There they

[1] Herzfeld, *Sakastan* p. 20.

[2] See Chap. VI p. 233, Chap. VIII pp. 320 *sqq.*, and App. 16.

[3] Franke p. 61.

[4] Franke p. 67. Chang-k'ien found the K'ang-kiu north (say, rather, north-west, as Herzfeld, *Sakastan* p. 22) of Ta-yuan (Ferghana); Hirth p. 95 §22.

[5] A. Herrmann, *Sacaraucae* in PW, identified the Sai-wang with the Sacaraucae; often followed, but it will not work in that absolute form.

set up the Saca, or rather nomad, government which Chang-k'ien found in 128 (see p. 308); they are represented as distinct from the K'ang-kiu but on good terms with them.[1] It was easy at this time to occupy Ferghana: Eucratides had just overthrown the Euthydemid dynasty, he himself with his army was in India, and in 159 he met his death; the government in Bactria, whatever it was—possibly for a time Mithridates—can in the years after 160 have had no troops to spare for the north; in or just after 159 the Sai-wang could have set up their rule in Ferghana with impunity, and Heliocles, preoccupied first with the recovery of Bactria and then with the invasion of India, must have let this outlying province go. It is of course possible that Saca rule in Ferghana was not set up till *c.* 130; but it is impossible to see what body of Sacas could then have occupied it, while *c.* 159 it is easy. There may have been Sacas in Ferghana since Darius' day (p. 475); but if so they had seemingly long ceased to be nomads, and what Chang-k'ien describes is a ruling stratum of nomads imposed upon an agricultural population.[2]

We must now turn to Chang-k'ien.[3] He was sent in 138 by the Han emperor, Wu-ti, as his envoy to the Yueh-chi to solicit their alliance against the common enemy, the Hiung-nu. Where the Yueh-chi were at the time, and what route Chang-k'ien took, are not recorded, but it is generally supposed that he followed the northern route through Chinese Turkestan to Kashgar; thence he would have taken the route by Irkishtam and the Terek pass to Ferghana (p. 84), which probably shows that he expected to find the Yueh-chi still north of the Jaxartes. On his way through Chinese Turkestan he was captured by the Hiung-nu and kept in more or less honourable captivity for some ten years; finally he escaped with his attendants and proceeded on his mission as though nothing had happened, a fact which illustrates the man's force of character. He reached Ta-yuan (Ferghana); the Saca government passed him through to the K'ang-kiu and they in turn to the Yueh-chi,[4]

[1] Ssu-ma Ch'ien says that a little later (106–101 B.C.) the K'ang-kiu were their allies in their war with China; Hirth p. 113.

[2] There is a difficulty (discussed p. 308) in making out from Ssu-ma Ch'ien exactly what the political position was in Ferghana when Chang-k'ien saw it in 128; but Pan-ku deliberately corrects the difficulty, and as both historians had the same evidence (Chang-k'ien's Report) I follow him.

[3] See generally the Life, Wylie pp. 66 *sqq.*; and Hirth p. 93. There is a good account of Chinese expansion in Asia under the Han in Grousset pp. 208 *sqq.*

[4] Hirth p. 94 §9; Wylie p. 66.

then camped between Samarcand and the Oxus. This shows that part of the K'ang-kiu, who had perhaps received an accession of strength from the Sai-wang, had, like the Yueh-chi, crossed the Jaxartes and now lapped Ferghana round on the north-west and west; probably the Yueh-chi had driven part of the horde across before them, for Chang-k'ien says that the K'ang-kiu to the south of the river were 'under the political influence of' (*i.e.* subject to) the Yueh-chi as those north of the river were to the Hiung-nu.[1] They may possibly have extended to the Samarcand country,[2] though if they did it was probably later. But the reason that Ta-yuan entrusted Chang-k'ien to their safe-conduct, which would mean for him a considerable détour to the westward, more probably was, not merely that they were vassals of the Yueh-chi, but that Samarcand was still maintaining itself in some sort of quasi-independence and blocking the direct road; the nomads had no chance of taking a properly fortified town by assault, and could only bring it to terms by ravaging its lands year by year till it agreed to pay tribute for them, as some cities in Ionia had bought off the Galatae. Chang-k'ien failed to obtain the alliance of the Yueh-chi, who told him that they were tired of fighting and trekking and only wanted a peaceful life in the rich country which they had at last secured, and returned to China by the more difficult southern route from Badakshan over the Pamirs and so through Chinese Turkestan; he was again captured by the Hiung-nu, but after a year's captivity he reached China in 126. In 115 he was sent on a mission to the Wu-sun, then apparently about Lake Issyk Kul (pp. 276 *sq.*) and from there sent out subordinate envoys to visit the Western Countries up to and including Parthia, a country he himself never saw. He died in 114, a year after his return to China.

His Report to the emperor on the western countries which he discovered, and the use made of it by Ssu-ma Ch'ien and Pan-ku, are noticed in Appendix 20. But, though Ssu-ma Ch'ien professedly gives his Report, the question arises how far the Report so given is really

[1] Hirth p. 96 §27, where 'east' must really be north or north-east; 'east' would be Ta-yuan and the Yueh-chi.

[2] Herzfeld, *Sakastan* p. 23, and his map facing p. 24 (following de Groot pp. 106–8, see p. 307 n. 4). But Herzfeld's whole scheme is coloured by his mistake about Ta-yuan (App. 10), and there is nothing in the sources to show that *at this time* the K'ang-kiu were southward of Ferghana at all: the accounts both of Ssu-ma Ch'ien (Hirth p. 95 §20) and Pan-ku (Wylie p. 44; de Groot p. 109) represent Chang-k'ien as putting them *northward* of it, and this is a passage in which Pan-ku is correcting a mistake of Chang-k'ien's on another geographical point (p. 477).

Chang-k'ien's own, and I have not succeeded in finding any study of this subject.[1] Pan-ku says that the subordinates whom Chang-k'ien sent out from the Wu-sun country in 115 did not get back to China till after his death;[2] Chang-k'ien's Report therefore should only contain such information as he acquired in 128. But it is certain that the Report *as we have it* in Ssu-ma Ch'ien includes information obtained in 115. In 128 the great Saca invasion of Parthia was in full swing.[3] But in the Report An-si (Parthia) is bounded on the north by the An-tsai (Aorsi)[4] who lay round the Aral northward and eastward; this means that Parthia was suzerain of the whole Massagetae country up to the Aral and the lower Oxus, which was only the case from the time when Mithridates II (who became king in 124) had overcome the invasion to his death in 87 B.C. Again, in the Report Merv is Parthian;[5] but in 128 it was in the hands of the Saca invaders, and was never Parthian till, as part of the liquidation of the invasion, it was taken for Mithridates II by the Suren who struck the 'campaign' coins (p. 499), again later than 124. Finally, the Report says that the people of Parthia wrote on parchment in horizontal lines;[6] this looks like the observation of an eye-witness, but Chang-k'ien himself never saw Parthia. If then Pan-ku be right about Chang-k'ien's lieutenants, Ssu-ma Ch'ien has supplemented the Report himself and included in it information obtained in 115. But it will be noticed that all the above instances relate to Parthia alone, which Chang-k'ien never visited but which by the time Ssu-ma Ch'ien is supposed to have written had become very important to China

[1] Some Japanese scholar may have done one.

[2] Wylie p. 70.

[3] Dates: Tarn, *SP Stud.* pp. 14 *sqq.*; *CAH* IX pp. 583 *sqq.*

[4] Hirth p. 97 §37; see Tarn, *CAH* IX p. 585.

[5] Hirth p. 97 §34, An-si is 'close to the Oxus' ('extends to the Oxus', Wylie p. 39; 'lies on the Oxus', de Groot p. 93); this can only mean that Merv was already Parthian. Whether the name An-si itself be Antioch (Merv), or (spelling it An-sik) Arsak, has been much discussed. All the countries in the Report are names of *peoples*, and there is therefore no reason for supposing that in one case a king's name was used, especially as the Report knows nothing of the Parthians proper, the aristocracy; but it has not been noticed that the *Ch'ien-han-shu* is conclusive in favour of Antioch. It says that to reach An-si from O-ik-san-li (Seistan, see p. 347) you go north and then somewhat east (de Groot p. 92), which exactly describes the great road from Seistan by Herat to Merv; to Pan-ku therefore An-si was originally Antioch-Merv, Parthia being a derivative meaning. This is confirmed by Merv (Mou-lou) being called Little An-si in the *Hou-han-shu* (Chavannes, *T'oung Pao* VIII p. 177).

[6] Hirth p. 97 §37; Wylie p. 40.

on account of the through trade. It does not follow therefore that Ssu-ma Ch'ien did more than supplement the An-si section; and the things which matter to Greek history, the accounts of Ta-hia and Ta-yuan, I have taken—I have found nothing to the contrary—to represent Chang-k'ien's own observation.

For what he saw himself his evidence is excellent, but the things he only heard are not necessarily in the same category. No doubt he could speak the Yueh-chi language, for it was apparently customary in China for officials destined for any country to be taught its language before starting;[1] but outside of the Yueh-chi he may have depended on such interpreters as they could provide (as the Wu-sun in 115 provided interpreters for his subordinates),[2] and they themselves were new arrivals in a strange world, as he was. At the same time, if the leading Yueh-chi clans spoke Saca, as is now the dominant belief (p. 287), then Chang-k'ien could himself more or less understand the peoples he met with; this is reflected in his statement that from Ferghana to Parthia, though there were dialectical variations, the people could all understand one another.[3] His one real mistake was that sometimes, over the relative positions of peoples, he got the points of the compass wrong,[4] a mistake easy enough to make in a new world; Pan-ku, by whose time a mass of information on the subject was available, occasionally corrects him.[5] One thing however the Yueh-chi could not provide, and that was an interpreter for Greek: from first to last he never notes the existence of Greeks[6] though he records their works, just as neither he nor his subordinates ever discovered the Parthian aristocracy. He distinguishes most carefully, as any Chinaman of experience would, between nomads like the Yueh-chi and the K'ang-kiu, who followed their flocks, and settled countries like Ta-yuan, Ta-hia, and An-si (Parthia), where the people had 'fixed abodes' and practised agriculture. The strange thing about his Report *as we have it* is that it never

[1] Wylie part 2 p. 89; de Groot pp. 127–8. But what Wylie translates as 'Academic Institute' de Groot calls a park full of strange animals. Would officials learning a language really be sent to the Zoological Gardens?

[2] Wylie p. 69; de Groot p. 27.

[3] Hirth p. 108 §101. Cf. Eratosthenes in Strabo xv, 724.

[4] If all the points of the compass given in Chang-k'ien's Report in Ssu-ma Ch'ien be taken out, it will be found impossible to make them all fit each other.

[5] An important instance in App. 10.

[6] It is conceivable that such as remained were bilingual, but not very likely as early as 128.

mentions the Sacaraucae and Massagetae and their invasion of Parthia; this was going on while he was among the Yueh-chi and he must have heard of it. But by the time Ssu-ma Ch'ien wrote it was ancient history; direct intercourse by caravan between China and Parthia was well established, and if Ssu-ma Ch'ien edited the An-si section he may have omitted some reference to the invasion as being now meaningless; he does not give the Report as a separate formal document but incorporates its substance in his own work. But one cannot analyse from translations as though they were Greek texts, and the work must be left to Chinese scholars.

I have said that Chang-k'ien is quite clear that the conquest of the Ta-hia (Bactria proper) was the work of the Yueh-chi.[1] But almost every modern writer known to me attributes that conquest to 'Sacas' driven southward by the Yueh-chi, who are supposed to have occupied the country until the Yueh-chi expelled or subdued them. Chang-k'ien, who was there, knows nothing about this, and no scrap of evidence for it exists; it arose originally from a misunderstanding of a simple passage in Strabo, and for many years one writer has just copied it from another, till it has become an obsession; every form of 'Saca'—Sacaraucae, Sai-wang, even Tochari—has been pressed into service, and the theories to which this belief has given rise have done more than anything else to obscure the history of the time. Certainly Strabo says that the Sacas occupied Bactria;[2] but the most cursory perusal of the context shows that throughout the whole section he is talking, not of the second century B.C., but of a time long before that—he calls it Achaemenid, but it was really the seventh century—the time of the great Saca invasion, well known from Assyrian sources, which had played its part in the fall of Nineveh and had penetrated as far as Armenia and Cappadocian Pontus.[3] An attempt has indeed been made since the theory was started to found the supposed Saca conquest of Greek Bactria a little more plausibly by citing a passage in Trogus, but as a matter of Latin Trogus' text will not bear the interpretation put

[1] Hirth p. 96 §29, and the parallel passage Wylie p. 41; de Groot p. 95.

[2] Strabo XI, 511, τὴν Βακτριανὴν κάτεσχον. The latest quotation of this theory is by Konow, *CII* p. xxi, who has made it the basis of his scheme in *JIH* XII, 1933, p. 1. Herrmann, *Sakai* in PW col. 1788, has been exceptional in recognising that Strabo refers to the seventh century B.C.

[3] A good commentary on the Strabo passage is E. H. Minns, *CAH* III pp. 188 *sqq.* and especially 190. See also J. Junge, *Z. f. Rassenkunde* III, 1936, p. 68.

upon it.[1] There is in fact no reason of any kind for thinking that Chang-k'ien was mistaken;[2] and whatever happened to outlying parts of the Bactrian kingdom, the supposed Saca conquest of Greek Bactria proper is a myth.

It is time to consider the Greek writers.[3] Apollodorus attributes the conquest of the Bactrian kingdom to four nomad peoples, Asii, Pasiani, Tochari, and Sacarauli;[4] 'Trogus' source' formally attributes it to two, Asiani and Saraucae,[5] though subsequently he mentions the Tochari (p. 286). Taking 'Trogus' source' first, one of his two names must represent Chang-k'ien's Yueh-chi; and as the Saraucae (Sacaraucae), of whom something is known (p. 291), are out of the question, the Yueh-chi are the Asiani. The form Asiani is an (Iranian) adjectival form of Apollodorus' Asii, which is the substantival form; the Asii therefore are the Yueh-chi, whether (as some have supposed) the two words be identical, or not.[6] From 1918 to 1936 it was further believed that a Central Asian text gave the name of a people Arsi who spoke toχrī (Tocharian) and who were the Greek Asii;[7] the Arsi were accordingly supposed to be the Yueh-chi (or the dominant stratum of the Yueh-chi, which I shall come to) and much has been written about them. It has now been argued, with an impressive wealth of evidence, that Central Asian texts know no such people as the Arsi.[8] Naturally I do not know myself if this will win general acceptance, but to avoid questions I shall use the name Asii, though in quoting from others I must give the form they use, Arsi.

[1] *Prol.* XLI, Saraucae et Asiani Bactra occupavere et Sogdianos, which has been taken by Marquart (*Ērānšahr*, *Gött. Abh.* III, 1901, p. 205), Konow (*CII* p. xxii, *JIH* 1933 p. 6), and Herzfeld (*Sakastan* p. 26), to mean that the Saraucae occupied Bactria and the Asiani Sogdiana. A Latin writer who meant this would have said so; Trogus' sentence, from its form, can only be a perfectly general statement. Herrmann, *Sakai* in PW col. 1617, properly rejected Marquart's view.

[2] The movements of the Sai-wang have been already dealt with.

[3] I considered all these names in 1930 in *SP Stud.* §1, in the light of what was then known, but there have been many important developments since.

[4] Strabo XI, 511. There can be no possible doubt that Apollodorus is Strabo's source, though he is not named; there is no one else.

[5] Trogus, *Prol.* XLI. Saraucae for MSS Sarancae is certain.

[6] On the various attempts to explain the name Yueh-chi see Konow in *CII* pp. lviii *sq.*; P. Pelliot, *JA* 224, 1934, p. 25 n. 2.

[7] E. Sieg, *Berlin SB* 1918 p. 560; F. W. K. Müller, *ib.* p. 578. A clear account of the history of the question is given by P. Pelliot, *JA* 224, 1934, p. 23.

[8] H. W. Bailey, *Ttaugara*, *BSOS* VIII, 1936, pp. 883, 905 *sqq.* He makes ārsi = Sanscrit ārya. Pelliot, *T'oung Pao* XXXII, 1936, p. 265, finds the rejection of the name Arsi convincing.

It has, however, not been noticed that the Hellenistic world knew a people called Arsi, even if Central Asia did not. The name occurs in a very curious list of peoples in Pliny. In chapter 16 (18) of book VI (46 *sqq.*) Pliny describes the lands from Hyrcania to Bactria; he gives first Hyrcania, then Margiane, then 'Caucasus', which he describes as extending from Margiane to Bactria, inhabited by the Mardi (of the Elburz) and some unknown peoples; beyond (*ultra*) comes the list in question (48); then a city in Aria; then the Derbices (a Massagetae clan) on the Oxus, and some unknown names; finally Bactria. His own ideas of this part of the world were therefore very hazy; but he thought that he was going eastward, and by *ultra* he meant east of Margiane and 'Caucasus', though we should really have to translate it 'somewhere in the East'. For the list which is *ultra* is not one of his usual strings of unknown names, but is a refuge for a number of well-known peoples from all over Asia whose names were in his note-books but whom he did not know where to place—the Matiani from Armenia, the Cadusii from Gilan, the Chorasmii from the Aral,[1] the Gandari from India (Gandhāra), the Sarangae from Seistan,[2] the Paricani from Ferghana or Gedrosia,[3] and the Arsi from—where? The name *proves* nothing; but it *suggests* that he had got the native name of the Asii, and, not knowing where to place them, put them in his 'refuge' list, just as Ptolemy got the name Tochari in connection with Bactria and, not knowing what to do with them, made them a Bactrian tribe.[4]

The name Asii, then, represents the Yueh-chi. But very many scholars, from Richthofen to Herzfeld, have held that the Tochari were the Yueh-chi;[5] and to-day that is certain, from the now known occurrences of the name Tochari. It has been identified with the Thagouroi of Ptolemy on the Silk Route who had a city Thogara;[6] the Chinese

[1] Or from Parthia proper (App. 11), if he took this name and Gandari from Herod. VII, 93, where the two are brigaded together.

[2] Given again twice over, as Drangae and as Zarangae, in their right place, VI, 94; the spelling Sarangae is from Herod. III, 93. Pliny has reproduced names from three different sources without suspecting their identity.

[3] Gedrosia has been the usual view. Ferghana: Herzfeld, *Memoirs of the Arch. Survey of India* XXXIV, 1928, p. 6.

[4] Ptol. VI, 11.

[5] Müller and Sieg, *Berlin SB* 1916 p. 395, said that no one had ever doubted this. If only that were true (see pp. 295 *sq.* for the other theory about the Tochari) how much unnecessary trouble and confusion would have been saved.

[6] Ptol. VI, 16, 5 and 8, from the Maes Titianus itinerary, early second century A.D. See F. W. Thomas, *JRAS* 1931 pp. 834–5; A. Herrmann, *Θαγοῦροι* in PW,

knew of remnants of the Togara in Kan-su in the second century B.C.;[1] the name occurs in or about Kan-su in Thibetan texts;[2] and the same name, ttaugara, for a town in Kan-su, is found in a document in Khotan Saca as late as A.D. 800.[3] It follows that the Tochari, who as we know from Apollodorus came to Bactria in the second century from somewhere else, came from Kan-su; but the Chinese historians show that what did come from Kan-su to Bactria at that time were the Yueh-chi. Again, we know from Apollodorus and Pliny (fully given p. 84) that, while there were no Tochari in the Tarim basin in the reign of Euthydemus (died about 190 B.C.), there were Tochari there later at the date of some source of Pliny's; and here again Chinese historians show that part of the Yueh-chi (the Little Yueh-chi) came and settled there at some time not long after 174 B.C. (p. 276); and Indian writers called both the Great and the Little Yueh-chi by the same name, Tukhāra (Tochari).[4] Finally Ptolemy, all unknowingly, locates Tochari in several places where the Yueh-chi are known to have been on their journey (see App. 21, p. 517), which alone would be conclusive. In fact, wherever we meet Yueh-chi from the Chinese side, we also meet Tochari, whether the evidence comes from texts in Greek, Chinese, Indian, Thibetan, or Saca; that suffices.

The Yueh-chi horde, therefore, was composed of two different peoples, who appear in Greek as Asii and Tochari. 'Trogus' source' gives the relationship: reges Thocarorum Asiani—the Asii are lords of the Tochari.[5] That is, at the time of the conquest of Bactria the Asii were the dominant or ruling people,[6] however the horde may have originally taken shape. The idea occasionally put forward that the Asii conquered the Tochari *after* the conquest of Bactria may be summarily dismissed. Had Trogus meant this, he (or any other Latin writer) would have said so, and would not have used a phrase of unexampled ambiguity and clumsiness for its (supposed) purpose; while the fact that the Chinese had the Tochari name in the second century B.C., but

1934; Bailey *op. cit.* p. 885. See further App. 21. Both Thomas and Herrmann have noticed that the identity *must* follow.

[1] Bailey *op. cit.* p. 885.

[2] Thomas *loc. cit.*, see Bailey *ib.*

[3] Bailey *op. cit.* p. 884.

[4] Lévi, *JA* 1897 i p. 10, 1933 p. 26; de la Vallée-Poussin pp. 336 *sq.* One modern theory brings Kanishka from the Little Yueh-chi.

[5] Trogus, *Prol.* XLII.

[6] So Müller, *Berlin SB* 1918 p. 579: the Arsi were the ruling caste of the Tochari.

nevertheless called the horde which migrated from Kan-su not Tochari but Yueh-chi, shows that that horde, before it quitted Kan-su, already contained something more than Tochari, *i.e.* that the combination of Asii and Tochari into one horde had already taken place.

The race and language or languages of the composite Yueh-chi horde have been the subject of much discussion, chiefly philological.[1] A few years ago the dominant belief was that the Asii (Arsi) were a Turki people,[2] but to-day it is thought that they were Iranian Sacas;[3] I may perhaps venture the remark that Asia is getting very full of Sacas, even if Pliny (VI, 50) did call them 'innumerable'. One must take the Kushans as representing the Asii or say rather the dominant element among the Yueh-chi,[4] whether the Kushans were a tribe or sept or whether Kushāna was not a tribal name but a family or dynastic title;[5] and it is a strong argument that when the Kushan language was first reduced to writing on their coins, it was apparently the north-Iranian dialect now called Saca and not the Sogdian dialect of

[1] For the literature see the discussions in *CII* pp. xlix *sqq.*; Grousset p. 213; de la Vallée-Poussin pp. 303–8.

[2] The reasons are collected in *CII* p. l. There seems to be some evidence for Turki septs on the Jaxartes much earlier; see Kiessling, *Hunni* in PW col. 2599, and a communication by Nöldeke to Gutschmid (*Gesch. Irans* p. 2 n. 1) pointing out that the name Carthasis in Curt. VII, 7, 1 is Turki.

[3] *CII* pp. li *sqq.* and references; Grousset *op. cit.* p. 59 and references; O. G. von Wesendonk, *Klio* XXVI, 1933, p. 337 (who connects the name Arsi with the Iranian stem aršan, man or hero, seen also in aršaka). I gather from de la Vallée-Poussin (pp. 301, 303), who has seen the MS, that this will be the view of F. W. Thomas in vol. II of *CHI.*

[4] I need not consider a new theory (Konow, *JIH* XII, 1933, pp. 8–14) which makes of the five Yueh-chi princes (the Kushan chief being one) five Saca princes of Bactria conquered by the Yueh-chi. It is claimed that Pan-ku is ambiguous; on this ground the plain account in the *Hou-han-shu* is thrown overboard, though Fan-ye must have known, and, as the Chinese always call the Kushans Yueh-chi, it is said that they were mistaken. The theory is one more unhappy offshoot of the elementary blunder over Strabo which started the belief in a Saca conquest of Greek Bactria (p. 283). Another version of the same theory, open to precisely the same objections, makes the five princes Ta-hia = Tochari: P. Pelliot, *JA* 224, 1934, pp. 38 *sqq.*; on the impossible equation of Ta-hia and Tochari see p. 296.

[5] A tribe or sept: J. Kennedy, *JRAS* 1912 p. 670; Baron A. von Staël-Holstein, *Berlin SB* 1914 p. 645, *JRAS* 1914 p. 79; A. Herrmann, *Sacaraucae* in PW col. 1613; E. J. Rapson in *CHI* p. 583; de la Vallée-Poussin p. 306; Konow in *CII* pp. xlvi, xlix *sq.*, though later he has called it a family name, *Ep. Ind.* XXI, 1931, p. 59. A title: J. F. Fleet, *JRAS* 1914 pp. 369–81, 413; F. W. Thomas, *JRAS* 1915 p. 532; B. Laufer, *Language of the Yueh-chi* 1917 (not seen). A personal name: K. P. Jayaswal, *JBORS* XVI, 1930, p. 256.

Bactria.[1] But language and race are not identical things. To Greeks, who were not scientific ethnologists, the matter was simple: if a horde spoke Saca it was a Saca horde. It is not so simple to-day; the one assurance we have is that every great horde must have been a racial mixture, whatever might be the preponderating element. No philological arguments can make some of the Kushan portraits look like Iranians or any other 'Indo-European' people;[2] and I have felt trouble myself—no one else seems to have done so—over the number five of the five Yueh-chi princes (*yabghu*), for five is not a typically Iranian number and one cannot well separate the five princes of the Yueh-chi from the five of the Turki Hiung-nu. But five was a dominant number in China,[3] where it occurs with the same monotonous regularity as does seven in astrology; and it may be that both hordes had merely borrowed from China,[4] with which they had long been in contact, and had passed the number on to others.[5] But this is a guess, and the number where it occurs *might* indicate a Turki custom and a Turki element; the word *yabghu* is Turki. Be this as it may, the right view about the Asii in Bactria, I think, is to say that they probably *spoke* Saca, but to refrain from dogmatising about their racial quality.

The race and language of the Tochari are a most difficult problem;[6] I would gladly pass it over if I could, for I feel much diffidence in saying anything at all. It was once supposed that they brought with them

[1] Eratosthenes called Bactria and Sogdiana *ὁμόγλωττοι παρὰ μικρόν*, Strabo XV, 724. H. W. Bailey, *op. cit.* p. 893, referred 'Bactria' here to the Kushans, on the ground that Strabo wrote a century after the conquest of Bactria. The passage was in fact written by Eratosthenes about a century *before* the conquest.

[2] Note the strong resemblance between the portrait of Wima Kadphises, *BMC* Pl. XXV, 6, and those of Ephthalite Huns in Whitehead *NNM* Pl. XII, 1 and *ASI* 1915–16 Pl. XXVI nos. 46 to 50.

[3] A large number of instances are collected by R. Wilhelm, *A short history of Chinese civilisation* (Eng. trans.) pp. 71, 86. See also Chavannes, *Les mémoires historiques de Se-ma Ts'ien* III p. 409, five governors of heaven assisted by five planets (Iran has four governors); the number five is said to be common in Chinese astrology.

[4] Wesendonk *op. cit.* p. 337 says that the Turkish title *yabghu* of the five Yueh-chi princes was borrowed from China.

[5] The K'ang-kiu had five princes, Wylie p. 44, de Groot p. 105, which they cannot have got from China. But they *might* have copied the Hiung-nu.

[6] For the history of the problem see P. Pelliot, *Tokharien et Koutchéen*, *JA* 224, 1934, p. 23. Other recent studies of importance are S. Lévi, *Le 'Tokharien'*, *JA* 1933 p. 1; H. W. Bailey, *Ttaugara*, *BSOS* VIII, 1936, p. 883; Pelliot, *A propos du 'Tokharien'*, *T'oung Pao* XXXII, 1936, p. 259.

from Europe, and spoke, the famous *centum*-language with Italo-Celtic affinities, discovered in Chinese Turkestan, which used to be called Tocharian. To-day this language is no longer called Tocharian, and we are told that it is certain that its two forms, called Dialects A and B, were the languages of two states in the northern part of Chinese Turkestan, A of Agni-Karachar (with Turfan) and B of Kucha;[1] and we are also told that neither dialect could have been (*i.e.* represent) the language of the historical Tochari who invaded Bactria, because their name is aspirated while Dialects A and B have no aspirates.[2] None of this is much help to the historian of Greek Bactria, for it belongs to a later world: the known history of Agni and Kucha begins later than the conquest of Bactria,[3] and the known remains of Dialects A and B belong, I understand, to the eighth century A.D.[4] But *centum*-languages did not grow of themselves in Central Asia, the Indo-European languages of Asia belonging to the *satem* group; it would seem that the two dialects, or rather their parent form, must originally have come from Europe and must have been brought to Agni and Kucha by some definite people before they could become the languages of little states in those localities; and granted that the two dialects are full of loan-words from other languages, that does not alter the fact that they are *centum*-languages at bottom, just as Roumanian, though said to be full of loan-words, is none the less a Romance language. The only people at present known who could have brought a *centum*-language from Europe to Chinese Turkestan—no other has ever been suggested—are the Tochari; not the Tochari who as part of the Great Yueh-chi invaded Bactria, but the Tochari element in the Little Yueh-chi who after 174 B.C. moved into Chinese Turkestan.

Certainly it is not known what language was spoken by the second-century Tochari,[5] for apparently those in Bactria at some period after

[1] A: Bailey *op. cit.* pp. 896 *sqq.* B: Lévi, *JA* 1913 p. 311; 1933, p. 1. Pelliot, *T'oung Pao* XXXII p. 265, prefers the form Yen-ki or Yen-yi to Agni. Konow, *Asia Major* IX, 1933, p. 455 (and more briefly *JIH* XII, 1933, p. 7), argued that 'Tocharian' was originally the language of the Arsi, and was not called toχrï till the Arsi had conquered the Tochari; but his article is based on the impossible Tochari = Ta-hia theory, p. 296.

[2] Lévi, *JA* 1933 p. 5; Bailey *op. cit.* p. 916.

[3] Kucha is said to be *mentioned* in 102 B.C., Bailey *op. cit.* p. 904.

[4] It is now claimed that there are remains of another dialect, C, from the third century A.D., which helps to bridge the gap: T. Burrow, *JRAS* 1935 p. 667. See p. 519.

[5] See Lévi, *JA* 1933 p. 5.

the conquest adopted the Saca speech of their Kushan overlords; and though Bactria after the fourth century A.D. bore their name, Tocharistan, it is now said that the language called toχrī (toχarī or toγarī) in Central Asian documents was the Saca speech of the Kushans of Tocharistan and nothing else.[1] It seems to me probable, however, that whatever the Tochari spoke in the second century B.C. it was not an Iranian dialect like the speech of the Asii; for unless there had been two completely different languages spoken in the Yueh-chi horde it is difficult to see how two contemporary, or all but contemporary, Greek historians could have distinguished the two components of that horde as sharply as they did, seeing that they were not scientific ethnologists and must have gone largely by language; and that means that unless the Tochari, who had originally come to Kan-su from somewhere else,[2] spoke Turki, one is thrown back for their language upon the West. One thing however is definite, the numerous and varied Greek forms of the name of this people, which are considered in Appendix 21; the analysis there given seems to me to put a somewhat different complexion upon the question of the aspirate in the name and to suggest that further investigation might be desirable before it be laid down as certain that Dialects A and B cannot have been, or represent, the language of the Tochari. The whole problem is shifting sand; but at the moment I can see no conclusive reason why anyone who so desires may not continue to hold—as theory, of course, not as fact—the once so attractive belief[3] that a large element among the conquerors of the Bactrian Greeks was a people with Italo-Celtic affinities who had trekked from Europe to the Chinese border, marking their road north of the Tien-shan with their grave-mounds,[4] and some of whom at a later time, when their culture had flowered, are represented by the blue-eyed people of the amazing frescoes from Turfan, with the men looking like Italians of the Renaissance and the women in dresses which would have been in place at Venice in her prime.

[1] Bailey *op. cit.* pp. 891–2, and on the form pp. 889–90; Pelliot, *JA* 224, 1934, pp. 34, 53, *T'oung Pao* XXXII p. 260.

[2] Bailey *op. cit.* p. 885 n. 3.

[3] A. von Le Coq, *Auf Hellas Spuren in Ostturkestan* 1926 p. 4 and *passim*; (see especially p. 114, the dresses, and Plates 13 and 36); *Von Land und Leuten in Ostturkestan* 1925 pp. 153 *sq.* For possible earlier traces of the Tochari in art see R. Fick, *Die Buddhistische Kultur und das Erbe Alexanders des Grossen*, Morgenland XXV, 1934, pp. 21–2, and the fine head, like a Viking, of Abb. 6.

[4] What is really needed is excavation of these grave-mounds; but that is impossible.

Next to be considered are the Sacarauli or Saraucae, names which undoubtedly represent the Sacaraucae (Saka Rawaka). These were the Sacas *para Sugdam* ('beyond Sogd') of the trilingual gold tablet of Darius I,[1] that is, the Sacas with pointed caps and the Amyrgian Sacas (if they were not identical) of the Naks-i-Rustam list (see on this App. 10); indeed the names Saka Rawaka and Saka Haumavarga have been connected.[2] In Darius' day these Sacas, who were his subjects, lived 'beyond Sogd' (southern Sogdiana) in the country to the south of and along the Jaxartes, whatever its extent; Ptolemy correctly gives the original seat of the Sacaraucae as south of the Jaxartes,[3] but in the second century B.C. they may have been a confederacy of the steppe peoples westward of Chodjend. The Sacaraucae had long been known to the Greek world. They had furnished 1000 mailed horsemen to the army of Darius III at Gaugamela,[4] and Alexander had recruited some of them, as he did Bactrians and Sogdians, to fill up his depleted cavalry prior to his invasion of India.[5] Two modern views, one that they were the Sai-wang[6] of the Chinese, the other that they were the K'ang-kiu,[7] have found much acceptance, and both views contain elements of truth, though not in that absolute form (pp. 278, 307); but for the moment the Sacaraucae must be treated by themselves. As the Yueh-chi crossed the Jaxartes westward of Ferghana they must have fallen on them; the Sacaraucae went, or were driven, southward to Bokhara; the Yueh-chi took the direct way towards Bactria by Samarcand; and the K'ang-kiu of Tashkent, crossing or driven across the river (as we have seen), occupied the grazing grounds of the Sacaraucae, the Yueh-chi having passed on. The natural road across the Oxus from Bokhara has at all times led to Merv,[8] and while the Yueh-chi conquered Bactria the Sacaraucae must have taken Merv.[9] Bokhara and Merv were their share of the conquest of the Bactrian kingdom, and from Merv they played their part in the great invasion of Parthia in 129 (in which they and the

[1] Sidney Smith, *JRAS* 1926 p. 435; E. Herzfeld, *Memoirs of the Arch. Survey of India* XXXIV, 1928, p. 1.

[2] A suggestion of Markwart's, quoted by Wesendonk *op. cit.* p. 337.

[3] Ptol. VI, 14, 14.

[4] Arr. *Anab.* III, 8, 3; 11, 4; 13, 4.

[5] Arr. *Anab.* V, 12, 2.

[6] A. Herrmann, *Sacaraucae* in PW.

[7] Gutschmid p. 71.

[8] W. Barthold, *Turkestan down to the Mongol invasion* 1928 p. 82.

[9] So Herrmann *op. cit.* col. 1618.

Massagetae were undoubtedly the chief actors), following the road Merv-Herat-Seistan.[1] It has already been seen (p. 278) that they had absorbed a Sai-wang element; but at this time they were a separate horde from the K'ang-kiu,[2] who were to absorb some of them later (p. 307).

One part of the story of the conquest of the Bactrian kingdom has always been omitted by modern writers; no one has really considered Apollodorus' fourth people, the Pasiani,[3] who happen to be important, for it was they who a century later put an end to Greek rule in India. As Asiani is the (Iranian) adjectival form of Asii, so Pasiani would be the similar adjectival form of, and would imply, a name *Pasii or *Pasi; and there can be no doubt that this name is the Parsii (Πάρσιοι) of the Greek geographers. For the same stem occurs again in southern Iran, and the known Greek variants on the word Pasargadae (the usual form in Greek writers), namely Passagadae[4] and Parsagadae,[5] make the equivalence *Pasi-Parsii certain;[6] they may also suggest that the word Parsii was really not Saca but Persian. The adjectival form of Parsii occurs again, alongside of the substantival form, in the names of the villages Parsia and Parsiana in Ptolemy (p. 332), Parsiana being identical with Pasiani.

As a place has to be found for the Parsii in the Bactrian kingdom, and as the Yueh-chi and the Sacaraucae between them account for Bactria proper, southern Sogdiana, and Merv, the only possible locality for the Parsii is farther to the west; their first conquest must have been

[1] Tarn, *CAH* IX p. 583. The Parthian reconquest, as the 'campaign' coins show, followed the same line in the reverse direction: Tarn, *SP Stud.* p. 17, *CAH* IX p. 585.

[2] To Chang-k'ien, the K'ang-kiu in 128 were not a very large horde; Hirth p. 96 §27.

[3] I discussed the Pasiani, but only up to a point, in *SP Stud.* pp. 11 *sqq.*

[4] Anaximenes of Lampsacus *ap.* Steph. *s.v.* See Herzfeld, *Klio* VIII, 1908, p. 26.

[5] Ptol. VI, 8, 12; see Herzfeld *ib.* p. 19.

[6] In *SP Stud.* p. 11 I used the identity Asii-Arsi; it is really the other way round. The instances given by F. W. K. Müller, *Berlin SB* 1918 p. 579, to prove this identity have been criticised by P. Pelliot, *JA* 224, 1934, pp. 29–31; he admits however that the Chinese Po-sse for Persia (Parsa) would imply a form *Pasi, were it not fifth-century A.D. and too late to use. But the Greek form Passagadae, used by an Alexander-historian of the fourth century B.C., removes Pelliot's objection; and indeed it is possible that Po-sse in the *Wei-shu* may mean not Persia but the Parsii (reasons in *SP Stud.* p. 12). The certain equivalent *Pasi-Parsii therefore guarantees Asii-Arsi, which in view of Pliny (p. 285) may still be required.

the one-time Bactrian satrapies west of the Arius, Tapuria and Traxiane,[1] that is, a large part of what had once been the kingdom of Antimachus, assuming that Merv, from its geographical position, must have fallen to the Sacaraucae from Bokhara. This would explain why Apollodorus named the Parsii among the conquerors of the Bactrian kingdom while 'Trogus' source' seemingly did not; Tapuria and Traxiane had long been Bactrian but were no longer so at the date of the Yueh-chi conquest, having been taken from Eucratides by Mithridates I (p. 219), and so it was possible for two well-informed writers to take different views about them; 'Trogus' source' must have reckoned the Parsii among the invaders of Parthia.

Who were these Parsii? The word seems to be the Old Persian Parsua,[2] which means Persians. The Persians of Persis called themselves Parsā; but the form Parsua is old—it has been suggested that it was the Median form of Parsā—and had already played a part in the history of the Iranian invasions as the name of a people who had reached north-east Iran and south Armenia and appear in Assyrian records;[3] of the known original Iranian tribes[4] they belonged to the Parsā-Parsua-Persian tribe. The Parsii of Apollodorus and Ptolemy, then, were a branch of the Persian people who had remained behind when their kinsfolk went south. But if they remained behind, where did they live? In Persian tradition the original Iranian 'home', that is, the centre from which the Iranian peoples set out on their conquests to the southward, was called Ērānvēj, and Ērānvēj has recently been identified with Chorasmia (Kwarizm).[5] Now Kwarizm, sandwiched between the Sacaraucae and the Massagetae, is too important a country not to have played *some* part in the second-century invasions; and my suggestion—naturally it is only conjecture—is that the Parsii-Parsua had stayed

[1] For the conquest of these two provinces by 'Scyths' and their recovery later by Parthia see Strabo XI, 515, βιασάμενοι τοὺς Σκύθας. A comparison with 517 shows what part of Bactria is meant; see Tarn, *SP Stud.* p. 20.

[2] The identity Parsii-Parsua was suggested by Marquart, and by Ed. Meyer, *Gesch. d. Alt.*[5] I, ii p. 898 n., merely as a query; see A. Christensen, *Die Iranier* 1933 p. 232 n. 4. But the history of the Parsii given here and in Chap. VIII has not been worked out before.

[3] For these northern Parsua see now E. Herzfeld, *Arch. Hist. of Iran* 1935 pp. 9 *sqq.*, 26 *sq.*, and Christensen *loc. cit.* Herzfeld thinks they were the Persians of Persis before they went south. For the land Parsuas in Armenia see *CAH* III pp. 169, 174 and *ib.* chaps. I and II, *passim.*

[4] Herzfeld *op. cit.* p. 9.

[5] E. Benveniste, *BSOS* VII, 1934, p. 265. Cf. Herzfeld *op. cit.* p. 7.

behind in Ērānvēj-Kwarizm when their kinsfolk originally went south. Unless I am entirely wrong in my interpretation of Stephanus,[1] the Parsii were at this time members of the great Massagetae confederacy (as would be almost inevitable from their geographical place in the invasion, which has already been considered); and, as I see the facts relative to the Chorasmii given in Appendix 11, the Chorasmii, who were also members of the Massagetae confederacy, were a tribe or section of the Parsii; after the latter people come on the scene they are not again mentioned. The Parsii were an important people, as is shown by Apollodorus naming them beside the Yueh-chi and the Sacaraucae; and the identification of them as Parsua, who might feel themselves different from their Saca neighbours if only because they doubtless spoke a form of Persian while the Saca speech was North Iranian, would explain the fact (which will play a considerable part in the subsequent story) that, when a large part of the Sacas who invaded Parthia passed on into Sind, the Parsii did not go with them but took a line of their own (App. 9). Though (if I am right) the Parsii were not strictly speaking Sacas (in the sense that probably they did not speak Saca), I shall, when we come to their kingdom of Ghazni-Kabul, sometimes have to use the term Saca for them; for the coins of this kingdom with Greek and Kharoshthi legends are known to numismatists as Saca, and any other course would lead to much confusion.

The identification of the Parsii gives one very important chronological indication. The real beginning of the Saca invasion of Parthia can be dated to 129 (apparently the first body crossed the frontier in 130),[2] and the bulk of the invaders were Massagetae and Sacaraucae; the Sacaraucae followed the Merv-Herat road, but the Massagetae might have advanced on a broad front farther to the west, as they always did when raiding.[3] Apollodorus' mention of the Parsii links up, as is common sense, this invasion of Parthia with the conquest of Bactria; it was one and the same upheaval of the steppes, set in motion by the advent of the Yueh-chi, and therefore, as between the limits of 141 and 128 for that conquest, it must fall about 130; the date usually taken, *c.* 135, arrived at by splitting the difference between 141 and 128, is too early.

Whether in the invasion of Parthia the Parsii went as far south as

[1] Namely, that *s.v.* Ἀραχωσία he identifies them as Massagetae; see App. 9.

[2] Chronology: Tarn, *CAH* IX pp. 281 *sqq.*

[3] Strabo XI, 511.

Seistan with the Sacas cannot be said, but they are presently found following Alexander's route through Arachosia by Ghazni and so to Kabul (App. 9), where we shall meet them later (Chap. VIII). Strabo (XI, 508) knows of a settlement of Parsii among the Anariakae of the Elburz, but it may be a question whether this was a deposit of the invasion of the second century B.C. or that of the seventh (p. 283), which Strabo says reached Armenia,[1] just as an Armenian story made the effects of the second invasion also felt in that country.[2] And we probably have a Greek notice of a short-lived kingdom founded at this time by some of the invaders, whether Sacas or Parsii, in Traxiane, between its conquest by the Parsii and its recovery by the Parthians some time before 115. Ptolemy gives among the towns of Bactria one named 'queen of Ebousmos' or 'of Tosmos'.[3] His co-ordinates place it somewhere in the Kasaf Rud valley,[4] *i.e.* in the satrapy of Traxiane,[5] whose capital was the important town of Tōs;[6] they may point to a dynast 'Ebousmos' (whatever his real name) ruling in Tōs who had renamed the place after his queen, Ptolemy's information coming from some merchant who had noted that he had visited a place called after Ebousmos' queen but had not given her name.

These were the invaders who put an end to the Greek kingdom of Bactria; and one must now turn to Chang-k'ien's description of the country just after the conquest. First, what is the meaning of his name for Bactria proper, Ta-hia? Before coming to what I think is the true view, two older explanations,[7] which will die hard, must be noticed. The one most widely spread is that the Tochari were not the Yueh-chi

[1] Strabo XI, 511, τῆς Ἀρμενίας κατεκτήσαντο τὴν ἀρίστην γῆν, afterwards called Sacasene.

[2] J. Kennedy, *JRAS* 1904 p. 309.

[3] Ptol. VI, 11, 8 Ἐβουσμουάνασσα ἢ Τοσμουάνασσα. Tomaschek, *Baktriane* in PW, emended this to *Εὐθυδήμου ἄνασσα*, an instance of the bad habit of substituting a known name for an unknown one where no reason exists.

[4] Berthelot p. 185 gives the fact, but his explanation of *ἄνασσα* is impossible.

[5] Tarn, *SP Stud.* pp. 23 *sq.*

[6] Arrian's Susia; Hysia, *βασίλειον Παρθυαίων*, of Artemidorus *ap.* Steph. *s.v.*, which means 'in Parthia', or perhaps 'in Parthyene', Tarn *ib.* p. 23 n. 1. On the importance of Tōs, where there is a great ruin-field of later times, see Herzfeld, *Arch. Mitt. aus Iran* I, 1929–30, p. 106.

[7] A third, Ta-hia = Dahae, is meaningless jingle; the Dahae did not live in Bactria. Other things apart, that is now shown by the Persian province-lists; the Dahae do not appear in any of Darius' lists, but they do appear in that of Xerxes (p. 80 n. 4), presumably as a new conquest, and were therefore quite separate from Bactria.

at all, but were the Ta-hia,[1] a theory which has worked utter confusion in the story. The modern form of the theory is that the Tochari came from Chinese Turkestan and conquered Bactria before the Yueh-chi, and were the Ta-hia whom the Yueh-chi subsequently conquered; and some scholars have accepted Ta-hia as a possible phonetic equivalent of Tocharia. But it has now been stated that this was not possible in the pronunciation of the second century B.C.;[2] and now that it has been shown that the Chinese in that century had the Tochari-togara name[3] its whole basis is gone. There is not, and never has been, one scrap of evidence for the identification Tochari = Ta-hia except this alleged phonetic equivalence, and, even were that possible, all it would prove would be, not that the Ta-hia were the Tochari, but that philology, though a good servant to the historian, can be a bad master. The matter is simple. The conquest of Bactria, we have seen, lies between 141 and 128, and was almost certainly *c.* 130. The well-informed Apollodorus, in whose lifetime the event took place, said that the Tochari at the time were nomads.[4] Chang-k'ien, who saw the Ta-hia in 128, said that the Ta-hia were communities of unwarlike traders living in walled towns.[5] A conquering horde of nomads does not, in two or three years time, turn into communities of unwarlike traders living in walled towns; there is nothing else which need be said,[6] except to regret the waste of labour and learning lavished on erecting theories upon such a basis.

The other explanation is that -hia is the first syllable of Yavanas, 'Ιάϝονες, and that Ta-hia means Greeks.[7] One might well enquire how Chang-k'ien came to hear either of the Sanscrit word Yavana or of the archaic Greek word 'Ιάϝονες; but in fact, had he somehow managed

[1] Started in its modern form by J. Marquart, *Ērānšahr* pp. 204–10; followed by E. Chavannes, *T'oung Pao* VIII p. 187; A. Kiessling, *Hunni*, and A. Herrmann, *Sacaraucae*, in PW; de Groot p. 10 and *passim*; Konow, *CII* p. liv and *passim*. Even Sir A. Stein inclined to believe it, *Serindia* I pp. 286–9, though he says (p. 287) that history must reckon with the fact that in historical times the Tarim basin has been utterly unsuited to nomad migrations.

[2] Communicated by Karlgren to Konow; see *Asia Major* IX, 1933, p. 463.

[3] H. W. Bailey *op. cit.* pp. 885–6.

[4] Strabo XI, 511, τῶν νομάδων... Τόχαροι.

[5] Hirth pp. 97–8.

[6] I said what was necessary in *SP Stud.* pp. 7–9. Herzfeld, *Sakastan* p. 27, dismissed the theory in a couple of words: it contradicts the sources. See also Franke pp. 31 *sqq.*

[7] E. H. Minns, *Scythians and Greeks* 1913 p. 129; Herzfeld, *Sakastan* p. 28. De Groot spells the word Ta-ha.

to get at a word for what we call 'Greek', what he would have got, as his compatriot Wen-chung did a little later, would have been Ἰωνακός (Yonaka) in some form (pp. 417*sq*)., and he would have transliterated this into Yung-kiu (Jong-kü, Jong-k'ut) as Wen-chung did (pp. 340 *sq*.).

The true explanation is very different. Already in 1904 it had been shown that the name Ta-hia occurs in Chinese texts long before the time of Chang-k'ien;[1] and though this was at first taken to mean that the Chinese had known the Tochari in the twelfth century B.C.,[2] it has since been explained[3] that, though the name Ta-hia may once have represented some real people in the north, in the third and second centuries B.C. the Ta-hia had become a people of fable on the western edge of the world,[4] and that when Chang-k'ien reached Bactria he thought he had found the mythical Ta-hia.[5] The fabulous nature of these Ta-hia comes out clearly in the story of the envoy sent to them to fetch bamboos for the emperor; the bamboo grew freely in China, but these were magical bamboos which, apart from their size, could only grow in fairy-land, seeing that he who owned a pipe made from them was privileged to hear and imitate the twelve notes of the song of the mythical phoenix, six sung by the male and six by his mate.[6]

Chang-k'ien's recognition of these legendary Ta-hia can be paralleled in his own time and country by the emperor Wu-ti's recognition of the 'heavenly horse', which will be noticed later and which seems to make the explanation certain; and indeed there are a couple of well-known parallels in the modern atlas. When the Happy Isles of the Greeks, floating in the unknown West, had been finally pinned down to the Canaries, their place in men's imagination was taken by a new island Antilia, which appeared on the fringe of the western ocean in many pre-Columban maps; to-day it is the Antilles. Such maps also showed

[1] Franke pp. 33–40.

[2] Franke in *Festschrift für Fr. Hirth* (*Ostasiat. Z.* 1919–20) p. 117.

[3] G. Haloun, *Seit wann kannten die Chinesen die Tocharer oder Indogermanen überhaupt?* 1926.

[4] *Ib.* pp. 198 *sqq.* Haloun says that Ta-hia is good Chinese, hia being the old dynastic name Hia, pp. 192, 201.

[5] *Ib.* p. 202. This conclusion was accepted by H. Maspero, *JA* 1927 p. 144. Herzfeld, *Sakastan* p. 28, called it 'recht unwahrscheinlich', but gave no reasons and did not consider either the bamboos or the parallels here given.

[6] *Ib.* pp. 157 *sqq.*, 180, 183. The Chinese 'phoenix' is no relation of the phoenix of Herodotus, whatever lay behind it (if anything did). A recent suggestion (Hon. M. U. Hachisuka, *JRAS* 1924 p. 585) is the rarely-seen ocellated pheasant. But pheasants do not sing.

in the far West another unknown island called Brazil,[1] that mysterious island of the red dye-wood which had replaced the Purple Islands of Pliny (VI, 202); and when the red dye-wood was discovered in Cabral's new Land of the Holy Cross, that land forthwith received, and still retains, the name of the mythical Brazil. It is very natural that what happened when Spain and Portugal discovered one new world in the far West should already have happened when China discovered another.

Chang-k'ien's account of the Ta-hia,[2] who are the people of Bactria proper, is that they had fixed abodes (*i.e.* were agriculturists, not nomads) and lived in walled towns and regular houses like the people of Ta-yuan; they were shrewd traders but poor fighters, so they had become subject to the Yueh-chi; their numbers he estimates at over a million. He calls their capital Lan-chi, *i.e.* Alexandria (Bactra, p. 115 n. 1), and was struck by its bazaars; he says however that they had no great king or chief, but that everywhere the cities and towns had, or were accustomed to set up, their own petty chiefs (see p. 122).[3] Most of the Ta-hia wore beards; and from Ferghana to Parthia, though the dialects differed, the people could understand each other[4] (the beards and language are Iranian). One other statement which Chang-k'ien makes[5] once provoked some discussion: 'they place high value on women, and husbands are guided in their decisions by the advice of their wives.' All it means, I think, is that he had heard of some local phenomenon, one that has been common at many periods and in many lands; probably no racial deductions can safely be drawn from it, but it might very

[1] I do not know what its connection may be with the Hy-Bresil of Celtic myth.

[2] Hirth pp. 97–8. There is no formal section on the Ta-hia in the *Ch'ien-han-shu*, they being included under the Yueh-chi, as that people had meanwhile occupied Bactria.

[3] Hirth p. 97 §48. So in the *Ch'ien-han-shu*; Wylie p. 40, 'were accustomed to set up petty chiefs over their cities'; de Groot p. 95, 'Die Städte setzten vielfach kleine Obmänner ein'.

[4] Hirth p. 108 §§101–2; so Eratosthenes in Strabo XV, 724, ὁμόγλωττοι παρὰ μικρόν. The *Ch'ien-han-shu* reproduces the statement about the language, but only mentions the people of Ta-yuan as having beards. One must follow Ssu-ma Ch'ien.

[5] Hirth p. 108 §102; Wylie p. 46. De Groot, p. 35, has gone most curiously astray here; he translates: 'Das Volk achtet die jungen Frauen hoch und die von ihnen ausgesprochenen Meinungen, die kräftigen Männer treffen darauf die Entscheidung.' This is the famous passage in Tacitus on the Teutonic virgins (*Germ.* 8, 5) transferred to an alien world. Franke notes the error and gives once again the real meaning.

possibly be a pre-Iranian survival.[1] His statement that the Ta-hia were poor fighters is doubtless only his compliment to his Yueh-chi hosts: but one may suppose that the warlike elements had been destroyed or driven out, for certainly what he saw was a country more or less derelict: the central government had been destroyed and not yet replaced by another (for the Yueh-chi did not actually occupy Bactria till later),[2] and every town had to shift for itself. Those Ta-hia who did not wear beards would be Greeks; but as even some Greek kings occasionally wore beards—the Seleucids Seleucus II and Demetrius II, and Strato I in India—there may have been more Greeks left than Chang-k'ien's statement would suggest.

The important thing in his account is of course the 'walled towns' and their government, the majority of these 'walled towns' being, as we have seen (pp. 121 *sq.*), fortified villages. In such few cities as existed the 'petty chiefs' would be either magistrates or the city-governors, ἐπιστάται, formerly appointed by the Greek king and now left masterless; on the analogy of the Parthian empire the city-governor might sometimes combine the two functions of representative of the royal power and head of the magistracy (p. 25) and, judging by what happened in Syria and Parthia, might sometimes take advantage of the absence of effective supervision to make himself tyrant or dynast. But in the mass of walled villages the 'petty chief' would be the head of the village community. This most important piece of observation has been discussed at length in chapter III, to which I must refer (pp. 120–4); the light thrown on the nature of the Bactrian village is Chang-k'ien's outstanding service to Greek history.

It should now be possible to form some idea of the conquest.

The Saca outbreak in the seventh century B.C. had been due to overpopulation. The same conditions obtained again in the second century, and the Saca lands, when the Yueh-chi appeared, were overpopulated and in a condition of unstable equilibrium; the impact of the Yueh-chi set up a series of movements which, after Parthia had dammed the flood on the west, were only to end with the Saca conquests in India

[1] M. Rostovtzeff has suggested (*CAH* XI, 1936, p. 92) that the part played in social and political life by the women among those half-Iranian Sarmatian tribes who were γυναικοκρατούμενοι came from the pre-Iranian Maeotian element in them.

[2] Chang-k'ien found them north of the Oxus, Hirth p. 96 §29, but they had crossed into Bactria before Ssu-ma Ch'ien wrote, *ib.* p. 94 §10, a passage in which Ssu-ma Ch'ien has antedated the crossing.

(Chap. VIII), conquests carried out by a people clearly far more numerous than the Greeks in India had ever been. But all barbarians were not merely barbarous; the Sacas in India, like the Parni in Iran, did not destroy the work of the Greeks but used it for their own advantage (p. 243); and the Yueh-chi, too, may not have been mere destroyers. The legendary Ta-hia, like other fairy peoples, presumably lived in a fairy land, and if Chang-k'ien thought that he had found them in Bactria, Bactria must still have been the fertile garden of the earth which it had been before; it had not been essentially damaged, and that is borne out by Chang-k'ien's account of the keenness of the people to trade. We must bear in mind Justin's statement that Bactria bled to death; the fighting forces of the last Greek king can hardly have been equal to those with which Demetrius had invaded India; indeed it is possible that after her defeat by Mithridates in 141 Bactria was weak enough to attract an invader. On the other hand, the military strength of a nomad people was out of all proportion greater than that of any settled people of the West with the same population.[1] The regular Chinese reckoning for nomads was that each family supplied one horseman to the general levy;[2] Chang-k'ien put the Yueh-chi levy in 128 B.C. at 100,000 horse archers,[3] and though this was far below their original strength, it was nevertheless a force with which the Bactrian Greeks had no chance whatever of coping; one recalls Rome's failures in the first century B.C. against far smaller numbers of Parthian horse archers. Whether in addition the Yueh-chi aristocracy fought in mail on partially mailed horses, as did the Saca aristocracies, is unknown. Probably one battle, fought north of the Oxus, sufficed for the Yueh-chi to overthrow the Greek government and the aristocracy, entailing a minimum of damage to Bactria itself; one battle had sufficed to make the much weaker Galatae masters for a time of the much stronger

[1] I say 'of the West', for Pan-ku gives to some of the little settled states in Chinese Turkestan more warriors than families. He takes a very high average for the number in a family there, even as high as 7, against one of 5 for Sacas (K'ang-kiu, Ta-yuan) and 4 for the Yueh-chi.

[2] Pan-ku's reckoning for the Yueh-chi, the K'ang-kiu, and the Saca rulers of Ta-yuan (de Groot pp. 95, 103, 109).

[3] Ssu-ma Ch'ien puts the Yueh-chi levy at from 100,000 to 200,000 horse-archers. But Chang-k'ien never gave such a margin of error for a people among whom he had lived; his figure for 128 B.C. was 100,000, as Pan-ku gives it, and 200,000, wherever it came from, must originally have referred to the Yueh-chi in Kan-su, before the loss of the Little Yueh-chi and of the fraction which stayed in the Lake Issykul country and the wastage due to forty-six years of fighting and trekking.

Macedonia. But the nomad cavalry were helpless against walls, and the walls even of the villages fulfilled their purpose; the 'walled towns' Chang-k'ien saw some two years later were untouched and were carrying on for themselves by means of their own organisation without a central government, though possibly they paid the Yueh-chi tribute.

Some lower class Greeks, traders and shopkeepers (so far as that class were Greeks), were undoubtedly still there, though Chang-k'ien seemingly did not distinguish them from the more numerous Bactrians, unless by his remark about beards; it may well be that, in spite of his knowledge of the bazaars in Bactra, he was never himself inside one of the Greek cities. These Greeks must have remained till, their government gone, they were absorbed in the native population. As to the upper class, the larger part undoubtedly perished. A few may have retired into India, but there is no trace in that country of any great accession of Greek strength. One section—a very small one—is known to have been exterminated: the Greek coinage of Bactria remained fine to the end, and then the great Bactrian artists vanished from the world; no trace of their peculiar skill in portraiture ever occurs again, in India or anywhere else. The likeliest supposition is that one battle sufficed to destroy most of the Greek aristocracy, just as in Britain the Northumbrian nobility was destroyed by the Picts at Nectansmere. The great Bactrian barons, if they still existed, presumably shared the same fate; they can never have been a numerous class. Chang-k'ien never mentions them at all; but no deductions can be drawn from his silence, for neither he nor the Chinese historians mention the aristocracy of Parthia.

But a few members of the aristocracy, Greek and Bactrian, must have escaped to the hills and taken refuge in the high valleys, beyond reach of the horsemen of the plains; such, or descendants of such, might be one or two of the very obscure kinglets known only from coins.[1] Some of these refugees may for a time have ruled petty semi-Greek kingdoms, which ultimately merged in the native element; it may be worth notice that Greeks had various stories of small Greek

[1] See p. 305 n. 2. Sapadbizes, for instance, wears Eucratides' helmet with Seleucus' badge and has an Indo-European face (*BMC* Pl. XXIV, 14, 15). The more important Hyrcodes, however, of whose silver issues many barbarous imitations exist, looks like a Kushan (*ib.* Pl. XXIV, 9), in spite of his Greek-sounding name; and 'King Antiochus', on the Indian side of the mountains (p. 323), is bearded and looks rather like a Parthian.

communities (though not in Bactria) being cut off and becoming 'barbarised',[1] and Plutarch has a fanciful account,[2] possibly based on a traveller's tale, of a body of Greeks thus cut off in another world beyond the Ocean stream who lost their nationality and language but miraculously recovered them. The Greeks who thus took refuge in the hills were the basis of the Alexander-descents of various hill chieftains on the Bactrian side of the great mountain wall formed by the Mustagh and the Hindu Kush (see App. 3). I have never seen a complete list of these descendants of Alexander; some were swept away in modern times by the Afghans, and if any still survive to-day they are Soviet citizens, but among them used to be the ruling families in Karategin, Darwaz, Roshan, Shignan (extinct), Wakhan (extinct), Pokhpu,[3] and, most important, the now extinct family of the Mirs of Badakshan, celebrated by Marco Polo,[4] whose very horses descended from Bucephalus[5] and whose Greek heirloom, a famous silver patera not later than the third century A.D.,[6] is now in an English museum.[7] Whether the hill-men in the period before Islam really retained any memory of Alexander or not (and it is possible), what lay at the bottom of the claim to descent from him was that fictitious Seleucid pedigree (App. 3) which, as we have seen, played such a part in the history of the Bactrian Greeks and under which not only the Seleucids but both the Greek houses who successively ruled Bactria traced their descent from the great Macedonian; it must be so, for that pedigree was demonstrably the origin of the Alexander-descents in the West (App. 3).

As regards these Bactrian hill-states, it means that somewhere in the pedigrees of their original ruling families[8] there was, or was supposed to be, a Bactrian Greek, whether a man or (more probably) a woman;

[1] A. D. Nock, *C.R.* XLIII, 1929, p. 126.

[2] *De facie in orbe lunae*, 941 A and C.

[3] See Yule, *Marco Polo*, 2nd ed. I p. 168, 3rd ed. I p. 160.

[4] Marco Polo I, chap. XXIX.

[5] Yule *op. cit.* 2nd ed. I p. 170, 3rd ed. I p. 162, suggested a connection between this story and the Chinese story of the heavenly horse (pp. 308 *sqq.*). He was probably right, though not quite as he meant: the origin of both the Badakshan and Ferghana horses must have been one of the great Parthian war-horses. See p. 308 n. 4.

[6] M. Rostovtzeff, *Seminarium Kondakovianum* VI, 1933, p. 171.

[7] O. M. Dalton, *The treasure of the Oxus*, 2nd ed. 1926, Pl. XXVII. Date not later than the third century A.D.: Rostovtzeff *op. cit.* p. 173.

[8] I do not mean that every little state had a separate descent. Some must have acquired it by marriage with a house that possessed it. But one can only speak in general terms.

and whether that Greek was actually of the royal blood of Bactria or not, he or she would certainly have soon become royal in the family tradition and therefore Alexander's descendant. There are still traces to be got, I believe, of these descents in the period before Islam: when in 614 Omar's general conquered Badakshan its king Bahram Shah was a descendant of Alexander;[1] and Marco Polo found a bit of the fictitious pedigree—the story that Roxane was a daughter of Darius III—current in Badakshan in the thirteenth century[2] as it had been current in the later Greek period (App. 3). Islam, which made Dhulcarnein one of its heroes, strengthened these beliefs—Marco Polo (I, XXIX) says that every ruler of Badakshan took the name Dhulcarnein; but it did not create them. Once the belief was established, a change in the ruling house would make little difference; conquerors or usurpers usually annexed the women of the conquered, and even if they did not they would annex any worth-while legend, just as the modern Mirs of Badakshan, who only went back to the seventeenth century, possessed both the legend and the heirloom. Provided people remain illiterate, such legends may run for ever; they are preserved in the memories of the women, which prior to printing were the world's marriage registers and books of pedigree. Indeed one amazing story exists of a name-memory which may, and seemingly must, have run for nineteen centuries from the period treated in this chapter: it is said that a century ago a dilapidated monument on the southern shore of Lake Issyk Kul was still called by the natives 'Chang-k'ien's Tablet',[3] and no one will accuse those natives or their forefathers of reading Ssu-ma Ch'ien. This, as I see it, is the history of the Alexander-descents.

For a considerable period after the conquest the coinage of the invading Yueh-chi consisted of more or less barbarous imitations of Greek coins, sometimes of those of Euthydemus but more usually of those of Heliocles;[4] as the nomads could not possibly coin for themselves till they began to adopt a settled life, and as it cannot be said when that was, these coins must have been struck by Greeks or Bactrians. Three classes of these imitations are known, one with Greek legends only, one with mixed legends of rude Greek and Sogdian letters, and one with

[1] G. W. Leitner, *Dardistan in 1895* (1895), Supp. p. 18. This pamphlet gives much information about Badakshan and its Mirs.

[2] I do not know whether this could have been got from some Arab writer.

[3] Hirth p. 138.

[4] *CHI* pp. 461, 557.

Sogdian letters only.[1] It would be natural to see in them the progressive loss of the Greek language, but it might also be that the divergences represent not different periods of time but different localities; much of their interest resides in the fact that they are early specimens of the Sogdian language,[2] which had therefore been reduced to writing under Greek rule. They *may* also indicate that in some towns native Bactrians had been in the service of the mints, like the Indian mint-officials in some of the late Greek kingdoms in India (pp. 356 *sq.*); but this more probably took place after the break-up of Greek rule, seeing that the last Greek king, Heliocles, did not employ native mint-officials in India. These coins also show that, whatever may have been the case under Greek rule, coins were now being produced elsewhere than in the royal mint at Bactra; these imitations, though made by people who still knew enough to give Heliocles a new type which he had never used himself,[3] cannot well have been struck at Bactra, for that mint could not suddenly have become barbarised unless Bactra had been sacked, and such was certainly not the case: Chang-k'ien's reference,[4] just after the conquest, to its 'markets for the sale of every sort of merchandise' show that it was undamaged. The nomads had no chance of taking such a strongly fortified city by military operations, but they could bring it to terms by ravaging its lands year after year; and Bactra must have made terms. No doubt for a considerable time it stood to the Yueh-chi in the same sort of quasi-independent relationship as Seleuceia for long did to the Parthians, paying however tribute for its land; in the nature of the case, nomads could not make a city their capital, *i.e.* the seat of their government, till they ceased to be nomads and adopted a settled life, and Bactra does not in fact appear as the Yueh-chi capital till much later.[5] The process may have been perfectly peaceful, like the 'peaceful penetration' of the Greek cities of the Bosporan kingdom by the Sarmatians.[6]

It is strongly held that the Saca speech of the Kushans was reduced

[1] R. Hoernle, *Ind. Ant.* XXVII, 1898, p. 225. I take it that the writing he calls Bactrian is Sogdian; see next note.

[2] Allotte de la Fuye, *Rev. Num.* 1925 p. 34.

[3] *BMC* p. 22.

[4] Hirth p. 98 §51.

[5] First mentioned as such in the *Hou-han-shu* (Chavannes' translation, *T'oung Pao* VIII p. 187). In the *Ch'ien-han-shu* the Yueh-chi 'capital' is still north of the Oxus, Wylie p. 40, de Groot p. 95; but as Pan-ku is not giving the later history of the Yueh-chi this gives no help over the date.

[6] Rostovtzeff, *CAH* XI p. 96.

to writing in Bactria,[1] and as it was written in Greek letters this could hardly have taken place before the Yueh-chi acquired Bactra as their capital. Various obscure rulers are known who probably belong to the century after the conquest and whose coins exhibit Greek elements;[2] some may have ruled bits of the one-time Greek kingdom, probably in the hills, or even ruled in some Greek city as vassals of the Kushans, but of more importance is the Kushan Miaos (or Heraos), the first chieftain among the Yueh-chi to issue a Greek coinage. He will be considered in a later connection (App. 17 and p. 342); but if the suggestion there made be well founded, his coinage must have been struck (or modelled) for him in Kapisa, not in Bactria, and the question may therefore arise whether it was not at Kapisa that the Saca speech of the Kushans was reduced to writing. The use in that language of the Greek symbol for *sh*, the sign *þ* (App. 18), gives no help; for though this sign occurs much earlier in north-west India than the coinage of the Kushan kings—it is found on the coins of Miaos (in the form P) about 50 B.C., and on some of those of Spalirises (p. 509) in the latter part of the first century B.C.—that does not prove that it was not also used in Bactria. *A priori*, the reduction of the Kushan language into Greek writing is more likely to have taken place at their capital Bactra than at Kapisa; but I can see no certainty. Though the Greek *language* must have soon perished, Greek *script* lasted on in Bactria (Tocharistan), and apparently in Shignan and Chitral also, for centuries, and even appears on Ephthalite coins[3] (fifth century A.D.); and it has been supposed that Hsüan Tsiang's reference to an alphabet of twenty-five letters in use in Tocharistan in his day (seventh century) means the Greek alphabet, twenty-four letters and *þ*.[4] The much earlier disappearance of Greek script in India (p. 356) may have been partly due to the competition of Kharoshthi.

[1] F. W. Thomas, *JRAS* 1913 p. 1016, 'nearer a certainty than a conjecture'.

[2] Hyrcodes (*BMC* p. 117; R. Hoernle, *JASB* 1899 vol. LXVIII part 1, extra no. 1 p. 26; Allotte de la Fuye *op. cit.* p. 151); Spabāris (*ib.* p. 155); Sapadbizes (?), who wears Eucratides' helmet (*BMC* p. 119; query, is he Spabāris?); and Phseigacharis (*ib.*), who must be later, as his coins have square phi and sigma. Hyrcodes issues Greek pieces and also pieces with Sogdian legends, but his face resembles that of Miaos and the Kushans. The obscure Sanabares (*BMC* p. 113) can hardly belong to this class, as his coins, unlike the others, have Greek monograms and were therefore struck in a recognised Greek mint.

[3] H. W. Bailey *op. cit.* pp. 891–2; Whitehead *JRAS* 1933 p. 220.

[4] Most recently by Bailey, *ib.*

The end of the Sacaraucae horde must be noticed here, because of its possible bearing on the dating of the important historian whom I have called 'Trogus' source' (p. 48). So far as one can rely upon Trogus' Prologues, the 'perishing' of the Sacaraucae was the latest incident in regard to Bactria which he related;[1] how far he may have gone in India has been considered elsewhere (*ib.*). The Sacaraucae are last mentioned by name as bringing Sinatruces to the Parthian throne in 77 B.C.,[2] though it has been supposed that they were the 'Scythians' with whom Phraates IV took refuge when expelled by Tiridates in 27 B.C.;[3] but this latter date need not be considered, for it is certain enough now that Phraates IV was restored by the Suren from Sacastene.[4] It seems an inevitable deduction, though it has not been drawn, that it was also the Suren who brought Sinatruces to the throne in 77 B.C.; this is far more likely than that it should have been done by nomads from Bokhara, and it would agree with the now known political orientations of the house of the Suren. Consequently we have no mention which can be trusted of the Sacaraucae as an independent horde later than the conquest of Bactria *c.* 130 B.C. and the associated invasion of Parthia in 129. Trogus clearly couples his account of the 'perishing' of the Sacaraucae with his account of the composition of the Yueh-chi horde; and as his source can only have given the latter account in connection with the conquest of Bactria, the 'perishing' of the Sacaraucae cannot be too far removed in time from that event.

It is perhaps not difficult to see what happened. The Sacaraucae, after taking Merv, joined in the invasion of Parthia. Some may have remained with their kinsfolk in Sacastene, and a large body, doubtless the majority, went on into India in conjunction with other Sacas; but part of the horde, between 124 and 115, were rolled back northward by the Suren when he liquidated the Saca invasion (p. 499)[5]; he took Merv and drove them back across the Oxus, whereon they 'perished'. But the 'perishing' of a horde does not mean that it was exterminated; it means that it ceased to exist as a separate horde by being absorbed into another horde, just as the Massagetae (that is, those of them who had

[1] *Prol.* XLII, Additae his res Scythicae (*i.e.* an excursus). Reges Thocarorum Asiani interitusque Saraucarum.

[2] Pseudo-Lucian, *Macrobii* 15. Herzfeld, *Sakastan* p. 27, consequently put the *interitus* after 77. But Pseudo-Lucian is hardly impeccable evidence on such a point.

[3] Justin XLII, 5, 5. Herrmann, *Sacaraucae* in PW, consequently (col. 1620) made the *interitus c.* 20 B.C., at the hands of the Yueh-chi.

[4] Herzfeld, *Sakastan* pp. 73–4.

[5] See further *CAH* IX p. 585.

remained in their original country) were absorbed soon afterwards; most of them had gone on into India, but those in the south of their original territory were seemingly absorbed by the Dahae[1] and those in the north by the Aorsi; the latter body were, with the Aorsi, ultimately absorbed by the Alans. In the same way, those of the Sacaraucae who were driven north were absorbed by the K'ang-kiu, who had occupied western Sogdiana behind them (pp. 280, 291); this may of course have been preceded by a destructive defeat, which left what remained of the Sacaraucae helpless between the victorious Parthians and the victorious K'ang-kiu. To Chang-k'ien, the K'ang-kiu in 128 were only a moderate-sized horde and not even fully independent,[2] but they appear in the Ch'ien-han-shu with a great accession of strength,[3] for which their absorption of the returning Sacaraucae would account; it is supposed that their territory now stretched from Tashkent to Bokhara and from eastern Chorasmia to Samarcand,[4] and Pan-ku not only makes them stronger than the Yueh-chi[5] but dilates on their pride and insolence in a way which shows that the Chinese found them very difficult to handle.[6] One reason why 'Trogus' source' gave prominence to the end of the Sacaraucae as a separate people would be that they had long been well known to the Greek world; but it may also very well be that they had supplied the leaders for the invasion of Parthia. In any case, their 'perishing' does not conflict with the date already deduced for 'Trogus' source' (p. 50).

There remains one country yet to notice, Ferghana (Ta-yuan), which had formed part of the kingdom of Euthydemus (p. 83 and App. 10). It was the first 'western country' which Chang-k'ien reached after escaping from the Hiung-nu; he found[7] a settled agricultural land like Bactria with 'walled towns' and 'postal roads', where the people made wine from grapes and stored it for years, and from which the vine

[1] Herrmann, *Massagetai* in PW col. 2129, though he puts it much too early. If this be right, the Dahae did not join in the invasion of Parthia; this might well be so, as they were Parthia's mother-people.

[2] Hirth p. 96 § 27, 80,000–90,000 archers, and a small territory, the southern part being under the political influence ('in der Gewalt', de Groot p. 15) of the Yueh-chi and the northern part under that of the Hiung-nu.

[3] Wylie p. 42, de Groot p. 103; 120,000 horse-archers.

[4] De Groot pp. 15, 106–8; he identifies their capital Pi-tien with Samarcand, on the distances given. Herzfeld (see *ante* p. 280 n. 2) has put this too early.

[5] 120,000 horse-archers as against 100,000.

[6] Wylie p. 43; de Groot p. 104.

[7] Hirth pp. 95 § 18 *sqq*., p. 108 § 99; Wylie p. 44; de Groot p. 109.

and the alfalfa were subsequently brought to China. His account, as given by Ssu-ma Ch'ien, is however not at all clear as to the political position in Ta-yuan; he may have passed through in a hurry, as he was only ten days distant from the Hiung-nu and may have felt unsafe till he could reach the Yueh-chi; but his statement that the people shoot arrows on horse-back is inconsistent with a purely agricultural land of the Ta-hia type, and the parallel passage in the Ch'ien-han-shu, which reproduces exactly the same account, makes it clear that there was a nomad people (or a people of ex-nomads) superimposed upon and ruling the agricultural population;[1] and in 106–101 the king of Ferghana bore the Saca name Mu-ku'a[2] (Mauakes-Maues, see p. 496).

Chang-k'ien *heard*[3] of the special horses of Ferghana, the great Parthian chargers[4] who were said to be descended from the 'heavenly horse', the *tien-ma*, and 'sweated blood' (whatever the Chinese word really means),[5] and fed on the alfalfa of the country; but the sequel makes it clear that he never *saw* them and did not know what they were, another proof that he hurried through the country.[6] But the emperor

[1] Pan-ku (Wylie p. 44, de Groot p. 109) gives first his own formula for Saca nomads (families x, population $5x$, warriors x) and then the same account of a settled agricultural people as Ssu-ma Ch'ien; seemingly he is making more precise what the earlier writer left somewhat vague.

[2] Hirth p. 112.

[3] Hirth p. 95 §19 (Chang-k'ien's Report).

[4] On the Parthian and Ferghana horses and the 'heavenly horse' see Tarn, *Military Developments* 1930 pp. 77 *sqq.* For the Doura graffiti of Parthian chargers see *Fourth preliminary report of the excavations at Dura-Europos* 1933 Pls. XXI, XXII, and *CAH* vol. of Plates IV p. 26 *c* (1934).

[5] Hirth p. 140 suggested that the word, han-huï, might be a transcript of some foreign sound.

[6] There are two Chinese accounts of what follows. Pan-ku in Chap. XCVI (Wylie pp. 44–5) makes Chang-k'ien himself tell Wu-ti of the Ferghana horses, *i.e.* in 126, and Wu-ti thereon sends an envoy to Ta-yuan who is put to death and the military expeditions of 106–101 follow at once; this cannot be right, for if Wu-ti was sufficiently interested to burst into poetry, twenty years delay is incredible. Ssu-ma Ch'ien (Hirth pp. 109–13) and Pan-ku in the Life (Wylie pp. 70–2) put the whole thing after Chang-k'ien's second mission in 115, and I have followed this in my text; it implies that Wu-ti never knew what the Ferghana horses were really like till *after* he had got the Wu-sun ones which Chang-k'ien brought home in 115, and that therefore Chang-k'ien, though he *heard* of the Ferghana horses in 128, never *saw* them and thought they were like the Wu-sun horses. The latest modern account is that of W. P. Yetts in *Eurasia Septentrionalis Antiqua* IX, 1934, p. 231; but he has not considered the difficulty discussed in this note (does it therefore only exist in the translations?) and does not refer to the great Parthian war-horses.

Wu-ti was interested when he heard of them, as he had found an oracle in the Book of Changes which said that 'the heavenly horse will come from the North-West'[1]—indeed it appears that an apparition of the creature had recently been recorded[2]—and when Chang-k'ien, on his second journey westward in 115, brought back some horses from the Wu-sun[3] which were stronger than any known in China, Wu-ti thought that these were the horses he had heard of, descendants of the 'heavenly horse', and named them 'heavenly horses'.[4]

But after Chang-k'ien's death in 114 he got information—it is not recorded how, but doubtless from one of Chang-k'ien's lieutenants—of the real nature of the Ferghana horses, and sent mission after mission to purchase some; on the arrival of the first ones he transferred the name 'heavenly horses' to them from the Wu-sun horses[5] and himself wrote a poem to celebrate the arrival of the 'heavenly horse' in China;[6] the type of these great chargers can subsequently be traced in Chinese art.[7] But he then heard from some young men attached to one of the missions[8] that the king of Ta-yuan, Mu-ku'a, had even finer horses in his city of Ir-shi[9] than those which he had got, and he sent an envoy to buy some; the murder of this envoy by Mu-ku'a, who thought he was out of reach, led to China's war with Ta-yuan, which was allied with the K'ang-kiu. There is no need to give details; after more than one fruitless attempt a Chinese army in 101 actually reached Ir-shi and took

[1] Hirth p. 103 §79.

[2] The first of the two poems given by Ssu-ma Ch'ien (*below*, n. 6), apparently in Wu-ti's reign.

[3] Hirth p. 102 §73.

[4] *Ib.* p. 103 §79; so Wylie p. 70 (from the Life).

[5] *Ib.*

[6] For the two poems see Chavannes' translation, *Les mémoires historiques de Se-ma Ts'ien* III pp. 236–7. It is the *second* poem (not the first, as Chavannes thought) which is Wu-ti's, as Ssu-ma Ch'ien shows clearly by Ki-Yen's remark. But this poem must be in or before 112, when Ki-Yen died (see Chavannes' note); therefore the first of the Ferghana horses reached China in or before 112 ('Le cheval céleste est arrivé'), and this confirms the version which I have adopted; Chavannes, in transferring the Ki-Yen incident from the second poem to the first, was misled by the belief that no Ferghana horses came till 101. It does not appear that the horse whose apparition is the subject of the first poem ('Le cheval céleste est descendu') was ever brought to Wu-ti at all; it was merely part of the 'heavenly horse' legend.

[7] Tarn *op. cit.* App. II.

[8] Hirth p. 109 §105.

[9] Hirth's spelling. Other versions have been Eul-che and Ni-se; de Groot calls it Dsi-su. Identified in later Chinese writings with Uratube.

the lower city, but could not reduce the citadel because, although they had cut off its water supply, there was in it a 'man from Ts'in' who knew how to dig wells;[1] finally the Chinese general, fearing the K'ang-kiu whom the besieged had threatened to call in, agreed to a compromise under which he retired after the besieged had killed Mu-ku'a, accepted China's suzerainty, and handed over a few of the horses.

I have related the story of the 'heavenly horse' because the recognition of this legendary creature and its offspring in the flesh by Wu-ti is such a valuable parallel to the recognition of the legendary Ta-hia by Chang-k'ien; but the story contains one other point of interest for the Greek historian, the man from Ts'in. Though the name Ts'in for China may be usually later, there are said to be cases in the Han period of the expression 'men of the Ts'in' meaning Chinese,[2] and the favourite interpretation has naturally been that the 'man from Ts'in' was a Chinese deserter;[3] it may be so, but my difficulty is that Ssu-ma Ch'ien has shortly before mentioned Chinese deserters quite explicitly in another connection,[4] and if he had meant the same thing in the passage in question he would presumably have said so. Another meaning of Ta Ts'in, later than Ssu-ma Ch'ien, is the Greek Orient generally, which by the time that the expression came into use meant in practice Roman Syria,[5] for the term never included An-si (Parthia); but in 101 B.C. Parthia already extended to the Euphrates, and the presence of a Syrian engineer in Ferghana at the time of the final break-up of Seleucid rule in Syria is too remote a possibility to be worth considering. But there still remains one other meaning of the word: a definite part of the Greek Farther East. In the Chinese translation of the Milindapañha Menander says that he was born in Ta-Ts'in,[6] when he had in fact been born in the Paropamisadae; and his capital Cho-kie (Sāgala) is said in one place to be in India[7] and in another 'in the kingdom of Ta-Ts'in, in the regions of the North';[8] that is, Ta-Ts'in is here used to

[1] Hirth p. 113 §122. De Groot, p. 40, makes it plural, 'men'.
[2] B. Laufer, *Sino-Iranica* 1919 p. 569.
[3] Hirth pp. 113, 150; de Groot p. 40; Yetts *op. cit.* p. 234.
[4] Hirth p. 108 §103, with note 5: some Chinese deserters settled in the western countries and taught the people the art of casting iron.
[5] The regular use in the *Hou-han-shu*, which begins at A.D. 25.
[6] Demiéville p. 168 §CVIII.
[7] Demiéville p. 90 §XXII.
[8] *Ib.* §XXV.

signify the Yavana country,[1] the country of the Bactrian Greeks. The 'man from Ts'in' in Ferghana *might* therefore be a Greek engineer of the Farther East, and this is certainly suggested by the wells, which are a parallel to the great wells of the Periplus near Barygaza, memorials of the Greek occupation of Surastrene (p. 148); in both the Greek and the Chinese accounts 'wells' mean deeper wells than the native inhabitants could dig for themselves. Nothing therefore prevents us from believing, if we wish, that the 'man from Ts'in' who foiled the Chinese army was the last Greek of the Bactrian kingdom to be mentioned in history.

As we have travelled far in Chang-k'ien's company, it is only fitting that the last word should be of him. The man who, by force of personality and not of arms, had opened up to China a new world in the west, gained the affection of the barbarians,[2] and enabled regular trade communication to be started between China and Iran along the subsequently famous Silk Route, was not forgotten in his own land; indeed he became something of a legend.[3] It is not clear to me either from Ssu-ma Ch'ien or Pan-ku that he brought the vine and the alfalfa from Ta-yuan to China himself—it would seem that he showed the way and that they were first actually brought by others[4]—but in any case later writers attributed to him not only the introduction of these two plants but that of many others which ultimately reached China from Iran; a whole list of legendary 'Chang-k'ien plants' is known.[5] And for years after his death Chinese envoys to the West always stated, as their passport to foreign peoples, that they were his countrymen, 'the mention of his name', says Ssu-ma Ch'ien, 'being regarded as a guarantee of good faith'.[6]

[1] So P. Pelliot, *JA* 1914 p. 401, on the passage last cited.

[2] Hirth p. 95 §13; Wylie p. 67.

[3] Laufer *op. cit.* p. 190. Yetts, *op. cit.* p. 231, speaks of the Chinese making of him a 'culture-hero'. See also K. S. Latourette, *The Chinese* I, 1934, p. 109.

[4] Laufer, *op. cit.* pp. 190, 210, 221, assumes that these two plants *were* brought by Chang-k'ien. But Ssu-ma Ch'ien ascribes their introduction to 'Chinese envoys', Hirth p. 108 §100, and Pan-ku to a subsequent Chinese mission, Wylie p. 45, de Groot p. 111. Pan-ku says later, in his own summing up (Wylie part 2 p. 113): 'The reports regarding the celestial horse and grapes led to the opening up of communication with Ta-yuan'; in his view then, as regards the vine, Chang-k'ien only brought back a *report*.

[5] Laufer *op. cit.* p. 190 and under Chive, Coriander, Cucumber, Fig, Pomegranate, Safflower, Sesame, Walnut.

[6] Hirth p. 103 §77; so Pan-ku, Wylie p. 70.

CHAPTER VIII

GREEKS AND SACAS IN INDIA

WITH the death of Menander the little thread of literary information which has been our guide through the maze breaks off, and except for one episode the story of Greek rule in India can be taken no further from written history. In places that rule lasted for well over a century after Menander's death, and a large number of kings are known: taking Bactria and India together, and assuming that the first Diodotus took the royal title, we know from literature and coins of thirty-six kings and one queen, Agathocleia;[1] a Kharoshthi inscription has added one more name, Theodamas.[2] The labours of numismatists[3] have succeeded in producing a broad outline of events, and some points of interest can be recovered, notably as regards the revival a generation before the end; that is all, for no Greek historian seems to have taken the story of the Farther East further down than the death of Mithridates II in 87 B.C. (pp. 45, 48). Putting it very roughly, until the coming of the Sacas the house of Eucratides ruled most of the country between the Hindu Kush and the Jhelum, though we may meet some Euthydemid kings to the west of that river, and the houses of Euthydemus and Menander ruled from the Jhelum to Mathurā; somewhere about 80 B.C. the Sacas, who had previously established a kingdom in Sind and the Greek sea-provinces to the southward, came up the Indus, occupied Taxila and Gandhāra, and drove a wedge in between the two realms or state-groups. To which house or group the greater number of the known kings belong has been

[1] In alphabetical order: Agathocleia, Agathocles, Amyntas, Antialcidas, Antimachus (2), Apollodotus (2), Apollophanes, Archebius, Artemidorus, Demetrius (2), Diodotus (2), Diomedes, Dionysius, Epander, Eucratides (2), Euthydemus (2), Heliocles, Hermaeus, Hippostratus, Lysias, Menander, Nicias, Pantaleon, Peucolaos, Philoxenus, Plato, Polyxenus, Telephus, Theophilus, Zoilus (2). I do not include Hermaeus' queen Calliope, as she did not reign alone.

[2] *CII* p. 6 no. III; see p. 323. For the supposed mention of some of the later kings in the *Yuga-purāna* see App. 4.

[3] For the coins of these later kings see especially *BMC* under their names; Whitehead *NC* pp. 294 *sqq.* and *Lahore Cat.*; *CHI* pp. 552 *sqq.*, 557 *sqq.*, 586 *sqq.* Two kings, Peucolaos (Whitehead *NC* p. 324) and Polyxenus (*Lahore Cat.* p. 53), were discovered after the publication of *BMC*.

elucidated from their coin-types,[1] and these, together sometimes with identical monograms, furnish the only safe ground; attempts to group the kings by artistic considerations[2] do not, in my opinion, take us very far, for the method is subjective and is open to the accident of a better engraver turning up in some town. Some of the known names are probably sub-kings.

In the western group, Heliocles was succeeded by Antialcidas, who must have begun to reign, or reign alone, not later than *c.* 130. He was a king of some power: he certainly ruled from the Hindu Kush to the Jhelum, as his silver coins show the full type of Alexandria-Kapisa[3] and the inscription on the Besnagar column[4] in Vidisā proves that he reigned in Taxila; the possibility that he still retained some footing north of the Hindu Kush has already been noticed (p. 273) in connection with his title 'the Victorious', and on the Besnagar column he is 'the Great King'. His known rule in Taxila, and the *pilei* of the Dioscuri on his copper coins, furnish the reason for the belief that henceforth the *pilei* were the type of Taxila. He was evidently related to Heliocles,[5] but how is unknown. His date depends largely on the Besnagar inscription, which shows him sending an ambassador, Heliodorus son of Dion, to a Sunga king Bhāgabhadra in Vidisā, then in the fourteenth year of his reign. This inscription is very important for another matter, to be noticed later; here it need only be said that the list of Sunga kings in the Purānas[6] knows no Bhāgabhadra, and he is generally identified with the last king but one of that list, Bhāga or Bhāgavata, whose fourteenth year is supposed to fall round about 90 B.C.,[7] though it has been put much earlier.[8] A reign of some forty years is possible enough, but there are considerable difficulties, which we shall come to later, in taking Antialcidas down to *c.* 90 B.C.; for five kings in Gandhāra have to come

[1] This is the basis of Rapson's scheme in *CHI*, which is much the best, and which, with certain alterations and additions, I follow in outline till near the end.

[2] Whitehead's scheme of three groups, west to east, according to the quality of the art. Certainly on the whole the west is rather better than the east, though I sometimes cannot follow his grouping as regards individual kings. But a recent discovery has borne out his view about Zoilus' two coinages (p. 319).

[3] *BMC* pp. 25–6, Zeus enthroned holding Nike on his hand, and before him a small elephant or the forepart of one.

[4] Published by Sir John Marshall, *JRAS* 1909 p. 1055; cf. J. Ph. Vogel, *ASI* 1908–9 p. 126. Much discussed since. See further pp. 380, 406.

[5] They use a common type, not found elsewhere: *CHI* pp. 559, 590.

[6] Given in *CHI* p. 518.

[7] *Ib.* p. 521.

[8] V. A. Smith made it 108 B.C.

in between Antialcidas and Maues, and the Saca (Parsii) occupation of Kabul, which was definitely before 87, was almost certainly after Antialcidas' death (see p. 472); it might therefore be better either to identify Bhāgabhadra with some earlier king or to suppose that Bhāga was earlier than the Purāna chronology makes him, and date the inscription not later than *c.* 100 B.C.

A difficult problem is the 'joint' coin of Antialcidas and Lysias.[1] Lysias on his own coins used the type of Demetrius, Heracles crowning himself; he sometimes wore Demetrius' elephant-scalp,[2] and adopted Demetrius' title ἀνίκητος; that he was a descendant, presumably a grandson, of Demetrius seems self-evident. But Antialcidas certainly belonged to the rival line of Eucratides, as his type '*pilei* of the Dioscuri' shows; and the 'joint' coin is so difficult that the view has been put forward that (for once) Lysias' types have not their natural meaning but are merely local.[3] But ἀνίκητος cannot be local, and that title, combined with the elephant-scalp, leaves no doubt who Lysias was, for the combination of these two things had been of the very essence of Demetrius' royalty (pp. 131 *sq.*). The important thing is that at some period Lysias was able to coin in a Greek mint, but all the mints known were in the hands of Antialcidas or Strato; at the same time the elephant on Lysias' coins (which might, however, be the elephant of Taxila), and more especially the little elephant on his aegis (which cannot well refer to Taxila), have been interpreted—in the latter case there seems no alternative—to mean that he regarded himself as under the protection of the elephant god of Kapisa.[4]

I see only one way to fit these facts together. It must be supposed that when Heliocles recovered Bactria some son of Demetrius, either Demetrius II or Agathocles, had survived and had continued to maintain himself in some of the hill provinces, cut off from the great road, the capitals, and the mints; as he had no mint, no trace of him during this period would remain. Lysias was his son,[5] and his 'joint' coin with Antialcidas refers to a rapprochement, probably a treaty of permanent peace, between the two factions, the end of the long feud of the rival

[1] *BMC* p. 166: obv., βασιλέως ἀνικήτου Λυσίου and bust of Heracles; rev., Maharajasa jayadharasa (victorious) Amtialikidasa and *pilei* of the Dioscuri.

[2] *BMC* Pl. X, 6. On one of this series he wears instead the flat kausia of the Euthydemids: *Lahore Cat.* p. 31 no. 156.

[3] Rapson in *CHI* p. 559.

[4] Whitehead *NC* p. 326 no. 4.

[5] His face is not old enough for him to have been Demetrius' son.

houses;[1] Lysias must have kept his hill kingdom but become in some form an associate—it could not here be sub-king—of Antialcidas, as he henceforth coined in his mints. For all four of Lysias' monograms appear on Antialcidas' coins[2] (though the latter has a couple of others also), which is decisive proof that they shared the same moneyers; there are arguments for both Kapisa and Taxila as the mint,[3] and probably Lysias used both. The 'joint' coin of course does not express the treaty, though it refers to it; it is not a joint coin at all, but a coin of Lysias, who (though Antialcidas was probably the more powerful) has naturally allotted to himself the obverse and the Greek legend; probably there were coins of Antialcidas with the position reversed. This treaty may be the reason why coins exist which show Antialcidas wearing the flat kausia of the Euthydemids[4] and Lysias wearing the helmet of Eucratides;[5] and an unexplained coin of Antialcidas, on which the elephant-god and his elephant are *marching*,[6] might relate to the same event, which would doubtless have been celebrated with some sort of a display or procession. The reason for such a reconciliation is obvious: the Saca menace was already coming into view.

Antialcidas was the last king to rule all the three kingdoms west of the Jhelum—Taxila, Gandhāra, Paropamisadae; on his death his realm was divided, or broke up, into its component parts. His successor in Taxila was Archebius, who struck a certain number of tetradrachms[7] and was certainly succeeded by the Saca Maues;[8] his coinage is better artistically than that of his contemporaries,[9] which means that a better engraver had appeared in Taxila. In Gandhāra five kings are known between Antialcidas and Maues:[10] Diomedes, Epander, and Philoxenus all use the humped bull of Pushkalāvatī; Peucolaos may be 'king Peucela' (pp. 244 *sq.*) and exhibits the Fortune of Pushkalāvatī on his rare

[1] There is a famous precedent in the treaty of permanent peace between Antigonus Gonatas and Antiochus I, which stood for generations.

[2] Cf. *BMC* p. 29 and Pl. XXXI, 2 with pp. 25–8.

[3] This depends on analysis of the monograms. I need not give it.

[4] *BMC* Pl. VII, 11, 13; *Lahore Cat.* p. 32 nos. 167–83.

[5] *BMC* Pl. VIII, 7. It might also explain why on two coins (*BMC* Pl. X, 10, 12) Strato too wears Eucratides' helmet with the bull's horn and ear.

[6] Whitehead *NC* p. 325 no. 21, Pl. XV, 5; he calls it a 'march past'.

[7] Thirty were found in 1917 in the Kabul hoard, Whitehead, *NC* p. 315.

[8] Rapson in *CHI* p. 559; his reason is conclusive. See Herzfeld, *Sakastan* p. 97.

[9] See for example the coin figured in *CHI* Pl. XXX *d*.

[10] *CHI* p. 557.

coinage;[1] Artemidorus' rule in Pushkalāvatī is certain both from his name and his types, and it is quite certain that his immediate successor was Maues.[2] The coins of Peucolaos and Artemidorus are extremely rare, and indicate very short reigns. As all coined in Pushkalāvatī, we cannot suppose a number of little kingdoms in the separate satrapies of Gandhāra; but some might have been sub-kings. The matter is complicated by Artemidorus' and Philoxenus'[3] use of the title ἀνίκητος, which may signify some connection with Lysias; it is likely enough that, if I am right about the peace between Antialcidas and Lysias, the two houses were intermarrying, as they did later (p. 337), and in fact Philoxenus uses the type of Antimachus II, 'King on prancing horse'.[4] It seems probable, therefore, that the one-time simple division—house of Eucratides west of the Jhelum, house of Euthydemus east of it—needs a good deal of qualification.

One thing may, I think, be left out of the question. Owing to the fact that the system of sub-kings has not been understood, the large number of the later Greek kings in India has been explained as meaning much civil war and one king ousting another.[5] There seems little trace of this, and less probability. Only one usurper, I think, can be detected—Telephus. Only one overstrike, so far as I know, occurs—that of a coin of Apollodotus II by Zoilus II Soter[6] in the eastern Punjab; and though overstriking is the usual accompaniment of conquest, every overstrike does not necessarily mean a war, unless we have some other reason for supposing one. There had been civil wars enough in the middle of the second century; but once we get to the first century B.C. they are very difficult to credit. The Greeks in the north-west of India, with Bactria, Seistan, and the sea-provinces all lost, had become politically isolated in a vast world of 'barbarism', and its dead pressure must have tended to hold them together, as the pressure of the coloured

[1] Whitehead *NC* p. 324 no. 20; *Lahore Cat.* p. 80 no. 642. The British Museum has a specimen.

[2] *CHI* p. 558 (conclusive); see Herzfeld, *Sakastan*, p. 97.

[3] There is a coin of Philoxenus with the legend badly blundered, Whitehead *JASB* VI, 1910, Num. Supp. XIV p. 559 no. 8, which cannot have been struck at Pushkalāvatī; he may have tried to coin in some province, unless it be a later imitation.

[4] *BMC* pp. 56, 55; cf. Pl. XIII, 6 with 3. I am not using von Sallet's 'joint' coin of Archebius and Philoxenus, as its genuineness is said to be doubtful: Rapson, *Indian Coins* 1897 p. 6.

[5] Whitehead *NC* p. 308.

[6] *Ib.*

population in South Africa is tending to unite Briton and Boer. The threat of the Saca invasion from the south was already apparent; such a peace treaty as I have supposed between Antialcidas and Lysias falls logically enough into its place. Had the Yueh-chi not been so tired of fighting and so anxious for a quiet life, Greek rule would probably have ended before it did; as it was, the Greeks were for the time safe from the side of Bactria.

It will be best to defer considering the Paropamisadae for the present and to turn to the eastern group. It has been noticed that Menander was succeeded by his widow Agathocleia as regent for their son Strato. She was the first woman actually to bear rule in any Hellenistic kingdom, though the rule of queens had not been unknown in old Macedonia; Parthia of course promptly copied, and when Mithridates I died in 138–7 he left his queen Ri..nu regent for his young son Phraates II;[1] subsequently the rule of women became common among the Ptolemies, and one queen of Ptolemaic blood, Cleopatra Thea, virtually ruled what remained of the Seleucid empire. Strato I is shown by his coin-portraits to have had a very long reign,[2] associated at the end with his grandson Strato II; in middle age he wore a beard, as two Seleucid kings had done (p. 299). A group of three kings, Apollodotus II Philopator, Dionysius, and Zoilus II Soter, show a common and peculiar monogram on their coins, some of which were therefore all struck by the same moneyer in one mint;[3] a hoard found on the upper Sutlej contained coins of these three kings and of no others,[4] and a hoard of 200 coins of Zoilus was found near Sāgala (Sialkot).[5] Another king, Apollophanes, whose coins are extremely rare but show Euthydemid types, certainly belongs to the same group, as another peculiar monogram which he shares with Zoilus II and Strato again shows that at one time all three shared a common moneyer;[6] these monograms mean that these four kings—Apollodotus II, Dionysius, Zoilus II, and Apollophanes—were sub-kings, or perhaps in some cases successors, of Strato. Yet another king whose coins are extremely rare, Polyxenus,

[1] A. T. Clay, *Babylonian records in the library of J. Pierpont Morgan* II p. 53; on the date, E. H. Minns, *JHS* XXXV, 1915, p. 34.

[2] Rapson in *Corolla Numismatica* 1906 p. 245.

[3] *CHI* p. 553. The monogram in question is shown in *BMC* pp. 37 no. 7, 51 no. 1, 52 no. 3.

[4] S. P. Noe, *A bibliography of Greek coin-hoards*, *NNM* 1925 p. 180.

[5] Whitehead *NC* p. 308.

[6] For this monogram see *BMC* pp. 54 no. 1, 52 no. 6, 40 no. 7.

should from his types be a member of this group.[1] All the kings here mentioned (including Agathocleia) use Menander's regular type of Athena Alkis on their coins, and must therefore, it would seem, have either belonged to his family or governed some part of his one-time kingdom. A peculiar statement in Plutarch (p. 48 n. 5) may mean that after Menander's death the eastern capital was shifted from Sāgala to Bucephala, which appears later as (probably) the capital of Hippostratus (p. 326).

How Strato governed Sind and Surastrene, or whether these provinces had broken off prior to the Saca conquest, is quite unknown; nothing of their history can be recovered. But as the later Saca rulers in Surastrene and Malva, Nahapana and Castana, seem to have copied the coins of Apollodotus II,[2] they at any rate had them to copy, and this king, who from his name was presumably a descendant of Apollodotus I Soter, may therefore have had something to do with the government in the southern provinces which Apollodotus I had originally conquered; he was not in the direct line, and may have been quite content to serve Menander's son, who *was* in the direct line, as Antimachus II served Menander (p. 230). But there are two considerable difficulties about Apollodotus II. A hoard of 221 coins was found at Amarkot near Dera Ismail Khan on the Indus which consisted solely of drachmae of the two kings named Apollodotus—82 of Soter, 96 of Philopator, 43 too worn to say.[3] If this hoard stood alone, few would doubt that, as the older numismatists believed, Soter and Philopator were the same person. But it seems certain that they were not: Philopator's monograms, and notably his Kharoshthi letters, suffice. The hoard *might* furnish some further reason for supposing that Philopator governed Sind and the southern provinces; but the absence from the hoard of all coins of any king but these two, who were apparently a good distance apart in time, is inexplicable on any ordinary grounds, and one must suppose that it was a freak collection made by somebody who claimed kinship with the line of Apollodotus and collected only the coins of the two kings of that name. The other difficulty concerns his date. It has been seen that the reigns of Dionysius, Zoilus II, and himself, or parts of them, must fall within the lifetime of a single

[1] *CHI* p. 588 = *Lahore Cat.* p. 53 no. 371. On another coin, no. 372, he uses the Gorgon's head of Demetrius and Menander.

[2] Rapson, *Indian Coins* p. 20.

[3] W. Vost, *JASB* v, 1909, Num. Supp. xi.

moneyer, and Apollodotus II should come before Zoilus II, as Zoilus overstruck one of his coins; this would agree with the natural supposition that he was a grandson of Apollodotus I and Zoilus II a grandson of Zoilus I (*below*). But there exists a coin of Apollodotus II which has been overstruck by Azes[1] with the 'naval victory' type with which he overstruck coins of Hippostratus when he put an end to Greek rule in the eastern Punjab (p. 349); and this would *prima facie* make Apollodotus II a contemporary of Hippostratus, reigning till about 30 B.C. But this is so impossible to reconcile both with the Zoilus overstrike and with the fact that none of the coins of Apollodotus II show the square omicron that it must be taken to mean that Azes after his victory, till he could reorganise things, overstruck any older coins he could get, as Euthydemus had once done in Bactria (p. 104).

It was the discovery of the great Bajaur hoard[2] which has added to the list of kings the second Zoilus.[3] This hoard consisted of nearly new coins of three early kings, Apollodotus I, Menander, and Antimachus II, with a single coin of Zoilus which had obviously belonged to the man who actually buried the hoard. A hoard like this was probably buried during some invasion, and there is a choice of two dates, Heliocles' invasion of Gandhāra between 150 and 140 B.C., or the Saca conquest of Gandhāra round about 70 B.C.; without doubt the earlier date is the right one. There was then a Zoilus connected with Gandhāra just after Menander's death. It had been pointed out before the discovery of this hoard that Zoilus had two distinct currencies, clearly distinguished in style, legends, types, and monograms, one of which suggested the eastern Punjab while the affinities of the other were with Gandhāra;[4] and the two currencies show different titles, Soter and Dikaios. It has been seen that Zoilus Soter belonged to the eastern group of kings connected with Strato; and Zoilus Dikaios, who is connected with Gandhāra, must be earlier, perhaps one of the missing sub-kings of Menander, whom he evidently survived. Had he been merely driven across the Jhelum by Heliocles into Strato's sphere, his monograms and the style of his coins would naturally have changed, but no reason is apparent why he should have changed his types, still less his title; and

[1] *Lahore Cat.* p. 123 no. 244.

[2] M. F. C. Martin, *JASB* XXIII, 1927, Num. Supp. XL p. 18. See p. 229.

[3] Coins: *BMC* pp. 52–3.

[4] Whitehead *NC* p. 308. The two coins *BMC* Pl. XII, 10 and 11, show the difference clearly.

it must I think be supposed that there were two kings of the name,[1] Soter being a descendant—presumably grandson—of Dikaios.

The beginning of the end for all the Greek kingdoms in India was the Saca conquests. After the Suren, whom Mithridates II had put in command of the country east of the Persian desert (p. 499), had broken the Saca invasion of Parthia and had recovered the country from Herat northward to Merv, the larger body of the invaders, driven by Parthian pressure, had entered India from Seistan (p. 321 n. 4), while the victorious Parthians brought into subjection the previously existing Saca state in Sacastene on the lower Helmand. The victories of the Suren took place somewhere between 124 and 115 (p. 281), and the Saca invasion of India may have begun any time after *c.* 120. The route of the main body of the invaders is unknown, but if they started from Sacastene they probably took the usual road which Craterus had once followed, by Kandahar and the Bolan or the Mulla pass, and if so their first conquest from the Greeks would have been the satrapy of Abiria on the Indus, which is known to have been theirs. They had come steadily southward since leaving the Jaxartes and the Caspian steppes, and southward from Abiria they still went, conquering Patalene and the Greek sea-provinces of Cutch and Surastrene; Indian tradition remembered their conquest of Sind, and how they went down the Indus in ships to the conquest of Kathiawar.[2] This kingdom, extending from Abiria to Surastrene, was their original kingdom in India and remained in that shape long enough to find its way into Greek tradition; it is Ptolemy's 'Indo-Scythia' and may be roughly dated *c.* 110 to *c.* 80 B.C. (p. 233).

The loss of Patalene and Surastrene meant to the Greek kings the loss of political control over the sea-ports which gave access by sea to the western world, but the sea-ports themselves may not have been much affected. Demetrias-Patala, we shall see, remained a Greek city for some time longer, and its position under Saca rule doubtless resembled that of the Greek cities in Parthia, as Seleuceia or Susa, under the rule of the Parthians (p. 30). The political forms at Barygaza while it was under Greek rule are unknown. If the old shrines or temples (*ἱερά*) in the neighbourhood mentioned in the Periplus (p. 148) were Greek, as that work implies, then Barygaza was presumably a Greek *polis*, the missing capital of Surastrene; but one does not know how far one can

[1] As Martin suggested, *op. cit.* p. 19. But he did not notice Whitehead on Zoilus.

[2] K. P. Jayaswal, *JBORS* XVI, 1930, pp. 233–4; Sten Konow, *JIH* XII, 1933, pp. 18–19.

rely on the archaeological knowledge of the merchant who wrote that work, and it is safer to draw no deductions from these temples. But there must at any rate have been a considerable settlement there of Greek traders—even in the middle of the first century A.D. the town was still using the currency of Greek kings—and that settlement still continued in being under Saca rule, for there is a clear indication of its existence in the reign of Augustus. A king Pandion or Porus (? king of the Pāndhya kingdom in Southern India) sent an embassy to him with a letter written on parchment in Greek,[1] and on the way the embassy picked up a gymnosophist, who accompanied them; this man belonged to Barygaza,[2] so it must have been in Barygaza that the envoys got their letter written. Greek then was still a living language there about the Christian Era, and may have persisted for some time as a *lingua franca* for traders from the West; one may recall that the women of Surastrene long continued to use the Greek salutation *χαῖρε* or *χαίρειν* (p. 235). But whether the Yavanas mentioned in an inscription of A.D. 106[3] had much to do with the Bactrian Greeks may be doubted.

With the further conquests of the Sacas in the south, outside of the Greek provinces, I am not at the moment concerned. But somewhere about 80 B.C. they started northward from Abiria up the Indus[4] to attack the Greek centres in the north, under a leader whose name in Greek was Maues or Mauakes, in Kharoshthi Moa or Moga (p. 496). The same name, Mauakes (Mu-ku'a), had been borne by the Saca king of Ferghana in 101 B.C. (p. 308); if I am right in my belief that the Saca rulers of Ferghana at this time belonged to the Sai-wang (pp. 278 *sq.*), Maues may have belonged to the same people, some of whom, we have seen, must have come south with the Sacaraucae; Maues' power would explain the insistence of the Chinese sources on the Sai-wang ultimately reaching and ruling 'Ki-pin' (see p. 277 n. 6).

The early coins of Maues bear the simple legend 'Of King Maues'. It would be tempting to ascribe these early coins of his to the kingdom of 'Indo-Scythia' and to suppose that they were struck in Demetrias-

[1] Nicolaus of Damascus in Strabo xv, 686, 719.

[2] Nicolaus' *Βαργόση* must be Barygaza, though Strabo did not recognise it. Renou, *La géographie de Ptolémée* 1925, Index *s.v.* *Βαρυγάζα*, made the identification.

[3] De la Vallée-Poussin p. 216.

[4] Cunningham's view that they came up the Indus and not through the passes is now generally accepted: Thomas, *JRAS* 1906 p. 216; Rapson, *CHI* p. 567; de la Vallée-Poussin p. 235; Herzfeld, *Paikuli* pp. 38 *sq.*; Konow, *CII* p. xxxi. But no one seems to have noticed that Ptolemy is conclusive on the matter.

Patala, which was still a Greek city in the third quarter of the first century B.C.[1] and, though there is no trace of a royal mint there, could doubtless have produced them; but this must be rejected, for Maues cannot have led the original invasion from Sacastene (that might mean a reign of sixty years or more), and if his early coins belonged to 'Indo-Scythia' there should also be coins of his predecessor in rule, which do not exist. The early coins must be taken to be Maues' first coins after he got control of the Taxila mint; as one shows the Apollo and tripod of Apollodotus,[2] another an exact copy of the elephant's head of Demetrius,[3] and a third the trotting horse which had first appeared on later imitations of the coins of Heliocles,[4] they indicate a comprehensive claim on the part of Maues to all the Greek dominions west of the Jhelum. He was in possession of Taxila before but not long before *c.* 77 B.C. (App. 16); the conquest of Gandhāra cannot be put much before 70, as there are five kings to come in between Antialcidas and himself, or much after, as time is required for the subsequent events in the Paropamisadae (*post*). After the occupation of Taxila, but later than the Taxila copper-plate of *c.* 77 B.C., Maues took the title 'Great King of Kings' in imitation of Mithridates II; doubtless he was emphasising a claim to be as good a man as the king who had expelled his people from Parthia.

One detail of the Saca conquest has survived on the coinage: Maues' fleet defeated a Greek fleet on the Indus, which gave him control of the river and opened the way to Taxila. This victory must have been a decisive event, as it is the event which Maues celebrated on his coins. One coin shows Poseidon with his trident—the usual symbolism of a naval victory—trampling on a river-god;[5] on another Poseidon, while he still tramples on the river-god, hurls his thunderbolt at a small figure clinging to an *aphlaston*, the stern erection of a (presumably sinking) galley.[6]

[1] This is shown by the cave inscription Nasik 19, see p. 257 n. 3.

[2] *BMC* p. 72 no. 6; Cunningham, *Coins of the Sakas* (the fullest catalogue), *NC* 1890 p. 132 no. 14.

[3] *BMC* p. 68 no. 1; Cunningham *ib.* p. 131 no. 6.

[4] *BMC* p. 72 no. 28; Cunningham *ib.* p. 133 no 15.

[5] *BMC* p. 70 no. 15; Cunningham *ib.* p. 134 no. 22, cf. nos. 25, 26; *Lahore Cat.* p. 100 no. 20.

[6] *BMC* p. 71 no. 17, Pl. XVII, 2; Cunningham *ib.* pp. 106, 134 no. 23; *Lahore Cat.* p. 101 nos. 23, 24; *ASI* 1912–13 p. 47 no. 15, 1928–9 p. 65 no. 13 (both from Taxila).

Maues' conquest of Taxila and Gandhāra cut off the Greeks of the eastern Punjab from those of the Paropamisadae; but it is likely that a few Greeks, instead of coming under Saca rule, were driven, or retreated, up into the hills, and that petty Greek princelets, cut off from cities and mints and not always able to coin,[1] maintained themselves in the hill valleys till their race merged in some native line and nothing remained but the legend of the descent of various native rulers from Alexander (p. 408), just as seems to have happened on the Bactrian side of the mountains (pp. 302 *sq*.). One such princelet may have been the ancestor of the 'King Theodamas' who has left no coins but whose signet, with his name in Kharoshthi, was found in Bajaur,[2] and who apparently lived in the first century A.D.; another, whose published coin is said to have come from the Paropamisadae and who was therefore probably later than the loss of that country by the Greeks, used the legend 'King Antiochus', whether that was his name or whether he was emphasising his Seleucid lineage.[3] So far as can be traced, no Greek king ever became a Saca vassal. The Sacas, however, like the Parthians, whom they seem to have resembled, were not mere destroyers, but were ready to take advantage of and utilise the superior civilisation of the conquered Greeks; they retained the Greek provincial administration (pp. 241 *sqq*.) and coined in the Greek mints with a similar bilingual coinage, while the Greek cities, what few there were, kept some autonomy (p. 352 *sq*.). The Sacas simply stepped into the shoes of the Greeks; Indian writers regularly classed them with the Yavanas, and regarded them, as they regarded the Yavanas, as imperfect Kshatriyas (p. 173 n. 6).

But Maues could not, or did not, conquer the Greeks of the eastern Punjab; they seem to have held the line of the Jhelum successfully (p. 329), which implies that the Indian peoples immediately concerned were still on their side. But before Maues came, the eastern Greeks had already lost Mathurā and the country between Mathurā and the eastern boundary of the Madras, the Ravi. According to the coins, the last Greek king to rule Mathurā itself was Strato I in conjunction with his grandson Strato II,[4] a fact which seems to indicate that the eastern

[1] There is a class of round bronze coins (*BMC* p. 112) with debased Greek and Kharoshthi legends, both illegible, and types a humped bull and a Bactrian camel. Could these be coins of refugee princelets northward of Gandhāra?

[2] *CII* p. 6 no. III.

[3] A. von Sallet, *Z. für Num.* XX, 1897, p. 219, who compares it in style to the Hyrcodes coins, p. 305 n. 2. Legend ΑΣΙΛΕΩΣ ΝΤΙΟΧΟΥ, and Greek letter K.

[4] *CHI* p. 575.

kingdom remained in one hand as long as Strato I lived. As we have seen, he was a young boy when Menander died between 150 and 145; allowing for his long life and for the fact that at the end his grandson was associated with him in the kingdom, Mathurā cannot well have been lost before 100 B.C. or thereabouts, and a date for its loss of *c.* 100 B.C., or possibly a little later—anyhow before 90 B.C.—would agree very well with all other indications.[1]

How the Greeks came to lose these provinces east of the Ravi is unknown, except that it had nothing to do with the Sacas; they contained no Greek centres, they were perhaps lightly held, and granting that Greek rule may have been acceptable to this or that Indian people in 180 B.C., circumstances might well have altered eighty years later. Most of the peoples east of the Ravi already noticed as within Menander's empire (p. 239)—Audumbaras, Trigartas, Kunindas, Yaudheyas, Ārjunāyanas—began to coin in the first century B.C.,[2] which means that they had become independent kingdoms or republics; but the coins do not all tell the same story. Those of the two southernmost peoples begin somewhere about 100 B.C. and bear the legends 'Victory of the Ārjunāyanas' and (on their copper issue) 'Victory of the Yaudheyas', which point to their having won independence by the sword. With them, from its position, must have gone Mathurā itself, and its vassal kings became independent monarchs; it is tempting to see in the change of style on their coins from the king's name alone to that name with the addition of the title rājan[3] their declaration of independence. Of the Trigartas nothing seems known, but the Audumbaras and Kunindas may not have been lost till somewhat later. The coinage of the former,

[1] The *Purānas*, except the *Yuga-purāna*, all give eight kings of the Yavanas in India (there were of course far more) but the names and duration of rule differ (Lévi, *Quid de Graecis* p. 11). These lists are valueless; the one said to be the oldest and usually quoted, that of the *Vayu-purāna* (p. 133 n. 3), is in utter confusion chronologically and is not true for any one place in India. But the figure, eighty-two years, for the duration of Yavana rule which Cunningham cited, *NC* 1872 p. 185, as it is not a round number, might be a real tradition for some particular place; if so, that place must be Mathurā, as the figure is far too small for anywhere else unless Sind or Surastrene, and they cannot come in question because later Puranic history is confined to the United Provinces and Bihar (*CHI* p. 307). This would make the loss of Mathurā shortly after 100 B.C., which agrees well enough with the view in the text, based on coins.

[2] See the Introduction to and catalogue in *BMC India* under the respective names.

[3] *Ib.* p. cx.

to whom their trade was of importance, starts somewhere in the first century B.C.; as they occasionally imitate the types of Demetrius and Apollodotus I, one wonders whether their king Mahādeva's assumption of the title 'King of kings' on his coins,[1] which is said to be very early for an Indian king,[2] was copied from Eucratides. Later in the first century a ruler of the Kunindas, Amogabhūti, issued a silver coinage 'which would compete in the market with the later Indo-Greek silver';[3] both these peoples had been somewhat affected by the Greeks.

About 60 B.C., probably before Maues died, the Sacas conquered Mathurā, and the Indian kings are followed by Saca satraps, the best known being Hagāmasha and Hagāna;[4] they in turn were followed by a Saca Great Satrap, Rājuvula (once read Rañjubula) of the coins,[5] Rājuvula or Rājula of the inscriptions,[6] who imitated the money of the two Stratos; the change in style may have some connection with Azes' conquest of the eastern Greek kingdom (p. 349). The dates mean that the Sacas reached Mathurā quite independently of their advance up the Indus, perhaps from Malva across Rajputana by Ajmer. Attention has already been called to their numbers; their invasion differed from that of the Greeks in being a regular conquest, and their strength is shown by the manner in which some of the states they founded lasted far into the Christian Era.[7] There is nothing to show that when the Sacas reached Mathurā *c.* 60 B.C. the eastern Greeks had lost Sāgala; they still ruled everything between the Jhelum and the Ravi.

The Greek kings of the eastern group cannot be arranged in order, but one or more must have bridged the gap between Strato I and the last pair of eastern kings, Hippostratus and Nicias, about whom a certain amount of information can be recovered. Hippostratus' coins[8] show both the round and the square omicron, and the bearing of this upon his date must be considered. The square omicron had appeared

[1] *BMC India* p. 123. [2] *Ib.* p. lxxxv.

[3] *Ib.* p. ciii.

[4] *CHI* p. 527; Whitehead, *NNM* p. 45; *BMC India* pp. cxi, cxvi, 183–4, where Allan dates the first Saca satrap of Mathurā to about 60 B.C.; this cannot be far out.

[5] Coins in *BMC*; see p. xxxix, and *CHI* pp. 527, 575; Whitehead, *NNM* pp. 45–6; *BMC India* pp. 85–9. In 1853 ninety-six coins of Strato were found together with Rājuvula's money in Mathurā, Noe *op. cit.* p. 126.

[6] Rājula on the Mathurā Lion Capital, *CII* no. xv. Rājuvula, *ib.* p. xxxiii, and see *BMC India* p. cxiii, where Allan now reads Rājuvula on the coins also.

[7] Grousset pp. 60–1: they held Seistan till the reign of Bahram II, A.D. 276–93, and Kathiawar and Gujerat till the fifth century.

[8] *BMC* pp. 59 *sq.*; Whitehead, *NC* p. 338; *Lahore Cat.* p. 75.

sporadically at Athens from the third century B.C.,[1] and there is an isolated occurrence of it at Susa in an inscription of 98 B.C.;[2] but its regular appearance upon the Parthian coinage begins at some period in the reign of Orodes II,[3] who reigned from 55 to 38/7 B.C., and this decided Professor Rapson to date its appearance in India to *c.* 40 B.C.,[4] a little later than the probable time of its appearance in Parthia, though he has entered a caveat that as regards the dating of the square letter-forms generally in India questions of different local usages may come in.[5] I think it may be taken that, if a king has a reasonably abundant coinage and that coinage regularly shows both forms of omicron (no king's coinage I think shows the square form alone), part of his reign anyhow should be later than *c.* 40 B.C.; but perhaps one can get a little closer than this. If I am right about the Chinese evidence (pp. 337 *sqq.*)—and no alternative explanation is apparent—Hermaeus was reigning somewhat before 48 B.C. and somewhat after 32 B.C. His reign then may be called *c.* 50–30 B.C., and his coinage shows a mixture of both forms of omicron, which helps to date Hippostratus; for as Hippostratus' coins show the same mixture he must roughly be contemporary. But on a coin of Spalyris, who was dead before Hermaeus' accession (pp. 341 *sq.*), there is the square omicron,[6] though he generally uses the round one;[7] the square omicron, therefore, is no bar to Hippostratus having begun to reign some years earlier than 50 B.C.,[8] should other indications point to that; the abundance of his tetradrachms suggests a reign of substantial length.

The naval symbolism on the coins of Hippostratus and Nicias, a new phenomenon among the Greeks of India, not only renders it impossible to separate them, but connects them both with one of the Punjab rivers. On some of Hippostratus' coin-series, both silver and square bronze, there occurs the Fortune of a city—the sole appearance of this type on the coins of any of the eastern group of kings—and the city can only be Bucephala, the one *polis* known so far to the east; his 'city' coins must therefore have been minted there—doubtless it was his capital—and as one series of his 'city' coins shows as type Triton holding a dolphin

[1] Cumont, *Fouilles* pp. 352 *sq.*

[2] *SEG* VII, 6.

[3] *BMC Parthia* pp. 73 *sqq.* Its regular occurrence at Susa begins with *SEG* VII, 12, in the reign of Orodes' successor Phraates IV.

[4] *CHI* p. 572.

[5] *JRAS* 1905 p. 811.

[6] *BMC* p. 100.

[7] *Ib.* pp. 98, 173.

[8] In fact another letter-form, the square omega, appeared in India before it appeared in (western) Parthia, p. 327 n. 7.

and rudder,[1] the river with which he is connected can only be the Jhelum. All the 'city' coins are distinguished by a peculiar monogram, that of his mint-master in Bucephala, found again frequently on the money of his conqueror Azes but nowhere else, and as it does not occur on his other coins he had at least two mints; the other was presumably Sāgala. Most of his coins are said to come from Punch or Hazāra, and a hoard of his tetradrachms has been found in Punch.[2] It must be remembered that that part of his kingdom alone which lay between the Jhelum and the Chenab, with its extension into the hills, was considerably larger than that of Alexander's powerful opponent Porus; and his realm may have been strengthened by Greek refugees from the lost eastern provinces.

Nicias can only have been a minor king, since, except for his unique drachm, he only strikes square bronze coins;[3] some have the round omicron, some the square form and in addition the square sigma[4] and an intermediate form of omega,[5] which do not appear on any other Indo-Greek coins. The square forms of these three letters together with a square phi appear regularly on the coins of Gondophares, whose rule began in A.D. 19[6] and whose huge realm had its capital at Taxila; his coinage is the most extreme example in India of the square lettering,[7] which died out as Greek ceased to be a living tongue in India and is entirely absent from the more conventional forms on the Kushan coinage after Kadphises I. But, in spite of the square letters, one cannot put Nicias later than Hippostratus, because of the round omicron; and the two are closely associated both by their naval symbolism, which points to similar circumstances, and by their common use of the type of Antimachus II, 'King on prancing horse'; they should therefore be his

[1] *BMC* p. 60 nos. 11–13.

[2] Whitehead, *NC* pp. 336, 338.

[3] Coins, *BMC* pp. 58, 171; Whitehead, *NC* p. 334.

[4] This form first appears in Parthia with Mithridates III (*BMC Parthia* pp. 61 *sqq.*) who reigned 56–55 B.C., and then regularly from the latter part of the reign of Orodes II (*ib.* pp. 73 *sqq.*). This suits my dating of Nicias well enough.

[5] *BMC* p. xlvi n.

[6] *CHI* p. 576; Herzfeld, *Sakastan* pp. 91, 96, 101.

[7] As his reign is A.D. 19–45 plus, and as the square omega first appears in Parthia under Vardanes, A.D. 41–5 (*BMC Parthia* p. 153), he introduced this form; that is, some district in India, probably Taxila, was experimenting for itself *after* Greek rule had ended. But the intermediate omega of Nicias, unknown in Parthia, shows that experiments had begun somewhere *before* Greek rule ended. The square forms of phi, theta, and rho appear at Susa earlier than Gondophares, with a square omicron but with a round omega: *SEG* VII, 12, 13.

descendants. Hippostratus' coinage shows that he was the more important; they may have been father and son, with Nicias his father's sub-king or associate. If it was known that Alexander's Nicaea still existed—there is no evidence[1]—one would emphasise the possibility that Nicias was 'king Nicaea' (with the name adapted to the common Greek form) and ruled Bucephala's bridge-head on the Saca bank of the Jhelum, an outpost of Hippostratus' kingdom, and also the possibility that the square letters other than the omicron were especially favoured in the country between the Indus and the Jhelum which was dominated by Taxila. In any case, Nicias' coins are usually found in the Jhelum district and his kingdom was somewhere on that river; his coins are of poor style, which may point to an improvised mint. There is a third king, Theophilus (p. 164), whose extremely rare coins show a square theta[2] and who might therefore belong to the same group; he uses Demetrius' type of Heracles standing[3] and was therefore probably a Euthydemid, but it is impossible to say where he ruled.

The reason for one's interest in the obscure Nicias is a square bronze coin of his which shows on the obverse a head of Poseidon with his trident and on the reverse a dolphin twined round an anchor,[4] recalling the Triton holding a dolphin and rudder of Hippostratus. That this coin celebrates a naval victory seems certain enough: Poseidon had not appeared on any Greek coin in the Farther East since the first Antimachus had used the type to celebrate his naval victory on the Oxus (pp. 90 *sq.*). It might be suggested that, if Nicias was a descendant of Antimachus I through Antimachus II, he was merely copying his type; but even if he had it to copy, which would be very doubtful, it is far too remote in both time and place, and moreover the two types are very different.[5] Nicias' Poseidon and trident must have its usual meaning on Greek

[1] It has been tentatively suggested that the type Nike on various Greek, Saca and Pahlava coins in India may refer to Nicaea (*CHI* pp. 551, 588, 592); but I think myself that Nike is too common a type everywhere to have a local meaning. Ptolemy does not mention Nicaea; but he is not professing to give a complete list of towns west of the Jhelum as he does east of it.

[2] Not used by Gondophares or in Parthia; but it had occurred at Athens, Cumont *loc. cit.*, and is found at Susa, *SEG* VII, 12 (between 36 B.C. and A.D. 1) and 13 (A.D. 1). It seems to show that the Greeks in India were in communication with Susa up to the end.

[3] *BMC* p. 167 no. 1.

[4] Whitehead, *NC* p. 334 no. 53, Pl. XVI, 14.

[5] Nicias has 'head of Poseidon' only, Antimachus I a full-length figure.

coins: he had defeated a Saca fleet on the Jhelum. In a sense he is imitating Maues' coin, but his Poseidon tramples on no river-god; to the invading Sacas the rivers were hostile barriers, but to the Greeks on the defensive the Jhelum played its traditional rôle of friend and would-be-helper to the defence.[1]

If this requires confirmation it can be found in the dolphin twined round an anchor. This type had never before been used in the East, but it was known in the West, in Alexandrian or rather perhaps Phoenician art; it occurs on a mosaic in the House of the Trident at Delos, done by a Phoenician artist not later than the end of the second century B.C., and subsequently at Pompeii, and it has been interpreted to mean 'prosperous voyage'.[2] At Delos it seems to be connected with the Phoenician merchants established there, and merchants must have brought it to Bucephala; it need not have come from Phoenicia direct, for there were 'Syrians' settled in Merv (p. 15) and Susa (p. 29) and a large body at Seleuceia (p. 18); Phoenician merchants had followed Alexander to India, Phoenicians formed a settlement called Tyre in that country,[3] and it was Phoenicians who had passed this symbol across Asia. On Nicias' coin the symbol meant that his victorious fleet had had a 'prosperous voyage'. The Triton with dolphin of Hippostratus must refer to the same victory; doubtless Nicias had been actually in command of the joint fleet, but the ultimate importance of the victory is shown principally by the fact that Hippostratus, on one of his silver issues, assumes the title 'Great King',[4] which no Greek in the Farther East had done on his coinage before him[5] except Eucratides. But as the dolphin twined round an anchor became Nicias' usual reverse type on his bronze coins,[6] associated with his head on the obverse, the victory must have been won early in his reign, and might be anywhere from about 60 to 50 B.C. (pp. 326, 336).

Unquestionably the vanquished were the Sacas. Maues had struck a

[1] Porus against Alexander, which reappears later in strange circumstances. Nonnus, who knew little or nothing of India but the Alexander-story, makes the Hydaspes (Jhelum) and not the Indus the principal river in his India; it is the father of the Indian leader Deriades and itself fights against Dionysus.

[2] Ch. Picard, *Syria* XIV, 1933, pp. 318–20.

[3] Steph. *s.v.* *Τύρος*; see p. 10.

[4] *BMC* p. 59 nos. 3 *sqq.*; *Lahore Cat.* p. 75 nos. 610–15.

[5] Antialcidas is called 'the great king' in the Besnagar inscription, but not on his coins.

[6] *BMC* p. 58 no. 2.

coin with well-known types of both Eucratides and Demetrius,[1] showing that he claimed to be the successor of both kings; but he never used Menander's characteristic Athena Alkis, and therefore never ruled any part of Menander's home kingdom east of the Jhelum. Whether it was his fleet which was defeated, or whether he was already dead, cannot be said; it might suit best to suppose that his fleet was defeated in an attempt to open a way up the Jhelum to Bucephala as it had opened a way up the Indus to Taxila, and that he died soon after. For the victory, as will be seen, was certainly followed, though not necessarily at once, by a period of peace, or rather perhaps cessation of hostilities, between Greek and Saca; and as this cannot have been due to one reverse—the Sacas were too strong for that—it may imply Maues' death. It will be suggested later that his death was in 58 B.C.

The notable thing about Hippostratus' reign is the appearance of his tetradrachms in considerable abundance.[2] Tetradrachms in India are supposed to have been issued for the use of the Greek rather than the Indian community;[3] and this must be right, for the Kushans, with masses of Indian subjects, got on quite well without any silver coinage at all except such punch-marked and Greek pieces as might still be in circulation. After Menander, tetradrachms of the kings west of the Jhelum are not common,[4] and of the kings east of the Jhelum none are known at all[5] except a few of Agathocleia and of Strato I;[6] then at the very end of Greek rule come a large number of those of Hippostratus and a still larger number of those of his contemporary Hermaeus in the Paropamisadae. As Greeks in India were certainly not increasing—they may have been considerably diminished by the Saca war, and had certainly lost a great deal of territory—the phenomenon can only mean an increased trade with the western world, and that in turn must mean that both kings for a time enjoyed an interval of peace, which must

[1] *BMC* p. 70 no. 14, Cunningham *NC* 1890 p. 136 no. 7; obv., Eucratides' 'Kapisi' type, with forepart of elephant before Zeus; rev., Demetrius' type of Heracles standing and crowning himself.

[2] Whitehead, *NC* p. 304; *NNM* p. 26.

[3] Whitehead, *NC* p. 303.

[4] They were thought very rare (Whitehead, *NNM* p. 25; *NC* p. 304) till ninety-seven came to light in the Kabul hoard in 1917 (Whitehead, *NC* p. 315), the most numerous being thirty of Archebius.

[5] *Ib.* p. 303.

[6] Twenty-three in the Kabul hoard, and a few in the Tatta hoard, P. Gardner, *NC* 1887 p. 181.

primarily have been due to Maues' death. We have seen how the flourishing period of Greek rule in India coincided exactly with a great outburst of prosperity in Seleuceia on the Tigris (p. 261); one is inclined to ask whether a new increase in the Indian trade may have been one cause of the increase of coining in Parthia about this time—of drachms after Phraates III had re-unified the empire (66 B.C.) and of tetradrachms from the middle of the reign of Orodes II (57–38/7 B.C.).[1] The matter is too obscure to be considered here. But it is of interest that these last fractions of the Greek empire in India should not only have been still trading with the West but should have been able to increase that trade, and that a new symbol should have reached India from the Phoenician world, and a new letter-form from Susa (p. 328 n. 2). It is known that Hermaeus and Hippostratus were in touch (p. 337); and though no doubt they could have maintained communication through the hills northward of the Saca kingdom, still the Sacas held the great road and for effective trade purposes Hippostratus could only reach Hermaeus and the West across Saca territory, which again shows that there must have been an interval of peace (I shall come back to this): Hippostratus would not have coined tetradrachms in quantities had he not been in communication with the West through the Alexandria-Kapisa gateway, and it is worth notice that in a collection of coins recently formed in the Paropamisadae he and Nicias are the only kings east of the Jhelum after Menander who are represented,[2] save for a solitary coin of Strato.

I come at length to the Paropamisadae. Hermaeus cannot have ascended the throne later than about 50 B.C. (p. 337), and it is certain that another known king, Amyntas, was his father, for the monograms show that they had the same moneyer,[3] and both used a peculiar type of unknown meaning, a bearded male bust, radiate, in a Phrygian cap (p. 334). But there is nothing in Amyntas' coins to suggest a long reign, and even if Antialcidas could be brought down as late as 90 B.C., which seems very unlikely (pp. 313 *sq.*), there must still be a considerable gap between him and Amyntas, with no Greek king to fill it but Telephus, the extreme rarity of whose coins points to a very short reign. It is difficult to make out what was happening in the Paropamisadae between Antialcidas and Hermaeus, but far the likeliest hypothesis is that, till the advent of Maues, most of the country was in the hands of the 'Sacas'

[1] McDowell, *Coins of Seleucia* pp. 170–1.

[2] The unpublished Hackin collection in the Bibliothèque Nationale in Paris.

[3] Whitehead, *NC* p. 332 no. 44.

of Kabul, the Parsii, who have already been considered[1] and who after the invasion of Parthia had separated from the main Saca body and had gone north-eastward by Alexander's route via Alexandria-Ghazni to Kabul, which was in their hands some little while before 87 (on the date see App. 9); presumably they took it when Antialcidas died, and they may have had something to do with the break-up of his kingdom after his death. There is evidence that, with Kabul, they occupied some part of the Paropamisadae, for Ptolemy places them there and also gives two villages of theirs in that country, Parsia and Parsiana.[2] It has been suggested that a people called Parsus, mentioned by Pānini as somewhere in the Paropamisadae, were the same as Ptolemy's Parsii.[3] No one can say whether this were so or not; were it true, then the reason why the Parsii made for the Paropamisadae rather than Sind might have been that they had kinsfolk there, a deposit from one of the earlier invasions. To these Parsii of Kabul (Kophen, Ki-pin), whom in conformity with usage I shall sometimes have to call Sacas, belong the kings or rulers Spalyris (Spalahores), his son Spalagadames, and Spalirises.[4] Like all the Saca kings they struck a bilingual coinage, Greek and Kharoshthi; the find-spots of their coins point to a continuing connection with Arachosia, the one province outside of India and the Paropamisadae where Kharoshthi legends might occur,[5] and probably the centre of their power was Ghazni and Kabul (App. 9), a combination not uncommon in later history. I shall return to these rulers later; here I only want to point out that during the interregnum in the Paropamisadae the Parsii of Kabul may have occupied a good deal of that country.

Another factor in the story of the Paropamisadae is that at some period Maues was certainly ruling and coining in Kapisa, and the monograms show that his immediate predecessor or successor was Telephus (App. 16). As Maues' conquest of Gandhāra cannot be put much later than *c.* 70 (p. 322), the commencement of his rule in Kapisa is probably to be dated between 70 and 60 B.C. It does not necessarily mean that he was ever there in person—he ruled a vast kingdom; but he had a governor there.

[1] See Chap. VII, pp. 293 *sqq.*, and App. 9.

[2] Ptol. VI, 18; see p. 469.

[3] S. Beal, *Hsüan Tsiang, Si-yu-ki* II p. 285 n. I suppose Parsu *might* represent the form Parsua (p. 293).

[4] F. W. Thomas, *JRAS* 1906 pp. 208 *sq.*, had doubts whether these three names, though Iranian, were Saca. As I see it, these kings were not Sacas but Parsii, whose language was presumably some form of or allied to Persian.

[5] *CHI* p. 569.

Telephus, who for a little while ruled in Kapisa (App. 16), adds to the general obscurity. His extraordinary coin-types[1] may suggest that he was not even a Greek, in spite of his name; he does figure one Greek god, the 'Zeus enthroned' which had become the type of Kapisa, but he does not use the types of any known Greek king, a fact which might indicate a usurper.[2] It is a commonplace that the coinages of the Greek kings in India down to the end show Greek sobriety in the types used—Greek gods and the old types of the rival houses—but that on the Saca and still more on the Kushan coinages there appears a great multiplicity of types and that the Greek or semi-Greek artists who worked for these foreign kings let their imaginations run riot. They have run riot on Telephus' scanty coinage; among the types on his bronze are an Indian fakir squatting,[3] and his silver issue (p. 496 n. 8) shows on the obverse a serpent-footed giant and on the reverse a radiate king or god facing a male figure with horns, a group which might belong to Iranian mythology.[4] The giant suggests that the artist of the coin had seen the Pergamene frieze, another sign that intercourse with the West was maintained till the end; if we knew why the giant occupies the place on the coin normally filled by the king's head we might know who and what Telephus was.[5] Later, in the art of the Roman empire, the serpent-footed giant figures as the opponent of the Sun-god or of Juppiter and is thought to symbolise the Powers of Darkness;[6] but even a barbarian usurper could hardly put the symbol of the Powers of Darkness on a coin where his own head should be. Probably Telephus preceded Maues: in the confusion of the times he seized Kapisa for a little while and Maues dethroned him.

[1] *BMC* p. 171; Whitehead, *NC* pp. 336 *sqq.*

[2] Usurpers sometimes changed their names; Diodotus in Syria called himself Tryphon, and the Hyrcanian governor of Phraates II in Babylonia, when he seized the crown, called himself Himerus; it is an inevitable deduction from E. T. Newell's study, *NC* 1924 p. 175, that the Greek word ἵμερος was not the man's real name.

[3] Whitehead, *NC* p. 336 no. 58.

[4] It might be the Sun-god Mihira (Mithras) and the Moon-god Mao (said to be Zend, *BMC* p. lxiii), the horns being his crescent, who are so common on the coins of Kanishka and especially Huvishka; the two together on a gold coin of Huvishka, *BMC* p. 141 no. 42.

[5] Skythes has been suggested for the giant. But it is not known that Skythes was half a snake, though his mother was; and in any case he belongs to the Scythians of Europe. O. Stein, *Telephos* 4 in PW, 1934, compares the giant to the Tritons of Hippostratus and of Gandhāra art.

[6] M. P. Nilsson, *Arch. f. Religions-Wiss.* XXIII, 1925, pp. 175, 181; M. Dunand, *Le musée de Soueida* 1934 p. 31 no. 36. I owe these references to Prof. Nock.

There were still plenty of Greeks in the Paropamisadae, for when the Kushan Kujula Kadphises invaded that country some generations later, he thought it worth while trying to get them on his side in his conflict with the then Pahlava rulers (App. 17); but if any independence remained in the confused period after Antialcidas' death it must have centred in the two Greek cities, Alexandria and Cartana-Bamyan, with their grip on the regular route to Bactra and the West. As Maues, however, ruled for a time in Kapisa, no doubt Alexandria then had to accept his overlordship, which would mean that the city probably retained a certain autonomy in the usual way but that he appointed an *epistates* (city governor),[1] who might however be a citizen. But as we next meet Alexandria in the hands of Amyntas, Maues' governor must have been expelled by a Greek rising led by that prince, perhaps with the help of barbarian auxiliaries; unless, as is possible, Amyntas himself was Maues' *epistates* and revolted. Beside the Chinese evidence (p. 339), Amyntas' rule in Alexandria is attested by the 'Zeus enthroned' on his coins;[2] but who he was is unknown. Some facial resemblance has been detected between him and two of the kings of Antialcidas' house, Archebius and Peucolaos;[3] this is not worth much on Indo-Greek coins, but he *may* have been a member of that line. If we could explain an unexplained coin-type used by him and his son Hermaeus, the head of a god bearded and radiate who wears the pointed Phrygian cap (not the Saca cap with flaps),[4] we might know more about him.

The rising which placed Amyntas on the throne can hardly have

[1] The relationship is shown on a coin of Maues struck in Kapisa, *Lahore Cat.* p. 99 no. 15; obv., Zeus enthroned; rev., a turreted city Fortune standing to front (Alexandria).

[2] His Zeus occasionally carries Athena on his hand instead of Nike, Whitehead *NC* p. 332 no. 4. The significance of this is unknown; perhaps she was the city-goddess of Alexandria, or she may have symbolised the Greek recovery (cf. p. 68).

[3] Whitehead, *NC* p. 332.

[4] *BMC* pp. 61 nos. 4, 5, 66 nos. 51–5; *Lahore Cat.* pp. 78 no. 637, 84 no. 679. Sabazios is often bearded and wears a Phrygian cap (Eisele, *Sabazios* in Roscher IV 245 fig. 4, 247 fig. 7; *ib.* the Copenhagen relief, also in A. B. Cook, *Zeus* I, facing p. 392; Schaefer, *Sabazios* in PW I A 2, *op. cit.* 1548–50) but is never radiate (Eisele, *ib.* 263). Sozon, however, identified with Sabazios by Ramsay, Perdrizet, Cumont, and Höfer (PW *ib.* col. 1282), though others dispute the identification, is radiate. But it would be a *very* long shot to suggest that the type might be a conflation of Sabazios and Sozon and that Amyntas or some ancestor might have come from Anatolia; though the type cannot be meant for the heads of Amyntas and Hermaeus themselves (as Whitehead in *Lahore Cat.* takes it) for several reasons.

taken place during Maues' lifetime; it would be natural to suppose that it followed promptly upon his death, which provided an opportunity; possibly too it was inspired by, or connected with, the Greek victory on the Jhelum. Now Hermaeus conquered the Paropamisadae before 48 B.C. (p. 342) and cannot therefore have come to the throne *later* than about 50; Maues was certainly dead before Hermaeus' conquest, and the most likely *a priori* chronology would be that Maues died and Amyntas came to the throne in Alexandria somewhere round about 60 B.C.

So far I have been deducing the chronology from the coins, with the help of the Chinese evidence which will be considered later; but there is another line of evidence which I think establishes the exact year of Maues' death, and on that several other things depend. In Indian tradition,[1] after the Sacas had conquered Ujjain they were defeated and driven out in the year 58 B.C. by the Indian king Vikramāditya, who established the first Indian Era, the Vikrama Era, as from that year, doubtless in imitation of the Era of the defeated Sacas;[2] the Jain tradition makes this (the first) Saca rule in Ujjain last four years only.[3] If we suppose, as many have done, that the tradition enshrines a fact—and anyhow the Vikrama Era is a fact—then the first Saca conqueror of Ujjain can only have been Maues, and the date of Maues' death is 58; and this fits so closely with the *a priori* chronology already worked out on other grounds that I have no hesitation in assigning Maues' death to that year.[4] (I must note that if the Vikrama Era related to the recapture of Ujjain from the Sacas, that is, was a Malva Era,[5] that might support the view that the Saca Era of A.D. 78 was also a Malva Era and was instituted by the Western (Saca) Satraps;[6] it would commemorate their independence and their retaking of Ujjain.)

[1] *CHI* p. 168; *CII* p. xxvii.

[2] *CII* p. xxviii.

[3] *Ib.*

[4] It is interesting that Marshall, *JRAS* 1914 p. 977, and Rapson, *CHI* p. 571, once inclined to think that the Vikrama Era might mark Azes' accession, which, on the view that Azes succeeded Maues, would mean that Maues died in or about 58 B.C. (so Marshall, *ASI* 1912–13 p. 7). But it is now practically certain that Azes was much later, as will be seen.

[5] By Malva Era I mean one which originated in Malva and not in the North, not one invented by the Mālavas.

[6] De la Vallée-Poussin pp. 353–4; Konow in *CII* p. cxiii. But I would sooner, if I could, treat A.D. 78 as Kanishka's Era, for I do not believe in Konow's date for Kanishka (see p. 352).

This dating for Maues' death brings coherence into the whole story. The rising which expelled Maues' governor from Kapisa and brought Amyntas to the throne of Alexandria was in 58, immediately upon the news of Maues' defeat and death, and Hippostratus and Nicias won their victory upon the Jhelum about the same time; these things, combined with the defeat which lost Ujjain, are pointers which show (as it appears that the story necessitates) that Maues' swiftly won empire broke down, or broke up, on his death, which gives point to the Indian king's Era; that empire evidently depended on a single personality and had not yet had time to become consolidated. The Chinese noticed that the Sacas were composed of various peoples and normally formed separate kingdoms,[1] which means that anyone who attempted to weld them into an empire would have to reckon with strong fissiparous tendencies; and if Maues really belonged to the Sai-wang (p. 321), who cannot have been very numerous in India, he may have supplied one more instance of the ruler of a small tribe only holding the larger tribes to a precarious allegiance because his command alone gave promise of victory.[2] There is in existence an autonomous gold coin of the city of Pushkalāvatī,[3] which shows that at some time the city was independent; one would like to suppose that its brief independence was also won on Maues' death (Azes subsequently coined in Pushkalāvatī) but it is difficult to suppose that a *gold* coin with a Kharoshthi legend on the *obverse* can belong to this period, though precedents for either alone perhaps exist;[4] it is, however, equally difficult to suppose that Pushkalāvatī, even if still a *polis*, achieved independence in the period when imported gold was being freely coined by the Kushan kings. I must leave it unexplained. One point may be added about Maues' date: even though his conquest of Taxila was not long before *c.* 77, his death

[1] De Groot, p. 87, from the Ch'ien-han-shu: 'Das Volk der Sak bestand aus Teilen die zerstreut lebten und in der Regel verschiedene Reiche bildeten.' See on this Herzfeld, *Sakastan* p. 18.

[2] The stock example is Vercingetorix.

[3] *CHI* p. 587 Pl. VI, 10; obv., Fortune of Pushkalāvatī wearing a mural crown and holding a lotus, with her name in Kharoshthi; rev., humped bull with Greek legend ταῦρος and a Kharoshthi word. Also given by Whitehead, *NNM* Pl. XXIX, 15; *BMC* p. 162. No one, I think, has assigned a date to it.

[4] Agathocles' *Hirañasame* coin (p. 160) has Kharoshthi legends on both sides. There is a little gold piece in the Lahore Museum with the unknown name Athama (*Lahore Cat.* p. 145 no. 399; Rapson *JRAS* 1905 p. 783) which Whitehead, *NNM* p. 32, thinks is possibly Saca; and an early gold coin of Taxila exists (p. 104).

in 58 still gives plenty of time for his coinage; before he died he controlled at least three Greek mints, if not more.

Unless I am entirely wrong about the Chinese evidence which follows, the accession of Hermaeus falls between two points, the first appointment by China of a general of the western *limes*, which is said to have been in 59,[1] and the accession of the Han emperor Yuan-ti in 48; and as by the latter date Hermaeus was already in possession of the Paropamisadae, then if Amyntas began to reign in 58 Hermaeus' accession was quite certainly not later than 50 and probably not much earlier. Numismatists seem agreed that his reign exhibits a curious revival of Greek power; his large and widespread coinage should attest a substantial kingdom, though any fresh influx of Greeks or mercenaries from the West seems at this time quite out of the question. It has even been suggested that his rule extended to the Jhelum.[2] One would like to believe this, and it would certainly suit very well with his relations with Hippostratus; but it seems incredible that he could have been strong enough to take Gandhāra and Taxila from the Sacas, and against it is the fact that, on the Chinese evidence, he can only have taken what was under the rule of the Sacas of Kabul, and they were not ruling Gandhāra. It must be supposed that he ruled all the Paropamisadae, but no more. He was, however, certainly in touch with the kingdom of Hippostratus on the Jhelum; his queen Calliope, on the silver coins which show their jugate busts,[3] appears at his side wearing the diadem and is named with him in the legend and should therefore, as usually supposed, have been a princess in her own right, but whether that be so or not, she can only have come from Hippostratus' kingdom, for these coins bear the type of Hippostratus and Nicias, 'King on prancing horse',[4] which Hermaeus himself did not use. The idea that the last descendant of Eucratides married the last descendant of Euthydemus is very attractive; but the old feud may have been healed long before (p. 314) and in any case there is no certainty that Hermaeus *was* descended from Eucratides.[5]

[1] Gutschmid p. 109.

[2] Gutschmid, *ib.*, Gandhāra and part of the Punjab; Whitehead *NC* p. 340, from Kabul to the Jhelum, on the ground that several monograms appear for the first time on his coins (looking at the long interregnum, they naturally would; there would be new moneyers). *Contra*, Sir J. Marshall, *JRAS* 1914 p. 981.

[3] *BMC* p. 66 nos. 1, 2.

[4] *CHI* p. 560; originally Cunningham's deduction.

[5] He sometimes wears Eucratides' helmet (P. Gardner, *NC* 1887 p. 181—the Tatta hoard—Pl. VII no. 9); but so does Strato, *ib.* no. 6.

Many Kharoshthi letters appear on Hermaeus' coinage, but always in company with a Greek monogram; they point to native mint officials. Kharoshthi letters are common on the coinages of the later Euthydemid kings east of the Jhelum (pp. 356 *sq.*), but had so far never appeared west of the Jhelum or on the coins of any descendant of Eucratides. They might perhaps be an argument that Hermaeus did not belong to Eucratides' line; but they are more likely to mean that he was seeking to strengthen his revived kingdom by a large enfranchisement of Indians.[1] Hermaeus' abundant tetradrachms, like those of Hippostratus, witness to an increased trade with the West; and Hippostratus may have got his silver from the Panjshir mines in Hermaeus' kingdom. Indeed trade in Hermaeus' reign must have been brisk all round; a coin of his has even been found in Chinese Turkestan,[2] and there has also come from Khotan a much defaced piece which apparently bears his name and has a legend in half-obliterated Chinese characters.[3] It was doubtless of local manufacture;[4] but his traders may have travelled far, and it would seem that in some way his sphere and that of China may have been in contact.

Beside Hermaeus' own coinage, some issues exist which connect him with the first Kushan king, Kujula Kadphises (Kadphises I).[5] The five chiefs of the Yueh-chi have already been mentioned; Kadphises, the chief (*yabghu* or *yavuga*) of the Kuei-shuang tribe or section, the Kushans proper, conquered the other four chiefs and made himself king of the whole people, thenceforth known to history as Kushans. The event is recorded in the Hou-han-shu, and as that history professedly starts from the events of A.D. 25 it is recognised that the date at which Kadphises seized the supreme power cannot be earlier. But it is also certain that Hermaeus did not live till A.D. 25 or anywhere near it, and it is now generally recognised that Greek rule had ended long before Kadphises I invaded and conquered the Paropamisadae.[6] The old belief that these coins were a joint issue of Hermaeus and Kadphises I has in consequence been universally abandoned,[7] for it is recognised that a

[1] One might compare the large enfranchisement of Asiatics, for a special purpose, at Pergamum in 133 B.C.

[2] Sir A. Stein, *Serindia* III p. 1340.

[3] *BMC* p. 172 no. 4; P. Gardner, *NC* 1879 p. 274.

[4] It cannot be Hermaeus' own, as he apparently bears the title rajadirajasa (see App. 17), though only the first four letters can be read.

[5] For these coins, and this section generally, see App. 17.

[6] I think *CHI* pp. 561–2 expresses the general belief.

[7] Konow in *CII* p. lxiv still inclined to think that they meant an alliance between

considerable interval of time separated the two kings; but nothing else has taken its place. I see no reason to doubt that, like other coins we have met with—coins of Antimachus and Agathocles (App. 3) and of Eucratides (Chap. v)—these are *pedigree* coins (App. 17): an ancestor of Kadphises, probably his grandfather, had married a relative of Hermaeus, and Kadphises was commemorating his relationship to the last Greek king. The reason is obvious: in his struggle with the then Pahlava rulers of the Paropamisadae he was trying to get the Greeks on his side by proclaiming that he was no foreign conqueror but their legitimate king, relative and heir of Hermaeus, whose power he magnified accordingly. The ancestor of Kadphises in question must have been Miaos (his name is uncertain), the only Kushan before him to issue a Greek coinage; he is considered in Appendix 17.

We now have several questions to answer. How did it happen that, with Greek independence in the Paropamisadae so near its end, Hermaeus suddenly managed to extend his rule and his power in the way he did? Why did he give a relative in marriage to a barbarian, the contemporary Kushan chief? And why does there exist a suggestion of relations between him and China? Fortunately we have here, for the last time, the help of the written word. There is a story in the Ch'ien-han-shu, the story of the first and last intervention of the elder Han dynasty south of the Hindu Kush, which will answer all these questions, if it relates to Hermaeus; and the fact that it will explain Hermaeus' situation and no other situation is very strong evidence that it does relate to him, for the story is dated.

The story[1] runs that W'ou-ti-lao king of Ki-pin killed some Chinese envoys, a pastime seemingly in favour with kings who thought themselves beyond the reach of China's very efficient arm (cf. p. 309). After his death, his son (whose name is not given) dispatched an envoy to China with gifts, *i.e.* to make his peace, and Wen-chung, the Chinese general at the Barrier, the *limes* west of Kan-su,[2] was sent to escort the envoy home. W'ou-ti-lao's son plotted to kill Wen-chung, but Wen-chung discovered this and allied himself with Yin-mo-fu, son of the king of Yung-kiu; the two attacked Ki-pin and killed W'ou-ti-lao's

Hermaeus and Kadphises I, some time after A.D. 25; but he has now abandoned this untenable view, *JIH* 1933 p. 29.

[1] Wylie p. 36; Franke p. 63; de Groot p. 88.

[2] On the discovery of some stations along the Barrier see Sir A. Stein, *Serindia*, Chaps. XIV–XX *passim*, and *Geogr. Journ.* 1925 p. 428.

son, and Yin-mo-fu was installed as king of Ki-pin, receiving the seal and ribbon of investiture; that is, Wen-chung installed him as king but as a vassal of China. Wen-chung, be it noted, played the leading part, though he had no Chinese troops, for it is expressly stated at the beginning of the story that Ki-pin was too far away for Chinese troops to go there. Subsequently Yin-mo-fu himself, in the reign of the emperor Yuan-ti (48–33 B.C.), killed the escort of a Chinese envoy and sent an envoy to China to excuse himself; but Yuan-ti took no thought for such a distant land. In the reign of Ching-ti (32–7 B.C.) other envoys came (*i.e.* from Yin-mo-fu), but the emperor was advised not to notice them, the ground alleged for this advice being that they were not real envoys but only traders seeking trade.

Very various interpretations,[1] which need not detain us, have been given offhand of this story, often with little regard to circumstances or dates. The only real attempt to consider the several factors has been von Gutschmid's,[2] and I have no doubt that his explanation is correct: Yin-mo-fu is Hermaeus; Ki-pin here is Kophen;[3] Yung-kiu is Yonaki, 'Greek-town'.[4] W'ou-ti-lao he did not explain beyond saying that he was a Saca; for no king with a name the least like W'ou-ti-lao is known. But in fact a perfectly good explanation of the name had already been given by Wylie, though von Gutschmid did not know this: it is the word ἀδελφοῦ (adelphou) on the coins of Spalyris.[5] This explanation has gained enormously in probability since it was put forward, for

[1] Lassen, II² p. 409, said W'ou-ti-lao was Gondophares, now known to have been more than two generations later. Cunningham, *NC* 1888 p. 52, made Yin-mo-fu Miaos; J. Kennedy, *JRAS* 1912 p. 685, made him Kanishka or a viceroy of his. A. Herrmann, *Sakai* in PW, made him Maues, Maues being to him an Amyrgian Saca who came in from the north-west *c.* 60 B.C., while he said that 'no one can doubt' that W'ou-ti-lao was Agathocleia, nearly a century earlier. Franke p. 63, de Groot p. 88, and Konow *CII* p. xxiv relate the story without explanation; but Konow p. xxv has some pertinent criticism of Herrmann and thinks that Yin-mo-fu was not a Saca.

[2] Pp. 109–10 (in 1888). Followed by F. O. Schrader, *Die Fragen des Königs Menandros* 1907 p. xiv.

[3] On Ki-pin, at this time Kophen-Kabul, see App. 9.

[4] See the discussion of Yonaka and Ionaca in the Excursus pp. 417 *sq*. Franke, p. 63, renders the word as Jung-k'ü, and de Groot, p. 88, as Jong-k'ut, which is even nearer; for I gather (de Groot I p. ix) that the g in ng was not sounded in speaking and that in some words the final t was mute.

[5] Wylie p. 36 n. (in 1881). He thought W'ou-ti-lao a near phonetic approach to ἀδελφοῦ. Karlgren (*CII* p. xxiv n. 4) says that the old pronunciation of W'ou-ti-lao would be uo-d'au-lâu, which is very near ἀδελφοῦ.

Professor Herzfeld has brilliantly shown that the name Phraotes, which Apollonius in Philostratus gives to the king of Taxila, is *apratihata*, one of Gondophares' predicates in the Kharoshthi legend on his coins;[1] and if part of one king's title could be turned into a king's name, so could that of another. The other Saca ruler who called himself on his coins *βασιλέως ἀδελφοῦ*, the 'king's brother', Spalirises,[2] cannot come in question, for he did not die but became successively Great King and Great King of Kings; and Spalyris[3] (Spalahores in the Kharoshthi) did have a son Spalagadames[4] who presently succeeded him.[5] It is true that Spalyris on his coins does not appear as king, while W'ou-ti-lao is called king; but Pan-ku's source, which can only be Wen-chung's Report, was merely mistranslating the words *ἀδελφοῦ τοῦ βασιλέως*, 'brother of the king', in Spalyris' title as 'Adelphou the king'. It must be remembered that, so far as is known, Wen-chung was the first Chinaman to come into actual contact with Greeks or the Greek language. He probably knew Saca,[6] but that might not help him much if the Parsii of Kabul still spoke some form of Persian; and he cannot have failed to get some very muddled interpreting. Besides Adelphou as the king's name, he never got the name Alexandria but only the adjective *Ἰωνακή* (Ionake, 'Greek') which he took for the name of the city; he was not the only person in the Farther East to make that particular mistake.[7]

One may now attempt to put together the story of Hermaeus. W'ou-ti-lao was Spalyris, Saca governor of Ki-pin (at the time Kabul) and of as much of the Paropamisadae as the Sacas of Kabul held; his son and successor was Spalagadames. Yin-mo-fu, son of the king of 'Greek-town', was Hermaeus,[8] son of Amyntas, king of Alexandria and of whatever went with Alexandria; and as Wen-chung allied himself

[1] *Sakastan* p. 113.

[2] *BMC* p. 100 no. 1, obv., *βασιλέως ἀδελφοῦ Σπαλιρίσου.*

[3] *BMC* p. 100, nos. 1–3, obv., *Σπαλυρίος δικαίου ἀδελφοῦ τοῦ βασιλέως.* See p. 345.

[4] Kharoshthi legend on reverse of the last-mentioned coin.

[5] *BMC* p. 99.

[6] It was the Han custom that officials going to a country should be taught its language (p. 282 n. 1). What Wen-chung would have known would probably have been the Yueh-chi form of the Saca language.

[7] The merchant, or whoever it was, from whom Ptolemy took the name Ionaca for Antioch-in-Persis (Bushire) made precisely the same mistake. See p. 418.

[8] If Yen-kao-chen is Wima (*Οοημο*) Kadphises, which everyone accepts as certain, Yin-mo-fu can perfectly well be Hermaeus.

not with the king of 'Greek-town' but with his son, Amyntas was unable to act, perhaps dying, as Yin-mo-fu is thenceforth treated as king; and as he was king before Yuan-ti's accession in 48 B.C. we have a *terminus post quem non* for Hermaeus' accession, and one substantially in accord with the date deduced from the use of the round and square omicron successively on his coinage. The prime mover in the conquest of Ki-pin-Kabul from Spalagadames was Wen-chung; he had no troops of his own, but the whole prestige of the Han was behind him, and he must either have had allies or been able to secure them. At some period which cannot be ascertained but which was later, perhaps very much later, than the death of Chang-k'ien in 114, China had succeeded in securing what Chang-k'ien had sought in vain, a perpetual alliance with the Yueh-chi;[1] whether the alliance still existed in Wen-chung's day cannot be said, but an indication remains of help rendered to China by that people at some unknown time or times,[2] and it was the help of one of their princes which Wen-chung obtained[3] against the Kabul Sacas. Of the five Yueh-chi princes, the Kushan chief Miaos, who was in the country between Chitral and the Panjshir district,[4] was the nearest to Alexandria; he supplied the necessary force, presumably for a consideration, Spalagadames was defeated and killed, and Hermaeus was installed by Wen-chung as king in Kabul. Doubtless Hermaeus, whose abundant silver coinage shows that the Panjshir mines were working well, paid Miaos in cash, precisely as the kings of Macedonia or Per-

[1] Wylie, part 2 p. 85, 'When the Han sent an envoy to Woo-sun, the envoy passed southward to Ta-wan and the Yue-she, forming a perpetual alliance with these nations.' The statement is given by Pan-ku as though between the years 114 and 110, but is certainly out of place. The Yueh-chi had recently refused Chang-k'ien's request for an alliance for a reason which made it unlikely that they would change their minds till some considerable time had elapsed. Ssu-ma Ch'ien knows nothing of this alliance, and it is not alluded to in his account of China's war with Ta-yuan, 106–101. It must at any rate therefore be later than 101 and later than Ssu-ma Ch'ien. De Groot unfortunately neither translated nor noticed the passage; it is part of the section of text on p. 125 'mit Stillschweigen übergegangen' because he had already translated the parallel section from the *Shi-ki*. But this particular passage is not in the *Shi-ki*.

[2] The obscure sentence in Pan-ku's account of the Yueh-chi, which de Groot (p. 96 and Franke's note) first translated 'Alle (*i.e.* the Yueh-chi and Ta-hia) werden sie mit Befehlen der Han-dynastie versehen' (which Franke preferred), and subsequently 'Gemeinsam verleihen sie den Gesandschaften von Han ihren Beistand'.

[3] This follows, as a fact, from the Hermaeus-Kadphises coins; see App. 17.

[4] On the location of the Kuei-shuang at this time see Konow in *CII* p. lvi, and de Groot p. 100 (Kafiristan).

gamum had been used to hire a tribe of Gauls for cash; but he also gave the Kushan a relative in marriage, who was probably his sister rather than daughter, seeing that he had only just come to the throne. The hand of Wen-chung can be seen here: Kushan help might be needed again, and it was the regular practice of the Han, as can be read in the Ch'ien-han-shu, to bestow an Imperial princess in marriage upon a barbarian ruler whose help or alliance might be useful; indeed if no Imperial princess was available they made one,[1] as bees can if necessary make a queen. In this way Hermaeus got the whole of the Paropamisadae, but as China's vassal. Subsequently, as the emperor Yuan-ti took no interest in the remote West, he virtually threw off his (rather nominal) allegiance by putting to death the escort of a Chinese envoy, but was still interested in trade; hence the coin with his name and Chinese characters found on the road to China. He was still alive after 32 B.C., when Ching-ti succeeded; but he certainly did not reign till anywhere near A.D. 19, the date of the accession in northern India of the Parthian Gondophares. The foreign lords of the Paropamisadae after his death continued to copy his coinage;[2] finally came the Kushan Kadphises I, Miaos' descendant, who claimed and conquered the Paropamisadae as the representative by blood of Hermaeus (App. 17). The whole story fits together extraordinarily well.

The Greek revival in the Paropamisadae then was directly due to the intervention of China, and Hermaeus began his reign as China's vassal. To what the successful stand on the Jhelum was due cannot be said, unless to a considerable influx of Greek refugees into Hippostratus' kingdom. The period of peace or of cessation of hostilities which followed Maues' death and enabled the Greek revival probably lasted till well after 40 B.C., to give room for the coinages of Hermaeus and Hippostratus with the square omicron and especially for their numerous tetradrachms, and that must mean that Maues' realm broke up on his death, as has already been argued for other reasons; but though this might have saved the Greek kings from further attacks for the time being, it would hardly have given that security of trade communication between Hippostratus and Hermaeus along the great road through Taxila and Gandhāra which, as we have seen, their coinages demand.

[1] See two instances, de Groot pp. 126, 127, 'erhob...zur kaiserlichen Prinzessin', which is clearer than Wylie part 2 pp. 87, 88.

[2] *CHI* pp. 561–2.

We must therefore look a little more closely at this period of peace, and that will entail the examination of an obscure class of coins which bear the name Vonones[1] and which show that a Vonones, called Great King of Kings, was suzerain of the Saca (Parsii) rulers of Kabul—Spalyris (Spalahores), Spalagadames, and Spalirises.[2] There can be no certainty as to what these coins mean, and any theory must entail difficulties;[3] I must give what seems to me the probable solution, though I am aware that it presents difficulties in turn. It seems certain from his name that Vonones was a Parthian. The Parthian survey reproduced by Isidore shows that, after the defeat of the Saca invasion, Mithridates II claimed that the Sacas of Sacastene and the Parsii of Arachosia were vassals of the Parthian realm, which means that with the virtual establishment of two Parthian realms they became vassals of the Suren in Seistan, if he could enforce his authority. He may have continued to enforce it over the Parsii of Arachosia and Kabul; and even though the Saca kingdom of Maues in India was completely independent, the Surens must have preserved a claim that that kingdom was only an offshoot of Sacastene and that consequently they were its rightful overlords, for that claim was fully enforced later when in A.D. 19 the then Suren Gondophares[4] brought the Saca domains in India under his direct personal rule.

The best solution I can see is that Vonones was the Suren, or rather

[1] *BMC* pp. 98 *sqq.*, 173. Mostly from Ghazni, Kandahar, and Seistan, with a few from Kabul: Cunningham *NC* 1890 p. 106.

[2] The Vonones coin mentioned by Herzfeld, *Sakastan* p. 92, which has on the reverse the legend rajadirajasa mahatasa Ayasa, cannot show that Vonones was Azes' suzerain, for Azes' title Great King of Kings forbids the supposition. I do not know where, or what, the coin is, but it naturally suggests a coin overstruck by Azes at a later date.

[3] The principal theories are those of Rapson in *CHI* Chap. XXIII, with which my own has certain affinities, and the very different one of Herzfeld in *Sakastan*, who identifies Vonones with the Arsacid king of Parthia who reigned A.D. 8–11 (as does Konow, *CII* p. xliii) though their coin-types are entirely different, and consequently gets everything very late. He starts from two wrong datings: our fixed points, he says (p. 91), are that the history of the Saca kingdom in India lies between Isidore, 1 B.C., and the date of the *Periplus*; for this (p. 89) he takes the Kornemann-Schur dating, A.D. 90–100, which has been refuted since he wrote, p. 148 n. 4. It really lies between the date of the Parthian survey which Isidore is reproducing, *c.* 110–100 B.C., and the true date of the *Periplus*, the middle of the first century A.D. (*ib.*); what matters is not Isidore's own date but the date of his information.

[4] Herzfeld, *Sakastan* p. 98 to end, a most enlightening study.

the ruler of the Suren's realm, for the time being;[1] he cannot have been Maues' successor, as his name is Parthian, not Saca. The Suren who in May 53 had won the battle of Carrhae for Orodes II of Parthia had been put to death by him soon afterwards, perhaps the same year;[2] as he was under thirty he cannot have left a grown son, and Vonones might have been a kinsman, left to govern the East while the Suren was engaged in the West, or even an usurper. In either case he acted as though completely independent and took the title Great King of Kings left vacant by Maues' death, which shows that what he was thinking of was dominion over the Sacas in India. He was safe from interference from the Arsacids in the West, for down to the failure of Antony's invasion in 36 B.C. they were fully occupied in fighting or watching Rome; Orodes had no opportunity to attend to the East, and it agrees with this that no Suren took part in the resistance to Antony.[3] As for Vonones' vassals, Spalyris, the ruler of Arachosia and Kabul, on some coins[4] acknowledges Vonones as his suzerain and does not call himself king, but on another series,[5] which does not mention Vonones, he calls himself 'king's brother'; he cannot (as I see it) have been really Vonones' brother,[6] as Vonones was a Parthian, and it was probably merely a title of honour, since 'brother', implying brother of the king, was a known title of honour at Hellenistic courts;[7] though the view has been taken (I think wrongly) that it means brother-in-law.[8] Spalyris' son Spalaga-

[1] This really agrees with Rapson, *CHI* p. 572, 'suzerain over the kingdoms of eastern Iran'; for he wrote before Herzfeld had shown that that suzerain was the Suren.

[2] Plut. *Crass.* 33, οὐ μετὰ πολὺν χρόνον after Carrhae; it was early enough to prevent a Parthian invasion of Syria in 52, Tarn, *CAH* IX p. 612.

[3] If he had, he must have commanded; he could not have been subordinated to Monaeses, who we know did command. M. Rostovtzeff, *CAH* XI p. 114, suggests that Monaeses belonged to the Suren clan, which I find difficult to believe, but does not (if I understand him) suggest that he was the Suren, *i.e.* the ruler of eastern Parthia; the difficulties would be great, but need not be considered here.

[4] *BMC* pp. 98, 173.

[5] *Ib.* p. 100 nos. 1–3.

[6] Rapson, *CHI* p. 574, makes him his brother.

[7] *OGIS* 138 and further instances in Dittenberger's note 8. Many Hellenistic court titles were in use in Parthia, and the Parthian king himself was 'Brother of the Sun and Moon'.

[8] Herzfeld, *Arch. Hist. of Iran* 1935 p. 64. He makes it part of the Saca rule of succession, under which the crown went to the dead king's sister's son (the so-called Pictish or matriarchal rule of succession). But he gives no evidence that the Sacas *had* matriarchal succession (if such a thing really existed); Abdagases was Gondo-

dames does call himself king on his coins[1] but also acknowledges Vonones' suzerainty. If Vonones grasped independence and took his title in the winter of 53–2, there is room for the coins before Hermaeus killed Spalagadames and took Kabul, which need not have been before 49; Spalyris might have governed Arachosia and Kabul for years as Parthian governor or vassal without coining and might only have begun to coin when Vonones seized power. For Vonones' title shows that he was thinking of something much bigger than Kabul: the explanation of the peace and of the trade communication between Hippostratus and Hermaeus must be that he did succeed in asserting his authority over the Sacas in India, at any rate over Gandhāra and Taxila, though he did not apparently transfer his seat of government to India, as Gondophares was to do. The peace then was a Parthian peace, and attacks on the Greeks by the disunited Sacas ceased; Vonones may have even favoured the Greek states—many Parthians were Philhellenes—as a useful counterpoise to the ambitions of his Saca vassals. After the death of Spalagadames Vonones' vassal ruler in Arachosia was Spalirises, who on his early coins[2] called himself 'king's brother'.

If the period of peace lasted till well after the year 40 B.C., as seems probable, Vonones can hardly have died before that date. The next ruler of eastern Parthia, whoever he was, seems to have reversed his policy and returned to the traditional rôle of the Surens as supporters of the Arsacids, for in 27 B.C. he received Phraates IV when driven out by the usurper Tiridates and restored him to his throne (p. 306). He can have played no part in the East outside of his own kingdom of Seistan; perhaps he did not seek to, or perhaps Spalirises revolted and defeated him; in any event Spalirises seized what of Vonones' power he could, took the title of Great King, and conferred the same title on his son Azes.[3]

Support for this theory concerning Vonones' successor seems forthcoming from the Chinese side. It has been seen (see also App. 9) that down to, and at the time of, the installation as king of Yin-mo-fu (Hermaeus) about 49 B.C. the term Ki-pin meant to Pan-ku Kabul and

phares' nephew, but was probably a brother's son (*Sakastan* p. 105), and anyhow they were Parthians, not Sacas. And Spalagadames did *not* succeed Vonones.

[1] *BMC* p. 99.

[2] *BMC* p. 100.

[3] *BMC* p. 102: obv., Spalirises, Great King; rev., Azes, Great King. There seems no doubt that it means father and son. Rapson, *CHI* p. 573, thought that these coins were struck in Vonones' lifetime; it is possible.

whatever of the Paropamisadae the Parsii of Kabul ruled; consequently his general description in the Ch'ien-han-shu of Ki-pin as the Saca realm refers to a time later than 49 B.C., and as his history ends with A.D. 24 the time referred to is that of the Azes dynasty; Maues is too early. But side by side with Ki-pin Pan-ku describes another kingdom, O-ik-san-li[1] (pp. 14, 204 n. 1), which was bounded on the east by (the Saca kingdom of) Ki-pin, on the north by (the Kushan realm of) Bactria, and on the west by Li-kan (Media) and Tao-ki (Babylonia), and was therefore the Suren's kingdom of Seistan, whatever it exactly comprised besides Seistan proper. It was suggested long ago that O-ik-san-li was Alexandria,[2] and that seems now certain;[3] but it has not been asked where an Alexandria could be found in Seistan. One can now see that it was the official name of Prophthasia, Alexander's capital of Seistan (pp. 14, 49), which has perished in the Greek tradition;[4] the Chinese named the country from its capital. The point is that Pan-ku knew that under the Azes dynasty the Saca realm (Ki-pin) was independent of the Parthian Suren in Seistan (O-ik-san-li), just as I have worked it out for Vonones' successor; this independence ended in A.D. 19, when the Suren Gondophares again brought Ki-pin under Parthian rule.

Spalirises and his son Azes were then joint kings. Coin-finds, notably coins buried beneath the foundations of stupas, connect Azes with Taxila, and the humped bull of Pushkalāvatī is common among his types, and therefore Spalirises, whose coins come chiefly from Arachosia,[5] must have ruled in the west of his realm with Azes as co-ruler in the east—the regular Seleucid system once more. Subsequently both father and son appear with the title Great King of Kings.[6] Since Azes must have had that title by 30 B.C. at the very latest;[7] since it was Spalirises who put an end to Hermaeus' kingdom (p. 350); and since

[1] Wylie p. 38; de Groot p. 91. Wylie spelt it Woo-yih-shan-le.

[2] Wylie p. 38 n. He thought of Alexandria-Herat, which probably did belong to the Suren's kingdom (Alexander had once conjoined Seistan and Herat), but cannot be O-ik-san-li, for the reason given in n. 4 (*below*).

[3] De Groot p. 92 seems conclusive.

[4] O-ik-san-li was the terminus of the road to the south, Wylie p. 39, de Groot p. 92; this makes it certain.

[5] Mostly from Kandahar, with a few from the Punjab: Cunningham, *NC* 1890 p. 109. Also from Kabul: Wilson, *Ariana Antiqua* p. 316.

[6] Spalirises, *BMC* p. 101; Azes, coins *passim*.

[7] His enormous coinage, and also those of Azilises (which is plentiful) and Azes II, have to come in before A.D. 19.

Hermaeus was ruling well after 32 B.C. (p. 350); the only solution of the chronological problem seems to be that father and son were both Great King of Kings at the same time, as they had been Great King at the same time; when Spalirises took the title Great King of Kings he conferred the same title on his son and co-ruler, Azes, just as Azes subsequently did on his own son Azilises.[1] There is no lack of precedents for father and son being co-equals, whether in title and fact, like Antigonus I and his son Demetrius the Besieger, or in title and theory, as in the Seleucid practice; the only thing which makes it seem strange is the title Great King of Kings conferred upon a son, and even for that there is a famous parallel. At the Donations of Alexandria in 34 B.C. Antony had conferred the title Queen of Kings upon Cleopatra and the title King of Kings on her son and (in theory) co-ruler in Egypt, Ptolemy Caesar;[2] news travels fast in the East, and Antony's action may have prompted that of Spalirises. Doubtless the Parsii were by this time thoroughly mixed with Saca blood, but they were Persians at bottom, and father and son may have felt themselves superior to the Saca tribes about them.

This too might be the reason why Azes did not use the old Saca Era which had been used by the Saca Maues (App. 16), though Sacas themselves used it much later when under Parthian rule.[3] It is now believed that the Era of Azes used by some individuals in the Kushan period to date their donations was the Vikrama Era of 58 B.C.[4] (p. 335), and the explanation might be that Azes, finding two Eras already current in his realm, emphasised the fact that he was not a Saca and that his house and people had never been subject to Maues by adopting the Indian Vikrama Era in preference to the Saca one. But it would remain strange that Azes' name should have become attached to an Indian Era,

[1] *BMC* p. 173 nos. 1, 2; coins of Azes, obv., Azes, Great King of Kings; rev., Azilises, Great King of Kings. The coins which have Azilises on the obverse and Azes on the reverse are those of Azilises reigning jointly with *his* son Azes II; the reigns of the three kings of this dynasty therefore overlap to an unknown extent. That there *were* three kings, not one, see App. 16.

[2] See Tarn, *CAH* x p. 80.

[3] The Taxila duck vase, see p. 500.

[4] The Taxila silver scroll, *CII* p. 70 no. XXVII, and the Kalawān inscription, *JRAS* 1932 p. 949, *ASI* 1930–4 p. 163. Some scholars, including Marshall and Rapson, have always thought this most probable (references *CII* pp. 70–1); and Konow, who formerly refused to believe that *ayasa* in *CII* XXVII was Azes, now in the light of the Kalawān inscription regards this as unavoidable, *JRAS* 1932 pp. 950–2; *JIH* XII, 1933, pp. 1–4; see p. 502.

and possibly it was not the Vikrama Era that he used but one of his own creation, dating like the Vikrama from Maues' death in 58 B.C. and indicating that he claimed not only to have succeeded to Maues' empire but that that empire, though it had lapsed *de facto*, had never lapsed *de jure*. For in any case it does not mean that Azes came to the throne in 58 B.C. It used to be believed that he followed Maues immediately; but the reasons for a considerable interval between Maues and himself are much too strong,[1] as has been seen.

The advent to power of Spalirises and his son heralded the end of Greek rule. As soon as Azes felt strong enough—probably about 30 B.C., though a somewhat earlier date may be possible—he attacked Hippostratus. The Saca fleet avenged its previous defeat on the Jhelum and gave Azes control of the river and a crossing; Poseidon with his trident appears on one of his coins,[2] and Poseidon with his trident trampling upon a river-god on another,[3] and it was with the latter type that Azes overstruck some of Hippostratus' coins,[4] a fact eloquent of the end of the kingdoms of Hippostratus and Nicias; that end is further attested by the appearance upon Azes' coins of the Athena Alkis of Menander[5] and the monograms of all Hippostratus' moneyers.[6] But Azes' type of Poseidon trampling on a river-god is copied from the similar type of Maues (p. 322); he therefore already regarded himself as Maues' destined successor, and in the north of India at any rate he was to restore Maues' empire.

Hermaeus' kingdom may or may not have lasted a year or two longer. The deterioration of his later coins with the square omicron has been said to witness to the difficulties which surrounded him;[7] if so, it might mean that the conquest of his kingdom was a slow process and that his best engravers, like the great Bactrian artists, fell fighting. Somewhere between 48 and 33 B.C. China under Yuan-ti had ceased to take any interest in the Paropamisadae, which was relegated to the list

[1] It has already been suggested that Azes may not have followed Maues immediately: Konow, *JIH* XII, 1933, p. 20.

[2] *BMC* p. 77 no. 55; Cunningham, *NC* 1890 p. 142 no. 7.

[3] *BMC* p. 89 nos. 101–4; Cunningham, *NC* 1890 p. 144 no. 1.

[4] *BMC* p. 89 n.; another specimen, *Lahore Cat.* p. 122 no. 246. See *CHI* p. 572.

[5] *BMC* Pl. XVIII, 2, 3; clearly Alkis, not Promachos. Pl. XVIII, 4, *might* be meant for Promachos; it is uncertain.

[6] *CHI* p. 572. His coins show all three of Hippostratus' monograms, the distinctive one of the Bucephala moneyer being very common.

[7] *CHI* p. 561.

of 'unregistered and impracticable' lands; Wen-chung had no successor, and Hermaeus paid for his virtual repudiation of China's suzerainty with the loss of her support (he might have lost it in any case), which may also have entailed the loss of the support of her Kushan allies. After a new emperor, Ching-ti, had in 32 come to the throne, Hermaeus sent envoys to him, officially to ask for pardon, but really in a desperate effort to obtain China's help, which attests his altered circumstances; Ching-ti's advisers however were hostile to the idea of interfering in a land which Chinese troops could not effectively reach across the mountains, and it is the long memorandum on this subject presented by Tu-k'in to the Emperor which shows that in reality Hermaeus had sent to ask for help.[1] Ching-ti on a trivial pretext (p. 340) refused to receive the envoys, and Hermaeus was left to his fate; after all, his last dealing with China had consisted in putting to death the escort of a Chinese envoy. Spalirises conquered the Paropamisadae[2] and the 'Zeus enthroned' of Alexandria-Kapisa appears on his coins;[3] the Zeus is sitting full face, and it has been noticed for a century that his 'Zeus enthroned' is a copy of that of Hermaeus;[4] also the sign *þ* for *sh*, which (as P) had appeared on Miaos' coins presumably minted in, or copying patterns made for him in, Kapisa (App. 17), now sometimes appears on those of Spalirises (p. 509). But he cannot long have survived his conquest—his coins, though not rare, are said not to be very numerous—for the monogram of one of Hermaeus' moneyers appears on coins of Azes.[5] Hermaeus' death cannot be put much later than 30 B.C., indeed it cannot really be said whether he or Hippostratus fell first; but however that may be, with the deaths of these two kings almost everything in Asia between the Euphrates and the Jumna which Greeks had once ruled had now passed into the hands of peoples from the northern steppes.

[1] For this story, from the *Ch'ien-han-shu*, see Wylie pp. 36 *sqq*., Franke pp. 63 *sq*., de Groot pp. 88 *sqq*. See p. 473.

[2] *CHI* pp. 562, 574.

[3] *BMC* p. 101, Pl. XXII, 4; *CHI* Pl. VII, 38.

[4] First by Wilson, *Ariana Antiqua* p. 315 (1841). See the two side by side, *CHI* Pl. VII, 37, 38.

[5] Whitehead *NC* p. 340.

CHAPTER IX

THE GREEKS AND INDIA

THE end of Greek rule east of the Hindu Kush closely and rather dramatically coincided in date with two linked events in the Mediterranean world, the end of the last Hellenistic kingdom in the West, Egypt, and the establishment of the Roman empire of Augustus; as Augustus entered Alexandria on the first of August 30 B.C., it is conceivable that one or even both of the two remaining Greek kingdoms in India was actually the last Hellenistic kingdom to survive in independence. The reign of Augustus, though he had nothing much to do with the world east of the Euphrates, forms a convenient line of division both in India and in the Parthian empire, though not in the same way. For the Greeks of Parthia it marks, very roughly, the time when the period of achievement passes over into the period of decay, though in some places, as Seleuceia on the Tigris and Seleuceia on the Eulaeus (Susa), the latter process was perhaps not very marked till the second century A.D. In India, however, the period of achievement seems to have ended with Menander's death, though that may be an illusion due to the fact that the succeeding half century is to us a blank; but in any case it will appear that the process of Indianisation of the Greeks cannot have well begun later than the early part of the first century B.C. The division which Augustus' reign makes in India is a hard and fast division in the nature of our *evidence*. The knowledge, principally of Northern India, obtained by the Greek invaders is carried no further, but is replaced by information about the coasts and the ports derived from merchants of the Roman empire, men of every nationality, who now began to visit the harbours of Southern and of Farther India and even of China, giving Greek names to the little nameless islets where they found anchorage or water;[1] they learnt much about the coasts, but little or nothing about the interior of Northern India, with which they were not concerned. Much information about their doings survives in the Periplus, in Pliny, and in Ptolemy, and has been worked up in modern books; this has to be separated carefully from the fairly abundant Hellenistic information in Ptolemy and Pliny,

[1] Such names are too common throughout Ptolemy book VII to list.

and the Hellenistic historian must avoid drawing on it unless he has some definite reason, for it has nothing to do with the story of the Bactrian Greeks in India.

As in this chapter I shall sometimes have to refer to Kanishka and other Kushan kings, it may be convenient to some readers to have an indication of the dating. The five Kushan kings (or principal kings) in order are Kujula Kadphises I, Wima Kadphises II, Kanishka, Huvishka, Vasudeva. The reign of Kujula, the conqueror of the Paropamisadae, is from somewhere after A.D. 25, the date at which the Hou-han-shu begins, to *c.* A.D. 50. Professor F. W. Thomas tells me that his chronology in the Cambridge History of India for the next two reigns will be Wima (the conqueror of Northern India) *c.* 50 to 78 (the so-called Saca Era),[1] Kanishka 78 to *c.* 103. The date of Kanishka's accession has been one of the most disputed points in history, four theories having found support:[2] the Vikrama Era, 58 B.C.;[3] A.D. 78; *c.* A.D. 100; second century A.D. To-day the question seems to lie between 78 and 128 (Dr Sten Konow's date).[4] I do not believe in 128 myself; even if it should turn out that, as some believe, 78 is a Malva Era (see p. 335) and not the Era of Kanishka by which the later Kushans dated, that would not make Kanishka second century. To avoid begging questions I generally (after Kujula) refer to reigns, not dates.

Little remained in India which could in any sense be called distinctively Greek after about the middle of the first century A.D., or say roughly the establishment of the Kushan empire which replaced in the North-West the rule of the Parthian Gondophares and his successor Pacores. Such cities as were Greek *poleis*—they were very few—lived on under Saca and Parthian rule in the same sort of quasi-autonomous relationship to their Iranian overlords as can be traced in the relationship of Seleuceia to the Arsacid monarchs; the unique coin of Pushkalāvatī (p. 336) shows that that city, like Seleuceia for a time in the first century A.D., was at some period completely independent. The number

[1] Sir J. Marshall, *ASI* 1929–30 (pub. 1935) pp. 55–7, has recently given reasons for believing that the Kushans, *i.e.* Wima Kadphises, took Taxila between A.D. 60 and 64.

[2] A convenient list of the writers who have supported each of these theories will be found in Winternitz, Eng. trans. II pp. 612–13.

[3] I had supposed this view was obsolete; but D. N. Mukherji, *Indian Culture* I, 1935, p. 477, has adduced some astronomical calculations in its support.

[4] In *CII*. A specific argument against this date, breaking fresh ground, is given by L. Bachhofer, *Ostasiat. Z.* XVI, 1930, p. 9.

of representations of the Fortune of some city (*i.e.* the city itself) with her mural crown on Saca coins[1] tells its own story; most illuminating is a coin of Zeionises,[2] nephew and satrap of the Parthian Gondophares (A.D. 19 to 45 *plus*), which shows the Fortune of some city, undoubtedly Pushkalāvatī, confronting the king as a separate and obviously quasi independent entity. Literature gives little help here. The Periplus in the middle of the first century A.D. mentions Bucephala,[3] which probably, though not necessarily, means that it was still surviving as a city; the second part of the Milindapañha twice mentions Alexandria of the Caucasus (p. 421 n. 4), but that document may not be later than the end of Greek rule, and in any case the name may simply have been borrowed from the first part. Fortunes of cities never appear on the Kushan coinage, and there can be little doubt that the cities, if not destroyed, had by the end of the first century A.D. become to all intents and purposes Indian, though that does not mean that some people may not still have understood the Greek language. This general result is borne out by the Greek monograms on the coins, for as long as they persist they show that Greek moneyers were still operating or controlling the city mints. On the coins of Azes and his dynasty Greek monograms are so numerous and varied that it seems as if Azes must have opened some fresh mints. They occur on the coins of Gondophares (who was still reigning in A.D. 45) and of his nephew and subking Abdagases, but not on those of Gondophares' successor Pacores, or later; that is, we meet no Greek moneyers, as we meet no Greek cities, after about the middle of the first century A.D.

The question of whether Greek remained a living tongue in India as late as the reign of Kanishka was argued at a symposium of the Royal

[1] Maues: *BMC* pp. 68 no. 4 and 70 nos. 12, 13, Pl. XVI, 3, 9; *NC* 1890 pp. 131 no. 7 and 134 no. 21; *Lahore Cat.* p. 99 no. 15; *ASI* 1914–15 p. 46 no. 12; *NC* 1923 p. 340 no. 66. Azes: *BMC* pp. 82 nos. 109–11 and 90 nos. 191–9, Pls. XVIII, 10, 11, XX, 1. Azilises: *ib.* p. 94, Pl. XX, 9–11; Cunningham *NC* 1890 Pl. VIII, 6; *ASI* 1914–15 p. 31 no. 26; an unpublished type *ASI ib.* no. 24; and see *CHI* p. 588. Whether the seated figure on a Saca coin, Cunningham, *NC* 1890 p. 154 no. 6, be really the Fortune of a city may be doubted; it is difficult to see the turreted crown on the plate.

[2] *BMC* p. 110 nos. 1, 2, Pl. XXIII, 4. An inscription, *CII* p. 81 no. xxx, shows that Zeionises (Jihonika) also ruled in Taxila; but Taxila was not a *polis*, and the city on his coins is certainly Pushkalāvatī, cf. *CHI* pp. 582 n., 588.

[3] *Periplus* 47. The writer, who knew nothing about Northern India, wrongly put it in *Προκλαΐς*, which here and in 48 is obviously not Pushkalāvatī, as it is in Ptol. VII, 1, 44, but the province, Peucelaïtis.

Asiatic Society in 1913, and the supporters of the negative view, led by Professor F. W. Thomas, had the best of the argument.[1] I am not going over that ground again; but several things are clear to-day which were unknown or not clear in 1913, and they are worth looking at. I must premise that the *sh* sign, Þ, on coins of Kanishka and his successors has nothing to do with it; that sign had appeared long before on the coins of Miaos and Spalirises (App. 17, 18). Greek was alive in the time of Kujula Kadphises; the square letter-forms and the different mistakes in the legend on his coins prove that much. But the coins of Wima Kadphises exhibit correct Greek written in the orthodox way except for the lunate sigma; *prima facie*, his moneyers were copying a dead language. Are there any signs of life? The significance of the verbal form τυραννοῦντος on the coins of Miaos, contemporary with Hermaeus, is noticed elsewhere (App. 17), and on the coins of Gondophares' sub-king Abdagases the verbal form occurs again as βασιλεὺς βασιλεύων, 'under the rule of king Abdagases';[2] and as the use of βασιλεύοντος on the pedigree coins of Antimachus and Agathocles (App. 3) shows that it was regarded as the proper word to express the position of a sub-king, it follows that in Gondophares' reign there were Greeks who still understood very well the distinction between βασιλεύς and βασιλεύων.[3] This in itself takes us no further down than the Fortune of a city on Zeionises' coins has already done; but βασιλεύων occurs again in the regular legend on the widespread coinage of the 'Nameless king'.[4] This shows that to some of his moneyers Greek was still alive, and also shows that he was a sub-king of some sort; and as the Hou-han-shu says that Wima Kadphises governed his Indian possessions through a viceroy, and as it has usually, though not universally, been supposed that that viceroy can only have been the Nameless king,[5] this *may* take us down nearly to the reign of Kanishka.

For Kanishka's reign itself the question must turn on his Greek title

[1] Reported at length in *JRAS* 1913 pp. 627 *sqq.*, 922 *sqq.*

[2] *BMC* pp. 107–8.

[3] In Philostratus' *Life of Apollonius* II, 32, Gondophares himself is made an Indian who talks Greek and reads the *Heracleidae* of Euripides. Any Parthian king *might* have known Greek; but Philostratus' story was merely invented for the sake of Apollonius' remark, II, 33, about the 'return of the Heracleidae'.

[4] *BMC* pp. 114–16: βασιλεὺς βασιλεύων σωτὴρ μέγας.

[5] J. Kennedy, *JRAS* 1913 p. 664; de la Vallée-Poussin p. 312; Konow in *CII* pp. lxviii–ix. Cunningham possessed a coin which connected the two, *NC* 1892 pp. 55, 71 no. 14. It is noteworthy that a gold coin of Wima is now known (*NC* 1934 p. 232, *BM Quarterly* VIII p. 73) which gives him the title βασιλεὺς βασιλέων σωτὴρ μέγας.

βασιλεὺς βασιλέων Κανέρκου, 'Kanishka king of kings', where a nominative, βασιλεύς, is in agreement with a genitive Κανέρκου. To Professor Thomas in 1913 this appeared to be an unintelligent copying of a dead language;[1] Dr Sten Konow in 1928 compared it with an idiom from Chinese Turkestan,[2] which I understand obtained in more than one language there. This no doubt is a possible origin, especially if Kanishka, as some believe, came from Chinese Turkestan; but there does seem now to be a simpler explanation. Inscriptions from Doura have given us some knowledge of the sort of Greek, alive enough but vulgarised, spoken by the less educated classes in the decay of what had once been a Hellenistic city, and its most marked feature is the substitution of genitive for nominative and the use of the two in agreement.[3] We may believe that in Kanishka's time educated Greeks and educated Greek were alike extinct in India; but some of his moneyers could evidently still speak Greek in a vulgarised form, whatever else they spoke also—incidentally an argument for not dating this king too late. As the coins of the Kushan kings after Kujula Kadphises show no moneyers' marks, neither Greek monograms nor Kharoshthi letters, a thing which must reflect royal orders, we are deprived of our best means of judging what Kanishka's moneyers were. There were still people with Greek names, and the father of Menander the wrestler[4] must have had *some* Greek feeling if he named his son after the great Yavana king. The 'slave Agesilas'[5] who was the architect of Kanishka's stupa near Taxila and made his relic casket may have been anything from a skilled Greek slave imported from the West to a subject of Kanishka[6] with little Greek about him but his name; as he worked in the Gandhāra style the latter is more probable. After Kanishka no question arises.

[1] *JRAS* 1913 pp. 1013–14. [2] *CII* p. liii.

[3] Cumont, *Fouilles* p. 351. His instances are confined to γυναικός for γυνή, but instances of other words from later finds are *SEG* VII, 683, 685, 688, 696–8, nominative and genitive in agreement; 374, 488, genitive for nominative. So on a coin of Gotarzes of Parthia, A.D. 41–51, *BMC Parthia* p. 165.

[4] *CII* p. 134 no. LXX, late Kushan period, from Peshawur. It is remarkable that the name, Minamdra, keeps the Greek nu; but *l* and *n* could run parallel in Prakrit (p. 238 n. 2), and the *n* does not prevent the inscription being late.

[5] *Ib.* p. 135 no. LXXII, Agisala.

[6] If 'slave' be used either in the Persian (Achaemenid) sense of any subject not royal, or in the Graeco-Parthian sense of any subject not *āzāt*, a member of the privileged Parthian nobility (Rostovtzeff and Welles, *Yale Class. Stud.* II p. 52; H. W. Bailey, *BSOS* VI, 1932, p. 953), which in Greek was rendered by ἐλεύθερος; hence the strange idea in some Roman and modern writers that Surenas took an army of slaves against Crassus.

Greek legends cease to appear on the coins; Saca written in Greek letters continues till the reign of Vasudeva, and then even Greek script vanishes from India.

We can now return to the period of Greek rule and gather up what indications remain of what the Greeks in India did. The provincial organisation of the Greek empire in India at its fullest extent has already been examined (Chap. VI), and Indian citizens of one Greek *polis* at least, Demetrias in Sind, have been traced at a date which cannot be much later than 50 B.C. (p. 257 n. 3). The Kharoshthi letters on some of the Greek coins,[1] which from their relation to the Greek monograms are clearly the initials of an Indian moneyer, enable us to confirm these Indian citizens. These letters are for some time confined to the group of kings who ruled east of the Jhelum, the kings of the houses of Euthydemus and Menander, which for all purposes of policy were identical in fact as, except for Menander himself, they were in blood; Kharoshthi letters are common on the coins of Strato I, Zoilus II Soter, and Apollodotus II, and occur on those of Apollophanes and Dionysius, but are never found on coins of Menander and his contemporaries, *e.g.* Antimachus II, or for a little while after his death (Agathocleia and Zoilus I Dikaios); we may say roughly that they begin with the last quarter or last third of the second century B.C. They never occur on coins of any king known to be of the house of Eucratides, or on the coins of Lysias, who, though a Euthydemid, coined in Antialcidas' mints (p. 315). Except on the late base silver of Strato I they are, prior to Hippostratus, confined to the copper currencies, and the usual rule is that they never appear alone but always in association with a Greek monogram. In the Seleucid mint at Antioch it was the rule for two moneyers to sign the coins, one being a permanent mint-master and the other a changing city magistrate.[2] I do not know whether an examination of every coin with a Kharoshthi initial on it (which I cannot make) would show if these Indians were ever magistrates; but there is one simple case in which the Kharoshthi letter certainly represents a permanent official of the mint, and that is the 'city' coins of Hippostratus, minted in Bucephala (p. 245), a Greek *polis*. All his 'city' type coins, both bronze and silver, bear the same very distinctive Greek monogram and the same Kharoshthi letter; these were his two mint-masters at

[1] *BMC* under the various kings here mentioned; cf. Whitehead, *NC* p. 314. On the monograms generally see App. 1.

[2] E. T. Newell, *The Seleucid Mint of Antioch* 1918 *passim*.

Bucephala. It is known from Plutarch that Perseus had two mint-masters at Pella (p. 437), and I have traced the two in Bactra in the great period (App. 1); what is not known is whether, when there were two, they were colleagues with equal authority, or whether one was subordinate; this in Hippostratus' mint would be the Indian. The latter is more probable, for we see the Indian moneyer at first signing copper money only before being at the end promoted to signing the silver also. But in one mint we find an Indian mint-master already in control by about the beginning of the first century B.C.: on some late silver of Strato, called semi-barbarous, and on some bronze of Strato, Zoilus II, and Apollodotus II, there is no Greek monogram at all but only two Kharoshthi letters, showing that the mint in question had two Indian mint-masters; the mint in question was probably Sāgala, which, unlike Bucephala, was not a Greek *polis*. The fact that Kharoshthi letters are comparatively rare on coins of Maues[1] is one more sign of his early date, for throughout the Saca and Parthian (Pahlava) coinages from Azes to Pacores such letters are common. Very rarely, and very late, one Kharoshthi letter appears alone; this occurs only on some 'uncertain' bronze coins, which I have thought might belong to kinglets driven into the hills (p. 323 n. 1), and on the second series of the 'Hermaeus' coins of Kujula Kadphises (App. 17); he was an invader issuing proclamations, and had to get his propaganda money struck as best he could.

That these Indian mint-officials who signed the coinage were citizens where they occur in a Greek *polis* is certain, for they could not possibly have been anything else. And as it cannot be supposed that Sāgala under Strato or Bucephala under Hippostratus was incapable of supplying two Greeks to manage the mint, we must see in this admission of Indians to office a deliberate act of policy. The evidence of the coins takes us a good deal further back than that of the cave inscriptions, and no doubt by the last quarter of the second century the Euthydemids, whether from choice or by force of circumstances, were coming to rely more and more upon their Indian subjects; but the coins do not supply evidence for the time of Demetrius and Menander. Seeing, however, that the rule of these two kings was based on the idea of a sort of partnership, Indians must from the first have been admitted to citizenship; indeed it is not apparent on what other lines a place like Demetrias in Sind could ever have been a *polis*, as it certainly was from its dynastic name. The kings of Eucratides' line, like Eucratides himself, may have

[1] Instances are Cunningham *NC* 1890 pp. 133 no. 19, 135 no. 24.

held different views; we do not know. But the only king west of the Jhelum on whose coins Kharoshthi letters occur, and the only king therefore to admit Indians to office, was Hermaeus, and it is quite uncertain if he did belong to the house of Eucratides; in any case he may have turned to his Indian subjects, as at the end he turned to China, in an attempt to stave off the inevitable.

That is as far as one can get with the cities, though it seems obvious that if there were Indian officials of the mints they were not likely to be the only officials who were Indians; it has already been pointed out that the great loosely hung satrapies could only have been worked by the retention of much of the existing Indian arrangements. The one Indian governor mentioned, an unnamed meridarch, seems to belong to the early Saca period;[1] but undoubtedly it must be supposed that, while the Seleucids occasionally fitted an Iranian official into their own Greek system, the Euthydemid provincial administration in India was essentially Graeco-Indian. Still it must not be forgotten that the undivided empire of Demetrius and Menander was in form a Hellenistic kingdom, one that had originally branched off from the Seleucid kingdom though it had taken a somewhat different complexion; and the Greek satrapies, with their *strategoi* and meridarchs, became so firmly impressed on the country that the Sacas took over the Greek provincial organisation with even less change than the Parthians made when they took over the Seleucid, while the four satrapies into which the Greeks had divided Sind lasted, with whatever boundary modifications, far down into Indian history as the four traditional divisions of that land. Other things too, for a time, were firmly impressed by the Greeks upon that part of India which they ruled. The bilingual coinage, with legends in Greek and Kharoshthi, was continued by Sacas, Parthians, and the earlier Kushans, though with the passing of Greek rule its meaning and significance had passed also; the Kharoshthi legends were first discontinued by Kanishka.[2]

[1] *CII* p. 4 no. II, from Taxila, dated by Konow about the second half of the first century B.C. It reads: 'By...the meridarch, together with his wife, the stupa was established in honour of his mother and father, for the presentation of a respectful offering.' The name is lost; but it is said that Indian Buddhist texts always say 'women and men', putting the woman first (Rhys Davids I p. 83 n., II p. 127 n. 1), and in fact the phrase 'in honour of mother and father' is very common in Kharoshthi inscriptions, *CII* nos. XX, XXIII, XXVII, XXXVI no. 6, LXXXV, LXXXVI; also mother comes before father in other phrasing, *ib.* nos. XIII, XXXI, XCII. This makes this Buddhist meridarch an Indian, for it is incredible that a Greek would have named his mother before his father.

[2] A solitary bilingual coin of Kanishka is known, *BMC* p. 175 no. 1.

Another thing was the Greek calendar. It has already been mentioned (p. 64) how that great invention the Seleucid Era, model for the Parthian and for the Roman provincial Eras, swept Asia west of India; and it is certain that the half-Seleucid Euthydemids used it in Bactria, for they could not possibly have used anything else, in view of the trouble they took to proclaim that they were Seleucids; as to the house of Eucratides, Plato's dated coin is definite proof (p. 209). Demetrius of necessity took the Seleucid calendar (in its Macedonian, not its Babylonian or semi-Babylonian, form)[1] to India with him, and there it gave birth to many other Eras;[2] kings or dynasties of alien blood might desire to set up Eras of their own, but they were all copies; the *idea* of reckoning time from a date fixed once for all came to India with the Greeks. Sacas and Kushans copied so closely that nothing differed but the initial year, and their calendars have been called Indo-Macedonian;[3] they kept the same subdivisions, the Macedonian months, and the Macedonian names of these months in place of the Indian names often appear in the datings of Kharoshthi inscriptions of the Saca and Kushan periods.[4] Indeed, though Brahmi inscriptions normally use the Indian month-names, a Sanscrit inscription recording a donation is now known, written in Brahmi and found as far afield as Mathurā, which is dated in the reign of the Kushan Huvishka in the 28th year of the Era of Kanishka on the first day of the Macedonian month Gorpiaios.[5] It has however been suggested that the donor must have come to Mathurā from the North-West.[6]

The one town in the Greek sphere which has been excavated, Taxila, was unfortunately not a Greek *polis*. Hellenistic Taxila has already been noticed (p. 179); but the town on Sirkap now so well known from the excavations is essentially the Parthian town of Gondophares, one

[1] I must refer back to pp. 64 *sq.* It should be obvious now, apart from the evidence given p. 47 n. 2, that the Euthydemids could only have used the same form as the Seleucids themselves.

[2] Konow's discussion of the Eras, *CII* pp. lxxxii *sqq.*, overlooks this obvious fact.

[3] Konow, *CII* p. lxxxix.

[4] *CII* nos. XIII, LXXIV, LXXIX, LXXXII, LXXXVI; one Saca period, four Kushan.

[5] Jayaswal, *JBORS* XVIII, 1932, p. 4; Konow, *Ep. Ind.* XXI, 1931 (pub. 1934), p. 55; H. K. Deb, *IHQ* 1932 p. 117, who points out that the Indian and Macedonian months were readily interchangeable, both being lunar. The Macedonian months could as well be fitted to the Indian year as they were to the Roman year at Nineveh, *CIG* 4672.

[6] Konow, *IHQ* IX, 1933, p. 147.

of his capitals, and the bulk of the jewellery and small objects found, which are very numerous, illustrate Parthian culture in the middle of the first century A.D.[1] Sir John Marshall's comparisons of the details revealed by excavation with the account of Taxila in Philostratus' Life of Apollonius[2] have shown that Philostratus, however much he may have romanced in other ways, had before him a tolerably accurate account of the external aspect of Taxila itself, given by some traveller who visited it in Gondophares' reign; and though the ground-plan of Hellenistic Taxila was fairly regular, Philostratus remarks on the narrow and irregular streets of the Parthian town, which are compared to those of Athens.[3] The palace, a plain unadorned building in the middle of the town, probably Saca or Parthian, is frankly an Assyrian palace; it has been compared to Sargon's palace at Khorsabad.[4]

The one definitely Greek public building which has been discovered did not belong to the Hellenistic city. It is a little Ionic temple of the Parthian period at Jandial,[5] which in form is a Greek temple; the column drums were ground together in the Greek way, but it was covered with the common shell stucco and built on to it was a square tower; it is thought that this may have been a Tower of Silence and that the temple was built by a Greek architect for the Iranian community. There is a square Parthian tower also at Tel Umar (Seleuceia on the Tigris),[6] the so-called 'Ziggurat of Opis'; what the relation, if any, between the two may be I do not know. Jandial attests the presence, shortly after the Christian Era, of a Greek or semi-Greek architect who still understood Greek methods of work; this naturally suggests the former existence of Greek architecture in Bactria, but it does not follow, and nothing can be known till excavation be possible in that country. But one other

[1] *ASI* 1929–30 p. 57.

[2] *ASI* 1912–13 pp. 8, 30, 34, 37 and part I p. 13; the passages cited are from Philostratus II, 20, 23, 25.

[3] *ASI* 1912–13 p. 8; Philostratus II, 23, *φασὶ δ' ὡς ἀτάκτως τε καὶ 'Αττικῶς τοὺς στενωποὺς τέτμηται*. The narrow winding streets of Athens, never remodelled, were long famous in a world which had adopted Hellenistic town-planning.

[4] Sir J. Marshall, *ASI* 1913–14 part I p. 16; *A Guide to Taxila* pp. 68–70.

[5] *ASI* 1912–13 pp. 35–9; 1913–14 part I pp. 16–17; 1914–15 part I p. 14. Patches of the stucco, *λίθου κογχυλιάτου* of Philostratus, still remained. Some remarks on Jandial in Benjamin Rowland Jr., *AJA* XXXIX, 1935, pp. 493–6; he thinks Ionic capitals disappeared from India with the Greeks, to be replaced by Roman Corinthian. His chronology however is not always correct.

[6] L. Waterman in *Second Preliminary Report upon the Excavations at Tel Umar* pp. 75–8, cf. Preface p. vi.

building at Taxila reinforces my conclusion that *c.* A.D. 50 is the period after which we cease to find anything which can really be called Greek. A little Buddhist building of the late first century A.D. (early Kushan period), inside the Kunāla stupa, shows that its architect had heard of, and had tried to apply, the Greek principle of *entasis*, that is, giving a slightly convex curve to parts of the building instead of a flat line in order to correct certain optical illusions; but he did not really understand the matter, and though he knew that there ought to be curves he has made his own curves concave instead of convex, thus increasing the optical illusion which the curves were intended to correct.[1] In other words, understanding of this principle of Greek architecture was dead; all that remained was the knowledge that there once had been some principle.

In addition, so far as Greeks go, Taxila has supplied a few pieces of Greek sculpture, the best known being the head of a Dionysus and the child with its finger to its lips;[2] various small objects of art and also seals, some with Greek engraving and two or three bearing Greek names written in Kharoshthi (p. 389); and a great number of coins, including new ones of the Parthian and Kushan periods,[3] sometimes of value for chronology because of the stratification of the finds. But the great value of the excavations to the Greek historian lies in their revelation of the fact that the capital which Demetrius built for himself was an Indian city and not a Greek one (p. 179).

Something must now be said about trade. Trade between India and the West did not start in the reign of Augustus;[4] a considerable trade had been going on since the Greek conquest, and though it is only now and then that details can be obtained, the main fact is unquestionable. Certain things have already been noticed; the new outburst of prosperity at Seleuceia, which coincided almost exactly in date with the great period of Greek rule in India from Demetrius' conquest to the death of Menander, is the most notable (p. 261), but almost equally so are the enormous quantities of Indian ivory and spices exhibited by

[1] Sir J. Marshall, *ASI* 1914–15 part I pp. 13 *sq.*

[2] *ASI* 1912–13, Pl. XX; *CHI* Pls. XXXI, XXXII. Often figured.

[3] Published year by year in *ASI*; many are noticed throughout this book. On one group see *CHI* pp. 580–1.

[4] For the trade between the Roman Empire and India, which is a separate matter, see Warmington (the fullest account); also M. P. Charlesworth, *Trade routes and commerce of the Roman Empire* Chaps. IV, VI.

Antiochus IV in his triumph at Daphne in 166.[1] Parthia grew wealthy on the land trade which poured through her, and towards the end of the second century B.C. Chang-k'ien, or rather perhaps Ssu-ma Ch'ien (p. 281), referred to the long distances both by land and water which the merchants of that empire (*i.e.* Parthian subjects, whatever their nationality) were accustomed to travel.[2] Even towards the end of Seleucid rule in Syria, when politically the kings appear to us to have been little but leaders of mercenaries and northern Syria to have been in a state not far removed from anarchy, trade between Syria and the East still went on, as is attested by the number of late Seleucid coins found in the hoards from Mandali,[3] east of the Tigris, and from Teheran;[4] but the commercial revival already noticed under the last Greek rulers Hippostratus and Hermaeus was connected with the establishment by Rome in 64 B.C. of settled rule in Syria, for Crassus' invasion of Parthia in 53 was too local and transitory to disturb the main trade route from Seleuceia to Syria for more than a year or two.

These facts suggest that what was important to the Greeks of Bactria and India was trade with the Seleucid empire through Seleuceia, for there do not appear to be any corresponding facts with regard to Egypt. This trade was essentially a trade *with* Seleuceia, which passed the goods on overland to Syria and the Phoenician ports; the great city which had taken the place of Babylon was clearing-house and middleman by whatever route goods came from the Far East, whether by the main land road which ran Bactra-Hecatompylos-Ecbatana-Seleuceia, or by the southern land route through Seistan to the Gulf of Ormuz (App. 12) and so up the Persian Gulf, or directly by sea from Barygaza and Demetrias-Patala to the Gulf of Ormuz (App. 12). More will be known about the trade between India and Seleuceia if the Greek centre and mart on that Gulf, Harmozia-Omana, the 'harbour of the Macedonians', be ever located and excavated; its merchants were certainly important as middlemen, for Seleucid coins have rarely been found in India, and those apparently only certain pieces of Antiochus I and II.[5]

[1] Polyb. XXX, 25, 12, 800 tusks; *ib.* 26, 1–2, spices, of which the cinnamon and nard anyhow came from India.

[2] Hirth p. 97 § 35.

[3] E. T. Newell, *NC* 1924 p. 141.

[4] M. Dayet, *Aréthuse* 1925 p. 131.

[5] Sir G. Macdonald, *JHS* XXIII, 1903, p. 108; S. K. Chakrabortty, *IHQ* XI, 1935, p. 244, who argues that certain specimens lighter than the Attic standard were struck on an Indian standard for trade purposes; *sed quaere*.

Some of the Hellenistic information in Ptolemy with regard to India and the Farther East generally, which I have attempted to separate from that part of his information which dates from the Roman empire, was ultimately derived from the itineraries of merchants who went thither from the West, and the amount he knew witnesses to the number of his informants, that is, to a very lively trade intercourse. I may add that if an embassy from India came to Augustus as early as 26 B.C.,[1] rulers in India must for some time have been accustomed to follow the course of events in the Mediterranean world.

Of the spread of trade eastward in the Greek period we do not get too many indications. With the nomad conquest of Bactria and the loss of Bactra, whose equipment of markets was duly recorded by Chang-k'ien,[2] the Greeks lost control of the half-way house where met the land routes from India and China and the trade was gathered up, though it is evident from the coinages of Hippostratus and Hermaeus that the Yueh-chi no more interfered with trade with the West than did the Parthians at this time. But the loss of Bactria meant that when in 106 B.C.[3] the Chinese sent their first caravan through from China to Parthia *via* Bactra, the Greeks, now confined to India, had no part in this through trade or anything to do with the import of Chinese silk which grew up along what was to be known as the Silk Route. The most definite things which can be traced to the time when Greeks still held Bactria are the import of nickel from China at the end of the reign of Euthydemus (p. 87), an Alexandrian glass vase with a head of Athena of the second century B.C. found in Honan,[4] and Bactrian and Syrian cloth, perhaps as early as the late second century, found by the Koslov expedition at Urga in Mongolia,[5] which had travelled along the route to Mongolia of which something has already been said (p. 109); whether it was at this time or later that the Greek word diadem reached Mongolian[6] through Sogdian I do not know, nor do I know the date of the famous white bronze mirror of the Han period with Graeco-Bactrian designs.[7] The failure of the people of Ferghana to get into

[1] Warmington p. 36. [2] Hirth p. 98 § 51. [3] Hirth's date, p. 133.

[4] M. Rostovtzeff, *Social and Economic History of the Roman Empire* p. 513.

[5] W. P. Yetts, *Burlington Magazine* 1926 p. 168; M. Rostovtzeff, *Mon. Piot* XXVIII, 1925–6, pp. 171–2 (some Bactrian, some Syrian, end of second or first century B.C.), and *The Animal Style in South Russia and China*, 1929, Pl. XXIV A and p. 85.

[6] B. Laufer, *Sino-Iranica* p. 573.

[7] In the Victoria and Albert Museum. See S. W. Bushell, *Chinese Art* I,[2] 1910, fig. 60.

touch with China and their anxiety to do so, recorded by Chang-k'ien in 128 B.C. (p. 87), may show that the difficulties had been very considerable till China opened up the way; and the things which China received from the Graeco-Iranian world—the pomegranate and other 'Chang-k'ien' plants (p. 311), the heavy equipment of the cataphract,[1] the traces of Greek influence on Han art[2]—are probably all later than 106 B.C., as were her own exports of silk, furs,[3] and the high-class iron which came to Parthia through Merv;[4] and if China got the vine (p. 311) and the great war-horse (p. 309) earlier, it was still not till after the fall of the Greek kingdom of Bactria; the Greeks lost Bactria too soon for the Chinese trade. Doubtless in the first century B.C. the Greeks in India imported for themselves silk and other articles from China, for Chinese jade[5] and a Japanese scallop-shell[6] (the earliest known indication that Japan existed) were found at Taxila, and later we hear of a regular trade route from Bactra to Barygaza;[7] but what the ancient world really found lucrative was transit trade,[8] and it cannot be supposed that silk, instead of going to Seleuceia, would travel all the way to Barygaza to be shipped to the West till direct voyages to Egypt became usual, and by that time the Greeks had lost Barygaza and their Indian ports.

Two slight indications may exist of communication, not of course direct, between the Greeks of India and the Indo-Chinese peninsula. One, already noticed, is the occurrence of Menander's name in Indo-Chinese tradition (p. 267); the other is an object dug up at Taxila (Sirkap), the head and shoulders of a gorilla-like figure.[9] Sir John

[1] Laufer, *Chinese clay figures* 1914 p. 217; M. Rostovtzeff, *Mon. Piot* XXVI, 1923, p. 135; *The Animal Style* p. 107.

[2] Hirth, *Ueber fremde Einflüsse in der chinesischen Kunst* 1896; Rostovtzeff, *Mon. Piot* XXVIII, 1925–6, pp. 171–3 and references, *Inlaid bronzes of the Han dynasty* 1922 pp. 58 *sqq.*, who thinks (*L'art gréco-iranien*, *Rev. des Arts Asiatiques* 1933 p. 218) that it was exercised through that form of Graeco-Indian art which he calls Greco-Sakian, *Seminarium Kondakovianum* 1933 p. 169. *Contra*, O. Fischer, *Die chinesische Malerei der Han-dynastie* 1931 (not seen): Han art purely indigenous.

[3] Pliny XXXIV, 145; *Periplus* 39.

[4] Seric iron was called Margian in 53 B.C. because it reached Parthia through Merv, Orosius VI, 13, 2 combined with Plut. *Crassus* 24. The widespread theory that Seric iron came from the Cheras of southern India (Warmington pp. 157 *sq.*) cannot stand against this fact. Pliny XXXIX, 15 says that Seric iron was better than that produced in Parthia.

[5] *ASI* 1919–20 part I p. 19.

[6] *Ib.* 1926–7 p. 118 no. 14.

[7] *Periplus* 48, 64.

[8] Tarn, *Hell. Civ.*[2] p. 220.

[9] *ASI* 1929–30 p. 91 no. 111.

Marshall has pointed out that it is hollow like many Hellenistic statuettes, and that the modelling is much superior to that of objects from the Saca-Parthian and Kushan strata; and as it came from one of the Hellenistic strata it is probably Greek work. No Greek in India can have known the gorilla, but the figure certainly suggests that the artist had seen, or had had a description of, an orang; and if a polar bear reached Alexandria,[1] an orang may well have come to Taxila. In addition, the Greek word for mustard, *σίναπι*, is supposed to have come from Farther India,[2] but that has nothing to do with the period under consideration, for the word was known at Athens in the fifth century B.C.;[3] though how it got there is a mystery, as it is said not to occur in Persian.

What India, whether Greek or Indian, did try to do was to get into touch with China through Khotan, independently of Bactria. We have seen that the Greeks were trying to do this in the reign of Hermaeus (p. 338); in the latter half of the first century B.C. Indian-speaking traders had got as far as the Chinese *limes*,[4] and in the first three centuries of the Christian era there appear to have been settlements of Indian or Indian-speaking traders in Chinese Turkestan, more especially in the Khotan district,[5] with a view to the Chinese trade; but the communications of that country with India, whether with Gandhāra or Kashmir, were across difficult passes, and it is not known how much it really means. The Greek words found in documents of this period from the Khotan country have already been considered (pp. 85 *sq.*); but to these settlements must belong the clay sealings found at Niya and other places near Khotan[6] which occasionally show Greek or Graeco-Roman types, sometimes on the same documents as Chinese sealings; a number of clay sealings of the sort, once also attached to documents, have been found in India at Besnagar.[7] Sir Aurel Stein said comprehensively in 1907 that all these classical seals from the Khotan country were Roman work,[8] of the third or at earliest the second century A.D., and certainly most of them came from the Roman empire; some

[1] Athen. v, 201 c, *ἄρκτος λευκὴ μεγάλη μία*.
[2] J. Przyluski and C. Régamy, *BSOS* VIII, 1936, p. 703.
[3] Aristoph. *Eq.* 631, in the form *νᾶπυ*; see Athen. IX, 367 a.
[4] Sir A. Stein, *Asia Major* (Hirth Anniv. volume) 1923 pp. 367, 372.
[5] De la Vallée-Poussin pp. 321–2 and references.
[6] Published by Sir A. Stein in *Ancient Khotan* 1907, and *Serindia* 1921.
[7] *ASI* 1914–15 part I p. 20; see D. R. Bhandarkar, *ib.* 1914–15 p. 77.
[8] *Ancient Khotan* p. 357.

correspond to types on Roman Imperial coins, as the supposed Eros to the *Genius populi Romani* on coins of Diocletian,[1] or Ganymede feeding the eagle of Zeus to a similar type on coins of Marcus Aurelius and Commodus.[2] But it is also possible that this or that one might have come from Seleuceia, or those with a Kharoshthi legend, like the Athena Promachos,[3] from India, or some might even be copies made locally; dating by seals is rather delusive work, for a signet ring might pass from father to son for generations. It is certain however that the Turkestan seals are essentially later than the period treated in this book, and I have only mentioned them to bring out that point, since they are rather famous.

With trade between India and the West[4] in the period of Greek rule we reach firmer ground. Earlier times need not detain us here. The export from India of ebony and other woods,[5] of peacocks, and doubtless of some spices, was very old, and in the third century under the Mauryas there must have been a regular export trade to the Greek West, though it cannot be said how large it was: Indian ivory continued to reach the Aegean till Ptolemy II threw enough African ivory on the market to break the price and secure the trade for himself;[6] Indian spices came to Egypt; Ptolemy II exhibited Indian dogs and cattle in his triumph.[7] So long as Egypt held the Phoenician ports the overland commerce from the East through Seleuceia partly enured for her benefit; to this period may belong the epitaph, once seen at Harūnabad near Kermanshah in Media, of a Greek merchant from Samaria in the Fayûm who was working the land-route.[8] But what needs considering here is the increase of trade after Northern India passed under Greek rule, and

[1] L. C. Woolley in *Serindia* I p. 216; figured Pls. XX, XXVII (N. XIII. ii. 10).

[2] Woolley in *Serindia* III pp. 1250, 1260; Pl. V (F. VII. 002).

[3] *Serindia* I p. 258, Pl. XX; frontispiece to *Ancient Khotan*. Several impressions of her were first given by Stein in *Sandburied ruins of Khotan* 1903. She is Greek enough.

[4] Most of the literature on the Indian trade in the Hellenistic period relates to Egypt. See M. Chwostow, *History of the eastern trade of Graeco-Roman Egypt* 1907 (in Russian; results in M. Rostovtzeff, *Arch. f. Pap.* IV, 1908, p. 298); H. Kortenbeutel, *Der ägyptische Sud- und Osthandel in der Politik der Ptolemäer und römischen Kaiser* 1931; Rostovtzeff, *Foreign Commerce of Ptolemaic Egypt*, *Journ. of Econ. and Business Hist.* IV, 1932, p. 728 (largely the Arabian part); E. Leider, *Der Handel von Alexandreia* 1933 pp. 57 *sqq*.

[5] Warmington p. 213.

[6] Tarn, *Hell. Civ.*[2] p. 226 (references).

[7] Callixenus in Athen. v, 201 b, c.

[8] Fr. Sarre and E. Herzfeld, *Iranische Felsreliefs* 1910 p. 226, reproduced from an old copy, which, though very imperfect, shows the earlier form of sigma, Σ.

especially certain things which happened round about 100 B.C.; the caravan which came through from China in 106 B.C. was not the only phenomenon of importance at the turn of the century. One must first get clear about the sea-route.

Indian vessels were coasting along Gedrosia to Arabia and the Persian Gulf before the time of Alexander, for Nearchus got a guide in Gedrosia who knew the coast as far as the Gulf of Ormuz;[1] but from those points Arab peoples had a monopoly.[2] The chief Indian export for some time must have been spices, which Arabs distributed to the western world along with their own spices; the Arabs of Gerrha on the Persian Gulf supplied Seleuceia, so far as the trade did not come overland, and after the Ptolemies lost their Phoenician ports at the end of the third century they were thrown back for spices exclusively upon their Arab middlemen—Sabaeans, Minaeans, Lihyanites; Alexandria knew so little about the trade that even in the second century B.C. she believed that cinnamon came from Arabia or Somaliland. Egyptian records testify to the importance of the spice trade at this time, and when the Greek Eudoxus of Cyzicus made the first (Greek) through-voyage from Egypt to India *c.* 120 B.C. (p. 370) it was with spices and precious stones that he loaded his ship for the return journey;[3] and Demetrius may for a time have held the spice-land of eastern Gedrosia (p. 94). But the wealth of Antiochus IV in Indian products shows not only that the Seleucids, after they acquired all Phoenicia, probably began to gain on the Ptolemies, but that there was now a large increase in the ivory trade: the 800 elephant tusks from India which that monarch exhibited in his triumph at Daphne were presumably meant to overtrump, in the eyes of the world, the 600 African tusks which had been carried in the triumph of Ptolemy II.[4] The position in Menander's reign has already been described (pp. 260 *sq.*): ships from the Greek ports in India were following Nearchus' route along the Gedrosian coast to the Greek centre on the Gulf of Ormuz (App. 12), whence the goods went by water to Seleuceia; what is not known is when the Greek centre on that gulf began to compete with Gerrha as intermediary between India and Seleuceia,[5]

[1] Arr. *Ind.* 27, 1.

[2] For what follows see generally Tarn, *Hell. Civ.*² pp. 213 *sqq.* and references.

[3] Poseidonius in Strabo II, 98, ἀρώματα καὶ λίθους πολυτελεῖς.

[4] Callixenus in Athen. V, 201 a.

[5] There may already in Persian times have been a centre on this gulf intermediate between India and Babylonia, for Nearchus changed guides there, his second guide being a Persian, Arr. *Ind.* 37, 2.

and how Gerrha, which was badly placed, stood the competition. This route, in which ships from Barygaza hugged the coast the whole way, calling at Demetrias-Patala, is the first of the four stages described by Pliny. It is now necessary to date those stages, for the second and third have usually, in defiance of Pliny's own language, been put far too late; and as I shall need these stages to explain the Yavana merchants of the cave inscriptions, I must not at this point use those inscriptions.

Pliny's four stages[1] are stages of the voyage from Egypt to India, the gradual utilisation of the south-west monsoon; no information remains as to the use of the north-east monsoon for the voyage westward, but I shall assume that when ships began to cross open sea on the way to India they soon learnt to cross it on the way back also. As Nearchus was told of, and waited for, the north-east monsoon,[2] Indians had known of it long before Greeks, though they had only used it for coasting voyages;[3] had they learnt to cross the open sea, Greeks in the second century must have copied them. Pliny's four stages are (1) coasting all the way;[4] (2) cutting across a bit of open sea from a point in Arabia which he calls Syagros to Demetrias-Patala;[5] (3) cutting out Demetrias (this is the important matter) by sailing direct from the Arabian coast (and *a fortiori* from the Persian Gulf) to a port he calls Sigerus, somewhere south of Barygaza (and naturally therefore to Barygaza also);[6] (4) cutting out Arabia altogether and sailing direct from the Somali coast to Muziris and other ports in the extreme south of India.[7] He gives certain time-indications. The fourth stage was in use when he

[1] Clearly done in Warmington, pp. 45–6 and map; but in dating stages 2 and 3 he has not considered what Pliny says. See also (more briefly) E. Kornemann, *Janus* I (*Festschrift für C. F. Lehmann-Haupt*), 1921, p. 56, who puts the third stage in Augustus' reign. The possible bearing of the cave inscriptions on the matter has not been considered.

[2] He left Patala when the 'Etesian winds', the S.W. monsoon, stopped, late September or early October, Arr. *Ind.* 21, 1. He waited a month in 'Alexander's harbour' till he got the N.E. monsoon, November; Arr. *Anab.* VI, 21, 3, *παρέμενε τὴν ὥραν τοῦ παράπλου*, shows that he knew it was coming.

[3] Evidence for Indian voyages, W. H. Schoff, *Periplus* pp. 228 *sq.*; but the use of a 'shore-sighting bird' does not prove ocean voyages. I am speaking only of Greeks and Indians at one particular period; Polynesians and Malays have crossed great expanses of ocean in their canoes both before and since.

[4] Pliny VI, 96–100, ending sic Alexandri classis navigavit.

[5] *Ib.* 100, postea...aestimatione.

[6] *Ib.* 101, secuta aetas...diuque ita navigatum est.

[7] *Ib.* 101, donec compendia invenit mercator...106.

wrote but had not been in use very long;[1] doubtless the usual date for its commencement, A.D. 40–50, is approximately correct. The second stage was very short, for he says that the next generation, *secuta aetas*, passed to the third; the second then did not last more than thirty years. By contrast, he says that the third stage, after the *secuta aetas* adopted it, lasted a long time, *diu*, and 'a long time', as specifically contrasted with a generation, cannot mean less than a century and might mean more; from the way he puts it, he is clearly describing what, to himself, had seemed to be the permanent way of the world till quite recently. Taking then a century for the third stage, which would make it begin *c.* 60–50 B.C., and thirty years for the second stage, we get from Pliny a date of *c.* 90–80 B.C. for the first use of the south-west monsoon (otherwise than for coasting). But we happen to know from other sources that *something* important connected with the Indian Ocean had happened before 78 B.C. and after *c.* 111 B.C., say *c.* 100–80 B.C., and this cannot well be anything but the first use of the south-west monsoon.[2] The two lines of evidence then agree as well as may be; that means that the third stage cannot have begun later than *c.* 50 B.C. and may have begun *c.* 70 or even a little earlier. It does not seem possible to put the beginning of the second and third stages in the Roman Imperial period.

I have carefully avoided mentioning the much discussed and variously dated Hippalos, the traditional 'discoverer' of the south-west monsoon, for it matters nothing to me which stage he inaugurated or even whether he was not a man at all but either a sailors' name like Davy Jones or a personification of the monsoon,[3] as Greeks had personified other winds as Boreas or Zephyrus. And I have also not mentioned

[1] Pliny VI, 101, nunc primum certa notitia patescente.

[2] Some have put the whole thing much later, *e.g.* Warmington, and M. P. Charlesworth, *Class. Quarterly* XXII, 1928, p. 92. But the inscription given in Preisigke, *Sammelbuch* 2264 = Schubart, *Klio* X p. 54 n. 2, dated 78 B.C., and followed by *OGIS* 186 (62 B.C.) and 190 (51 B.C.), which all make the *epistrategos* of the Thebaïd *epistrategos* of the Indian Sea as well as of the Red Sea, shows that some important new thing relating to the Indian Ocean had happened prior to 78 B.C., and W. Otto, *Hippalos* 3 in PW, was clearly right in making this the first use of the monsoon, which he therefore put *c.* 100 B.C.; see also E. Kornemann, *Janus* I p. 55, and R. Hennig, *Terrae Incognitae* 1936 p. 228. Then H. Kortenbeutel took the matter further (*op. cit.* p. 48) by giving 111 B.C. as the *terminus ante quem non* on the strength of *P. Lond.* II, 13 (*i.e.* Sir F. G. Kenyon, *Greek papyri in the British Museum* 1898), which is substantially right (see his discussion); Kenyon's actual words were 'safely dated about the years 116–111'. Leider *op. cit.* p. 58 follows Kortenbeutel.

[3] Hippalos is the monsoon in Pliny VI, 100, 104.

'direct' voyages, because the first man who went right through from India to Egypt or *vice versa* could have done it as well coasting as in any other way. One Indian[1] and perhaps a second,[2] who cannot be dated, appeared in Egypt in the Ptolemaic period, but the first man actually recorded to have gone all the way by sea was the Indian captain who in the reign of Ptolemy Euergetes II was picked up half-dead in the Red Sea, having lost his crew (? killed by Arabs);[3] and the first Greek recorded as having gone all the way was Eudoxus of Cyzicus, who sailed under that Indian's guidance to Demetrias or Barygaza.[4] Eudoxus got back to Egypt before Euergetes' death in 116, but his subsequent activity was under that king's successors; his voyage therefore was *c.* 120, and he presumably coasted. After him a few ships in the late Ptolemaic period went right through from Egypt to India,[5] but the extreme rarity of Ptolemaic coins in India shows that to the end the Ptolemies really relied on their Arab middlemen.

Having now dated Pliny's third stage I can turn to the pepper trade,[6] for the export of pepper from India on any scale certainly began in the period of Greek rule. It has been thought that Indian pepper in small quantities—packets passed from one people to another—may have found its way to Greece and been used as a medical drug as early as the fifth century B.C., but I am not clear about this. Certainly in the fourth century there was something called pepper to be bought in Athens;[7] but the 'pepper' with which the epicures of the fourth and third centuries stuffed their sucking pigs is specifically called 'Libyan',[8] which means that it came from Carthage, and as Indian pepper would hardly

[1] Buddhist gravestone at Alexandria discovered by Sir F. Petrie, see *JRAS* 1898 p. 875.

[2] It may have been an Indian who gave thanks for a safe journey in Pan's temple at Edfu (inscription in note to *OGIS* 72, see U. Wilcken, *Arch. f. Pap.* III p. 320, *Grundzüge* I p. 264); but the words Σόφων Ἰνδός are only Wilcken's emendation of a meaningless word. It may be right; but no other Indian seems known who took a Greek name.

[3] Strabo II, 98 (Poseidonius).

[4] Poseidonius' story of Eudoxus is *F. Gr. Hist.* no. 87, fr. 28=Strabo II, 98–102. One need not doubt the voyage, even if Poseidonius does display ignorance of the Ptolemaic regulations concerning imported spices.

[5] A disputed matter; but Strabo II, 118 and 101 are explicit, and XVI, 798 is not against it. See U. Wilcken, *Zeits. f. ägypt. Sprache* 1925 p. 88.

[6] For the pepper trade in Roman times see Warmington *passim* and Schoff, *Periplus* pp. 213–16.

[7] Athen. II, 66 d, e.

[8] Ophelion in Athen. *ib.* d.

have gone from Phoenicia to Carthage and thence back to Athens, it was undoubtedly the so-called African pepper; it can only have come in very limited quantities, as it is only known as a luxury for gourmets. Alexander's expedition found out nothing about Indian pepper, for Theophrastus, who regularly reflects the botanical results of that expedition, only knew pepper as a medical drug and only included it among some medical odds and ends in the very last chapter of his History of Plants;[1] he knew nothing about its growth or its country. Certainly Indian pepper did not come to Egypt on any scale in the third and second centuries B.C., or there must have been some hint of it by now in the papyri; and there was no longer a Carthage to send it after 146 B.C. Then comes a casual notice in Plutarch,[2] which shows that in the year 88 B.C. Aristion, at the moment tyrant in Athens, had so much pepper in his house that he could use *two quarts* of it for an extremely base practical joke. That fixes the beginning of the substantial export of Indian pepper not later than *c.* 100 B.C., and it might be a good deal earlier, for though Eudoxus brought back no pepper on his voyage of *c.* 120, that does not actually prove that export had not yet started; still, somewhere between 120 and 88 B.C. is the most likely date. The probable beginning of the pepper trade then is not far from the probable beginning of the use of the monsoons, but I think this is only coincidence, for pepper seemingly did not as yet go to Egypt; it went to Seleuceia and overland to Syria, and the Romans first made its acquaintance after they had annexed Northern Syria in 64 B.C., and for a time thought it came from Syria or Arabia.[3]

Here at last the Yavanas of the cave inscriptions, whom we have already met (pp. 254 *sqq.*), can be brought in—wealthy Indian merchants[4] who were Greek citizens and who appear in the country behind Bombay. One, Indragnidatta the Yonaka, is known to have been a citizen of Demetrias-Patala, and all must have been citizens either of Demetrias or of Theophila (whatever its Indian name was), as no other Greek *poleis* in the south are known. The chaitya halls at Nasik and

[1] Odds and ends, *Hist. of Plants* IX, 19, 4; medical drug *ib.* IX, 20, 1 and περὶ πνιγμοῦ fr. 166, both cited in Athen. II, 66 e, f.

[2] *Sulla* 13.

[3] Vitruvius VIII, 3, 13.

[4] O. Stein, *Indian Culture* I, 1935, p. 343, has pointed out that some of these Yavanas belonged to corporations. Probably this means trading companies; the 'companions' of some of the Kharoshthi inscriptions (*CII* nos. XII, XIV, XVIII, XXV, XXVIII) might be the same thing. Cf. the guilds of the Taxila coinage, p. 161 n. 1.

Karli are first-century B.C., when Demetrias and Surastrene were under Saca rule, and on archaeological grounds are said more probably to belong to the later than to the earlier half of the century;[1] while Indragnidatta's own inscription,[2] on internal evidence, can be dated to about 50–30 B.C. Indragnidatta had come to Demetrias from the north; and there can be little doubt that these merchants' inscriptions belong to the period of the cessation of hostilities between Greeks and Sacas already described (pp. 343 *sq.*), that is, roughly between *c.* 50 and *c.* 30 B.C., the time which saw a revival of Greek trade in the north under Hermaeus and Hippostratus (see generally Chap. VIII). The main route from southern India northward came to Ujjain, where it met the road from Barygaza going eastward; it then continued northward from Ujjain by the way Apollodotus had once taken, passing through his foundation Theophila and so to Demetrias. This was the road taken by the produce of southern India going northward; and the most important product of the South was pepper, of which one district in Malabar had something approaching a monopoly.[3] When therefore a genuine export trade started, pepper had to make a laborious land journey northward to Demetrias; and even if it went to the sea at Barygaza (not of course through Ujjain, but by some road branching off from the southward) all ships going westward had to call at Demetrias, as Pliny shows; that city was the first centre of export.

Then came Pliny's third stage, with direct voyages from Sigerus south of Barygaza (and *a fortiori* from Barygaza also) to the coast of Arabia or the Persian Gulf, cutting out Demetrias altogether—that is the point I have already emphasised; and pepper shortened its journey to the Persian Gulf and Seleuceia by going direct across the sea from one of those two ports. Nobody knows where Sigerus was,[4] but it must have been somewhere in the neighbourhood of Bombay; the five Yavanas of the Karli cave, and some of the Indians, came from an unknown seaport Dhenukākā (p. 258) which may be the equally unknown Sigerus. Now Pliny's third stage, as we have seen, began *c.* 70–50 B.C., and it obviously has some connection with the appearance of these Yavana merchants in the south not long after 50 B.C. What

[1] Sir J. Marshall, *CHI* p. 637.

[2] Nasik 19; on the date see p. 257 n. 3.

[3] *Periplus* 56.

[4] Warmington, p. 45 and map, makes it Jaigarh, which is about the location required.

happened seems now tolerably clear. The cutting out of Demetrias threatened the pepper merchants there with ruin; Indragnidatta and his friends left the city, went south to the country behind Bombay, and got on to the new pepper route to the sea; their donations show that they prospered greatly, as their enterprise deserved. Ultimately it was pepper, the 'passion of the Yavanas' as a much-quoted Tamil poem calls it,[1] which brought about Pliny's fourth stage, when ships went direct to the pepper country of Malabar; but I need not describe the enormous dimensions which this trade was to reach, except to notice that the insatiable desire of the Roman world for pepper in the first century A.D. had a later parallel in the desire for pepper which arose in western Europe after Vasco da Gama had opened the sea-route round the Cape and had for the second time in history made Malabar easily accessible to the West.

One would expect to find in the Greek period a brisk trade in the export of parchment to India, for since in the early second century Eumenes II of Pergamum had started its manufacture on a great scale in his slave factories it had become the common writing material of Asia west of India, and at the end of that century Chang-k'ien or his lieutenants had noted its regular use throughout the Parthian empire (p. 281); it may have been the knowledge they brought back to China that there were better things to write upon than silk and split bamboo which ultimately led in A.D. 105 to Ts'ai Lun's great invention—paper. But the only actual indication of parchment which I have found in India is the Greek letter written on that material to Augustus from Barygaza (p. 321), and that is not enough to argue from. The Greeks in India must however have had *some* writing material—their words for pen, ink, and book passed into Sanscrit (p. 376)—and it is not likely to have been anything else.

But one other trade must, I fear, be carried back to Greek times, one that thrusts roughly on our notice the shadow-side of all ancient civilisations, that slave basis of which the historian must never lose sight. Among a dry list of articles for which there was a ready market at Barygaza the Periplus lists certain things which the king would buy, and one of them is 'good-looking virgins for concubines';[2] and the

[1] Yavanapriya. A list of the commodities beginning with Yavana, all of the Roman Imperial period, was given by Lévi, *Quid de Graecis* 1890 p. 25 and by A. Weber, *Berlin SB* 1890 p. 912; often repeated since.

[2] *Periplus* 49, παρθένοι εὐειδεῖς πρὸς παλλακίαν.

way it is put indicates a well-known thing, a 'standing order' in that market. In some plays of Kālidāsa (fifth century A.D.) the king is represented as accompanied by a body of women called Yavanas;[1] these Yavana women had already appeared in the plays of Bhāsa in the first century A.D.,[2] and a name and tradition that could last so many centuries must have been old and well established, which takes time. It would seem, too, that the tradition was true. In Kālidāsa's play Mālavikāgnimitra, Agnimitra has a brush on the Sindhu river with some Yavana cavalry, a story which is certainly a genuine tradition (p. 228), as usually supposed; and if Kālidāsa's use of the word Yavana goes back in one case to the second century B.C., doubtless it goes back to the Greek period in the other case also. It might perhaps be argued that these Yavana women merely meant 'westerners', seeing that there seems to be evidence in Ptolemaic times for an export of girls from Syria;[3] but in view of the meaning of Yavana in the Mālavikāgnimitra this would be difficult to support. Certainly these Yavana women only make it *probable* that an export of Greek girls to India was going on under Greek rule; but there is confirmation from the Greek side, for Poseidonius says that Eudoxus shipped some girls—singing girls or 'flute-girls'—for his attempted voyage to India round the Cape[4] (end of the second century B.C.), and Poseidonius' testimony to this traffic is valid even should we regard his story of the Gades ship which doubled the Cape and inspired Eudoxus' attempt as not proven. Earlier back than the period of Greek rule in India this particular traffic can hardly go, for Megasthenes says that Chandragupta's girls were Indians, bought from their fathers.[5] Certainly in the third century Ptolemy II was importing Indian girls into Egypt along with Indian dogs and cattle,[6] and it has been thought that the high tax in Egypt in the first century A.D. on girls for prostitution imported from the East by the sea-route might

[1] Weber, *op. cit.* p. 910, already connected this with the *Periplus*; often repeated.

[2] A. B. Keith, *The Sanscrit Drama* 1924 p. 61 n. 2.

[3] A. Andréadès, *Des droits de douane prélevés par les Lagides sur le commerce extérieur* 1934 (from *Mélanges Glotz*, vol. 1), p. 28 n. 4.

[4] Strabo II, 99, μουσικὰ παιδισκάρια. 'Flute-girl' was a euphemism, as 'actress' once was in English.

[5] Strabo XV, 710. The girl in the second mime of Herondas (third century) is a Greek, but there is nothing to show that she was meant for export.

[6] Callixenus in Athen. V, 201 a. His parrots were not necessarily Indian, as has been supposed.

go back to, and witness to, their import in Ptolemaic times;[1] but we may believe that the better-class Greek would feel some difference between importing 'barbarian' girls and exporting girls of his own race to 'barbarians'. If however this export of Greek girls to India be a fact, it is difficult to disconnect its origin from the vast increase in slave-trading, with Delos as its centre, which took place in the Mediterranean in the late second and early first centuries B.C. after Rome had broken the Hellenistic Powers, and if this be so, the mixture of nationalities among the merchants of Delos would show that the traffic was largely in the hands of foreigners, who were not likely to be particular about the nationality of their wares.

We can now leave trade and turn to the relations between Greeks and Indians. Two peoples can hardly live side by side in the same country for a long period without a certain amount of mutual borrowing; but speaking generally, we know far less than we could wish of the interaction between the civilisation of the Greeks and the civilisations which they met with in Asia and Egypt. A number of people in Asia Minor, in Syria, in Judaea (till the movement was quenched in blood)—that is, in the lands whose natural outlet was to the Mediterranean—borrowed a good deal from Greek civilisation and became, as we say, hellenised, or partially so; but if we except the religious sphere—the effect upon Greeks of the religions of Asia and Egypt and the invasion of the Mediterranean world by those religions—it seems that the only people who really affected Greeks in turn were the Babylonians (Chap. II). The interaction between the civilisations of Greece and India, which is what concerns us here, produced certain interesting effects for a time, but (leaving the Buddha-statue out of the question for a moment) they were not lasting, and what we see is rather one-sided: we see what little Indians took from Greeks because we have the Indian literature, but it is not so easy to see what Greeks took from Indians, because the Greek literature is lost. Indian civilisation was strong enough to hold its own against Greek civilisation, but, except in the religious sphere, was seemingly not strong enough to influence it as Babylonia did; nevertheless we may find reason for thinking that in certain respects India

[1] The tariff of Koptos of A.D. 90, *OGIS* 674 (γυναικῶν πρὸς ἑταιρισμόν); L. Fiesel, *Gött. Nachr.* 1925 pp. 96 *sqq.*; cf. Andréadès *op. cit.* p. 17 n. 1. Fiesel, p. 101, asks if the import tax, more than five times that on a soldier's 'wife', was meant to be prohibitive; it might only mean that the traffic was extremely lucrative and could stand a high tax.

was the dominant partner. It must be emphasised that Greeks were not in India for the purpose of hellenising Indians, and there is no sign that they ever attempted to do so; they had come to India for a definite purpose, which had failed, and they stayed there to rule what they could because there was nothing else they could do. An Indian who was a citizen in a Greek *polis* was bound to some small extent to hellenise himself; he would have to learn enough Greek for purposes of daily life and understand something of Greek civic forms, but hellenisation in the proper sense—the adoption of Greek culture as one's own culture—is not likely often to have happened. A few of the educated, we shall see, read a little Greek literature and were slightly affected by it, but it did not go very far: we get no trace of the 'culture-Greek' of the West, or even of Indians taking Greek names, as was common enough among some Asiatic peoples; the Indian Yavanas of the cave-inscriptions, who were Greek citizens, kept their Indian names and culture, though one had been slightly affected by Greek custom.[1] The two peoples merely lived side by side on good terms; had the terms not been good, Greek rule could never have lasted as it did and there could not have been any Gandhāra school of art. Two Greek kings, Demetrius and Apollodotus, were taken up into the great Indian epic, the Mahābhārata (p. 165), which was still receiving additions; and except in the extreme East (p. 324) Greek rule everywhere was overthrown, not by any action by Indians, but by a new and more numerous body of foreign invaders. We must look more closely at the borrowings for their own sake; but, except for the Buddha-statue, the history of India would in all essentials have been precisely what it has been had Greeks never existed.

Literature must have first place. A few common Greek words found their way into Sanscrit, terms for pen and ink and book (which tell their own story), a horse's bit, a mine used to sap a fortress wall,[2] and a camel;[3] the mine, *syrinx*, may show that Indians had something to learn from Greeks in the matter of besieging 'fenced cities'. That Sanscrit should have borrowed the name camel is interesting, for India

[1] Nasik 19: Indragnidatta, a Buddhist, in his dedication uses the Greek 'father and mother' instead of the regular Buddhist 'mother and father' (p. 358 n. 1).

[2] Weber *op. cit.* pp. 911–14: melā (μέλαν), kalamo (κάλαμος), pustaka (πύξινον), khalina (χαλινός), surungā (σύριγγα); now commonplaces. On kampana (campus, κάμπον) see B. Liebich, *BSOS* VI, 1931, p. 431; O. Stein, *ib.* VII, 1933, p. 61; not before A.D. 100 anyhow. For syrinx cf. p. 15, *ante*.

[3] Kramēla or kramēlaka, Liebich *loc. cit.*; said to be fairly widespread.

already possessed both the camel and a name for it, *ustra*; a new name, in these circumstances, *ought* to indicate a different animal. The camel[1] of India, as of China, was the two-humped camel of Central Asia, the so-called 'Bactrian' camel, which at this time was *not* the camel of Bactria; the Bactrian Greeks had used the camel of Iran, the one-humped Arabian camel which by Alexander's day had already been domiciled about the Persian desert; whether it was Persians or Greeks who brought it to Bactria is not known, but it was the one-humped camel which the Yueh-chi found and used in Bactria.[2] One would have expected, from the Sanscrit word, that the Greeks had brought their one-humped camels to India with them,[3] but of this there is no sign; all the camels on coins in India from Menander to the Kushans are the two-humped species,[4] and this particular borrowing remains a mystery. On the other side, the Greeks must have used some common Indian words, as the English in India do to-day, but the only ones which reached the West were terms for 'camp', 'army', and 'general', preserved by a Greek lexicographer;[5] they illustrate the native armies of the Greek kings.

Apart from Alexandria and the old Greek cities, Greeks of the Hellenistic period settled in Asia or Africa did not as a rule produce literature unless they were reacting against some definite threat to their Greekhood, like foreign rule. In Egypt they only wrote letters and epitaphs; for a long time their Greekhood was not threatened and they left literature to Alexandria, which was not Egypt. The western part of the Seleucid empire was much the same, until the late flowering of poetry in Syria when Seleucid rule was dying and Greekhood seemed likely to go down before the Arab and the Jew. But when the Parthians took over the Seleucid empire east of the Euphrates there was an outburst of literature in the Greek cities of Parthia (Chap. II); it was their

[1] On the distribution of the two species at this time cf. Tarn, *Military Developments* App. III.

[2] Wylie p. 40; de Groot p. 95.

[3] Cf. Liebich *loc. cit.*

[4] Menander, *BMC* p. 169 no. 4, Pl. XXXI. Round bronze coins, uncertain (p. 323 n. 1), *ib.* p. 112. Azes, *ib.* Pl. XIX, 9; *NC* 1890 p. 145 no. 2; *Lahore Cat.* p. 129 nos. 305–7; *ASI* 1914–15 p. 30 no. 20. Kujula Kadphises, *ASI* 1912–13 p. 52 no. 51, 1914–15 p. 34 no. 40, 1928–9 p. 66 no. 19; Cunningham, *NC* 1892 p. 66 nos. 1–5. Naturally also on some Indo-Chinese coins from Khotan, *JASB* 1899 vol. LXVIII part I, extra no. 1 p. 16. A two-humped camel on an early ring-stone from Mathurā in the Indian Museum, Calcutta: *ASI* 1930–4 p. 261.

[5] Hesychius: *βαιστήνης· παρ' Ἰνδοῖς τὸ στρατόπεδον. βαίστηνος· ὁ στρατός.* Cf. O. Stein *op. cit.*, and add *μαμάτραι· οἱ στρατηγοὶ παρ' Ἰνδοῖς.*

response to the challenge of the foreign conquest, the assertion of their continuing Greekhood in the now dominant world of Iran. And in the same way, though almost all the evidence is lost, we can still get traces of the literature written by the Greeks in India, the assertion of their Greekhood against the heavy pressure of the civilisation of India. We have traced at least two Greek poems, one a lyric and one in hexameters or elegiacs, written in Menander's empire (pp. 246–9); and a Greek original of part of the framework of the first part of the Milindapañha, which reached Alexandria, is about as certain as any work can be which is not actually mentioned anywhere (see Excursus). And the Indian author of Part I of the Milindapañha gives us our best idea of the attitude of a well-educated Indian to Greek literature. He knew the current Hellenistic Greek of the East and had evidently read a little current literature; the idea that he may have had some knowledge of Plato, though quite in the air, is not impossible, for Egypt has shown that Plato was a favourite enough author with Greeks abroad. But the man himself, his thoughts and beliefs, were not touched in the least; had no Greek ever existed, his treatise on Buddhist doctrine would still have been written without a thought or a word being altered, save for the omission of the Greek allusions. But it would not have been written in quite the same form or in quite the same setting. And this, we shall find, is what any borrowing from the Greeks of our period seems to mean in almost everything (unless possibly medicine); it is a matter of external *form*, but very rarely of substance.

I have said 'very rarely', for there may have been one Indian writer who borrowed more than form. The bit of chronicle in the Yuga-purāna which narrates the Yavana conquest (App. 4) is unlike anything Indian, for no Indian wrote or understood history; their minds did not work that way, and they left the historical sense and the independent discovery of historical writing to be among the great possessions of China. I have no doubt that Dr Jayaswal was right[1] in seeing behind these sections of the Yuga-purāna a chronicle written soon after the events described, written by an Indian, and written in Prakrit, for the Sanscrit still has the form Dharmamita for Demetrius instead of Dharmamitra.[2] If this be so, the original Indian author wrote under the influence of Greek historical writing, whether it was the mere knowledge that there was such a thing or whether there was once

[1] *JBORS* XIV, 1928, p. 398; see App. 4.
[2] For an occurrence of the form Dharmamitra in Sanscrit see p. 118.

a Greek account of the conquest, perhaps used later by Apollodorus also.

There is a bare possibility that another Indian writer may have been influenced, not by any particular Greek writing, but by the knowledge that there existed a certain Greek literary type, and that is the author of Part II of the Milindapañha, who drew a picture of an ideal Buddhist city, the city of all wise and faithful men.[1] It has been called the only Utopia known in Indian literature,[2] and it has been suggested that the author may have read Plato.[3] There is no need to go to Plato, for the fourth and third centuries abounded in Greek Utopias, but the Indian Ideal City is not in the least like any Greek Utopia which has survived; it is more like the New Jerusalem, and its bazaars sell Buddhist virtues. The most that could be suggested is that the author had heard that Greeks wrote Utopias, and even that is somewhat discounted by his citing a lost Indian work as his model.[4] And in fact there is said to be another description in Buddhist literature which has also been compared to the New Jerusalem of Revelation and which cannot be far in time from Part II of the Milindapañha: that is the paradise of Amitābha, the Buddha of measureless light, one of the antecedent Buddhas of the Mahāyāna, where men live in unbroken happiness till they attain Nirvana.[5]

There is a statement in the rhetorician Dio Chrysostom that Indians possessed and used a translation of Homer into their own language.[6] It has no chance whatever of being true,[7] for nowhere in the Hellenistic world has there been found any translation of any piece of Greek literature into any language except (at the end) Latin; and now that it appears that some Greeks probably knew the Mahābhārata (pp. 380 *sq.*), the suggestion[8] that Dio really meant the Indian epic has gained greatly in probability. The interest of Dio's statement is that it has been used as

[1] Rhys Davids II pp. 211–43.

[2] Mrs Rhys Davids, *The Milinda Questions* 1930 p. 133.

[3] *Ib.* p. 137. A connection of the author with Plato on general grounds was suggested long ago by Weber, *op. cit.* p. 927. It has not received support, though *comparison* has been common enough.

[4] Rhys Davids II p. 232 (342).

[5] Sir Charles Eliot, *Hinduism and Brahmanism* II, 1921, pp. 29–30; written about the Christian Era, p. 181.

[6] LIII, 6, *μεταλαβόντων αὐτὴν εἰς τὴν σφετέραν διάλεκτόν τε καὶ φωνήν.*

[7] It does not improve matters to cite Aelian, *V.H.* XII, 48, a story that there was not only an Indian translation but a Persian one also; for Aelian indicates plainly enough that he did not believe it.

[8] Weber, *Ind. Stud.* II p. 162; R. Pischel, *Die Indische Literatur* 1906 p. 195. See Winternitz III p. 627.

the basis of a theory that the Indian Dohā metre grew out of the Greek hexameter[1] (though a translation would probably not have exhibited the hexameter). The Dohā metre, which is dactylic in structure, belongs to the group of literary languages called Apabrança[2] which are neither Sanscrit nor Pali, and the earliest remains of this group are said to be the language of the Abhīras (p. 171), who in Menander's reign were in his satrapy of Abiria on the Indus; but more recently the connection of the Dohā metre with the hexameter has been denied on the ground that it can easily be explained from Indian sources.[3] I do not presume to discuss the matter, but if anyone should again desire to connect the two metres he could base his theory on something more to the point than Dio; for the Abhīras were Menander's subjects and Greek hexameters were being written in Menander's kingdom (pp. 248 *sq.*).

Plutarch's statement, however, that some Indians worshipped Greek gods[4] is on another footing: it is not rhetoric but simple fact, for Indian citizens in Greek cities of necessity took part at certain times, even if only outwardly and for conformity, in the official city worship.

But much more important than the things to which I have referred are the traces which show that some Greeks probably—one might almost say certainly—knew the Mahābhārata; for Hellenistic Greeks as a general rule took no interest in the language or literature of the Asiatic peoples with whom they were in contact (p. 59),[5] and this illustrates once more the fact that their attitude in India differed somewhat from that in other parts of Asia. The inscription which Heliodorus son of Dion, ambassador from Antialcidas to some Sunga king of Vidisā, set up on a column at Besnagar (p. 313) concludes with the words, inscribed on the reverse side of the pillar, 'Three immortal precepts when practised lead to Heaven—Restraint, Renunciation, Rectitude';[6] and these words have been identified as a concise rendering of two passages in the

[1] H. Jacobi in *Αντιδωρον*, *Festschrift Wackernagel* 1923 pp. 127 *sqq.*

[2] Jacobi *op. cit.*; A. B. Keith, *A history of Sanscrit Literature* 1928 pp. 32–3.

[3] Keith *op. cit.* pp. 370–1.

[4] Plut. *de Alex. fortuna aut virtute* 328 c. The whole passage, of which other items are noticed where they belong, attributes to Alexander in the usual way things which happened later. Plutarch no doubt would have said that they were due to his original impulse.

[5] The most amazing instance is that the well-informed Strabo (xvi, 760–1) had never even heard that Jews possessed a great literature, though the Greek Septuagint translation was available to him.

[6] Raychaudhuri's translation (next note). L. D. Barnett, *JRAS* 1909 p. 1093, rendered it 'Selfrestraint, selfsurrender, and diligence'.

Mahābhārata.[1] Heliodorus called himself a Bhāgavata, a devotee of the reformed worship of Vishnu-Krishna as the Supreme Being; and it has been suggested, independently of the words cited above, that he may have known the Bhagavadgītā,[2] one of the philosophical chapters tacked on to the epic. The quotation by itself is perhaps not quite conclusive for his personal acquaintance with the Mahābhārata, as it *might* have been found for him by an Indian secretary, if he had one; but if the inscription means that he is pledging himself to these three virtues[3] then it *is* conclusive, as would in any case be the natural interpretation. Another instance is supplied by the occurrence in Ptolemy and in the Bassarica of Dionysius of the name of the Pāndava-Pāndus,[4] who are not known to have played any part in, or been mentioned in, history during any period in which Greeks were acquainted with India; they were only a people of the epic, and the ultimate common source of Ptolemy and Dionysius can only have been a Greek who had read the Mahābhārata and taken the name directly from it.[5] It may be connected with this that, as has often been noticed, Ptolemy's names for the rivers of the Punjab are nearer the Sanscrit forms than are the Greek names in use since Alexander's day, and suggest as their ultimate source a Greek acquainted with Sanscrit. Another case of a Greek knowing some Indian literature has already been noticed (p. 47): 'Trogus' source' knew the Jain dating for Chandragupta's accession (it may have been through him that the name 'Jains' found its way to the West),[6] and can only have got it from some Greek who read Jain writings, unless, as is not impossible, he could read them himself.

After literature, one naturally turns to the drama. The days when it could be suggested that the classical Sanscrit drama of the Gupta period was in any sense derived from the Greek drama are long past; no one now doubts that the Indian drama was a native growth precisely as the Greek drama was, though it may be matter of debate whether its origin was religious or secular, and what part was played by different elements.[7]

[1] H. Raychaudhuri, *JASB* XVIII, 1923, pp. 269–71; V. Battacharya, *IHQ* VIII, 1932, p. 610.
[2] De la Vallée-Poussin p. 190.
[3] Sir J. Marshall, *JRAS* 1909 p. 1056: 'pledges himself to the three' cardinal virtues.
[4] For this name and the evidence see App. 19.
[5] Conceivably 'Trogus' source', p. 47.
[6] Hesychius, *Γεννοί· οἱ Γυμνοσοφισταί*. Query if *Γεννοί* represents *Ϝεννοί*.
[7] There is a large literature on the Indian drama; but Winternitz III pp. 160–83, and the exhaustive discussion by A. B. Keith in part I of *The Sanscrit Drama* 1924, will give all that is here necessary.

But the much-canvassed question of whether, during its formative period, it underwent any or what Greek influence is another matter. Details have now been so thoroughly examined that there is no need to do it afresh,[1] even were I able; I need only give just what appears to myself. The fragments of Bhāsa's plays, first century A.D., and the fragments of Buddhist dramas discovered in 1911 by Professor Lüders, have brought the Indian drama far nearer to the period of Greek rule than are the plays of the Gupta period; and if Professor A. B. Keith be right, and there was already a nascent Indian drama in the second century B.C. or at latest early in the first century,[2] then there must have been *contact* of some kind between the two arts. For the argument that we do not know that Greek plays were acted in India is worthless. There were Greek *poleis*, and a *polis* of any pretensions without a theatre is unthinkable (cf. p. 17); the one at Babylon has been excavated.[3] And Egypt has at least taught us that whatever other works Greeks might take with them to foreign lands they would certainly take Homer and Euripides.[4] There is no need to doubt Plutarch's statement that Euripides and Sophocles were acted at Susa,[5] for it is known that Sophocles reached India: on a fragment of a vase found near Peshawur and now in the Punjab Museum at Lahore is the scene from the Antigone where Haemon begs Creon for Antigone's life,[6] and as the vase was of local manufacture[7] it proves at the least that somebody in Gandhāra was interested in Sophocles, and there is therefore no reason to doubt a knowledge of Euripides also at Pushkalāvatī or any other important Greek centre. Contact, then, there must in all probability have been.

Before going further, a word must be said about the mime, for Reich's view that the Indian drama was influenced not by the Greek

[1] On the alleged Greek influence, Winternitz III pp. 175 *sqq.* and Keith *op. cit.* pp. 57 *sqq.* will give the literature and arguments; I have not met with anything more recent which is material, except as regards the mime (*below*). There is a sensible discussion by Wecker, *India* in PW, 1916.

[2] *Op. cit.* pp. 45, 72.

[3] R. Koldewey, *Das wieder erstehende Babylon*[4] 1925 pp. 293–9.

[4] Cf. C. H. Oldfather, *Greek literary texts from Graeco-Roman Egypt* 1923 pp. 66, 67, 70.

[5] *Mor.* 328 D. On the possibility that *SEG* VII, 3 implies that the Dionysiac artists visited Susa see Fr. Cumont, *CR Ac. Inscr.* 1933 p. 268 n. 4. There is no reason why they should not have visited India, if mime-actors did.

[6] Sir J. Marshall, *JRAS* 1909 pp. 1060–1; *ASI* 1914–15 p. 11 n. 2.

[7] Marshall in *CHI* p. 646.

drama but by the Greek mime[1] has had a certain amount of support.[2] Little is known of the Greek mime, in the sense of a regular *ὑπόθεσις* or stage-play; knowledge of that seems largely confined to the Roman form.[3] But the mime was of Greek origin, and numerous notices of mime-actors in the Greek world have been collected from inscriptions;[4] mimes *were* acted in the Seleucid empire, for Antiochus IV included some in his triumphal celebrations at Daphne;[5] and it would seem that companies of mime-actors did visit India. Perhaps the extant parody of the Iphigeneia in Tauris, in which the barbarian king is an Indian and talks pseudo-Indian gibberish,[6] may bear on this; but in any case it seems to follow from the much-discussed Yavanikā, the curtain against which Indian plays were acted.[7] The word, to my mind, cannot merely mean 'Yavana cloth', because the Yavana name occurs three times in, or in connection with, the classical dramas, and as we have seen that the Yavana cavalry and the Yavana women embody true traditions come down from the period of Greek rule (p. 374), it seems inevitable that the Yavana curtain must also represent a tradition going back to the same period. Now Greek dramas were not acted against a curtain, but Roman, and therefore presumably Greek, mimes usually were;[8] and the Yavanikā must be, as Reich thought,[9] the *siparium* of the mime players. Reich brought out some likenesses between the classical and Indian mime,[10] and perhaps the curtain does make a case for Indians being

[1] H. Reich, *Der Mimus*, 1903, I ii chap. VIII p. 694.

[2] It convinced Professor Körte, *Neue Jahrb. f. d. klass. Alt.* XI, 1903, p. 539, 'überzeugend'; and Winternitz, III p. 180, thought it possible that the mime *had* some influence, and that the question was not yet decided. But the majority of scholars have rejected it; see E. Wüst, *Mimos* in PW, 1932, col. 1762, and Winternitz *ib.*

[3] Christ-Schmid[6] II i p. 181.

[4] L. Robert, Ἀρχαιολόγος, *Rev. Ét. Gr.* XLIX, 1936, p. 235, who stresses the Greek origin; see esp. p. 243. Cf. Cumont, *L'Égypte des Astrologues* 1937 p. 82.

[5] Polyb. XXX, 26, 7 = Athen. V, 195 f. See also Athen. I, 19 c; Suidas, *προδείκτης*; Wüst *op. cit.*

[6] *P. Oxy.* III, 413; the papyrus is second-century A.D., but the piece itself might be older. On the language see J. U. Powell and E. A. Barber, *New Chapters in the history of Greek literature* II, 1921, p. 215.

[7] For the Yavanikā see Lévi, *Quid de Graecis* p. 25, and many since; Keith *op. cit.* p. 61.

[8] Cases occur in the Roman period of a more elaborate background with doors, Robert *op. cit.* p. 250.

[9] *Op. cit.* pp. 706–7.

[10] The most important is the correspondence (p. 701) of the sutradhāra and sutradhāri with the Greek archimimus and archimima.

borrowers,[1] though I feel some doubt about this. But if Indian mime-actors did borrow more than the curtain from the classical mime, which is quite uncertain, what could it come to as regards the serious drama? The answer must be, very little; *perhaps* a stock character like the fool, where he occurs; nothing that goes to the root of the matter. When we talk of Shakespeare, we are not usually thinking of the clowns or the prologue to the Taming of the Shrew; and Reich himself admitted that in Kālidāsa's most important play, Sakuntalā, there is no trace of the influence of the mime at all.[2]

To return to the two dramas. Contact, as we have seen, was probable; but contact does not necessarily mean influence. Certain parallels between Greek and Indian plays have been put forward, but nothing convincing in this respect; human minds, working on the same subject, have a tendency to work on parallel lines. I shall not attempt to go beyond the view that we cannot deny the possibility of Greek influence but that there is no evidence;[3] perhaps however I can make two points a little more precise than hitherto. On the analogy of the Milindapañha, if there was any Greek influence it would have been a matter of *form* only, of outward shape; the substance is as Indian as it can be. No one, I think, can read a play like Sakuntalā, which in a less sophisticated age than our own took London by storm as it did Goethe, without realising that he is in a totally different world from anything which he has ever met with in Greek literature. And my second point concerns that same substance. The strongest argument of those who have believed in substantial Greek influence has always been that Kālidāsa's plays contain recognition scenes, and these were the stock-in-trade of the Athenian writer of comedies, Menander. Why Menander should be brought in is obscure to me, for any contact is much more likely to have been with Euripides;[4] even Philostratus knew that much.[5] But in any case the argument is easy to disprove. Ancient civilisations, whatever their merits, usually gave far less individual security than we expect

[1] Reich p. 740 thought that a woman actor in India, being against Indian canons (in serious drama), must have been borrowed from Greece. But the archimima was equally against the canons of classical Greece in serious drama, so the argument fails. The mime in fact was a thing apart and a law to itself.

[2] *Op. cit.* p. 739.

[3] Keith *op. cit.* p. 68.

[4] Oldfather, *op. cit.* pp. 66, 67, 70, shows that in Egypt Euripides was much the more popular of the two.

[5] *Life of Apollonius* II, 32 (the *Heracleidae*); see p. 354 n. 3.

to-day, and in any country, not only in Greece or India, recognitions of lost wives or daughters were the most obvious of all the material which lay to the hand of the dramatist. We possess an old Peruvian play (and a very good one) called Apu Ollantay,[1] composed in the reign of the Inca Tupac Yupanqui and written down after the Spanish conquest. That play turns entirely on two recognitions, the first by the imprisoned princess of her lost daughter, and the second, through the child's instrumentality, of the prisoner herself by her husband and her brother the Inca; but the most hardened Diffusionist would scarcely suggest that the author, who had never heard of the Old World or of reading or writing, was borrowing from Menander.

In another form of literature modern study has entirely shifted its ground. No one would now ask whether India derived her fables and folktales from the Greeks, for it has been recognised that each individual story presents its own problems and must be treated on its own merits;[2] one may have originated in India or even in China[3] and travelled to Greece, another may have originated in Greece and travelled to India, while others may have started in Babylonia or Egypt or Iran and spread in any or every direction. Tracing the paths of these stories, which range over many centuries, is a fascinating pursuit, but has nothing to do with what we are considering.

We come for a moment to science. Except for mathematics, the bent of the Indian mind was almost entirely towards religion and philosophy, the matters of the spirit; it no more wanted Greek science than it wanted Greek history. The Babylonian astronomer might meet the Greek astronomer on equal terms and put his knowledge at his disposal, but nothing of the sort seems to have happened elsewhere in the world. Nearly everything connected with scientific relationships is of necessity matter for the expert, and I can be very brief. There are said to be some analogies between Greek and Indian medicine which necessitate the conclusion that India took over some Greek medical learning,[4] in

[1] A rendering into English, with a history of the Spanish text and a bibliography, will be found in Sir Clements Markham, *The Incas of Peru* 1910.

[2] Winternitz III pp. 294–311; A. B. Keith, *A History of Sanscrit Literature* 1928 chap. XVII; W. R. Halliday, *Indo-European Folktales and Greek legend* 1933. The *Bericht* on the Greek fable by W. Port in *Bursian-Münscher* vol. CCXL, 1933, does not deal with India.

[3] Like the story of the Magnet-rock which holds ships, R. Hennig, *Arch. für Kulturgeschichte* XX, 1930, p. 350. The story comes in Ptolemy VII, 2, 31.

[4] Winternitz III p. 554.

return supplying Greek physicians with some valuable drugs; but it has also been held that no conclusion on the subject is possible.[1] Some Indian astronomers of the Gupta period are generally supposed to have made an attempt, which failed, to introduce Alexandrian astronomy into India;[2] but even this has been denied,[3] and in any case is far outside my period, as is the relationship, if any, between Greek and Indian mathematics, in which science India, by the invention and positioning[4] of numerals, ultimately made possible advances which could not have been reached by the purely geometric methods of Greece. Certainly India, though she might not want Greek science, knew and admired it, more especially medical science; the Yavanas appear in the Mahābhārata as 'all-knowing',[5] and there is an Indian story that the Greek physicians of Bactra and Taxila were so skilful that they could give sight to the blind,[6] a story which no doubt grew out of some real operation for cataract, just as the similar story in Greece that the physician Asclepiades once raised a man from the dead is known to have grown out of the fact that he once recognised that a man being carried out to burial was only in a state of catalepsy.[7] It was therefore natural and inevitable that after Greeks had vanished from India legend should credit them with magic powers, as has happened to other vanished peoples; in the Kashmir poet Ksemendra (eleventh century A.D.) Yavanas can make and fly aeroplanes.[8] As to the pseudo-science of astrology, Indians had long known something about it, and most of such contacts with Greek knowledge as can be traced are again much later than the Christian Era; but it is now said that one thing did come from Babylon to India during the Hellenistic period, the art of foretelling the future by means of the stars.[9]

[1] Keith *op. cit.* pp. 513–14.

[2] The fullest account I have met is G. R. Kaye, *Hindu Astronomy*, in *Memoirs of the Arch. Survey of India*, XVIII, 1924. For the literature generally see W. Gundel's *Bericht* on Astronomy and Astrology in *Bursian-Münscher* vol. CCXLII, 1934, ii, pp. 115–21.

[3] Sukumar Ranjan Das, *IHQ* IV, 1928, p. 68.

[4] It is now said that Babylon had what was practically a positioning system, with base 60 instead of 10, many centuries before India: O. Neugebauer in *Studien zu Gesch. d. Mathematik*, by B. Datta and others, II i, 1930; see *JHS* 1931 p. 130. But seemingly nothing came of it.

[5] Lévi, *Quid de Graecis* p. 23. Often quoted.

[6] Przyluski, *Açoka* p. 107.

[7] Cf. Pliny VII, 124 with Celsus II p. 38 l. 15, and see Tarn, *Hell. Civ.*[2] p. 272.

[8] Lévi *op. cit.* p. 15, and in many books.

[9] J. Scheftelowitz, *Die Zeit in der indischen und iranischen Religion* 1929 pp. 1–10, which I only know in the citation by Gundel *op. cit.* p. 119.

But the real strength of Greece lay not in science but in philosophy, and here Greek and Indian met on equal terms. That is the meeting we would know about; and there is not a word that can be said.[1] The Greeks in India may not have been the most likely soil to develop philosophers, though one cannot imagine a Hellenistic kingdom without them; but communication with the West was free enough, and there was the Stoic school at Seleuceia (p. 42), which doubtless held to the Stoic tradition that they must do more than sit and wait for men to come to them: they must go to men. We may, if we will, let fancy play round some meeting of Stoic and Buddhist, and seek to interpret for ourselves how far each would understand the other's point of view. But it is only fancy; we *know* nothing—nothing but a little Greek ivory pendant from Taxila, which bears on each of its two faces the head of a philosopher.[2]

We may turn now to a matter more important to the Greek historian, the influence of India on her Greek invaders. Eratosthenes[3] instanced, as the best 'barbarians' whom Greeks had met, Romans and Carthaginians in the West and eastern Iranians and Indians in Asia—the peoples who when he wrote were about to be included in Demetrius' empire. Of the Bactrians and their cognate peoples in eastern Iran we know nothing; but it has already been indicated that the Greek attitude with regard to Indians was not quite the same as their attitude with regard to Asiatic peoples farther west. For one thing, many more Greeks relatively knew some Indian language. In other Hellenistic kingdoms, though there must always have been some officials who knew the language of the subjects, the mint officials needed only Greek, but in India the mint officials from the start had to know some Prakrit and be able to write Kharoshthi. And there is the matter of inscriptions. The fact, often emphasised, that India has yielded no Greek inscriptions means nothing; no place where Greek inscriptions are likely to be found has yet been excavated, and it will be time enough to draw deductions from their absence when Bucephala or Pushkalāvatī has been thoroughly dug out; I say 'thoroughly', for the excavation of Susa had lasted for nearly a generation before the workers came upon a pocket of Greek inscriptions. Taxila, the one town in the Greek sphere in India which has been excavated, was never a Greek city, and so far

[1] For suggestions see Winternitz III p. 478.

[2] *ASI* 1912–13 part I p. 14.

[3] Strabo I, 66.

as I know, no cemetery of the Greek period has been unearthed anywhere. But it *is* important that we possess a number of inscriptions by Greeks written in Kharoshthi (and even in Brahmi), though unfortunately they give little or no information about the second century B.C., the time we want to know about; just as in the Seleucid empire we now know more about the Parthian period than about the constructive reigns of Seleucus I and Antiochus I, so in India we get material for the first century B.C. which is denied us for the age of Demetrius and Menander. But these inscriptions, which are chiefly dedications and votive offerings, do tend also to show the special place which India held in regard to Greeks, for no Greek votive inscriptions or *proskynemata* have, I believe, been found in any other Oriental language, like Aramaic or Egyptian.

Of the inscriptions dated in the period of Greek rule, that of Heliodorus on the Besnagar column is probably the earliest; it is not likely to be later than 100 B.C. and may even be a little earlier (pp. 313 *sq.*). He was the Greek ambassador of a Greek king, but he does not use Greek for his inscription; he proclaims himself the adherent of an Indian creed, quotes an Indian epic, and sets up his record in Brahmi. It might be argued that there were no Greeks in Vidisā to read it, or that he wished to pay a compliment to the state to which he was accredited, though even so a bilingual inscription would have been indicated. But such considerations do not in any case apply to the very important Kharoshthi inscription, on a vase from Swat, of the Greek meridarch Theodorus.[1] Dr Konow put this inscription not *later* than the middle of the first century B.C.; but his whole scheme of historical dating in the Corpus, some of which he has now abandoned (p. 495), is later than the one worked out in this book, and this inscription is probably early in the century, and might well be even as early as that of Heliodorus. Theodorus was a Buddhist, and his dedication deals with a matter which by his time must have been of interest, or even of importance, to many more Greeks than himself, the establishment of (that is, the provision of a stupa to contain) some relics of Buddha; but his dedication is in Kharoshthi alone, not in both languages, and he therefore assumed that every Greek in Gandhāra who was interested in Buddhism would know Prakrit and could read Kharoshthi.[2] One must

[1] *CII* p. 1 no. 1.

[2] It might be objected that, as the vase would be enclosed in the stupa, the inscription would not show. But the 'enclosed' inscriptions on the gold plates

suppose therefore that by the earlier part of the first century B.C. many Greeks in Gandhāra were becoming bilingual. The only other material inscription from the period of Greek rule, that of the Buddhist Theodorus Datiaputra of about 42 B.C., will be noticed later (p. 391).

The Kharoshthi inscription of the wrestler Menander (see p. 355 n. 4), who may not have had much that was Greek about him, is of the Kushan period. But we get two Greeks of about the Parthian period, the first half of the first century A.D., who used the Indian forms of their names, King Theodamas on his signet-ring found in Bajaur,[1] and Theodorus son of Theoros on two silver bowls from Taxila.[2] Theoros, though sufficiently attested as a Greek name,[3] was a tolerably rare one and not one that an Indian would adopt, even if Indians did take Greek names; there is no evidence that they ever did, and as we have seen there is some evidence that they did not (p. 255). Theoros then, round about the Christian Era, really was a Greek, which is interesting; but his son, evidently a well-to-do man, put his name on his votive offering[4] not in Greek but in Kharoshthi.

Lastly come three names which have not been or cannot be dated: two on signet-rings, Timitra (Demetrius) from Besnagar[5] and Denipa (Deinippos) from Taxila,[6] and the feminine name Saphā, the donor in an inscription now lost,[7] which Dr Konow suggested might be Σοφή (Sophe). This seems fairly certain,[8] for though Σόφη is apparently not actually known,[9] the masculine form Σόφος occurs as a man's name in

used as foundation deposits for Darius' palace at Persepolis are trilingual; and it is possible that copies of 'enclosed' inscriptions were exhibited, perhaps in a non-permanent form.

[1] *CII* p. 6 no. III.

[2] *Ib.* p. 98 no. XXXVII, 1, 2: Theütaras(y)a Thavaraputras(y)a. Konow sought to explain Thavara from Sanscrit, but there can be no doubt what it is; as to the 'v', Theoros would be Thavara just as Theos is Deva. O. Stein's sweeping deduction from Thavara as an Indian name (*Indian Culture* I, 1935, p. 353) was unfortunate.

[3] Two instances in PW, one in Preisigke's *Namenbuch* (Egypt), several in Pape. The feminine Theoris also occurs.

[4] Marshall, *ASI* 1929–30 p. 68, gives reasons for thinking that Theodorus was making a donation of these bowls; Konow also translates (Gift) of.......

[5] D. R. Bhandarkar, *ASI* 1914–15 p. 77 and part I p. 20.

[6] *CII* p. 101 no. 7; J. Charpentier, *Ind. Ant.* 1931 p. 78.

[7] *CII* p. 114 no. XLVII.

[8] O. Stein *op. cit.* p. 354 tried to make Saphā the feminine of 'the Indian name transliterated as Sophon' in *Σόφων 'Ινδός* (p. 370 n. 2). But *Σόφων 'Ινδός* is only a conjectural emendation, and Sophon is not an Indian name but a well-known Greek one; Susemihl I p. 878 and Ditt.[3] 1021 may suffice here.

[9] I have not searched among recent inscriptions.

papyri,[1] and that should suffice, seeing that Greeks in the East had some fancy for similar names.[2] One other name, however, is far too late to consider, that of the *bhikku* Dharmamitra from Nagara; for though Dharmamitra had been used for Demetrius (pp. 178, 455) and Nagara had been Dionysopolis, the inscriptions are fifth-century A.D. and both the monk and his name were certainly Indian.[3]

The conclusion then must be that from about the beginning of the first century B.C., speaking very roughly, the Greeks, or many Greeks, in India were becoming Indianised. The conclusion can only be tentative, for we do not really know what was happening in the Greek cities; but on existing material it seems the only conclusion possible, and we shall meet with other things which bear it out.

I doubt if mixed marriages played as much part in this result as might be supposed, at any rate so long as Greek rule lasted; the general question has already been considered for the Middle East, and there it was found impossible to envisage mixed marriages on any considerable scale till after the Christian Era (pp. 35 *sqq.*). Naturally there would be *some* mixed marriages in India in the first century B.C., for Greeks had not the faintest feeling about what among English-speaking peoples to-day is called the 'colour-bar'; but they had a good deal of pride in their Greekhood, and must have attempted, at any rate for a time, to keep themselves as Greek as possible (p. 38), whatever the attractions of Indian *religions*. There are said to be statements in Buddhist literature that among the Yavanas, if a man met with a sudden death, he might not be buried till the king was told,[4] obviously to give the opportunity for an enquiry; it seems to point to some care on the part of the kings to keep up Greek numbers—the life of a Yavana was not a thing to be wasted. I think there was another factor, apart from mixed marriages, to which a good deal of weight must be given. British children are not

[1] *P. Lond.* III, 1213 a l. 4, 1214 a l. 5; *P. Ryl.* II 150 l. 2 (A.D. 40); Arcadius, περὶ τόνων p. 84 (Barker), who says that, as a name, the word is paroxytone. I owe these references to Professor Last.

[2] With Sophe, 'Wise', compare Dikaios, 'Just', the name of two different youths in the ephebe list from Babylon of 109–8 B.C., *Klio* IX, 1909, p. 352 no. 1. Dikaios as a name has survived into modern Greek, while Sophe, in the form Sophie, Sophia, has become common in many languages.

[3] *CII* pp. 95, 96, XXXVI nos. 5, 8.

[4] Lévi, *Quid de Graecis* p. 23. By 'king' one must understand the proper official. It must mean something more than a mere register of deaths such as there apparently was in Egypt under the Romans.

brought up in India to-day, not so much because they cannot be reared (though in some places they may grow up sickly) as because there is a tendency that at their impressionable period some of their native characteristics may weaken and they may acquire a mentality somewhat nearer akin to that of the Indian, and not the highest type of Indian; continue the process among the Greeks for several generations—it would work like compound interest—and the resulting Indianisation would be obvious. The Greeks in India may have ultimately vanished, not because they became Eurasians, but because they became Indians.

Somewhere I have met with the whole-hearted statement that every Greek in India ended by becoming a Buddhist. Some no doubt did, though a good many must have ended by being killed in the Saca wars; but in fact at present there are only five Greeks whose religious predilections are known or can be deduced, and three of these were not Buddhists. Heliodorus the ambassador was a Bhāgavata, a worshipper of Vishnu-Krishna as the supreme deity; the legend on the seal of Timitra from Besnagar has been interpreted as referring to a Brahmanic sacrifice which he instituted;[1] and the Greek who read Jain literature and passed a piece of his information on to 'Trogus' source' (p. 47) was, if not actually a Jain, at any rate interested in the doctrines of that sect. Theodorus Datiaputra, whose inscription, found in Swat, was most probably written *c.* 42 B.C.,[2] was certainly a Buddhist, as he dedicated a tank 'in honour of all beings', which is said to be a common Buddhist formula; and though one interpretation of Datiaputra (see p. 125 n. 2) would make him by descent not a Greek but a hellenised Bactrian, this is unlikely. Lastly, Theodorus the meridarch, who established some relics of Buddha 'for the purpose of the security of many people', was undoubtedly a Buddhist; for had he merely been carrying out an order of his Government he must have said so and not taken all the credit to himself. If, however, we meet Greeks of different creeds, it must at any rate speak to a good deal of general interest in the religions of India, while the Gandhāra school of art, of which I shall have to say something

[1] D. R. Bhandarkar, *ASI* 1914–15 p. 77.

[2] *CII* p. 65 no. XXIV. It is dated in the year 113 of some Era, which Konow, I think rightly, made the first Saca Era, that of the Moga copper-plate. The year 113, on his reckoning in *CII*, was A.D. 29; on mine (see App. 16) it would be *c.* 42 B.C., which is preferable; for at that time the Sacas were ruling in Gandhāra, while in A.D. 29 they were not. Konow, however, has now abandoned the *CII* dating for inscriptions dated in the old Saca Era (see *JIH* XII, 1933, pp. 1–4, and App. 16) and his new dating would fall during Saca rule.

presently, is probably evidence that this very limited analysis, though the best one can make, does injustice to the position of Buddhism among the Greeks of the North-West; Buddhism to them must have been far the most important religion, if only for the political reasons already considered (Chap. IV), and the kings must always have depended a good deal on Buddhist support.

If we had enough Greek names from India, something might perhaps be learnt in this connection from the nomenclature; but only thirteen are known[1] beside the twenty-seven names of monarchs, omitting those kings who came from Bactria. However, even these scanty names do show one phenomenon which attracts attention and may be noticed for what it is worth. Among the royal names are four compounded with the names of Greek gods,[2] few enough, perhaps; but among the names of commoners there is only one, Heliodorus, and that is uncertain, for the Helios may well be Sūrya. Four of the commoners are, naturally enough, named after kings, but three of the others bear the same name, Theodorus; and if the late kings Theophilus and Theodamas be added, no less than five names in our scanty list, all later than 100 B.C., are compounded with the indeterminate Theos.[3] That may mean that the Greek father, while willing to be pious, was not going to specify what god was the object of his piety; he was not clinging to the gods of Greece, but was ready to come under other influences. It would seem that the Greek gods in India, though they remained as official coin-types or material for artists, had little enough to do with the religion of the people, at any rate in the first century B.C. Menander's adoption of the purely Greek Athena *may* have helped her to keep some hold, as she did at Seleuceia (p. 68), though only one slight indication remains (p. 334 n. 2); but it cannot be said how far Heracles and Dionysus were merely Krishna and Siva, and certainly Zeus was almost always the elephant-god of Kapisa.

[1] Demetrius and Antiochus from the *Milindapañha* (see Excursus), Timitra (Demetrius), Menander (the wrestler); Heliodorus (son of Dion); Dion, Theoros, Deinippos, Sophe, Agesilas; Theodorus the meridarch, Theodorus Datiaputra, Theodorus son of Theoros. All have already been referred to.

[2] Omitting Apollodotus II as a hereditary name and Artemidorus as probably formed from the non-Greek goddess of Pushkalāvatī (*CHI* p. 558), they are Apollophanes, Diomedes, Dionysius, Hermaeus; and Dionysius might only refer to Siva.

[3] It might be argued that Theodorus is only Devadatta. But the first two of the name were Buddhists, and could hardly have borne the name of Buddha's implacable enemy, who pursued him through all his existences.

This does seem to have some bearing on the relationship of the Greeks generally, or of many Greeks, to Indian religions and primarily of course to Buddhism, once Indianisation had begun after *c.* 100 B.C.; and in fact it was, as we shall see, about this time that something took place which is without parallel in Hellenistic history: Greeks of themselves placed their artistic skill at the service of a foreign religion,[1] and created for it a new form of expression in art. Nothing can be more eloquent of the Indianisation which was taking place and of the attitude of Greeks generally to Buddhism; it has been well said that the art of Gandhāra was born of Buddhist piety utilising Yavana technique.[2] If Greeks elsewhere made statues of foreign deities, it was because they wanted them themselves; for example, they made statues of Isis, not for the benefit of the religion of the native Egyptians, but because sections of the Greek world were taking Isis to themselves as their own and wanted statues of her. But what happened in India was a different matter, whether some of the Greek artists of Gandhāra were or were not actually Buddhists; it might sometimes be difficult to say, for very many people gave Buddhism some sort of intellectual assent without joining the Order, just as in Russia to-day only a small minority of those who assent to Communism are members of the Order, the Communist Party. But Buddhists or not, these Greeks worked for the Buddhist world; and the school of Gandhāra, in that sense, is unique.

With that school, considered as art,[3] I am not concerned; I only want the chronological history of an idea. A great mass of sculptures and reliefs is now known, and the Gandhāra art extended all over

[1] Greek kings elsewhere, from motives of policy, might build or restore temples to a foreign deity and employ some Greek work-people; but that is a very different matter.

[2] Grousset p. 80.

[3] There is a large literature, which I need not set out. The standard work is A. Foucher, *L'art gréco-bouddhique de Gandhāra* 1914 (2 vols.); such of the later special literature as is known to me and is material to my subject will be mentioned in its place. Accounts will be found in all general works on India, like those of R. Grousset, L. de la Vallée-Poussin, and P. Masson-Oursel and others, *Ancient India and Indian Civilisations*, 1934. For later influences in Central Asia see primarily the works of Sir A. Stein and A. von Le Coq; for those in the Paropamisadae, the memoirs of the French archaeological Mission, notably J. Barthoux on Hadda and A. Godard and J. Hackin on Bamyan. None of this is material to the particular question with which I am alone dealing. A recent study has sought to deny Greek influence altogether and to connect Gandhāran art with Mohenjodaro, the gap being only some three millenniums: Fr. H. Heras, *Journ. R.A.S., Bombay Branch*, XII, 1936, p. 71.

the Greek North-West; practically everything is an illustration of the life and the previous lives of Buddha, very few pieces being known which do not relate to him,[1] and the Gandhāra influence has been traced into Central Asia and, some would say, still farther east, as well as in the later Buddhist art revealed at Hadda and Bamyan. The content of the art is purely Buddhist; the form at the start is largely Hellenistic Greek, and commonplace Greek motives are freely used as decoration; as time passed the style steadily became more and more Indian and less and less Greek. This Graeco-Indian art is distinct from the purely Greek pieces found in north-west India, like the Athena of the Lahore Museum, which represent the art of the Greeks for themselves; some of these pieces are said to belong to the second century B.C., but some have been placed in the first century,[2] so that the two arts may have overlapped. There are affinities between the Greek decorative motives of the earlier Gandhāra pieces and the coins; the Tritons[3] recall Hippostratus' coinage of *c.* 60–50 B.C. onwards (p. 326), and the so-called gigantomachy,[4] which shows the influence of Pergamum, is a parallel to the serpent-footed giant on Telephus' coin of *c.* 70–60 B.C. (p. 333), which also connects with Pergamum; it seems probable that an occasional artist came out from the West.

The beginnings of the Gandhāra school have been dated everywhere from the first century B.C. (which was M. Foucher's view) to the Kushan period and even after it; and the late date, which one had hoped had died with Vincent Smith, is now becoming fashionable again (pp. 397 *sq.*) and is supported by postulating that in the Kushan period there was a large influx of artists into India from the Graeco-Roman West. There is indeed said to be a class of gems found in India which suggest that in the first and second centuries A.D. a strong wave of artistic *influence* from Asia Minor did reach India;[5] but whether these gems were engraved in India or whether, like the Turkestan seals, they themselves

[1] H. Hargreaves published two in *ASI* 1926–7 p. 232 and said there was only one other then known.

[2] Marshall in *ASI* 1912–13 p. 27 assigned the Dionysus to the second century B.C. but the statue of the child to the first century.

[3] Foucher I pp. 241 *sqq.* figs. 120–4. Fig. 124, from Pushkalāvati, is a two-tailed Triton, as is the Triton on Hippostratus' coins, *BMC* Pl. XIV, 6, with which Foucher p. 242 compares it. On the two-tailed Triton see Dressler in Roscher v, 1156, 1166.

[4] *Ib.* p. 245 fig. 125. But the giant of the fight is really a two-tailed Triton.

[5] Marshall in *CHI* p. 648.

came from the Roman world I do not know. But the builder of the little chapel inside the Kunāla stupa (p. 361) did not come from the West. The only people we actually know of who did come to India from the West in the Roman Imperial period were, on the one hand, the numerous merchants who frequented the ports of Southern and Further India and gave Ptolemy his information about these coasts and who certainly had nothing to do either with art or with north-west India, and, on the other hand, an occasional traveller like the one whose description of Taxila under Gondophares was reproduced by Philostratus (p. 360); and if it be supposed that the powerful Kushan kings did import artists on a considerable scale from Graeco-Roman Asia Minor, it is strange that these men, instead of working in their own Graeco-Roman style, should have proceeded to start a school of Indo-Greek art, and even stranger that no information about the Kushan kings or the Northern India of that period ever came back to Roman Asia or to the West at all. Gandhāra art, much Indianised, *flourished* under the Kushans because an art-current will last after the people who started it have vanished; but to date its *beginning* at a time when Greeks were dying out and Greek influence in India was over is an historical impossibility, and certainly no trained Greek historian will ever believe it [1] unless something very much more to the point can be adduced than has yet been done. I have already pointed out (p. 134), with the terrible example of the Victory of Samothrace always before me, the danger of trying to found chronology upon different writers' different and perhaps subjective views upon style; no doubt style is sometimes useful as a support to or illustration of chronology, but the style-sequences must themselves be properly founded first, or else one is merely arguing in a circle.

My reason for considering the chronology is on account of a matter of great importance to the story of the Greeks in India, the origin of the Buddha-statue and the controversy of late years regarding that origin; for there seems to be a definite and very material chronological

[1] The only Greek historian known to me who has noticed the matter is E. Cavaignac, who said in 1933 that *somehow* the Gandhāra school *must* be connected with the Bactrian Greeks (*Indian Art and Letters* VII p. 125), *i.e.* the Bactrian Greeks in India. This is the view for which Sir J. Marshall for long contended, *e.g.* *JRAS* 1909 p. 1060; and in 1914 A. Foucher (II, 443) made it the dominant view for a good many years. But Marshall, under the influence of the hellenised art of Parthian Taxila, has now changed his view and puts the origin of Gandhāra art in the period of Parthian rule, first century A.D.: *ASI* 1930–4 (pub. 1936) p. 151.

fact of which, so far as I can find, no account has been taken, and which in my view should be conclusive. Before coming to it I must just sketch in outline the conflicting views on the matter; and I had better state once again that the real question at issue is not one of style or stones but of the genesis of an idea.

For centuries Indian Buddhists, as is well known, had felt a deep-seated repugnance to depicting Buddha in human form; they represented him only by symbols. In Indian art from the third to the first centuries B.C., at Bodh Gaya, at Bharhut, at Sanchi, Buddha had never appeared in person; his presence was indicated by the Bo-tree or the Wheel of the Law, by his footprints or his umbrella, by an empty throne. But in the Greek or semi-Greek art of Gandhāra he *was* represented in human form, while on the other hand at Mathurā there have been found purely Indian statues of Buddha[1] as a man which show no trace of Greek influence; something—what it was may be rather the question—had therefore occurred which had overcome the repugnance of Indian Buddhists to portray him or see him portrayed as a man. Twenty years ago M. Foucher's view was generally credited: the portrayal of Buddha as a man was due to the semi-Greek art of Gandhāra, and the great mass of Buddha-statues which have existed for many centuries and exist to-day all over eastern Asia ultimately go back to the Gandhāra Buddhas, though all traces of Greek influence have long died out. But to-day the Indian Buddhas of Mathurā have come into prominence, and it is being argued that the Gandhāra Buddhas had only local influence or no influence at all, and that the later Buddha statues all derive from the purely Indian art of Mathurā. It is a big question; it was summed up by Dr E. Waldschmidt in 1930[2] in the telling phrase that the battle-cries now are 'Gandhāra and Greece' or 'Mathurā and India'.[3]

[1] First detected by Dr Ph. Vogel. His latest and fullest work on the art of Mathurā, with magnificent plates, is *La sculpture de Mathurâ* 1930 (= *Ars Asiatica* XV).

[2] *Die Entwicklunggeschichte des Buddha-bildes in Indien, Ostasiat. Z.* 1930 p. 273.

[3] There is an excellent exposition of the question and arguments in de la Vallée-Poussin, pp. 244 *sqq.*; I have however ventured to take it my own way. The question has sometimes been mixed up with the very different question whether Indians made statues of their gods before Greeks came, *i.e.* before Alexander. I think the evidence is sufficient that they did; but this has not, and cannot have, any bearing on the question of the Buddha-statue, for Buddha was still being represented by symbols at Sanchi (first century B.C.).

No one has ever put the Mathurā Buddhas before the Christian Era,[1] and usually they are assigned to the late Kushan period, second century A.D., the association of the Kushan Huvishka with artistic activity at Mathurā being indisputable.[2] The champions of Mathurā are therefore in some difficulty, and are not certain whether to meet it by dating the beginning of the Gandhāra school very late (a matter to which I have already referred) or by positing two separate and unconnected creations. Dr L. Bachhofer[3] for example, who dates the first Gandhāra Buddha not later than the Christian Era, has said that soon after Kanishka's accession Mathurā did over again for itself what Gandhāra had already done; that is, he believes in two independent origins of the Buddha-statue. Waldschmidt, whose view has been much supported,[4] also dated the first Gandhāra Buddha to about the Christian Era, and the first Indian Buddha of Mathurā, uninfluenced by Gandhāra, about a century later; he makes Greek influence reach Mathurā twenty years later still (which is odd, seeing that Greeks had ruled there from *c.* 175 to *c.* 100 B.C.) and die out again, leaving the path clear for the classical Buddhas of the Gupta age and all subsequent Buddhas to derive from the art of Mathurā. Dr W. Cohn, who has maintained since 1925 that on internal grounds the Buddha-statue must be a purely Indian invention even though this be only a theory resting on hypotheses,[5] also believes that the Buddha-image was evolved twice and independently, and has said that the time will come when Mathurā will stand forth as the sole place of origin of the Buddha-statue, *even though it cannot be proved*[6]—a

[1] It is difficult to separate the Buddha-image at Mathurā from the Jina-image; and according to Ramaprasad Chanda, *ASI* 1925–6 p. 124, all the Jain images of the Mathurā group are dated, and dated in the Kushan period, except one figure on a tablet of homage, which *may* be as old as the Christian Era.

[2] Ph. Vogel, *ASI* 1906–7 p. 79.

[3] *Die frühindische Kunst* 1929 p. 116. I have been unable to see this book and rely on W. Cohn's summary, *Ostasiat. Z.* 1930 p. 286.

[4] *Op. cit.* p. 277. His view is cited as being now the general opinion of 'Indologie'—hardly that, unless in Germany—by R. Fick, *Die buddhistische Kultur und das Erbe Alexanders des Grossen* 1934 p. 23.

[5] *Buddha in der Kunst des Ostens* 1925 pp. xxvi–xxvii, and see a valuable review by him of recent literature in *Ostasiat. Z.* 1930 p. 285. I have not seen Scherman, *Die Buddhadarstellungen des Münchner Museums für Völkerkunden* 1928, who I understand supports Mathurā.

[6] In a review of Fick in *Ostasiat. Z.* 1934 p. 139 (my italics). In *Buddha in der Kunst des Ostens* p. xxvi he had looked forward to it being one day proved 'klipp und klar'.

remark which deserves to live. (By 'influence' these writers mean influence upon style.)

On the other hand Dr A. K. Coomaraswamy, who has always championed Mathurā, has seen that it is really putting too much strain on people's credulity to ask them to believe that a Buddha-image was created afresh and quite independently at Mathurā a century or more after it had already been created in Gandhāra (a point which Dr Vogel has often emphasised), and he has always made the two creations take place simultaneously; in 1926 he declined to fix a date,[1] but in 1927 he put the date in the middle of or early in the first century A.D.,[2] and in 1931 he repeated that the Gandhāra Buddha must be later than the Christian Era.[3] Other writers also, as already noticed, have thought to solve the problem by dating the Gandhāra school late, since the Mathurā Buddhas could not be put early. Mr C. de B. Codrington, who found the Greek side unintelligible both in fact and chronology[4] and therefore turned to the Indian side, has said that Foucher's chronology does not contain a single fixed point and that there is no reason to antedate Gandhāran art in order to provide a borrowed origin for the Buddha image.[5] L. Bachhofer in 1925[6] argued that Gandhāra art *must* be late because no coins earlier than Azes I were found under excavated stupas without coins of Azes I also, which is not even true to the facts[7] and also neglects to notice that under many stupas there were no coins at all; and in 1931[8] he argued that, as the heads from Hadda look like Hellenistic work of the second century B.C. and in fact belong to the fourth–fifth centuries A.D., the earlier any Gandhāra work looks the later it actually is; one would have expected a critic of his experience to have had some inkling of the explanation.[9] Dr Sten Konow,[10] after finding that on his own chronological scheme all *dated* statues of

[1] *The Indian origin of the Buddha image*, *JAOS* XLVI, 1926, p. 165.

[2] *History of Indian and Indonesian art*, 1927 p. 60.

[3] Reviewing Bachhofer, *JAOS* LI, 1931, p. 58.

[4] *Ancient India* 1926 pp. 50–1. I do not blame him.

[5] *Op. cit.* p. 55.

[6] *Zur Datierung der Gandhāra-Plastik* 1925 pp. 8 *sqq.*

[7] Under stupa U^1 at Taxila, *ASI* 1915–16 p. 2, the latest coin found was one of Spalahores (Spalyris), who died *c.* 50 B.C. (before 48 B.C.), some twenty years before the reign of Azes; see Chap. VIII.

[8] In *Studia Indo-Iranica* (*Ehrengabe für W. Geiger*) 1931 p. 39.

[9] The stucco heads were cast in old Hellenistic moulds and then attached to the fourth-century A.D. bodies; see A. Foucher, *Mon. Piot* XXX, 1929, p. 101, who says that the very beautiful head in the Musée Guimet which he is considering is good enough to have been by Lysippus.

[10] *Berlin SB* 1928 p. 565.

Buddha are very late, has made the Gandhāra school begin *after* the Kushan period, *i.e.* at a time when Greeks and everything Greek had completely vanished from India; and finally Dr E. Herzfeld has put the Gandhāra monuments 'later by many centuries' than the Graeco-Bactrian empire.[1] It is a fact that there is nothing to be made of the dated Buddha statues; the earliest, the Loryan Tangai Buddha, is dated 318,[2] and even if the earliest possible dating, the hypothesis that the figures refer to the Seleucid Era, be taken, that only makes it A.D. 6; in fact it is quite uncertain in what Era it is dated. And though the Bimarān casket in the British Museum was found with some coins of Azes I, that only means that it is probably not earlier than *c.* 30 B.C. and may be a good deal later; his big coinage may have long remained in circulation.

It seems evident that some of the writers I have cited are confusing two different things, history and psychology. What history desires to know is who made the first statue of Buddha, and when. But this school is so impressed with the belief that Indians ought, as a matter of psychology, to have made the first statue of that revered figure and that they alone would have possessed the necessary religious vision[3] (this I think is in one aspect true and I shall return to it later), that they argue that what ought to have happened must have happened, a very dangerous procedure. It has led one writer to the statement that 'the essential thing is to prove' what he wants to believe;[4] it has led others to the hypothesis that if Greeks made statues of Buddha they must have been copying Indian work and that therefore we must postulate earlier Buddhas of wood or ivory which have perished without trace,[5] a hypothesis admittedly unsupported by evidence and definitely contradicted by the fact that on the Gandhāra statues Buddha's hair is not shaved and his head is really the head not of an ascetic or a monk but of a king.[6] Clearly what is wanted is not more theories but some definite piece of chronological evidence which shall decide whether the Gandhāra Buddha be early or late; and that evidence exists.

[1] *Archaeological History of Iran* 1935 p. 58. [2] *CII* p. 106 no. XL.

[3] Cf. Cohn, *Buddha in der Kunst des Ostens* pp. xxvi–xxvii; Codrington *op. cit.* p. 47; V. Goloubew, *BEFEO* XXIII, 1923, p. 451. [4] Goloubew *op. cit.* p. 451.

[5] Cohn *op. cit.* p. xxiii; H. v. Glasenapp in *G.H. Ohje Commemoration Volume* 1935 (not seen; I rely on *Ostasiat. Z.* XXI, 1935, p. 231).

[6] A. Foucher, *The beginnings of Buddhist Art* (trans. by L. A. Thomas and F. W. Thomas) pp. 131–3. For the assimilation of Buddha's funeral to that of a Chakravartin king see p. 264.

It exists in the representation of a Buddha statue on a coin of Maues;[1] for that Maues reigned from *c.* 80 to *c.* 58 B.C. seems now certain enough (Chap. VIII)—his reign may have begun somewhat earlier but cannot have ended later—and no one can ever again place this king near the Christian Era without first explaining away the definite fact of the identical Telephus-Maues monograms at Kapisa (see App. 16), which will take some doing. The high probability (we shall find it is a certainty) of there being a representation of Buddha on a coin of Maues was pointed out in 1914 by Mr Longworth Dames,[2] to whom the credit belongs; but it was done in a review, which might easily escape notice, especially in 1914, and as the review was later than the three numismatic works professedly dealing with the Saca coinage, those who consult those works naturally find no trace of the matter; I have in fact only met one reference to it, and that did not appreciate its significance.[3] Longworth Dames was not considering the controversy over the origin of the Buddha-statue, for in 1914 it was not in view; he was merely interpreting a particular coin, which must now be examined.

The coin is one of a pair with identical obverses, which cannot be separated; but I will leave the second coin[4] for the moment, merely saying that the humped bull on its reverse shows that both were minted at Pushkalāvatī, the capital of Gandhāra. The types on the first coin were said by the older numismatists to be, obverse, elephant running with wreath in trunk; reverse, king to front seated cross-legged on a cushion with a sword across his knees.[5] I will take the reverse first.

[1] *BMC* p. 70 nos. 20–24, Pl. XVII, 5; Cunningham *NC* 1890 p. 133 no. 17, Pl. III, 17; *Lahore Cat.* p. 102 nos. 29–31, Pl. X, 31.

[2] In a review of vol. I of Whitehead's *Lahore Catalogue*, *JRAS* 1914 p. 793, he said: 'A close examination of the plates and of three specimens in my possession fails to confirm the presence of a sword, the horizontal line to the right being probably part of the seat. The attitude of the figure seems to justify its identification as a seated Buddha, very like the seated Buddha on Kanishka's coin', *BMC* Pl. XXXII, 14. 'If this attribution is correct it is probably the earliest appearance of Buddha in coinage.' I note that V. A. Smith, *India Mus. Catalogue* p. 40, left it open whether the figure is a king or a god.

[3] Codrington *op. cit.* p. 38 n. 2, who merely said that if Longworth Dames was right it was 'the earliest Buddha figure known'.

[4] *Lahore Cat.* p. 102 no. 32. A second specimen has recently been dug up at Taxila, *ASI* 1929–30 (pub. 1935) p. 88 no. 22.

[5] Both obverse and reverse are enclosed in a square frame of fillet pattern, but this is merely ornament, not enshrinement, as similar frames occur on other Saca coins where no such meaning is possible; see *Lahore Cat.* pp. 124 no. 255, 143

First, the cushion. The object supporting the Maues figure is not a cushion, for it does not go down in the middle and up at the ends as a real cushion does if a man sits on it;[1] it is solid, that is, it is a pedestal or throne of some kind. Then as to the sword. The plates and coins accessible to me[2] show clearly that Longworth Dames was right about the line: it does not go across the figure as a sword would, but there is a line on the figure's left (our right) and apparently a tiny bit of line on the figure's right;[3] the figure interrupts the line and there is no trace of a sword-hilt. It is therefore the back of the throne, and the figure is seated on one of the thrones with a back which occur so frequently as supports of statues of Buddha.[4] It is material here that the latest numismatist to describe the coin, Mr Whitehead in the Lahore Catalogue, does *not* mention a sword or any other object across the knees or the figure; in fact it has its hands folded in its lap in a well-known attitude of seated Buddhas, and I do not envisage a Greek artist giving a king a sword for him to fold his hands meekly over it. It hardly needs to be added that a sword is a most unlikely object for a Saca king to hold, seeing that the weapons of the steppes were bow and spear. This can be illustrated from another Saca king, Azes I. The horseman on the obverse of one series of his coins, who can only be himself, carries a couched spear;[5] and another coin-series shows on the obverse a king, undoubtedly Azes himself, seated cross-legged[6] and holding across his knees the butt end of the great spear of the cataphracts, the κοντός[7]—

nos. 386–9, *BMC* Pl. XXI, 12 (Spalyris); *Lahore Cat.* p. 144 no. 397, *BMC* Pl. XXII, 2 (Spalirises).

[1] This can be seen in the case of the cushion on which Kanishka's Buddha is seated, *BMC* Pl. XXXII, 14.

[2] Of actual coins I have only been able to see the series in the British Museum.

[3] This second bit of the line is shown in *Lahore Cat.* Pl. X, 31. I cannot see it on the British Museum specimens, all somewhat worn.

[4] For the square throne of the Buddha statues see Foucher II pp. 315, 439, 679, 687, 691, etc.; one with back and side-pieces, p. 493, and another such unadorned, Vogel *op. cit.* Pl. XXXIII *b.* Some of those with backs are elaborately carved, as Vogel Pls. XXVI, XXVII.

[5] *BMC* Pl. XVIII, 10, 11; *Lahore Cat.* Pl. XII, 292; *ASI* 1929–30 p. 89 no. 26.

[6] *BMC* p. 83 nos. 115–20, Pl. XIX, 1; Cunningham *NC* 1890 p. 147 no. 9; *Lahore Cat.* p. 118 nos. 188–208.

[7] *BMC* sword, Cunningham sceptre, *Lahore Cat.* sword or mace. It has no resemblance to any of these objects, and there can be little doubt what it is, though I believe no explicit illustration of a κοντός has been found (the Doura graffiti only show a line). For the figure of (possibly) another king of nomad race with a spear see *The Excavations at Dura-Europos, 2nd season,* 1928–9 p. 196 (M. Rostovtzeff).

the part for the whole, there not being room to get in the whole spear; it lies across his knees because his raised right hand is already occupied and a κοντός presumably required both hands. Lastly there comes the placing of the figure on the Maues coin, which is most important. The cross-legged king Azes is of course on the obverse of his coin, that being the king's place on coins. Were the Maues figure a king, it could only be Maues himself; but it is on the *reverse*, which on coins is not the king's place but the god's place.[1] No Greek engraver could have put Maues, the conquering ruler of a large empire, on the reverse of his own coinage.

The placing of the figure, then, on the reverse should alone be conclusive that it represents Buddha, or rather, from the throne and the attitude, a statue of Buddha; but whether it be conclusive or not is not actually material, for the obverse of the coin, 'elephant running with wreath in trunk', clinches the matter. The elephant is *not* running: he has both his forefeet high in the air, and any Indian Greek knew well enough that elephants do not run like that. The creature is *dancing*, dancing on its hind legs and offering a wreath to the seated figure. Here the second coin comes in; it has precisely the same obverse type, elephant dancing and offering a wreath, but on the reverse the place of the seated figure is taken by the humped bull of Pushkalāvatī. Elephants may offer wreaths[2] to kings or gods, but they do not offer wreaths to humped bulls, and what the bull, Siva's bull, therefore represents is clear enough: it is Siva himself, the god's symbol for the god, who in fact does not appear in person on coins till those of the Kushans; there is an earlier instance in India of an elephant offering a wreath to a god, the Zeus of Kapisa, on a coin of Antialcidas.[3] This settles the question of the seated figure. The dance of the elephant, on both coins, is a religious dance before his god, like that of David before Yahweh and many another instance; he is performing an act of reverence or worship

[1] Kanishka's Buddhas are naturally on the reverse, *BMC* Pls. XXVI, 8, XXXII, 14. The Buddha of Kujula Kadphises (p. 403) is on the obverse because there *is* a god, the Zeus of Kapisa, on the reverse, and Buddha was the more important of the two.

[2] The literature on wreaths is collected by L. Deubner, *Arch. für Religionswiss.* xxx, 1933, p. 70 n. 1. For the offering of wreaths to gods see Ganszyniec, *Kranz* in PW, cols. 1592–3, 1600–1.

[3] *BMC* p. 25 no. 2, the elephant *hands* it to Zeus. A rare coin of Antialcidas (*Lahore Cat.* Pl. IV, 212; *ASI* 1929–30 p. 86 no. 9) has obv. bust of the king, rev. elephant standing and holding wreath; it *may* mean he is offering it to the king.

before the two beings (I must not here call Buddha a god)[1] who represented the two religions which divided the allegiance of Pushkalāvatī, those of Buddha and of Siva.[2]

Whether the elephant represents Maues' Indian kingdom,[3] or whether it be the elephant of Taxila (pp. 163 *sq.*), symbolising his capital —there is no third alternative—is not very material, for in either case the meaning is clear: Maues, having conquered Gandhāra, is at pains to assure his new subjects in the usual way that he will respect both their religions; coins of this kind, as I have said before, are only the dead residuum of what were once living proclamations and acts of State. It is material here that there is a series of coins struck by Kujula Kadphises[4] after the conquest of the Paropamisadae which show on the obverse a seated Buddha with one hand raised in benediction, and on the reverse a standing Zeus, which must be the Zeus of Kapisa; these coins afford a close parallel to the Maues coins, for in each case Buddha is associated with the god of the city of minting, in the one case the elephant-god of Kapisa and in the other Siva of Pushkalāvatī; it may be worth notice that Wima Kadphises after his conquest of Gandhāra called himself a follower of Siva.[5] It was a standing difficulty when M. Foucher wrote[6] that the earliest Buddha-statue on a coin was that on a coin of Kanishka,[7] which is fairly late; we now have a regular sequence—Maues, Kujula Kadphises, Kanishka.

Maues' conquest of Gandhāra was not much earlier or much later than 70 B.C. (p. 322), and the Buddha-statue must have been well established before he issued his coin; that dates the Gandhāra Buddha

[1] If not actually a god on Maues' coin, he is very near one, as on Kanishka's coins; for the latter see Foucher II p. 439, de la Vallée-Poussin p. 323.

[2] This can have nothing to do with Siva as Nataraja, Lord of the Dance, a motive which seemingly does not occur in art before the sixth century A.D.; E. B. Havell, *A handbook of Indian Art* 1920 p. 176.

[3] A gold stater of Wima Kadphises represents him riding on an elephant to commemorate the conquest of his Indian realm, *Brit. Mus. Quarterly* VIII, 1932, p. 73; J. Allan, *NC* XIV, 1935, p. 4. No other king, Greek, Saca, Pahlava, or Kushan, rides an elephant.

[4] *ASI* 1912–13 p. 52 nos. 52–4 (6 specimens), 1914–15 p. 33 no. 38, 1915–16 p. 34 nos. 18, 19. By combining the coins Marshall read the legend on the obverse (*ASI* 1912–13 p. 44) as yavugasa Kujula Kasasa Kushanasa, 'Of the chief Kujula Kadphises the Kushan'.

[5] Foucher II p. 519; de la Vallée-Poussin p. 312.

[6] See Foucher II p. 442.

[7] *BMC* Pl. XXXII, 14; *ASI* 1915–16 p. 34 no. 20.

to early in the first century B.C. *at latest*, and that agrees with the already noticed parallelism of some of the Greek ornamentation of Gandhāra art with coins of Telephus and Hippostratus. This means that Foucher's chronology for the beginning of the Gandhāra school was substantially right.

The Gandhāra Buddha is then at least a century, and perhaps nearer two centuries, older than the Indian Buddhas of Mathurā; by the time the latter started, statues of Buddha had been common for generations in the North-West of India, the original Greek territory, and Mathurā, situated on the great high-road, the most frequented road in India, which ran from Pātaliputra and the Ganges country through Mathurā, Taxila, and Pushkalāvatī to Kapisa and so to the West, could not possibly have remained ignorant of them. I shall not instance the pieces at Mathurā which show Greek motives unintelligently applied by some Indian artist commissioned to do something which he did not understand;[1] but Greeks had ruled Mathurā for three-quarters of a century, down to somewhere about 100 B.C., and therefore, whenever Mathurā first received Greek artistic *influences*,[2] it is idle to suppose that people there did not *know* what the Greeks were doing—quite a different matter—or that there could have been in that town a second creation of the Buddha image bearing no relation at all to the first creation.

I am only concerned with chronology, and the long priority of the Gandhāra Buddha is now, I think, proved by a definite piece of evidence; but I should like to sketch what, in my opinion, must have been the course of events.[3] The Greek, as we have seen, was becoming Indianised from about the beginning of the first century B.C., and therewith was born the Gandhāra school, which *must* from its date be in the line of development of the Greeks who came to India from Bactria; the Indian Buddhist, influenced by Bhakti (p. 406), wanted the story of the life and previous lives of Buddha cut in stone, and the Greek was

[1] Heracles strangling the Nemean lion, the so-called Silenus, and the Bacchanalian scene; this last has been dated to the first century B.C. by Ramaprasad Chanda, *ASI* 1922–3 p. 167. Vogel I think has not dated these pieces, but would, I imagine, on his argument, put them later; see generally his articles *ASI* 1906–7 p. 137, *ib.* 1909–10 p. 63, and *La Sculpture de Mathurâ* p. 82.

[2] Vogel has always contended that they came through the medium of the Gandhāra school.

[3] It has been suggested to me by Professor A. D. Nock that there is in a measure a parallel to be found in Mithraic iconography, as last studied by Fr. Saxl, *Mithra* 1931.

now, as he might not have been in the time of Demetrius and Menander, ready to respond. The first Greek artist had to decide what to do with the perpetually recurring central figure. He may or may not have known, or cared, whether Gautama had been a man or a god; being a Greek, he only knew one way of representing either, and therewith was born, in the mind of some unknown and obscure Greek sculptor, the idea of representing Buddha in human form. The Greek artists took their own Apollo type and Indianised it; the steps from the Greek Apollo to the Graeco-Indian Buddha have often been traced.[1] But their Buddha went no deeper than their Apollo; he was just a beautiful man; you may search these suave faces[2] in vain for what should have been there, the inner spirit of the great Reformer.

So some Indians ultimately felt.[3] It can only have been dissatisfaction with the established Gandhāra type of Buddha which first produced the Indian type at Mathurā. It was recognised that it was now far too late to represent Buddha in any way but as a man; but they wanted a Buddha of their own, not a Greek Apollo. How far at the start any question of spirituality entered into the matter may be doubtful; something may have been due to the Kushan king Huvishka's patronage of Mathurā art; in any event the light ladies who figure as Yakshīs on some Buddhist monuments there[4] do not suggest any excessive spirituality among the Buddhists of Mathurā. Their first essays at making Buddhas of their own produced, according to Dr Vogel, only mediocre figures, gauche and heavy and of an astonishing uniformity.[5] But Indian artists had to learn how to express themselves, which took time; they were struggling toward something better.

Most writers who regard the Indian Buddhas of Mathurā as earlier than the Gandhāra type have not attempted to explain, though it urgently calls for explanation, how the Indian came to discard the old rule of only representing Buddha by symbols, which had lasted for

[1] Beside Foucher II pp. 283–4, see a number of images of Buddha arranged to show the transition from the Apollo type by A. H. Longhurst, *Illustrated London News* 1929 i p. 394 (March 9th); also the development arranged on Pl. VII in P. Masson-Oursel and others, *Ancient India* 1934.

[2] What I mean can be illustrated from various figures in Foucher, vol. II: p. 291 fig. 445, the Buddha in the Guides' Mess, Mardān; p. 303 fig. 449 (Peshawur Museum); p. 309 fig. 452 (Lahore Museum). Also *ASI* 1915–16 Pl. XX *d*.

[3] Cf. E. B. Havell, *A handbook of Indian art* 1920 p. 152.

[4] Vogel, *La Sculpture de Mathurâ* p. 32 Pls. XVIII, XIX.

[5] *Ib.* p. 39.

centuries, and to make of him a human figure; an interesting view however *has* been put forward, which at first sight seems as though it might provide an alternative to the explanation that it was due to Greek example, and that is that it was due to the penetration of Buddhism by Bhakti.[1] But the chronological difficulty is considerable. Bhakti, which means devotion, has been defined as 'passionate self-oblivious devotion to a deity' (say rather, a supreme personal Being) 'who in return bestows his grace';[2] its scripture is the Bhagavadgītā, which was added as an episode to the Mahābhārata and which enjoins the worship of a personal god.[3] When Bhakti began to penetrate Buddhism seems unknown, but it substituted devotion to the person of Buddha for the original idea of Buddha as a teacher, and was one of the factors which led to the divine Buddha of the 'Great Vehicle', the Mahāyāna. But Bhakti penetrated other religions also: it created the new Vishnuism, the personal cult of Vishnu-Krishna as an all-embracing god, the Bhāgavat whose worshippers were called Bhāgavatas.[4] Possibly the new Vishnuism did originate at Mathurā, the traditional birthplace of Krishna, but it is far older than the Mathurā Buddhas; it is said to be mentioned in Pānini,[5] and also in a Brahmi inscription of the second century B.C.,[6] and indeed it rather looks as if Bhakti, generally speaking, may have been partly the reaction of the Indian mind to, or against, the foreign invasions, Persian and Greek. By about 100 B.C. the Bhāgavata religion was well established in places as far distant as Taxila and Vidisā, as is shown by the column at Besnagar of Heliodorus the Bhāgavata from Taxila (p. 381) and by another column two miles away at Bhilsa,[7] set up by a man named Bhāgavata in connection with the temple of Bhāgavat and dated in the reign of the Sunga king Bhāgavata (the names explain themselves); while in the course of the first century B.C., besides the occurrence of the word in inscriptions,[8] a king of the Audumbaras in the eastern Punjab called himself a Bhāgavata.[9]

[1] Ramaprasad Chanda, *ASI* 1925–6 p. 125; Konow, *Berlin SB* 1928 p. 570, who quotes to the same effect (p. 566) a study by A. K. Coomaraswamy in 1927 which I have not seen. Cf. de la Vallée-Poussin pp. 255–6.

[2] Sir Charles Eliot, *Hinduism and Buddhism* II, 1921, p. 180. See also Winternitz, Eng. trans. II p. 435.

[3] Eliot *op. cit.* pp. 180, 200; Winternitz *op. cit.* p. 437.

[4] Eliot *op. cit.* p. 182.

[5] Not later than 300 B.C., *CHI* p. 113.

[6] Eliot *op. cit.* p. 197, referring to no. 6 in Lüders' list of Brahmi inscriptions.

[7] D. R. Bhandarkar, *ASI* 1913–14 p. 190.

[8] Eliot *op. cit.* p. 197, citing no. 1112 in Lüders' list.

[9] *BMC India* pp. lxxxv, 123, on coins of Mahādeva.

Though it is not known when Bhakti first began to affect Buddhism, it seems impossible to separate this by any long interval from the origins of the Bhāgavata religion, which probably gave the impulse[1] and which was well established in the Buddhist North-West by or before *c.* 100 B.C.; and where Bhakti may come in over the question of the Buddha statue is not in relation to the Mathurā Buddhas at all but in relation to the creation of the Gandhāra Buddha in the early first century B.C.;[2] it may have been the reason why the Buddhists of the North-West began to want the lives of Buddha glorified in stone and why they acquiesced in and took up the methods of their Greek artists, who could only represent Buddha, as they represented their own gods, in human form. The Indian artists of Mathurā discarded the old rule of representing Buddha only by symbols, not because of Bhakti, but because for generations that rule had vanished from the Graeco-Buddhist art of the North-West and they could not fall behind; it was too late to do anything else.

Ultimately the Indian artist reached what he sought, a spirituality which the Greek Apollo type could never have given him. Beside the writers whom I have been quoting, Sir John Marshall has pointed out[3] that, in the great Buddhas of the Gupta period, we get a spiritual quality in the Indian conception of the Divine which could not have arisen in a school based upon classical tradition; and I may perhaps refer to the wonderful and saintly face of a Buddha-statue in the Lahore Museum,[4] where the bones, outlined through the starved flesh, bring vividly before us one who had suffered deeply with and for suffering humanity. But all that Indian artists did—and it is immaterial here whether, as regards *style*, all subsequent Buddhas derive from the Indian Buddhas of Mathurā or from the Buddhas of Gandhāra—originated in a reaction against the established Greek type of Buddha. What they might have done had the Greek type not existed is bootless speculation; in the way that things did happen as matter of history, all the Buddha-statues in Asia with all their implications—and the Buddha-statue played its part in that conversion of Buddha from a man into a

[1] Ramaprasad Chanda, *op. cit.* p. 125, who, however, says 'evidently', not 'probably'.

[2] Winternitz suggested this, Eng. trans. I p. 255; it is much the most satisfying theory chronologically.

[3] *ASI* 1907–8 p. 40, quoting Havell; *CHI* p. 649.

[4] Figured in Foucher II p. 439.

god which took place in the Mahāyāna[1]—are there because some nameless Greek artist in Gandhāra, who had to earn his living, first portrayed Buddha in the only way he knew of. I have been tracing the history of an *idea*, the idea of representing the founder of Buddhism as a man; and that idea originated, not with India, but with Greece. It was the one great mark which the Greeks set upon India; and they did it by accident.

But far-reaching as the Greek mark may have been, and deeply as it has influenced many countries in Eastern Asia which Greeks never knew, it no longer influences India: Buddhism has long since vanished from the land of its birth. The Greeks, as we have seen, did to some small extent affect Indians while they were in India, and were also to some extent affected by them; but there was nothing that was to be permanent there, not even the Buddha-statue. What I said earlier in this chapter, that (except for the Buddha-statue) the history of India would have been essentially what it has been had Greeks never existed, only needs now one very trifling qualification—the Alexander-descents of some hill rulers. I have already considered the origin and meaning of these when writing of Bactria (Chap. VII), and the part played in them by the fictitious Seleucid pedigree; the only thing which need be added here is to call attention to the fondness of Indians of all classes for keeping pedigrees, which with them, as the Purānas show, really took the place of history.[2] As in Bactria, so also in India, I have never met with a complete list of the Alexander-descents, but a recent writer[3] has given an interesting account of two of these hill rulers, Shah Sikander Khan, Mir (or Thum) of Nagir, who likes visitors to remark on the resemblance of his profile to that of the heads on some Greek coins (which happens to be true), and his elder brother Sir Mohamed Nazim Khan, Mir (or Thum) of Hunza; those who like picturesque links across the ages may find one in the fact that Hunza is to-day ruled by a descendant of Alexander who bears a British title. And that is all. It might serve as a text for yet another sermon on the vanity of human wishes that, while all else which Greeks did or sought to do in India has long vanished from that country, the one thing which still survives there in living form is a legend based on a fiction.

[1] The Gandhāra statues of Bodhisattvas show that Mahayanism was already beginning in Gandhāra art.

[2] Winternitz III p. 81.

[3] R. C. F. Schomberg, *Between the Oxus and the Indus* 1935, esp. pp. 106, 145.

CONCLUSION

MUCH was lost to the history of Hellenism when the Greek accounts of their empire in Bactria and India which once existed were allowed to perish. The story of the Greeks in the Farther East is notable in two aspects, first as the history of a march state and secondly as a unique chapter in the dealings of Greeks with the peoples of Asia; and to omit the Euthydemid dynasty from Hellenistic history, as has usually been done, and to confine that history to the four dynasties which bordered on the Mediterranean—one of which, the Attalids, was of very secondary importance—throws that history at least out of balance. A few words may be said by way of conclusion about these two aspects of the Graeco-Bactrian empire.

Professor Toynbee in his great work has dealt once for all with the characteristics of the march state at large[1] and has given many instances of how such a state, under the stimulus of external pressure, might be expected to develop such strength that it would not only master the pressure but would have plenty of energy over for other purposes. It might perhaps be said that in the Greek world Macedonia had been such a state: exposed to barbarian pressure from the North and to the pressure of Olynthus and Athens from the side of the sea, the little country developed such amazing vitality that it not only mastered both pressures and for two centuries shielded Greece from the barbarism of the Balkans but was able also to conquer the great empire of Persia. But however that may be, Bactria under the Euthydemids was a perfect illustration of the history of a march state.

When in the middle of the third century B.C. the hand of the Seleucid slackened on the dangerous north-eastern frontier and a body of Parni from the steppes broke in and set up the little kingdom which Greeks called Parthian, Bactria not only stood in the gap and shielded the Graeco-Iranian world from the nomads for over a century, but the

[1] A. J. Toynbee, *A Study of History* II (2nd ed. 1935) pp. 112–208, 'The Stimulus of Pressures'. A march state was a state on the boundary of the community to which by race and culture it belonged, and as such acted as the shield of the interior against pressure from some alien community, in the case of Bactria the northern nomads. The classical instance is Brandenburg as the Teutonic outpost against the Slavs.

story of Macedonia repeated itself, line upon line, in the Farther East: Euthydemus was Philip II, Bactria was Macedonia, the derelict Mauryan empire was the Persian empire, and Demetrius was a second Alexander. As Philip had completed the making of Macedonia and the welding of its feudal princes and its tribes into a people actively aware of its unity, so Euthydemus was able to complete the process—others may have begun it—of turning Bactria, with its Iranian barons, its Greek settlers, its serf peasantry, into a real state, which promptly developed such strength that while it held off nomadism with one hand it was able to annex most of Northern India with the other. Alexander had had difficulty enough in conquering the powerful Iranian barons of the marches, and as he knew that mere conquest was useless unless you could find a way of living with the conquered afterwards, he had sought to reconcile them by marrying into their class. Whether by accident or design, Seleucus had also married the daughter of a march baron, which may—we do not know—have favourably affected the fortunes of her son Antiochus I in the North-East. But in some way Euthydemus did succeed in doing what Alexander had meant to do; he did reconcile the great landowners and secure their co-operation. That no doubt was always possible, on terms; but what is extraordinary is that he did it while at the same time he was also transforming the peasantry and substituting for the open serf village of Alexander's day the quasi-autonomous communities in large walled villages which Chang-k'ien found in Bactria. We would give much to know his secret; what it meant to unite Bactria can be seen by looking at the complete failure of the Seleucids in regard to the rest of Iran, which fell away from them almost automatically as soon as the Parthians made it possible, while in Bactria the Parthians could never get a footing. Alexander had seen that ruling Iran was going to be the real difficulty, and before he died he had decided that the only solution was frankly to take her into partnership and create a Graeco-Iranian state. Whether even his genius and driving power could have carried this through against the opposition of the old-fashioned Macedonians was never to be put to the test; but Euthydemus, aided by the ever-present danger from the nomad world, was able to do it in Bactria.

Demetrius took the ideas of Alexander and of his father to India, and the kingdom he established there was not Greek but Graeco-Indian, some sort of a partnership. He had several advantages; one was the political position so skilfully exploited by himself and his lieutenants, which threw a good deal of India on to his side from the start; another was the fact that the attitude of Greeks, or of some Greeks, towards Indians differed somewhat from their attitude towards other 'barbarians'; they regarded them more as their equals. He was quite consciously copying Alexander: he meant to sit on the throne of the Mauryas as Alexander had sat on the throne of the Achaemenids. But there had been two Alexanders, the conqueror and the dreamer; and Demetrius' idea of an empire which was to be a kind of partnership between Greek and Indian was inspired by the Alexander who had dreamt of a human brotherhood. How much with Alexander may have been sentiment we do not know; he was great enough to indulge in all the sentiment he pleased, did he desire to. But naturally one does not attribute sentiment to Euthydemus and his son; what *they* wanted was a great empire, but they thought that in the world of their day co-operation between Greek and Asiatic, such as Alexander had envisaged, offered the best chance of making one. Something of their strength is shown by the fact that Demetrius' general Menander, who was not of his blood, carried on his policy wholeheartedly after his death; none of Alexander's generals had done as much.

If we look at the state-forms of the Hellenistic kingdoms in their prime, say in the third century, we see in Ptolemaic Egypt absolute monarchy unfettered by any other element in the state; we see in Antigonid Macedonia a monarchy limited by the age-old rights of the Macedonian people under arms; we see in Seleucid Asia a monarchy limited by the rights of many more or less autonomous cities, rights which in most cases they had themselves created. All three state-forms could be traced back to some aspect of Alexander's monarchy; all three dynasties could claim to be carrying on something which he had done. But there was another element in the matter, the huge mass of native subjects of the Alexander-monarchy; and we see no monarchy in the West which (putting religion aside) was subject to limitation, voluntary limitation of course, by the rights of its native subjects, though one does not know what Cleopatra VII might have done had she come at the beginning of Ptolemaic history instead of at the end.[1] But Hellenistic history would be imperfect had no dynasty made some sort of an attempt to put into practice, as the Stoics in some sense put into theory, not

[1] It is interesting, in connection with Demetrius as King of Justice, to compare the conception in the Cleopatra prophecy of the justice she is to bring to the world; Tarn, *JRS* XXXII, 1932, pp. 136, 139.

anything which Alexander had *done* but the greater thing which he had *dreamt*; and that is the importance of the Euthydemid dynasty during the three generations of its power (for politically Menander may be called a Euthydemid). The banishment of that dynasty from Greek to Indian history has been a sad impoverishment of the Hellenistic story.

But the successes of Euthydemus and his son were bought at a price. Naturally we do not know exactly what the co-operation of Greek and Asiatic meant in their hands, or how far, if at all, they limited their own autocracy by rights conferred upon their native subjects. But dim as is our sight in the historical twilight which is all that has been vouchsafed to us, two things stand out sharply enough: that some Indians saw in Demetrius something resembling the ideal King of Justice of their own traditions, and that many of Demetrius' Greek subjects were not in sympathy with his policy, just as many of Alexander's Macedonians had disliked his policy with regard to Persia. The result was seen when Antiochus IV sent his cousin Eucratides to attack Demetrius. Apart from their traditional feeling of loyalty toward the Seleucid, many of the Greeks of Bactria undoubtedly preferred the simple nationalist policy of the hellenising Antiochus to what they must have considered the pro-native policy of Demetrius; Demetrius is not the only king in history who has fallen because his ideas were too advanced for the majority of his subjects to follow them. The most important fact in the history of the Greek East is that something not very unlike the modern struggle between nationalism and co-operation was fought out two thousand years ago under the shadow of the Hindu Kush.

Perhaps I may be permitted here one moment of pure fantasy. There is in existence, I believe somewhere in the United States, a slab of stone brought from Swat on which a Greek artist has carved two figures. I have not sought to trace it, as it is not historical evidence; but the figures have appeared in a very remarkable work of fiction,[1] and one who saw the slab before it was sold has assured me that the description of them there given is entirely accurate. One of the figures is a Greek Victory, and facing her is a strange composite creature with the head of a Greek Zeus and the body, repulsively rendered, of a native; and it pleases me to imagine that some Greek nationalist was here giving his views of the Indian empire of Demetrius and Menander: '*This* then is the result of our victories—this mongrel monstrosity.' It is but a fancy; and his

[1] A story, *ad veritatem ficta*, called *The Silver Hand of Alexander*, by an anonymous author, in Blackwood's *Tales from the Outposts*, vol. 1, 1932.

view would assuredly not have been the only one, though it played its part.

Unfortunate as were the results of Antiochus' attack for the future of Greek civilisation in the East, one must in fairness admit that he had plenty of provocation. It may speak well for the Greeks of the Farther East that, both in Bactria and in India, they were never, except in the extreme east of their Indian realm, ousted by the peoples they ruled; but nothing ever prevented Greeks themselves from tearing each other to pieces so long as they had the power, and, as in the West, so in the East, they had fallen victims to themselves before they fell victims to the foreign conqueror. The weakened march state of Bactria itself was destroyed by a sudden blow. But its defence against its own domestic barbarians, the peoples it knew, always held good, like that of Macedonia. The Macedonian defence was broken once for a moment, but by a strange race from the distant North Sea; and when the Bactrian defence failed at the end it was broken by an unknown people from the borders of China, who not only possessed irresistible numbers but had perhaps been rendered desperate by their long failure to find any land where they could settle in peace. Had Fortune allowed Demetrius to consolidate Bactria and Northern India into one empire, it should have been strong enough to withstand even the Yueh-chi; but the lot fell otherwise.

The story of the Euthydemid dynasty is then, in one sense, the story of a courageous experiment which failed, though there is nothing to show that it need have failed but for external interference. But the experiment is only one aspect of it. In our mechanical age to-day, when the hopes, or the fears, of many are that the future will be a future of men thinking and acting in droves, at the mercy of mass belief and mass propaganda and little less mechanised than the machines they serve, it may please a few here and there to go back for a moment to a simpler and less sophisticated world, a world of wonderful chances for the individual, where great risks might still bring great prizes for those who ventured. It is with some such thoughts in mind that I have attempted to see what could be recovered, if only in barest outline, of the lost story of the Greeks in the Farther East and of the dynasty which so nearly led them to amazing success. For one thing about that story is sure; win or lose, succeed or fail, it is the story of a very great adventure.

EXCURSUS

THE MILINDAPAÑHA AND PSEUDO-ARISTEAS

The Milindapañha[1] or Questions of Milinda is the one extant work professedly dealing with any of the Greek monarchs in the Far East; for Milinda, beyond any question, is the king Menander.[2] It exists in a Pali version and, in part, in a Chinese translation of the fourth century A.D. of which two recensions are extant. The Pali work falls into two well-marked divisions; the first comprises pp. 1–89 in Trenckner's edition of the Pali text, being books I–III inclusive;[3] the second and longer part comprises all that follows. It is now generally agreed that Part II is later than Part I and the work of a different hand,[4] and it is also generally agreed that Part I (or perhaps I should say the original of Part I) cannot be placed too long after Menander's death; but I need not quote the datings suggested, for none of those who have professedly dealt with the work have investigated Menander's chronology and have usually put him near the end of the second century B.C. or even in the first century. The Chinese translation includes Part I and a few pages of Part II.

The work is cast in the form of a dialogue between Menander and a Buddhist sage Nāgasena, with an introduction in which Menander, at his capital Sāgala, appears as a great king fond of learned disputations, together with his 500 Yonakas, four of whom play a part in setting the scene for the dialogue proper. In the first part Menander's professed object is not the

[1] I cite this work in Rhys Davids' translation of the Pali version, 2 vols. = *Sacred books of the East* vols. XXXV–VI, 1890, 1894; I give his pages and in brackets the pages of Trenckner's Pali text; Part I is vol. I pp. 1–136. I have also consulted L. Finot, *Les questions de Milinda* 1923 (translation of Part I); O. F. Schrader, *Die Fragen des Königs Menandros* 1905; Winternitz II, 1920, pp. 139 *sqq.* (II pp. 174 *sqq.* of the English translation, 1933); P. Pelliot, *Les noms propres dans les traductions chinoises du Milindapañha*, *JA* 1914 p. 379; Mrs Rhys Davids, *The Milinda Questions* 1930. I have been unable to see R. Garbe, *Der Milindapañha, ein kulturhistorischer Roman* 1903, and A. Gueth, *Bhikku Nyanatiloka, Die Fragen des Milinda* 1919. For the Chinese translation I have used Demiéville's exhaustive study, who gives (pp. 75 *sqq.*) a French translation *sub tit. Sûtra du bhikshu Nagasena.* A bibliography of the literature relating to the Chinese version is given by Siegfried Behrsing in *BSOS* VII, ii, 1934, p. 335, and of that relating to the Pali version *ib.* p. 517.

[2] See now Pelliot *op. cit.* pp. 380–5, and for the interchange of *l* and *n* Sylvain Lévi, *JA* 1915 p. 101.

[3] It concludes with 'Here ends the answering of the problems of the questions of Milinda', Rhys Davids I p. 136.

[4] Rhys Davids (against the general belief) argued for a single author, as does Mrs Rhys Davids *op. cit.* I cannot believe myself that the very different pictures of Milinda himself in Parts I and II are by the same hand.

pursuit of knowledge but a dialectical victory over Nāgasena, though he does not in fact keep his end up very well. In the second part, in which Menander gives Nāgasena a succession of dilemmas to solve, the king has become a Buddhist devotee humbly seeking knowledge, who at the end forsakes his throne and the world and enters the Order. Part II, notwithstanding its merits as literature—has it not preserved for us the Song of the Two Fairy Birds?—has no pretensions to be history; what I shall have to say deals with Part I. The charm with which the whole work is written and its importance for Buddhist doctrine—it stands just outside the Tripitaka, the Pali Canon of Buddhist Scriptures[1]—has led to it being much treated by Indian and Buddhist scholars, but chiefly of course for its doctrinal content; and it has been asserted, in all good faith but without sufficient knowledge from the Greek side, that it has no value for history and contains no trace of anything Greek.[2] It has never been examined by any Greek scholar, and it is time that this should be done. With Buddhist doctrine I am not concerned; my aim is to try to get the relation of Part I to Greek rule in India.

Kings who liked disputations were a commonplace in Indian tradition, as were philosophical discussions in Indian life; some sage, arriving at a village, would challenge all and sundry to dispute with him, the conclusion being that the vanquished became the disciple of the victor,[3] as at the end of Part II Milinda becomes the disciple of Nāgasena. Also, with the Dialogues of the Buddha, the dialogue had become in India a well-established literary form for the conveyance of instruction in religion or philosophy. What was *not* known in Indian literature—what had never happened before and was not to happen again—was that the interlocutor in a dialogue should be a foreign king and that the aim of the interlocutor should be a dialectical victory; for the interlocutors in the Dialogues of the Buddha, like those in the Dialogues of Plato, are only an agreeable piece of machinery for eliciting the opinions of Buddha or Socrates. The model of the Milindapañha has often been sought in one of the Dialogues of the Buddha, the Sāmaññaphala Sutta;[4] but though it is pretty certain that one section of the introduction to the Milinda echoes the introduction to the older dialogue,[5] the scheme of the two works is totally different. In the Sāmaññaphala Sutta the king Ajātasattu, who really wants to know, asks one reasoned question, naming various learned men (some of them known to be historical) who have been unable to give him the answer, and the Buddha then makes a long reply; there is no working

[1] For the Canon see Winternitz II chap. I and *CHI* pp. 192 *sqq*.

[2] *E.g.* Winternitz II p. 141 n. 1 (Eng. trans. p. 176 n. 2), also citing Garbe *op. cit.* p. 114; Mrs Rhys Davids *op. cit.* p. 21. It is a commonplace.

[3] Rhys Davids, *Buddhist India* 1903 pp. 247–8, *Buddhism* 1896 p. 98. The *Upanishads* also give cases of kings instructing Brahmans (L. H. Gray, *Enc. of Rel. and Ethics* VII p. 721), but that is a rather different matter.

[4] Translation by Rhys Davids in *Dialogues of the Buddha* I, 1899, p. 65 (= *Sacred Books of the Buddhists* II).

[5] Rhys Davids (*Milinda*) p. 8 n. 2.

out of the argument by question and answer. But though Indian scholars may be reminded of the Sāmaññaphala Sutta or the Upanishads, any Greek scholar who looks into the Milinda will at once be reminded of something very different, a Hellenistic work in which the writer makes a foreign king put a large number of questions to the wise men of the writer's own race and creed, the whole work being designed to do for the religion of the Jewish writer what Part I of the Milinda was designed to do for the religion of its Buddhist author: the Letter of Pseudo-Aristeas. I shall come to this work presently; I hope that it may help to resolve one or two of the problems which the Milinda presents to the Greek scholar.

There are however two preliminary points. It has been suggested that certain passages in the Pali text of book I of the Milinda are interpolations;[1] but, if they are, it happens that none of them are material for what I want, so this need not be considered. More important is the widespread belief that the Pali text is not the original, but is a translation of a work written either in Sanscrit or some northern Prakrit.[2] Part of the argument for this is philological and must be left to Pali scholars, but there has also been a desire to account for differences in the Pali and Chinese versions by supposing both to be translations from a common original. This supposition does not commend itself to me.[3] It is hard to believe that a Chinese translator some five centuries later, dealing with a foreign language and a long forgotten geography, would be bound to reproduce his original unaltered, even if (a large assumption) he desired to do so (one could find many analogies); and it is said that the Chinese text itself has been subject to revisions and modifications,[4] which must surely affect the question. The question then whether the Pali text be original or derivative is one for philology, but it does not affect what I have to say, which, put briefly, is this: there are in the Pali Milinda as we have it certain small but quite definite Hellenistic Greek elements which cannot be explained on any current theory. I must now examine these and see whither they lead us. These Greek elements can more or less be dated; to date the Pali text of Part I is not my province, but reason may appear for suggesting a *terminus post quem non*.

The first thing is the word Yonaka, used for a Greek; it is used twice of Greeks generally,[5] and twice of Menander's 500 Yonakas; except for Milinda Part I the word seemingly only occurs once again in India, in inscription 19 from the Nasik cave (p. 257 n. 3).[6] The ordinary Sanscrit word for a Greek

[1] Winternitz II p. 143 n. 2 (Eng. trans. p. 178 n. 1).

[2] Rhys Davids I p. xi, II p. xii; Pelliot *op. cit.* p. 380; Winternitz II p. 142 n. 1; Demiéville p. 4; Mrs Rhys Davids *op. cit.* p. 5; J. Rahder, *Groot-Indië*, cited by Behrsing *op. cit.* p. 343.

[3] Neither did it to Rhys Davids, II p. xii, though he believed in an older original on philological grounds.

[4] Demiéville pp. 3, 4.

[5] Pp. 2 (1), 105 (68).

[6] I have found no clear statement that it never occurs elsewhere; but the only earlier Pali writings are the books of the Buddhist Canon, which are not likely to

was Yavana[1]. This is the Greek Ἰάϝων, and it certainly came to India through Achaemenid Persia, for in the Old Persian of Darius' inscriptions the form used is always Iauna,[2] which was also the colloquial form.[3] The fact that Hebrew made of it Javan (Yawan) and the Hittites Yevanna has led to a suggestion that it came to India not through Persia but through Semitic Babylon;[4] but this seems impossible, for in the Babylonian version of Darius' inscriptions the form used is always ia-ma-nu or ia-a-ma-nu,[5] corresponding to a form Yamanim in a document from Ras Shamra,[6] and this cannot possibly make Yavana. The Prakrit word, used in the third century B.C. in Asoka's inscriptions, is Yona. I have never seen its relation to Yavana discussed, so it is probably unknown; the obvious supposition is that Yona stands to Yavana as Ἴων to Ἰάϝων (the relationship of the two Greek words is also unknown)[7] and that it was derived directly from Ἴων, for no similar Persian word has been cited and the third century is late for a borrowing from Persia.

Yonaka also did not come through Achaemenid Persia,[8] as it corresponds to nothing in classical Greek; it is not Ἰωνικός (which incidentally does not mean Ionian), but implies a form Ἰωνακός, unknown to classical Greek; and the appearance of the word is far too late for a borrowing from Persia, for no one would put Part I of the Pali Milinda *earlier* than the late second century B.C., and the Nasik cave inscription is probably not earlier than the

refer to Greeks, and neither Lévi in *Quid de Graecis* nor Weber in *Berlin SB* 1890 pp. 907 *sqq.*, who give every mention of Yavanas they can find, gives any other instance of Yonaka. I thought I had discovered another in B. C. Law, *Some Kshatriya tribes of ancient India* 1923 p. 250, who among his ancient sources cites a passage containing the word Yonaka from a work called *Sāsanavamsa*; but I found that this work was written in Burma in 1861 (Winternitz II p. 176)—not the only time in this period that a modern work has been quoted by somebody as ancient authority.

[1] Lévi, *Quid de Graecis* p. 3, n.: Yavana Sanscrit, Yona Prakrit. That Yavana in this period usually, though not always, means Greek has long been settled by many lines of evidence. O. Stein's recent contention (*Indian Culture* I, 1935, p. 343) that it never means Greek is mere paradox; he examines one line of evidence only, and from the Greek side inadequately.

[2] F. H. Weissbach, *Die Keilinschriften der Achämeniden* 1911: Behistun §6; Persepolis e §2; Naks-i-Rustam §3. So in the inscription from Darius' palace at Susa; Kent, *JAOS* LIII, 1933, p. 1, ll. 33, 42, 48, who gives it as Yaunā.

[3] *Ἰαοναῦ* in Aristophanes, *Ach.* 104.

[4] C. C. Torrey, *Yawān und Hellas*, *JAOS* XXV, 1904, p. 302.

[5] See note 2, *above*.

[6] E. Cavaignac, *Mélanges Bidez* I, 1934, p. 86.

[7] Busolt, *Griech. Gesch.* I[2] p. 283; Ion (*Ἴων*) 3 in PW (Eitrem). See Addenda.

[8] Weissbach, *Ionaka* in PW, says 'wahrscheinlich = altpersisch iaunaka'; but as he gives no reference for 'iaunaka' I take him to mean that this would be the O.P. form and not that such a form actually existed. It makes no difference either way to my argument.

middle of the first century B.C. (p. 257 n. 3). The questions to be answered are, where did the author of Part I of the Pali Milinda find the word Yonaka, and why did he use it instead of either of the current terms, Yavana or Yona? Where he found it is not in doubt; for the form Ἰωνακός, though unknown to classical Greek, existed at this time in the current Hellenistic Greek of the Farther East, one instance being certain and another almost certain. One of Ptolemy's innumerable sources gave him the phrase Ἰωνακὰ πόλις, 'Greek-town', for a city on the Gulf of Bushire, presumably Antioch in Persis;[1] and the word seemingly occurs again in the Ch'ien-han-shu. The story of Yin-mo-fu who ruled in Yung-kiu in the time of the Han emperor Yuan-ti (48–33 B.C.) is dealt with elsewhere (p. 339); all that need be said here is that the story as Pan-ku gives it must have been taken from a report made by the Chinese general Wen-chung who played a part in it, for no other source for an incident in the remote Paropamisadae seems possible; and Wen-chung can only have got the name Yung-kiu (Jong-k'ut), which is Yonaki, 'Greek-town',[2] from people on the spot. Yonaka therefore was taken from the current Hellenistic Greek of the time,[3] whether from the spoken language or from some Greek writing, which means that in either case the author of Part I of the Milinda knew some Greek. This is confirmed by the fact that the wealthy Indian merchant who called himself a Yonaka in the Nasik inscription was a citizen of the Greek city Demetrias (p. 257) and as such probably knew some Greek also.

Why the author of Part I of the Milinda used the term Yonaka will, I hope, presently appear; but I must point out in passing that if the Pali work was derived from a Sanscrit or Northern Prakrit original it is difficult to see why the common Sanscrit or Prakrit word, Yavana or Yona, was not used; and it is equally difficult to see how, if the Hellenistic Yonaka *was* used, it kept its place in a translation, seeing that even in Part II of the Pali text it has been replaced by an explanatory term, as it has in the Chinese translation. In fact the word Yonaka is a considerable difficulty in the way of current beliefs.

I come to Menander's 500 Yonakas. They are introduced without any explanation of what they were.[4] That they were really his Council—the ordinary Council of every Hellenistic king, which in another aspect was his 'Friends'—is not in doubt; the number 500 is of course conventional and is fully explained elsewhere (p. 267). The author himself might perhaps have known what Menander's Yonakas were, but the point is that he assumes that his Indian readers will know also, a large assumption. He is supposed to

[1] Ptol. VI, 4, 2; see Tarn, *JEA* XV, 1929, p. 11 n. 4. It is not uncommon for Ptolemy to give, as a town, the description without the name, *e.g.* VI, 1, 5, κωμόπολις; VI, 7, 9, Ἀραβίας ἐμπόριον. See p. 13.

[2] On the various spellings and the sound see p. 340 n. 4.

[3] The word Jonaka is said to be still in use on the west coast of India for foreigners; K. R. Pisharoti, *Indian Culture* II, 1936, p. 575.

[4] Pp. 36–7 (22–3), the king is attended by 'the 500 Yonakas'. That is all.

have written in north-western India, and this assumption shows that the allusion to Menander's Yonakas was written at latest soon after Menander's death. Even so, it may have puzzled Indian readers, for later times at once felt the need of explanation; in Part II of the Pali text 'Yonakas' is replaced by 'ministers',[1] and a corresponding expression is used by the Chinese translator of Part I.[2] What emerges so far, then, is that the writer of Part I of the Pali Milinda knew some Greek and that the reference to the Yonakas was written very soon after Menander's death; even so, he asks rather much of his Indian readers.

In fact he asks still more of them. He himself seems to be so familiar with the four-square type of Hellenistic city—the type described by Polybius (VI, 31, 10) as cut into four quarters by two great roads crossing at right angles in the middle of the city, with four gates at the ends of the two roads—that he can use it as an illustration: Nāgasena says 'It is like the case of the guardian of a city who, when seated at the cross-roads in the middle of the city, could see a man coming from the East or the South or the West or the North';[3] and this is identical with what Strabo (XII, 566) says about the cross-roads of Nicaea in Bithynia, 'so that from one stone in the middle of the gymnasium a man could see the four gates'. Indians had their own system of town-planning, but their cities were not built like that.[4] It used to be said that we hardly knew a Greek city built like that either,[5] except Alexandria in Egypt and Nicaea in Bithynia; but this was due to the cities excavated having mostly been old cities in Asia Minor remodelled, and it now appears that enough cities in Syria which exhibit the four-square plan are known to warrant the statement that this seems to have been the usual plan of the new

[1] II p. 373 (419), 'the 500 high ministers of the king'.

[2] Demiéville p. 95 (xxviii), 'Les ministres de l'entourage du roi'. So pp. 90 (xxiv), 93 (xxvii).

[3] P. 95 (62). Finot's translation p. 107 is identical.

[4] K. Rangachari, *IHQ* IV, 1928, pp. 102–3: according to the *Silpasāstras*, if a city be square with four gates at north, east, south, west, the middle part must be a square with a temple at each corner and four roads connecting the four temples—a very different matter. (For his sources (one unpublished) see *IHQ* III, 1927, p. 813; the earliest *Silpasāstras* are supposed to be fifth or sixth century A.D., *i.e.* Gupta period.) For the normal square in the middle of the city, containing the temples, palace, and ancillary buildings, with four broad streets demarcating it, (compare *e.g.* the Parthian square at Hatra), see also B. B. Dutt, *Town Planning in Ancient India* 1925 pp. 258–64. One of these late writers, Mānasāra, is said to refer to towns with two large streets crossing each other at right angles in the centre (Dutt p. 124); but none such is known, and it might be a Greek or Roman echo; all these writers deal only with *theory*. The usual belief (Rangachari, *IHQ* III p. 824) is that in *fact* Indian towns grew up haphazard, like Delos.

[5] The two great cross-roads which appeared in the first air photographs of Seleuceia on the Tigris seem only to be lines between the tels. Excavation did not go far enough to show the plan of the city.

Seleucid foundations,[1] and it was of these that Polybius was thinking. Whether there was a Greek city in India built on the four-square plan is naturally unknown (once again, the location and excavation of Bucephala are badly needed); the nearest in distance to Sāgala actually recorded is Cartana-Tetragonis in the Paropamisadae (pp. 98 *sq.*). The author of Part I of the Milinda might have been a travelled man and might have seen such cities. But the point is that he expects his Indian readers to take his allusion, that is, to be familiar with the idea of treating Hellenistic cities of the four-square type as the normal type of city, rather than the Indian towns they knew. He could not really expect this; the probability therefore is that he just took his illustration from some Greek work because it was useful. For that the Greeks of India had been very familiar with the four-square type in Bactria-Sogdiana seems to follow from the fact that in Arab times the great cities there (except Bokhara) still retained the typical four gates.[2]

We have then two allusions in Part I of the Pali Milinda which are very near in time to Menander and which presuppose a knowledge of certain Greek things in the reader. Another Greek item is shown in a list of people which runs Yonakas, Kshatriyas, Brahmans, householders (bourgeois).[3] An Indian Buddhist writer would naturally put Kshatriyas before Brahmans, but no one but a Greek was going to put Greeks first of all; to Indians they were, at best, imperfect Kshatriyas (p. 173). This item, like the word Yonaka, is from some current Greek source, oral or written.

The next point is whether Menander's birthplace is historical or not. Seeing that the author of the Greek allusions in the Pali Milinda, whether he were the Pali writer or another, was very near in time to Menander, it would be absurd to reject his evidence about the birthplace; it is very much better than the evidence for most people's birthplaces in the Hellenistic world. In the Pali text Menander was born in a village called Kalasi not far from Alasanda (Alexandria of the Caucasus) and 200 yojanas from Sāgala;[4] I need not go into the distance, as Professor Rapson has said all that is necessary.[5] The *name* of the village has been doubted, because the Pali text also makes Nāgasena born in a village called Kajangala under the Himalayas, and as the only known village of that name was on the Ganges it has been suggested that a later interpolator added names at random;[6] but the argument is not a valid one, for it makes the untenable assumption that there cannot have been a second village of the same name. Another writer has proposed to correct Kalasi into Kapisa;[7] but an Indian author of the North-West would not have called Kapisa a village, and it is not scientific to turn an unknown name into a known one without some clear reason. In any case, whether the

[1] Fr. Cumont, *CAH* XI p. 634.

[2] W. (V. V.) Barthold, *Turkestan down to the Mongol Invasion*[2] 1928 pp. 78 (Balkh), 85 (Samarcand), 100 (Merv), 147 (Gurgānj).

[3] P. 105 (68).

[4] P. 127 (82–3).

[5] *CHI* p. 550.

[6] Demiéville p. 23 n. 1.

[7] A. Foucher, *JA* 1929, I, p. 244; *BSOS* VI, 1930–2, p. 344.

unknown name Kalasi be correct or not, we have the invaluable fact that Menander was born in a *village*. Hellenistic queens did not live in villages, neither were Hellenistic princes born in them; consequently—and this is the point which matters—Menander was born a commoner, and was not therefore a Euthydemid (see further p. 141).

This conclusion is not affected by the very different version of the Chinese translation several centuries later, which makes him born a prince.[1] He had already, in Part II of the Pali Milinda, become a prince, descended from a long line of Kshatriya ancestors;[2] it is usual enough, in the successive stages of a story, for a commoner who achieves fame to turn into a prince, but no one has ever known a prince turn into a commoner. That is simple; but the Chinese translator has gone on to alter the locality of Menander's birth. He describes Alasanda as 2000 yojanas from Sāgala instead of 200 (*i.e.* he makes it Alexandria in Egypt) and makes Menander born heir to the throne of a country near Alasanda beside the sea.[3] It is indeed unfortunate that a number of French scholars should have championed this as against the Pali version, and should have believed that Alasanda from the start meant Alexandria in Egypt and that the Pali writer altered an original 2000 into 200.[4] If the Pali text be the original, such a theory is of course indefensible. But even if not, the theory first violates the sound canon of historical criticism that the smaller number is to be preferred unless there be very good reason to the contrary, and then lands us in a historical absurdity; for where does anyone propose to find, near Alexandria in Egypt about 210–200 B.C., a country on the sea ruled by a Greek dynasty? The matter is really free from difficulty. The Chinese translator had never heard of Alexandria of the Caucasus; if he had heard of the capital of the Paropamisadae at all, he would only know the name Kapisa (p. 433 n. 1 and App. 6); to him Alasanda meant, and could only mean, the only Alexandria he knew of, Alexandria in Egypt, and he altered 200 yojanas to 2000 accordingly, but he called attention to this by recording the distance in yojanas as well as in Chinese li, which should put anyone upon his guard. Also he knew nothing himself about

[1] Demiéville p. 79 (ix), 'naquit au bord de la mer comme prince héritier du roi d'un pays'; so p. 90 (xxiii).

[2] II p. 206 (329).

[3] Demiéville p. 168 (cviii) and see n. 1 above.

[4] Pelliot *op. cit.* pp. 413 17; followed by Demiéville p. 168 n. 2, Finot p. 157 n. 86, and Grousset pp. 55 n. 3, 58 n. 1. Lévi, *IHQ* XII, 1936, p. 126, also followed Pelliot in making all the mentions of Alasanda in the *Milinda* refer to Alexandria in Egypt. This is impossible. Beside the passage in Part I here discussed, the name occurs three times in Part II: Rhys Davids II pp. 204 (327), 211 (331), and 269 (359). In the last passage it is Alexandria in Egypt beyond question, as you cross the high seas to get there. But in the two former passages the name occurs in lists of places *in India*, and can only be Alexandria of the Caucasus; surely 211 (331), 'from Kotumbara and Mathurā, from Alexandria, Kashmir, and Gandhāra', is plain enough.

Menander, but he found that in the book he was translating he was called a great king, and that the second part of that book made him born a prince, so he inevitably made him born a prince also; and as he did know that Alexandria in Egypt was on the sea, and as Menander's birthplace was said to be near Alexandria, he naturally made him a prince of a country on the sea. It is very simple if taken in the proper order.

The next thing is the names of those four of Menander's Yonakas who play a part in the introduction or scene-setting to Part I of the Pali Milinda, Devamantiya, Anantakāya, Mankura, Sabbadinna; what is material is not so much the names, whether real or fictitious, as the nationalities. That the first two names are Demetrius and Antiochus has never been doubted, though they have seemingly been 'adjusted' to make some sort of sense in Pali.[1] It seems equally certain that the third name is Pakor (Pacorus).[2] Pacorus was a common Parthian name, occurring in India as Pacores, but Mankura can hardly have been a Parthian and must have been some other north Iranian, Bactrian or Sogdian; looking at the doubts whether the first Arsaces was a Parthian (Parnian) or a Bactrian the difference cannot have been great, and I understand that the two languages, Pahlavi and Sogdian, are closely connected, and that Sogdian borrows from Pahlavi.[3]

The fourth name, Sabbadinna, is unexplained, for one cannot take seriously suggestions like Sarapodotos or Pasidotos, the latter of which is not even Greek;[4] it has indeed been said that the name cannot be explained from Greek, Sanscrit, or Pali.[5] The Chinese translator gives no help, for it is supposed that he took the name literally as meaning 'endowed with everything' or something of the sort, and translated it by K'ien, 'the avaricious'.[6] The word Sabba- occurs in various Indian names, like Sabbamitra,[7] or Sabbakami, the Pali name of Ananda's disciple Sarvakama,[8] or the king Sambos-Sabbas of the Alexander story;[9] but I must suppose that Sabbadinna, which would presumably be Sarvadatta in Sanscrit,[10] makes no sense in either

[1] Rhys Davids I pp. xviii–xix, who suggests that Devamantiya might mean 'Counsellor of the gods' and Anantakāya 'having an infinite body'. For other such 'adjustments' see p. 458 n. 2.

[2] Pelliot p. 405; it is the Chinese Man-k'iu, the name of Pakor II in the *Hou-han-shu* (E. Chavannes, *T'oung Pao* VIII, 1907, p. 178).

[3] R. Gauthiot, *Mém. de la société de Linguistique* XIX, 1916, p. 126, with instances.

[4] If it were, it could only have the nonsense meaning of 'given to everyone', just as the real name Pasiphilos (*P. Cairo Zen.* III, 59454) means 'dear to everyone'.

[5] Mrs Rhys Davids *op. cit.* p. 26.

[6] Demiéville p. 100 (xl) and n. 4; if K'ien be really Sabbadinna, which is not clear to me. Why Demiéville calls the name Sabbadinna an 'appellation sans doute ironique' escapes me.

[7] Rhys Davids II p. 45 and n. 3; cf. Przyluski, *Açoka* p. 266.

[8] Przyluski, *Açoka* p. 51.

[9] Sambos in Arrian, Curtius, Diodorus, and the Metz Epitome; Sabbas, Plut. *Alex.* 64; Sabos, Strabo XV, 701.

[10] Sanscrit datta = Pali dinna = Greek dotos.

language, or this explanation would have been given long ago. Ptolemy (VI, 11, 6) gives an otherwise unknown tribe, Σαβάδιοι, in Bactria; but a connection with this would involve treating -dinna as a mere 'adjustment', to give the name an Indian look. More hopeful is the group of names which centre on Sabazios (Thracian Sabadios) and are allied, through the equation Sabazios-Sabaoth, to Jewish Sabbath-names;[1] for though a comparison with the Macedonian (? Thracian) name Sabataras[2] (probably connected with Sabadios) or with the common Jewish name Sabbataios-Sambathaios would involve the same difficulty about -dinna, a better suggestion can be offered which would make -dinna an integral part of the name. If Gressmann be right,[3] there was in Anatolia a goddess Sambethe-Sabba (the traditional name of the Chaldaean Sybil, Berossus' daughter) corresponding to the god Sabbatistes, worshipped by the well-known Sabbatistai of Cilicia;[4] and a name Sabbadotos, 'the gift of (the goddess) Sabba',[5] would be a normal Greek formation on the lines of Theodotos, Diodotos, Apollodotos, and would in Pali be Sabbadinna.[6] This would not of course make the man a Jew, any more than the Sabbatistai were Jews; he would be a more or less hellenised Anatolian. Menander, it seems, had some Anatolian troops (p. 250); and there would be no objection to an Anatolian being on his Council, seeing that under Antiochus III an Anatolian, the Carian Hermeias, was vizier. If this be well founded, Sabbadotos must have been the man's real name, for no Indian would have known of the goddess Sabba or been able to invent the name; he (and naturally the other three also) would therefore be historical. However that may be, since it has been seen that the Greek allusions in Part I of the Milinda must have been written soon after Menander's death, that work is at any rate good evidence that his Council was a mixture of nationalities, precisely as one would expect.[7]

Nāgasena has been investigated most thoroughly, and the conclusion reached is that he was an invented character; he has no known existence apart from the Milinda.[8] It seems therefore that the Indian Buddhist who wrote

[1] On this subject see Cumont, *CR Ac. Inscr.* 1906 p. 63.

[2] Ditt.[3] 267; cf. O. Hoffmann, *Die Makedonen* p. 164, connected with Sabadios-Sabazios.

[3] Gressmann, *Sabbatistai* and Beer, *Sambethe* in PW.

[4] *OGIS* 573.

[5] Somewhere I have seen it suggested that the Cappadocian name Ἄββατος (in the genitive) of Michel 546 should be Σάββατος.

[6] Cf. Devadinna, 'the gift of the god', in an inscription of Asoka's time; de la Vallée-Poussin p. 155.

[7] So the Parthian kings' Council, copied from Hellenistic usage (Fr. Cumont, *CR Ac. Inscr.* 1931 p. 245), must sometimes have included foreigners (Greeks), since Hestiaeus of Susa was a 'Friend', *SEG* VII, 1.

[8] Demiéville p. 67 concludes his examination by deciding that there is no mention anywhere of Nāgasena which is independent of the *Milinda*. Cf. Finot p. 12: Nāgasena is unknown to Buddhist tradition and is not historical. This is borne out

Part I of the Milinda, with a large selection of Buddhist monarchs and Buddhist sages to choose from, selected as the principal characters in his Dialogue a foreign king and a non-existent sage. Why? To answer that question, which goes to the root of the matter, I must leave the Milinda for the present and turn to Pseudo-Aristeas. The investigation, I fear, is going to take us right down one of the by-paths of Hellenistic literature; and I must begin by analysing Pseudo-Aristeas.

The Letter of Pseudo-Aristeas[1] tells the story of Ptolemy II inviting to Alexandria 72 Jewish Elders to translate their Scriptures into Greek—the legendary account of the origin of the Septuagint; there is an introduction or scene-setting explaining how Ptolemy was led to do it, and an account of his entertainment of the Elders. Among other things he gives seven great banquets, at which he puts a question to each of the Elders and the Elder answers it; there are ten questions on five nights and eleven on the last two. The author introduces throughout the work praise of the Jewish religion and customs, and it has been universally recognised that it is a propaganda work designed to commend the Jewish religion to Greeks. Another thing now universally recognised is that its date is very much later than the time of Ptolemy II; it has even been put after the Christian Era. Wendland dated it *c.* 90 B.C. or later; Thackeray put it about 120 to 80 B.C.;[2] Février merely put it before 30 B.C., that is, before the end of the Ptolemaic dynasty;[3] Momigliano, comparing various letters in I Maccabees, thought it was *c.* 110–100 B.C.;[4] the latest study known to me, a detailed examination of the language in the light of Hellenistic Greek, decides that the linguistic evidence so far as it goes supports an already well-known dating, *c.* 100 B.C.[5] Many arguments have been adduced to prove this or that dating which are not valid, but one was given by Wendland in his Introduction which seems to me pretty conclusive for a date not *earlier* than *c.* 100 B.C.,[6] and I have not been con-

by a wild Indo-Chinese tradition (G. Cœdès, *BEFEO* XXV, p. 112) which makes Nāgasena a pupil of Dhammarakkita (Asoka's missionary to the West) who lived in Asokagrāma (Pātaliputra) and had been Menander's teacher before Nāgasena.

[1] I use the text of P. Wendland, *Aristeae ad Philocratem Epistula* 1900, and cite by his paragraph numbers. A list (not quite exhaustive) of writings on the subject will be found in E. Bickermann's study, *Z. f. d. neutestamentliche Wissenschaft* XXIX, 1930, p. 280. Some I have not seen.

[2] H. St J. Thackeray, *The letter of Aristeas* 1917.

[3] J. G. Février, *La date, la composition, et les sources de la lettre d'Aristée à Philocrate* 1925.

[4] A. Momigliano, *Aegyptus* XII, 1932, p. 161.

[5] H. G. Meecham, *The letter of Aristeas* 1935. This date is that adopted by Wilamowitz, *Deutsche Literaturzeitung* XXI, 1900, col. 3320, and by Christ-Schmid[6] II, i, 1920, p. 621.

[6] Among the names of the 72 are Ananias and Chelkias, the latter a rare name; these are the names of the two Jewish generals of Cleopatra III in her war with Ptolemy Lathyrus.

vinced to the contrary by Dr E. Bickermann's attempt to fix the date between 145 and 127 B.C.[1] For the purposes of this Excursus I take the date as *c.* 100 B.C., though all that I really need at this stage is the certain fact that Pseudo-Aristeas wrote much later than the reign of Ptolemy II. For it has then to be asked why the Jewish author should have chosen as his protagonist Ptolemy II, a king long dead and done with; and perhaps if we can answer that question we shall know why the Buddhist author chose Menander.

Now, though Pseudo-Aristeas is late, there is one part of the work which is most obviously third century B.C.—the questions addressed by Ptolemy II to the Elders and their answers.[2] This document, except for some interpolations which I shall come to, is paragraphs 187–294 inclusive in Wendland, and I must have some distinguishing names; I shall therefore use 'Pseudo-Aristeas' for the late author of the Letter and those parts of the work which he wrote himself, and shall refer to the third-century document as 'the Questions of Ptolemy II' or simply 'the Questions'.

These Questions of Ptolemy II, though embodied by Pseudo-Aristeas in a Jewish propaganda work, are in no sense Jewish propaganda. A reference has been thought to be detected in 228 to the fifth commandment of Moses; but even if this be so it has no propaganda value, for many people beside Jews honoured their parents.[3] In 263 occurs a statement which is very close to James iv, 6, and I Peter v, 5, 'God resisteth the proud but giveth grace to the humble';[4] but attempts to find the source of 263 in the Old Testament have not been very successful,[5] and it is centuries earlier than the two

[1] Bickermann *op. cit.* His valuable examination of the formulae in the royal letters puts the work within the limits 145 to 100 B.C., though strictly speaking the facts he gives p. 289 n. 1 prove a date *c.* 100. His dating before 127 depends entirely (for on the sea-port matter Pseudo-Aristeas is self-contradictory) on the implication in a phrase of Pseudo-Aristeas that Idumea was not part of Palestine, 127 being the date of its annexation to the Maccabee realm. But Bickermann has himself shown that much of Pseudo-Aristeas' description of Palestine is simply a compound of the Old Testament and of ideas about the Ideal State, and one cannot, I think, pick odd items out of this farrago and say '*These* are dated history'; the independent Idumea is only O.T. Edom. He has not noticed that Pseudo-Aristeas was so ignorant about Palestine that he makes the Jordan encircle Judaea and then join another river near Egypt and run out to sea with it (116–17).

[2] Thackeray *op. cit.* p. xiii says that Ptolemy's questions in 187, 193, 194, 196 are late and indicate a tottering dynasty. The case is precisely the opposite: Ptolemy asks how he may be invincible in war and a terror to his enemies, and (twice) how he may keep his possessions unimpaired, *i.e.* the conquests made from the Seleucids and Antigonids by his father and himself. The writer knew Ptolemy II pretty well. I do not know of any other question which has been used to support a late dating except 250 (see p. 427).

[3] For Greeks, cf. the famous parabasis of Aristophanes' *Wasps*.

[4] 263, ὁ θεὸς τοὺς ὑπερηφάνους καθαιρεῖ τοὺς δὲ ἐπιεικεῖς καὶ ταπεινοὺς ὑψοῖ.

[5] Thackeray refers to *I Sam.* ii, 7; *Prov.* iii, 34. There are other passages also; but none is really very close.

Epistles. There is nothing else. The Questions never mention Jewish religion or customs or even the Jewish people; these were not the things on which, in that document, Ptolemy was seeking information. His questions are about himself and his own rule—the duties, privileges, ambitions of a king; and this is underlined in 294, where at the end he thanks the Elders, not for telling him anything about their own religion or ideas, but for giving διδαχὴν ἐμοὶ πρὸς τὸ βασιλεύειν, 'teaching me how to rule'. The document is in fact a περὶ βασιλείας or treatise on kingship,[1] but written by a hellenised Jew and not by a Greek. At the turn of the fourth-third centuries B.C., and right down the third, nearly every Greek philosopher wrote a περὶ βασιλείας as a matter of course;[2] the Hellenistic kingships were a new thing, and philosophy worked hard at shaping the theory of the new phenomenon, though most of the literature is lost. The Questions are full of the well-known third-century terminology of the matter:[3] beneficence,[4] equity,[5] good feeling towards all men,[6] and above all the famous φιλανθρωπία or love of one's subjects,[7] which is said (265) to be the most necessary possession of all for a king.

That all this belongs to a περὶ βασιλείας and must have been written in the third century, not the first, should need no demonstration; the document belongs to the period when the περὶ βασιλείας was a most active literary form. But in fact a precise demonstration of the date is given in 252—the king must judge petitions justly.[8] The Questions then belong to a time when the reigning Ptolemy might receive petitions. In the third century petitions were sent to the *strategos* of the nome, and some, though probably not the

[1] Bickermann *op. cit.* p. 285 saw that the Questions would some day have to be analysed on the lines of a περὶ βασιλείας. Momigliano *op. cit.* p. 169 refers to the difficulty caused by the insertion of a treatise περὶ βασιλείας, but does not go into it further. This Excursus was finished before I saw either of these articles; but in fact Bickermann and myself both go back to Professor Goodenough's illuminating study (next note).

[2] See generally on these treatises E. R. Goodenough, *The Political Philosophy of Hellenistic Kingship*, *Yale Class. Stud.* I, 1928, p. 55. Cf. Tarn, *Alexander the Great and the unity of mankind*, *Proc. Brit. Acad.* XIX 1933.

[3] See generally Max Mühl, *Die antike Menschheitsidee in ihrer geschichtlichen Entwicklung* 1928; E. Skard, *Zwei religiös-politische Begriffe: Euergetes-Concordia* 1932; Tarn *op. cit.*

[4] Εὐεργεσία or εὐεργέτης, 190, 205, 210, 249, 281; beside the above works, see the references to kings' letters in F. Schroeter, *De regum hellenisticorum epistulis in lapidibus servatis* 1932 p. 44.

[5] Ἐπιεικεία and ἐπιεικής, 188, 192, 207, 211, 263, 290.

[6] Φιλία to all men, 225, 228.

[7] 208, 257, 265, 290. On φιλανθρωπία see especially S. Lorenz, *De progressu notionis φιλανθρωπίας*, 1914; J. Kaerst, *Gesch. des Hellenismus* II² p. 321 and references; Schroeter *op. cit.* pp. 26 n. 1, 45.

[8] κρίσει κατευθύνων τὰ τῶν ἐντεύξεων.

majority, did reach the king himself; but by the beginning of the second century special officials had been appointed to deal with them, and none ever reached the king.[1] The Questions therefore are third century; and as they must obviously be earlier than the troubles between Ptolemy IV and the Jews, they belong to the reign of Ptolemy III, when Ptolemy II was still a great memory. The famous question in 250, πῶς ἂν ἁρμόσαι γυναικί, forms no objection to this. It does not of course mean, as it has been taken to mean, 'How can I get on with my wife?'—the writer had presumably no desire to court the fate of Sotades by putting such a question into a king's mouth;[2] it is impersonal, 'How can a man get on with his wife?'—a commonplace *aporia*.[3]

Now undoubtedly, in the original Questions of Ptolemy II, the king questioned 70 Elders, divided into groups of ten (I shall come to that), and not 72 as Pseudo-Aristeas makes him do; the join where the two numbers were fitted together can still be detected. If 72 were the number, the last two groups must contain eleven apiece, as in Pseudo-Aristeas they do; and when, in the last group but one, Ptolemy questions an *eleventh* Elder, Pseudo-Aristeas 273 volunteers as the explanation of this τὸν ἑνδέκατον ἐπηρώτα διὰ τὸ δυὸ πλεονάζειν τῶν ἑβδομήκοντα, 'he questioned the eleventh because there were two more than the 70',[4] that is, 'the 70' of the Questions which Pseudo-Aristeas is working into his book; otherwise the remark would be pointless, for he has already explained at length in his introduction that there were 72, and why there were 72, and given all their names. That 70 was the original number in the legend is presupposed both by the name Septuagint and by the obvious imitation of the 70 Elders of Exodus xxiv, 1, 9;[5] 72 does not occur before Pseudo-Aristeas, and was invented by him to make six from each of the Twelve Tribes, as Epiphanius says;[6] he therefore had to add two more questions to the original 70. I have already mentioned that there are certain interpolations in the Questions; beside these two questions and answers, there are the sections which mention Greek philosophers at the Court[7] and which have nothing to do with the original

[1] P. Collomp, *Recherches sur la chancellerie et la diplomatie des Lagides* 1926.

[2] It has been applied to Ptolemy II and Arsinoe II and to Ptolemy Euergetes II and Cleopatra II. Neither view requires comment.

[3] We shall meet many *aporiai*, commonplace 'hard questions' or (colloquially) 'stumpers' (see further p. 430 n. 6). They were not confined to Greeks, and were proper to kings; the Queen of Sheba tried her collection upon Solomon, *I Kings* x, 1, and see Plutarch's *Banquet of the Seven Sages* (p. 436). Though Plutarch there is very contemptuous about them, he was not above discussing them himself; see the essays *Mor.* 955 E 'Whether water or fire be the more useful' and 959 B 'Whether the creatures of the land are more intelligent than those of the water'.

[4] Thackeray's translation, 'for their number exceeded 70 by 2', misses the point of the definite article.

[5] See Thackeray's discussion of the numbers, *op. cit.* p. xviii.

[6] Thackeray *ib.* p. 115.

[7] 200–202, 235.

Questions. The reason for their insertion by Pseudo-Aristeas is obvious. Though writing propaganda himself, he was building his book round an older document[1] which had no propaganda value but which was useful as being probably well known among hellenised Jews and as vouching for good relations between the Jews and the greatest of the Ptolemies, and he tried to make propaganda of it by explaining (235) that the Jew could beat the Greek philosopher on his own ground. Josephus, when he incorporated much of Pseudo-Aristeas in his own work, showed better judgment by omitting the Questions altogether, as having no value for his purpose.

One other point needs explanation, another sign of the adaptation of the Questions to propaganda purposes. As they stand, the answer of the Jewish Elders to every one of the questions contains, at the end of the answer, a reference to 'God' (or in one or two cases to the 'Divine law'); and it will be noticed by anyone who cares to go through the answers that in practically every case the clause containing the word 'God' can be omitted from the answer without impairing the meaning in the least. The original Questions had nothing to do with the Jewish religion, and Pseudo-Aristeas has adapted them to his purpose by adding these references to 'God'. He himself has made it clear (235) what he was doing: the Jews, he says, could outrun the philosophers because they took God for their starting-point.

Now why did Ptolemy II, in the original Questions, go to the trouble of giving seven great banquets to the Elders in order to ask only ten questions each night, both questions and answers being very short? There must be some explanation of that number ten. The Jewish author of the Questions was steeped in Greek learning, as he knew about Greek treatises on kingship; had he before him some tradition, or some model, presumably Greek, which indicated that when a king questioned foreign wise men ten was the right number of questions for him to put? To answer that we shall have to do what one has to do sooner or later with so many Hellenistic problems and get back to Alexander.

There is no reason to doubt Arrian's story[2] that Alexander in India really

[1] Professor Nock tells me that the Orphic texts and the Sibyllines supply other instances of Jews of this period utilising existing material.

[2] Arr. *Anab.* VII, 1, 5–6, λέγουσιν. (On Arrian's use of this word see E. Schwartz, *Aristobulus* in PW, and E. Kornemann, *Die Alexandergeschichte des Königs Ptolemaios I* 1935 pp. 21–30.) Arrian's source here cannot be Callisthenes, who was dead, or Onesicritus or Megasthenes, who gave versions of their own (see in text), or the Cleitarchean vulgate, because Diodorus, Curtius, and Justin alike know nothing of a conversation between Alexander and any gymnosophists; and if Kornemann *op. cit.* p. 158 be right, it cannot be Aristobulus. Only Nearchus and Ptolemy therefore remain. Nearchus told the story of Calanus (Arr. VII, 3, 6), whoever else did also; but whether Arrian's source be Nearchus, or Ptolemy, or both, the *fact* of the meeting is very well attested indeed, even if Kornemann (p. 158) be right that the *conversation* had received some Stoic-Cynic colouring before it reached Arrian.

did meet and converse with certain recluses (though imperfectly, since at least two interpreters were needed);[1] for Calanus is historical enough, whatever his real name was, and the fact that he did accompany Alexander shows that some sort of meeting took place. The meeting to which Arrian here refers is that near Taxila, afterwards worked up by Megasthenes,[2] at which Calanus was present; Arrian subsequently relates it again from Megasthenes as though it were a different one. The incident caught the imagination of more people than Megasthenes, and, like various other things, developed after Alexander was dead. Onesicritus indeed put out a story[3] that Alexander had not talked to the men himself but had sent *him* to do it; but he could do no better than make one of his Indians give the ordinary Greek account of the Golden Age and the other talk a few Cynic commonplaces, and his version never exercised any influence.

What Alexander may actually have said to the recluses is not material here; what matters is the legend. Though the steps cannot be traced, our existing literature shows that, at some undefined period later than Megasthenes, two main versions of Alexander's conversation with the Indian gymnosophists had come into existence: one, which I will call Y, is represented to-day by the Metz Epitome,[4] Berlin papyrus 13044,[5] and (with slight variations) Plutarch;[6] the other, which I will call Z, is the version of the Alexander-Romance;[7] both represent Alexander as putting a number of questions, though other incidents may differ. It has been contended that the list of questions in the Metz Epitome and the papyrus (these two lists are identical) is the oldest form, Plutarch and Z being derivatives;[8] but I cannot see it quite like that. In Z Alexander comes to the Indians peaceably and is quite agreeable; in Y he is a tyrant who threatens them with death,[9] though he ultimately relents; in this respect Z agrees with the historical fact (Arrian) while Y is a tendencious invention, which should therefore be later. Again,

[1] Arr. VII, 1, 15 δι' ἑρμηνέων, and therefore two at least (Indian into Persian, Persian into Greek). Onesicritus, Strabo XV, 716, says three, which may be true, *i.e.* the Indian-into-Persian interpreter did not know the particular dialect of the recluses.

[2] Strabo XV, 718 = Arr. VII, 2, 2–4; to be distinguished from Arr. VII, 1, 5–6.

[3] Strabo XV, 715.

[4] Ed. O. Wagner, *Jahrb. f. klass. Phil.* Supp. Bd. 26, 1901, pp. 93, 109 §§79–84.

[5] Ed. U. Wilcken, *Berlin SB* 1923 p. 161, with a valuable examination of the whole subject.

[6] Plut. *Alex.* 64.

[7] The references for the questions in the four oldest versions are: A′, III, 6 (Kroll, *Historia Alexandri Magni* I p. 104); R. Raabe, *Ἱστορία Ἀλεξάνδρου* 1896, III σκγ′, p. 77 (the Armenian version); Sir E. A. W. Budge, *The History of Alexander the Great* 1889 pp. 92 *sqq.* (the Syriac version); Julius Valerius III, 11–12.

[8] Wilcken *op. cit.* p. 174.

[9] Cf. the story of Ahikar the Wise, where the king of Egypt threatens Sennacherib with war if he cannot guess his riddles; W. R. Halliday, *Indo-European Folktales and Greek legend* 1933 pp. 244 *sqq.* and references.

the question which in Z is 'Which is bigger, land or sea?' has become in Y 'Which rears the bigger animals, land or sea?' and the simpler form must be the older.[1] Y attempted to turn Alexander into a tyrant by shifting the time and the place of the questioning to Sambos' revolt, of which Z knows nothing; in Plutarch we still have the historical Sambos on the Lower Indus, but in the Metz Epitome Sambos has been shifted to the Malli; Plutarch therefore in this respect represents an earlier version of Y. As every account in both Y and Z begins with the same question, 'Which are more numerous, the living or the dead?' it is clear that both ultimately derive from a common original. Many variations of this must have come into existence,[2] but in some respects Z, however much its different versions may have been worked over, represents (as we have seen) an earlier form, *i.e.* stands nearer to the common original, than does Y. The common original must be early, for of the Y documents, though the Epitome and the papyrus generally agree as against Plutarch's variants, in one important point the papyrus agrees with Plutarch as against the Epitome;[3] and as the papyrus has been dated to *c.* 100 B.C. or perhaps a little earlier,[4] the original of the Y documents must be second-century at latest, and the common original of Y and Z earlier still.

A feature of Y, however, is that its three documents all represent Alexander as putting *ten* questions, a matter which they drive home by saying that there were ten Indians; one question is put to each, as it is also in Z, though Z never specifies the number of Indians. The common original then, it seems, must have made Alexander ask ten questions, and this becomes certain if Z be examined. Of the earlier versions of the Romance, the fullest list of questions is in the Armenian; the others have all become imperfect, A′ giving five questions only, the Syriac and Julius Valerius eight. The Armenian has eleven[5]—ten *aporiai*[6] and an added question τί ἐστι βασιλεύς; 'What is a king?' (βασιλεία in B′, *imperium* in Valerius, 'kingdom' in the Syriac), a question which goes straight to the root of the treatises on kingship. Undoubtedly therefore the common original of Y and Z contained, not

[1] Wilcken *op. cit.* pp. 166 *sqq.*

[2] Wilcken *op. cit.* p. 182.

[3] The seventh question in Plutarch and the papyrus is 'How can a man become a god?' while the Epitome has 'How can I be thought to be a god?' Wilcken p. 170 explains the Epitome version as a scribe's error; I feel no certainty about this.

[4] Wilcken p. 160.

[5] The Z versions all begin with an exclamation of Alexander's, τάφους οὐκ ἔχετε; That this is not one of the questions proper is shown by Leo (*Der Alexanderroman des Archipresbyters Leo*, ed. Fr. Pfister, 1913, III, 6) who belongs to the older group of recensions (*id.* p. 20) and who retains this exclamation, though he omits the questions (and much else) for the sake of brevity. The end of the list in the Armenian version, τῶν κτιστῶν τί ἐστι γλυκύτατον...τί δὲ πικρότατον; though separated, is only one question; so Kroll *op. cit.* p. 105 n.

[6] On *aporiai* see Wilcken pp. 166, 169, 179; also p. 427 n. 3 *ante*.

simply ten questions, but ten questions which were *aporiai*; and these presently began to be altered. Plutarch and the Epitome have six *aporiai*—five identical with the Z list and an altered one; they have two questions which have been substituted for *aporiai* to carry through the contention in Y that Alexander was a tyrant, viz.: 'How did you induce Sambos to revolt?' and 'Who has answered worst?' (for he was to be killed first); and for the two remaining *aporiai* have been substituted two questions relating to Alexander's kingship, (1) 'How can one be most loved?' and (2) either 'How can a man become a god?' (Plutarch) or 'be thought to be a god?' (Metz Epitome). As the Armenian version of Z has the complete list of ten *aporiai* and also a question about kingship, a question reproduced in the other (imperfect) versions of Z, it can be seen that what happened was this. There was an original list of ten *aporiai*, which in course of time became altered by the introduction of other questions of two types; one type, appearing only in Y, was substituted for some *aporiai* for the sake of Y's 'tendency'; the other type consisted of questions relating to kingship, which in Y were *substituted* for certain *aporiai*, but in Z were *added* to the list; and there can be little doubt that the ten *aporiai* extant in the Armenian version are the list of questions in the common original. The point however which I wanted to make has now made itself: the stereotyped number of Alexander-questions, from the common original onwards, was ten, however the actual questions might be shuffled about.[1]

There can be little doubt that when the author of the Questions of Ptolemy II made that king ask only ten questions a night he was following the tradition of the Alexander-questions. There is the further resemblance that while Alexander questions quite fictitious Indians, invented to be questioned—this appears from the location of the questioning in several different places and at different times[2]—the author of the Questions of Ptolemy II invented a body of quite fictitious Jewish Elders to make the responses to that monarch. What the relation may be between the questions about *kingship* put by Ptolemy II and those which found their way into the Alexander-questions I do not know, for it cannot be guessed at what time such questions first entered the Alexander-list; there may well be no relation at all, seeing what a much-discussed question kingship was in the third century, and indeed Plutarch's Banquet of the Seven Sages (p. 436) shows how easily a discussion of *aporiai* would slide into talk about kingship.

[1] Plutarch and the Metz Epitome divide the ten Indians into nine and a leader, who in Plutarch is umpire, and to whom is put the tenth question 'Who has answered worst?' This explains the title of a work Wilcken cites as agreeing with the Metz Epitome, *'Εννέα σοφῶν ἀποφθέγματα πρὸς 'Αλέξανδρον τὸν Μακεδόνα.* I have been unable to see it.

[2] Historically, near Taxila (Arrian). The Romance: directly after the battle with Porus and among the Oxydracae (where Alexander never was). Plutarch: on the lower Indus, after Sambos' revolt. Metz Epitome: in the Malli town where Alexander was wounded, Sambos being transferred to the Malli.

Now nobody can say that Ptolemy II may not at some time have conversed with some Jewish Elders; but those he is represented as conversing with are fictitious. Nobody can say that Menander may not at some time have conversed with a Buddhist sage; but the one he is represented as conversing with is fictitious. We can now see that Pseudo-Aristeas chose Ptolemy II as his protagonist because there was already in existence a document, the Questions of Ptolemy II, which made Ptolemy II converse with Jews; and the author of the Questions had chosen Ptolemy II because, for the Jewish world of that day, he was the greatest king of the time and the Alexander-questions showed that it was proper for great kings to converse with foreign sages. Let us suppose, in the same way, that the Buddhist author of Part I of the Milinda chose Menander as his protagonist because there was already in existence a document which made Menander converse with a Buddhist, and that the author of that previous document had chosen Menander because he was the greatest king of the time to the world about him and the Alexander-tradition showed that it was proper for great kings to converse with Indian sages. This would imply that the story of Alexander's conversation with Indian sages was, in some form or other, known in India; but if any Greek literature or tradition found its way to India at all, as it certainly did,[1] stories about Alexander in India certainly would. But if the author of Part I of the Pali Milinda had such knowledge of a previous document as Pseudo-Aristeas had of the Questions of Ptolemy II, that means that there was once in existence a Greek Questions of Menander based, like the Questions of Ptolemy II, on the Alexander-tradition—did not an eastern Greek, Apollodorus (pp. 143 *sq.*), compare Menander's conquests to Alexander's?—and conceivably also on some real conversation of Menander's, just as the Alexander-tradition goes back to a real conversation of Alexander's.

This hypothesis of a Greek Questions of Menander will explain a number of things, and is required in order to explain them. I have already mentioned the curious way in which the author of Part I of the Milinda takes certain things for granted—that his Indian readers would know what Menander's Yonakas were and would know that the lay-out of the four-square Hellenistic city was the normal one; if he was taking these things from a Greek work that would be explained, as would his use of the Hellenistic Greek word Yonaka and his placing of Greeks before Kshatriyas and Brahmans. His knowledge of Menander's birthplace and of the mixed nationalities on his Council he *might* have had himself, though it would be more natural to suppose that they were taken from the Greek work also; but if the names of Menander's four Yonakas are historical, and as we saw there is a possibility of this, they *must* have come from the Greek work; and if what I have said

[1] Pp. 376 (books), 378 (historical writings), 382 (Sophocles, and therefore *a fortiori* Euripides, cf. p. 354 n. 3); possibly mimes (p. 383). But in fact no one could fail to know that Demetrius claimed to be a second Alexander, which meant that Alexander-literature would be in vogue; see the legends cited p. 155.

in Appendix 6 be correct, the fact that Menander's birthplace is said to have been near *Alexandria* instead of near *Kapisa* is very likely due to the Greek work also.[1] The Greek work, too, if (*ex hypothesi*) it were suggested by one or more of the lists of Alexander-questions, must have contained some *aporiai*—as a matter of historical development it could not do otherwise—and that would explain the fact that the author of Part I of the Milinda represents Milinda in the Introduction as eager to score a dialectical victory, while in the body of the book he makes little attempt to do so. And it would explain, not only why the Indian author chose a Greek king as one protagonist, but also why he chose an invented character, Nāgasena, for the other: Nāgasena came from the Greek work, like the Yonakas, and was invented as the Indians in the Alexander-questions were invented.

There is also a curious remark in the Milinda which can only be explained if we suppose that the Alexander-questions *were* known in India. When Milinda and his Friends are discussing how many of the brethren Nāgasena shall bring with him, Sabbadinna says 'Let him come with ten', and sticks to his point till the king has said three times that Nāgasena shall bring as many as he likes.[2] This number only has meaning in reference to the ten of the Alexander-questions, and presumably comes from the Greek Questions of Menander (which no doubt, like the Questions of Ptolemy II, were not confined to ten questions); what Sabbadinna in effect says is 'You ought to follow the Greek tradition' and Milinda says 'No'.

So far, the existence of a Greek Questions of Menander has been deduced as an astronomer deduces the existence of an invisible body in the heavens, from its disturbance of other bodies; but there is one fact still to come which I think goes far towards providing direct evidence. Pseudo-Aristeas begins as the Milinda begins, with an introduction which sets the scene. In the introduction to Pseudo-Aristeas four Friends of Ptolemy II play a part—Demetrius the librarian, Aristeas, and Archias and Sosibius the ἀρχισωματοφύλακες; and the principal part is given to Demetrius. In the introduction to the Milinda four Friends of Menander play a part—Demetrius and three others whom I have discussed; and the principal part is given to Demetrius. Coincidences do occur, but one must not reckon upon their occurrence; the natural explanation is that one of these schemes was borrowed from the other. But certainly neither the Questions of Ptolemy II nor Pseudo-Aristeas

[1] This would explain why the Chinese translator turned the word into Alexandria in Egypt; he only knew the capital of the Paropamisadae as Kapisa, whether, as is likely, the Alexandria-name had perished by his time, or not. The appearance of Alexandria of the Caucasus twice in a list of Indian cities in Part II of the *Milinda* (p. 421 n. 4) may be taken from Part I, but may also mean that Part II cannot be much later than about the end of Greek rule.

[2] P. 47 (30). Ultimately Milinda silences Sabbadinna by saying 'Does he think we are not capable of feeding so many?' One thinks involuntarily of Ptolemy feeding seven times ten Elders; but there cannot be any connection.

would be known in India; they are not likely to have circulated much beyond the circle of hellenised Jews, and in the Hellenistic period Jews are not heard of farther east than Susa (p. 29). And certainly the Pali Milinda was not read in the West, besides being probably too late. But a copy of a Greek Questions of Menander, written in India soon after Menander's death (which was between 150 and 145), could have reached the library at Alexandria *via* Babylonia, the great clearing-house between East and West, and reached it in plenty of time for Pseudo-Aristeas *c.* 100 B.C. to read it; he was obviously interested in kings' questions, and would have read it had he found it. It looks as if it were the Greek Questions of Menander which gave him the idea of resurrecting Demetrius the librarian (who was Demetrius of Phalerum, dead before the time of Ptolemy II) so that he might have a Demetrius to play the principal part in his own scene-setting. There is of course no difficulty about a Greek work being written in Menander's kingdom; we have already (Chap. VI) met with conclusive indications of at least two Greek poems written there.

And if the author of Part I of the Pali Milinda could and did read Greek, it does help out what some Pali scholars have felt about that work taken as a whole. Rhys Davids (I p. xii) called it 'the only prose work composed in ancient India which would be considered, from the modern point of view, as a successful work of art'. Finot (p. 14), after observing that the vivacity and sobriety of the dialogue resembled the Socratic dialogues rather than anything Indian, said 'On serait même enclin à reconnaître dans cette forme originale et presque insolite une influence hellénique'. Winternitz (II p. 141) said that it was so alive and fresh that it well supported comparison with the Dialogues of Plato.[1] Evidently some Pali scholars have felt about the Milinda much as most people have felt about Ecclesiastes, that at some time the author had read Greek literature and breathed Greek air; and if this be true, Part II cannot be later than the first century B.C., seeing that Greek rule ended altogether about 30 B.C., and the earlier in that century the better (see also p. 433 n. 1). It would be interesting to know how it is proposed to reconcile this Greek atmosphere of the Pali Milinda with the common belief that it is a derivative document from an Indian original (p. 416); a translator could hardly maintain that atmosphere if he found it or create it if he did not. I venture to think my own explanation preferable.

The conclusion is that certain things in Part I of the Pali Milinda and certain resemblances to Pseudo-Aristeas can only be explained by postulating a short Greek Questions of Menander, in which Menander questioned an invented figure, the Buddhist sage Nāgasena; the questions must, as a matter of the historical development of this form of literature, have consisted largely

[1] Winternitz however (*ib.*; Eng. trans. p. 176) rejected Weber's suggestion (*Berlin SB* 1890 p. 927) of an actual connection with Plato. I note a recent attempt to show that Plato knew the Dialogues of the Buddha; C. Fries, *Rh. Mus.* LXXXII, 1933, p. 145.

of *aporiai*, though there may have been others. This work, like the various versions of the Alexander-questions, must have had some sort of introduction or scene-setting, from which the Pali author took the Yonakas and their names; the parts of the introduction to the Pali work dealing with the previous existences of Milinda and Nāgasena and so forth were naturally not in the Greek work. From the Greek work came the fact that Sāgala was Menander's capital, and probably the details of his birthplace; but that and the reference to the four-square Hellenistic cities might have come from some other Greek source. We have seen (p. 249) that some Greek in India may have written a Praise of Menander, and that in any case there was some Greek poem which mentioned him. There may in fact have been a regular Menander literature; and we seem to possess traces of another bit of it, an Indian Avadāna intermediate in time between the Greek Questions of Menander and the Pali Milinda. It survives in a Chinese translation made in A.D. 472 by a sramana from the West, and is called 'Avadāna of the discussion between the king Nan-t'o (Nanda) and Nāgasena'.[1] It has been pointed out that the Indian original must have been older than the Pali Milinda because the name Nanda still kept the first *n* of Menander;[2] but there is more than that. The first three of the four questions asked by Nanda-Menander are serious questions relating to Buddhism; but the fourth is merely two commonplace *aporiai* on the Greek model, 'Why is summer hot and winter cold? And why is a summer day long and a winter day short?'[3] These *aporiai* show that the work stood nearer to the Greek Questions of Menander than did the Pali Milinda, from which *aporiai* have completely vanished.

The end was that, just as Pseudo-Aristeas saw in the Questions of Ptolemy II a useful peg on which to hang a tractate on Judaism, so some Indian Buddhist saw in the Greek Questions of Menander a setting which could conveniently be utilised for a treatise on Buddhism. We have seen that the Greek work, assuming that it existed, must have been written very soon after Menander's death and, if it reached the library at Alexandria, must have reached it by or before 100 B.C.; and as Part I of the Pali Milinda (or the Indian work of which it is a translation, if it really be a translation) has to fall in the period when Greek was colloquially spoken in India and Indians might know Greek works, I do not see how it can be much *later* than 100 B.C., which would give ample time for intermediate developments. It might be earlier; it must surely be before the Greeks in India began to be Indianised (Chap. IX) and the Sacas began to break up the Indo-Greek world.

One further point. The earliest list of Alexander-questions could consist

[1] Given as part 3 of an article by Dr J. Takakusu on the Chinese version of the Milinda, *JRAS* 1896 p. 17: *The Samvukta-ratna-pitaka Sūtra*. This sūtra contains 121 stories in eight books; the Avadāna in question is no. CXI in book 8.

[2] Pelliot *op. cit.* p. 380. Cf. Takakusu p. 17, 'a comparatively early date'.

[3] Takakusu *ib.* p. 21.

solely of *aporiai* because it was only a small incident in a long story; but it is hard to conceive of a Greek writing a Questions of Menander with a formal introduction merely to make the king put *aporiai* to a Buddhist sage. The Questions of Ptolemy II is a serious enough document, even though it has not got rid of *aporiai* altogether;[1] and the Greek Questions of Menander must surely have contained serious questions as well as *aporiai*, questions not perhaps specifically connected with Buddhism, but at least concerned with such commonplaces of philosophy as might interest both peoples. If so, the legend of Menander as a great Buddhist monarch might not be purely Indian; Greeks might have played a part in its formation. But that would not prove that the Menander of history took a personal interest in Buddhism (see pp. 268 *sq.*).

I must conclude by referring to the Banquet of the Seven Sages, as in that work Plutarch, at a later day, summed up this business of kings' Questions. He starts from a list of *aporiai* supposedly sent by the king of Egypt to the king of Ethiopia to guess, to which Thales casually supplies the right answers; and Plutarch, through his mouthpieces, says that Greeks were once fond of these things (153 E), but now they are no better than children's riddles (154 A), though they may do for kings (153 F) (see p. 427 n. 3). But when, on two occasions, the Seven are prevailed upon to give *their* opinions on a question, these are concerned, the first time with kingship (152 A, B) and the second time with another form of polity (154 D–F). So far as Plutarch goes, there is nothing which disagrees with what I have written.

Early in this book (p. 39) I suggested that we might find that the Greek culture-sphere, which extended at any rate to Susa, did in the second century B.C. embrace the Greeks in India. I trust that this Excursus, together with Chapter IX, has now shown that this must have been the case.

[1] Two at least: 213, 'How can one sleep without dreaming?' and 250, 'How can a man get on with his wife?' Later on, *aporiai* may have been finally dropped from kings' Questions; see a Hermetic fragment, in which a king questions a prophet named Tat about doctrine, in Reitzenstein, *Poimandres* p. 354, XVII. I owe this reference to Professor Nock.

APPENDIX 1

MONOGRAMS AND FIND-SPOTS

In order to save much repetition in the text, the principles followed in this book on these two matters are set out here.

It has been widely believed that the monograms on the Greek coins from Bactria and India, or most of them, denoted mint-cities;[1] and even to-day, I understand, it is thought that some of them must be mints, though one numismatist has stated that they may sometimes 'denote the name of the local magistrate under whose authority the coin was struck'.[2] Yet Cunningham's laborious effort to work out the mint-cities from these numerous monograms was a complete failure, and it is admitted that, after many years of study, no single monogram of any mint has been identified, while on the other hand the *types* of at least two mint-cities, the 'Zeus enthroned' of Alexandria-Kapisa and the humped bull of Pushkalāvatī, are perfectly certain.

Why it was ever supposed that the Greek kings in the East would make such a radical breach with Seleucid custom I cannot imagine;[3] the continuity between the eastern Greek kingdoms and the Seleucid realm is as marked as that of other Seleucid Succession states, indeed in many ways more so; this book has, I trust, shown the trouble taken by both houses, that of Euthydemus and that of Eucratides, to prove that they were Seleucids. No one seems ever to have doubted that the Seleucid monograms represent moneyers,[4] and the Seleucid system of monograms at the Antioch mint has been elucidated by Mr E. T. Newell;[5] the monograms are those of continuing mint-masters and changing city magistrates. There is literary evidence for mint-masters in one kingdom, Antigonid Macedonia;[6] and it is admitted that the monograms on the coinage of Parthia, the principal Seleucid Succession state, are usually

[1] *BMC* p. lv; *CHI* p. 443 (very definitely). But the last word of Cunningham, the protagonist of this view, was that not one half were mint-cities; *NC* 1888 p. 205.

[2] Whitehead, *NNM* p. 26.

[3] This is where Cunningham went wrong; he thought he was dealing with 'eastern kings', not Hellenistic states, *NC* 1888 p. 205.

[4] P. Gardner in *BMC Sel.* p. xxxii; Sir G. Macdonald, *JHS* XXIII, 1903, p. 101.

[5] *The Seleucid Mint of Antioch* 1918; see the instances of long tenure of office on p. 10, and generally pp. 44, 54, 68–9, 80, and the résumé pp. 129 *sqq.*

[6] Plut. *Aem. Paul.* 23, *τοὺς ἐπὶ τοῦ νομίσματος* at Pella (two men). An earlier mint-master of Perseus, Zoilus, is known: A. Mamroth, *Z. f. Num.* XXXVIII, 1928, p. 4. For a case of a mint-master moving from Tarsus to Pella see E. T. Newell, *The coinages of Demetrius Poliorcetes* 1927 p. 83.

those of moneyers.[1] That the Bactrian and Indian monograms must also be, anyhow as a general rule, those of moneyers—mint-masters or city magistrates—seems to me almost too clear for argument; the Kharoshthi letters (instead of monograms) on some of the later Greek coins in India (p. 356) should alone be conclusive. The contrary belief would mean that some princelets were operating as many mints as Alexander ever did; that the Saca Azes, whose monograms and letters are very numerous, was operating several times as many; and that Eucratides' twenty-stater gold piece, of finest Bactrian work, was struck in the same mint as some of the very inferior coins of his bitter enemy Menander in the eastern Punjab.

It is becoming clear that both Seleucids and Parthians operated only a few mints, serving large areas; and so far as can be made out there were very few regular Greek mints in the Farther East. Only four are at first certain: Bactra, Alexandria-Kapisa, Pushkalāvatī, and one in Menander's home kingdom in the eastern Punjab, presumably at the capital, Sāgala. A fifth, Taxila, is morally certain; and it is possible that there was always a second mint in the eastern Punjab, at Bucephala,[2] though it only becomes certain under Hippostratus (p. 326). It is possible, though it cannot be proved, that there was for a time a mint in Antimachus' sub-kingdom of Margiane, either at Antioch-Merv or possibly at Susia-Tōs; but this is very speculative, for his famous portrait was certainly engraved in Bactra (p. 75) and his coinage may have been struck for him there also (p. 440). There seems no trace to be got, so far, of any Greek mint either in Arachosia-Seistan or in Sind, where stood two of Demetrius' name-cities, though later the Sacas struck, or got struck for them, a rude coinage in Seistan itself (p. 502). No doubt any city with a Greek community could produce coins of some sort if the political position necessitated this; but I am talking of the regular royal mints.

One reason alleged for the belief that the Bactrian and Indian monograms represent mint-cities must be noticed—that certain monograms appear over such long periods of time that they cannot be moneyers.[3] There is nothing in this. None of the mint-cities possessed an overflowing population of Greeks, and no doubt the office of mint-master was often hereditary,[4] as was

[1] Wroth, *BMC Parthia* pp. lxxix *sq.* and a certain instance p. lxxxiii; McDowell, *Coins from Seleucia* p. 168 (the tetradrachms). It is noteworthy that Professor P. Gardner, who in 1879 said that many of the Bactrian and Indian monograms might stand for mints (*BMC* p. lv), had in 1877 maintained that to call the Parthian monograms mints was to go altogether beyond the evidence (his *Parthian Coinage* p. 23).

[2] It has been suggested that Menander's ox-head was meant for the type of Bucephala.

[3] *BMC* p. lv; *CHI* p. 443.

[4] Macdonald *loc. cit.*: the monograms show that 'the magistracies attached to the mint (at Alexandria Troas) were held in succession by members of the same family or families, a practice that we know to have been followed in other parts of the Hellenic world'.

the office of *strategos* at Doura.[1] Let me give an instance from a city which *had* a numerous Greek population, Athens. During a large part of the third and part of the second centuries B.C. the office of *paidotribes* at Athens was hereditary in the family of Hermodorus of Acharnae; the inscriptions show the name Hermodorus as *paidotribes* spread out over about a century, whether there were two or three men of the name, *i.e.* whether we are dealing with three or five generations.[2] Suppose that that family, instead of being hereditary *paidotribai* in Athens, had been hereditary mint-masters in Alexandria-Kapisa; we should get the Hermodorus monogram spread out over about a century, and we might get it over the whole century and a half of Greek rule in that city.

That should suffice for possibilities. While not asserting that all Bactrian and Indian monograms *must* necessarily represent moneyers—an alternative might be that some represented *officinae*,[3] workshops, of which a great city might have more than one—I see no reason to suppose that they ever denote mint-cities.[4] And I am not sure if any monogram occurs which is sufficiently stereotyped to denote an *officina*.[5]

It may be worth looking as an illustration at one common Bactrian monogram, ℞; for as this monogram also occurs on a group of copper coins of Seleucus I found at Seleuceia[6] it quite certainly represents a man and not a place. It is dominant during Bactria's great period. It begins on the later coinage of Euthydemus,[7] and appears on coins of Demetrius, Antimachus, Euthydemus II, Agathocles (twice), and the first issue of Eucratides[8] before he took the title 'Great King'; then it ceases. It is certainly connected with the mint at Bactra, since it is one of the only two monograms on the money of Euthydemus II; its appearance on two of the pedigree coins of Agathocles shows that they were struck for him in Bactra, as would be natural in the case of a sub-king; the same applies to the other sub-king in

[1] Jotham Johnson, *Dura Studies* 1932 pp. 17 *sqq.*

[2] The inscriptions are set out by W. S. Ferguson, *Athenian Tribal Cycles* 1932 pp. 104 *sq.*; on the dating see also Tarn, *JHS* LIV, 1934, p. 30. Ferguson got the inscriptions into three generations; I inclined to five, with three men named Hermodorus. The principle is the same in either case.

[3] Suggested by Wroth as regarded the Parthian coinage, *BMC Parthia* pp. lxxxiv *sq.*

[4] Such minor variations of type in a series as are referred to in *CHI* p. 443 might of course be due to different mints or *officinae*, *i.e.* different die-cutters. But I do not know what relation, if any, such things bear to the monograms.

[5] McDowell, *Coins from Seleucia* p. 169, makes the attractive suggestion that the stereotyped monograms on later Parthian drachmae, which for long reproduced those on the money of Phraates III, were at the start moneyers' monograms which became stereotyped to mean certain mints.

[6] McDowell *op. cit.* p. 6 no. 9 and Pl. I no. 6.

[7] *BMC* p. 5; *CHI* p. 443.

[8] *BMC* pp. 6, 8, 10, 12, 13; for Demetrius see also *NC* 1904 p. 321, 1935 p. 1.

the list, Antimachus. The fact that this monogram does not appear on the earlier coins of Euthydemus, on the later coins of Eucratides, or on any of those of Heliocles, is further proof that it cannot represent a city or a workshop; it is, beyond any question, a man's signature. This man then held office from about 200 B.C. (certainly not earlier) to 167—say thirty-three years at the outside; he was therefore a mint-master. There is no reason whatever against his holding office for thirty-three years; two mint-masters are known at Antioch who held office for twenty-two and twenty-eight years,[1] and a case is known of a man being *paidotribes* at Athens for thirty-four years at the least;[2] not to mention Sosibius, who held high office under the third and fourth Ptolemies, first as *dioecetes* and then as vizier, for forty-one years.[3] If we like, we may see in [monogram] the mint superintendent who was largely responsible for enlisting the services of the artists who made the Greek coinage of Bactria such a wonderful portrait-gallery. His colleague or vice-official ɸ,[4] the other monogram on the coins of Euthydemus II, which appears also on the coins of Demetrius, Agathocles (including a pedigree coin), and Eucratides (including the Heliocles-Laodice coin), held office from about 190 to, at latest, Eucratides' death in 159, say perhaps thirty-one years. That these two men went over to Eucratides may illustrate the strength of his appeal (Chap. v).

The same monogram [monogram] in India on twenty-two coins of the Bajaur hoard,[5] composed of coins of Apollodotus, Menander, and Antimachus II (p. 229), must be another man, whose monogram also appears on coins of Menander's son Strato I; and a third man, possibly a grandson of the first, signs coins of two later members of the house of Eucratides, Antialcidas and Archebius, with the same monogram. What little is known of Greek names in India apart from the kings points to certain favourite names being often repeated (p. 392). This seems to be the story of one common monogram, and it has nothing whatever to do with mint-cities. But it is to be hoped that it may one day be possible for numismatists to work out the Bactrian and Indian mints as the Seleucid and Parthian mints are being worked out.

Much use has been made by some writers of the find-spots of coins in determining where this or that king reigned, but it is not a satisfactory form of evidence; I have sometimes been forced to use it in default of better, but

[1] Newell, *The Seleucid Mint of Antioch* p. 10.

[2] Abascantus: *IG* II^2 2086 l. 115 and 2097; see W. B. Dinsmoor, *The Archons of Athens* 1931 p. 94; J. Kirchner, *Gnomon* 1932 p. 453.

[3] Tarn, *JHS* LIII, 1933, p. 66.

[4] Two contemporary mint-masters are met with at Antioch (Newell, *op. cit.* p. 10) and at Pella (Plut. *Aem. Paul.* 23); whether they were colleagues or whether one was subordinate to the other cannot be said. So far as I know, this monogram never occurs again.

[5] M. F. C. Martin, *JASB* XXIII, 1927 (pub. 1929), Num. Supp. XL pp. 18, 20. It is unfortunately not stated on whose coins this monogram occurs, but some twenty-five years will cover the whole.

coins travel in trade and almost any other kind of evidence is preferable. In many cases too the find-spots are unknown; at best we have only a very partial picture. The following rules seem sound. If a king has an abundant coinage which is found in many places over great distances, like the coinages of Apollodotus and Menander, that is evidence of a widely extended rule, but not evidence that he ruled in all the places where his coins are found. If the coins of a king with a very large coinage are never found in a particular district, that creates a presumption, in the absence of other evidence, that he did not rule there; but if the coinage be small, no presumption is created; and in both cases, large and small coinage, the absence of coins in a district cannot be set up against other evidence that the king in question ruled there. If only a few isolated coins of a king be known, the find-spots afford no real evidence for the locality of his rule. The belief that find-spots of *copper* coins are good evidence of rule, because they do not travel far from the place of issue, is unfounded; copper coins must have circulated regularly over all the country served by the mint of issue, which might be very extensive, and a good deal more than that can be demonstrated. There have been found in Susa 143 copper coins of Seleuceia on the Tigris,[1] and sixty chalkoi of an unknown king Tigraios, who if I am right ruled at Omana on the Gulf of Ormuz (p. 485); large numbers of copper coins of Kadphises I have been found at Taxila, where probably he never ruled;[2] and copper coins of the Ptolemies have frequently been found, not only all round the Mediterranean,[3] but even at many places in Britain.[4]

Account must also be taken of known centres of trade; for example, the great mass of coins of many kings which Masson got about Begram reflects the fact that Alexandria-Kapisa was the gateway of the trade between India and the West, but does not necessarily show who ruled there. It also has to be borne in mind that the coins of some kings continued to be struck after their deaths. Eucratides was not long in India, but Masson picked up his copper coins at Begram by the thousand; Euthydemus was almost certainly dead when Demetrius conquered Seistan, but his copper issues are said to be the only money which has been found in that country in any quantity; the copper money of both must have continued to be coined after their respective deaths. The most curious instance, for which the evidence is unimpeachable, is that the money of both Apollodotus and Menander was circulating in Barygaza in the middle of the first century A.D. (p. 149), two centuries after their deaths, though Surastrene had long been lost to the Greeks. It must be supposed that the great trading port, having found that these coins were good media of exchange, continued to copy them indefinitely for trade purposes; the Saca rulers would not desire to interfere with what was presumably a lucrative procedure.

1 *MDP* xx, 1928, pp. 37–40; xxv, 1934, pp. 62–3. 143 altogether.
2 *CHI* p. 584; Marshall, *ASI* 1929–30 p. 57.
3 J. G. Milne, *JRS* 1932 p. 247; and see p. 149 n. 6.
4 List of places in *NC* 1930 p. 338.

APPENDIX 2

THE NAMES IN *-HNH*

The form of name ending in -ηνη (or -ιανη) which is proper to the Seleucid eparchies has been considered in Chapter I. But as in Chapter VI I have made use of this form as a test with regard to certain passages in Ptolemy's account of India, it is necessary to consider the converse question: granted that the -ηνη form is the most characteristic form for the names of the Seleucid eparchies and for the satrapies of Seleucid Succession states or of states which were influenced by and copied the Seleucid (or, what comes to the same thing, the Parthian) organisation, do we find, eastward of the Euphrates, -ηνη (or -ιανη) forms which mean something other than such eparchies or satrapies; or, to apply it to the particular case in question, when we meet Greek -ηνη forms in Ptolemy's (or anyone else's) description of India, a country which at the period in question (second century B.C.) had never been under Seleucid or Parthian influence, are we justified in treating these names as the names of the provinces of a Greek kingdom? I have tried to collect any seeming exceptions I can find in the relevant Greek literature and must now go through them; I am not of course noticing the mass of such forms in Strabo, Ptolemy, and elsewhere which are obviously either eparchies of a known satrapy or satrapal provinces of a known kingdom. To avoid misconception, I must emphasise once more that I am only here dealing with Asia east of the Euphrates, the new world which the Greeks settled and which never became Roman, though in fact Pontus, Cappadocia, and Armenia Minor exhibit the same phenomena. I am not considering Syria, which is a world by itself,[1] and in particular I am not considering Asia Minor west of the Halys. I do not know what its organisation in this respect was, and no one has worked it out; when Strabo talks of Cyzicene or Amisene I do not know if he means eparchy or city territory; the names might, for all that is yet known, be related to the old Greek city-names in -ηνη like Mytilene, Priene, Cebrene. All this has nothing to do with the matter in hand, which is Ptolemy upon India.

Three so-called towns in the Peutinger Table—Pantyene, Tazarene, Thybrassene—are really eparchies of Carmania and Gedrosia; it has long been recognised that in this part of Asia the Table gives provinces as towns.[2] Doubtless this is another of those traces of the Seleucid survey which Tomaschek detected in the Table.[3]

[1] U. Kahrstedt, *Syrische Territorien in hellenistischer Zeit* 1926; O. Leuze, *Die Satrapieneinteilung in Syrien* 1935.

[2] Müller, *GGM* I, xcv, 'Deinde (after Media and Persis) Tab. Peut. non oppida sed regiones memorat usque ad Besten'; K. Miller, *Itineraria Romana* 1916 col. 786 and map.

[3] *Wien SB* CII, 1883, p. 145.

Stephanus (*s.v.*) gives a town Barene in Media near Ecbatana. In Isidore's list of the Parthian satrapies (Seleucid eparchies) in Media along the great road he omits (§6) the name of the province between Gambadene and Rhagiane in which Ecbatana stood, merely calling it ἡ Μηδία ἡ ἄνω. Barene is not a town, but is the missing name of this eparchy.

The Periplus (48) and Ptolemy (VII, 1, 62) both call the city of Ujjain Ὀζήνη. This has nothing to do with the -ηνη names; it is merely someone's transliteration into Greek letters of the sound of the Indian name Ujjahini. It suggests however that other similar transliterations may exist.

The Periplus (62) gives a region Dosarene on the coast of Orissa, where a Greek name is impossible. It is not given in Ptolemy, who only gives a town Dosara and a river Dosaron (VII, 1, 77). The author of the Periplus, in the middle of the first century A.D., was an unlearned trader who knew nothing about the long-vanished Seleucid eparchies; but he knew that in Asia a great many names of districts ended in -ηνη, and he just coined Dosarene from Dosara as a likely reproduction of the sound of the Indian name Dacharna.[1] I shall return to Dosarene, which is much later than the Hellenistic period.

The 'regio Attene' near Gerrha of Pliny VI, 148 is identical with Polybius' Χαττηνία, the third χώρα or province of the Gerrhaeans.[2] That the Gerrhaeans, who were closely associated with the Seleucids throughout, would organise on the Seleucid model, as did the Nabataeans, is obvious.

Two names may be dismissed offhand. Maikene (Strabo XVI, 767) is a province of Characene, and Bubacene (Curt. VIII, 5, 2) is an eparchy of Sogdiana.

Gouriane, a town in Margiane, is Ptolemy's one mistake, if it be a mistake, for it appears from Polybius that the proper Greek name of the place was τὰ Γουρίανα.[3] What probably happened is that the native name was something like Ghurian (a name existing to-day, but farther southward);[4] Ptolemy's source, an unlearned trader, turned it into Gouriane, not knowing any better, and Ptolemy, usually careful in this respect, overlooked it. Beside Ὀζήνη, there is a sort of parallel in Eratosthenes' term Ariana for the Iranian plateau, which is not an -ιανη name but only the Pahlavi āryān[5] in Greek letters.

Pliny VI, 43 gives the Median Apamea, which was really in Choarene,[6] as 'Apamea Rhagiane cognominata'; this is only an adjective, Apamea 'the Rhagian',[7] like his Antiochia Syria, 'the Syrian'.[8]

1 Cited by Müller *ad loc.* from Lassen as the Sanscrit form.

2 Polyb. X, 9, 1–3 = Steph. *s.v.* Λάβαι and Χαττηνία.

3 On the identification of Gouriane (Ptol. VI, 10, 4) and τὰ Γουρίανα (Gutschmid's certain correction of the MSS Ταγουριαν in Polyb. X, 49, 1) see *CAH* VIII p. 141 n. 1.

4 Kiessling, *Guriane* in PW.

5 Herzfeld, *Sakastan* p. 37.

6 Isidore 8; unless there were two cities of the name.

7 Strabo XI, 514 calls it περὶ τὰς Ῥάγας.

8 Pliny VI, 47; see p. 15 n. 1.

I come now to the two real difficulties, which are in Hyrcania, a country where the town-names are so hopeless that not even Professor Kiessling has tried to straighten them out; no one of the lists we possess bears any recognisable relation to any other. Polybius gave a town Ἀχριανή,[1] and Patrocles, a century earlier, gave one called Σαμαριανή.[2] I have found nothing to throw light on Achriane; it may be a transcript of a native name ending in -ān, but that is guesswork. Samariane of course looks like 'Samaritan'. There is a story, given only by Orosius (III, 7, 6) and other late writers, that Artaxerxes Ochus deported some Jews to Hyrcania;[3] but even if he did, they would not in the fourth century B.C. have named their town after the hated Samaria. There are later legends which identify Gog and Magog, shut up behind the mountains, with the Ten Tribes;[4] but one can hardly bring this into relation with Patrocles, neither did Assyrians really deport Samaritans to the Elburz, far outside their empire.[5] A Greek epitaph of a 'Samarian', Eumenes, is said to have been seen near Kermanshah in Media (see p. 366 n. 8), but as his wife was named Arsinoe he presumably came from Samaria in the Arsinoïte nome (Fayûm) in Egypt. A colony from Samaria in Palestine, settled by Alexander or some Persian king, is conceivable, but none such is known. Patrocles got his information through interpreters, and the name may be his own rendering in Greek of what he understood an interpreter to say; but what it means I do not know.

Lastly I must notice Ἀραρηνή in Arabia, as it comes in Strabo, and is instructive. Strabo (XVI, 781) says that Aelius Gallus, after leaving Leuce Come, went south through the land of Obodas' kinsman Aretas and then through a land of nomads, largely desert, called Ararene, under a king Sabos. The Nabataean state, though never Seleucid, had the Seleucid province-names, like Saracene (the first occurrence of the name Saracen), but in the first century B.C. and later the southward boundary of that state was at Hegra,[6] a little north of Al-'Ula, and Ararene was far beyond its bounds. But Ararene was not east of the Euphrates and is a late name, belonging to the reign of Augustus; it is the first example of a process, due to the -ηνη termination having become so usual throughout Asia, whereby under the Roman Empire that too familiar termination tended to be applied loosely to any territorial district; examples are the already mentioned Dosarene of the Periplus and the later Palmyrene. But this late usage has nothing to do with the second century B.C., and (Dosarene apart) I have only met with two instances of it east of the Euphrates. Writers of the Roman

[1] Steph. Ἀχριανή, πόλις Ὑρκανίας. Πολύβιος δεκάτῳ.

[2] In Strabo XI, 508.

[3] See on this story A. R. Anderson, *Alexander's Gate, Gog and Magog, and the Enclosed Nations* 1932 p. 59.

[4] Anderson *op. cit. passim.*

[5] As Anderson p. 58 suggests. For the real location of Gozan (Guzana) see Sidney Smith in *CAH* III p. 6 and Map 1.

[6] Tarn, *JEA* XV, 1929, p. 23.

Empire, even Strabo, sometimes misused two particular words and wrote Bactriane and Parthyene for Bactria and Parthia;[1] but this is a mere mistake, due to the cause mentioned above, and cannot affect the general result arrived at for the Hellenistic period.

The conclusion for that period then is that we have found two difficulties, perhaps exceptions, in Hyrcania and one lapse in Ptolemy. Looking at the great number of *-ηνη* and *-ιανη* names known, this is little enough in the literature of a people who were often careless about, and perhaps even disliked, the consistent use of technical terms in the modern fashion, and, in the particular case of India, is little to set against the fact that Ptolemy, but for his one lapse, is always careful in his usage. Moreover the eparchy- or province-names in the Paropamisadae seem certain (pp. 96 *sq.*); and though prior to the second century B.C. that country had belonged rather to the Iranian than to the Indian system, it could not fail, from its position on the Indian side of the Hindu Kush, to be something more than a half-way house to India. It seems then that such exceptions as I have succeeded in finding do not provide any alternative to the view that the nine province-names collected in India—seven from Ptolemy and one each from Pliny and Arrian—and discussed in Chapter VI must have the same connection with the Seleucid terminology as is exhibited in the nomenclature of all the other Seleucid Succession states, that is, that they were provinces of the Greek kingdom in India.

[1] Isidore shows that there was a Parthian satrapy (Seleucid eparchy) called Parthyene; perhaps therefore there was also a Bactrian satrapy (Seleucid eparchy) called Bactriane.

APPENDIX 3

AGATHOCLES' PEDIGREE COINS

In the first century B.C. there was in existence a fictitious pedigree of the Seleucid house which derived the descent of the dynasty from Alexander.[1] The fact is clearly shown in a series of inscriptions[2] set up by Antiochus I of Commagene below the representations of his ancestors, each inscription giving the name and patronymic of the corresponding figure; these inscriptions professedly give the respective pedigrees of his father, going back to Darius, and of his mother Laodice Thea Philadelphos, who was a Seleucid princess, a daughter of Antiochus VIII Grypus; and his mother's pedigree is the ordinary Seleucid pedigree[3] but begins with Alexander.[4]

How was Alexander brought into the Seleucid pedigree? I must emphasise that the Commagene inscriptions mean that some member of the direct Seleucid line was (supposed to be) a *lineal descendant* of Alexander. This member could not be the first Seleucus and the story could not have originated in his reign, as a great many people knew that he and Alexander were contemporaries and much of an age. Professor Rostovtzeff in an interesting paper[5] has suggested that the explanation is that in 306 Seleucus was trying to connect himself with Alexander by connecting his own mother Laodice with Alexander's mother Olympias. The method suggested is not too convincing, seeing that Laodice was a Macedonian name and Olympias was an Epirote; however, his quotation from Libanius may be taken to show that Seleucus I, like Ptolemy I and Antigonus I, did claim some connection with the Argead line. But a claim by Seleucus I to be connected with the Argeads has no bearing at all on the question, how did some member of the direct Seleucid line later than Seleucus I come to be considered a *lineal descendant* of Alexander? I answered that question in 1929,[6] but I can now take it further.

There is a story preserved in almost identical language by Livy and Appian,[7] which therefore (I think no one will dispute this) originally came from Polybius; and as it concerns people who lived in Polybius' own city, Megalopolis, during his own youth, it is extraordinarily well attested and

[1] I must refer to my paper *Queen Ptolemais and Apama*, *Class. Quarterly* XXIII, 1929, p. 138.

[2] *OGIS* 388–401.

[3] *Ib.* 399–401.

[4] *Ib.* 398.

[5] ΠΡΟΓΟΝΟΙ, *JHS* LV, 1935, pp. 56, 63–5.

[6] I gave it briefly, as being a simple case of two and two making four; but as Professor Rostovtzeff thinks my answer 'far-fetched' (*ib.* p. 65 n. 24) I must now give every link in the chain with (I fear tedious) minuteness.

[7] Livy XXXV, 47, 5 = App. *Syr.* 13.

the details must be taken as trustworthy. The story is that in 192 B.C. there was living in Megalopolis as a citizen a Macedonian named Philip who boasted that he was a descendant of Alexander, and 'to gain credence for his story' he named his two sons Philip (after Alexander's father) and Alexander, and named his daughter Apama. In Megalopolis at that time, therefore, it was believed (or some believed) that there had been an Apama who was a very close relative of Alexander's in the sense that his father Philip was a very close relative; for the man who wanted 'to gain credence for his story' would surely have named his daughter after Alexander's mother Olympias or his sister Cleopatra had it not been believed that there had been a woman named Apama who was at the very least as close a relation as they. Now as matter of history it is certain that Alexander had no relative named Apama, and tolerably certain that that rare name is Achaemenid[1] and not Macedonian at all. But though there was no Apama connected with Alexander, there was a very well-known woman of that name connected with Seleucus: at Susa in 324 he married an Apama who was a daughter of the Sogdian baron Spitamenes[2] and almost certainly an Achaemenid on her mother's side, and she bore him a son, Antiochus I. We have accordingly now got to find two things: an Apama who shall be (supposed to be) a very close relative of Alexander's, and a woman through whom some Seleucid king prior to the second century could claim *lineal descent* from Alexander (it has to be a woman, as the male line back to Alexander's contemporary Seleucus I was at the time accurately known to everybody); and as the name Apama is rare, and no Apama is known in the period of Alexander and the Successors except Seleucus' queen, the conclusion is inevitable that the answer to both questions is identical—Seleucus' queen Apama became a daughter of Alexander, and the fictitious Seleucid descent from Alexander was traced through her as (the real) mother of Antiochus I.

The fictitious Seleucid pedigree thus established is the key to several things in the Farther East, and the first is the coin-series of Agathocles. He struck a series of tetradrachms which bore on the obverse the head (or device) of some former king with his name and cult-title or legend, and on the reverse the characteristic type of that king, with the legend *βασιλεύοντος Ἀγαθοκλέους δικαίου*, 'Under the rule of Agathocles the Just'.[3] The coins known give the names of Alexander, Antiochus Nikator, Diodotus Soter, Euthydemus Theos, and Demetrius Aniketos;[4] the Alexander coins (there are two in the British Museum) of course have the head not of Alexander but of Heracles (or Alexander as Heracles) wearing the lion's scalp, and the

[1] Tarn, *op. cit.* p. 140; see Rostovtzeff *op. cit.* p. 65 and n. 24.

[2] Arr. VII, 4, 6 (from Ptolemy I).

[3] On *βασιλεύοντος* see further p. 354.

[4] The first four coins: *BMC* p. 10 nos. 1–3, Pl. IV, 1–3, and p. 164, Pl. XXX, 5; the Diodotus and Euthydemus coins also in *CHI* Pl. IV, 1 and 2. The new Demetrius coin: *NC* 1935 p. 1.

Antiochus coin, from the characteristic reverse type, is certainly Antiochus II.[1] These coins used to be called memorials of former rulers (which is meaningless), though more recently one numismatist did utter, very doubtfully, the word 'relationship';[2] they are in fact Agathocles' pedigree. The exact resemblance of this coin-series to the series of inscriptions in which Antiochus I of Commagene gave his mother's pedigree—both begin with Alexander and continue through the Seleucid line—shows that the nature and purpose of the two series must be identical, and as the Commagene series is professedly a pedigree, so must that of Agathocles be: he is giving the Euthydemid pedigree back to where it branches off from the Seleucid pedigree, followed by the fictitious Seleucid pedigree from that point back to Alexander. Some inscriptions are missing from the Commagene series, and two coins—Antiochus I and Seleucus (or Seleucus and Apama)—from Agathocles' series; but as the Demetrius coin only came to light in 1934 specimens of the others may yet be found. As Agathocles' pedigree passes backward through Diodotus to Antiochus II, it proves, as stated in Chapter III, that Diodotus married a daughter of Antiochus II and Euthydemus a daughter of Diodotus by the Seleucid princess; Agathocles was a Seleucid on the distaff side. The reason why he desired to proclaim that the Euthydemid family were Seleucid collaterals is given in Chapter V.

Antimachus published his pedigree at the same time as Agathocles; it was of course the same from Euthydemus backwards, but only the Diodotus and Euthydemus coins are known;[3] they show (see pp. 75 *sq.*) that Antimachus was a son of Euthydemus. The coins follow the same plan as those of Agathocles, but bear on the reverse the legend *βασιλεύοντος* Ἀ*ντιμάχου θεοῦ*, 'Under the rule of Antimachus the god'; naturally the two series were issued by the two kings in collaboration, and for the same reason.

There are several things to be said about the fictitious Seleucid pedigree. I think Yule was the first, though not the last, to suggest that the Alexander-descents of the Hindu Kush country were connected with the Bactrian Greeks;[4] it was a wonderfully brilliant guess, for now that it is known that the Euthydemid kings (and the house of Eucratides too, for that matter) claimed to go back to Alexander little doubt seems possible. These descents are discussed in Chapters VII and IX; here I need only point out that one of them further defines the position of Apama. Marco Polo relates that in his

[1] The first three kings named Antiochus have all been proposed, but there is no doubt at all. See *CHI* p. 450.

[2] Whitehead, *NNM* p. 16.

[3] The Diodotus coin, *BMC* p. 164, Pl. XXX, 6. The Euthydemus coin, long known to be in the hands of an Indian dealer, is now in the British Museum.

[4] Yule, *Marco Polo*, 2nd ed. 1874, vol. I p. 169 (p. 160 in the 3rd ed.), 'probably due to a genuine memory of the Graeco-Bactrian kingdom'. He did not consider the claim to Greek ancestry real. Recently given by W. P. Yetts, *Eurasia Septentrionalis antiqua* IX, 1934, p. 234, 'an outcome of the Greek conquest of this region and the establishment of hellenised states'.

day the (now extinct) family of the Mirs of Badakshan claimed to be descended from Alexander and a daughter of King Darius.[1] Alexander did marry Darius' elder daughter, Barsine, at Susa in 324;[2] but it is not Barsine who is meant, for Marco Polo also says that when he was at Balkh (*i.e.* Bactra) 'the people of the city tell that it was here that Alexander took to wife the daughter of Darius'.[3] The wife Alexander *did* marry at Bactra was Roxane, daughter of the Bactrian baron Oxyartes; and in Bactria therefore she had become Darius' daughter, just as she is in the Greek Alexander-romance[4] and some other Greek sources.[5] Apama then in the fullest version of the legend became a daughter of Alexander by his wife Roxane daughter of Darius III; the fact that the real Apama *was* an Achaemenid, and that she and the real Roxane both belonged to the Bactrian nobility,[6] doubtless helped, as perhaps did the legendary story that (beside Alexander IV) Roxane did have another child who died.[7] Naturally the makers of legend were not troubled by the trifling fact that the two women must in reality have been much the same age; legend, like law, cares not for trifles. One Hellenistic instance must suffice. When Antigonus I sent to Polyperchon a boy to play, under the name of Heracles, the part of an illegitimate son of Alexander, he chose (doubtless for some facial resemblance) a boy nearly six years too young for the alleged occasion of his birth;[8] but the discrepancy did not trouble the common man at the time, and has troubled few historians since.

The fictitious Seleucid pedigree played its part in the West no less than in the East. Apart from Megalopolis and Commagene, another Alexander-descent has come to light in the Greek city of Teos,[9] and others may follow; for an Alexander-descent implies attachment in some form or other to the

[1] 1 chap. XXIX in Yule; p. 56 in A. Ricci's translation from the text of L. F. Benedetto, *The travels of Marco Polo* 1931.

[2] Arr. VII, 4, 4 (from Ptolemy I).

[3] 1 chap. XXVII in Yule; Ricci p. 54.

[4] *Historia Alexandri Magni*, ed. Kroll, p. 92 l. 2, and often; and in some later versions.

[5] Suidas *s.v.* *Δαρεῖος*; Syncellus p. 264 B, given as Porphyry in *FHG* III p. 693 fr. 3 (1), but not so in *F. Gr. Hist.* Porphyry in fact, *F. Gr. Hist.* no. 260 fr. 3 (2), gave an intermediate version: Roxane was daughter of Oxyartes, king of the Bactrians.

[6] Sir A. Stein, *Innermost Asia* II p. 886 n. 2, made the attractive suggestion that Roxane was the same word as Roshan (which would make Roshan Oxyartes' fief), and then withdrew it on the ground that classical literature knows other Roxanes. But, so far as I know, other occurrences of the name are all much later than Alexander and therefore quite immaterial, being merely taken from his queen's name.

[7] Berve, *Das Alexanderreich* II p. 347.

[8] Tarn, *JHS* XLI, 1921, pp. 24, 27.

[9] *SEG* II, 581, second century B.C., a long catalogue of names of citizens of Teos, with patronymics but no other descriptive words, in the middle of which appears the entry *Διονύσιος Πυθέου ὁ ἐξ 'Αλεξάνδρου*.

Seleucid pedigree, and doubtless there were people in the Greek world who traced their lineage, real or reputed, from a concubine of this or that Seleucid king; compare the one-time descents from Charles II in England. Whether there was once a version in the West which made Apama a daughter of Barsine, not of Roxane, cannot at present be said; but certainly in the second century B.C. the legend that Apama was Alexander's daughter was well known from Megalopolis to Merv.[1]

It is tempting to try and guess when this legend originated. The coin-series of Antimachus and Agathocles can be accurately dated to 168 or 167 B.C. (Chap. v), but we can go back much further than that in the West. Apama of Megalopolis married king Amynander of Athamania in 192. In that year the claim of her family to descend from Alexander was known far beyond the bounds of Megalopolis, for it was known to Antiochus III: he held out to Apama's brother Philip, as a bait for his services, the hope of the crown—his 'ancestral' crown—of Macedonia.[2] If Apama married in 192 she was probably born round about 212–210, and she had two elder brothers; her father's claim then must have been in existence about 220, and might of course be older than that. We have then to seek an occasion of origin earlier than about 220; and as obviously the origin could not fall in the reigns of Seleucus I or of Apama's son Antiochus I, we are restricted, speaking roughly, to the reign of Antiochus II or Seleucus II. The establishment by Antiochus II of the cult of the πρόγονοι (ancestors) of the dynasty[3] might have prepared

[1] Apama underwent yet another transformation in Augustan literature; in Livy XXXVIII, 13, 5 she is Seleucus' *sister*.

[2] Livy XXXV, 47, 7; App. *Syr.* 13, ἐπελπίζων—playing with him.

[3] Rostovtzeff *op. cit.* In his text, pp. 59 *sqq.*, he calls the founder Antiochus III, on rather slight grounds, but in the later note on p. 66 he inclines to return to Antiochus II, the usual opinion. But I do not believe in the suggestion (p. 65) that there was an earlier cult of πρόγονοι under Antiochus I which included Alexander and the Achaemenids, and that Antiochus III (or II) 'eliminated' them 'from the list of his πρόγονοι'. Rostovtzeff (see p. 62) is going on the reference by the Ionian League to the policy of the πρόγονοι of Antiochus I in *OGIS* 222, a much-discussed expression, most recently treated by C. B. Welles, *Royal Correspondence in the Hellenistic period* 1934 p. 81. Now the *policy* is an essential part of the business; and if the references given by Rostovtzeff in the notes to p. 62 be examined, it will be found that there is only one real parallel to the phrase in *OGIS* 222, but that is a very exact parallel indeed. In l. 17 of Ditt.[3] 434/5 (Chremonides' decree of 267 B.C.)—a document of the same generation as *OGIS* 222—Chremonides makes Ptolemy II, in showing zeal for the liberation of Greece, follow τεῖ τῶν προγόνων καὶ τεῖ τῆς ἀδελφῆς προαιρέσει, the policy of his πρόγονοι and of his sister (Arsinoe II); both inscriptions refer to the *policy* of the πρόγονοι, and no one, I think, has ever doubted that in Chremonides' decree the word means Ptolemy I and no one else at all; the official pedigree of Ptolemy II as it was in 267 is well known from Satyrus and Theocritus (Tarn, *JHS* LIII, 1933, p. 57), and does not include either Alexander or anyone else who could have had a policy about Greece except Ptolemy I. It follows that the πρόγονοι of Antiochus I in *OGIS* 222

the ground, for the common man might not know very well whom this might include, while he probably did know that the state cult of the rival Ptolemies started with Alexander. But this cult was not the origin of the popular belief, for it did *not* start with Alexander.[1] It is clear, from the proceedings of Antiochus III in 192, that, though he knew of the alleged Seleucid Alexander-descent, he did not believe it; we may assume therefore that the Euthydemid kings did not believe it either. But the fictitious pedigree was used as propaganda by Agathocles and Antimachus in order to influence the common man at a time when they were fighting for their lives (Chap. v); it may therefore be supposed that it originated in some Seleucid extremity in order to influence the common man, and that it did influence him. If so, the fictitious pedigree first saw the light about 246–5, when Ptolemy III was overrunning the Seleucid empire in the name of the alleged rightful heir and the young Seleucus II was fighting for the very existence of his dynasty; 'we Seleucids are the true sons of Alexander' would have been no bad battle-cry. His sister took the fabrication eastward with her when she married Diodotus and it passed to her Euthydemid descendants; Bactrian local patriotism did the rest. As on the coins of Agathocles and Antimachus the dead kings of Bactria, Diodotus and Euthydemus, appear with cult names, it is conceivable that the Euthydemids had a state cult of their own, running back through the Seleucids to Alexander (see p. 201 n. 3).

should mean Seleucus I and no one else. Rostovtzeff's article really does not bear at all on the point considered in this Appendix—how came the Seleucid dynasty to be made *lineal descendants* of Alexander?

[1] *OGIS* 245, 246.

APPENDIX 4

THE YUGA-PURĀNA OF THE GĀRGĪ SAMHITĀ

The Gārgī Samhitā is an astrological work of uncertain date (it has been dated anywhere from the Christian Era to the third century A.D.), one of whose chapters, the Yuga-purāna, contains an historical account of (among other matters) the Greek advance to Pātaliputra, written as usual in the form of a prophecy. The existing texts of the Yuga-purāna are written in Sanscrit with (it is said) traces of Prakritisms; in the opinion of the late Dr Jayaswal, who devoted special attention to this work,[1] the extant account must go back to a historical chronicle,[2] written either in Prakrit or in mixed Sanscrit-Prakrit, which he dates in the latter half of the first century B.C. on the ground that it mentions no dynasties later than the Sacas. Historians of India have usually considered the historical account of the Yavanas in the Yuga-purāna as valuable, an opinion shared by Jayaswal, who regards the work as the earliest known Purāna and as exhibiting an independent tradition; occasionally someone has dissented from this view,[3] but the manner in which the accounts of the Greek Apollodorus and of the Yuga-purāna complement each other (Chap. IV) ought to be conclusive for the Yavana sections, as the two are presumably independent.

The history of the Yuga-purāna in modern times is peculiar. H. Kern in 1865 first brought it to notice in the preface to his edition of the Brihat Samhitā;[4] he possessed a single MS, apparently rather broken, and he gave a translation[5] of the greater part (not all) of what are §§5 and 7 in Jayaswal's translation (p. 453). Of §6 he merely said that it contains complaints against heretics, presumably Buddhist monks.[6] Nothing more was published, and what was known of the Sanscrit text so far as it related to the Greeks was confined to these parts of §§5 and 7, which Weber subsequently reprinted,[7] and to one line of §6 which Kern had quoted; except for Lévi,[8] §6 has gone unnoticed, though many writers have quoted or paraphrased Kern's trans-

[1] K. P. Jayaswal, *Historical Data in the Gārga-Samhitā and the Brahmin Empire*, *JBORS* XIV, 1928, p. 397. This is his publication of the text of the *Yuga-purāna*, with a translation.

[2] The worthlessness of the other Purānas on the Yavanas (pp. 133 n. 3 and 324 n. 1) makes this, to me, quite certain.

[3] As J. F. Fleet, *JRAS* 1914 p. 795, who called it historically worthless, but gave no reasons.

[4] H. Kern, *The Brihat-Sanhitá of Varáha-Mihira*, vol. XLVIII of the *Bibliotheca Indica* of the Asiatic Society of Bengal; Calcutta, 1865.

[5] *Ib.* pp. 37–8 of the preface. [6] *Ib.* p. 38.

[7] A. Weber, *Indische Studien* XIII, 1873, p. 306.

[8] P. 456, *post*.

lations of parts of §§5 and 7. I am informed by Dr L. D. Barnett of the British Museum that the MS used by Kern has been lost; consequently the bits of Sanscrit text mentioned above are of some value. It is also of interest that, on the strength of the historical passage, Kern dated the Gārgī Samhitā to *c.* 50 B.C.,[1] that is, he agreed very nearly with Jayaswal's dating of the original, for that he should confuse the date of the Gārgī Samhitā itself with the date of certain information contained in it was in 1865 inevitable; even to-day it is unhappily not uncommon to find statements preserved by some secondary Hellenistic writer assigned to that writer's own date.

This was the position till quite recently, when Jayaswal discovered two other MSS of the Yuga-purāna, one in the possession of the Asiatic Society of Bengal, the other in the Government Sanscrit College of Benares; these he has edited with a translation,[2] of which I reproduce the material part. A third MS also exists in Paris, and Lévi sent Jayaswal a list, which he published,[3] of the readings in which it differs from his edition; I gather that the variants, which in the Yavana sections are few, have as regards those sections no historical importance and that, speaking generally, the Paris MS confirms his results, but naturally I cannot be sure.

Jayaswal has conveniently divided his translation into fifteen sections, and I now give his translation of §§5 to 7; the section headings are his own.

'§5. [The Greek invasion and the Battle of Pushpapura.]

'After this, having invaded Sāketa, the Pañchālas, and Mathurā, the viciously valiant Yavanas (Greeks) will reach Kusumadhvaja ("the town of the flower-standard"). Then the thick mud-fortification (embankment) at Pātaliputra being reached, all the provinces will be in disorder, without doubt. Ultimately a great battle will follow with tree (-like) engines.[4]

'§6. [Condition of the people at the end of the Kali age.]

'In the end of the Yuga there will be non-Aryans following the religious practices of the Aryas. The Brahmanas, the Kshatriyas, the Vaisyas as well as the Sūdras will be low men. They undoubtedly will dress themselves all alike and will have conduct all alike. In that end of the Yuga men[5] will be united with heretical sects; they will strike friendships for the sake of women. This is without doubt. Without doubt there will be in this world Bhiksukas (religious mendicants)[6] of the Sūdra caste, wearing Chīra (Buddhist religious cloth) and bark, wearing matted hair and bark. At the approach of the end of the Yuga in this world, the Sūdras will offer oblations to fire with hymns proclaimed with *omkāra* and (will be) keepers of the three fires with little

[1] *Op. cit.* p. 40.

[2] P. 452 n. 1.

[3] *JBORS* xv, 1929, p. 129; the variants, usually single words, are only given in Sanscrit, with one exception which is translated; if that be the most important, the others are presumably, to the historian, negligible.

[4] The *Arthasāstra* mentions that on the walls of a city there should be engines of war (Jayaswal's note).

[5] *I.e.* the orthodox (W.W.T.).

[6] Buddhists (W.W.T.).

hesitation.[1] Without doubt in the end of the Kali age there will be Sūdras who will address with 'Bho!' and Brahmanas who will address others with 'Arya!' They will be alike in dress and conduct.

'§7. [Exactions of Dharma-mita, and Greek retirement from Madhadesa.]

'The *tamā*-elders of Dharma-mita will fearlessly devour the people. The Yavanas (Greeks) will command, the Kings will disappear. (But ultimately) the Yavanas, intoxicated with fighting, will not stay in Madhadesa (the Middle Country); there will be undoubtedly a civil war among them, arising in their own country,[2] there will be a very terrible and ferocious war.'

I now give for comparison a translation, kindly made for me by Dr Barnett, of those parts of §§5 and 7 which Kern gave and of which the Sanscrit text of his lost MS survives; it will be seen that it differs from Jayaswal on one important point, the definite statement that the Greeks took Pātaliputra.

'§5. Thereupon advancing to Sāketa, the Pañchālas, and Mathurā, the Yavanas, wickedly valiant, will win Kusumadhjava. Thereon, when the goodly (?) Puspapura has been gained... [Kardame prathite are unintelligible], all regions will become disturbed, without doubt.

'§7. The Yavanas furious in battle will not stay in the Middle Country; there will be without doubt mutual conflicts [reading samgrāmā for sembhāva]; out of their own circles will arise an awful and supremely lamentable strife.'

Before going further, I must mention one later study. Diwan Bahadur Professor K. H. Druva,[3] after premising that in all the MSS all the lines but twelve and many proper names are corrupt and many lines misplaced, has reconstructed the story with liberal alteration of proper names and, as he admits, free use of conjecture, inference, and 'guesses at truth';[4] his ideas of Greek history are somewhat antiquated, and the result, I fear, is too arbitrary to be of any use to the historian. But he has made one or two acute suggestions, which will be noticed where they belong.

Certain points about the document must now be considered. Jayaswal points out, as is clear if the Yuga-purāna be taken as a whole, that to the author the history of India centres on Pātaliputra;[5] he has in fact no further interest in the Greeks once they have quitted the Middle Country. It seems to me equally clear that the document as we have it speaks from the Brahman standpoint and rather dislikes Buddhists, Sūdras, and foreigners, whether Greeks or Sacas. But this was by no means an inevitable feature of a historical document written from the point of view of Pātaliputra, where Buddhism was strong; and in fact the work contains two curious exceptions to this dislike of the Greeks. One is the name Dharma-mita. Undoubtedly Jayaswal

[1] *I.e.* Sūdras will usurp the functions of Brahmans (W.W.T.).

[2] *I.e.* not in India (W.W.T.).

[3] *Historical contents of the Yuga-purāna*, *JBORS* XVI, 1930, p. 16.

[4] *Ib.* p. 59.

[5] *Op. cit.* (1928) p. 415.

is right that this name is yet another transcript of Demetrius,[1] but he has not noticed that it has been 'adjusted' in order to make the word Dharma part of the name, 'Friend of Justice', and thus recall the phrase Dharmaraja; that is, Demetrius is made a King of Justice. The allusion to Demetrius is dealt with elsewhere (pp. 178, 411). The other exception is the characterisation of the civil war between the Greeks which was to damage the Euthydemid power in India so badly as 'supremely lamentable'. The original chronicle or document, therefore, on which the Yuga-purāna as we have it was based was probably favourable to the Euthydemids, and the tone has been somewhat altered in transmission by the later author. As to the *tamā*-officials, Jayaswal has pointed out that the word is unknown and has suggested a connection with *ταμιεῖον*;[2] certainly 'tax-collectors' gives the sense required. The objection to the tax-collectors might find a place in the original document, even if it was favourable to Demetrius; few people love taxes.

Jayaswal thinks that §5 means that the Greeks did not take Pātaliputra.[3] But even in his MSS the first two lines of §7 show that Demetrius and the Yavanas had the supreme power, which entails the occupation of the capital, and Kern's MS gave its capture; the translations of both Lévi[4] and Barnett (above) are clear as to that. There is no doubt that in actual fact the Greeks did take Pātaliputra, from the passage of Apollodorus given on p. 144, a passage which has not found its way into the stock Greek quotations available to the Orientalist and is therefore usually overlooked.

Section 8 says that after the Yavanas have perished by the power of the Age seven kings will reign in Sāketa, and then with §§9 and 10 we come to the advent of the Sacas. I mention this because Jayaswal, by certain synchronisms with the Sunga kings which I am not competent to check, has reached the date of *c.* 100 B.C. for the coming of the Sacas, which is very much the dating I have adopted on quite other grounds.

In §11 are mentioned five Mlechchha kings, greedy and powerful, who will destroy the four castes: (1) red-eyed Amlata, the invincible; (2) Gopalobhama, reigning one year; (3) Pushyaka the just, one year; (4) Savila the invincible, three years; (5) Viknayas a non-Brahman, three years. Jayaswal suggests that the first four are the Greek kings Amyntas, Apollophanes, Peucolaos, Zoilus. I think this most improbable. These Greek kings have nothing to do with the story of Pātaliputra; their coin-titles, except perhaps in the case of Peucolaos, do not agree with those given to the kings of §11;[5] and Zoilus *δίκαιος* and Peucolaos are certainly, and Zoilus *σωτήρ* probably,

[1] For a list of the known transcripts of the name see p. 458 n. 2. This form, as Dharmamitra, occurs again as the name of Demetrias in Sogdiana; Lévi, *JA* 1933 p. 27 n. 1, and see p. 118.

[2] *JBORS* XIV, 1928, p. 128.

[3] *Ib.* p. 417.

[4] *Quid de Graecis* p. 17; he translates 'deinde capta urbe Puspapuro'.

[5] On the coins Amyntas is *νικάτωρ* and the two kings named Zoilus are *δίκαιος* and *σωτήρ* (see Chap. VIII); none are *ἀνίκητος*. Peucolaos is *δίκαιος* and *σωτήρ*.

earlier than Amyntas. These Mlechchha kings are well down in the Saca period; I fortunately do not have to guess who they are.

Finally §6, which Kern so tantalisingly omitted. Lévi's brief paraphrase in 1890[1] of this section, based I suppose on Kern's indications, was 'tunc pravae religioni addicti populi (Buddhistae scilicet) imperabunt', and a section in this sense would have been invaluable to the historian; but Jayaswal's full translation has nothing in it about ruling. What the section seems to mean is that the world will be turned upside down, distinctions of caste will vanish, and low-caste Sūdras will do many things which they have no business to do. The reference to Sūdras becoming Buddhists seems to me meaningless, as Buddhism knew no castes and equally accepted Brahman and beggar; it *may* be a way of saying that Buddhism will get the upper hand, but I do not so read it. But whether this picture is meant for the result of the Greek conquest at all may be doubtful; the section begins 'In the end of the Yuga', the Age, and it looks as if Druva might be right in transferring the whole section to the final period of destruction which will follow all the wars and close the Yuga. Also this section clumsily cuts in half the chronicle of the acts of the Yavanas and looks like an interpolation; it may be that the destruction of caste was a common-form accusation which could at any time be brought against any foreign ruler, as it is against the Mlechchhas in §11. One thing is clear: a Greek historian could only use §6 with the greatest reserve, and I am not using it.

[1] *Quid de Graecis* p. 17. It will be understood that this need not necessarily have been Lévi's opinion later.

APPENDIX 5

DEMETRIUS IN THE HĀTHIGUMPHĀ INSCRIPTION OF KHĀRAVELA

Few inscriptions have evoked so much discussion as the long document in the Hāthigumphā cave (Cave of the Elephant) in Orissa which records the acts of Khāravela, king of the Kalingas.[1] It ought to be a valuable historical record, but it is said to be so defaced and so difficult to decipher that almost everything about it seems to be matter of controversy or conjecture, including its date; for though the dominant opinion has been, and is, that it belongs to the middle of the second century B.C. (the reasons for this belief have differed considerably at different times), this opinion has not passed undisputed; there are archaeological difficulties for one thing,[2] and if an eminent scholar could declare in 1930 that on epigraphical grounds it must be very much later than 150 B.C.,[3] a layman cannot regard the date as settled. What interests the Greek historian, however, and the reason why this Appendix has to be written, is the fact that of recent years this inscription has been supposed to contain, and may contain, a reference to Demetrius.

In 1919 the late Dr Jayaswal and the late Professor R. D. Banerji made a fresh examination of the rock, and Jayaswal announced that he had read the word Yavanaraja, followed by the proper name Dimata; he has stated that he found the syllable -ma- clear and ultimately with great difficulty read Dimat[a.[4] This reading, and its interpretation as the Greek king Demetrius, were accepted both by Banerji[5] and by Dr Sten Konow.[6] Konow however said of his own reading: 'I can see Yavanaraja, as read by Mr Jayaswal, and of his Dimata the -ma- is quite legible'; he did not say if he could see the supposed faint traces of the rest of the word. Finally, in a joint article in 1930,[7] Jayaswal and Banerji, after saying that -ma- was distinct and that the first and third syllables could be read with great difficulty, added that the Greek king Demetrius called himself Dime[tra on his coin legends. The inscription is in Prakrit, and Dimata might therefore, I suppose, replace Dimetra; but though Dimetra might have passed in 1919, when nothing was

[1] Bibliography of the large literature in *CHI* p. 683, supplemented at considerable length by de la Vallée-Poussin pp. 193–4. Accounts of the inscription in *CHI* pp. 534 *sqq.* and de la Vallée-Poussin pp. 193 *sqq.* On the various datings proposed see also Sten Konow, *Acta Orientalia* I, 1923, p. 12.

[2] Sir John Marshall in *CHI* pp. 639 *sq.*

[3] De la Vallée-Poussin p. 198; Khāravela must be 'après, beaucoup après 150', probably early first century A.D.

[4] *JBORS* XIII, 1927, pp. 221, 228. [5] *Ib.*

[6] Konow *op. cit.* p. 27.

[7] *Ep. Ind.* XX, 1929–30, pp. 76, 84.

known of the Kharoshthi version of Demetrius' name on his rare bilingual coins but the letters Dime-, it should not have been put forward in 1930, seeing that in 1923 Mr Whitehead had published[1] the bilingual tetradrachm (p. 77), now in the British Museum, which gives (in the genitive) the full Kharoshthi reading of Demetrius' name, Demetriyasa. There is however among the transcriptions of the Greek name Demetrios[2] a seal from Besnagar which reads 'Of Timitra', and which would I suppose suffice to make Dimata a quite possible Prakrit form.[3] But on the facts above stated it would appear that there is an element of conjecture in the reading.

There is also, I apprehend, an element of conjecture in the decipherment of the sentence which states what the Yavanaraja did, as the translations of Jayaswal and Konow (I have not found any other) differ considerably. Konow's version[4] in 1923 was: 'And through the uproar occasioned by the action [*i.e.* incidents of Khāravela's invasion of Magadha] the Yavana king Demetrius went off to Mathurā in order to relieve his generals who were in trouble.' Jayaswal's version in 1927[5] was: 'On account of the report (uproar) occasioned by the acts of valour [*i.e.* the capture of a fortress etc. previously mentioned] the Greek king Demet(rios) drawing in his army and transport retreated to abandon Mathurā.' Then in 1928 Jayaswal put forward a totally different view:[6] what the inscription refers to, he said, is the Greek king (he does not say Demetrius) being beaten off from Pātaliputra when he attacked it and retreating to Mathurā. He had evidently discarded the *abandonment* of Mathurā (which is wise), and on this theory Khāravela does not come into the business at all.

It appears then (unless there be something later which I have missed) that all we can get at, taking the most favourable view, is that a Greek king, who may have been Demetrius, retreated to Mathurā. So much is known from other sources: the Yuga-purāna records the withdrawal of the Greeks from the Middle Country (App. 4), while Ptolemy and the coins show that Menander subsequently ruled in Mathurā (pp. 227, 228 n. 2, 245). Certainly the reason

[1] *NC* 1923 p. 317 no. 2.

[2] Transcriptions. Dattāmitra (Patañjali and *Mahābhārata*), Devamantiya (*Milindapañha*), Dharma-mita (*Yuga-purāna*, App. 4); these three are 'adjusted' to look like Indian words. Demetriya (on the bilingual tetradrachm), Timitra (on a seal from Besnagar, *ASI* 1914–15 i p. 19, ii p. 77). Add Damtāmitīyaka or Datāmitīyaka (Nasik 19, see p. 257 n. 3) for an inhabitant of Demetrias, and Dharmamitra-Demetrias, Lévi in *JA* 1933 p. 27 n. 1 (see p. 118). Note that Demetriya, though Prakrit, has retained the *r*.

[3] The substitution in Prakrit of *t* for the Greek δ can be seen on the coins in the usual Kharoshthi form of Artemidorus, Atrimitora, and in the two variants of Diomedes, Diyamedesa and Diyametasa, Whitehead *NC* p. 333. On one tetradrachm of Artemidorus the Kharoshthi has dropped the *r* but kept the *d*, Atimidara; Martin, *JASB* XXIII, 1927, Num. Supp. XL p. 20.

[4] *Op. cit.* p. 27.

[5] *JBORS* XIII p. 228.

[6] *JBORS* XIV p. 417.

for this withdrawal given or implied in the inscription—that the Greeks were frightened away by the invasion of Khāravela, though *ex hypothesi* he was attacking their enemy Pushyamitra—cannot be right; it may have pleased Khāravela to think so (if the inscription really be his and not of a later time), but one must follow the Yuga-purāna, which is explicit that the Greeks left the Middle Country because of Eucratides' invasion. It is true that this statement of the Yuga-purāna cannot be checked; but as the account given in the Yavana sections of that document is supported by the Greek Apollodorus where we possess him (Chap. IV), one feels confidence in its statement about the Greek withdrawal, though no fragment of Apollodorus on the subject has survived. But the inscription, though its somewhat conjectural decipherment affords no firm ground to the historian, may be right about the fact of the withdrawal, even though the reason be wrongly given.

One further point must be briefly noticed. Konow has put forward the view that, if the Khāravela inscription really mentions Demetrius (note the 'if'), then Demetrius was the king of the sieges of Sāketa and Madhyamikā mentioned by Patañjali,[1] which would mean (among other things) that it was he and not Menander who led the Greek advance south-eastward and he and not Apollodotus who led the Greek advance southward of Sind. Had the relations between Demetrius and his lieutenants ever been worked out, such a theory could never have been put forward; the evidence given in Chapter IV is too strong to give it a chance. But quite apart from that, the inscription can have no bearing at all on the Greek *invasion*, as I have been at pains to explain (pp. 146 *sq.*). What it might show is that Demetrius was in the Middle Country when the news came of Eucratides' attack, and ordered the withdrawal from Pātaliputra; but at present it is not possible to rely on this as attested by evidence, though the course of events (see Chaps. IV and V) renders it probable enough in itself.

[1] *Op. cit.* p. 35. Jayaswal has followed him, *JBORS* XIV p. 127.

APPENDIX 6

ALEXANDRIA OF THE CAUCASUS AND KAPISA

The relation of these two towns to each other is a problem. The Alexander historians make it clear that Alexandria was meant to be the capital of the Paropamisadae, and the references to it in the Milindapañha (p. 421 and n. 4) show that it was existing in the second century B.C., in the flourishing period of Greek rule, and probably in the first century also; and there is a Chinese mention of it round about 50 B.C. (p. 340). The literary evidence is then perfectly clear. But the evidence of the coins is equally clear that Kapisa was the Greek capital, for the coins of Pantaleon and Agathocles which show the Zeus of Kapisa holding Hecate *τριοδῖτις* on his hand prove beyond any doubt that (among other things) Kapisa was successively the seat of these two sub-kings (see on this p. 158). I need not enlarge here on the importance of Kapisa; this book should have sufficiently shown it, and Kapisa continued to be a capital for centuries after the name of Alexandria was forgotten.[1] Now it is unthinkable that there should have been at the same time two Greek capitals of the Paropamisadae; and a solution of the difficulty must be attempted.

In the absence of excavation there can naturally be no certainty about the site of Alexandria; all the sites so far proposed—the most favoured has been the ruin-mounds at Opian near Charikar—are mere guess-work, and the French archaeological mission declined to locate it.[2] There is however no reason to doubt the statement that it was in Opiane,[3] for Alexander founded it on his way northward by the Seistan-Ghazni-Kabul route, which would take him through Opiane on his way to the passes of the Hindu Kush; this means that it stood somewhere to the *west* of the united Panjshir-Ghorband river. We are also told that it was close to the Hindu Kush,[4] that it was the gateway to India,[5] and that it stood at the meeting-place of the three routes which crossed the Hindu Kush from Bactra (p. 139), the *τρίοδος ἐκ Βάκτρων* which was in the Paropamisadae. This last is shown by a comparison of the two surviving versions of the bematists' account of Alexander's march. Pliny (VI, 61) names as stages along the route the town of 'the Arachosians' (see App. 9), Ortospana (certainly Kabul, p. 471), and Alexandri oppidum, Alexander's city, *i.e.* Alexandria. In Eratosthenes[6] the name 'the Arachosians'

[1] On Kapisa see generally Foucher, *Afghanistan* pp. 266, 281 *sqq*.

[2] *Ib.* p. 274.

[3] Alexandria no. 5 in Stephanus, *ἐν τῇ Ὀπιάνῃ κατὰ τὴν Ἰνδικήν*, see p. 96.

[4] Curtius VII, 3, 23, in radicibus montis.

[5] Diod. XVII, 83, 1, *κατὰ τὴν εἰσβολὴν τὴν φέρουσαν εἰς τὴν Ἰνδικήν*.

[6] Strabo XI, 514. Eratosthenes adds that the *τρίοδος* was in the Paropamisadae, XV, 723.

is followed by the sentence *εἶτ' εἰς 'Ορτόσπανα ἐπὶ τὴν ἐκ Βάκτρων τρίοδον δισχιλίους*. As his version and Pliny's alike go back ultimately to the bematists' account they must agree on the stages, and Ortospana-Kabul was nowhere near the *τρίοδος*; for as, of the three routes across the Hindu Kush, one followed the valley of the Ghorband river and another that of the Panjshir, the *τρίοδος*, as everyone has seen, can only be at or near the point of junction of the two rivers.[1] This being so, something has fallen out in the text of Strabo XI, 514 after *'Ορτόσπανα*; the sentence should read *εἶτ' εἰς 'Ορτόσπανα* [figure, *εἶτ'*] *ἐπὶ τὴν ἐκ Βάκτρων τρίοδον*.[2] The *τρίοδος* then in Eratosthenes is the same stage as Alexandri oppidum in Pliny; Alexandria therefore stood at (or near) the *τρίοδος*, *i.e.* at or near the junction of the two rivers.

But what did stand at the *τρίοδος* was Kapisa; the above-mentioned figure of Hecate *τριοδῖτις* on the hand of the god of Kapisa is conclusive (see p. 158). Kapisa then stood at somewhere about the same place as Alexandria, and its history leaves no doubt that it was in fact the gateway of India, as Alexandria was said to be. The Milindapañha (*ante*) forbids the assumption that in the second century B.C. Alexandria had ceased to exist and that Kapisa had taken its place. And a physical identification of the two towns is impossible, for Alexandria stood in Opiane, to the *west* of the united Panjshir-Ghorband rivers, and Kapisa stood in Kapisene[3] to the *east* of them. There is no doubt about this, for Kapisene was Kafiristan or part of it; the province could only have lain to the east of the united rivers, because the province to the west of them, Opiane, is fixed by the modern name Opian; and in fact it has been suggested that Kapisa and Kamboja, the name of the people of Kafiristan, must be the same word.[4] Doubtless the native town of Kapisa was in existence long before Alexander's time.[5]

One further point. It has sometimes been stated that Kapisa is represented by the modern Begram, and this was the view of the French archaeological mission,[6] the reason being that Masson found vast quantities of Greek coins about Begram, including thousands of those of Eucratides, who is known from one of his coin-legends to have ruled in Kapisa (p. 212). But Begram is on the *west* side of the united rivers, in what was once Opiane. What

[1] Eratosthenes in Strabo XV, 723; *ἡ μὲν ἐπ' εὐθείας διὰ τῆς Βακτριανῆς καὶ τῆς ὑπερβάσεως τοῦ ὄρους εἰς 'Ορτόσπανα ἐπὶ τὴν ἐκ Βάκτρων τρίοδον ἥτις ἐστὶν ἐν τοῖς Παροπαμισάδαις*. The words *εἰς 'Ορτόσπανα*, which have got in from XI, 514, make nonsense and should be omitted; the meaning is quite simple, 'the direct road through Bactria and across the Hindu Kush to the *τρίοδος* in the Paropamisadae'.

[2] I am deliberately not considering the distance figures, as I only need the names of the stages. By Pliny's time more than one version of the bematists' figures had grown up, VI, 62.

[3] Pliny VI, 92, Capisene habuit Capisam urbem.

[4] Lévi, *JA* 1923 ii p. 52.

[5] Pliny VI, 92 implies this.

[6] Foucher, *Afghanistan* p. 269.

the mass of coins found about Begram therefore shows is that the mint (or principal mint) and trading centre of the Greek rulers of Kapisa lay *west* of the united rivers, *i.e.* in Alexandria.

There seems only one solution. Alexandria-Kapisa was a double city; the Greek Alexandria stood on the west bank of the united Panjshir-Ghorband rivers near the confluence, facing the native Kapisa on the east bank, and the two formed one city; and what Begram, a name meaning 'the city',[1] really represents is not so much Kapisa as Alexandria. Greeks *may* have tended to call the double city Alexandria and Indians Kapisa,[2] but there was no clear rule, for the name Alexandria appears in the Milinda and the name Kapisa in one of Pliny's sources. For consideration of what such a double city might mean I must refer to the text (p. 98); others of course are known. On the evidence of literature and the coins, which is all we have, there seems to be no other explanation; but it is to be hoped that some day it may be possible to test it by excavation.

[1] Mazumdar in Cunningham, *Geog.* p. 672.

[2] *E.g.* Mahāmāyūri ll. 83, 94 (Lévi, *JA* 1915 pp. 52, 55) and the Kharoshthi inscription on one of Eucratides' coin-series (p. 212). But it is said not to be mentioned in any Sanscrit text.

APPENDIX 7

ANTIOCHUS IV AND THE TEMPLE OF NANAIA

Did Antiochus IV attack the temple of Artemis-Nanaia in Elymais and suffer a repulse, or is the story a doublet of the story of Antiochus III attacking the temple of Bel in Elymais and losing his life?[1] The sources are Polybius XXXI, 9 (11); I Maccabees vi, 1–4; II Maccabees i, 13 *sqq.* and ix, 1 *sqq.*; Josephus, *Ant.* XII, 354–9; Appian, *Syr.* 66; Porphyry, frs. 53, 56 in *F. Gr. Hist.*; Eusebius I, 253 (Schöne); Jerome on Daniel x, pp. 718, 722. Of these, the two early sources, Polybius and the author of I Maccabees (whose story is independent of Polybius and is reproduced by Josephus), know nothing of any attack on a temple.

What Polybius says[2] is that Antiochus wanted money and proposed to attack the temple; it does not follow that he had information as to what Antiochus had in mind, and the statement might mean no more than that Antiochus had his army with him. Polybius does not say either that he then attacked the temple or that he was beaten off; he goes on to say that he was deceived of his expectation because the barbarians of the place would not agree to the proposed transgression of law (or custom). As Polybius could not possibly say that the natives did not agree to being attacked—a mere absurdity—the only thing which his rather obscure *παρανομίᾳ* can mean is that Antiochus made some proposal to the temple authorities which they rejected as unlawful or sacrilegious; and as he begins by saying that Antiochus wanted money, doubtless what it means is that the king demanded of the temple authorities money in some form, perhaps as (nominally) a loan which he may or may not have intended to repay. He was refused, and nothing further happened; when we come to the circumstances, it will be obvious that nothing further *could* happen.

The story in I Maccabees is that Antiochus heard of a wealthy city called Elymais in Persia in which was a wealthy temple; he attacked the city but was beaten off and fled to Babylon where he died. This, as we shall see, is fiction, but the point is that the writer knew nothing of any attack upon, or intention to attack, a *temple*; the king attacks a *city*. This story is repeated by Josephus, who has added the name of the temple as that of Artemis.

[1] Herzfeld, *Sakastan* p. 39, goes further than the doublet suggested by Bouché-Leclercq and says that Antiochus IV was never in Elymais at all. But, sources apart, he cannot have come to Gabae from the north-west, as Herzfeld suggests; he would have been going away from his objective, Parthia, and for no apparent reason.

[2] *βουλόμενος εὐπορῆσαι χρημάτων προέθετο στρατεύειν ἐπὶ τὸ τῆς Ἀρτέμιδος ἱερὸν εἰς τὴν Ἐλυμαΐδα. παραγενόμενος δ' ἐπὶ τοὺς τόπους καὶ διαψευσθεὶς τῆς ἐλπίδος διὰ τὸ μὴ συγχωρεῖν τῇ παρανομίᾳ τοὺς βαρβάρους (τοὺς) οἰκοῦντας περὶ τὸν τόπον, ἀναχωρῶν κ.τ.λ.*

It is worth notice in passing that neither Strabo's sources nor Josephus know of any attack upon the temple. Strabo, in his account of Susa and Elymais,[1] gives the attacks on temples there made by Antiochus III and Mithridates I of Parthia; had he found in his sources an attack by Antiochus IV, who comes between these two kings, he could hardly have omitted it. Josephus, in his criticism of Polybius, blames him for connecting Antiochus' death with a *wish* to plunder a temple which (he says) he did not in fact plunder.[2]

Before going further, the actual circumstances must be considered, which means answering the question 'What was this temple of Nanaia-Artemis?' It has been known since 1931 (earlier writers on the subject could not know) that the Elamite nature-goddess Nanaia was the great goddess of Greek Susa, and that her temple was at Susa and was, for some purposes at any rate (*e.g.* manumissions), used by the Greeks of Susa as their city-temple (see p. 29). It is also clear from Strabo and Pliny that there was no other temple of Nanaia (*i.e.* no other of importance) in Elymais at all;[3] this temple at Susa is the one Strabo calls τὰ Ἀζάρα,[4] and this is the temple of the Antiochus story. It may be that Polybius knew this, though he has contrived to give the false impression of a temple in Elymais; the one writer who certainly knew that the temple stood in a great city is the author of I Maccabees (Josephus merely copies him). I do not know whether Nanaia's temple stood within or without the wall of Susa;[5] but as regarded the city it was a little temple-state with its own treasury, a state within a state, as the temple of Artemis at Ephesus had been prior to the reign of Lysimachus, and as many other Asiatic temples were, *e.g.* at Babylon and Uruk; and exactly as the Ephesians (before Lysimachus) nevertheless treated the Artemision as their own temple, so the Greeks at Susa regarded the temple of Nanaia. They sometimes called Nanaia Artemis, and it seems that by the latter part of the second century she, like Ishtar-Artemis of Uruk, had appropriated from Ephesus Artemis' bee (p. 6); and the importance of this temple of Nanaia is shown by the fact that the Parthian king Phraates II, whose father Mithridates I had conquered Elymais, occasionally put her bee on the royal coinage.[6] Now Susa was Antiochus' city—the inscriptions show that it was Seleucid throughout the reigns of Seleucus IV and Antiochus IV;[7] con-

[1] Strabo XVI, 744.
[2] *Ant.* XII, 358, βουληθέντα.
[3] Strabo XVI, 744; Pliny VI, 135, who shows it was at Susa.
[4] Strabo XVI, 744.
[5] If it be identical with the temple of Anaïtis mentioned by Aelian where tame lions lived in the precinct, it was probably outside; but the identification is guess-work.
[6] For the bee see Allotte de la Fuye, *MDP* XXV, 1934, p. 10.
[7] Seleucus IV: *SEG* VII nos. 17 and 2. Antiochus IV: *ib.* nos. 24 (see Fr. Cumont, *CR Ac. Inscr.* 1932 p. 285) and probably 15. It may be a question whether no. 18 belongs to the reign of Antiochus III, whose rule is known from Polybius (so Cumont and Holleaux, on the letter-forms, *CR Ac. Inscr.* 1931 p. 287), or of Antiochus IV (E. Cavaignac, *BCH* LVII, 1933, p. 416).

sequently the temple of Nanaia was Antiochus' own temple. And Hellenistic kings did not sack their own temples;[1] that is first principles. But though Nanaia's temple was a state, it was not a large territorial state like some temple-states in Asia Minor, but a city-temple like the Artemision at Ephesus; and had Antiochus really desired to sack it, the 'barbarians of the place', that is, the Elymean priesthood and personnel of the temple, would have had no chance of resisting his army, as very late writers make them do.

It follows from this that the story in I Maccabees, that Antiochus attacked his own city of Susa, cannot be true, and also that the two late versions which grew up—that of Appian (second century A.D.), that he did sack his own temple, and that of Porphyry fr. 53, that he tried to sack it and was beaten off—cannot be true either, apart from the fact that these late stories cannot be set up against Polybius. They belong to a time when the facts about Nanaia's temple and its connection with Susa were no longer known in the West (Porphyry fr. 56 apparently puts the temple on the summit of a holy mountain called Saba); and probably they all grew either out of Polybius' unhappy phrase προέθετο στρατεύειν or out of the fact which itself gave rise to Polybius' phrase and to the story in I Maccabees, the fact that Antiochus did march his army to Susa as a stage on the road to Parthia; I have given his route elsewhere (pp. 213 *sq.*). Whether Polybius understood what Antiochus was doing is very doubtful; but we cannot go behind him, and whatever be the dealing between Antiochus and the temple authorities which is concealed beneath the obscure phrase μὴ συγχωρεῖν τῇ παρανομίᾳ, the words can only indicate some peaceful dealing and not an attack. Whether the *late* story of the attack may be a doublet of the story about Antiochus III is quite immaterial.

I need hardly notice the two inconsistent stories in II Maccabees. In i, 13 Antiochus enters the temple of Nanaia peacefully to wed the goddess—that is taken from his marriage to Atargatis—and is murdered by the priests, which Polybius shows to be untrue. In chap. ix he attacks a temple in *Persepolis*, is beaten off, flies to Ecbatana, and dies 'eaten of worms' on his way to Judaea. Polybius shows the latter part to be untrue; but the story has this amount of interest—it knows that Antiochus *was* at Persepolis with his army, as he must have been on the road he was following (p. 214).

The story then that Antiochus IV sacked or tried to sack the temple of Nanaia is very late and demonstrably untrue; but there is still one point to notice, and that is that Elymais, in the sense of the kingdom of Elymais, does not come into the story at all, though both the early sources use the name. Whether that kingdom sometimes included Susa or not,[2] it did not do so in

[1] It has been thought that Antiochus III at Ecbatana was an instance to the contrary; see Holleaux in *CAH* VIII p. 140. I think myself that it proves that, as some have supposed, Ecbatana was at the time Parthian.

[2] The notices are most confused. Weissbach, *Elymais* in PW, thought that Elymais and Susiane were 'im Grunde' identical; Cumont, *CR Ac. Inscr.* 1932 p. 248 argued that Susa was never subject to the kings of Elymais. I need not go into the question here.

the reign of Antiochus IV, as the inscriptions show that Susa was his city. It cannot be said for certain whether the first king of Elymais, Kamnaskires I, threw off Seleucid rule after Magnesia or after the death of Antiochus IV; Strabo would suit either view,[1] but the former is more probable, for Diodorus (? from Polybius) implies that when Antiochus III reached Elymais it was both independent and organised;[2] moreover, while Kamnaskires I on his drachms does not bear the title 'Victorious', on his tetradrachms he does,[3] which could be interpreted to mean that it was only after the repulse of Antiochus III that he took that title and began to coin tetradrachms. But there is no certainty. It is however certain that if Elymais had a king, or whoever was its king, during the reign of Antiochus IV, that king was Antiochus' vassal; for Eucratides, who was responsible, could never have gone eastward leaving behind him an independent rebel of considerable power[4] at the very gates of Susa. And with the temple of Nanaia at Susa that king had no concern. I have mentioned Elymais because of one curious little fact bearing on Antiochus' story: when Kamnaskires II, whose date (82–1 B.C.) is known from his dated coins, revolted from Parthia in the break-up which followed the death of Mithridates II in 87 and again made Elymais independent, he put on his coinage, not the Seleucid Apollo of Kamnaskires I, but the well-known type of Antiochus IV, Zeus enthroned holding Nike on his hand.[5] There was no hostility to the memory of Antiochus IV in Elymais.

[1] XVI, 744: Elymais had refused to be subject to the Seleucids as it refused to be subject to the Parthians.

[2] Diod. XXIX, 15: Antiochus III said that the Elymeans began 'the war' against him, which implies organisation.

[3] Hill *op. cit.* pp. clxxxvi–vii. The coins are dated by their style to the first half of the second century B.C.

[4] Strabo, *ib.*, δύναμιν κεκτημένος μεγάλην.

[5] Hill *op. cit.* pp. 245 *sq.*; Pl. XXXVIII, 1–4.

APPENDIX 8

A SEALING FROM SELEUCEIA

Among the seal-impressions found in excavating Seleuceia on the Tigris is one which differs considerably from the ordinary run of impressions made by seals of local or western manufacture;[1] it is the head of a man, between youth and middle age, who wears the flat kausia of the Euthydemids known from the coins of Antimachus and Demetrius II,[2] and the portraiture is so strong and vivid that to my mind there can be little doubt that the seal was engraved in Bactria by one of the good artists.[3] Mr McDowell, in publishing it, called it Timarchus,[4] but I see no possibility of it being Timarchus; the head is not diademed, and bears not the least resemblance to the head of Timarchus on his coins,[5] quite apart from the Bactrian kausia. If, after the death of Antiochus IV, Eucratides, as seems certain enough, acknowledged no allegiance to the Seleucid Demetrius I and stood with the rebel Timarchus (p. 218), Demetrius I cannot have been badly disposed towards Eucratides' enemies; and it might therefore be conceivable that the portrait in question was that of some member of one of the Euthydemid families who had escaped the slaughter of his house by Eucratides and found refuge in Seleuceia after the accession of the Seleucid Demetrius I.

It was common enough for Hellenistic kings to give asylum to other states' exiles, who might one day have their uses; one need only recall the number of the dispossessed who had found shelter in their time at the courts of Lysimachus and Ptolemy II. But if some Euthydemid prince did escape in 167, his natural refuge would not have been Seleuceia, which was closed to him and was to remain closed for another four years till Antiochus IV died, but Apollodotus or Menander in India; and the discovery of the Bajaur hoard has made it more than probable that a son of Antimachus,

[1] McDowell, *Stamped objects*, Pl. I, 10 and p. 46.

[2] Two coins of a 'King Antiochus', with a head-covering something like a kausia, have been found at Seleuceia: McDowell, *Coins from Seleucia* pp. 17, 18 nos. 39, 40; but it cannot be said that it is the same as the Euthydemid kausia. There is also a head of 'King Diodotus' in a flat kausia, *Lahore Cat.* p. 10 no. 4. But these earlier instances are not really material, for I am going on the portraiture, not the kausia.

[3] McDowell, *Stamped objects* p. 218, thought of some connection with Bactrian art, but did not draw the obvious conclusion.

[4] *Ib.* pp. 214 *sqq.*

[5] *BMC Sel.* p. 50. McDowell *ib.* p. 217 sought to meet this objection by saying that the head on Timarchus' coins is not himself but Antiochus V. But the head is that of a middle-aged man, while Antiochus V at his death in 162–1 cannot have been over twelve, the earliest possible year for his birth being 174.

afterwards Antimachus II Nikephoros, did escape to Menander (p. 229). As both Menander and the Seleucid Demetrius I were natural enemies of Eucratides, it is therefore conceivable that Menander, during his struggle with Eucratides, sent this Antimachus (not yet his sub-king) to Seleuceia as his envoy to Demetrius I and that he is the prince of the seal-impression who wears the flat kausia of the elder Antimachus; the portrait of Antimachus II happens to be unknown, as when king he did not put his head on his coins.[1] If so, another similar Seleuceia sealing, an excellent portrait of an older man whom McDowell calls Heracleides,[2] would be some official who accompanied Antimachus on his mission.

This theory would imply that the prince of a rude coin-mould found at Seleuceia,[3] who wears both kausia and diadem, is not identical with the prince of the seal-impression, with whom McDowell was inclined to identify him.[4] The identity seems to me more than questionable; so far as can be judged by the coin-mould as illustrated, the features of the two men bear little resemblance, and the half-obliterated type of the coin-mould is certainly not the well-known type of Demetrius, Heracles standing upright and crowning himself, as McDowell thought;[5] the club over the left shoulder is absent, and the figure is not standing upright at all but *leaning* on some object (? a pillar) as large as itself; it is no known Graeco-Bactrian type. The prince of the coin-mould might be some refugee to whom some Seleucid gave a little principality for his living, as Ptolemy II did to Ptolemy 'the Telmessian'[6] or Antony to Monaeses;[7] but it is entirely obscure.

[1] No doubt his coin-type, 'king on prancing horse' (*BMC* Pl. XIII, 3), is meant for himself. On *ib.* p. 55 this king's head-dress is called a kausia; but nothing on the plate suggests that it was the flat kausia.

[2] *Op. cit.* Pl. I, 11.

[3] *Ib.* Pl. VI, 115, 116.

[4] *Ib.* pp. 217 *sq.*, 249 *sq.*

[5] *Ib.* p. 250, where his references are to Demetrius' type, though he does not name it.

[6] *OGIS* 55.

[7] Plut. *Ant.* 37; Dio XLIX, 24, 2.

APPENDIX 9

KI-PIN (KOPHEN) AND 'ARACHOSIA'

The controversy whether the Chinese Ki-pin in the Kushan period meant Kapisa or Kashmir is now, or ought to be, ancient history; there is no reasonable doubt that the word meant the Kushan empire, which included Kapisa and Kashmir and much else; if you went to either place you went to Ki-pin.[1] But the Chinese had the word long before the Kushan period; and its earlier meaning has its bearing on the story of the Greeks in India.

It was seen long ago that the word Ki-pin imports a Greek place-name Kophen[2] or Kophene, obviously connected with the Kophen (Kabul) river. Cunningham, in the belief that this place-name does not actually occur in Greek (Kophene does not), gave the name Kophene, a properly formed eparchy name, to the district south of the lower Kabul river of which Purushapura (Peshawur) was the capital,[3] thus making it one of the satrapies of Gandhāra; and in fact, though the names of several of the Gandhāra satrapies are known (p. 237), that of the Peshawur satrapy is missing (unless it were part of Peucelaïtis and not a separate satrapy). But this cannot be right, for, though the province-name Kophene does not occur in Greek, a town-name Kophen does, and it cannot be Peshawur. Stephanus gives the name and identifies it with a town Arachosia 'not far from the Massagetae';[4] his source for the identification is not given. By 'Massagetae' here he can only mean the people called Parsii (Pasiani of Apollodorus)[5] who after the overthrow of the Bactrian kingdom had joined in the great Saca invasion of Parthia; his statement means that at the time of the invasion the Parsii were members of the Massagetae confederacy,[6] for no other Massagetae had anything to do with Kophen. After the defeat of that invasion the Parsii had separated from the main body and had worked northward through Arachosia by the regular route which Alexander had once followed, by Ghazni to Kabul;[7] this is clear from Ptolemy, who has preserved so much information from the Greek period in India (Chap. VI), and who, perhaps ultimately from 'Trogus' source', records the Parsii by name as being in the Paropamisadae (which they could not have reached in any other way) and also gives two villages of theirs in that country, Parsia and Parsiana.[8]

[1] Lévi concluded long ago (*JA* 1915 p. 102) that the Chinese mixed up Kapisa and Kashmir in their Ki-pin.

[2] Lassen, 1^2 p. 29 n. 1; Gutschmid p. 109.

[3] *Geog.* pp. 38, 43, and see his Map 3.

[4] *s.v.* Ἀραχωσία: Ἀραχωσία, πόλις οὐκ ἄποθεν Μασσαγετῶν, ἥτις καὶ Κωφὴν ἐκαλεῖτο.

[5] For the Pasiani-Parsii see pp. 292 *sqq.*

[6] For another case of a particular member of the Massagetae confederacy being called 'Massagetae' compare Arr. IV, 16, 4 with Strabo XI, 513 (given p. 479 n. 1).

[7] Tarn, *SP Stud.* pp. 14 *sqq.*; *CAH* IX pp. 583 *sqq.*

[8] Ptol. VI, 18; Parsiana is the adjectival form, like Pasiani, p. 292.

One must first try to be clear about this town Arachosia, for no serious examination of the difficult geography of the Arachosian satrapy has been made since Droysen. Stephanus' town Arachosia is the town Arachosia of Pliny VI, 92 and the Arachotos of Ptolemy VI, 20, and is also 'the Arachosians' of Eratosthenes in Strabo XI, 514[1] and of Pliny VI, 62, two notices which both go back to Alexander's bematists and give their distances; the name 'the Arachosians' indicates the Persian capital of the Arachosian satrapy. 'The Arachosians' has nothing to do with any Alexandria, or with Kandahar or Ghazni; we have the bematists' figures, and Droysen[2] proved conclusively that 'the Arachosians' was somewhere in the neighbourhood of Kalat-i-Gilzai, a natural enough situation for the seat of the Persian satrap who had to govern both the plains of Seistan and the hill country to the north and east. But Alexander separated Seistan from the Arachosian satrapy and left that satrapy nothing but the hill country, identical with the later Parthian satrapy of Arachosia in Isidore 19; and 'the Arachosians' ceased to be a good centre for government. Alexander, therefore, who had already provided for Seistan by the foundation of Alexandria-Prophthasia (p. 14) on the Hamun Lake, proceeded to found, much farther to the north than Kalat-i-Gilzai, an Alexandria which was to be capital of the hill country; the foundation of this Alexandria is recorded in Arrian III, 28, 4 as made *before* Alexander crossed the Caucasus into the Kabul valley but when he was already in the hills and in a district where the people were 'Indians' (*ib.* III, 28, 1); without any doubt therefore it is now represented by Ghazni. This Alexandria is the *μητρόπολις* 'Αραχωσίας of Isidore 19, which Droysen rightly saw was Ghazni;[3] Isidore, in calling the Parthian satrapy of Arachosia 'White India', recalls Arrian's 'Indians'. It is also Alexandria 'among the Arachosians', no. 12 in Stephanus' list, and may also be no. 15, 'beside the Arachosians (or "the Arachosians") but bordering on India'.[4]

This shows that the corruption in Isidore 18 and 19 goes deeper than has

[1] Stephanus *s.v.* *'Αραχωτοί*, citing Strabo XI, *i.e.* 514, calls 'the Arachosians' a city of India, which can only mean Isidore's 'White India' (p. 53). As Isidore's phrase belongs to the time of the Azes dynasty, *c.* 30 B.C.–A.D. 19, Stephanus shows that the name Demetrias had been lost and the old name had come back by that date, which agrees roughly with the period when the name Demetrias in Sind went out of use, p. 257 n. 3. The rest of the notice in Stephanus, for which he also cites Strabo XI, *εἰσὶ δὲ καὶ ἄλλοι ('Αραχωτοὶ) πλησίον Μασσαγετῶν*, has (as *ἄλλοι* shows) nothing to do with 'the Arachosians' or the city Arachosia; it is merely the *'Αραχωτοί* on the Oxus of Strabo XI, 513, an obvious error for Apasiacae, see p. 91 n. 3.

[2] *Hellenismus* III, 2, pp. 217–20 (second German ed., 1877).

[3] *Ib.* III, 2, p. 720. Writers since Droysen have usually called it Kandahar, and I fear I have done this myself; but it will not work once it is looked into.

[4] *Παρὰ τοῖς 'Αραχώτοις, ὁμοροῦσα τῇ 'Ινδικῇ*. This may be a duplicate of Alexandria no. 12, *ἐν 'Αραχώτοις*, from another source, or perhaps a duplicate of no. 5, Alexandria (of the Caucasus) in Opiane.

been supposed;[1] the name of the metropolis of Arachosia in 19 must be Ἀλεξάνδρεια, not Ἀλεξανδρόπολις, and Ἀλεξάνδρεια should not come in 18 at all but only Ἀλεξανδρόπολις, near (πλησίον) Sacastene (not *in* Sacastene, as Droysen *loc. cit.* and Tscherikower, p. 103 give it). Alexandropolis near Sacastene can only be Kandahar, and this settles the question of its foundation, for a place called Alexandropolis cannot have been a city founded by Alexander (p. 7), and in fact there is no record that he founded Kandahar; Alexandropolis at best was a military colony which (possibly quite correctly) attributed its settlement to him. I need not consider the conflicting opinions about the *name* Kandahar, whether it be derived from Alexander (Iskandr), from Gandhāra (for which there seems no historical reason), or (most probably) from the Parthian Gondophares (Gundofarr). It must however be supposed, for reasons given elsewhere (p. 94), that the old Persian capital, 'the Arachosians', was the point at (or representing) which Demetrius founded his name-city Demetrias.

Stephanus' notice of the town Arachosia and the Massagetae is therefore absolutely right. But his further identification of the town Arachosia with Kophen cannot be right, for Kophen cannot be separated from the Kophen (Kabul) river; what the identification does show is that there was some connection between the town Arachosia and Kophen, and this is shown again by Pliny VI, 94, who makes the Kophen a river of Arachosia, though he places on it a town with an Indian name.[2] Returning to the bematists' route from Seistan to the Paropamisadae *via* Ghazni, there is no doubt that Ortospana, as universally believed, is Kabul,[3] this being its Iranian name;[4] and as the town Kophen has to be connected both with the town Arachosia and the Kophen river there is no place which it can be except Kabul, for there is no other place of importance on the route Seistan—Arachosia (Demetrias)—Ghazni (Alexandria)—Kabul (Ortospana)—τρίοδος (Alexandria) whose Greek name is missing.[5] Kophen therefore is Ortospana-

[1] In 18 (Sacastene) he has *καὶ πλησίον Ἀλεξάνδρεια πόλις καὶ πλησίον Ἀλεξανδρόπολις πόλις*, and in 19 (Arachosia) he has *Ἀλεξανδρόπολις, μητρόπολις Ἀραχωσίας*. It has long been recognised that one of the two names in 18 must go out; and Arrian III, 28, 4 makes it certain that the name in 19 (Isidore is reproducing an official survey) should be *Ἀλεξάνδρεια*. *Ἀλεξάνδρεια* therefore has been transferred from 19 to 18, and must go out of 18 and back to its place in 19, which has been filled by *Ἀλεξανδρόπολις*, taken from 18. The real reading then of 18 is *καὶ πλησίον Ἀλεξανδρόπολις πόλις* and of 19 *Ἀλεξάνδρεια, μητρόπολις Ἀραχωσίας*.

[2] Condigramma, which is Sanscrit -grāma; see other cases p. 244.

[3] Pliny VI, 61 (from the bematists), fifty Roman miles from Alexandria, *i.e.* from the *τρίοδος*, a fixed point (see App. 6); it is near enough. On the right reading of Strabo XI, 514, see p. 461: the distance between Ortospana and the *τρίοδος* has fallen out.

[4] Ptolemy has similar Iranian names in VI, 8, 13, *Πορτόσπανα* in Carmania, and VI, 4, 4, *Πορυόσπανα* in Persis.

[5] I cannot use Hsüan Tsiang's Hu-pi-na as evidence for the name Kophen, for opinion has always been divided as to whether Hu-pi-na was Kabul or whether

Kabul, and Kophene, though the actual word does not occur, must have been the Greek name of the Kabul eparchy of the Paropamisadae satrapy under the Seleucids; several eparchy names in that satrapy are known (pp. 96 *sq.*), but the Kabul name is missing. Stephanus' mistaken identification of the town Arachosia with Kophen (Kabul) arose therefore, not merely from the fact that the two towns were stations on the same great route from Seistan to Alexandria-Kapisa, but from the fact that in Demetrius' reign both were for a time under the same sub-kings (Pantaleon, Agathocles, see pp. 157 *sq.*) and both subsequently formed part of the kingdom of the Parsii, a kingdom known to some source of Ptolemy (presumably 'Trogus' source'), if his Gazaka or Gauzaka[1] be the native name of Alexandria-Ghazni;[2] for he puts this place in the Paropamisadae, which (as Ghazni was certainly in Arachosia) here means the kingdom ruled from Kabul.

It can now be seen what happened. After the Parthians, somewhere between 124 and 115, broke the Saca invasion, the invaders, who comprised more than one people, entered India not by one route but by two. The movements of the main body, who ultimately came up the Indus to Taxila, are noticed elsewhere (Chap. VIII). But another body, the Parsii, went north from Sacastene through Arachosia by Alexander's route—we have been looking at the record—and ultimately took Kophen-Kabul from the Greeks. From their first contact with China dates the origin of the name Ki-pin.

Ki-pin was originally Kophen-Kabul.[3] The name Ki-pin is unknown to Chang-k'ien and also to Ssu-ma Ch'ien, who is supposed to have finished the Shi-ki about 99 B.C. or somewhat later[4] (Chap. CXXIII, which alone concerns us, contains information of the year 101); the name had therefore not reached China by *c.* 100 B.C. It first occurs in the Ch'ien-han-shu, written by Pan-ku late in the first century A.D. That work states that the first relations of China with Ki-pin (*i.e.* China's first attempt to reach any land south of the Hindu Kush) began in the reign of the Emperor Wu-ti,[5] who died in 87 B.C.; Kabul therefore was in Saca hands before that date, and the natural supposition is that the Sacas took it when the kingdom of Antialcidas, who must have been a king of some power, broke up on his death (p. 315); incidentally this furnishes another reason for supposing that he was not alive

it represented Opian, and there can be no certainty. See the discussion in T. Watters, *On Yuan Chwang's travels in India* II, 1905, p. 266, with the itinerary p. 342 of V. A. Smith, who preferred Opian, and add to Watters' references Wylie p. 34 n., who preferred Kabul.

[1] Ptol. VI, 18, 4, *Γάζακα ἢ Γαύζακα.*

[2] E. Benveniste, *JA* 226, 1935, p. 143, reading *Γάνζακα.* This town has not the same co-ordinates as Alexandria (Ghazni), VI, 20, 4, but that means little; Ptolemy's habit of making two places out of one is notorious (pp. 231 *sq.*).

[3] Lassen suggested Ki-pin might be Kabul, but it has never been worked out; Wylie pp. 33–4 assumed it.

[4] Hirth p. 91.

[5] Wylie p. 36; Franke p. 63; de Groot p. 88.

as late as 90 B.C. (p. 314). Wu-ti's communication was certainly not with Antialcidas himself: the Chinese could never have been given, or obtained, the name Kophen as the name of Antialcidas' extensive realm, for to the Greeks Kabul was of very secondary importance. At the same time, the great Saca state in northern India created by Maues had not formed by 87 (Chap. VIII); Wu-ti's Ki-pin therefore was Kabul and whatever the Sacas (Parsii) of Kabul ruled at the time, which may have been a large part of the Paropamisadae (p. 332). This too is the meaning of Ki-pin in the story of Yin-mo-fu given in the Ch'ien-han-shu (set out pp. 339 *sq.*), which Pan-ku must have taken from Wen-chung's Report, no other source being possible. But shortly after this episode communication with the Paropamisadae was abandoned by the Emperor Yuan-ti (48–33 B.C.), and a memorandum drawn up by Tu-k'in for the next Han Emperor Ching-ti (32–7 B.C.) said that it was impossible to reach that country effectively and that it was best to leave it alone (p. 350); Wen-chung was probably the last Chinese official to visit it.

The name of this the first Saca state south of the Hindu Kush with which the Chinese had become acquainted was transferred, by a natural process, to the great Saca realm which soon afterwards absorbed it, and that is what it meant to Pan-ku himself, writing about a century later than that absorption; probably he did not know what Wen-Chung's Ki-pin was, but he transcribed faithfully and gave us the chance of knowing. To Pan-ku personally Ki-pin meant the Saca realm in India;[1] later writers transferred the name to the realm of the Kushans who ultimately replaced the Sacas. It has been truly said that the Chinese never got clear ideas about this great kingdom of 'Ki-pin' in Saca times.[2] Pan-ku did not follow his usual rule of giving the numbers of families, of inhabitants, and of warriors, but merely said that the numbers were those of a great kingdom, his formula for states of which he knew little, and his own formal account of Ki-pin[3] is a mixture of elements drawn from different parts of it and not necessarily all trustworthy; for its alleged currency[4] numismatists have sought, and will seek, in vain.

I venture to think that the story of the name Ki-pin is now tolerably complete.

[1] So Herzfeld, *Sakastan*, p. 32 (cf. p. 35): Ki-pin must be treated as 'die politische Einheit des Sakareichs'. Pan-ku, having transferred the Ki-pin name of Kabul to the Saca kingdom, introduced a new name for Kabul (Ko-fu, Kao-phou, Ko-hu) and wrongly made it the domain of one of the five *yabghus* of the Yueh-chi; the author of the *Hou-han-shu* pointed out the error (see de Groot pp. 101–2). The evidence given in this Appendix and in Chapter VIII shows that the *Hou-han-shu* is right.

[2] Franke p. 59; cf. de Groot p. 86.

[3] Wylie pp. 33 *sq.*; de Groot p. 87; Konow, *CII* pp. xxiii *sq.*

[4] Wylie p. 35; de Groot p. 87; gold and silver coins with obv. a man on horseback and rev. a man's face.

APPENDIX 10

TA-YUAN

The Greek occupation of Ta-yuan[1] (Ferghana) has not always been accepted,[2] and one must consider the evidence. Certain things may be ruled out at once. Naturally I agree with those who have said that Ta-yuan does not mean 'the great land of the Yavanas'; it is enough that the Ch'ien-han-shu knows of a 'little Yuan', Siao-yuan, in the Tarim basin, which had nothing to do with Greeks.[3] The vine and the alfalfa grew in Ta-yuan, and a considerable number of scholars have believed that the Chinese terms for these plants, p'u-t'ao and muk-tuk, were respectively *βότρυς* and Μηδική (*πόα*), but I do not see how this belief can survive Professor Laufer's analysis.[4] Certainly, though Laufer said that the vine was native all over Iran and was not brought to Ferghana by Greeks,[5] he could produce no evidence for it in Ferghana itself earlier than the Annals of the Ts'in dynasty, fourth century A.D.,[6] which is not in point. But his evidence for the vine in Margiane and Bactria (the nearest countries) is from Strabo, who never mentions Ferghana; so, for all we know, the vine may have been native there or may have been introduced by Greeks or by anybody else; it is no evidence for anything. The habit of keeping wine in jars for years was of course a Greek custom; but unless it be proved that it was not a native custom in Iran also (as to which I know nothing) it cannot be asserted that Greeks introduced it.[7]

This narrows the question down to two points. Ssu-ma Ch'ien says that Chang-k'ien travelled through Ta-yuan on 'postal roads'.[8] Persians made

[1] See generally Chang-k'ien's description of Ta-yuan in Ssu-ma Ch'ien (Hirth pp. 95–6), reproduced in the *Ch'ien-han-shu* (Wylie p. 44, de Groot p. 109), and further Chapter VII.

[2] I think the only writer who has really considered it was V. V. Barthold, *The Graeco-Bactrian State and its spread to the North-East, Bulletin* (*Izvestiya*) *of the Imp. R. Acad. Sc.* 1916 pp. 823–8 (in Russian); he rejected it, but apparently solely on the wine question, and that is not the evidence at all. Professor E. H. Minns kindly supplied me with a synopsis of the main points in this article.

[3] Wylie p. 28, de Groot p. 64 (Sao-wan). The latter (p. 12) says there is no traceable connection between Ta-wan and Sao-wan; all the less likely, therefore, is it that yuan (or wan) should be Yavana.

[4] Vine: B. Laufer, *Sino-Iranica* 1919 pp. 225–6; alfalfa, *ib.* pp. 212–13. Barthold *op. cit.* had rejected the equation p'u-t'ao = *βότρυς* three years previously. O. Franke (note in de Groot p. 35) says that muk-tuk (mu-su, buk-suk) must be derived from some unknown Iranian word.

[5] Laufer *op. cit.* pp. 221 *sqq.*

[6] *Ib.* p. 221.

[7] Barthold *op. cit.* said that there are no Greek words for wine-making in the east-Iranian tongues.

[8] Hirth p. 94 §9.

post roads before Greeks did, but it cannot be shown that the Persians ever ruled Ferghana. The 'Sacas' of the earlier lists of Darius' empire (Behistun and Persepolis) were in the last list, that of Naks-i-Rustam, divided into their two components, the Sacas wearing pointed caps and the Amyrgian Sacas (haumauarga, 'preparers of Haoma'),[1] the new province-list of Xerxes[2] agreeing in this respect with that of Naks-i-Rustam; but Herodotus, in his reproduction of Xerxes' army list, specifically identifies the two,[3] and even if not identical they cannot therefore have lived far apart; I know no reason for Professor Herrmann's view that the Amyrgian Sacas lived on the Pamirs[4] (which cannot possibly have belonged to Darius), and the Hellanicus fragment, the source of which must be Persian, says that they lived on a plain.[5] It is now known from Darius' gold plate[6] that the Sacas he ruled, who must be these two bodies, lived para Sugdam, 'beyond Sogd', *i.e.* in the country between the mountains north of Samarcand and the Jaxartes; and the question is whether the expression 'Saca-land beyond Sogd', primarily no doubt the Chodjend country and the land to the westward, would also include Ferghana. (It would be no objection that Ferghana was an agricultural country; some Saca clans were no longer nomads.) I cannot answer that question; but it is certain that if Ferghana was ever Achaemenid it had been lost before Alexander's day; he could not have left an outlying Persian province without either occupying it himself or sending a force to do so, and also Ptolemy's Sogdiana does not include Ferghana.[7] But supposing that Darius *had* ruled Ferghana and *had* made post roads, is it conceivable that the local population would have kept them in order for nearly four centuries till 128 B.C., when Chang-k'ien saw them? These roads are good evidence for the Greek occupation of Ferghana, but they are not actually conclusive.

What is conclusive is that Chang-k'ien found the country, as he found Bactria, full of 'walled towns'; he gives 'fully 70' in Ferghana alone, a small country. What they were has already been explained (pp. 121 *sq.*); most were large native villages walled round. But the phenomenon, precisely as in Bactria (which Chang-k'ien compares with Ferghana throughout), means Greek occupation and nothing else; for eastern Iranians did not build towns

[1] O. Leuze, *Die Satrapieneinteilung in Syrien und im Zweistromlande von 520–320*, 1935, p. 250 [94], seems to me conclusive that it was such a division and not a new conquest.

[2] E. Herzfeld, *Arch. Mitt. aus Iran* VIII, 1936, p. 58 ll. 26, 27. The list is before 480 B.C.

[3] Herod. VII, 64, the Sacas wearing pointed *κυρβασίαι* are called by Persians Amyrgian Sacas.

[4] A. Herrmann, *Sakai* in PW; see Marquart's criticism, *Untersuchungen zur Geschichte von Eran* II, 1905, p. 140. See however p. 477.

[5] In Stephanus: *'Αμύργιον· πεδίον Σακῶν.*

[6] S. Smith, *JRAS* 1926 p. 435; E. Herzfeld, *Memoirs of the Arch. Survey of India* XXXIV, 1928.

[7] Cf. on this Berthelot p. 191.

and did not wall-in villages. This comes out clearly enough in the Alexander-story. There is one exception in that story, and it is given as something exceptional—the seven fortresses which the Achaemenids had built to guard the Jaxartes frontier against nomads.[1] These were military fortresses, not villages. Yet six of them had only low mud ramparts,[2] and Alexander took them as he pleased; only of the largest one, Cyropolis, is it stated that it had a 'higher wall',[3] compelling him to bring up his siege train. If there was one place in eastern Iran in Alexander's day large enough to be called a town it was Bactra itself; and Bactra was not walled. When Spitamenes attacked it behind Alexander's back,[4] the commandant in the place had only a few details and the sick; on the other hand, Spitamenes had only light Sogdian and Saca horse, useless against walls. Had there been a wall, the commandant only had to close the gates and Spitamenes was helpless; instead, he led out what men he had and they were naturally annihilated; therefore there was no wall, and Spitamenes could have taken Bactra but for Craterus' timely arrival. Spitamenes, just before, had taken one of the border forts which guarded the Bactrian frontier;[5] if his horsemen could take it, it had nothing but a low mud rampart, at best. It was Greeks who turned Bactra into a great fortress and filled Bactria with 'walled towns' which nomad horsemen could not take (see generally Chap. III); and no one else could have done the same thing in Ferghana.

It will be seen that I follow the opinion which, prior to Professor Herzfeld's Sakastan, was universally held, that Chang-k'ien's Ta-yuan was Ferghana (though, as will appear, it was larger than Ferghana proper), as Ta-yuan admittedly is in Chinese literature from the fourth century A.D. onwards.[6] Herzfeld however has argued[7] that Chang-k'ien meant by *his* Ta-yuan not Ferghana but the Pamirs; but though he has rightly pointed out elsewhere that what Chang-k'ien saw and what he heard are different things, he has here omitted what Chang-k'ien saw in Ta-yuan and has based his argument solely on the relative positions by points of the compass which Chang-k'ien gives for the several peoples he mentions, a thing over which a stranger in a strange and unknown world might easily make mistakes; indeed if one considers the mistakes made by Ptolemy, with all the sources of information which he had at his disposal,[8] it would be extraordinary if Chang-k'ien had *not* made any. And when Chang-k'ien put the Yueh-chi west of Ta-yuan[9] (which is what

[1] This story is in Arrian IV, 2 *sqq.*

[2] *Ib.* IV, 2, 3, τῷ τείχει γηΐνῳ τε καὶ οὐκ ὑψηλῷ ὄντι.

[3] *Ib.* IV, 3, 1, τετειχισμένη...ὑψηλοτέρῳ τείχει ἤπερ αἱ ἄλλαι.

[4] *Ib.* IV, 16, 6 *sqq.*

[5] *Ib.* IV, 16, 4–5.

[6] For this later evidence see de Groot p. 109.

[7] *Sakastan* pp. 22 *sqq.* and plan on p. 23.

[8] *E.g.* he puts the Massagetae east of Sogdiana instead of west (VI, 13), and Sogdiana both east (VI, 11) and west (VI, 12) of Bactria, both being wrong.

[9] Hirth p. 95 §22.

Herzfeld is going on) he did just make a mistake (or Ssu-ma Ch'ien made one in transcribing his Report); this is shown clearly enough by Pan-ku, who in transcribing the same passage quietly corrected 'west' to 'south-west' or 'south',[1] and this is one of those cases in which the later historian, who had at his disposal much new information collected by Chinese envoys and caravans, is bound to be right.

But the real point is that, apart from its Saca rulers, Chang-k'ien describes Ta-yuan, which he had seen, as a settled country exactly like Ta-hia (Bactria),[2] with the same soil, climate, productions, and customs,[3] which must mean highly organised agriculture like the Bactrian. He says that the people grew not only wheat but rice,[4] which means irrigation and a hot summer climate (he does not mention rice in Bactria, though he had heard that it grew in Chaldaea),[5] and that the vine and alfalfa grew well in Ta-yuan,[6] and that like Bactria the country was full of 'walled towns', whose number he gives as 'fully 70';[7] the Chinese subsequently planted an agricultural colony there.[8] Was there really on the Pamirs a highly organised agricultural state with wheat-fields and rice-fields,[9] clover-fields and vineyards, and seventy walled towns? Any description of the desolate and windswept Roof of the World will suffice to negative the supposition.

It may however be taken as certain that Chang-k'ien's Ta-yuan, as a state, was larger than Ferghana proper and extended up the river valleys to the Pamir watershed. He says that Ta-yuan borders to the east upon two states, Hau-mi (U-bi), a very small place, and Yu-tien (Hu-tin, Khotan), and that in Yu-tien all the rivers run eastward but that westward of it (*i.e.* in Ta-yuan) they all run westward.[10] The Saca rulers of Ta-yuan, then, ruled up to the watershed, and may in part have lapped round the Yueh-chi country on its eastern side; and the people in the high valleys may, for all we know, have been part of the Amyrgian Sacas. But this is not what Herzfeld meant (see his plan p. 23); and it is not what Herrmann meant either.

[1] Wylie p. 44 (south); de Groot p. 109 (south-west). South-west will serve. The Yueh-chi had not moved in the meanwhile except to extend *southward* across the Oxus to occupy Bactria; their capital was still north of the Oxus.

[2] Hirth p. 97 §47.

[3] Wylie p. 44, de Groot p. 109.

[4] Hirth p. 95 §19.

[5] *Ib.* p. 97 §41.

[6] *Ib.* pp. 95 §19, 108 §99.

[7] *Ib.* p. 95 §20.

[8] *Ib.* p. 116.

[9] On the Indian side, some inferior rice is said to be grown to-day in the Gilgit valley, about 5000 feet up. But Gilgit is very far from being the Pamirs, which have an average height of 13,000 feet and are under snow for at least half the year.

[10] Ssu-ma Ch'ien (Hirth p. 95, de Groot p. 12). The parallel passage in the *Ch'ien-han-shu*, Wylie p. 30, de Groot p. 69, shows that the statement is Chang-k'ien's.

APPENDIX 11

CHORASMIA

The name Chorasmia is never given by any Greek writer, but only a people Chorasmii. It is always assumed that this people lived in Chorasmia, *i.e.* Kwarizm, Khiva, the fertile country south of the Aral on the lower Oxus. It may be well to test this assumption and see whither that leads us.

The Chorasmii are first mentioned by Hecataeus[1] as living in a land, partly plain partly mountain, eastward of the Parthava; this land is not Kwarizm, where there are no real mountains and which was not eastward of the Parthava. In Herodotus also the land of the Chorasmii is partly plain partly mountain, their neighbours being Hyrcanians and Parthians (Parthava), but in his day they had lost the plain to the Persian kings;[2] they were subject to the Persians, and in Xerxes' army list they are brigaded with the Parthava and with no other people.[3] Herodotus then agrees with Hecataeus, except that the Chorasmii had lost the best of their land. He puts them in the 16th satrapy with the Parthava, Arians, and Sogdians; the passages cited above show that this is correct for the Chorasmii, even though 'Sogdians' here are impossible.[4] Darius' three lists of lands give no help, as the eastern lands are not in any geographical order and moreover the position of the Chorasmii differs in the Behistun and Naks-i-Rustam lists; but in the inscription relating to the building of the Apadāna at Susa Darius obtained some substance from Chorasmia which, if the translation 'turquoise' be correct,[5] agrees with Hecataeus and Herodotus, for turquoise could not come from anywhere but the famous mines in Khorasan; but as there are other translations this cannot be stressed. Lastly Arrian, describing the 'Taurus-Caucasus' line of mountains from an unknown source (? Eratosthenes), makes it run from Armenia by the Parthians and *Chorasmians* to Bactria and the Hindu Kush.[6] So far, then, the Chorasmii are a people in the Hyrcanian-Parthian satrapy, and as Darius' land-lists name them separately they differed recognisably from the Parthava, but they were apparently Iranians[7] and not a pre-Iranian people like the Tapuri. It would seem therefore probable that Darius I never ruled Kwarizm.

[1] Athen. *II*, 70 b. [2] Herod. III, 17. [3] *Ib.* VII, 66.

[4] *Ib.* III, 93. I am not concerned here with the Sogdians; but Herat and Samarcand cannot have been governed by the same satrap when the Bactrian satrapy, which included Margus (Merv), cut communication between them.

[5] Kent's translation, *JAOS* LIII, 1933, p. 1 l. 39. Scheil however gives haematite and Herzfeld grey amber; see Kent's note and p. 103 n. 5.

[6] Arr. v, 5, 2.

[7] Pseudo-Lucian, *Macrobii* 4; not the best of evidence.

By the time Alexander arrived the state of things had changed. The Chorasmii were now no longer subject to Persia; there are none in the army of Darius III. Instead, they had become members of the Massagetae confederacy,[1] though that does not locate them; but something may be learnt from the visit of their king Pharasmanes to Alexander.[2] Arrian makes him say that his kingdom bordered on the Colchians, a wild impossibility doubtless arising out of an interpreter's blunder;[3] but his offer to guide Alexander to the Euxine shows that he knew, or knew of, the trade route which ran through the land of the Aorsi north of the Aral and Caspian to the Black Sea,[4] which certainly suggests that he and his people were at the time in Kwarizm. The Chorasmii then in the late Persian period had moved north, whether to escape Persian rule or because they had lost their best land; but the important thing is that their king should have had a good Persian name.[5] Two other pieces of evidence belong to the time between Alexander and the nomad conquest of Bactria; Ptolemy[6] puts the Chorasmii on the Oxus, *i.e.* in Kwarizm, and the Mihr Yast (§14) implies the same. It says that Mithras beholds the broad navigable waters hastening towards Mouru (Merv), Harôyu (Aria), Gava-Sughdha (Sogdiana), and Hvâirizem (Chorasmia).[7] The three first rivers are obviously the Margus, Arius, and Oxus; and the fourth must also be the Oxus on its way to Kwarizm,[8] for no large river hastened towards the Parthian satrapy. Once we get to the time of the nomad conquest of Bactria, the name Chorasmii does not occur again in Greek sources.

We now have to ask why the Chorasmii migrated from south to north against the general direction of all known Iranian migrations, and why they, a people living in northern Iran, had a king with a Persian (south Iranian) name. The hypothesis put forward in Chapter VII pp. 292 *sqq.* (to which I

[1] Strabo XI, 513. Strabo adds that Spitamenes took refuge with the Chorasmii, while Arrian IV, 16, 4 says that he went to the country of the Massagetae; the Chorasmii therefore were already part of the Massagetae confederacy in Alexander's day.

[2] Arr. IV, 15, 4.

[3] Droysen I, 2, p. 66 (ed. 1877) saw that it was nonsense; and the Chinese evidence and that of Strabo XI, 506 as to the Aorsi lying round the heads of the Aral and Caspian is conclusive. U. Wilcken, *Alexander der Grosse* p. 162, has a most interesting idea: Pharasmanes (who had just given asylum to Spitamenes) was challenging Alexander to fight the nomad world.

[4] Strabo XI, 506.

[5] It must be the same name as Pharismanes, son of the satrap Phrataphernes, Arr. VI, 27, 3.

[6] Ptol. VI, 12, 4; doubtless ultimately from the Alexander-story.

[7] Darmesteter's translation, *Sacred Books of the East* XXIII, 1883, p. 123, does not give 'navigable', but only 'wide-flowing rivers'. 'Broad navigable waters' is the recent translation of A. Christensen, *Die Iranier* p. 216.

[8] So Darmesteter *loc. cit.* The Atrek flows *away from* Parthia proper.

must refer) regarding the Pasiani-Parsii of Apollodorus will answer these questions: the Parsii (Parsua) were Persians who had stayed behind in Kwarizm when the rest of the Parsua-Persians went south, and the Chorasmii must have been a section or tribe of the Parsii. That is why the Chorasmii went *north* to Kwarizm; they had once migrated from it to the south and were now returning to their own people. That is why their chief had a Persian name; like the Parsii, they must have spoken some form of Persian. That is why they were in the Massagetae confederacy; the Parsii were members (p. 469). That is why their name died out in Greek writers; they were included in the Parsii. Though the Greeks had never had a name for the country of the Chorasmii, the Persians had; and that name, as the Mihr Yast shows, followed the Chorasmii to Kwarizm. I believe that my hypothesis covers all the facts at present known.

APPENDIX 12

ORMUZ: A LOST KINGDOM

Of all the Seleucid satrapies Carmania is the least known; it seems to have no history. Strabo (xv, 726) has scarcely a word more recent than Onesicritus and Nearchus; his notices of the mines and the gold-bearing river are explicitly ascribed to Onesicritus; the head-hunters *might* be new, but as they come between references to Onesicritus and to Nearchus they are probably taken from one of them. Except for some names in Ptolemy, the only writer with any new information is Pliny in book vi, and it can be isolated by first taking out the old information. The mines and the gold-bearing river (vi, 98) are from Onesicritus, as a comparison with Strabo xv, 726 shows; the distance (*ib.*) of the crossing from the 'promontory' of Carmania (Cape Jask)[1] to Macae (Ras Mussendam) in Arabia is shown by the name Macae to come from Nearchus,[2] though Pliny's 'five miles' must be a corruption, for it is neither the actual distance nor Nearchus' 'one day's voyage'. The statement (vi, 110) that beyond the 'promontory' are the Harmozaei is from Nearchus.[3]

Deducting these passages, and omitting for the moment vi, 152, Pliny's information later than Onesicritus and Nearchus is as follows. vi, 107, the country about the Amanis river is fertile, with fields and vineyards, and is called Armysia (this variant on Harmozaei should indicate a new source); the towns are Zetis and Alexandria (the latter, near Gulashkird, comes in the Alexander-historians). vi, 110, after mentioning the Harmozaei, and giving a parenthesis to what 'quidam' say, he goes on 'ibi (among the Harmozaei) Portus Macedonum et arae Alexandri in promunturio'; that is, his source knew of a Graeco-Macedonian harbour town on the Gulf of Ormuz[4] and altars on C. Jask attributed to Alexander, who was never near the place (Nearchus, who was, built no altars). This information is from Hellenistic sources. Next vi, 149: Juba (he says) omits to mention two places, Batrasasave the town of the Omani, and Omana, which earlier writers ('priores', *i.e.* some Hellenistic writer) made a much frequented harbour of Carmania. Pliny here is following Juba down the Arabian coast southwards from Gerrha, and he himself thinks that Omana, like the Omani, was in Arabia. This is immaterial, for the Periplus (36) is clear that Omana was in Carmania on the Gulf of Ormuz, as Juba probably knew also from his Hellenistic 'priores'; Pliny has confused Omana with the Omani on the Arabian side, whose name survives in Oman; doubtless the same people were, or had been, active on

[1] The ἐν Βάδει χώρῳ of Arr. *Ind.* 32, 5.

[2] *Μάκετα* in Arr. *Ind.* 32, 7.

[3] Arr. *Ind.* 33, 2.

[4] Nearchus found no town at the Amanis mouth; but this does not prove that Portus Macedonum was a new Greek foundation, for it need not have been actually at the river mouth. I have, for once, got little from Kiessling, *Harmozeia* in PW.

both sides of the narrow strait (see p. 485). Omana then was a much frequented harbour of Carmania in Hellenistic times, as it was to the author of the Periplus; this means that for once the Periplus can be used for the earlier period.

Ptolemy VI, 18 adds little; native names apart, he gives three towns in Carmania—Alexandria, Carmania Metropolis (certainly Kerman), and Harmouza (? Harmozia); this last is doubtless Pliny's Portus Macedonum among the Harmozaei, and, as will presently appear, it was probably Omana. Ptolemy's Harmouza is the Harmoza Regia of the Ravennate geographer; this ought to mean that it was once somebody's capital. Of course neither Harmozia nor Portus Macedonum (p. 13) was its official name.

We have then in Pliny bits of some Hellenistic account of a settlement about the Amanis (Minab) river country reaching roughly from Alexandria-Gulashkird to the sea, with a harbour town on the Gulf of Ormuz which did a large trade. There seems to be no other place along the Carmanian coast where a settlement on any scale could be made; and this district, not Kerman, was the essential 'Carmania'. 'Alexander's' altars on C. Jask are like 'Alexander's' attempt to establish agriculture in Gedrosia (p. 260): both refer to some Hellenistic ruler. Pliny's Zetis (not noticed by Tscherikower) is not another town but only a nickname for Harmozia;[1] it is a corruption of a transliteration of ζήτησις[2] (or perhaps ζητεῖς) made in Pliny's usual fashion,[3] and is a parallel to Prophthasia (p. 14); as the latter city was nicknamed 'Anticipation' (not of course by Alexander) in allusion to Alexander's anticipation of Philotas' conspiracy, so Harmozia was nicknamed 'The Search' in allusion to Nearchus' search for Alexander. The name Portus Macedonum should show that the place was hellenised.

Before going on I must notice Naumachaeorum promunturium in Pliny VI, 152, the projecting land which forms the northern horn of the Gulf of Ormuz as C. Jask does the southern; Pliny calls it 'over against Carmania', a good instance of the use of 'Carmania' for the Amanis river country. Naumachaeorum is another of these mistaken transliterations (n. 3, *below*); it is ναυμάχων[4] or ναυμαχούντων or something of the sort turned into a tribe, the reference being to Numenius' sea-fight in the next sentence. This took place

[1] Zetis and Alexandria in Pliny must be Harmouza and Alexandria in Ptolemy. On nicknames see chap. I.

[2] Droysen, 2nd German ed. III, 2, p. 326, already wondered whether Zetis might not be connected with Nearchus' search.

[3] Besides Zetis and Naumachaeorum here given, I have noticed the following. Pliny VI, 50, ibi Napaei interisse dicuntur a Palaeis = λέγονται ὑπὸ παλαιῶν ('ancient writers' have become a tribe). VI, 92, praefluens Parabesten Arachosiorum = παρὰ Βεστήν (Bestia desolata of the Peutinger Table). VI, 92, Cataces, *v.l.* Cateces, a tribe in Paropamisadae = κάτοικοι (p. 99). VI, 96, Xylinepolis ab Alexandro condita (repeated by various modern writers) = ξυλίνη πόλις, 'a town built of wood' (p. 244). Doubtless a search would reveal others. There is a famous one in Ptol. III, 2, 27, noticed by Nobbe: town Σιατούτανδα = Tac. *Ann.* IV, 72, ad sua tutanda.

[4] See Athen. IV, 154 f.

while Mesene (Chaldaea) was still Seleucid, and belongs to the reign of Antiochus III, probably to some movement in Persis after Magnesia; Numenius was his eparch of Mesene[1] and also commanded his squadron on the Persian Gulf whose fleet station was in Mesene, probably Antioch-Charax. But how he had a *sea-fight* with Persians of Persis, unless some Greek cities were helping them, is utterly obscure.

I have pointed out (p. 261) the need in the second century B.C. for some trading intermediary between India and Babylonia on the Iranian coast (Gerrha being on the wrong side of the Persian Gulf), as the southern Arabs formed a trading intermediary between India and Egypt; for this was the time when trading vessels from Barygaza still hugged the Gedrosian and Carmanian coasts.[2] The natural point for such an intermediary, as it was in the Middle Ages, would be the Gulf of Ormuz, and the Periplus, which can be used here, describes the trade activity at Omana (36); there was a regular ferry to Arabia run by hand-sewn native coracles, and in exchange for Indian wares they shipped to India spices brought from Arabia, gold,[3] and various other products; the place was also a centre of the pearl trade. Whoever ruled there may well have ruled on both sides of the strait. Probably too in Hellenistic times Indian goods came overland to Omana as well as by sea. Though Strabo thrice mentions a road from Babylonia and Susa by Persepolis to 'the middle of' Carmania,[4] he never carries it on to Seistan; probably therefore most of the caravan trade from India by the southern route through Seistan did not in Hellenistic times go overland to Babylonia by Persepolis but came to sea at the Gulf of Ormuz, again as in the Middle Ages. This was perhaps the return route taken by the Hyrcanian envoys to Nero in A.D. 59, who had to avoid Vologases of Parthia and who started somewhere on the Persian Gulf;[5] it would have been far shorter for them to go by Ormuz to Seistan than to go round by Patala and the Indus. The Peutinger Table, some items of which in the East may go back to the Seleucid survey, appears to know this route between Seistan and Ormuz and names as a half-way house a place Arciotis in the Jiruft basin, possibly Marco Polo's Camadi, whose ruins have furnished some Hellenistic seals.[6]

What now was the political position on the Gulf of Ormuz after the Greeks had occupied Barygaza and got the Indian end of the great sea-route to Babylonia? After the Seleucids had lost Seistan, Persis, Elymais, and Characene, a process begun after Magnesia and completed at latest soon after the death of Antiochus IV in 163, they cannot have retained the then isolated

[1] Niese II, 401 rightly saw that it was Antiochus III. Under Antiochus IV the eparch of Mesene was Hyspaosines.

[2] See Chap. VI p. 260 and references.

[3] Gold from the Hyctanis in Carmania, Pliny VI, 98; gold mines on the Arabian side, *ib.* VI, 50.

[4] II, 79; XV, 727, 744. It goes to τὰ μέσα of Carmania, *i.e.* Kerman.

[5] Tac. *Ann.* XIV, 25; cf. Herzfeld, *Sakastan* p. 87; *CAH* X p. 764.

[6] Tomaschek, *Wien SB* CII p. 175; Sir A. Stein, *Journ. Geog. Soc.* LXXXIII, 1934, pp. 125, 128.

Carmania. But this province was not at the time included, so far as is known, in the Bactrian or Parthian realm; two centuries later Persis ruled the Kerman country,[1] but that is not in point. The general of the Carmanian satrapy, like others, must have done something for himself in the universal break-up, but no record remains; Carmania in the second century B.C. is a lost land. And by a curious coincidence the British Museum possesses a lost coin.[2] It is a well-executed Greek copper coin, showing jugate heads, both diademed, of a king Bellaios and his queen, whose name is effaced; the reverse type is the prow of a Greek war-galley, and 'the strongly bevelled edge recalls Seleucid influence'. It ought then to belong to some Seleucid Succession State on the sea, but it will not fit any place whose coinage is known. The name Bellaios appears to be Macedonian.[3]

My suggestion is that the Hellenistic notices of the Amanis country in Pliny, the need of an intermediary on the Iranian coast for the India-Babylonia trade, the epithet Regia applied to Harmozia, the account of Omana, the unknown fate of the Carmanian satrap, and this unique coin, are all connected, and that Bellaios, sometime general of the Carmanian satrapy (or that general's descendant), ruled a little kingdom on the Amanis river with a good sea-port and capital on the Gulf of Ormuz, a kingdom which must sooner or later have become a vassal of Parthia and had apparently foundered before the date of the Periplus (middle of the first century A.D.). There may be other traces of it beside the coin.

Stephanus *s.v.* calls Carmania 'a country of India'. It was never ruled from India; the notice is one of a class in Stephanus, like 'Gerrha, a city of the Chaldeans' or 'Barygaza, the emporium of Gedrosia' (p. 260), which refer to close trading connections; it shows that at some time Carmania (the Amanis country) was neither Seleucid nor Parthian (*i.e.* was independent) and was an emporium for the Indian trade, as I have worked out.

Isidore of Charax knew a king Goaisos who died at a great age in his own lifetime and therefore lived in the first century B.C. and who ruled 'the spice-land of the Omani'.[4] There was no such place, for the Omani, opposite

[1] *Periplus* 33. [2] Sir G. F. Hill, *NC* 1928 p. 15 no. 41.

[3] The name *Βελλαῖος* in Egypt, second century B.C., *BGU* II no. 601 l. 20; the form *Βελλεῖος* both in Egypt (Preisigke, *Namenbuch s.v.*) and in Macedonia (*SEG* III 499–501); the form *Βελλέ(ου)*, query *Βελλε(ίου)*, at Doura, *SEG* VII 452. The name *Βιλλαῖος* (Nonnus XXVI, 217) is merely that of the river Billaios (Ap. Rhod. II, 793) or Billis (Pliny VI, 4) in Asia Minor and can hardly be connected with *Βελλαῖος*; it is more probably the same as the Ionian *Βιλλᾶς*, on which see L. Robert, *BCH* LVII, 1933, p. 476 n. 4. There was in Illyria, probably *c.* 167–153 B.C., a princelet named *Βαλλαῖος* who coined (Head[2] p. 317); but he cannot be connected with *Βελλαῖος*, for, beside the different spelling, he had nothing to do with the Seleucids. Could his name be connected with the Illyrian town *Βύλλις*, on which see Robert, *BCH* LII, 1928, p. 433?

[4] Pseudo-Lucian *Macrob.* 220, *'Ομανῶν τῆς ἀρωματοφόρου βασιλεύσας*. There is no need to suppose that this is from Pseudo-Isidoros (p. 54).

Omana, were far from the nearest frankincense country; τῆς ἀρωματοφόρου means, in the usual way, the depot for spices, which to a native of Charax would be Omana, just as Egyptian Greeks regularly called Somaliland ἡ κινναμωνοφόρος because it was for them the depot for cinnamon from the Far East. Goaisos therefore probably ruled on both sides of the strait. He can hardly have belonged to the Greek dynasty; he was probably an Arab who (or whose predecessors) ousted (or succeeded) the Greeks, like the Arab line of the Abgars in the same century in the formerly Seleucid Osrhoene. If Goaisos were an Arab king ruling also in Omana, Pliny's belief that Omana was in Arabia would be explained, and there is evidence to show that somewhere in the Hellenistic period some kingdom must have embraced both sides of the straits;[1] even to-day the coastal population of the Gulf of Ormuz is said to be mainly Arab. It would also explain the Arab name Omana; the Arab dynasty, doubtless sprung from the Omani, had given a name taken from their own land and race to the Hellenistic harbour-town and capital which we have met under the names of Harmozia, Zetis, and Portus Macedonum. Whatever the Greek official name of this town may have been, it has perished as have the official names of Hekatompylos and many other towns (p. 13).

There is still another unknown king who may belong to the same dynasty as Goaisos. In 1935 J. M. Unvala published sixty chalkoi from Susa with the legend 'Of king Tigraios',[2] which incidentally revealed that a coin of this king from Susa was already known though the name was corrupt.[3] The reverse types include the Ptolemaic eagle, an Artemis, a term, a winged thunderbolt, a boar's head, and a palm, some of which are Seleucid, while the last three are also Graeco-Indian of the second century B.C. Unvala's hypothesis that Tigraios was Molon has nothing to recommend it; apart from the silence of Polybius, Molon could not have taken and used a barbarian name. The coin-types point to an international trade centre having definite relations with Greek India;[4] and as coins from Omana would naturally appear at Susa, Tigraios is probably another of the lost kings of the Amanis kingdom, earlier than Goaisos.

[1] Stephanus, *s.v.* *Μάκαι* (which is Ras Mussendam), an ἔθνος between Carmania and Arabia; and *s.v.* *Ὤγυρις* (the island Khism), whose ethnic he forms on Arabian analogies. Stephanus' source for these notices is not given, but for this part of the world his usual source is Marcianus, and these notices may therefore ultimately be Hellenistic. Grohmann, *Makai* in PW, leaves it open where this people came from; Kiessling, *Gedrosia* in PW, makes them Gedrosians who had migrated to Arabia across the strait.

[2] *Rev. Num.* 1935 p. 158; *βασιλέως Τιγραίου*, and king's head on obverse.

[3] Allotte de la Fuye, *MDP* XXV, 1934, p. 25 no. 56; *βασιλέως ΙΠΑΙΟ*.

[4] This, and the Ptolemaic eagle, seem to forbid any supposition that Tigraios might have been a king of Characene filling the gap in the dated coinage after A.D. 71–2; it would be much too late for the types.

APPENDIX 13

ΣΑΓΑΛΑ Η ΚΑΙ ΕΥΘΥΜΕΔΕΙΑ[1]

Renou[2] in his edition of Ptolemy's Indian books prints Εὐθυδημία. His note is: "Εὐθυδημία scripsimus: εὐθύδη X, εὐθημία Γ, εὐθυμηδία ω, -μέδια ά.' His text is based on X (Vaticanus 191, thirteenth century) which all editors seem agreed is the best MS; Γ (Vatic. Palat. 388, fifteenth century) is said to exhibit some curious and erratic readings; ω is Renou's sign for the general body of MSS, and ά for the *editio princeps* of 1533 (Bâle) which Müller rated highly; it is based on Γ but has various divergences. The Latin versions all have -media. One MS of the group ω (Vat. Urbin. 82) is eleventh-century; -μηδία therefore is actually the oldest reading known, for what that may be worth.

It might be held that εὐθύδη of X warrants Εὐθυδημία, but Renou did not explicitly put it on that ground; there is little doubt from his note (scripsimus) that he adopted Bayer's old conjecture Εὐθυδημία because most writers since have done so. The historical considerations which make Εὐθυδημία impossible are dealt with in my text (pp. 247 *sq.*); here I am only considering Ptolemy's text.

The corruption of -μηδία into -δημία would be easy and obvious; Εὐθυδημία makes such good sense so long as one does not think about it, and the reasons which have affected the modern writer are precisely those which would have affected the ancient scribe. But if the original text gave the obvious Εὐθυδημία, no reason can be found for its alteration in almost every MS into the meaningless Εὐθυμηδία. It is just possible that Εὐθυμηδής was a (very rare) Greek name;[3] but cities were not named after commoners, and though a military colony might be (pp. 6, 11), no one would suggest that Sāgala was a military colony. No modern writer has in fact adopted Εὐθυμηδία. It is clearly a corruption; but one cannot suppose almost universal corruption of anything so obvious as Εὐθυδημία.

We must therefore follow the rule *praestat lectio difficillima* and turn to Εὐθυμέδια. This cannot possibly be a corruption of Εὐθυδημία; and it is not easy to see how Εὐθυμηδία, composed apparently of two words well known to any scribe, could become Εὐθυμέδια, while -μέδια would infallibly become -μηδία owing to the mental pull of the well-known name Μηδία. Now Εὐθυμέδια as it stands is not only meaningless but wrongly accented; place-names ending in -ια after a short vowel are paroxytone,[4] and it ought

[1] Ptol. VII, 1, 46. [2] L. Renou, *La géographie de Ptolémée, l'Inde*, 1925.

[3] The one possible instance is Euthymedes of Pliny XXXV, 146, with a *v.l.* Euthymides.

[4] As Ἀρμενία, Μακεδονία, Καππαδοκία, and many others.

to be Εὐθυμεδία. The accent shows that the right form must have been Εὐθυμέδεια. This could easily be corrupted on the one hand into Εὐθυμέδια and on the other into Εὐθυμηδία; for Μηδία (the country) was sometimes spelt (and accented) Μήδεια,[1] and the corruption therefore ran Εὐθυμέδεια—Εὐθυμήδεια—Εὐθυμηδία. That Εὐθυμέδεια *would* have been corrupted is certain, for no scribe would have understood it. I have not traced the first appearance of this word, but prior to Renou's edition it was generally supposed that it had MS authority; one must take it from Renou that this is not so. It is a properly formed feminine name, one of a class (p. 248 n. 2); but it has been generally discarded for Εὐθυδημία because writers could not explain it. I gave the right meaning long ago,[2] but did not know enough at the time to account for it; it is now extremely obvious (p. 248). Ptolemy then wrote Σάγαλα ἡ καὶ Εὐθυμέδεια.

I must however notice one further point. Renou actually supported the conjecture Εὐθυδημία by an appeal to Nonnus XXVI, 338, not in his critical note, certainly, but in his index;[3] a misleading statement which took in Przyluski[4] and might take in others. Nonnus never mentions the word.[5] The MSS of XXVI, 338 (see Ludwich's edition of 1911 *ad loc.*) give the line as *λαὸς εὐκρήδεμνον* Ἐριστοβάρειαν *ἐάσας*. Of course Eristobareia is meaningless; Nonnus' 26th book, the gathering of the Indian army, is full of meaningless names which he invented himself. But de Marcellus, in his edition (1856) of Nonnus for the Didot series, went steadily through book XXVI altering meaningless names into names he happened to have heard of, sometimes regardless of scansion, and among others he altered Ἐριστοβάρειαν into Εὐθυδήμειαν, producing the marvellous hexameter *λαὸς εὐκρήδεμνον* Εὐθυδήμειαν *ἐάσας*. He gave no reasons; his note[6] merely says that Eristobareia, a meaningless word, 's'évapore devant l'Euthymédie de Ptolémée, qu'il faut lire Euthydémie'. It is a pity that such rubbish should have found a place in Ludwich's apparatus,[7] as well as in Renou.

The whole story of the word Εὐθυδημία (see further, p. 247) has been a lamentable example of how *not* to write history.

[1] Stephanus *s.v.* Ἀρσακία. [2] *JHS* XXII, 1902, p. 274.

[3] P. 80: 'Εὐθυδημία I, 46; [Εὐθυδήμεια Nonnus 26, 338].'

[4] *JA* 1926 p. 21 n. 1: Rapson (he means Macdonald) thinks Euthydemia conjectural, but 'cf. toutefois la leçon *Εὐθυδήμεια* (Nonnus XXVI, 338) citée par Renou, *La géographie de Ptolémée* p. 80'.

[5] In fact Nonnus himself did not know a single name from the Indo-Greek period; for *Κασπείρων* of XXVI, 167, if correct (all MSS have *καὶ σπείρων*), was certainly merely taken, like so many other names, from the *Bassarica* of Dionysius (see Stephanus *s.v.* *Κάσπειρος*). His few genuine Indian names are taken from the Alexander story.

[6] P. 118 n. 84.

[7] His note is: '*ἐριστοβάρειαν* LΩ; *Εὐθυδήμειαν* m. "Num *Ἀριστοβάρειαν?*" k*' (*i.e.* Koechly). 'm' is de Marcellus' edition.

APPENDIX 14

THE SUPPOSED OXO-CASPIAN TRADE-ROUTE

This route from India to the West by the Oxus and the Caspian, sometimes called the northern route, is supposed to be given twice by Strabo[1] and once by Pliny;[2] there is nothing else, for Solinus 19, 4 is merely copied from Pliny. The correct explanation was given by Professor Kiessling in 1914,[3] but it was given in a couple of sentences in the middle of a very long article on Hyrcania and has never been taken up or followed; and the whole subject has been such a mass of misunderstanding that it is worth setting out the formal proofs.

Strabo II, 73. A comparison with XI, 509 shows both that this is from Patrocles and that it is not Eratosthenes' version of Patrocles; it may therefore be taken to be what Patrocles said himself. The literal translation is: 'The Oxus is sufficiently navigable for the Indian trade to be carried across to it and to be easily brought down the river to the Hyrcanian (sea)[4] and the

[1] Strabo II, 73: *καὶ τὸν Ὦξον δὲ τὸν ὁρίζοντα τὴν Βακτριανὴν ἀπὸ τῆς Σογδιανῆς οὕτω φασὶν εὔπλουν εἶναι ὥστε τὸν Ἰνδικὸν φόρτον ὑπερκομισθέντα εἰς αὐτὸν ῥᾳδίως εἰς τὴν Ὑρκανίαν κατάγεσθαι καὶ τοὺς ἐφεξῆς τόπους μέχρι τοῦ Πόντου διὰ τῶν ποταμῶν.* Strabo XI, 509. Aristobulus says that the Oxus is the greatest river he himself saw in Asia, except the Indian rivers: *φησὶ δὲ καὶ εὔπλουν εἶναι καὶ οὗτος καὶ Ἐρατοσθένης παρὰ Πατροκλέους λαβών, καὶ πολλὰ τῶν Ἰνδικῶν φορτίων κατάγειν εἰς τὴν Ὑρκανίαν θάλατταν, ἐντεῦθεν δ' εἰς τὴν Ἀλβανίαν περαιοῦσθαι καὶ διὰ τοῦ Κύρου καὶ τῶν ἑξῆς τόπων εἰς τὸν Εὔξεινον καταφέρεσθαι.*

[2] Pliny VI, 52 (*i.e.* Varro), Jahn's text: Adicit idem (Varro) Pompei ductu exploratum in Bactros VII diebus ex India perveniri Iachrum ad flumen quod in Oxum influat, et ex eo per Caspium in Cyrum subvectos, et V non amplius dierum terrano itinere ad Phasim in Pontum Indicas posse devehi merces. This as it stands is neither grammar nor sense; the whole passage is framed on the words exploratum posse merces and governed by posse, and subvectos therefore ought to be subvectas and the following et should be omitted; subvectas, to agree with merces, is guaranteed by the subject of *περαιοῦσθαι* in Strabo XI, 509 being 'goods'. Read therefore 'in Cyrum subvectas V non amplius' etc.

[3] Kiessling, *Hyrkania* in PW, the best thing on Patrocles. Kiessling makes two points: (*a*) col. 465, Pliny no less than Eratosthenes depended on Patrocles; (*b*) col. 467, Patrocles said that goods *could* easily come down the Oxus to the Caspian and so to the Cyrus, and this was turned into a statement that they *did* come. That, in a nutshell, is the whole of the matter.

[4] *ἡ Ὑρκανία* is only used for the Hyrcanian *sea* when the context is clear, as Strabo II, 129 and XI, 519; Arr..V, 26, 2; Ptol. V, 13, 6. As it must certainly mean the sea here—that was the point of getting a report at all—we have not the whole context.

places beyond as far as the Black Sea by way of the rivers', *i.e.* the Cyrus and the Phasis. This sober statement is part of Patrocles' report to Antiochus I, and in Greek, as in English, it can mean two things: (1) that the Indian trade was being brought down the Oxus to the Caspian and beyond, and (2) that it was not being so brought but easily could be. The word 'easily' shows that (2) is the real meaning of Patrocles' report; he told Antiochus that it would be easy to make a trade route. Be it remembered that, when he was exploring the Caspian, he had taken the mouth of the Atrek for that of the Oxus[1] and had therefore supposed that the Oxus entered that sea.

Strabo XI, 509. Aristobulus is probably only cited here as an authority for the Oxus being *εὔπλους*, for it is unlikely that he wrote late enough to use Patrocles; however, it does not matter if he did use him, for that would only mean that he understood the report as Eratosthenes did. What follows is Eratosthenes' version of Patrocles: 'Eratosthenes, citing Patrocles, says that the Oxus is navigable and brings down many goods from India to the Hyrcanian sea; thence they cross the sea to Albania and are carried by way of the Cyrus and the places beyond to the Black Sea.' Note that Eratosthenes has altered the whole sense by turning 'easily' into 'many goods'. This makes it clear, first that Strabo II, 73 *is* Patrocles' own version as given in his report, and secondly that Eratosthenes understood that report in sense (1) above (*i.e.* misunderstood it) and, perhaps quoting from memory, made an alteration in the report which confirmed his own misinterpretation. Strabo, who had himself later knowledge (*e.g.* from Apollodorus), duly repeats Eratosthenes' version, though, after giving Eratosthenes' views generally on this part of the world, he says impatiently (XI, 510) that Eratosthenes tries to reconcile a lot more things of the sort but that he has given quite enough; it may not have escaped his notice that what Eratosthenes says is in direct conflict with his (Strabo's) own statement that the Caspian was not navigated and not used,[2] for which he proceeds to give his reasons (he means of course serious navigation, not native fishing boats and so on). The only other point worth notice is the fact that you could not have a regular commercial route across, or rather coasting round, a large expanse of water without also having ports, both for shipping and money-changers; and no port, Greek or native, anywhere on the Caspian is ever mentioned by anybody.

I come to Varro (Pliny VI, 52). Varro says that it was found out (not 'explored') on Pompey's expedition that in seven days goods came through (or could come through) from India to the river of Bactra, which ran into the Oxus, 'and from the Oxus these goods, carried (or "if carried") across the Caspian to the Cyrus, can be brought down the Phasis to the Black Sea with a land porterage not exceeding five days'. The India-Bactria time-table might come from anywhere and does not concern this Appendix, while the

[1] Kiessling *op. cit.* col. 464.

[2] XI, 509, *ἄπλους τε οὖσα καὶ ἀργός*. Improved upon by Mela, III, 5, 3: it was too full of monsters for navigation.

overland porterage between Cyrus and Phasis was a well-known thing[1] and may be left out; what remains is the statement 'Indian goods can be brought from Bactria *via* the Oxus, Caspian, Cyrus, and Phasis to the Black Sea'. This *is* Patrocles' report, for like that report it is put in a shape which could mean two things: (1) goods are brought, (2) goods could be brought, but are not. It would be too much of a coincidence to suppose that independent reports were made to Antiochus I and to Pompey, each of which was drawn up in language legitimately susceptible of two meanings. Pompey was never near the Caspian, and the man he commissioned to find out for him merely quoted Patrocles, adding the well-known land porterage; probably it was the only thing he could do. But one point is clear; had there been a trade-route in active operation, Pompey would not have called for a report on its feasibility.

There was never then in existence more than one independent statement about an Oxo-Caspian trade-route, Patrocles' report to Antiochus I, and the word 'easily' shows that its real meaning was, 'You can easily make a trade-route from Bactria across the Caspian to the Black Sea if you like.' This is confirmed by Strabo's ἄπλους and by Pompey's enquiry whether such a thing was feasible. There is no evidence at all that, in Greek times, any such trade-route from India ever existed.[2]

[1] Strabo XI, 498. Seleucus' alleged intention to connect the Caspian and the Black Sea by a canal (Pliny VI, 31) meant connecting the Cyrus and the Phasis by a waterway to do away with this land porterage and avoid breaking bulk. The Soviet government to-day have a plan to connect the Caspian and the Sea of Azov by a ship canal (the Manych canal) a long way to the north of the Cyrus (N. Mikhaylov, *Soviet geography* 1935 p. 192 and Plan p. 185); but this goes far beyond anything which Seleucus can have dreamt of, and would traverse country unknown to him.

[2] There was in existence in Strabo's own time (XI, 506) a trade-route from the East to the Black Sea which passed *northward* of the Caspian, the Aorsi (who had by now absorbed the remnant of the Massagetae) being the middlemen, and which became important later; but this has nothing to do with the supposed Oxo-Caspian route.

APPENDIX 15

THE OXUS QUESTION TO-DAY

No competent person to-day believes that the Oxus ever entered the Caspian bodily in historical times. The dominant modern theory about the Oxus in the Greek period, as put forward by Professor A. Herrmann,[1] is that the river itself entered the Aral, as to-day, but that before reaching the Aral it threw off a branch into the huge Sary Kamish depression south-west of the Aral, and that that branch issued southward from Sary Kamish, flowed down the Uzboi channel, and entered the Caspian at Balkan Bay, admittedly the only point where a lost river could enter the Caspian. He relied on two things: (1) a study by W. (V. V.) Barthold[2] of Arab evidence of the thirteenth to the sixteenth centuries, and (2) an article in German by W. Obrutschew,[3] who explored the Uzboi and published his results in Russian in 1890, of which book his German article is a summary.

Herrmann has envisaged a regular lost river, perennial and large enough to carry shipping, not an occasional spill-way, though Obrutschew called it an overflow channel for Sary Kamish when it got full; but both were rather obsessed by the belief that they had got to explain the northern or Oxo-Caspian trade-route from India, which never existed (App. 14). It was unfortunate therefore that Obrutschew discovered two (dry) waterfalls on his line of route, which would necessitate unloading and reloading vessels twice, a point already rubbed in.[4] Herrmann claimed one of these waterfalls, that at Igdy, as a confirmation of his view, it being, he thought, the waterfall of Polybius x, 48; it may suffice to say that Obrutschew gives the fall at Igdy as 3 to 5 metres high, while that in Polybius shoots the river clear to such a distance that *a quarter of a mile* of dry ground is left between cliff and water, a feat which even Niagara makes no attempt to emulate. In fact, that chapter in Polybius, with its Oxus running into the Caspian near Hyrcania (the Atrek again), is only a couple of yarns, told as such to Polybius or to his source: nomads can cross the Oxus because *either* (*a*) there is a miraculous waterfall *or* (*b*) the river conveniently dives underground for a space. They crossed in fact as Turkomans have always crossed, swimming and holding on to their swimming horses. Herrmann's theory is reproduced without comment on E. Herzfeld's map in Sakastan and elsewhere, but naturally has

[1] *Petermanns Mitt.* 1913, ii, p. 70; 1930 p. 286; 1931 p. 75; *Gött. Abh.* xv, 1914 no. 4 (the principal exposition).

[2] In R. Stube's *Quellen und Forschungen zur Erd- und Kulturkunde* II, 1910.

[3] *Petermanns Mitt.* 1914, i, p. 87.

[4] By R. Hennig, *ib.* 1930 p. 288.

not escaped criticism;[1] for example, J. Kirste[2] has pointed out that Herrmann has neglected to notice the view of Fr. von Schwarz in his book Turkestan (1900) that the Uzboi was a salt-water channel connecting Aral and Caspian, which is why they were sometimes treated as a single sea (in fact, others beside von Schwarz have long believed in a salt-water connection); and R. Hennig[3] has recently collected examples of other rivers which were supposed in antiquity to discharge into, or send a branch into, some sea which they never in fact entered.

The scientific evidence is in a hopeless tangle. M. Konshin, who investigated the ground earlier than Obrutschew,[4] and F. Walther, who investigated it later,[5] gave results which on two different lines were incompatible with his and with a lost river; he in turn has declared that they are wrong, while Konshin has said that he is wrong.[6] There seems to be no later scientific evidence, or rather, if such exists in Russia, it has not been made available to the western world. One important point, however, appears to have been overlooked. The Oxus is recorded to have burst through into Sary Kamish more than once during the nineteenth century, but it did not seek the Caspian or go any farther. If then 2000 years ago a perennial river, fed by the Oxus and large enough to carry shipping, flowed from Sary Kamish down the Uzboi to Balkan Bay, it would seem that the Oxus must have carried a far greater volume of water than it has done in modern times; certainly it then received some tributaries which do not now reach it, but on the other hand much more was being drawn off in Bactria for irrigation than in the nineteenth century.

Here comes in Barthold's Arab evidence.[7] He says that only two Arab writers are independent witnesses, Kasvin in the fourteenth century and Kafizi-Abru in the fifteenth; both agree that in their day the Oxus entered the Aral by several mouths but sent a branch (whose route I cannot identify) over a waterfall and into the Caspian; and both state that in former times the whole river entered the Aral, the change having coincided with the appearance of the Mongols in the country. Now in Babylonia the Mongols utterly

[1] De Groot p. 16, on the Chinese evidence (which is conclusive that the Aral existed), calls Herrmann's views on the Aral grotesque; but this does not necessarily touch the question of a lost river.

[2] *Wien SB* CLXXXII, 1918, Abh. 2 p. 78.

[3] *Klio* XXVIII, 1935, p. 253; *Terrae Incognitae* 1936 p. 185.

[4] His results, published in Russian, are given by Moser, *À travers l'Asie Centrale* 1886 p. 228; E. Delmar Morgan, *Proc. R. Geog. Soc.* XIV, 1892, p. 236; Prince Kropotkin, *J. Geog. Soc.* XII, 1898, p. 306.

[5] *Petermanns Mitt.* 1898 p. 204; a good study.

[6] In a work of 1898 which I have not seen, probably in Russian.

[7] I have been unable to see his German article which Herrmann used, but a summary of his views, from the Russian, appeared in the *Journal of the Geographical Society* XXII, 1903, p. 328. I have not looked for recent work on these Arab writers; it is not material to the point I want to make.

destroyed the irrigation system. If they did the same in Bactria, then the Oxus *would* suddenly increase in volume and might seek a new outlet, though it would remain strange that the new water got as far as Kwarizm before finding one. What knowledge of antiquity these two writers may have had I have no idea, neither do I know if their statements have been subjected to the necessary critical analysis; but evidently they met with no tradition that the Oxus had ever done this before, and so far as they go they are therefore against Herrmann's view.

I am not saying here that Herrmann's theory for the Greek period is either right or wrong; no one can say that.[1] The Greek evidence does not support it, and the Arab evidence is *prima facie* against it; but that is not the point. The point, as I see it, is that it is not a question for scholars at all but for science, and that the only people who can settle it are the Russian Government; and apparently it may soon be too late. For it has been a Russian dream for centuries to 'turn the Oxus back into the Caspian'; and the Soviet Government are credited with a plan[2] to break up the Oxus and to take one branch across the Kara-Kum desert (for irrigation purposes) to a point east of Balkan Bay, and another branch, which will join it there, from a point in the Khiva country down the Uzboi, avoiding the saline expanse of Sary Kamish; the two together will then enter the Caspian at Balkan Bay, if there be any water left to enter it. We are not explicitly told how far the plan has gone—if the amount of water available has been calculated, if the Uzboi has been surveyed (it used to be said that there was difficulty about the levels), and what is to be done with the Aral when half-dry; but there are said to have been 'scientific expeditions' and the branch across the Kara-Kum is said to have been begun. It is greatly to be hoped that, before work be started on the Uzboi, scientific experts may investigate *all* the various lines of evidence and decide whether that channel formerly carried fresh water, salt water, or no water at all (unless this has already been done); for once a river be brought down it the evidence will be destroyed, and the 'Oxus question' will, for the Greek scholar, remain for ever the nightmare which it has always been.

[1] The *theory* might be right even if the actual course suggested be wrong.

[2] N. Mikhaylov, *Soviet Geography* 1935 pp. 130–2.

APPENDIX 16

THE ERA OF THE MOGA COPPERPLATE FROM TAXILA

The copperplate inscription from Taxila[1] which mentions 'the Great King, the Great Moga' (*i.e.* Maues (p. 496), subsequently Great King of Kings), is dated on the 5th day of the Macedonian month Panemos in the year 78 of some unknown Era. That Era has been the subject of many theories;[2] but I have to treat it afresh, for there is a definite piece of evidence which has not been utilised, and the date of Maues is vital to any understanding of the first century B.C. in India, including the problem of the Buddha-statue (Chap. IX). It is obvious that the inscription must come very soon after the Saca occupation of Taxila, for Maues was not yet Great King of Kings, as on the majority of his coins. It is possible to clear the ground somewhat at the start.

First, the Era was used by a Saca king and was therefore a Saca Era; theories like that of Mr Banerji[3] which make it a Parthian Era can be ruled out. Certainly it was for long believed that in India Sacas and Parthians (Pahlavas) were so closely associated that they could not be distinguished; but they *must* be distinguished, for they were perpetual antagonists,[4] and it is incredible that a Saca king would have used a Parthian Era. This also puts out of court the view of M. A. Foucher,[5] that this Era was the Arsacid Era with the hundreds omitted; moreover, apart from systems with omitted hundreds being open to damaging criticism,[6] the Arsacid Era is not known to have been used by the Pahlava kings in India, which means that it was not used in the east Parthian realm of the Surens of Seistan.

The Vikrama Era of 58 B.C.[7] can be ruled out; for, apart from the impossibility of a Saca king using an Era established through a Saca defeat, it would make Maues king in Taxila in A.D. 20, while it is a fixed point that Gondophares' reign there began in A.D. 19.

The suggestion that the Era might be that of Demetrius' conquest of India[8] may be ruled out. Such an Era would have started somewhere about 180 B.C., which would make Maues king in Taxila somewhere about 102 B.C., and would leave no room for Ptolemy's kingdom of 'Indo-Scythia'. Few would defend so early a date;[9] but the point, 'Indo-Scythia' apart, is that,

[1] *CII* p. 23 no. XIII.

[2] Some are discussed by de la Vallée-Poussin, pp. 267 *sqq.*, 272 *sqq.*, 367 *sqq.*

[3] *Ind. Ant.* XXXVIII, 1908, p. 67.

[4] I heartily agree with Konow as to this, *JRAS* 1932 p. 955. I trust that this book has brought it out.

[5] Foucher II p. 488.

[6] See *CII* p. lxxxiv.

[7] H. K. Deb, *JRAS* 1922 p. 42.

[8] J. Charpentier in a review, *Ind. Ant.* 1931 p. 78.

[9] For A. Herrmann's theory about Maues, which mixes up the first and second centuries B.C., see p. 340 n. 1.

looking at the trouble the Euthydemids took to prove to the world that they were Seleucids (Chap. v), Demetrius could not possibly have used any Era but the Seleucid, while Maues would not have used an Era of the conquered Greeks.

Sir John Marshall once thought it was an Era of Maues himself and dated the inscription to 17 B.C.,[1] but he has now abandoned that view for the one advocated by Rapson (p. 496).[2] There is no real doubt that it means an Era *used by* Maues.[3]

We come therefore to the group of theories which connect the Era with the Sacas of Seistan. Dr Sten Konow in the Corpus took the view that the Era celebrated Saca independence obtained on the death of Mithridates II in 88 B.C. (really 87) and that the date of the inscription was therefore 10 B.C.;[4] but the discovery of the Kalawān inscription[5] has led him to abandon this view and (substantially) to adopt that of Rapson,[6] which has also entailed abandoning the chronology of the Corpus for a number of other inscriptions dated in the old Saca Era.[7] There is in fact no reason for supposing that the Sacas of Seistan *did* obtain independence on the death of Mithridates II, though the Suren whose immediate vassals they were may have done so.

Dr K. P. Jayaswal[8] made the Era *c.* 120 B.C., which he took as the date of a revolt by the Sacas of Seistan against Mithridates II, and dated the inscription therefore *c.* 42 B.C. The legend he cites, if based on fact, certainly shows that they were at enmity with Mithridates; but the Saca invasion of Parthia was quite certainly in 129,[9] and if one can speak of a *revolt* in Seistan (I doubt it myself, see p. 500) it was probably then. As Mithridates was completely victorious, it does not seem a hopeful point for the start of a continuing Saca Era; but this dating will be considered later.

Professor E. Herzfeld[10] in 1932, after a long criticism, concluded with truth that there were only theories and no firm ground, but suggested that the date of the Taxila copperplate might be about 32 B.C. (arrived at by estimating the time required for the coins known prior to Gondophares) and the Era consequently about 110. This also will be considered later.

1 *ASI* 1912–13 p. 7; *JRAS* 1914 p. 986. Konow in *CII* p. xxxii said that Marshall took this date 'from archaeological reasons', which might have been important; but a reference to the passages I have cited shows that this was apparently a mistake, and anyhow Marshall has abandoned the dating. An Era of Maues was also advocated by Ramprasad Chanda, *JRAS* 1920 p. 319.

2 *ASI* 1929–30 (pub. 1935) p. 63, cf. p. 72.

3 First pointed out, I think, by Senart: de la Vallée-Poussin pp. 272–3.

4 *CII* p. xxxii.

5 Text, *JRAS* 1932 p. 949; *ASI* 1930–4 (pub. 1936) p. 163.

6 *JRAS* 1932 pp. 957, 964; *JIH* XII, 1933, p. 4.

7 *JIH* XII, 1933, p. 4.

8 *JBORS* XVI, 1930, pp. 231, 240.

9 Tarn, *SP Stud.* p. 14; *CAH* IX pp. 581–2.

10 *Sakastan* pp. 98–100.

The dominant theory to-day is that of the late E. J. Rapson in 1922;[1] both Sir John Marshall and Dr Sten Konow have abandoned their own late datings in its favour. It makes the Era *c.* 150 B.C.; what he says is that it 'may possibly mark the establishment of the new kingdom in Seistan after its incorporation into the empire by Mithridates I' and is 'probably of Parthian origin'. This makes the Taxila copperplate *c.* 72 B.C., and is very close to the dating arrived at in this Appendix. But, though I agree that the Era marks the date of the establishment of a new kingdom in Seistan, I cannot myself accept a Parthian origin for an Era used by a Saca king, apart from the fact that an inscription now calls a date in that Era 'Saka';[2] so I must attempt both to date the Era and to find an occasion when it could have been established by Sacas.

I must however first notice the name Moga of the inscription, generally supposed (as I believe myself) to be the king of the abundant coinage[3] whose name is given in Greek as Maues and in Kharoshthi as Moa, though doubts have occasionally been expressed.[4] I take it that the full form of the name sounded as Mauakes[5] to Greek ears, just as it sounded to Chinese ears as Mu-ku'a;[6] this would easily represent Moga. But I do not see how to equate Moga with Moa; there must therefore have been two forms of the name in Saca, a long and a short one. Greek writers record such double name-forms from other languages, e.g. Kynna-Kynane, daughter of Philip II and an Illyrian mother (? from Illyrian); Sabba-Sambethe, the 'Chaldean Sibyl' (presumably Anatolian); and Phraates-Phraatakes (from Parthian Pahlavi), an exact parallel in another North-Iranian tongue to Maues-Mauakes. Indeed there might be a parallel from Saca itself, if it be correct that Azes-Azilises are only short and long forms of the same name,[7] and if the language be Saca.

The point I want to make myself is one of which no theory has yet taken account, the close connection between Maues and an obscure Indo-Greek king called Telephus. Telephus' coins are very rare,[8] only nine specimens

[1] *CHI* p. 570; cf. *JRAS* 1930 pp. 186, 193.

[2] In the Jihonika inscription, *CII* p. 81 no. XXX (see p. 500), Konow says that F. W. Thomas and himself have now read 'Saka' before the number, 191: *JIH* 1933 p. 3.

[3] His coins: *BMC* pp. 68 *sqq.*; Cunningham *NC* 1890 pp. 130 *sqq.*

[4] J. F. Fleet, *JRAS* 1914 p. 797; and see now p. 502.

[5] Leader of the Sacas at Gaugamela, Arr. III, 8, 3.

[6] King of Ta-yuan in 101 B.C., Hirth pp. 109 *sqq.*; see p. 308.

[7] F. W. Thomas, *JRAS* 1906 p. 208; Herzfeld, *Sakastan* pp. 93, 97; Konow, *CII* pp. xxxix *sq.* This does not necessarily mean that Azes and Azilises were the same king (p. 498 n. 5); kings of the same name succeeding one another were as familiar to the ancient as to the modern world.

[8] His coins: Whitehead *NC* p. 337 nos. 58, 59 (four bronze pieces), cf. Whitehead, *JASB* VI, 1910, Num. Supp. XIV p. 561 no. 12, and another specimen, *ASI* 1912–13 p. 46 no. 7; and four specimens of the silver coin, *BMC* p. 171 Pl. XXXII, 7, *ASI* 1929–30 p. 74 no. 46 = p. 88 no. 21, and the two in Berlin, O. Stein, *Telephos* (4) in PW, 1934.

being actually known, but one of them gives a tiny picture of Mt Pīlusāra[1] like the well-known one on the 'Kapisi' coins of Eucratides (p. 213); that, and the type 'Zeus enthroned' on his bronze money, show that he ruled and coined in Kapisa. His coins show two peculiar monograms, which can only be those of his moneyers in that city (see App. 1); and these two monograms also occur on coins of Maues and are said to occur nowhere else.[2] Maues then not only coined in Kapisa—that could be deduced from his coins which show the 'Zeus enthroned' type of Kapisa[3]—but coined there with the same two moneyers as Telephus, and therefore either directly before or after him; as the extreme rarity of Telephus' coins points to a very short reign, Maues' date at Kapisa in either case is substantially the date of Telephus. What is that date?[4] Telephus' coins all show the round omicron alone, which *prima facie* puts him before *c.* 40 B.C. if not before 50 B.C. (p. 326); in fact no numismatist, on numismatic grounds, has ever classed him with the really late kings like Hippostratus, Nicias, Hermaeus. Now the round and the square omicron (p. 326) afford a good test for comparative dating *in the same locality*; and this makes it impossible to put Telephus after Hermaeus, who also ruled and coined in Kapisa. For Hermaeus' coins show both the round and the square omicron, and their abundance postulates a reign of some length; and on this ground alone he cannot well have come to the throne later than *c.* 50 B.C. or died before 30 B.C. (see generally Chap. VIII). Indeed if, as seems almost certain, he was Yin-mo-fu of the Ch'ien-han-shu (p. 340), then there is evidence that he came to the throne before 48 B.C. and was alive at some date after 32 B.C.; the end of Greek rule in the Paropamisadae, *i.e.* his death, falls about or soon after 30 B.C. (p. 350). But immediately before Hermaeus comes the reign of his father Amyntas (p. 331), of unknown

[1] No. 59 in Whitehead *NC* = Pl. VIII no. 640 in *Lahore Cat.*

[2] Whitehead's discovery in *JASB* 1910 (for reference see p. 496 n. 8); I rely on him for the fact of non-occurrence elsewhere. He pointed out (*NC* p. 337) that it implies a close bond in time between Telephus and Maues. The Telephus monogram on Whitehead no. 58 occurs on several coins of Maues given in *BMC*; that on no. 59 is on two coins of Maues in *Lahore Cat.* Pls. X, 20 and XV, 1.

[3] *Lahore Cat.* p. 99 no. 15; Cunningham, *NC* 1890 p. 134 no. 21, and p. 136 no. 27 = *BMC* p. 70 no. 14. This last is unmistakable: Zeus holds Nike on his hand and before him is the forepart of a small elephant, as on Eucratides' 'Kapisi' coins (p. 213). Cunningham *ib.* p. 104 says that Maues' coins are never found in the Kabul valley; but in fact some come in to dealers at Jalalabad (J. Hackin, *JA* 226, 1935, p. 290), and in any case the evidence of the type last mentioned, and of the monograms, is much too explicit to be overruled by any consideration of find-spots (see App. 1).

[4] O. Stein *op. cit.* only says first century B.C. He puts Maues before Hippostratus (which is right, but he gives no reasons) and Telephus before Maues, because Maues, he thinks, copied his coins. His date-sequence therefore is substantially mine, but it is done in a few lines.

length; keeping everything as late as possible, that still puts Telephus, and consequently Maues, not later than about 60 B.C. at latest.[1]

This should suffice; but other things bear it out. Debased or barbarous imitations of Hermaeus' money continued to be struck after his death[2] and down to the advent of Kujula Kadphises by those, whether Sacas or Pahlavas, who then ruled in Kapisa; this makes it almost impossible to postulate another Greek king in Kapisa after him, and in fact he has always been considered to be the last Greek king; and Kujula Kadphises, who was in a position to know, certainly treated him as the last Greek king in the Paropamisadae (App. 17). While these considerations forbid us to put Telephus after Hermaeus, an additional reason arises in the case of Maues, even leaving out of account the fairly good style of his coins and the absence from them of the square omicron. The accession of the Parthian Gondophares is fixed by an inscription to A.D. 19,[3] and there is good proof that his predecessor was named Azes.[4] Between Maues and Gondophares therefore must come in the coins of the three members of the Azes dynasty—Azes, Azilises, Azes II[5]—and also those of another Saca Great King of Kings, Azes' father Spalirises (p. 346), who is later than Maues, as his coins after he was Great King of Kings show the square omicron, while those of Maues have the round form only. Azes' large coinage, and still more the great number of letters and monograms on his coins, indicate a reign of substantial length; and this alone suffices to exclude the idea that Maues can be anywhere near the Christian Era.

On the other hand, even if Antialcidas be brought down as late as 90 B.C., which is very improbable (p. 314), there is still a time-gap of about a generation between Antialcidas and Amyntas, with no Greek king except Telephus who can be placed there; is seems obvious that the rule at Kapisa of Telephus and Maues must come somewhere in this gap, which cannot begin later than *c.* 90 or end later than *c.* 60. The monograms then are fatal to any attempt to

[1] In Chapter VIII reason is given for putting Maues' death and Amyntas' accession in the year 58. But, as that chapter presupposes and draws deductions from this Appendix, this Appendix has to be argued as though, as regards the dating of Telephus and Maues, those deductions did not yet exist; otherwise one would be arguing in a circle. But there is no need to repeat here what I have said in that chapter about the square omicron and the Chinese evidence; that could have come in either place.

[2] *CHI* pp. 560–1.

[3] *CHI* p. 576; Herzfeld, *Sakastan* p. 101.

[4] *CHI* p. 577; Herzfeld, *Sakastan* pp. 96–7.

[5] Herzfeld, *Sakastan* pp. 97–8, made all three the same man. But *the same engraver on the same coin* could not use the two forms Azes and Azilises for the same man; also the stratification at Taxila, where the coins of Azes II have generally been found nearer the surface, is regarded by Marshall as conclusive for two kings named Azes; see *JRAS* 1914 p. 979, *ASI* 1929–30 p. 72. N. G. Majumdar, *ASI* 1928–9 pp. 169, 171, has drawn the same deduction from Kharoshthi palaeography. See also p. 348 and n. 1.

date Maues in the latter part of the first century B.C., like Herzfeld's 32 B.C. or Jayaswal's 42 B.C.; and they show, therefore, that the Era of the Taxila copperplate cannot be later than the reign of Mithridates I of Parthia.

There is still one other consideration which seems to exclude the dates of Herzfeld and Jayaswal. The Era must be a Saca Era; and this cannot be reconciled with any dating of it in the reign of Mithridates II. For Herzfeld has brilliantly shown that Sacastene became the domain of the Suren[1]—a vassal state of one who was himself a vassal of the Arsacid; and he is certainly right in dating this event to the reign of Mithridates II. While he was showing this, I was showing that Mithridates II had entrusted the liquidation of the Saca invasion, in the countries east of the Persian desert, to some one whom I could not identify but who was needed to explain certain coins and whom I called the 'king of the campaign coins'.[2] If the two things be placed side by side, it will be seen at once that Herzfeld and myself were approaching the same thing from different points of view and that my 'king of the campaign coins' ('king' was a mistaken word to use) is his Suren. This makes the matter very plain. Mithridates II entrusted the campaign against the Saca invaders to the Suren (as Orodes II entrusted that against the Roman invaders to a later Suren), and after his success rewarded him with the conquered Sacastene as his fief. The 'campaign coins',[3] which as I pointed out were no part of the Parthian royal coinage, were struck by the Suren, or struck for him, to pay his army; the head is his, but the Arsaces of the coins is Mithridates II,[4] just as on the bilingual tetradrachm of Demetrius II the head and type are his but the name and legend are his father's (p. 78). This agrees with the fact brought out by Herzfeld, that prior to Gondophares the Surens had, so far as is known, no regular coinage.[5] The Suren then got Sacastene early in the reign of Mithridates II, and would certainly have kept it while that king lived. But an Era implies independence, and the Sacas of Sacastene would hardly have started one to celebrate the fact that they had been put under the rule of the Suren; we need a Saca, not a Parthian, Era. This bears out the conclusion from the monograms that we must look to the reign of Mithridates I and not to that of Mithridates II.

[1] *Sakastan* pp. 70–80.

[2] Tarn, *SP Stud.* pp. 16–18. McDowell, in assigning these coins to Sinatruces (*Coins of Seleucia* p. 211), has not considered Herzfeld on the Surens.

[3] The five coins with legends *καταστράτεια* (twice), Areia, Traxiane, Margiane.

[4] The legend on these coins, *βασιλέως βασιλέων Ἀρσάκου θεοπάτορος εὐεργέτου ἐπιφανοῦς φιλέλληνος*, is not one of those which Wroth in *BMC Parthia* assigned to Mithridates II, though that king employed the last three titles; *θεοπάτορος* (which need mean no more than the Kushan *devaputra*, 'Son of Heaven') is taken from the legend of his father Artabanus II (Artabanus I, Wroth). It means that Mithridates' titles were not yet settled and that the Suren's Greek engraver in the Far East gave him a good selection. On the confusion of the Parthian legends of this period and the gradual formation of the later stereotyped legend see Herzfeld, *Sakastan* pp. 46–8.

[5] *Sakastan* p. 98.

We are therefore compelled—there seems no alternative—to seek an occasion in the reign of Mithridates I which some Sacas, who must be connected with the Saca invaders of India, could have found opportune for establishing an Era. I have given elsewhere (p. 223) the reasons which seem to necessitate a supposition that Mithridates I settled some Saca allies or mercenaries in Sacastene, or that they settled themselves; the process must have been similar to the 'settlement' of the Galatae in northern Phrygia by Nicomedes of Bithynia and Mithridates of Pontus,[1] and Mithridates of Parthia may have had as little option in the matter as had his namesake; if there were already some Sacas in Seistan[2] (on which I express no opinion) that would help to explain their choice of that district. The newcomers need not have been very numerous; Isidore's Sacastene is not a large province, and the Galatae held up Asia Minor for years with only 20,000 men. The settlement can be roughly dated, by means of the date of Eucratides' death in 159, to *c.* 155 (p. 223)—a couple of years margin either way. Then the question arises, did these Sacas assert a *de facto* independence from the start, as did the Galatae, or not until Mithridates I died, leaving a minor to succeed him: that is, does the Era date from *c.* 155 or from 138–7? The former date would put the Moga inscription *c.* 77 B.C., the latter would date it 60–59. This latter date might perhaps be fitted in with Telephus; but, though no chronological argument can be drawn (as has sometimes been done) from Maues' title Great King of Kings, the earlier date is almost certainly correct. For there was one important difference between the settlement of the Galatae and that of Mithridates' Sacas. The Galatae only got, in Galatia, a poor country; but the Sacas got one of the richest, and safest, districts in Mithridates' empire. This proves that they virtually settled themselves; had he been able to settle them as subjects, he would have followed the usual course of settling them on a frontier to guard it. They can only therefore have dated their Era from their acquisition of a good new country; they were doubtless independent, or virtually so, till the Suren conquered them for Mithridates II. This does not necessarily mean that they *instituted* their Era *c.* 155; they may have done that much later, just as nobody knows when either the Seleucid or the Arsacid Era was actually instituted.

One other dating must be considered, that of the Taxila duck vase inscription (*CII* p. 81 no. xxx), which as already mentioned is dated under the satrap Jihonika (Zeionises) in 'Saka' 191. The vase was undoubtedly buried when the Kushans took Sirkap, an event now dated with fair certainty to A.D. 60–64;[3] but it is much worn, and Konow considers that it had had 20 to 25 years of usage before it was buried.[4] If the Saca Era be rightly put

[1] *CAH* VII pp. 104–6.

[2] F. W. Thomas, *JRAS* 1906 p. 181. Konow, who disagrees, points out that Darius does not mention Sacas in Zranka (Drangiana), *CII* pp. xviii *sq.* Neither do the Alexander-historians.

[3] Sir J. Marshall, *ASI* 1929–30 (pub. 1935) p. 55, where he gives his reasons.

[4] Konow, *JRAS* 1932 p. 957, *JIH* 1933 p. 3.

c. 155 B.C., the vase was made *c.* A.D. 36, in the reign of Gondophares, some 24 to 28 years before it was buried, which confirms the dating I have come to. The inscription shows that, though Zeionises was a Parthian, a nephew of Gondophares, Gondophares' Saca subjects still dated by their own Era.

This makes the first Saca Era *c.* 155, arising out of events for which definite reasons are given in Chapter v, and the date of the Moga inscription *c.* 77; as Maues naturally conquered Taxila before he could reach Kapisa, this agrees very well with the deduction already made that Telephus cannot be later than about 70–60. It agrees very well too with the history. The Saca state in Sacastene must have acted as a magnet to the Sacas of the North when they invaded Parthia in 129. The invasion was finally liquidated by the Suren somewhere between 124 (the accession of Mithridates II) and 115, by which date the Parthians were in possession of Merv (p. 281). The Saca invasion of Sind may then have begun any time after about 120; there was a halt after the conquest of the provinces between Abiria on the middle Indus and Surastrene, of unknown duration but long enough to find its way into tradition (p. 320); this was followed by a fresh move up the Indus from Abiria under Maues, which put Taxila into his hands by or shortly before *c.* 77.[1] Mithridates II rewarded the Suren, and tried to provide against Sacastene being again a danger point, by putting him and his house in charge of Sacastene and the East; if we neglect *names* (he was not yet a 'king') and look at *things*, it was one more offshoot of the Seleucid system of a joint-king governing the East. The ultimate result was a second Parthian realm in the East (Indo-Parthian or Pahlava of the numismatists) which for a time under Gondophares may have been more powerful than the Parthia of the Arsacids.

It only remains to notice two possible objections to the view here put forward. One is Herzfeld's: as the Saca Era of A.D. 78 is certain, a second Saca Era is improbable.[2] There is really nothing in this. The first Saca kingdom in India ended by everything that remained after the loss of Malva and Ujjain coming under the rule of the Parthian Suren Gondophares in A.D. 19; this put an end to the use for official purposes of the first Saca Era of *c.* 155 B.C., even if Gondophares' Saca subjects continued to use it. Malva and Ujjain had been lost in 58 B.C. to the Indian king Vikramāditya (whatever king this name represents), who commemorated this by the establishment of the Vikrama Era; and when the Western Saca Satraps retook Ujjain in A.D. 78 they may have set up a new Era of their own (see further, p. 335).

[1] Konow suggested that the Kharoshthi inscription from Maira in the Salt Range, *CII* p. 11 no. VIII, might belong to a year 58 of the same Era as the Moga inscription and might mention Moa (Maues), and might mark the progress of the Sacas up the Indus. But date and name seem to be really conjectural, and he said (p. xxxii) that it is 'too defaced to be utilised with confidence'. More recently however (*JIH* 1933 p. 19) he *has* utilised it with confidence, dating it *c.* 86 B.C. and using it as evidence that Maues began to reign about 90 B.C.

[2] *Sakastan* p. 99.

Both the Eras of *c.* 155 B.C. and A.D. 78, though set up in different kingdoms, would naturally be called 'Saca'. Suppose the Angles who invaded Britain had used Eras; there would have been a Northumbrian Era, and then when Mercia rose to power a Mercian Era; but both would have been 'Anglian'.

It also might be asked, if the Sacas were independent enough *c.* 155 to institute an Era like the Arsacids (Parni), why did they not also coin, as the Arsacids apparently did from an early period? There was a good reason for this. Neither Parni nor Sacas could at first coin for themselves; they depended on getting control of a Greek mint, or anyhow of a Greek city. The Parthians early secured Hekatompylos, which would explain the coins of the kings before Mithridates I (if the 'beardless' coins really belong to them). But in Sacastene the Sacas, as Isidore shows, did not control any Greek city; indeed there is no trace that there ever was a Greek mint at all in Seistan, which had continued to be served by Euthydemus' money (pp. 95, 164 n. 1). The Sacas did their best; they produced some barbarous imitations of Euthydemus' coins.[1] But they probably had no chance of instituting a proper coinage till Maues got control of the mint at Taxila; their first kingdom on the Indus, comprising Patalene and Abiria, seems to have left no numismatic record (pp. 321 *sq.*).

It will be seen that my date of *c.* 155 for the Era of the Moga inscription is much the same as Rapson's *c.* 150, but has been arrived at on other lines; and that it is in my view a Saca, not a Parthian, Era.

* * * *

An article by M. Govind Pai, *JIH* XIV, 1935, p. 309, only came to my notice after this book was finished. After a minute examination of the writing of the Taxila copperplate inscription (pp. 328–38) he discards the name Moga and for mogasa reads māgasa, 'of the month Māgha'; he decides that this relates to an intercalation of this month in 77–6 B.C., which makes the Era 155–4; he refers this Era however to the usual imaginary Saca conquest of Bactria (p. 283), which he puts between 162 and 140! I can only notice the strange coincidence with my own dating of the Era; his readings I must leave to Kharoshthi scholars, though I should be astonished to find an inscription in any language dated by 'the Great King, the Great' without giving the name. I note the similarity of his view to one once held by Dr Konow with regard to the Taxila silver scroll, *CII* p. 70 no. XXVII; in the Corpus Konow interpreted ayasa as referring to an intercalation of the (named) month Āshādha, but the form ajasa in the Kalawān inscription has led him to abandon this and to agree with Marshall and Rapson that ayasa, like ajasa, is Azes; *JRAS* 1932 pp. 950 *sqq.*, *JIH* 1933 p. 2.

[1] Rapson in *JRAS* 1904 p. 675 no. 5.

APPENDIX 17

THE HERMAEUS-KUJULA KADPHISES COINS

Hermaeus' Greek legend on his own coins, both silver and copper, which were struck in the Alexandria-Kapisa mint, is always *βασιλέως σωτῆρος Ἑρμαίου*, 'Of king Hermaeus, saviour', and the Kharoshthi legend is the corresponding Maharajasa tradatasa Heramayasa, with the 'Zeus enthroned' of Alexandria-Kapisa.[1] The Kadphises coins, which are of inferior style, resembling the debased copies of Hermaeus' money issued after his death, fall into two classes. The first class[2] has: obverse, bust of Hermaeus diademed and Greek legend *βασιλέως στηρος συ Ἑρμαίου* (often corrupted); reverse, Heracles facing with club and lion's skin, and a Kharoshthi legend signifying 'Kujula Kadphises, Kushan, *yavuga* (chief)'. This class has the square omicron but no other square letters. The second class[3] has: obverse, bust of Hermaeus diademed, and a Greek legend, usually mutilated, reading 'Kujula Kadphises, Kushan'; reverse, the same as the first class. This class, beside the square omicron, has the square sigma and phi which one associates with the coins of Gondophares; as both classes must be near in time, it is clear that the period is getting too late for letter forms to mean much chronologically. In addition, there is a third class which belongs here, a strange copper coinage:[4] obverse, bust of Hermaeus with a Greek legend *βασιλέως στηρος συ Ἑρμαίου*; reverse, Nike holding wreath and a Kharoshthi legend Maharajasa rajarajasa mahatasa Heramayasa, 'Of King Hermaeus, King of Kings, the Great', or 'Great King of Kings'. This class shows the round omicron, and no square letters at all. It cannot be Hermaeus' own coinage; he never uses such titles, nor could he, and the Greek legend is identical with that of the first class mentioned above. The round omicron therefore has nothing to do with the round omicron of the earlier coinage of Hermaeus himself, and that means that we are approaching the time when, on the Kushan coinage, the square letter-forms will have vanished from India and the round omicron will have become stereotyped. As, of the coins mentioned above, the first and third classes are connected by the identical Greek legend and the first and second by the identical reverse, all the coins

[1] *BMC* pp. 62–6.

[2] *Ib.* pp. 120–1. A number have since been found at Taxila: *ASI* 1912–13 p. 52 nos. 48–50, 1914–15 p. 33 nos. 35–7, 1929–30 p. 83 nos. 355–63.

[3] *BMC* p. 122. There are a number from Taxila among the coins of Kadphises I listed in *ASI* 1929–30 pp. 83 *sqq.* nos. 364–451.

[4] *BMC* p. 172; *Lahore Cat.* p. 85 nos. 682–92. I suppose that the coins found at Taxila with bust of Hermaeus and Nike are of this type, *ASI* 1929–30 pp. 74 *sq.* nos. 47 *sqq.*, but there is no further description of them.

must belong, roughly, to the same period, which can only be the reign of Kujula Kadphises I; his reign cannot have begun till somewhere after A.D. 25,[1] the date at which the Hou-han-shu begins, and probably went down to *c.* 50 (p. 352), so that these coins are at least some two generations later than the death of Hermaeus.

The late date of the third class, the copper coinage with the round omicron, is also shown by the words *στηρος συ* in the Greek legend. *στηρος* used to be treated as a corruption of *σωτῆρος*, but it occurs too regularly and consistently for this to be possible, and also such a corruption will not explain *συ*. Konow has explained *συ* as Kushan *shau*, *i.e.* Shah, king,[2] which in view of the seal from Bajaur with the inscription (in Kharoshthi) su Theüdama[sa][3] seems most probable; but he still took *στηρος* to be *σωτῆρος*. Many explanations of both words have been put forward;[4] I venture to think the view is certain enough which makes *στηρος* the same language as *συ*, and that the meaning must be related to the Kharoshthi legend on the copper coins of the third class with round omicron—'Great King' or something of the sort.

In any case there is little question as to what these coins are. Those of the third class, certainly in the Kharoshthi legend and probably in the Greek legend, make out that Hermaeus was a much more important king than he really was, that is, they are propaganda; the first and second classes are then propaganda also. But if Kadphises I used as propaganda the name and portrait of a Greek king who was dead some fifty years or more, and equipped him with extravagant titles which he never bore and which were not suited to his position, only one explanation is possible. We have in this book met with several undoubted pedigree coins or series of coins used as propaganda—those of Antimachus, Agathocles, Eucratides (Chap. v)—and these coins of Kadphises I are pedigree coins also: the Kushan, who was about to take or had just taken the Paropamisadae from its Pahlava rulers, is announcing that he is related by blood to Hermaeus in order to make himself more acceptable to the Greeks of that country; he is not a foreign conqueror but their lawful king. We get three steps in the process, though the sequence may be notional rather than temporal. The first (class 3) is that Hermaeus was a very great king. The second (class 1) stresses the relationship; Hermaeus has half—the more honourable half—of the coin. In the third (class 2) Hermaeus has less than half; he is falling into the background. Lastly come the coins of Kadphises alone, which I need not give. Neither of the Greek types on the coins here examined is a type of Hermaeus, any more than the legends are his; they are put on at random; Heracles[5] and Nike might always be well-pleasing to Greeks.

[1] One of his coins bears an imitation of the head of Augustus, Cunningham, *NC* 1892 p. 65 no. 7.

[2] *CII* pp. lxiii–iv. [3] *Ib.* p. 6 no. III. [4] Given *ib.* p. lxiii.

[5] Cunningham suggested that the Heracles was the Kushan god of death, *NC* 1892 p. 59. But what then was Nike?

This view of the coins, which seems to me inevitable, supports and is supported by a theory which has been put forward about Kadphises I. The name is spelt, in Kharoshthi, Kaphasa or Kapasa on coins of his found at Taxila,[1] and Lévi interpreted the name Kadphises to mean 'the Kapisa man',[2] which, as Konow has pointed out, might mean that his people considered that he had a title to the throne of Kapisa.[3] As we have seen, he himself did claim such a title through his relationship to Hermaeus.

I have given in the text of Chapter VIII (p. 343) the reasons for supposing that Hermaeus gave a relative—sister is more probable than daughter—in marriage to a Kushan chief who was ancestor, probably grandfather, of Kadphises I. He can I think be identified. A Kushan chief is known, prior to the time of Kadphises I, who struck a Greek coinage with a Greek legend: Miaos (or Heraos—the name is said not to be certain) who calls himself 'Kushan' on his coinage.[4] The obverse shows his head, while the reverse has the type of the Hermaeus and Calliope coins,[5] 'King on horseback'; but a flying Victory crowning the king, natural enough in the circumstances, has been added, a design repeated later on the coins of Gondophares. Miaos' coins are earlier than the Hermaeus-Kadphises coins, since for a monogram they bear the Greek letter B, while one class (class 2) of the Hermaeus-Kadphises coins has Kharoshthi letters but none have Greek letters. The portrait of Miaos bears a very strong resemblance to some of those of Wima Kadphises,[6] the son of Kadphises I, who if I am right was his great-grandson. The legend is ΤΥΡΑΝΝΟΥΝΤΟΣ ΜΙΑΟΥ (or whatever the name is) ΣΑΝΑΒ ΚΟΡΡΑΝΟΥ, with many variants in the spelling. The last word is certainly 'Kushan', the Ρ being the *sh* sign (see App. 18); this is its first appearance on coins in the Farther East, though it was soon followed by the *sh* sign on the coins of Spalirises (p. 509). The word *τυραννοῦντος* shows that Miaos was not a king, but a local ruler of some sort whose position was less than royal; *τύραννος* is regularly used in that sense by the author of the Periplus[7] about a century later, and *τυραννοῦντος* shows not only that the moneyer knew Greek as a still living tongue but that

[1] *ASI* 1912–13 pp. 44, 51. On the various spellings of the name see Konow, *CII* pp. lxiv, lxviii.

[2] *JA* 1923 p. 52.

[3] *CII* p. lxvi n. 3.

[4] *BMC* p. 116 (*s.v.* Heraüs); Cunningham *NC* 1888 p. 47 and more fully 1890 p. 111; Rapson, *Indian coins* 1897 p. 9; J. Kirste, *Wien SB* CLXXXII, 1918, Abh. 2 pp. 50 *sqq.*; *CII* p. liii.

[5] *BMC* p. 66.

[6] See especially *BMC* Pl. XXV, 6; the resemblance is most marked. There is no portrait of Kujula Kadphises.

[7] *Periplus* 24 is the best instance; see also 14, 16, 22, 23. J. Kennedy, *JRAS* 1913 p. 125, thought that *τύραννος* in the *Periplus* meant a local ruler who was probably a vassal, but the evidence does not go to show that vassaldom was of the essence of the meaning. Some have thought that the five Yueh-chi princes were vassals of some supreme overlord; there seems to be no evidence.

he could appreciate the distinction between τύραννος and τυραννοῦντος—not 'ruler' but 'under the rule of'; he probably had in mind βασιλεύοντος on the pedigree coins of Antimachus and Agathocles. The Kushan Miaos must in fact have been one of the five princes of the Yueh-chi, the *yabghu* (*yavuga*) of the Kuei-shuang, who at this time are said to have been somewhere between Chitral and the Panjshir country (p. 342); there is said to be tolerably easy communication by the Dorah pass between Badakshan on the Bactrian and Chitral on the Indian side.[1] The Greek moneyer did not attempt to render Miaos' title; perhaps he did not know very well what *yavuga* meant, and so used the indefinite τυραννοῦντος; on the later Kushan coinage *yavuga* was to be transliterated. So far everything agrees well enough with the view that Miaos was a contemporary of Hermaeus and ancestor of Kadphises I.[2]

The word ΣΑΝΑΒ is unexplained; but Cunningham was certain of the B on every coin he had seen. His own explanation, *tsanyu* (= *devaputra* of the Kushan kings), is hardly satisfactory; it neglects the B, and it may be doubted whether a Kushan chief at this time could have called himself 'Son of Heaven', whatever his Imperial descendants were to do.[3] The popular interpretation, Saka,[4] is equally unsatisfactory. It, also, neglects the B; Miaos coined tetradrachms, which no Saca king ever did;[5] above all, no known Saca or Kushan king ever calls himself 'Saca', and it is not, I think, even known whether the collection of peoples whom the Persians (followed by the Greeks and ourselves) called Sacas ever called themselves by that name, precisely as it is not known what the people whom Greeks and Romans called Parthians called themselves. One writer has sought to remedy the omission of the B by saying it is Middle Persian *ve*, 'and', and that the legend should read 'Saca and Kushan';[6] but Greek coin-engravers in India did not join two titles by καί and did not use Middle Persian words for simple Greek ones. ΣΑΝΑΒ remains unexplained.

Miaos' coinage, especially his portrait, is too good to have been struck anywhere but in a Greek mint, which, if I am right about his relations with Hermaeus, could only be Kapisa; the introduction of the *sh* sign could only have taken place in some regular Greek centre. On the other hand, the various coins we have show too many variations and blunders in the legend for the Kapisa mint at the beginning of the reign of Hermaeus. It may be that there

[1] Sir A. Stein, *Serindia* I pp. 25–6.

[2] Cunningham suggested 'father and predecessor', *NC* 1890 p. 114; but on the dates it must be 'grandfather' at the least.

[3] Cunningham (*ib.*) however claimed to have read *devaputra* on a copper coin in the (usually illegible) Kharoshthi legend.

[4] *BMC* pp. 116, xlvii; Kirste *op. cit.* p. 56; *CII* p. liii.

[5] Cunningham *NC* 1890 p. 114.

[6] Kirste p. 56. He suggested (p. 55) that ΚΟΡΡΑΝΟΥ really means, not Kushan, but 'conqueror of Kushans', instancing Germanicus. But Germanicus is not Germanus, as it would have to be on his argument.

was by now a good deal of difference between the mints in Greek Alexandria and Indian Kapisa. But the commonsense of the matter seems to be that Miaos' portrait was engraved, and coin-models made, for him in the capital, and that he then copied them, as best might be, in his own lordship. This would agree well enough with the story.

The conclusion, then, is that when Kujula Kadphises, a descendant of the Kushan *yavuga* Miaos who had married a relative of Hermaeus, invaded the Paropamisadae, he proclaimed to the Greeks that he came, not as a foreign conqueror, but as their lawful ruler by hereditary relationship to their last king Hermaeus; the coins here considered are the dry bones of that propaganda. It shows, incidentally, that in the first half of the first century A.D. there were still enough Greeks, or what passed as Greeks, in the Paropamisadae to be worth conciliating.

APPENDIX 18

SAN AND RHO

That the sign *þ* which appears in Greek legends on the Kushan coinage and on that of two earlier rulers has the value *sh* was remarked in 1872 by Cunningham,[1] who thought that the sign was a peculiar form of Rho. In 1887 Sir A. Stein[2] put forward the theory that it was a revival of the obsolete Greek letter San (which had the value *sh*), since the oldest minuscule form of San resembles, though apparently it is not identical with, the *þ* sign on the Kushan coinage. This has raised a good deal of discussion; on the one hand, various other origins have been suggested for the *þ* sign, including the Aramaean Tsade,[3] and on the other, much learning has been expended in an attempt to show that this sign had not the value *sh* at all but the value *r* (Rho),[4] while Professor F. W. Thomas has taken the view, which resembles Cunningham's, that the *sh* sign *þ* was derived from the *r* sign *ρ* (Rho),[5] and has also said that after the fifth century San only survived as a numeral[6] (and as a numeral it cannot come in question, for it was written with a totally different sign). But I have never seen the one enlightening Greek text on the subject quoted.

Athenaeus,[7] in discussing various substitutions of San (*sh*) for Sigma (*s*), says that Aristoxenus (end of the fourth century B.C.) frequently remarked on the tendency of singers to make that substitution; Aristoxenus' words as quoted (Kaibel's text) are *τὸ σίγμα λέγειν παρῃτοῦντο διὰ τὸ σκληρόστομον εἶναι...τὸ δὲ ῥῶ διὰ τὸ εὔκολον πολλάκις παραλαμβάνουσι.* Now the MS of Athenaeus, Codex Marcianus, in the second clause of the passage cited has *τὸ δὲ ρ̄*, which the Epitome, followed by Kaibel, has corrected to *ῥῶ* (see Kaibel's note). But that Aristoxenus *meant* San (the *sh* sound) is certain, not only from the manner in which Athenaeus quotes the passage in the midst of a discussion of San, but because the tendency of singers to sing San for Sigma had previously offended both Pindar[8] and his teacher Lasus of Hermione, who wrote an ode and a hymn without a Sigma in them[9] so as to give singers no excuse for singing the hated *sh* sound; and

[1] *NC* 1872 p. 181, 1890 p. 108, 1892 p. 54.
[2] *Academy* XXXII, 1887, p. 170.
[3] See F. W. Thomas, *JRAS* 1913 p. 642.
[4] J. Kirste, *Orobazes*, *Wien SB* CLXXXII, 1918, Abh. 2.
[5] *JRAS* 1913 pp. 1016, 1034. [6] *Ib.* p. 642.
[7] Athen. XI, 467 a, b.
[8] Fr. 79 b, *τὸ σὰν κίβδηλον ἀπὸ στομάτων.*
[9] Athen. X, 455 b, c; see in J. U. Powell, *New Chapters in the History of Greek Literature*, 3rd series, 1933, p. 49 (C. M. Bowra).

it is clear that it is this tendency to which Aristoxenus is alluding. This means that, *if* Athenaeus quotes Aristoxenus correctly and *if* Codex Marcianus represents Athenaeus correctly, San at the end of the fourth century was written *ρ̄* (Rho). But it is incredible that such a wonderful instrument as Greek in its prime should have made one sign do duty for both the *sh* sound and the *r* sound, even though the *sh* sound was no longer used in speaking. What Aristoxenus must really have written was not *ρ̄* but *ϸ*, which a copyist who no longer understood turned into *ρ̄*; there were two signs, *ϸ* (San) and *ρ* (Rho), perhaps with a very slight difference between them, *i.e.* the upper limb of San very short (compare the very slight difference in the German alphabet between the signs for *ʃ* and *s*); and in some times and places, especially where knowledge of Greek was imperfect or failing, much confusion might result; one might be used where the other should have been, sometimes perhaps owing merely to a slight error of an engraver's tool. But unquestionably the sign *ϸ* on the Kushan coinage is generally *sh*;[1] this is proved by the Indian pronunciation Kanishka of the Greek Κανεϸκι. The same is the case on some coins of the earlier Saca king Spalirises; his name is certain from the Kharoshthi Spalirisa, but in the Greek form, though the first letter is usually Sigma, it is also sometimes either *ϸ* or a form indistinguishable from a capital Rho;[2] actually the first instance in the East of a sign which looks like a capital Rho having the value *sh* appears on the Greek coins of the Kushan Miaos (App. 17).

Stein then should be right that on the Kushan coinage *ϸ* represents San; but it was not I think a *revival* of San. The Aristoxenus passage should solve the problem of how the 'obsolete' San ever reached the Farther East; the answer is that it was not entirely obsolete.[3] It was obsolete in classical *literature*; what kept it alive, ready to represent the *sh* sound in a foreign language if required, was not literature but music. Music formed part of the curriculum of the gymnasium, and gymnasia, as has been seen (p. 18), must have been universal in the Greek cities of the East; but there is more than that. Aristoxenus, says Athenaeus, spoke often (πολλάκις) about San. But Aristoxenus was famous; he was a learned Peripatetic and writer on the theory of music, and his works on the subject became classics in the Greek world; from him other writers on the subject took their start, and his writings must have been widely known. All the Hellenistic literature on music is lost, but there must once have been such a literature; one cannot suppose a blank between Aristoxenus in the fourth century B.C. and Aristides Quintilianus in the second century A.D., and indeed there is a reference to different schools of

[1] Kirste *op. cit.* pp. 12–17 makes rather a strong case for a Rho in OKPO on the coins of Kanishka and Huvishka.

[2] Set out *CII* p. xli. See Cunningham, *NC* 1890 p. 108.

[3] I make no reference to the horses branded with San in the fifth century (Aristoph. *Clouds* 122; Athen. XI, 467 b), for it is not known what the mark was or if the custom ever travelled to Asia.

thought having existed.[1] There was plenty of interest in music, and not only among intellectuals—the Syracusan Women of Theocritus proves that—and that this interest extended to the Farther East is shown by Herodorus' Ode to Apollo (p. 39) from Susa, where the unusual and intricate metre testifies to a corresponding study of music. All this must have kept alive the knowledge of San, because in music, unlike literature, the *sh* sound could not die; I understand that the tendency of some singers to sing *sh* (*e.g.* 'Ish' for 'Ich' in German) is as well-known in modern times as it was to Lasus and Aristoxenus. It is not necessary to say that a knowledge of San survived in *India* (though it may well have done so), for two art-motives travelled to India from Pergamum and the Phoenician sphere respectively shortly before the time of Miaos and Spalirises (pp. 394, 329), and there was perfectly good communication with the West in their day. And it seems certain that, if the *sh* sound could not die, the frequent comments on the subject of San by the most famous of Greek writers on music would not have been allowed to die either. And they did not die; some of them reached Athenaeus.

[1] The reference in Aristides Quintilianus to *οἱ συμπλέκοντες* and *οἱ χωρίζοντες*, on which see Susemihl II p. 223.

APPENDIX 19

PĀNDAVA-PĀNDU AND PĀNDHYA (see p. 381)

Ptolemy VII, 1, 6 calls the country between the Jhelum and the Ravi, with the cities of Bucephala, Iomousa, and Sāgala, ἡ Πανδοούων or Πανδαούων χώρα. The readings vary;[1] that of the best MS, X (Πανδόπων), is too corrupt to make anything of, and the others vary between Πανδούων, Πανδοούων[2] (which Renou prints), and Πανδαούων; the word is certainly Pāndava, the form last mentioned being an exact transliteration. The Latin versions give Pandanorum, Pandonorum, Pandorum, and Pandiana regio.

The location of the name, which is part of Ptolemy's Hellenistic material (Chap. VI), shows that it can have nothing to do with the kingdom of the Pāndhya in the extreme south of the Indian peninsula, which moreover only really came within the purview of the West about the time of Augustus, though the two names have sometimes been confused, both in the Latin versions of Ptolemy and in modern writers. The Pāndhya are the Πανδίονες of Ptol. VII, 1, 89, with a king Pandion (*ib.* 1, 11 Πανδίονος χώρας) whose capital (1, 89) was Μόδουρα, the 'southern Mathurā'. All the *v. ll.* without exception, both in 1, 11 and 1, 89, and whether Latin or Greek, retain either the *i* or the *n* or (more usually) both. Consequently, when the Latin versions of 1, 6 give the forms Pandanorum, Pandonorum, Pandiana regio, these readings have nothing to do with the name Pāndava, but are a confusion with, and are taken from, the Πανδίονες; Pandiana regio explicitly occurs in 1, 11 as a Latin rendering of Πανδίονος χώρα. The only Latin reading therefore of 1, 6 which belongs there is the form Pandorum; this is the reading of the majority of the Latin versions, and implies a Greek form Πάνδοι or perhaps Πάνδαι, which would represent the name Pāndu.

The Pāndya of southern India are mentioned in other classical writers.[3] Megasthenes (Arr. *Ind.* 8), who calls their country Pandaea (Πάνδαια), had heard dimly of them—that the Pāndya and not the Pāndus are meant is shown by the reference to their wealth of pearls—but had nothing else to tell about them except a foolish and unpleasant legend; the reference to this legend shows that they are also the gens Pandae of Pliny VI, 76, though he separates them from the king Pandion (*ib.* 105); probably Pandae here ought

[1] The readings throughout this Appendix are taken from the apparatus in L. Renou, *La géographie de Ptolémée, l'Inde*, 1925.

[2] *Γ* has *Πανδοούως*, which is obviously a mistake for *Πανδοούων*.

[3] Renou's Index attaches these passages to *Πανδοούοι* instead of to *Πανδίονες*, but does not cite Dionysius.

to be Pandaea, for Solinus, who usually copies Pliny, gives Pandaea gens (52, 15). That there has been a good deal of confusion is obvious. But there is one other notice which has been overlooked and which almost certainly refers, not to the Pāndya, but to the people of Ptolemy VII, 1, 6 (Pāndava-Pāndus). Dionysius in the Bassarica, in what survives of his list of the Indian peoples who followed Deriades (corresponding to book XXVI of Nonnus, who substantially copied him), has a name Πάνδαι,[1] which is not in Nonnus. Dionysius' date is quite uncertain[2] and he may have been earlier or later than Ptolemy; but all his names must *ex hypothesi* belong to northern India, like those of Nonnus, for Bacchus' conquest of India is merely a reflection of Alexander's, and with one exception (Πάνδαι apart) all his genuine known names, like those of Nonnus, are taken from the Alexander story. But he has *one* Hellenistic name, Kaspeiroi,[3] which Ptolemy also has; so the possibility of a real name outside the Alexander story is not ruled out. Now we have seen that the majority of the Latin versions of Ptol. VII, 1, 6 imply the existence of a name Πάνδοι or perhaps Πάνδαι; and this name is the Πάνδαι of Dionysius, whether he took it from Ptolemy or whether both ultimately go back to a common source.

We get then in northern India two versions of the name of the same people, Πανδοούοι or Πανδαούοι and Πάνδαι, connected by the form Πανδούοι (Pandui of one of the Ptolemy maps[4]); and these Πανδαούοι-Πάνδαι have nothing to do with the Pāndya of southern India but are the Pāndava-Pāndus of the Mahābhārata. Ptolemy must be wrong in fact in making the country between the Jhelum and the Ravi belong to this people (who in the epic are near Delhi), for, in the period when Greeks are concerned, the country between the Jhelum and the Chenab was Paurava country and that between the Chenab and the Ravi belonged to the Madras (p. 170); but that is not the point. The point is that the Pāndava-Pāndus do not appear in later history; they belong solely to the epic. The name therefore came to Ptolemy and Dionysius from some Greek who knew the Mahābhārata (see pp. 380 *sq.*); this was its ultimate source, and they could not have got it in any other way.

The possibility of a connection, legendary or otherwise, between the historical Pāndyas and the Pāndavas of the epic need not be discussed.

[1] Stephanus *s.v.* = fr. 21 in Müller, *GGM* II p. xxvii. The new fragments of Dionysius (*Arch. f. Pap.* VII p. 3; identified as Dionysius by R. Pleydell, *Phil. Woch.* XLIX, 1929, col. 1101) add nothing to the names of peoples already known.

[2] Christ-Schmid[6] II, 2, 1924, p. 672 can only say between A.D. 100 and 300.

[3] Steph. *s.v.* = fr. 16. See pp. 238, 487 n. 5.

[4] After Venetus 516 (R), in Renou. The location, on the sources of the Jhelum and the Chenab, does not agree with Ptolemy's text; but I only want the spelling.

APPENDIX 20

THE CHINESE SOURCES

The two main Chinese sources for the conquest of Greek Bactria are chapter 123 of the Shi-ki of Ssu-ma Ch'ien, who is said by Hirth to have finished his history about 99 B.C. (some put it rather later) and who reproduces Chang-k'ien's Report, more or less interwoven with his own narrative but in places apparently given verbatim; and chapters 96 (both parts) and 61 fols. 1–6 of the Ch'ien-han-shu (Annals of the Former Han) of Pan-ku, who died in A.D. 92 and whose history, left incomplete at his death and finished by his sister, runs from 206 B.C. to A.D. 24; chapter 61 fols. 1–6 contains among other things a Life of Chang-k'ien, largely drawn from himself, and chapter 96 is Pan-ku's own account of the Western Countries, based on Chang-k'ien's Report which is sometimes apparently quoted verbatim, but incorporating later material. Ssu-ma Ch'ien is supposed to be the more valuable source for what Chang-k'ien actually wrote, but it is not always easy to say what is Chang-k'ien and what is Ssu-ma Ch'ien; the latter writer brings in later material just as Pan-ku does, and for historical purposes chapter 123 of the Shi-ki requires the same kind of critical analysis as has been applied to many Greek historians;[1] I have done what little I can from a translation (see for example p. 281) but I do not pretend that it can be satisfactory. Pan-ku (who of course needs a similar analysis) had much new information at his disposal which Ssu-ma Ch'ien had not possessed, and his occasional corrections of the latter on matters like geography can be valuable. It is as well to explain that to accept a correction of Pan-ku's is not to prefer later evidence to earlier; it is like the case of two modern historians of whom the later in time has before him the same evidence as the earlier one and some additional evidence as well.

For Ssu-ma Ch'ien I use Dr Fr. Hirth's translation of chapter 123,[2] to the excellence of which many have testified. Taking Hirth's section numbers, Chang-k'ien's Report (or what professes to be his Report, see pp. 280 *sq.*) comprises § 18 (p. 95) to § 52 (p. 98) both inclusive and §§ 101–3 both inclusive (pp. 108–9); that §§ 101–3 are out of place where they come is proved by the sense running on without a break from the end of § 98 to the beginning of § 104, which must once have been contiguous (§§ 99–100 are a separate interpolation). These sections 101–3 ought to come between § 52 (end of the

[1] The need of this for Chinese historians generally was noted by H. Maspero, *Histoire et Historiens depuis cinquante ans*, 1876–1926, II, 1928, p. 531. If it has been done for chapter 123 of the *Shi-ki* I have not succeeded in finding it. It is a misfortune that Chavannes' great work did not reach that chapter.

[2] *JAOS* XXXVII, 1917, p. 89.

Ta-hia part of the Report) and § 53 (beginning of Chang-k'ien's memorandum for the Emperor on India, which is a different document). The An-si section of the Report has certainly been edited by Ssu-ma Ch'ien, for it includes information later than Chang-k'ien (p. 281). Some believe, as Professor W. P. Yetts kindly informed me, that chapter 123 of the Shi-ki was inserted by another hand after Ssu-ma Ch'ien's death, though I gather that no definite study of this question has appeared in print. I call the author of chapter 123 Ssu-ma Ch'ien throughout, without prejudice to any question (on which naturally I can express no opinion) as to whether it ought to be Pseudo-Ssu-ma Ch'ien. To the Greek historian it is probably immaterial whether it was Ssu-ma Ch'ien or another who preserved Chang-k'ien's Report; internal evidence I think shows that chapter 123 is anyhow much earlier than Pan-ku. The material thing would be to know how much really comes from Chang-k'ien, the contemporary eye-witness; on this I have found no help.

For the Ch'ien-han-shu I use the translations of A. Wylie[1] and J. J. M. de Groot, published in 1926 after his death by O. Franke.[2] Wylie's translation is severely criticised by de Groot (vol. I, p. v); but, except in the spelling of proper names and a few out-of-date explanations of them, I have found remarkably little difference in those parts of the two translations which I have had to study, while more than once without Wylie I should have been badly off.[3] On the other hand, Franke's corrections may indicate that de Groot's own translation is not always as faultless as he thought it was; and in one well-known passage it is, to use his own expression, 'hair-raising', for it introduces an alien set of ideas (p. 298 n. 5). If one knows something about the subject beforehand, there is much useful detail to be got from de Groot's commentaries; but his is a tiresome book to use, as the translation is scattered in snippets throughout the work and does not include quite everything (see the important omission noted p. 342 n. 1); and the historian must have everything that there is—that is first principles.

Beside the two main sources, an occasional item of information is added by chapter 118 of the Hou-han-shu (Annals of the Later Han) of Fan-ye, which carries on Pan-ku's history from A.D. 25; this chapter has been translated by E. Chavannes in *T'oung Pao* VIII, 1907, p. 149.

[1] *Journ. Anthropological Inst.* X, 1881, p. 20; XI, 1881, p. 83.

[2] *Chinesische Urkunden zur Geschichte Asiens*; zweiter Teil, *Die Westlande Chinas in der vorchristlichen Zeit* 1926.

[3] See for example, beside the omission noted p. 342 n. 1, my discussion of the name W'ou-ti-la-o on p. 340.

APPENDIX 21

THE GREEK NAMES OF THE TOCHARI

It is claimed (p. 289) that the Tochari who invaded Bactria cannot have spoken Dialects A and/or B, because their name was aspirated and these dialects have no aspirate. It seems advisable therefore to collect and examine all the Greek forms of the name, as this has not been done, and the Greek forms are much earlier than most of the Oriental ones.

Apollodorus, *c.* 100 B.C., has *Τόχαροι* (Tocharoi);[1] this form was popularised by Strabo and has passed into common use as this people's name. Ptolemy, VI, 11, 6, has this form in connection with Bactria, and also, VI, 12, 4, a form *Τάχοροι* (Tachoroi), with metathesis of the vowels, in connection with Sogdiana. In this form the aspirate comes in the second syllable, not the first. This placing of the aspirate is also found in the Sanscrit Tukhāra, and again in the name of Bactria (in various languages) from the fourth to the eighth century A.D., Tocharistan (presumably taken from *Τόχαροι*), and in forms derived from Tocharistan, like *toχrī* (*toχarī* or *toγarī*) which is found later in Central Asian documents as the name of the Saca speech of the Kushans of Tocharistan (p. 290), and Hsüan Tsiang's Tu-ho-lo (*Tuoχuâlâ*, Bailey) in the seventh century A.D.[2]

What form was used by the other Greek historian, 'Trogus' source', *c.* 85 B.C., can only be deduced, but certainly it was not *Τόχαροι*. The MSS of Trogus *Prol.* XLII give Thocarorum, Thodarorum, Thoclarorum, Toclarorum,[3] to which the best MSS add, in Justin XLII, 2, 2, the form Thogariis. It is possible therefore, but by no means certain, that this Greek historian's form had *th* and was Thocaroi or Thogaroi; that is, that the aspirate came in the first syllable, not the second. This position of the aspirate is found later in the much-quoted forms Θαγοῦροι (Thagouroi) and Θογάρα (Thogara) in Ptolemy (p. 285 n. 6) for a people and town in Kan-su on the way to Sera Metropolis, forms derived from agents of Maes Titianus and therefore second century A.D.; and again in the Thibetan forms[4] Tho-kar, Tho-gar, Thod-khar, Phod-kar, whose date I do not know, for a people in Kan-su. The form Phod-kar might guarantee Pliny's Focari[5] (in Chinese Turkestan), usually taken to be a corruption of Thocari; this passage in Pliny is most probably Hellenistic, and his form, and not the MSS of Trogus,

[1] Strabo XI, 511; see p. 284 n. 4.

[2] H. W. Bailey, *Ttaugara*, *BSOS* VIII, 1936, p. 887.

[3] This list from Ruehl's edition, 1886, p. lxii; O. Seel's recent edition, 1935, omits Thoclarorum. In the text of *Prol.* XLII Jeep printed Thogarorum, Ruehl Thocarorum; Seel prints Apollodorus' form, Tocharorum, which has no place in Trogus.

[4] F. W. Thomas, *JRAS* 1931 pp. 834–5.

[5] Pliny VI, 55, on which see p. 84.

is the likeliest evidence for the aspirated first syllable being Hellenistic.[1] The forms Thagouroi—Thogara show the same metathesis of the vowels as has already been seen in Tocharoi—Tachoroi.

There is still a third type of spelling which is almost certainly Hellenistic, and might well be as early as the form Tocharoi. Pliny VI, 22 says that a people called Tagorae[2] crossed the Tanais-Don from east to west with other 'Scyths', while across the Tanais had been another people called Inapaei who had utterly perished, viritim deletos; but in VI, 50 he puts this latter people among another set of 'Scyths' altogether, across (north of) the Tanais-Jaxartes—ibi Napaei interisse dicuntur. He has therefore confused, as is common enough, the two rivers called Tanais in antiquity, and has also confused two groups of 'Scyths' connected with the two rivers; it is uncertain therefore, from Pliny alone, whether the Tagorae lived east of and crossed the Don or lived north of and crossed the Jaxartes. Fortunately Ptolemy settles it. He knew of a people *Τακοραῖοι* (Takoraioi) north of the Imaos,[3] and gives them again as *Ταπουραῖοι* (Tapouraioi) living near the *Τάπουρα ὄρη*;[4] Professor Herrmann has conjectured *Ταγουραῖοι* (Tagouraioi) for *Ταπουραῖοι*,[5] but did not notice Takoraioi, which seems to make his conjecture certain. He identified the mountain chain near which the Tagouraioi lived (on the plains to the north of it) with the Alexandrovski range west of Lake Issyk Kul, and saw in the Tagouraioi that fraction of the Tochari-Yueh-chi who remained in the Sai-wang country when the Wu-sun and Hiung-nu drove out the main body of the Yueh-chi (p. 276) and who were ultimately absorbed by the Wu-sun, a brilliant explanation which may be gratefully accepted.

Certain sources, then, or a certain source, of Pliny and Ptolemy knew the Tochari as Tagorae or Takor(aioi) or Tagour(aioi), all unaspirated forms. But such source or sources also knew of the sojourn of the Tochari in the Lake Issyk Kul district and of their crossing the Jaxartes southward. The information here, then, in Pliny and Ptolemy does not come from merchants' itineraries or anything similar; it must go back ultimately to some historian who related the movements of the Tochari, and, as Apollodorus used the form Tocharoi, the only possible historian is 'Trogus' source', to whom, as this book has shown, a good deal in Ptolemy ultimately goes back; therefore, though it is only deduction, it is at least as likely that this historian, our best authority, used some unaspirated form like Tagorae as that he used the aspirated form Thocari or Thogari. If Professor Bailey's suggestion[6] that the Chinese in the second century B.C. were trying to copy a form *τογαρα* be right, the un-

[1] P. Pelliot, *T'oung Pao* XXXII, 1936, pp. 261–2, has expressed doubts about the existence of an aspirate in *Θαγοῦροι* and *Θροάνα* (p. 519), but did not apparently consider Trogus and Pliny. It would simplify matters if the first syllable of the word had never been aspirated, but there is a good deal of evidence.

[2] Apparently no *v.ll.*

[3] Ptol. VII, 2, 15.

[4] Ptol. VI, 14, 7–14, with *v.l.* *Ταπούρεοι*.

[5] A. Herrmann, *Τάπουρα ὄρη* in PW. The name can have nothing to do with the Tapuri, far away in Hyrcania and the Elburz.

[6] *Op. cit.* pp. 885–6.

aspirated form is very old, which supports the virtual certainty that the form Tagorae is Hellenistic. The form occurs again, as ttaugara, in a Khotan Saca document of *c.* A.D. 800.[1]

Before going on I must notice one thing about Ptolemy, as it is alluded to in my text (p. 286). I have described his method of work elsewhere (p. 231); he knew nothing about Central Asia himself, but he meant to get in all his (or Marinus') notes, and he has given five notices of the Tochari, belonging to different times and places and with different spellings—Thagouroi in Kan-su, Takoraioi north of Imaos, Tagouraioi near Lake Issyk Kul, Tachoroi in Sogdiana, Tocharoi in Bactria—without suspecting that he is recording the odyssey of one and the same people. It is very characteristic; but the point is that this odyssey is that of the Yueh-chi as given by the Chinese sources (Chap. VII), and it makes the identification of Tochari and Yueh-chi certain.

To sum up the Greek side. We have forms of the name with the second syllable aspirated but not the first, one of which is certainly Hellenistic; forms with the first syllable aspirated but not the second, one or more of which may be Hellenistic; and forms with no aspirate at all, one of which almost certainly is, and all may be, Hellenistic. Moreover each aspirated form has an unaspirated parallel; with Tocharoi—Tachoroi compare Takor(aioi); with Thagouroi compare Tagour(aioi); with Thogari, Thogara, compare Tagorae. Is this conclusive (as *ex hypothesi* it ought to be) that the name of the historical Tochari was certainly aspirated? I do not so see it, and one must consider what it means.

Will the known phenomena of metathesis and shifting of the aspirate account for all these forms? These phenomena are largely dialectical variations, as for example the several forms of the Thessalian name, and belong to the formative period of the Greek language; but in our case dialectical variations do not come in question, for we are dealing throughout with one form of Greek only, the Hellenistic Koine. As regards the Koine, the interchange of τ and θ is said to be common in Egypt and Asia Minor,[2] and would account for the variation T—Th in the initial letter of the Tochari name; the interchange of κ and χ is also said to occur in the same countries,[3] though I have not seen the evidence given.[4] Again, the variant Τόχαροι—Thocari would represent a known form of aspirate-shifting, like κιθών for χιτών, βάθρακος for βάτραχος, Φύτιος for Πύθιος,[5] though, once more, much of

[1] Bailey *op. cit.* pp. 884–5.

[2] Many instances in K. Dieterich, *Untersuchungen zur Gesch. d. griech. Sprache* 1898 pp. 84–5, and add *SEG* VI, 281, θέκνα for τέκνα (Phrygia); see also E. Schwyzer, *Griech. Grammatik* I (in Müller's *Handbuch* II i), 1934, p. 204.

[3] Schwyzer *ib.* p. 204. Dietrich p. 84 says it does not occur.

[4] A good case is *SEG* VI, 718 (Pamphylia), *Μαλάκου* and *Μαλάχου* (the same man). It is said to occur on Attic vase-inscriptions from the fifth century B.C. onwards (G. Meyer, *Griech. Grammatik*² 1886 p. 209), but that is hardly in point.

[5] Lists in R. Kühner, *Ausführliche Grammatik d. griech. Sprache* (3rd ed. by Fr. Blass) I, I, 1890, pp. 278–9; Meyer *op. cit.* p. 209; Schwyzer *op. cit.* pp. 268–9. Many are old, and in Kühner-Blass are given as variants between Attic and New Ionic. *Φύτιος—Πύθιος* is Hellenistic, Ditt.³ 710 D.

this is dialectical; and there are cases of interchange between κ and χ which are due to aspirate-shifting, like Χάλκας—Κάλχας, Καλχηδόνιοι—Χαλκηδόνιοι,[1] though the two forms may sometimes belong to different localities or dialects.[2] So far, the points to be noted are two. First, all these phenomena, so far as they appear in Hellenistic Greek—and we have to include yet another, the metathesis of the vowels—appear as single cases in some particular word and largely in inscriptions (or papyri); there is no authority for supposing that we can apply them all together to the same word, especially one known only from literary texts, and claim that they will explain the tremendous mix-up we find over the Tochari name, which appears to have no parallel in Hellenistic Greek.[3] And secondly, interchanges like that of τ with θ or κ with χ do not enable us to say in any particular case whether the aspirated form is the original one or not.[4]

But there are further considerations. One is the persistent γ in the Tochari name; I have found no suggestion anywhere that γ ever interchanges with χ. Another is the fact that an aspirate may just be introduced where no aspirate is; Attic has a tendency to turn unaspirated tenues into the aspirated form,[5] and the Koine in turn aspirates a good many words which are not aspirated in Attic.[6] I have come across two cases,[7] not in Egypt or Asia Minor and too recent to be cited in any grammar, where a certain κ has just been turned into χ; and there is the well-known instance of the Indian Pātaliputra becoming Παλίβοθρα in all Greek writers.[8] This is not the only case where the Greeks of the Farther East just inserted an aspirate; the *Sp* in the Iranian name Spalirises (Chap. VIII) is certain from all the Kharoshthi and most of the Greek legends on his coins, but there are coins (see App. 18) on which in the Greek legend it is spelt Shpalirises (*þ* for Sigma). Indeed it must be remembered that in common speech in many languages (and some of the Tochari-forms must come from unlearned traders) the aspirate is an unstable thing; Catullus' Arrius is own brother to John Leech's 'Arry. As regards the Greek evidence, then, this cursory examination may suggest that it is difficult to say offhand whether in the second century B.C. there *was* an aspirate in the Tochari name

[1] See last note.

[2] Cf. G. Daux, *Delphes* 1936 pp. 240 *sqq.*, on *Πλυγονεῖς* and *Φλυγονεῖς*, who in the second century B.C. were different peoples.

[3] One word in Greek has as many as eight variants, *βάτραχος* (list in Kühner-Blass I I p. 289), but they cannot be Hellenistic; of the first four, two are Ionic, and the last four, from Hesychius, must belong to different dialects, though no information is given.

[4] See the conflicting theories as regards old Greek in Meyer p. 209 and Kühner-Blass I I p. 277.

[5] Meyer pp. 209, 242; Kühner-Blass I I p. 111.

[6] Kühner-Blass I I p. 112.

[7] *SEG* VII, 142 (Palmyra, A.D. 81) *Σπασίνου Χάραχος*, for *Χάρακος* (spelt correctly in no. 135); J. Coupry and M. Feyel, *BCH* LX, 1936, p. 42 (Philippi, A.D. 41), χ(*ολωνίαι*) as a transliteration of coloniae.

[8] Schwyzer *op. cit.* p. 204 calls attention to this.

or not; and even if it be supposed that θ or χ or both really belong to the original name, we are faced with a further question: in the period under consideration (second century B.C. to second century A.D.) is it certain that θ φ χ in Greek *were* aspirated forms at all? The latest authority has pronounced the evidence on this point to be quite indeterminate.[1]

In fact, the Greeks never had a settled name for the Tochari (even the two contemporary historians use different forms) but only a medley of forms which fall into three classes; and the reason, whatever it was, must go deeper than such Greek linguistic phenomena as metathesis or shifting of the aspirate. It might mean that members of the horde themselves pronounced their name in different ways, and, if so, one possibility (there are probably others) would be that in the language of the Tochari we are dealing with a dying aspirate, as the *sh* sound died in classical Greek; compare the mute *h* in modern French, and the dying aspirate in *wh* in Britain to-day, where in the Gaelic-speaking Highlands one still hears 'which' and 'when', while in England it is common enough to hear 'wich' and 'wen'. A curious point may be noticed here. It has recently been claimed[2] that, beside A and B, a third 'Tocharian' dialect, C, existed in the Shan-Shan kingdom (near Khotan) in the third century A.D.; and some words contain the spirant *kh*, which would be equivalent to the Greek χ in Τόχαροι. Since A and B contain no aspirates, these words have been put down as foreign;[3] but I wonder whether in some cases they may not be the remains of a dying aspirate?

I must just mention that another name, Θροάνα, has been brought into discussion and claimed as the one relic, apart from their own name, of the speech of the historical Tochari.[4] But what Ptolemy does give is a *people* Θρόανοι somewhere on the Silk Route with a town Θροάνα;[5] and the Θρόανοι have been omitted from discussion. Θροάνα is said to be Sogdian drwʾʾn;[6] but unless some Sogdian document actually makes drwʾʾn a town of the Tochari, Ptolemy's sixth book is *prima facie* conclusive against any connection.[7]

I am not of course trying to prove anything in this Appendix; that is a matter for philologists. I am only pointing out that the Greek forms suggest that further investigation may be desirable before it be stated as an ascertained fact that the *centum* dialects A and B cannot represent the language of the historical Tochari.

[1] Schwyzer p. 205 sums up the evidence as 'teils positiv teils negativ'. He himself, not so long ago, would have written 'theils'.

[2] T. Burrow, *JRAS* 1935 pp. 667, 675.

[3] *Ib.* p. 669

[4] Bailey *op. cit.* pp. 888, 916; cf. Pelliot *op. cit.* p. 263.

[5] Ptol. VI, 16, 5 and 6.

[6] Bailey *op. cit.* p. 888.

[7] I suppose the occurrence together of the two names Θαγόρα (Tagora in some Latin versions) and Θροάνα in Ptol. VII, 2, 7, on the Great Gulf in Further India, near the equator, might be held to point to a connection. But what the names can mean here I have no idea, unless it is merely one of the usual cases where Ptolemy turns one place into two, see pp. 231 *sq.*

ADDENDA

THE GREEKS IN BACTRIA AND INDIA

In the *Times* of October 16th, 1937, to which Professor Adcock called my attention, there was announced the discovery, at Shinkot in Bajaur, of a relic casket with an inscription in Kharoshthi by the dedicator, an Indian Buddhist named Vijayamitra, dated on the twenty-fifth day of the Indian month Vaisakha in the fifth year of the reign of Menander. As Bajaur was the frontier province of Gandhāra to the northward, this furnishes proof of what I had previously deduced from the coin-hoards (see p. 229), that Menander recovered and ruled the whole of Gandhāra. Also it is the first instance in India of dating by the regnal years of a Greek king; that this should be done by an Indian Buddhist may bear on what I have written with regard to Buddhist support of Demetrius and Menander. Menander's fifth year most probably lies between 161 and 155 B.C.

P. 226. The latest possible date for Menander's death is 145, because Heliocles' conquests in India, which were after his death, took at least three years (p. 271) and were over by 141, a date fixed *aliunde*.

P. 417, n. 7. H. Bengston, *Philol.* XCII, 1937, p. 129, asserts that Ἴων is derived from Ἰάϝων, but his references do not bear this out. The difficulties have been investigated by P. Kretschmer, *Glotta* I, 1909, p. 14 n. 4, who suggested that they were parallel forms, and by A. Cuny, *Rev. E.G.* XXXIV, 1921, p. 155, who suggested that Ἰάϝονες was not Indo-European and was adopted in Asia by the Greeks. But no writer seems to have noticed the two similar parallel forms in India.

INDEX I

GENERAL

INDEX II

PRINCIPAL GREEK AND LATIN PASSAGES COMMENTED ON

(page numbers in brackets)

1.

2.

3.

4.

5.

6.

7.

8.

9.

10.

11.

12.

1. Euthydemus in old age.
2. Euthydemus on a pedigree coin of Agathocles.
3. Demetrius.
4. Antimachus.
5. Euthydemus II.
6. Demetrius II.
7. Demetrius II on his unique bilingual tetradrachm.
8. Pantaleon.
9. Agathocles.
10. Eucratides.
11. Eucratides (idealised).
12. Heliocles.

PEDIGREE[1] OF THE EUTHYDEMIDS AND EUCRATIDES

TO SHOW THE FICTITIOUS DESCENT FROM ALEXANDER

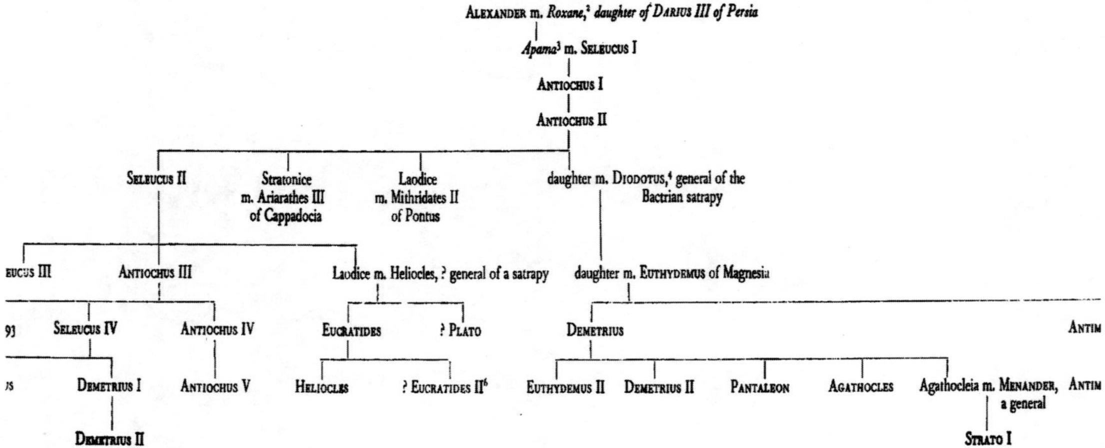

[1] Immaterial names are omitted. For the full Seleucid pedigree see *CAH* VIII.
[2] The historical Roxane, whom Alexander married, was a daughter of the Bactrian baron Oxyartes. He also married a daughter of Darius III, named Barsine.
[3] The historical Apama, whom Seleucus married, was a daughter of the Sogdian baron Spitamenes, but almost certainly an Achaemenid on her mother's side.
[4] Diodotus II can only have been Diodotus' son by a former marriage.
[5] Certainly of the royal house, and more probably Demetrius' brother than a collateral.
[6] Possibly Heliocles' son.

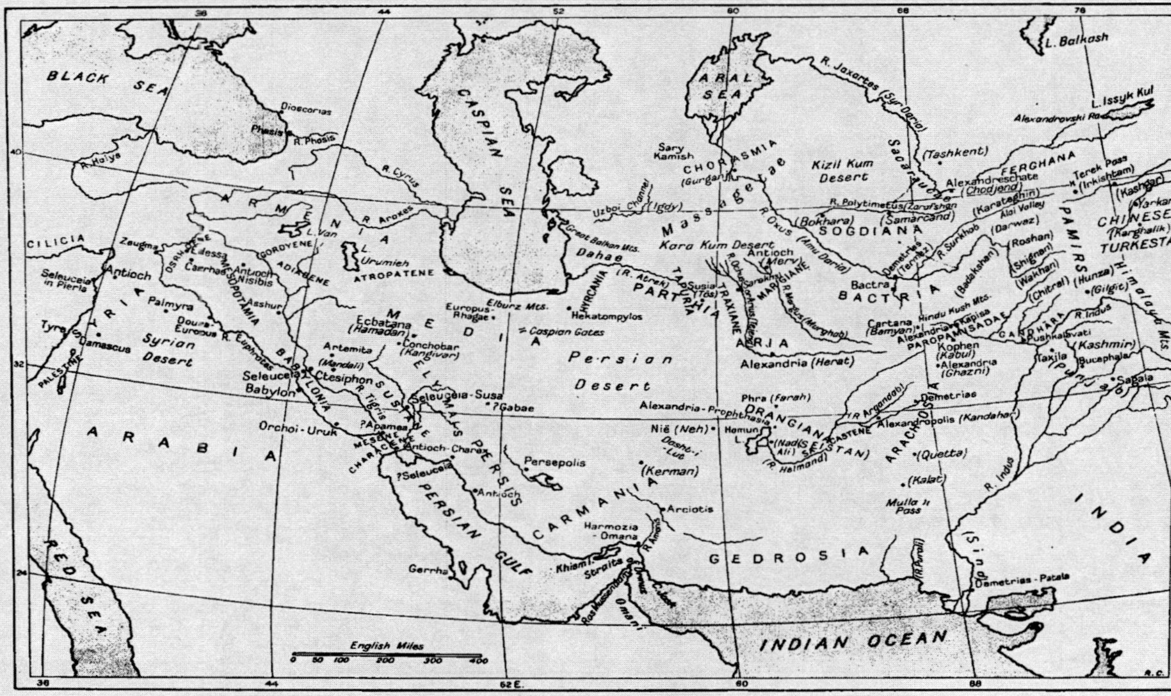
BLACK SEA
CASPIAN SEA
ARAL SEA
L. Balkash
L. Issyk Kul
Dioscorias
Phasis
R. Phasis
R. Halys
R. Cyrus
R. Araxes
ARMENIA
L. Van
L. Urumieh
ATROPATENE
CILICIA
Zeugma
Edessa
Carrhae
Antioch Nisibis
GORDYENE
ADIABENE
OSRHOENE
MESOPOTAMIA
Asshur
Seleuceia in Pieria
Antioch
SYRIA
Palmyra
Doura-Europus
R. Euphrates
Tyre
Damascus
PALESTINE
Syrian Desert
ARABIA
BABYLONIA
Seleuceia
Babylon
Ctesiphon
R. Tigris
Orchoi-Uruk
Artemita (Mandali)
Ecbatana (Hamadan)
Conchobar (Kangivar)
MEDIA
Europus-Rhagae
Elburz Mts.
Caspian Gates
ELYMAIS
SUSIANE
Seleuceia-Susa
?Gabae
?Apamea
MESENE
CHARACENE
Antioch-Charax
?Seleuceia
Antioch
PERSIS
Persepolis
PERSIAN GULF
Gerrha
CARMANIA
Harmozia-Omana
R. Amanis
Khiam I.
Straits
Ormuz
Ras Mussendam
Omani
C. Jask
Arciotis
(Kerman)
Dasht-i-Lut
Nië (Neh)
Persian Desert
HYRCANIA
Hekatompylos
Dahae
Great Balkan Mts.
(R. Atrek)
TAPURIA
PARTHIA
Susia (Tūs)
TRAXIANE
Uzboi Channel
(Igdy)
Sary Kamish
CHORASMIA
(Gurganj)
Massagetae
Kara Kum Desert
Kizil Kum Desert
R. Jaxartes (Syr Daria)
Sacaraucae
(Tashkent)
Alexandreschate (Chodjend)
FERGHANA
Alexandrovski Ra.
Terek Pass
(Irkishtam)
R. Polytimetus (Zarafshan)
(Bokhara)
(Samarcand)
SOGDIANA
R. Oxus (Amu Daria)
Antioch (Merv)
MARGIANE
R. Margus (Murghab)
R. Ochus
Sorakh
ARIA
Alexandria (Herat)
Bactra
BACTRIA
Demetrias (Termez)
R. Surkhab
(Karateghin)
Alai Valley
(Darwaz)
(Badakshan)
(Roshan)
(Shignan)
(Wakhan)
PAMIRS
(Chitral)
(Hunza)
(Gilgit)
(Kashgar)
(Yarkand)
(Karghalik)
CHINESE TURKESTAN
To Khotan
Himalaya Mts.
Hindu Kush Mts.
Cartana (Bamyan)
Alexandria-Kapisa
PAROPAMISADAE
Kophen (Kabul)
Alexandria (Ghazni)
GANDHARA
Pushkalavati
R. Indus
Taxila
(Kashmir)
Bucaphala
Sagala
(Punjab)
Phra (Farah)
Alexandria-Prophthasia
DRANGIANA
Hamun L.
(Nad Ali)
SACASTENE
(SEISTAN)
(R. Helmand)
R. Argandab
Demetrias
Alexandropolis (Kandahar)
ARACHOSIA
(Quetta)
(Kalat)
Mulla Pass
R. Indus
(Sind)
INDIA
GEDROSIA
(R. Purali)
Demetrias-Patala
INDIAN OCEAN
RED SEA
English Miles
0 50 100 200 300 400
36
38
44
52
52 E.
60
68
76
40
32
24
R.C.

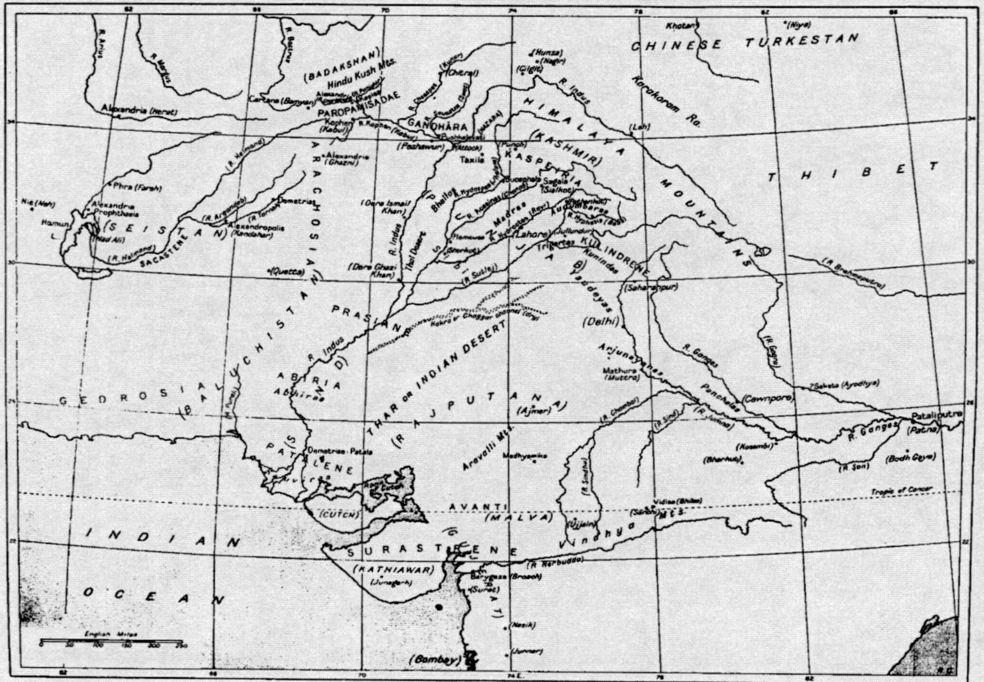

MAP 2
Northern Indi
after the
Greek Conque

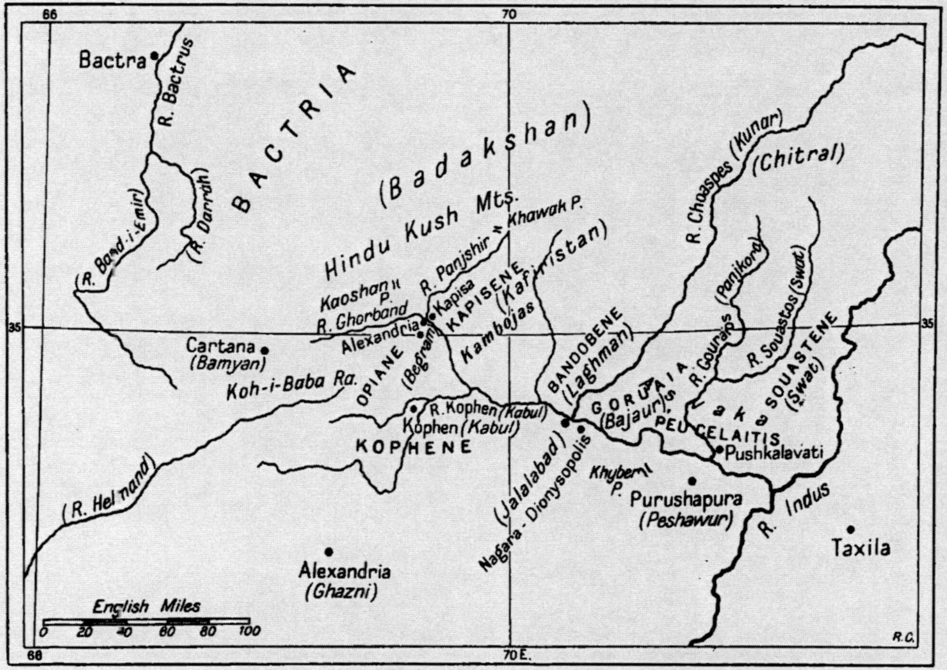

MAP 3
The Paropamisadae and Gandhāra (enlarged)